The Principles of

The Law of Property

IN SOUTH AFRICA

PRIVATE LAW

HANRI MOSTERT (Editor) | ANNE POPE (Editor)
PIETER BADENHORST | WARREN FREEDMAN
JUANITA PIENAAR | JEANNIE VAN WYK

OXFORD
UNIVERSITY PRESS
SOUTHERN AFRICA

SOUTHERN AFRICA

Oxford University Press Southern Africa (Pty) Ltd

Vasco Boulevard, Goodwood, Cape Town, Republic of South Africa
P O Box 12119, N1 City, 7463, Cape Town, Republic of South Africa

Oxford University Press Southern Africa (Pty) Ltd is a subsidiary of
Oxford University Press, Great Clarendon Street, Oxford OX2 6DP.

The Press, a department of the University of Oxford, furthers the University's objective of
excellence in research, scholarship, and education by publishing worldwide in

Oxford New York

Auckland Cape Town Dar es Salaam Hong Kong Karachi
Kuala Lumpur Madrid Melbourne Mexico City Nairobi
New Delhi Shanghai Taipei Toronto

With offices in

Argentina Austria Brazil Chile Czech Republic France Greece
Guatemala Hungary Italy Japan Poland Portugal Singapore South Korea
Switzerland Turkey Ukraine Vietnam

Oxford is a registered trade mark of Oxford University Press
in the UK and in certain other countries

Published in South Africa
by Oxford University Press Southern Africa (Pty) Ltd, Cape Town

The principles of the law of property in South Africa
ISBN 978 0 19 598404 0

© Oxford University Press Southern Africa (Pty) Ltd 2010

The moral rights of the author have been asserted
Database right Oxford University Press Southern Africa (Pty) Ltd (maker)

First published 2010

All rights reserved. No part of this publication may be reproduced,
stored in a retrieval system, or transmitted, in any form or by any means,
without the prior permission in writing of Oxford University Press Southern Africa (Pty) Ltd,
or as expressly permitted by law, or under terms agreed with the appropriate
designated reprographics rights organization. Enquiries concerning reproduction
outside the scope of the above should be sent to the Rights Department,
Oxford University Press Southern Africa (Pty) Ltd, at the address above.

You must not circulate this book in any other binding or cover
and you must impose this same condition on any acquirer.

Publisher: Penny Lane
Development editor: Mark Townsend
Project manager: Marguerite Lithgow
Editor: Rae Dalton
Indexer: Ethne Clarke
Proofreader: Jeannie van den Heever
Designer: Schalk Burger
Cover design: Oswald Kurtin/Schalk Burger
Set in 9.5pt on 12pt Utopia Std by CBT Typesetting and Design
Printed and bound by ABC Press, Cape Town
112647

Acknowledgements
The authors and publisher gratefully acknowledge permission to reproduce copyright material
in this book. Every effort has been made to trace copyright holders, but if any copyright
infringements have been made, the publisher would be grateful for information that would
enable any omissions or errors to be corrected in subsequent impressions.

Contents in brief

PART 1: GENERAL INTRODUCTION TO PROPERTY LAW

CHAPTER 1	PERSPECTIVE ON PROPERTY LAW	3
CHAPTER 2	PROPERTY AND THINGS: DEFINITIONS AND CLASSIFICATION	17
CHAPTER 3	RIGHTS	41
CHAPTER 4	POSSESSION	65

PART 2: OWNERSHIP

CHAPTER 5	CONTENT AND FORMS OF OWNERSHIP	89
CHAPTER 6	LIMITATIONS ON OWNERSHIP	115
CHAPTER 7	ACQUISITION OF OWNERSHIP	159
CHAPTER 8	PROTECTION OF OWNERSHIP	215

PART 3: SPECIFIC FORMS OF RIGHTS IN PROPERTY

CHAPTER 9	SERVITUDES AND RESTRICTIVE CONDITIONS	235
CHAPTER 10	MINERALS	265
CHAPTER 11	WATER	283
CHAPTER 12	REAL SECURITY	295

PART 4: OVERVIEW OF THE PRINCIPLES OF PROPERTY LAW IN ITS NEW CONTEXT

CHAPTER 13	PROSPECTS OF PROPERTY LAW	337

Contents

Contents in brief	v
List of authors	xv
Preface	xvii
About the book	xix

PART 1: GENERAL INTRODUCTION TO PROPERTY LAW

CHAPTER 1: PERSPECTIVE ON PROPERTY LAW — 3

1.1 Introduction — 3
1.2 Property: An evasive term — 4
    1.2.1 The use of 'property' in everyday language — 4
    1.2.2 What 'property' means to lawyers — 5
1.3 Context of property law: Framework and sources — 6
    1.3.1 Function of property law — 6
    1.3.2 Place of property law — 7
1.4 Roots of property law — 9
    1.4.1 Scope of property law — 11
    1.4.2 Sources of property law — 15
1.5 Mapping property law: The structure of this book — 17

CHAPTER 2: PROPERTY AND THINGS: DEFINITIONS AND CLASSIFICATION — 19

2.1 Introduction — 20
2.2 The characteristics and definition of things — 20
    2.2.1 Characteristics — 20
    2.2.1.1 Corporeality and incorporeality — 21
    2.2.1.2 Impersonal nature — 22
    2.2.1.3 Independence — 23
    2.2.1.4 Appropriability — 23
    2.2.1.5 Use and value — 24
    2.2.2 Definition — 24
2.3 The relationship between things, rights and property — 25
2.4 Classification of things — 28
    2.4.1 Classification according to negotiability — 28
    2.4.2 Classification according to nature — 32
    2.4.2.1 Corporeal and incorporeal things — 32
    2.4.2.2 Movable and immovable things — 33
    2.4.2.3 Single and composite things — 35
    2.4.2.4 Divisible and indivisible things — 38
    2.4.2.5 Consumable and non-consumable things — 39
    2.4.2.6 Fungible and non-fungible things — 39
2.5 Concluding remarks — 40

CHAPTER 3:	**RIGHTS**	**41**
3.1	**Introduction**	**41**
3.2	**Rights in respect of property**	**42**
	3.2.1 Conventional categories of real rights	42
	3.2.2 Real and personal rights	45
	3.2.2.1 Why the distinction between real and personal rights is important	46
	3.2.2.2 When the distinction is hard to draw	48
	3.2.2.3 Courts' approach to the distinction between real and personal rights	50
3.3	**The principle of publicity and the doctrine of notice**	**56**
	3.3.1 Publicity	56
	3.3.2 Doctrine of notice	58
	3.3.2.1 Successive sales	61
	3.3.2.2 Unregistered servitudes	62
3.4	**Concluding remarks**	**63**
CHAPTER 4:	**POSSESSION**	**65**
4.1	**What is possession**	**66**
4.2	**Nature of possessory rights**	**66**
4.3	**Elements of possession**	**70**
4.4	**Protection of possession**	**73**
	4.4.1 *Mandament van spolie*	75
	4.4.1.1 Circumstances for applicability	75
	4.4.1.2 Requirements	77
	4.4.1.3 Application of remedy to incorporeals	78
	4.4.1.4 Who can use the *mandament van spolie*?	80
	4.4.1.5 Relief available	80
	4.4.1.6 Defences	80
	4.4.2 Possessory action	83
	4.4.2.1 Circumstances for applicability	83
	4.4.2.2 Requirements	83
	4.4.2.3 Who can use the possessory action?	83
	4.4.2.4 Relief available	83
	4.4.2.5 Defences	83
	4.4.3 Interdict	84
	4.4.3.1 Circumstances for applicability	84
	4.4.3.2 Requirements	84
	4.4.3.3 Relief available	85
	4.4.3.4 Defences	85
	4.4.4 Delictual action	85
	4.4.4.1 Circumstances for applicability	85
	4.4.4.2 Requirements	85
	4.4.4.3 Who can use the delictual action?	86
	4.4.4.4 Relief available	86
	4.4.4.5 Defences	86
4.5	**Concluding remarks**	**86**

PART 2: OWNERSHIP
CHAPTER 5: CONTENT AND FORMS OF OWNERSHIP — 89

5.1	**Content of ownership**	**89**
	5.1.1 Definition of ownership	91
	5.1.2 Content and entitlements of ownership	92
	5.1.3 Limitations	95
5.2	**Forms of ownership**	**96**
	5.2.1 Individual title	96
	5.2.2 Co-ownership	96
	5.2.2.1 General elements and classes of common law co-ownership	97
	5.2.2.2 The undivided co-ownership share	98
	5.2.2.3 The commonly owned property	99
	5.2.2.4 Remedies	99
5.3	**Alternative forms of title**	**100**
	5.3.1 Sectional title schemes	100
	5.3.1.1 The nature of sectional ownership	101
	5.3.1.2 Management of a sectional title scheme	102
	5.3.2 Share block schemes	103
	5.3.3 Modified uses of share blocks and sectional title	104
	5.3.4 Communal property associations	105
	5.3.5 Indigenous land rights	107
	5.3.5.1 Pre-1991 tenure systems	110
	5.3.5.2 The Communal Land Rights Act 11 of 2004	111
5.4	**Concluding remarks**	**113**

CHAPTER 6: LIMITATIONS ON OWNERSHIP — 115

6.1	**Introduction**	**116**
6.2	**Types of limitations**	**117**
6.3	**Constitutional limitations: Section 25 of the Constitution**	**118**
	6.3.1 Constitutionality of interference with property	119
	6.3.1.1 Non-arbitrariness	123
	6.3.1.2 Law of general application	125
	6.3.1.3 Public purpose or public interest	126
	6.3.1.4 Compensation	127
	6.3.2 Proportionality of interferences	129
	6.3.3 Interferences that 'go too far'	130
6.4	**Private law limitations: Neighbour law**	**132**
	6.4.1 Nuisance	134
	6.4.1.1 Nuisance in the narrow sense	134
	6.4.1.2 Nuisance in the wide sense	137
	6.4.2 Traditional rules of neighbour law	139
	6.4.2.1 Encroachment	139
	6.4.2.2 Lateral support	143
	6.4.2.3 Party walls and fences	144
	6.4.2.4 Surface water	144
	6.4.2.5 Elimination of dangers, including collapsing buildings	145

6.5	**Public law limitations: Planning law**		**145**
	6.5.1	Structure of planning law	147
	6.5.2	The scope of planning law	148
	6.5.3	Content of planning law	149
	6.5.3.1	Land use planning	149
	6.5.3.1.1	Zoning	150
	6.5.3.2	Land use management	152
	6.5.4	Enforcement of planning measures	156
6.6	**Concluding remarks**		**156**

CHAPTER 7:	**ACQUISITION OF OWNERSHIP**		**159**
7.1	**Introduction**		**160**
7.2	**Original acquisition of ownership**		**161**
	7.2.1	Appropriation *(occupatio)*	163
	7.2.2	Accession *(accession)*	164
	7.2.2.1	General requirements	165
	7.2.2.2	Accession of movable property to other movable property	165
	7.2.2.3	Accession of movables to immovable property	167
	7.2.2.4	Accession of immovable property to immovable property	175
	7.2.3	Acquisition of fruits *(separatio* and *perceptio)*	175
	7.2.4	Manufacture *(specificatio)*	176
	7.2.5	Mingling and mixing *(confusio et commixtio)*	178
	7.2.6	Acquisitive prescription	179
	7.2.6.1	The requirement of possession	181
	7.2.6.2	The temporal requirement: Uninterrupted 30-year period	182
	7.2.6.2.2	Suspension	184
	7.2.7	Expropriation	188
7.3	**Derivative acquisition of ownership**		**188**
	7.3.1	Transfer of ownership as an abstract juristic act	190
	7.3.2	Requirements for a valid transfer of ownership	191
	7.3.2.1	The real agreement (subjective mental element)	192
	7.3.2.2	Sale of movables and transfer of ownership	194
	7.3.2.3	Delivery or registration (objective physical element)	197
	7.3.3	Delivery	197
	7.3.3.1	*Clavium traditio* (symbolic delivery)	201
	7.3.3.2	*Traditio longa manu* (delivery with the long hand)	201
	7.3.3.3	*Constitutum possessorium*	203
	7.3.3.4	*Traditio brevi manu* (delivery with the short hand)	204
	7.3.3.5	Attornment	206
	7.3.4	Transfer of immovable property – registration	211
	7.3.4.1	Publicity and certainty	211
	7.3.4.2	Effect of registration	212
7.4	**Concluding remarks**		**214**

CHAPTER 8:	PROTECTION OF OWNERSHIP	215
8.1	Introduction	215
8.2	**Real remedies**	**216**
	8.2.1 *Rei vindicatio*	217
	8.2.1.1 Requirements	218
	8.2.1.2 Defences against the rei vindicatio	219
	8.2.1.3 Limitations on the use of rei vindicatio	219
	8.2.2 *Actio negatoria*	226
8.3	**Delictual remedies**	**227**
	8.3.1 *Condictio furtiva*	227
	8.3.2 *Actio ad exhibendum*	228
	8.3.3 *Actio legis Aquiliae*	229
8.4	**Unjustified enrichment**	**229**
8.5	**Concluding remarks: How to choose a remedy**	**230**

PART 3:	SPECIFIC FORMS OF RIGHTS IN PROPERTY	
CHAPTER 9:	SERVITUDES AND RESTRICTIVE CONDITIONS	235
9.1	Introduction	235
9.2	**Definition and classification**	**236**
	9.2.1 Praedial servitudes	240
	9.2.1.1 Requirements	240
	9.2.1.2 Rights and duties	245
	9.2.1.3 Types of servitudes	246
	9.2.2 Personal servitudes	248
9.3	**Creation, termination and enforcement of servitudes**	**251**
	9.3.1 Creation	251
	9.3.2 Extinction or termination	253
	9.3.3 Enforcement	254
9.4	**Restrictive conditions**	**254**
	9.4.1 Definition and examples	255
	9.4.2 Nature, character and status of restrictive conditions	256
	9.4.3 Enforcement and defences	259
	9.4.3.1 Judicial remedies	259
	9.4.3.2 Statutory remedies	261
	9.4.3.3 Defences	261
	9.4.4 Removal or amendment of restrictive conditions	261
	9.4.4.1 Removal by court application	262
	9.4.4.2 Statutory procedures for removal	262
9.5	**Concluding remarks**	**263**

CHAPTER 10: MINERALS — 265

10.1 Introduction — 265
10.2 History of mineral law — 266
10.3 Ownership of minerals and petroleum under the MPRDA — 269
10.4 Important concepts used in the MPRDA — 273
10.5 Rights to minerals and petroleum — 274
    10.5.1 Nature of rights to minerals or petroleum — 276
    10.5.2 Content of rights to minerals or petroleum — 276
    10.5.2.1 Content of rights granted under the MPRDA — 277
    10.5.2.2 Activities and requirements — 278
    10.5.2.3 Competing rights of the surface owner — 278
    10.5.3 Transfer and encumbrance of rights to minerals or petroleum — 279
    10.5.4 Termination of rights to minerals or petroleum — 279
10.6 Social and environmental responsibility and liability of the mineral and petroleum industry — 280
    10.6.1 Environmental provisions of the MPRDA — 280
    10.6.2 Black economic empowerment and access to mining — 281
10.7 Mineral law as part of property law — 281
10.8 Concluding remarks — 282

CHAPTER 11: WATER — 283

11.1 Introduction — 283
11.2 Brief historical background — 284
11.3 The Water Act 54 of 1965 — 285
11.4 New water paradigm — 286
11.5 The Water Services Act 108 of 1997 — 287
11.6 The National Water Act 36 of 1998: A new approach — 288
    11.6.1 State acts as trustee — 288
    11.6.2 Access to and use of water — 288
    11.6.3 Servitudes — 289
    11.6.3.1 Servitudes in respect of water — 289
    11.6.3.2 Creation of servitudes — 290
    11.6.3.3 Rights and duties of relevant parties — 291
    11.6.3.4 Cancellation of servitudes — 291
11.7 Implications of the new water dispensation — 292
    11.7.1 Structural implications — 292
    11.7.2 Implications for the general public — 293
11.8 Concluding remarks — 294

CHAPTER 12: REAL SECURITY			**295**
12.1	Introduction		296
12.2	Personal and real security		297
12.3	Real security		298
	12.3.1	Categories of real security rights	298
	12.3.2	Functions of real security rights	298
	12.3.3	Nature of real security rights	299
	12.3.4	The security object	301
	12.3.5	The security parties	301
	12.3.6	The legal transactions	301
12.4	**Express real security rights: created by agreement**		**303**
	12.4.1	Special mortgage in immovable property	303
	12.4.1.1	Definition	303
	12.4.1.2	Constituting the mortgage	304
	12.4.1.3	Form and content of a mortgage bond	307
	12.4.1.4	Operation of a mortgage bond	309
	12.4.1.5	Types of mortgages	313
	12.4.1.6	Termination of the mortgage	314
	12.4.2	Pledge	314
	12.4.2.1	Definition	314
	12.4.2.2	Constituting a pledge	315
	12.4.2.3	Form and content	316
	12.4.2.4	Delivery	317
	12.4.2.5	Operation	319
	12.4.2.6	Termination of the pledge	320
	12.4.3	Notarial bonds	321
	12.4.3.1	General notarial bonds	322
	12.4.3.2	Special notarial bonds	322
12.5	**Tacit real security rights: created by operation of law**		**325**
	12.5.1	Tacit hypothecs	325
	12.5.1.1	Lessor's tacit hypothec	325
	12.5.1.2	Tacit hypothec of a seller under an instalment sale agreement	328
	12.5.2	Right of retention or lien	328
	12.5.2.1	Requirements	329
	12.5.2.2	Operation	330
	12.5.2.3	Types of liens	330
	12.5.3	Termination	331
12.6	**Judicial real security rights: created by court order**		**332**
12.7	**Concluding remarks**		**333**

PART 4: OVERVIEW OF THE PRINCIPLES OF PROPERTY LAW IN ITS NEW CONTEXT
CHAPTER 13: PROSPECTS OF PROPERTY LAW 337

13.1	Retrospect		337
13.2	Property law recontextualised		338
13.3	Principles and challenges		340
	13.3.1	Transmissibility	340
	13.3.2	*Numerus clausus*	341
	13.3.3	Publicity	343
	13.3.4	Abstraction	344
	13.3.5	Absoluteness	345
	14.3.6	Specificity	346
	14.3.7	Responsibility and trust	346
13.4	Concluding remarks		349

Bibliography 351

Table of cases 361

Table of legislation 373

Index 381

List of authors

Professor Hanri Mostert (Editor)

BA LLB LLM LLD (Stellenbosch University)
Hanri Mostert is a professor in the Department of Private Law at the University of Cape Town, where she teaches the law of property and the postgraduate course in comparative land law. She is also the UCT Law Faculty's Director of Research, and manages the Centre for Legal and Applied Research (CLEAR) at the University of Cape Town. Hanri has published widely on property law and related issues, and has a special interest in the public and constitutional law aspects of property law.

Ms Anne Pope (Editor)

Dip Lib (Stellenbosch University), BA LLB (Rhodes University), PG Dip International Research Ethics (University of Cape Town)
Anne Pope is a senior lecturer in the Department of Private Law at the University of Cape Town, where she teaches the law of property and courses on bioethics, HIV/Aids and the law, and research ethics. Anne's research interests include property and land law, including customary law, bioethics, research ethics, and family law, including customary law.

Professor Pieter Badenhorst

BLC LLB (University of Pretoria) LLM (University of the Witwatersrand) LLM (Yale University) LLD (University of Pretoria)
Pieter Badenhorst is an associate professor in the School of Law at Deakin University (Melbourne), where he teaches the law of property and land law. He is also an Attorney and Notary of the High Court of South Africa. Pieter has published widely on property law and mineral law.

Professor Warren Freedman

BCom LLB (University of the Witwatersand), LLM (University of Natal, now University of KwaZulu-Natal), PG Cert Higher Education (University of KwaZulu-Natal)
Warren Freedman is an associate professor in the Faculty of Law at the University of KwaZulu-Natal, where he teaches constitutional law and the law of property. He also teaches a postgraduate course in land use planning. Warren's research interests include the constitutional right to property, land reform, and coastal zone management law.

Professor Juanita Pienaar

BIuris, LLB, LLM, LLD (Potchefstroom University for Christian Higher Education, now the North-West University)
Juanita Pienaar is a professor and the Head of Department of Private Law at Stellenbosch University, where she teaches property law, advanced property law, and customary law. She is also an Acting Judge of the Land Claims Court. Juanita's research focuses on land law, land reform, and planning law.

Professor Jeannie van Wyk

BBibl (University of Pretoria), LLB (University of South Africa), LLM (University of the Witwatersrand), LLD (University of South Africa)

Jeannie van Wyk is a professor in the Department of Private Law at UNISA, where she teaches property law and the law relating to environmental management. She also teaches a postgraduate course in planning law at the University of the Witwatersrand. Jeannie is also involved in training environmental management inspectors.

Preface

This book grew out of a need, expressed by many South African property law teachers, for a text which provides an entry point to the law of property for law students, yet is sufficiently detailed to be useful to practitioners and researchers as a first point of reference. In addition, property law teachers want a text that gives active direction and assistance in highlighting and facilitating the acquisition of analytical, critical and problem-solving skills.

Our general attempt with this book is to present and discuss the law, to illustrate it innovatively, to critique it where appropriate, and to demonstrate critical engagement with the abstract notions of property law. In so doing, the purpose is to promote access to South African law of property in a contextually sensitive way, to inform and inspire new generations of property lawyers, whether they be students, teachers, researchers, or practitioners. Mere rote learning of legal principles and case names is insufficient for aspirant lawyers. Instead, well-honed skills of critical analysis and problem solving are indispensable. New generations of lawyers must be able to meet the additional challenge of being able to continue the development of sound jurisprudence based on constitutional principles, especially the values of the Bill of Rights. Given the importance of property, and the sensitivities that accompany land reform in particular, a sound understanding of basic principles of property law together with an ability to reflect on them are vital.

Furthermore, the idea was to collate the teaching experience of several teachers of property law to provide an approach that is harmonious and coherent, but is also varied and carries the mark of individual teachers. Teaching and learning take place in different ways for different people. This makes it desirable to demonstrate various approaches. We see this text as a tool for both law students and property law teachers. It can be used in the classroom to facilitate particular discussion, or at home to consolidate concepts and principles as they are applied in factual scenarios.

The goal is to empower rather than to dictate. Accordingly, the book provides distinctive didactic features in addition to its treatment of property law. These features include 'pause for reflection' boxes, 'counterpoint' boxes, and diagrams and other illustrative materials. A pause for reflection box contains information that either elaborates on or highlights particular aspects under consideration in the accompanying text. When there is uncertainty or controversy, specific points are discussed or an argument is presented to support a particular interpretation in counterpoint boxes. In addition, diagrams and other illustrative material appear in the text. The didactic features are explained more fully in the separate section entitled 'about the book'.

As an academic text, the aim of this book is to assist those wishing to study or engage with property law to understand the principles of the subject, and to encourage them to think critically and analytically about the implementation and impact thereof. For this reason, arguments developed on some points may deviate from the mainstream thinking in property law. As a didactic tool, this book aims to assist lecturers of property law to make this fascinating area of the law accessible to students, and to nurture the academic skills needed for students to master the subject. As a practitioner's companion, this book aims to provide an overview of basic property law principles, and their interpretation and implementation, alongside references to further sources of specialised property law knowledge.

This text is designed to complement the existing body of knowledge, to supplement it where necessary, and to provide commentary where appropriate. No attempt has been made to rewrite or to supplant existing textbooks. Instead, this book is written to be used either as a 'stand alone' text or alongside any recent, authoritative work on property law. However, from a didactic point of view, the recommendation is that it should serve as an entry point to the most recent standard works on property law. Allowing students to engage with and grasp the basic principles, but also to shift their attention to more detailed accounts of particular aspects of property law as provided by other more comprehensive texts, is good training for aspirant lawyers.

In addition, students should always be encouraged to engage with whole cases rather than only excerpts. It is only by reading and rereading whole judgments, including minority judgments, that a student develops a good feel for the discipline of law. The policy for a property law curriculum ought to be that fewer cases are studied in depth rather than many cases superficially. In-depth engagement promotes recognition of important principles at work, for example, precedent, distinguishing the role and weight of comparative and foreign law, as well as the justification (or lack thereof) for taking a different view from another (possibly binding) judgment. Excerpts can rarely be put to such diverse didactic uses.

The choice of cases for discussion in the text is governed by the value of the cases for teaching purposes. Naturally, any property law teacher would be free to substitute cases that better suit local conditions. However, where substitutions are made, it is strongly recommended that the general approach should remain the same: fewer cases, studied in depth, to permit development of analytical and problem-solving skills is preferable to learning lists of case names. In similar vein, to attempt to teach all content of this book to fledging law students would be a mistake. Depending on the structure of the curriculum, it is prudent to consider teaching the basic principles and separating the more advanced 'applied' areas to courses on a more advanced level. It is far more important that lawyers should have an excellent grasp of the basic principles of property law than that they should have covered as much territory as possible in the limited time allocated to the course.

The referencing policy adopted in this text is to refer to the most recent standard works on property law where detailed coverage of any particular aspect of property law appears. By implication, the sources relied on in these standard works are incorporated. 'Lean' referencing has been preferred over providing comprehensive lists of case law, detailed references to statutory law and similar practices. Thus, references are provided to be appropriately illustrative of recent judicial, or other, authority and to support the interpretation of certain principles. In general terms, references to the appropriate parts of recent standard works are included in pursuit of the recommendation outlined above.

In writing this book, we had the help and support of many people. In particular, the support of Penny Lane and Mark Townsend of Oxford University Press (SA) has seen this book through from conceptualisation to publication. Jacques Jacobs and Salona Lutchman of the University of Cape Town rendered excellent research assistance, and Bernard Heessen and the IT (Sharepoint) team of Stellenbosch University provided invaluable technical support. We also thank the University of Cape Town and the National Research Foundation for financial support, and Professor Tom Bennett and Professor Chuma Himonga of the University of Cape Town for advice on the relevance of customary law in modern property law. We are grateful to our friends and colleagues who provided the much valued support and encouragement that enriched the experience of producing this book. We pay special tribute to our co-authors who displayed patience, diligence, and a willingness to submit to editorial intervention which was generous in the extreme.

Hanri Mostert and Anne Pope
Cape Town
November 2009

About the book

The Principles of the Law of Property in South Africa is a pedagogically rich learning resource. This book is designed to form a strong foundation of understanding, to develop the skills to engage independently and judiciously with legal principles, and to create skilled and proficient lawyers.

Brief description of features

Pause for reflection boxes: These boxes may consider the policy ramifications of the law, how it works in practice, its logic and consistency with other principles, possible alternatives, and other key issues. This feature instils a broader and deeper understanding of the subject matter. It stimulates discussion, supports independent thinking, and develops the ability to engage meaningfully with relevant issues.

Counterpoint boxes: These boxes highlight specific criticisms of the law just described and identify reform options. They emphasise areas of controversy, problems with current law, and possible alternatives. This feature supports the ability to think critically and flexibly. It assists students to conceptualise legal issues from various perspectives, develops skills in formulating legal argument, and builds an awareness of various opinions about a particular principle.

Diagrams: These provide overviews and explain key concepts visually. This feature reinforces understanding, helps to clarify key concepts, and shows more clearly the interrelationship between distinct legal concepts and processes.

Tables: These are used to distinguish content, and assist with information management and conceptualisation.

PART ONE

GENERAL INTRODUCTION TO PROPERTY LAW

CHAPTER 1 Perspective on property law 3

CHAPTER 2 Property and things: Definitions and classifications 17

CHAPTER 3 Rights 41

CHAPTER 4 Possession 65

Chapter 1

Perspective on property law

'Without property there would be "no place for industry; because the fruit thereof is uncertain: and consequently no Culture on the Earth, no Navigation, or use of the commodities that may be imported by Sea; no commodious Building; no Instruments of moving, and removing such things as require much force; no Knowledge of the face of the Earth; no account of Time; no Arts; no Letters."'

Thomas Hobbes *Leviathan* part 1, ch 13, pp 64–65 (his capitalisation)

1.1	**Introduction**	3
1.2	**Property: An evasive term**	**4**
1.2.1	The use of 'property' in everyday language	4
1.2.2	What 'property' means to lawyers	5
1.3	**Context of property law: Framework and sources**	**6**
1.3.1	Function of property law	6
1.3.2	Place of property law	7
1.4	**Roots of property law**	**9**
1.4.1	Scope of property law	11
1.4.2	Sources of property law	15
1.5	**Mapping property law: The structure of this book**	**17**

1.1 Introduction

This book is about the law of property. It provides an overview of the most important principles of property law, and the way in which they are understood and applied in South Africa today. It does not propose to be exhaustive, nor does it attempt to be controversial. It mostly presents a conventional approach to the South African law of property through the prism of its Roman-Dutch law origins, and the new perspectives brought by constitutional and customary law, and land and resource reform. However, at some points, argument is developed that may perhaps be regarded as controversial rather than mainstream. The reason for this lies in the purpose of this book.

Property law is a highly abstract discipline, based on classical principles, tested by time and adapted where necessary. It is much more than simply a mildly interesting academic discipline. It is a core aspect of the law, and deals with such basic and everyday commercial activity that many legal practitioners derive their income mainly from practising in this field of law. Moreover, property law is also the battleground on which difficult socio-economic and political issues have to be resolved. All these may make a first experience of the subject daunting. This book aims to assist the initial encounter with South African property law.

The law of property has been expanded and adapted considerably over the past decades. Although we do not cover all its nooks and crannies, we provide a basis for studying, analysing and discussing this area of the law, and the manner in which it is being developed. Our focus is on the law of property as it stands today, with its shared historical roots and varied modern offshoots, its strict forms and its surprising inconsistencies.

1.2 Property: An evasive term

Property is a widely used term with many different connotations. Usually, the word 'property' refers to a particular object: 'her car', 'his house' or 'my farm'. In everyday life, no harm is done by referring to objects such as these as property. In the legal context, however, it is a more complex matter to use the word properly. In this section, we discuss the meaning of property in a broad, colloquial sense, before turning to its meaning in the law.

1.2.1 The use of 'property' in everyday language

On the street, one may hear the term used to refer to many different kinds of belongings. Usually, it involves the use of a genitive, or a possessive, pronoun: Susan may refer to 'her' property when she speaks of 'her' iPod; 'her' music collection that she bought online, and which is stored on the iPod; or 'her' song that she wrote herself and recorded at home. Jack may know that 'his' dog belongs to him in a way that 'his' daughter does not. Then, again, Heather, an estate agent, may talk about the 'properties' in her portfolio, meaning the homes that are for sale on the market and for which she seeks new owners.

The fact that people refer to an iPod, a music collection, a song, a home or a dog as property in everyday language does not mean that all these relationships are protected by the legal principles that we discuss in this book. Used in this sense, the term really is no more than a 'convenient expression',[1] denoting the claim of a particular individual to the item at hand.

The meaning of property is affected by the ideologies prevalent in the setting in which it is used. Property may refer to means to create wealth in a capitalist system. But it has a range of completely different meanings in a socialist or communist system[2] where, typically, a distinction is made between someone's personal belongings, 'people's property' (i.e. socialist property that belongs to everyone simultaneously and is administered by the state), and property used for practising a profession.[3]

In developing countries, such as South Africa, the term 'property' can also pertain to informal relations with land or other things. In other words, people regard their relations with certain things as property, even though such relations are not recognised or regulated by law. Because such relations are economically invisible, they have only limited potential to create wealth.[4] For instance, Nodyose buys a plot in Khayelitsha for R2 000 cash from someone who gives her his title deed and then disappears. She regards the plot as 'her' property, even though it is not registered in her name as required by law. She may be

---

1 Silberberg & Schoeman *Property* p 1.
2 Van Maanen, G 'Ownership as a Constitutional Right in South Africa – Articles 14 & 15 of the *Grundgesetz*: The German experience' (1993) 19 *Recht & Kritiek* 74 at 74.
3 See Mostert, H (2002) *The Constitutional Protection and Regulation of Property and its Influence on the Reform of Private Law and Landownership in South Africa and Germany – A Comparative Analysis* (Heidelberg, Springer) pp 535–542 for a discussion of the socialist example in East Germany before the Reunification of 1991.
4 De Soto, H (2001) *The Mystery of Capital: Why Capitalism Triumphs in the West and Fails Everywhere Else* (London, Black Swan) p 7.

surprised to learn that no bank is willing to grant her a loan to build a house on the plot. This is because she cannot offer the land as security for the loan if she is not the registered owner. Furthermore, if she wishes to sell 'her' land to Ayanda, she may learn that a complicated and expensive procedure involving a court order is necessary to substitute herself for the missing original seller as the registered owner. This substitution is necessary to enable her, in turn, to transfer ownership in the land legally to Ayanda. On the other hand, she may simply attempt another invisible hand-to-hand transaction, handing over the title deed against a cash payment, although that will place Ayanda in an equally precarious position.

Such examples illustrate the importance of understanding the legal meaning of property. This is discussed in the next section.

1.2.2   What 'property' means to lawyers

To understand exactly what is meant by the word 'property' in the law, many factors have to be considered. The nature and characteristics of the particular object referred to are important. So too is the relationship between the person and the object. Equally, the relationship between that person and other persons in respect of that object is relevant.[5] The weight that the economic and political system attaches to such an object and the relationships mentioned is also important. The extent to which the object can be regarded as a commodity may be relevant. Whether the Constitution acknowledges that such an object and the relationships involved deserve protection as property or should be regulated by the state, is another consideration that affects the understanding of the word 'property'.[6] Within the pluralistic South African context, cultural and ideological differences may influence its meaning in particular contexts. All these considerations feed into a definition of property as a legal term.

'Property' in the legal, technical sense of the word means rights: rights of people in or over certain objects or things.[7] Property is, therefore, a shorthand reference to someone's ability to undertake certain actions with certain kinds of objects. The term, however, does not only portray the relationships that exist in respect of various kinds of objects, but is also used to refer to the particular objects themselves. So, even lawyers use the term 'property' in many different contexts. They may use it to refer to any of at least three different concepts.[8] Sometimes, the term signifies the **right of ownership** in a legal object. This aspect is discussed further in chapter 5 below. In other circumstances, property simply refers to the **legal object** to which the right of ownership relates (of which there is a more detailed discussion in chapter 2). How the term is used depends on the specific context.[9] In some instances, it refers only to tangible objects, while in others it includes incorporeal objects. Furthermore, the presence of a clause protecting property as a fundamental right in the Constitution, gives property yet another meaning. Here it denotes all the **legal relationships that qualify for constitutional protection** under the constitutional property clause, even though they do not necessarily amount to either the right of ownership or the object to which ownership relates.[10] The rest of this chapter is devoted to explaining how property is defined and placed within the legal framework.

---

5   *Wille's Principles* p 406.
6   *Silberberg & Schoeman Property* p 1.
7   *Silberberg & Schoeman Property* p 9.
8   *Silberberg & Schoeman Property* p 1.
9   See e.g. *Samsudin v De Villiers Berange NO* [2006] SCA 79 (RSA) at para 45 where it was argued that, for purposes of the specific insolvency proceedings, references to 'property' in the relevant insolvency laws had to be interpreted to mean corporeal, movable property (rejected at para 54).
10 *Silberberg & Schoeman Property* p 1.

1.3 Context of property law: Framework and sources

We are all aware of the entrenched human habit of saying 'mine'![11] This is a word that you quickly learn as a toddler, and which you then use to assert your claims to your toys, your food, and your home. A while later, you learn to share. You learn how to behave towards others who may have claims to other toys, or another home, and how to behave towards those with whom you share your own toys. Property law formalises these behavioural patterns.

The relationships between people and objects form the basis of property law, which determines what people may and can do with the things that belong to them. It determines how they may protect their belongings. It also prescribes how people may acquire more things, or how they can dispose of these things. These considerations determine the place, function and scope of property law.

1.3.1 Function of property law

The formal function of property law is to harmonise different individual interests in respect of property; to guarantee and protect individual rights (and sometimes group rights) to property; and to control the relationships between natural or juristic persons, the things to which they are entitled, and the rights and obligations that arise from these relationships between different persons in respect of things. The fact that property enables these relationships between persons and objects, and persons and other persons on so many different levels induced the remark that 'man is not an island, he is more like a spaghetti junction'.[12] This cleverly summarises the basic result of the very existence of property, and it suggests that property law fulfils an important role in the web of relations spun around the basic, but all-encompassing, notion of property. Property law plays an important and dynamic role in the market economy, but it also acknowledges that property entails responsibilities.[13] The social function of property law is to manage the competing interests of persons who acquire and enjoy property interests, sometimes at the expense of one another. Of late, restrictions on the use of and trade in private property are on the increase.[14]

Property law protects private interests in property, but not in an absolute sense. Alongside the existing private law framework, the constitutional provisions operate to turn property law into a mechanism to determine the limits within which a person is free to deal with his property and that belonging to others. Hence, the law protects property and the freedom to enjoy it, but it also presumes that all who enjoy this freedom are bound by the duties it entails. So, for instance, Nelson may be free to own a car. The law prescribes, however, that he may use the car only under specific conditions, i.e. when he has a valid driver's licence. To obtain such a licence, he is expected to know the rules of the road, and be skilled enough to pass the driving test. When he uses the car, he is expected to abide by the traffic rules. In this way, the law ensures that the freedom to own and use a car does not interfere with the freedom of anyone else who also uses the road, or with the interest of the public in general in having safe roads.

---

11 The idea in this paragraph is articulated well in Cooke, EJ (2006) *Land Law* (Oxford, Oxford University Press) p 1, whence it is borrowed and adapted.
12 Cooke, EJ (2006) *Land Law* (Oxford, Oxford University Press) p 1.
13 *Silberberg & Schoeman Property* p 3.
14 *Wille's Principles* p 406.

1.3.2 Place of property law

Generally, private law is said to regulate the relationships between individuals. Public law regulates the relationships between the state and individuals. The two spheres of law are distinguished from each other with reference to whether they deal with relationships in the absence of or in the presence of state authority.[15]

The diagram below represents a conventional depiction of the place of property law in the South African legal system. Traditionally, property law is regarded as part of patrimonial law. Patrimonial law refers to the law that deals with the assets or estate of an individual. It comprises not only property law, but also the law of succession and the law of contract, among others. These disciplines in turn fall under private law.

Figure 1.1: Property law in the legal system

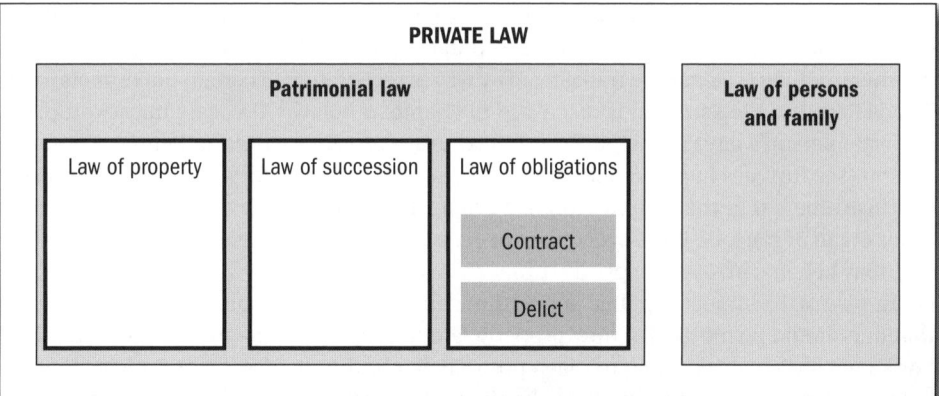

The reason for the classification lies in the formal function of property law. This is to regulate the relationships between individuals regarding certain objects; the relationships between individuals and such objects; as well as the rights and obligations that emanate from these relationships. This function typically falls within the ambit of private law as it draws upon the doctrine of subjective rights, which lies at the heart of private law. Essentially, this doctrine accords legal status to individuals and some types of social entities or associations of people.[16] The fact that the law affords human beings (i.e. natural persons) and some kinds of associations (i.e. juristic persons) legal subjectivity means that such persons bear capacities, rights, entitlements and duties. These capacities, rights and obligations can be exercised in respect of various types of 'legal objects'. A 'legal object' is anything in respect of which a person may hold a right. In property law, these rights and duties relate to a class of legal objects termed 'things' *(res)*. This term is analysed more closely below.[17]

A wide range of objects can be subject to property rights. For example, South African law has permitted the use of proprietary remedies to protect both tangible and intangible

---

15 Du Plessis, LM (1999) *An Introduction to Law* (Cape Town, Juta) pp 130–131.
16 Du Plessis, LM (1999) *An Introduction to Law* (Cape Town, Juta) pp 134–138; Davel, C and Jordaan, R (2005) *Law of Persons* 4 ed (Cape Town, Juta) pp 3–7.
17 See ch 2 below.

objects. Intangible shares[18] and the interest in a close corporation[19] have already been treated as property by the courts, and the rules applicable and remedies available to protect proprietary claims to real estate (land),[20] vehicles[21] and animals[22] have been invoked to protect these tangible objects as well. Objects may be protected because they are commodities and have a monetary value, or because they have sentimental value, i.e. they mean something to someone personally.

Although property law is classified traditionally as falling under private law, it cannot be divorced from public law. It is becoming ever more obvious that a diagram such as the one above represents only a part of what property law is really about. Some aspects of property law are regulated in the context of private law. For this purpose, the diagram is appropriate. Other aspects, which involve state authority, fall under public law. The diagram above does not deal with this important aspect of property law at all. The state plays an active role in many aspects of private life, also in arenas governed by property law. So, for instance, there are detailed ways in which the state (in the form of a municipality) may regulate building on land. (Building regulations are discussed in chapter 6 below.) The state prescribes the manner in which land may be transferred by way of registration of certain documents in the Deeds Registry. (Registration is discussed in chapter 3 below.) The state may expropriate a private person's land in the public interest, subject to compensation being paid to that person (see further chapter 6 below), or someone may have to forfeit property because it was instrumental in the commission of a crime. These are a few examples of how one or other organ of state, be it the executive, the legislature, law enforcement authorities or the like, may become involved in private property matters.

In view of the impact of public law on the scope and content of property law, we suggest that one should be mindful of how property law straddles both the private law and public law spheres when attempting to place property law within the legal system. The diagram below illustrates the place of property law in both the private law and public law spheres.

---

18 *Etkind v Hicor Trading Ltd* 1999 (1) SA 111 (W) at 125B–C. This decision has been criticised. See *Silberberg & Schoeman Property* p 199.
19 *Ben-Tovim v Ben-Tovim and Others* 2001 (3) SA 1074 (C).
20 *Badenhorst v Balju, Pretoria Sentraal, en Andere* 1998 (4) SA 132 (T).
21 *Khan v Minister of Law and Order* 1991 (3) SA 439 (T).
22 *R v Mafohla* 1958 (2) SA 373 (SR); *Reck v Mills* 1990 (1) SA 751 (A).

Figure 1.2: Property law in relation to private law and public law under the Constitution

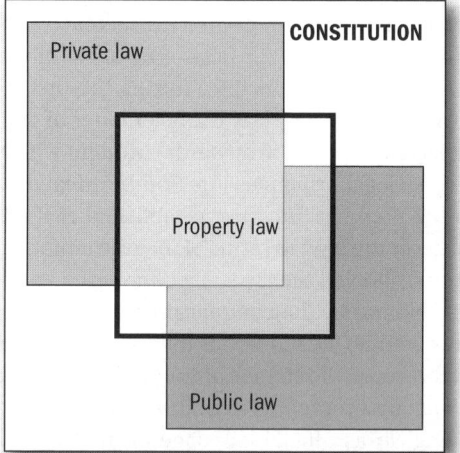

The fact that property law incorporates aspects of private law **and** public law needs to be factored into a discussion of the scope of this area of the law. In the sections below, we deal with this in more detail. It is necessary first to discuss the sources of South African property law by tracing its history.

1.4 Roots of property law

South Africa is home to one of the world's mixed legal systems. Two main Western or European legal cultures meet in the South African legal system, forming a blend of legal traditions.[23] The bipartite colonial history of South Africa had a profound influence on the eventual mixture of legal cultures prevalent in the legal system today.

On the one hand, South African common law originates from the legal tradition of the European continent. This is referred to as 'civil law' or the 'continental' or 'civilian tradition' and entails the legal rules upon which most of the legal systems of the formerly western part of the European continent are based. Essentially, these principles are derived from Roman law. There were, however, differences in the manner in which these principles were interpreted in the various continental jurisdictions of, for instance, France, Germany and the Netherlands. South African law is rooted in the civilian tradition because of importance attached to principles deriving primarily from Roman law. In particular, the South African common law is based on Roman law as it was understood and practised in the province of Holland in the mid-seventeenth century, the time when the first European (mainly Dutch) merchants travelled to and eventually settled at the Cape of Good Hope.[24] This is why South African common law is referred to as Roman-Dutch law.

---

23 Zimmermann, R 'Synthesis in South African Private Law: Civil Law, Common Law and usus hodiernus Pandectarum' (1986) 103 *SALJ* at 259–289; Du Plessis, JE 'The Promises and Pitfalls of Mixed Legal Systems: The South African and Scottish Experiences' (1998) 9 *Stell LR* 338 at 339.

24 Erasmus, HJ 'Thoughts on Private Law in a Future South Africa' (1994) 5 *Stell LR* 105 at 107. See Van Zyl, DH (1983) *Geskiedenis van die Romeins-Hollandse Reg* (Durban, Butterworths) pp 421*ff*; De Wet, JC 'Die Resepsie van die Romeins-Hollandse Reg in Suid-Afrika' (1958) 21 *THRHR* at 84*ff*; Pauw, P 'Die Romeins-Hollandse Reg in Oënskou' (1980) *TSAR* at 32*ff*.

On the other hand, South African law was also influenced significantly by English common law. This term refers to the legal rules applicable in England[25] and, more particularly, the rules applicable at the time when the second wave of colonisation of South Africa under British rule commenced at the beginning of the nineteenth century. Whereas the reception of Roman-Dutch legal principles during the first 150 years of white settler occupation in South Africa (1652-1795) was really a matter of chance,[26] the imposition of British colonial rule (especially from 1806 onwards) brought with it a more formalised, yet subtle, infiltration of English legal principles into South African law.[27]

The British allowed the Roman-Dutch law established at the Cape between 1652 and 1795 to continue as the law of the land in terms of the rule enunciated by Lord Mansfield in *Campbell v Hall*.[28] This rule allowed the laws of a conquered territory to continue in force until they were expressly altered by the conqueror. The power to introduce new laws was never used to abolish the Roman-Dutch law at the Cape completely, or to replace it with English law.[29] Gradually, however, the change of colonial power began to show an important and decisive effect on legal developments in South Africa. This was notable, for instance, in the introduction of English as official language of the Cape Colony and its courts. It contributed to the subtle infiltration of English concepts into the substance of the law.[30] English legal principles were introduced especially into mercantile law,[31] administrative law and procedural law through Acts of Parliament.[32]

Over time, a mixed legal system developed in South Africa. Influences from both the English common law and continental civil law traditions were incorporated in response to the governing political forces at various points in South Africa's colonial history. The impact of English common law and European civil law on South African common law varies among the different subdisciplines.[33] Property law is influenced strongly by civilian principles.[34] This implies a particular understanding of the relationship between ownership and other rights in respect of property. It also implies a particular understanding of the content of ownership and other rights to property.

---

25 The English common law is not to be confused with the South African common law, which refers to the legal rules received and applicable in South Africa.
26 During the first 150 years of settlement, formal colonisation of South Africa was not an objective. The Cape served merely as a refreshment post and half-way station for ships on mercantile travels between Europe and India. Until 1795, the territory was governed not by the government of the United Netherlands, but by the board of directors of the United East India Company (VOC). No explicit provision was made as to which legal principles were applicable. Because the earliest settlers had strong relations with the law of the province Holland, where the VOC was situated, these legal principles were generally applied to settle disputes. See Du Plessis, JE 'The Promises and Pitfalls of Mixed Legal Systems: The South African and Scottish Experiences' (1998) 9 *Stell LR* 338 at 340; Van Zyl, DH (1983) *Geskiedenis van die Romeins-Hollandse Reg* (Durban, Butterworths) pp 423-428.
27 Britain occupied the Cape temporarily from 1795 to 1803 to protect its interests against the onslaught of political changes brought about in Europe by the French Revolution. In 1806 it reassumed occupation of the Cape. This situation endured until South Africa gained independence from colonial rule in the twentieth century.
28 1774 1 Cowp 204 at 209, 98 ER 1045 at 1047.
29 Erasmus, HJ 'Thoughts on Private Law in a Future South Africa' (1994) 5 *Stell LR* 105 at 109.
30 Van Zyl, DH (1983) *Geskiedenis van die Romeins-Hollandse Reg* (Durban, Butterworths) pp 450, 453*ff*.
31 E.g. maritime and shipping law, insurance law and intellectual property law.
32 Erasmus, HJ 'Thoughts on Private Law in a Future South Africa' (1994) 5 *Stell LR* 105 at 110; Van Zyl, DH (1983) *Geskiedenis van die Romeins-Hollandse Reg* (Durban, Butterworths) pp 455*ff*; Du Plessis, JE 'The Promises and Pitfalls of Mixed Legal Systems: The South African and Scottish Experiences' (1998) 9 *Stell LR* 338 at 340.
33 Du Plessis, JE 'The Promises and Pitfalls of Mixed Legal Systems: The South African and Scottish Experiences' (1998) 9 *Stell LR* 338 at 340.
34 Van der Walt, AJ 'Tradition on Trial: A Critical Analysis of the Civil-Law Tradition in South African Property Law' (1995) 11 *SAJHR* 169; Zimmermann, R & Visser, DP (1996) 'Introduction: South African Law as a Mixed Legal System' in Zimmermann, R & Visser, DP (eds) *Southern Cross: Civil Law and Common Law in South Africa* (Cape Town, Juta) p 28.

For the greatest part of the nineteenth century, the Roman-Dutch basis of South African law was supplemented and reinforced by German Pandectism, for which an affinity existed among the Dutch scholars whose work was influential in the formative years of South African property law.[35] The Pandectist method entailed a particular historical interpretation and application of classical Roman law principles.[36] Its major contribution to modern South African property law is its account of property rights as subjective rights.[37] The doctrine of subjective rights still forms the backbone of the South African civil law concept of ownership, which is described as the pinnacle in a hierarchy of rights, because of the way in which it is enforced, and because of its broad content. Furthermore, the Pandectist method of scientific systematisation resulted in the depiction of ownership as a universal, timeless, abstract and logical concept.[38] This typification persists to this day, even though it is recognised as insufficiently mindful of the relativity of property rights and the responsibilities underlying such rights.[39]

This civil law-based understanding of property law, however, does not apply to all property relations in South Africa since people living under indigenous customary law and associated statutory arrangements adhere to a different system of distribution and protection of property. What is regarded as property might also differ in these settings. It is only recently that customary relations to property have begun to receive close attention as developments around land reform unfold. We discuss this in more detail in the following sections.

1.4.1 Scope of property law

'Property law' is often regarded as a synonym for 'the law of things'. The latter term is used pursuant to the Afrikaans term for the subject matter, '*sakereg*'. Yet, the terms 'property' and 'things' differ in meaning.

---

35 Van der Walt, AJ 'The South African Law of Ownership: A Historical and Philosophical Perspective' (1992) 25 *De Jure* 446 at 454, with reference to the first edition of Van der Merwe *Sakereg* (1979).
36 The work of the Pandectists typically involved a return to and expansion of the work of the classical Roman lawyers. This created the impression of the universality and timelessness of the principles discussed, which was further enhanced by the reflected authority of the notable Roman lawyers. This method was later exposed for disregarding the underlying and surrounding circumstances of certain legal principles and institutions, and their historical antecedents. Van der Walt, AJ 'The South African Law of Ownership: A Historical and Philosophical Perspective' (1992) 25 *De Jure* at 454.
37 Van der Walt, AJ 'Marginal notes on powerful(l) legends: critical perspectives on property theory' (1995) 58 *THRHR* 396-420; Van der Walt, AJ 'Tradition on Trial: a Critical Analysis of the Civil-Law Tradition in South African Property Law' (1995) 11 *SAJHR* 169-206.
38 Van der Walt, AJ 'The South African Law of Ownership: A Historical and Philosophical Perspective', (1992) 25 *De Jure* 446 at 455.
39 *LAWSA* Vol 27(1) at paras 297-298. See further ch 13 below.

> **PAUSE FOR REFLECTION**
>
> **Terminology**
>
> Afrikaans terminology is singled out here because of the important status that this language had, alongside English, as one of the official court languages during the twentieth century when many of the South African common law principles were developed. Afrikaans remains the only South African language, apart from English, in which scholarly work on property law has been published. There is no Afrikaans equivalent for the term 'property' as it is used here. The Afrikaans term '*eiendom*' may be equated with property in the sense of the object of a specific legal relationship. Yet, the Afrikaans term '*eiendomsreg*' refers only to the legal relationship of ownership, and is no equivalent for the English term 'property law'. The closest translation of the term 'property law' would be '*reg met betrekking tot eiendom*'. However, this is not a usual phrase in Afrikaans legal terminology.

The term property is used broadly to refer to a wide variety of patrimonial assets, not all of which are necessarily tangible or even protected as property in private law. The term things, however, is usually understood in a more restricted sense, referring only to tangible or corporeal objects.[40] The distinction is the result of differences in academic opinion about the characteristics of the legal object that is core to this field of law.[41] The term 'property law' is preferred here, because this area of the law covers not only private law relations in respect of particular types of legal objects that are corporeal or incorporeal, but also public law relations with a proprietary character, and the resultant rights and interests.

The system of rules that comprises property law regulates both factual and legal relationships with regard to things.[42] Hence it covers relationships such as possession of a toy or land, as well as ownership of such types of property. The law of property defines the legal object to which it applies, and classifies various types of property according to their nature and consequences. It further distinguishes different kinds of relationships in respect of property and classifies them, for instance, as real rights or personal rights. The law of property indicates how these rights differ from each other, and how one may distinguish between different kinds of real rights according to their scope and according to the holder of the right. How such rights may be acquired, lost and protected is also determined, as well as the consequences of factual proprietary relationships that do not qualify as rights, such as bare possession. The limitations that may be imposed upon these relationships by the law forms another important part of the overall scope of property law.

The scope of property law has always been influenced significantly by the host of statutory provisions that deal with special regulation of certain aspects of property. One of the oldest examples of such statutory development of common law principles is the imposition of a streamlined land registration system under the rule of Sir John Cradock,[43] and, later, the codification and unification of registration practices during the earliest decades of the twentieth century.[44] In particular, land law was (and remains) the playground of the legislature. During the twentieth century, statutory deviations from the common law

---

40 Van der Merwe *Sakereg* pp 20–23.
41 See Van der Merwe *Sakereg* p 21 and compare *Silberberg & Schoeman Property* p 3. See further *LAWSA* Vol 27(1) at para 195. For a more detailed discussion, see ch 2 below.
42 *Wille's Principles* p 406.
43 Proclamation on Conversion of Loan Places to Quitrent Tenure, 1813 (06.08.1813).
44 Deeds Registries Act 13 of 1918; Deeds Registries Act 47 of 1937.

system of private property law were effected to serve the purposes of high-finance property developments, upper-class housing and recreational and commercial real estate. These deviations became known as the 'new patterns of landownership'.[45] They were not aimed at serving the needs of the underprivileged, homeless, poor or dispossessed under the apartheid regime. At the lower end of the property market, the laws introduced hampered rather than promoted access to land, while embarrassed property lawyers turned a blind eye. The estimated 17 000 statutory measures issued by 1991[46] to regulate land control and racial diversity, and to give effect to the 'grand social experiment'[47] of spatial separation of races under apartheid, barely received so much as a mention in the textbooks on property and land law.[48]

Yet the area of land law witnessed the most far-reaching statutory changes to the common law of property during the twentieth century.[49] Some fifty years before the formal introduction of apartheid, indigenous black people were excluded statutorily from dealing with an overwhelmingly large part of the country's land.[50] Then, as South Africa began shedding the perceived constraints of European colonial domination, the infamous Group Areas Acts[51] fragmented the country into areas designated for the so-called white, Indian and coloured races. These laws gave rise to forced removals and evictions under apartheid.[52] Excessive law making and manipulation of existing notions of property resulted in the collapse of administrative and legal certainty and, moreover, massive underdevelopment. The network of primary and subordinate legislation that sustained the intricate web of statutory rights and obligations forming the backbone of apartheid[53] inevitably encroached upon common law and indigenous property rights.[54] These apartheid land laws resulted in a seriously compromised system of land rights. On the one hand, the existing Roman-Dutch-based common law was manipulated to protect rights in hierarchical fashion, affording best protection to ownership and registrable[55] real rights in land. In principle, these rights could be held only by the small white minority.[56] On the other hand, the system was used to preclude blacks from obtaining and holding land rights protected by the acclaimed

---

45 Cowen, DV (2008) 'New patterns of land ownership: the transformation concept of ownership as Plena in re Potestas' in Cowen, S (ed) *Cowen on law: selected essays* (Cape Town, Juta) pp 280-324.
46 Van der Merwe, CG & Pienaar, JM (1997) in Jackson, P & Wilde, DC (eds) *The Reform of Property Law* (Dartmouth, Ashgate) pp 334-336.
47 *Minister of the Interior v Lockhat* 1961 (2) SA 587 (A) at 602E-F.
48 Van der Merwe, CG & Pienaar, JM (1997) in Jackson, P & Wilde, DC (eds) *The Reform of Property Law* (Dartmouth, Ashgate) pp 348-349.
49 The Black Land Act 27 of 1913, the first in a long line of racially motivated land laws, provided the statutory basis for territorial segregation by dividing South Africa into the so-called 'black spots', on the one hand, and the 'non-African' areas, on the other. See maps and illustrations in Van der Merwe, CG & Pienaar, JM (1997) in Jackson, P & Wilde, DC (eds) *The Reform of Property Law* (Dartmouth, Ashgate) pp 336-337.
50 Murphy, J (1996) 'The restitution of land after apartheid: the constitutional and legislative framework' in Rwelamira, MR & Werle, G (eds) *Confronting Past Injustices, Approaches to Amnesty, Punishment, Reparation and Restitution in South Africa and Germany* (Durban, Butterworths) pp 113-122.
51 Act 41 of 1950; Act 36 of 1966.
52 Van der Merwe, CG & Pienaar, JM (1997) in Jackson, P & Wilde, DC (eds) *The Reform of Property Law* (Dartmouth, Ashgate) pp 334-340.
53 Eventually, fourteen different land control systems were in place in four national states, six self-governing territories and four provincial governments, restricting 80 per cent of the South African population to 13 per cent of the country's land. Bennett, TW (1996) 'African land – A history of dispossession' in Zimmermann, R & Visser, DP (eds) *Southern Cross: Civil Law and Common Law in South Africa* (Cape Town, Juta) p 65.
54 *Silberberg & Schoeman Property* pp 494-501.
55 This word is sometimes spelled as 'registerable' in the law reports and other texts. The dictionary spelling is 'registrable'.
56 Mostert, H (2003) 'The Diversification of Land Rights and its Implications for a New Land Law in South Africa' in Cooke, EJ *Modern Studies in Property Law Vol II* (Oxford, Hart Publishing) pp 4-6.

common law system of property and backed by the sophisticated and effective registration system.[57] Instead, the plethora of legislative and administrative measures forced blacks to resort to forms of land control that were not recognised, publicised or effectively protected. These 'lesser' rights included rights to tribal land[58] and rights in terms of statutes or permits.[59] Many South Africans did not enjoy any security of land title provided by the law, and, accordingly, could not rely on such relations to procure funds to improve their living conditions.[60]

By 1991, South African property law and, in particular, land law sported significant double standards. The acclaimed Roman-Dutch property law was cosmetically expanded to serve the needs of the higher (and whiter) end of the market (to enable apartment ownership, time-share rights and the like), while that same system was manipulated to restrict land control at the lower (or black) end of the market. Metaphorically, the magnificently developed 'façade of property law' hid the formalised inequality and institutionalised discrimination that made its 'backyard a dump'.[61]

Since the early 1990s, attempts have been made to reverse the discriminatory system of land law, a legacy of the apartheid era. To redress the imbalances that resulted from apartheid land law, a large-scale land reform programme was designed. This forms part of the constitutional reform that introduced the new democratic dispensation with the landmark elections of 1994. In the South African Constitution, property (which includes land) is protected as a fundamental right and the circumstances under which property may be regulated or expropriated in the hands of private owners are prescribed.[62] The constitutional property clause (s 25 of the Constitution) also contains extensive provisions that endorse the reform of land law. It provides for restitution in kind or in money to persons or communities dispossessed of property after 1913 as a result of past racial discrimination.[63] It further envisages that the state must ensure, within the bounds of its available resources, that people can gain equitable access to land.[64] It envisages legally secure tenure for those whose land rights were previously legally precarious because of apartheid.[65] In addition, the constitutional property clause enables the state to take steps to bring about reform of and equitable access to all natural resources.[66] Section 26 of the Constitution provides for access to housing as a separate fundamental right.

The constitutional mandate for land reform was translated into policy with the publication of the 1997 White Paper on Land Policy. This policy document sets out the overall targets for reform and provides guidelines according to which reform must occur. The White Paper poses fourfold objectives for reform: (1) to redress the injustices of apartheid; (2) to foster national reconciliation and stability; (3) to underpin economic growth; and (4) to improve

---

57   Mostert, H (2003) 'The Diversification of Land Rights and its Implications for a New Land Law in South Africa' in Cooke, EJ *Modern Studies in Property Law Vol II* (Oxford, Hart Publishing) pp 4–6.
58   Van der Walt, AJ (1999) 'Property Rights and Hierarchies of Power: A Critical Evaluation of Land Reform Policy in South Africa' in Du Plessis, LM (ed) 64 *Koers* (Potchefstroom University) p 262.
59   E.g. Group Areas Act 36 of 1966; Black Administration Act 38 of 1927; Proclamation succeeding the Regulations for the Administration and Control of Townships in Black Areas R293 *Government Gazette* 373 of 1962-11-16.
60   Nonyana, MR 'The Communal Land Rights Bill 2002 and related legislation' (December 2002) *Butterworths Property Law Digest* 4 at 7.
61   Van der Walt, AJ (1991) 'The Future of Common Law Landownership' in Van der Walt, AJ (ed) *Land Reform and the Future of Landownership in South Africa* (Cape Town, Juta) p 28.
62   Section 25(1)–(3) of the Constitution.
63   Section 25(7) of the Constitution.
64   Section 25(5) of the Constitution.
65   Section 25(6) and (9) of the Constitution.
66   Section 25(4)(*a*) and (8) of the Constitution.

household welfare and to alleviate poverty.[67] The White Paper addresses and defines the three separate but interconnected elements of the overall reform initiative, namely land restitution, redistribution of land, and tenure reform.[68]

In the wake of the White Paper, a host of laws dealing with issues of land reform have been promulgated. These laws are supplemented by legislative mechanisms pertaining to land administration and regulation[69] and, increasingly, also more explicit legislative endeavours to achieve economic empowerment.[70] The impact of the comprehensive land reform programme on the principles of land law in particular and property law in general, as well as the manner in which existing principles are used to move customary land tenure principles closer to the common law principles, are covered in various chapters throughout this book. By way of introduction, it may be indicated that the new constitutional dispensation (which supports property protection and regulation, mandates the land reform programme, provides basic rights to access housing and seeks to give equal recognition to common law and customary law principles) has already had a significant influence on property law. It has expanded the traditional sources of property law considerably as the next section indicates.

1.4.2 Sources of property law

The rules of South African property law are formulated in the common law, the mixed roots of which have been discussed above. As was indicated, Roman-Dutch principles of property law still form the backbone of the South African common law pertaining to property. They have been supplemented and expanded extensively by statute, as explained above. Case law (precedent) is a further source of property law where the courts interpret and develop the common law principles of property in South Africa.

Common law, precedent and statutory law hence were traditionally regarded as the sources of South African property law. Under the new constitutional dispensation, these sources can no longer be regarded as exhaustive. The Constitution of the Republic of South Africa is now the founding and directional document for the country's legal system. Since it came into force, all sources of law must be viewed in light of the Constitution. In particular, the Constitution allows for the protection of property, but also for the reform of property relations. Hence, the Constitution itself has become a source of property law. The Constitutional Court illustrated this fact in *Port Elizabeth Municipality v Various Occupiers*.[71] The case concerned the fate of a small group of unlawful occupiers. They had been settled for quite some time on unused, private, vacant land in the jurisdiction of the municipality, which applied for their eviction at the instance of the landowners and a large number of concerned neighbourhood residents. Essentially, the Constitutional Court had to decide whether the unlawful occupiers could be evicted under the particular circumstances. The court held that it could not endorse the eviction of the unlawful occupiers. In the course of the judgment, Sachs J articulated the 'new task' of the judiciary, namely to manage the counterpositioning of conventional rights of ownership against the new,

---

67 White Paper on SA Land Policy April 1997 at v.
68 Para 4 of the White Paper.
69 E.g. the Deeds Registries Act 47 of 1937, the Development Facilitation Act 67 of 1995 and the Land Survey Act 8 of 1997.
70 E.g. the Land Redistribution for Agricultural Development Plan (LRAD) introduced in April 2000.
71 2005 (1) SA 217 (CC).

equally relevant, right not to be arbitrarily deprived of a home, without creating hierarchies of privilege.[72] The judgment indicated that the legislative centrepiece relied upon for the eviction, the Prevention of Illegal Eviction from and Unlawful Occupation of Land Act[73] (PIE), requires the judiciary to 'infuse elements of grace and compassion into the formal structures of the law'. According to the court, both the Constitution and PIE confirm that 'we are not islands unto ourselves', and that competing interests must be balanced in a principled way to promote the constitutional vision of 'a caring society based on good neighbourliness and shared concern'. The court described the Bill of Rights specifically as 'a structured, institutionalised and operational declaration' of the South African society's 'need for human interdependence, respect and concern'.[74] This analysis represents a profound commentary on the way in which property law is to be understood in light of the Constitution.

In addition, the shift to a constitutional dispensation gives new impetus to sources of law such as customary law, which must now be given equivalent consideration, in appropriate circumstances, as is given to the existing common law, case law and statutes. The effect of the constitutional dispensation on the redefinition of the sources of property law is illustrated by the reasoning of the Constitutional Court and the Supreme Court of Appeal in the dispute between the Richtersveld community and the diamond-mining corporation Alexkor,[75] concerning the restoration of the ancestral lands of the indigenous Richtersveld community. The reasoning also demonstrates how the redefinition of the sources of South African property law affects the protection offered to relationships with land.

The community's claim to the Richtersveld, an area containing diamondiferous land, was brought in terms of the Restitution of Land Rights Act.[76] This Act is the statutory mechanism giving effect to the government's land reform-related restitution programme. An important aspect of the case was the community's assertion that they used the land according to their indigenous practices and customs. This claim was confirmed in both the Supreme Court of Appeal and the Constitutional Court and, on the basis thereof, the finding was that the land had to be returned to the community.

To determine what the customary law ownership of the land entailed, the Supreme Court of Appeal equated it with common law ownership, while the Constitutional Court indicated that the content must be ascertained by studying the customs and uses of the community. On completing this exercise, it was decided that the Richtersveld community's claim to the land incorporated a claim to the minerals in the land, and that the community's entitlement to both the land and the minerals in it had to be acknowledged and restored. This included the right of the community to claim compensation for the past exploitation of the land by the diamond-mining company and the state. The basis and content of indigenous land rights is discussed further in chapter 5 below.

---

72   *Port Elizabeth Municipality v Various Occupiers* 2005 (1) SA 217 (CC) at para 23.
73   Act 19 of 1998.
74   *Port Elizabeth Municipality v Various Occupiers* 2005 (1) SA 217 (CC) at para 37.
75   *Richtersveld Community v Alexkor (Pty) Ltd* 2001 (3) SA 1293 (LCC); *Richtersveld Community v Alexkor* 2003 (6) SA 104 (SCA); *Alexkor (Pty) Ltd and Another v Richtersveld Community and Others* 2004 (5) SA 460 (CC).
76   Act 22 of 1994.

PAUSE FOR REFLECTION	**Customary law and common law**

The *Richtersveld* decisions attempted earnestly to place both the customary dispensation and the common law rules regarding land on an equal footing as required in terms of the Constitution, which acknowledges the pluralistic character of the South African legal system. The approaches of the Supreme Court of Appeal and the Constitutional Court nevertheless varied starkly in this regard. Whereas the Supreme Court of Appeal attempted to reconcile the customary concept of landownership with the common law concept, the Constitutional Court indicated that these concepts are distinctly different.[77]

These different approaches illustrate a dilemma in the portrayal of the current principles of property, such as is attempted in this book. We acknowledge that the time has come to take legal pluralism seriously, and applaud the Constitutional Court's approach in (re-)defining the concept of landownership in view of the pluralistic setting. We also realise, however, that customary property relationships serve functions and purposes very different from those of property in a westernised or industrialised context. The former relationships are important in customary communities for various reasons, but in everyday commercial activity, the latter relationships are active and important. Our point of departure in this book is that the basic tenets of customary property differ so extensively from the principles of property applicable generally that it would be wholly inappropriate to attempt a large-scale reconciliation of these principles here. Where customary principles of property indeed interface with common law principles of property, we incorporate this into the discussion.

1.5 Mapping property law: The structure of this book

This book is divided into four parts. Part 1, to which this chapter belongs, contains a general introduction to property law and its most basic concepts: property and things; rights and possession. The discussion in this section attempts to provide a broad overview of how these basic concepts feature in the practice and theory of property law, and lays the foundation for further, more specialised discussion in other parts of the book.

Part 2 contains a discussion of the most extensive and prominent relationship between a person and property, namely ownership. It explores the content of this important concept in property law, and the forms of ownership acknowledged in South African law. It also discusses the limitations on ownership for, contrary to popular belief, ownership is unlimited only in theory. This part also deals with the manner in which ownership over property may be acquired, as well as the remedies available to protect ownership.

Part 3 presents a specialised discussion of various rights in property. It includes a discussion of rights with a limited content and which limit ownership, namely servitudes and restrictive conditions. The third part also deals with security of rights in property. It further contains wide-reaching discussions of specialised rights created by the reformative context of the new property law, namely those relating to minerals and water.

Part 4 provides an overview of the principles of property law as they are practised today, and in the new context of the extended sources that feed this area of the law.

---

77 See *Alexkor (Pty) Ltd and Another v Richtersveld Community and Others* 2004 (5) SA 460 (CC) at para 50.

Chapter 2

Property and things: Definitions and classification

'[T]he definition of a thing may become too vague to have any scientific value.'
PJ Badenhorst, JM Pienaar, H Mostert (2006) *Silberberg and Schoeman's Law of Property* p 18

2.1	Introduction	20
2.2	**The characteristics and definition of things**	**20**
2.2.1	Characteristics	20
2.2.1.1	Corporeality and incorporeality	21
2.2.1.2	Impersonal nature	22
2.2.1.3	Independence	23
2.2.1.4	Appropriability	23
2.2.1.5	Use and value	24
2.2.2	Definition	24
2.3	**The relationship between things, rights, and property**	**25**
2.4	**Classification of things**	**28**
2.4.1	Classification according to negotiability	28
2.4.2	Classification according to nature	32
2.4.2.1	Corporeal and incorporeal things	32
2.4.2.2	Movable and immovable things	33
2.4.2.3	Single and composite things	35
2.4.2.4	Divisible and indivisible things	38
2.4.2.5	Consumable and non-consumable things	39
2.4.2.6	Fungible and non-fungible things	39
2.5	**Concluding remarks**	**40**

2.1 Introduction

The legal objects at the centre of property law are things or property. In chapter 1 it was pointed out that the meaning attached to property in different settings makes a legal definition precarious. It was also pointed out how the terminological difficulties affect lawyers' understanding of the scope of property. In this chapter, the definition of these key terms is analysed more closely. Once one knows what may qualify as property or things, it is possible to understand the scope of property law better. A cumulative definition of thing allows one to determine exactly what is regulated by the law of property. This chapter thus explores the characteristics usually displayed by the things protected under the rules of property law. It deals with the various ways in which such things may be classified in law. It also deals with the relationships that may exist in respect of things, and how these relationships are seen and treated in law.

2.2 The characteristics and definition of things

The scope of property law is determined by the extent to which legal objects qualify as things. Roman jurists divided private law into three categories, namely the law relating to persons, the law relating to actions, and the law relating to things (i.e. *res*).[1] Everything other than persons and actions fell into this latter category of things. The understanding of the concept 'thing' (i.e. *res*) in Roman law was thus very broad. It included physical and non-physical (corporeal **and** incorporeal) legal objects, the latter referring to rights.[2] This broad definition was carried forward into Roman-Dutch law, and hence applies in the South African context.[3] However, because of the Pandectist influence on South African property law, some scholars, on dogmatic grounds,[4] reject the idea that incorporeal property (i.e. rights) can be regarded as things.

2.2.1 Characteristics

These different approaches render a clear definition of the core concept of property law problematic. Yet, it is necessary to understand which sorts of objects are governed by property law and which are not. As a point of departure, it is helpful to recognise what qualifies as property in the private law sense. Constructing a working definition of the concept of thing is thus necessary. The objective is to know when a proprietary remedy can be used and when not. If the object does not qualify as property in the private law sense, then no proprietary remedy lies. It should be noted, however, that in the constitutional and public law sense, a much broader notion of property applies.

The approach here is to examine more closely the characteristics of the type of legal object governed by property law. For now, the legal object is referred to by the term 'thing'. The discussion below indicates how these characteristics are to be employed to define the thing as a legal concept. Typical characteristics are corporeality, an impersonal nature,

---

1   The Roman jurist, Gaius, distinguished between the law relating to persons, things and actions respectively. Institutiones 1 2 12; D 1 5 1. *Silberberg & Schoeman Property* pp 2-3.
2   *Silberberg & Schoeman Property* pp 2-3.
3   *Silberberg & Schoeman Property* p 13.
4   Cloete, R 'Die historiese onderskeid tussen stoflike en onstoflike sake in die Suid-Afrikaanse sakereg: 'n Sinopsis' (2005) *De Jure* at 314; Van der Merwe *Sakereg* p 37; *Wille's Principles* p 412.

independence, appropriability, and use and value.[5] In other words, the distinction between property in private law, and an object that cannot be regarded as property in private law, is that the former nearly always has these characteristics.

2.2.1.1 Corporeality and incorporeality

Corporeality, as a characteristic of things, has proved to be controversial. An object can be labelled corporeal if it is tangible, i.e. if it can be felt or touched, or perceived by any of the five senses and if it occupies space.[6] Non-physical types of property (i.e. incorporeal property or intangible interests in property with a distinct economic value)[7] are, however, becoming increasingly important in the private, commercial and public spheres of life.[8] Intangible objects include forms of energy such as heat, light, sound, radioactivity or electricity. Incorporeal objects may also refer to rights. It is not yet settled in South African law whether energy may qualify as a thing.[9] Similarly, the question whether incorporeal objects can qualify as things has given rise to various academic opinions.

> **COUNTER POINT**
>
> **Incorporeals as things?**
>
> In the opinion of some authorities,[10] only corporeal objects may qualify as things. They advance the following reasons for excluding incorporeal objects from the definition of things:
>
> 1. Acknowledging incorporeals as things would render it difficult to distinguish between various kinds of rights as required by the doctrine of legal subjectivity.[11] The doctrine dictates that rights should be distinguished from one another according to their objects so that the nature of the object is decisive for the classification of the particular right.[12]
> 2. It would be illogical and jurisprudentially impossible to acknowledge that one right could be the object of another right (i.e. that a person may have rights over rights).
> 3. The nature of the relationship between a person with a real right and the thing itself does not permit incorporeality since this would conflict with the idea that a real right confers direct physical powers over the thing in favour of that person.
>
> Although all the above objections against including incorporeals in the definition of things are valid and dogmatically sound, they do not account for the pragmatic approach of the courts and legislature, which has been to include incorporeals in the ambit of things on various occasions.[13]

So, for instance, a right in other rights has been acknowledged by the courts and the legislature in the context of a usufruct in respect of mineral rights,[14] and real security rights in respect of real rights to land such as long leases, personal servitudes, mineral rights and

---

5 *Silberberg & Schoeman Property* pp 14-21.
6 *Silberberg & Schoeman Property* p 14.
7 Van der Walt *Constitutional Property Law* pp 65-66.
8 *Silberberg & Schoeman Property* p 532.
9 *Wille's Principles* pp 413-414.
10 Notably Van der Merwe *Sakereg* p 37; *Wille's Principles* p 412.
11 See p 7 above.
12 See further the explanation in *Silberberg & Schoeman Property* p 14.
13 Delport and Olivier *Sakereg Vonnisbundel* p 15.
14 *Ex parte Eloff* 1953 (1) SA 617 (T).

leases of mineral rights.¹⁵ A purchaser's personal right to a traded-in vehicle (forming part of the purchase price) in terms of his credit agreement with a third party was recognised as an incorporeal thing for purposes of a contract of sale.¹⁶ Furthermore, the courts have occasionally recognised (and occasionally rejected) the idea that one can possess incorporeals, and protect them with proprietary remedies.¹⁷

> **COUNTER POINT**
> **Things include incorporeals**
> Accordingly, some authorities argue in favour of incorporating incorporeals in the definition of things.¹⁸ Acknowledging that 'not all rights can function as things', these scholars nevertheless choose to view the many instances in which incorporeals were protected as things in the law not as exceptions, but as an indication that the definition of the legal concept at the core of property law should be flexible, rather than strict. This approach is justified with reference to the equally broad definition that was employed historically to describe the ambit of property law.¹⁹ These authors also point out that a strict dogmatic adherence to the requirement of corporeality in defining things excludes certain possibilities of interpretation of the distinction between real and personal rights.²⁰ Further justification for incorporating some types of non-physical property in the definition of the legal object of property law is found in constitutional property law theory (discussed below).²¹

Though some regard these instances as mere exceptions to the rule of corporeality, it is problematic to see all the many instances in which incorporeals are treated as property as exceptional. It is likely that the number of instances will increase as data stored electronically is commodified. The realities of legal practice thus demand that the characteristic of corporeality should not be regarded as an **essential** characteristic or prerequisite of property. Instead, corporeality should be seen as a **common** characteristic.

2.2.1.2   Impersonal nature

True to the doctrine of legal subjectivity,²² humans are not regarded as things.²³ They function as legal subjects, not objects. Slavery, which permitted humans to be treated as property, was abolished in South Africa in 1834.²⁴ All humans are regarded as having an inherent and inalienable right to dignity, as is enshrined in s 10 of the Constitution. Slavery is a gross violation of this right because it denies the humanity of the enslaved person.

---

15   Sections 56(1), 60 and 64(2) read with ss 64(1), 56(1), 68(2), 69(4), and 81 of the Deeds Registries Act 47 of 1937. See also the former s 71(5)–(6) of the Deeds Registries Act (as repealed by s 53 of the Mining Titles Registration Amendment Act 24 of 2003), which formerly enabled registration of security rights in respect of mineral rights and mineral leases. *National Bank of South Africa Ltd v Cohen's Trustee* 1911 AD 235; *Leyds v Noord-Westelike Koöperatiewe Landboumaatskappy Bpk* 1985 (2) SA 769 (A); *Bank of Lisbon and South Africa v The Master* 1987 (1) SA 276 (A); *Sasfin (Pty) Ltd v Beukes* 1989 (1) SA 1 (A) at 9H–J; *Land- en Landboubank van Suid-Afrika v Die Meester* 1991 (2) SA 761 (A) at 771C–F all demonstrate that a cession of personal rights for the security of a debt (*in securitatem debiti*) may take the form of a pledge.
16   *Janse van Rensburg v Grieve Trust CC* [1993] 3 All SA 597 (C) at 608d–e.
17   *Tigon v Bestyet Investments (Pty) Ltd* 2001 (4) SA 634 (N) at 641J; but compare *Telkom SA Ltd v Xsinet (Pty) Ltd* 2003 (5) SA 309 (SCA) at 314G–H.
18   Silberberg & Schoeman *Property* p 18.
19   Silberberg & Schoeman *Property* p 16.
20   Silberberg & Schoeman *Property* pp 16–17.
21   See ch 6 below.
22   See p 7 above.
23   Wille's *Principles* p 414; Silberberg & Schoeman *Property* p 19.
24   Wille's *Principles* p 414.

In similar vein, human body parts are not negotiable. However, advances in medical and dental science, together with the desire to live longer, have resulted in an increasing commodification of the human body. Blood may be extracted and used in transfusions. Organs are transplanted. Sperm and ova may be frozen and used for fertilisation in vitro or in utero. In each case, the human body parts are donated, rather than sold, which preserves the line between negotiability and non-negotiability. The National Health Act[25] deals with donations and use of human tissue, blood, and reproductive matter from living and deceased persons. It prohibits cloning of human beings. It also reaffirms the status of such tissue or body parts as beyond the parameters of commerce. However, renewable body parts may be dealt with in the open market under certain conditions. Hair may thus for instance be sold for wig making.[26]

2.2.1.3   Independence

A thing must have an independent legal existence. For example, a house generally does not exist separately and independently from the land upon which it is built and to which it is firmly attached. Also, a key by itself most often has no particular meaning, but has to be seen as an instrument of access to another object, such as a house, a post box or a vehicle.[27]

The law does not require that things be **physically** independent from their environment. Juridical independence suffices.[28] This means that the law may intervene by rendering independent something which otherwise would physically be part of another thing. So, for instance, land is rendered juridically independent once it has been surveyed and indicated on the diagram or general plan required to enable transfer of such land to an individual.[29] To return to the example of the house built upon land. The law has instituted mechanisms by which land may be separated and become negotiable by demarcation thereof, and by which parts of a building may be sectionalised and acquired by different owners as apartments upon compliance with certain statutory provisions.[30]

Components of a composite entity lack legal independence until they are physically or juridically individualised.[31] So, for instance, a house is usually alienated with all its fixtures and fittings. One may, however, exclude certain items in the contract of sale. For instance, a chandelier attached to a ceiling or a mirror attached to a wall may be contractually excluded and then removed (or it may be physically removed before the house is put up for sale). However, items that are built in, such as a bath or toilet bowl, and which can be physically removed only by damaging the fabric of the building, may usually not be excluded.

2.2.1.4   Appropriability

A thing must be susceptible to human control.[32] Control here refers to the possibility of enforcing and protecting the right in the thing. The sun, moon and stars thus will not qualify as things because they cannot be appropriated. The air that we breathe is also not

---

25 Act 61 of 2003.
26 *Wille's Principles* p 414.
27 *Silberberg & Schoeman Property* p 20.
28 *Silberberg & Schoeman Property* p 20.
29 Section 14 of the Land Survey Act 8 of 1997.
30 Sectional Titles Act 95 of 1986. More detail in Van der Merwe, CG (1996) *Sectional Titles, Share Blocks and Time-sharing* Vol 1 Chapter 2, pp 2–4.
31 *Wille's Principles* p 415; *Silberberg & Schoeman Property* p 20.
32 *Silberberg & Schoeman Property* p 21; *Wille's Principles* p 415; *LAWSA* Vol 27(1) at para 209.

susceptible to control. However, air compressed in a gas cylinder may function as a thing because it has been brought under human control.

2.2.1.5 Use and value

A thing must be of use and value to a person.[33] It may have an economic or a sentimental value. To determine use and value, the object must be considered in context: a dead leaf may not have any particular value to anyone, but a collection of dead leaves and other plant matter may be negotiable as compost.[34] Dangerous or unwanted objects, such as industrial or chemical waste, may also qualify as things, even though their value would be negative.[35]

> **PAUSE FOR REFLECTION**
>
> **The characteristics and the definition of things**
>
> Even with the requirements outlined above, there is no clear theory to explain what a thing is. There are at least two different approaches to defining the concept in South African law. On the one hand, there is a narrow or strict approach where all five characteristics mentioned contribute to the determination of whether a legal object qualifies as a thing.[36] On the other hand, there is a broader or more flexible approach where the five characteristics mentioned are regarded as guidelines rather than prerequisites in the determination of whether a legal object is a thing.[37]
>
> Of the five characteristics mentioned, corporeality is the crucially determinative consideration in distinguishing between these two approaches. From a practical perspective, it is really a matter of preference. If the general rule is that incorporeal property does not qualify as things for purposes of property law, then corporeality is an essential characteristic. Nevertheless, certain exceptions will be and are recognised.[38] If the view is that anything, whether corporeal or incorporeal, that is of use and/or value to persons and that is regarded as *intra commercium* (negotiable) is a thing,[39] then corporeality is a **common**, but not **essential** characteristic of a thing. For present purposes, we prefer the latter approach.
>
> The debate may be academic, but is nevertheless important. If something does not qualify as a thing, one cannot utilise a proprietary remedy to protect it or the rights held in respect of it. As will become clearer later, proprietary remedies are powerful and can be more effective than contractual remedies.

2.2.2 Definition

Based on the guidelines provided by the characteristics of things, one may define the concept of 'thing' as any independent object, whether corporeal or incorporeal, which does not form part of a human being, which may be controlled by humans, and is of use and value to them. Depicted diagrammatically, the elements of the definition are as follows:

---

33 *Silberberg & Schoeman Property* p 21; *Wille's Principles* p 415; *LAWSA* Vol 27(1) at para 205.
34 *Wille's Principles* p 415.
35 *Wille's Principles* p 415.
36 Van der Merwe *Sakereg* p 37.
37 *Silberberg & Schoeman Property* pp 18ff.
38 Van der Merwe *Sakereg* p 37.
39 *Silberberg & Schoeman Property* p 18.

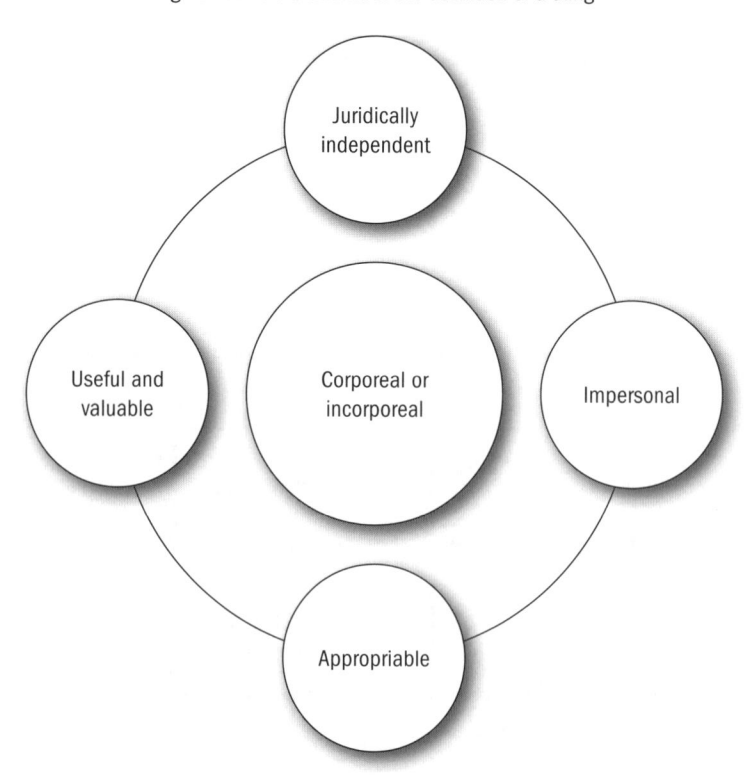

Figure 2.1: The elements of the definition of a thing

- Juridically independent
- Useful and valuable
- Corporeal or incorporeal
- Impersonal
- Appropriable

The definition provided above focuses on the characteristics that mark the legal object at the centre of property law, namely a thing. However, property law goes further than merely protecting and regulating things, which is its private law function. As indicated in chapter 1, the broader term 'property law' is preferred over the term 'law of things' because it encompasses a broader range of relations, including not only the object to which the law relates, but also the rights to such objects. It also includes the constitutional notion of property, which may be much broader than simply including the objects and/or the rights to such objects. This will be discussed in detail in chapter 6 below.

2.3 The relationship between things, rights, and property

The assets in a person's estate may be tangible, but need not be. For instance, a house, an iPhone or a Jaguar car may fall into Mick's estate in the same manner as would his copyright over the song he composed, or his claim against his friend Jerry for repayment of a loan. All these items may qualify as assets, and may act as the object of certain rights in terms of the doctrine of subjective rights.[40] Rights relating to the assets in one's estate are termed patrimonial rights. They may relate to tangible things, but also to other legal objects, such as immaterial property and performances in terms of a contractual or delictual obligation. The commonality between these rights is that they all have a patrimonial value.

---

40   Explained above, p 7.

However, not all the items forming part of one's estate qualify as things. Only those items displaying the characteristics discussed above[41] may fall into this category. So, for instance, the house, cellular phone and motor vehicle display the characteristics mentioned, but copyright is a form of immaterial property and the loan gives rise to a right to performance in terms of that contract. The diagram below demonstrates the different possible components of a person's estate.

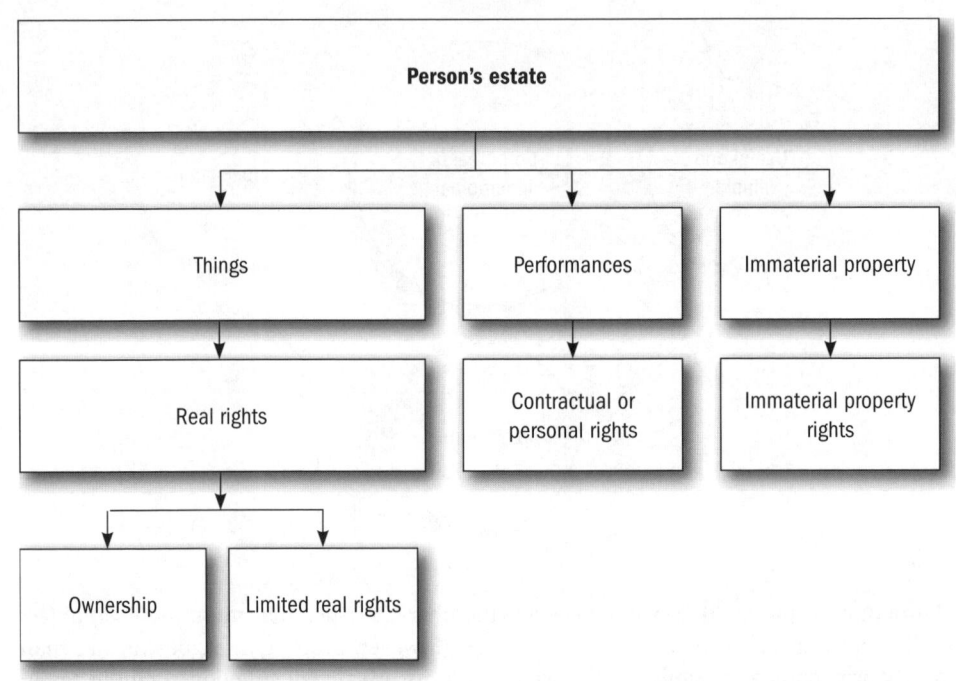

Figure 2.2: Components of an estate

```
                          Person's estate
         ┌───────────────────┼───────────────────┐
       Things            Performances      Immaterial property
         │                   │                   │
      Real rights     Contractual or       Immaterial property
                      personal rights            rights
      ┌────┴────┐
  Ownership  Limited real rights
```

In this book, our primary concern is with the category of patrimonial rights that flow from things. A considerable part of this book hence deals with real rights, of which the two main forms are ownership and limited real rights. Where it becomes relevant for purposes of property law, personal rights are also discussed.

As has been demonstrated, the notion of a thing is a core concept in property law. Nevertheless, it covers only some of the interests that may form part of a person's estate. By contrast, the concept of property has a much broader meaning.[42] It may refer to the legal object itself, in which case the term would be synonymous to thing. Property may, however, also refer to the right to a specific legal object. This use of the term then extends the notion to include the claims that a person may have against others, regarding her things.[43]

---

41 Explained above, pp 20–25.
42 *Silberberg & Schoeman Property* p 22.
43 *Silberberg & Schoeman Property* p 22.

Property is a term also used in the Constitution where s 25 guards against unconstitutional deprivation and expropriation of property. Since the function of the constitutional property clause differs from that of private law remedies which protect property, the definitional issues that arise in the constitutional context also differ from those in the private law context. For instance, the question whether property must be corporeal to be worthy of protection does not arise at all. In the constitutional sense, it is simply assumed that the term 'property' includes **any** patrimonial right to be protected or regulated.[44] Hence, until a different interpretation is advanced by the courts, one may assume that contractual rights will also qualify as property where the constitutional provisions have to be applied to determine whether an interference with such rights has occurred. The application of the property clause may even extend to statutory claims against the state regarding certain resources or performances, licences, permits and quotas. These claims are not necessarily based on contracts.

PAUSE FOR REFLECTION	Constitutional concept of property
	At this point, there is no closed description of exactly what the constitutional concept of property entails, and the courts are cautious not to restrict the constitutional definition of property.[45] Section 25 of the Constitution does not contain a comprehensive definition of property. It indicates only that, for purposes of constitutional protection, 'property is not limited to land'.[46] The courts will thus have to provide further clarity on the constitutional content and scope of property. The Constitutional Court is inclined to interpret the property concept generously, while being stricter when examining the justification for particular infringements on property. This means that the issue of the constitutional definition of the property concept is subsumed in the question of how property can be limited under the Constitution. Consequently, a more thorough discussion of this will follow in chapter 6 below.

As to the types of objects acknowledged as property under the Constitution, the Constitutional Court has indicated that the idea of property as corporeal, whether movable or immovable, will be a point of departure in determining the constitutional concept of property.[47] However, non-physical property should, in principle, qualify as property for purposes of constitutional protection.[48] The fact that constitutional protection of non-physical types of property is seen as unproblematic, confirms the approach, outlined above, that corporeality should not be regarded as a prerequisite characteristic of things. The justification for this approach may be expanded to include that constitutional property protection confirms the trend in private law to acknowledge the idea of incorporeal property. The open-endedness of the constitutional property concept certainly influences private law in the acknowledgement of more incorporeal, economically valuable assets as things.[49]

---

44 Silberberg & Schoeman Property pp 22, 531–540.
45 First National Bank of South Africa Ltd t/a Wesbank v Commissioner, South African Revenue Service 2002 (4) SA 768 (CC) at paras 48–49, 51–56.
46 Section 25(4)(b) of the Constitution.
47 In First National Bank of South Africa Ltd t/a Wesbank v Commissioner, South African Revenue Service 2002 (4) SA 768 (CC) at para 51 it was held that ownership of a corporeal movable must, like ownership of land, 'lie at the heart of our constitutional concept of property, both as regards the nature of the right involved as well as the object of the right' and that it must therefore be protected as property under the Constitution. This approach was followed in Zondi v MEC for Traditional and Local Government Affairs 2005 (3) SA 25 (N) at 34E, where it was held that livestock as corporeal movables qualified as property for purposes of s 25 of the Constitution.
48 Van der Walt Constitutional Property Law pp 65–66.
49 Van der Walt Constitutional Property Law p 67; Silberberg & Schoeman Property pp 532–533.

> **PAUSE FOR REFLECTION**
>
> **Conceptual severance**
>
> Because it is accepted that constitutional protection is afforded to intangible property interests, it is sometimes further argued that the various incidents of property are protected severally under constitutional property law.[50] This implies that the separate incidents that make up a property right may be protected individually, which restricts the possibilities of state limitation of property.[51] This approach is labelled 'conceptual severance'. Some authorities believe that the Constitutional Court decision in *First National Bank of SA Ltd t/a Wesbank v Commissioner, South African Revenue Service* contains tacit approval for such an approach.[52] However, this approach is particularly problematic when the issue of compensation for expropriation arises, and could place an intolerable burden on the state, 'causing abuse of the constitutional property clause and frustrating governmental reform efforts'.[53] It is unlikely that this approach of conceptual severance will be entertained in South African courts. First, it relies on a particular (Anglo-American) understanding of property as a bundle of rights, which does not enjoy much support in South African property law.[54] Second, conceptual severance arguments need a particular acceptance of the applicability of a doctrine of constructive expropriation to be effective, and, in South Africa, there has not been a conclusive decision about the applicability of this doctrine.[55]

2.4 Classification of things

Things may be classified in various ways. The classification of things is important in that it assists in determining the choice of rules or principles as regards the acquisition, protection and enforcement of rights in things, according to their nature. The function of a thing in particular circumstances determines its classification. The method of classification usually uses either the role of the thing in commerce (i.e. its negotiability in law), or its nature. The same thing may thus be classified in various ways.

2.4.1 Classification according to negotiability

If things are classified according to their place in commerce, the main distinction is whether they can be privately owned or not.[56] This is the distinction between *res in commercio* and *res extra commercium*: things that are in commerce (i.e. negotiable) and things that are out of commerce (non-negotiable). The diagram below demonstrates this classification.

---

50 Roux, T in Woolman et al. (2002) *Constitutional Law* pp 46–12*ff*, relying on *Geyser v Msunduzi Municipality* 2003 (5) SA 18 (N). See more detailed discussion in Van der Walt *Constitutional Property Law* pp 68–69; *Silberberg & Schoeman Property* p 533.
51 See further Van der Walt, AJ 'Subject and Society in Property Theory: A Review of Property Theories and Debates in Recent Literature: Part II' (1995) *TSAR* at 326*ff*.
52 Roux, T in Woolman et al. (2002) *Constitutional Law* pp 46–14*ff*, commenting on *First National Bank of South Africa Ltd t/a Wesbank v Commissioner, South African Revenue Service* 2002 (4) SA 768 (CC) at paras 100*ff*.
53 *Silberberg & Schoeman Property* p 533; Van der Walt *Constitutional Property Law* p 69.
54 The bundle of rights theory is discussed at p 93 below. It refers to the definition of ownership by relying on the various entitlements it may entail. It is rejected by Van der Merwe *Sakereg* p 174, who regards ownership as a unified concept that cannot be split into a variety of rights to be alienated separately. Van der Walt, AJ 'Unity and Pluralism in Property Theory – A Review of Property Theories and Debates in Recent Literature: Part I' (1995) *TSAR* at 15–41 challenges the approach of Van der Merwe, but relies on it in rejecting the idea of conceptual severance (Van der Walt *Constitutional Property Law* p 69).
55 Mostert, H 'The Distinction between Deprivations and Expropriations and the Future of the "Doctrine" of Constructive Expropriation in South Africa' (2003) 4 *SAJHR* at 567–592; Van der Walt *Constitutional Property Law* p 70.
56 *Silberberg & Schoeman Property* p 25; *LAWSA* Vol 27(1) at para 212.

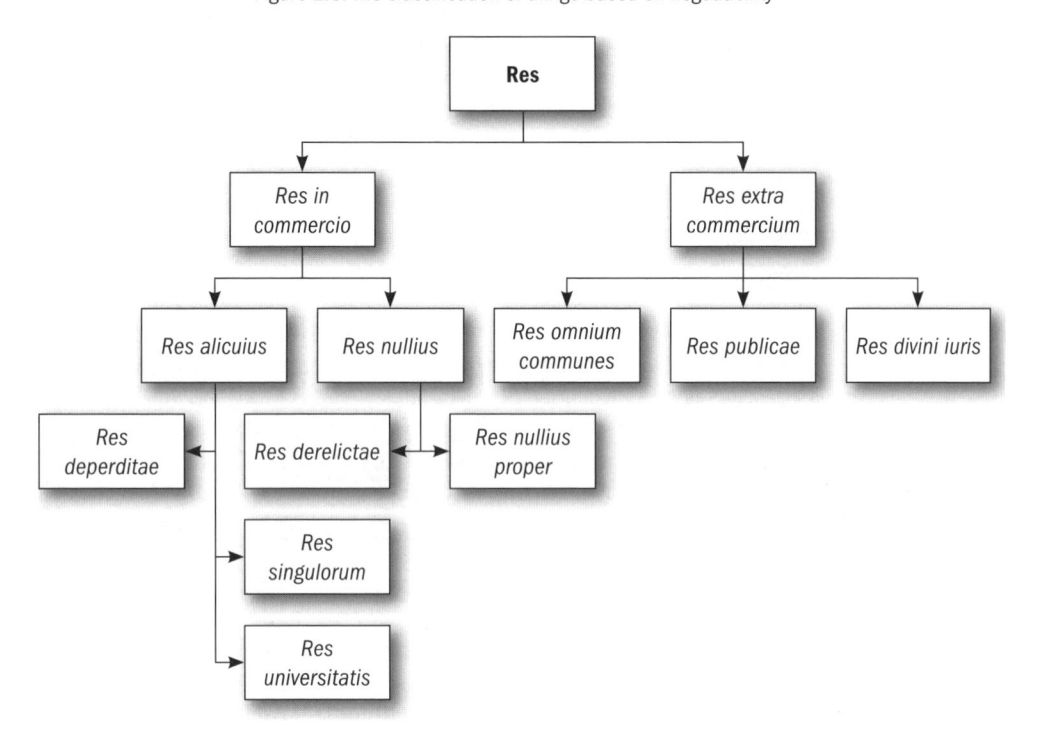

Figure 2.3: The classification of things based on negotiability

```
                                Res
                    ┌────────────┴────────────┐
              Res in                      Res extra
            commercio                    commercium
          ┌─────┴─────┐         ┌────────────┼────────────┐
      Res alicuius  Res nullius  Res omnium   Res publicae  Res divini iuris
          │             │         communes
    ┌─────┼─────┐       │
   Res   Res      Res nullius
deperditae derelictae  proper
          │
       Res
    singulorum
          │
       Res
    universitatis
```

If things can be privately owned *(res in commercio)*, the further distinction is between things that are currently owned *(res alicuius)* and things that are not currently owned *(res nullius)*. Things that are currently owned may be owned by individuals *(res singulorum)* or corporate bodies *(res universitatis)*. Examples of *res universitatis* include the university buildings belonging to the university; the public baths in Long Street, Cape Town, belonging to the City of Cape Town; the Union Buildings belonging to the state; and a church or graveyard that belongs to a particular congregation.

> **PAUSE FOR REFLECTION**
>
> **State held things and public access to private things**
>
> Modern law distinguishes clearly between things held by the state in its public capacity, and things owned by the state in its private capacity.[57] Things held by the state in its public capacity include, for instance, public buildings and state land. The state is, furthermore, also the custodian of mineral and petroleum resources, and water in South Africa. Such objects cannot be freely alienated, but are subject to applicable statutes, regulations and ordinances.

---

57   See *Silberberg & Schoeman Property* pp 31*ff*; *Wille's Principles* pp 416*ff*; *LAWSA* Vol 27(1) at para 214.

> Things owned privately, such as a restaurant or shopping mall, do not lose their private character merely because members of the public are generally invited to use them for designated purposes.[58] However, if members of the public have routine access, the landowner's power to exclude members of the public from the land may be compromised as it may clash with the constitutional right to freedom of movement.
>
> This does not mean that members of the public have limitless rights of free movement. The landowner is still able to protect its customer and business interests, and the physical integrity and security of its employees from unlawful conduct by members of the public. In *Victoria & Alfred Waterfront v Police Commissioner, Western Cape*,[59] the court found that, due to its location, size and composition, the Victoria and Alfred Waterfront in Cape Town is, for all practical purposes, like a suburb of Cape Town, even though it is in private hands. The attempts by the owners of the Waterfront to prohibit specific individuals (vagrants in this particular case) from being on the premises failed because the court found that excluding the vagrants from the area permanently would only be possible if there was no other way of achieving a lawfully justifiable goal.[60] This decision challenges preconceived ideas about the distinction between private and public property, and simultaneously demonstrates that private property may be subject to significant inroads due to the application of the fundamental rights under the Constitution.

Things that are unowned may be divided further into things that have never been owned (referred to here as *res nullius* proper), and things that were owned but later abandoned *(res derelictae)*. Things that have been lost *(res deperditae)*, however, still belong to someone because the owner has merely lost physical control, but has not intended to give up ownership. Lost things accordingly qualify as *res alicuius*.

Res nullius proper represents things that have never been owned. Examples include wild animals or birds, fish, and products of the sea. It is possible to establish ownership over such things by appropriation (i.e. by unilaterally taking control thereof), for instance by catching or taming a wild animal. Ownership of such an animal is lost if the animal escapes and regains its freedom, or where, despite being tamed, it escapes and does not return. Note, however, that legislation has changed the common law position in respect of many wild creatures and other natural resources. The Game Theft Act, for instance, criminalises the hunting or poaching of wild animals under certain circumstances.[61] In terms of this Act, if wild animals that are kept for hunting or commercial purposes are killed or captured, they cannot become the property of the hunter (as would have been the case under common law).[62] Instead, they remain the property of the person on whose land they are kept pursuant to a certificate issued in terms of the Act, or, alternatively, they become the property of the person on whose land they were captured. The Game Theft Act hence effectively excludes the common law rule that wild animals that escape from the control of their owners revert to being *res nullius*.

---

58 *Silberberg & Schoeman Property* pp 31–32.
59 2004 (4) SA 444 (C) at 451F–G, 585B–C.
60 *Victoria & Alfred Waterfront v Police Commissioner, Western Cape* 2004 (4) SA 444 (C) at 451I, 585D–E.
61 Game Theft Act 105 of 1991. See in particular the definition in s 1 of the Act, and the exclusions provided in s 2.
62 Van der Merwe *Sakereg* p 221. See also *Dunn v Bowyer* 1926 NPD 516.

In the category of things that cannot be privately owned *(res extra commercium)*, there is further division among things that are common to all *(res omnium communes)*, things that are public *(res publicae)*, and religious things *(res divini iuris)*. The latter category is obsolete in modern property law and the items associated with this category, e.g. graves, graveyards and tombstones, are privately owned[63] and protected from desecration by remedies in criminal law and delict *(actio iniuriarium)*.[64] This does not mean that the rights of others are completely denied. The Extension of Security of Tenure Act[65] acknowledges the right of occupiers of land in terms of the Act, to bury deceased family members on the land where they reside. This matter has been considered by the courts in recent years.[66] These rights may exist where an established practice of burial is discernible,[67] but they do not override other legislation or by-laws dealing with burials.[68]

Things common to all people *(res omnium communes)* belong to no one in particular and everyone at once. The air that we breathe, running water and the sea are examples of such things. They cannot be owned privately, but it is possible to acquire ownership of portions thereof by rendering them susceptible to control.[69] Compressing air in a gas cylinder would thus reduce the thing, comprised of the filled cylinder, to being negotiable *(in commercio)*.

Public things *(res publicae)* belong to an entire civil community, and are often referred to as state property.[70] This does not mean, however, that these things are in the (private) ownership of the state. Rather, the state holds the things for the benefit of its subjects. Examples include public roads, public rivers and harbours. Due to statutory intervention, the sea and seashore are regarded as public things in South African law.[71] Since the state assumes control over public things, this property may not necessarily be freely used by everyone. Mineral and petroleum resources have been placed in the custodianship of the state by recent legislation,[72] thus (arguably) bringing them within the ambit of *res publicae*. Use of these resources is strictly regulated.[73] For example, although anyone may apply for a prospecting or mining right, compliance with a strict set of requirements, most of which support the public interest in general, is required before the person is eligible to be awarded such rights. Similarly, water is now under the stewardship of the state in terms of the National Water Act.[74] This scarce resource must be managed and distributed so that the constitutional right of access to (potable) water can be realised progressively for all South Africans.[75]

---

63 Sonnekus, JC 'Eiendomsregte op grafte – en dan die gevolge daarvan?' (2000) *TSAR* 112*ff*.
64 *Wille's Principles* p 418; *Cape Town and District Waterworks v Executors of Elders* (1890) 8 SC 9 at 11-12.
65 Act 62 of 1997.
66 *Serole v Pienaar* 2000 (1) SA 328 (LCC); *Bührmann v Nkosi and Another* 2000 (1) SA 1145 (T); *Nkosi and Another v Bührmann* 2002 (1) SA 372 (SCA); *Nhlabathi v Fick* [2003] 2 All SA 323 (LCC); and see commentary in Janse van Rensburg, AM 'Access to Ancestral Burial Sites – Recent Decisions' (2002) *Obiter* 175-185; Kok, JA 'An Occupier's Right to Bury Relatives on Land' (2000) *De Jure* 161-174; Pienaar, JM and Mostert, H 'The Balance Between Burial Rights and Landownership in South Africa: Issues of Content, Nature and Constitutionality' (2005) 3 *SALJ* 633-660.
67 Section 6(2)(*dA*) of the Extension of Security of Tenure Act 62 of 1997.
68 *Silberberg & Schoeman Property* p 31.
69 *Silberberg & Schoeman Property* pp 25-26; *Wille's Principles* p 417; *LAWSA* Vol 27(1) at para 213.
70 *Silberberg & Schoeman Property* p 26; *Wille's Principles* pp 417-418; *LAWSA* Vol 27(1) at para 214.
71 Section 2(1) of the Sea-shore Act 21 of 1935. See analysis in *Silberberg & Schoeman Property* p 27.
72 Section 3 of the Mineral and Petroleum Resources Development Act 28 of 2002.
73 See discussion in ch 10 below.
74 Act 36 of 1998.
75 See discussion in ch 11 below.

2.4.2 Classification according to nature

Things may be classified according to their nature[76] into, for example, corporeals and incorporeals; single and composite things; movables and immovables, fungibles and non-fungibles; consumables and non-consumables; and divisible and indivisible things. Below is a diagrammatic summary of what is discussed in the following sections.

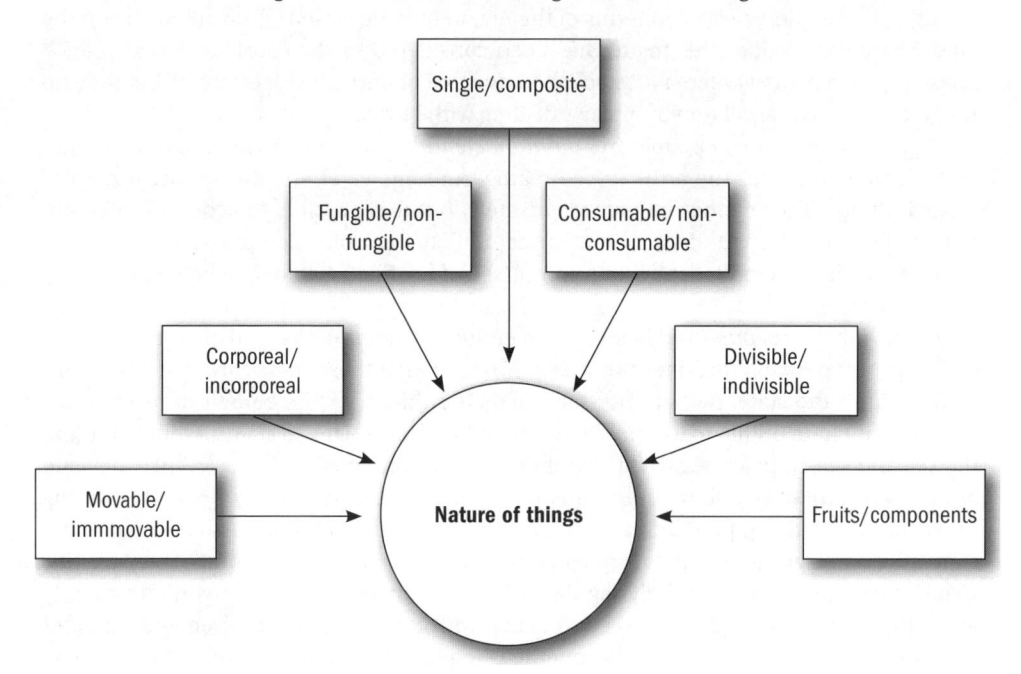

Figure 2.4: Classification according to the nature of things

2.4.2.1 Corporeal and incorporeal things

Things are classed as corporeals or incorporeals according to the convictions of the community, i.e. when they are tangible or can be perceived by the senses.[77] Incorporeals cannot be touched or perceived by the senses. 'They are abstract conceptions with no physical existence but an intrinsic pecuniary value.'[78] Examples of corporeals include land and houses, books, vehicles, technical equipment such as a computer or flash drive, food and clothing. Incorporeals include forms of energy, such as light, heat and sound, and also rights. When a **right** fulfils the same function as a **thing**, i.e. when it functions as an object in respect of which rights, duties and capacities can be exercised, it should be regarded as an incorporeal thing.[79] The law acknowledges, e.g. that a lease or usufruct can be mortgaged, and that rights can be attached in execution of a debt. In the past, a usufruct could also be

---

76 *Silberberg & Schoeman Property* pp 33*ff*; *Wille's Principles* pp 419*ff*; *LAWSA* Vol 27(1) at para 218.
77 Van der Merwe *Sakereg* p 24.
78 *Wille's Principles* p 419.
79 *Silberberg & Schoeman Property* p 34.

exercised over mineral rights and such rights could be leased.[80] The above types of situations are those in which rights (i.e. the mentioned lease, usufruct, rights attached, or mineral rights) function as incorporeal things.

> **PAUSE FOR REFLECTION**
>
> **Revisiting incorporeals as things**
>
> It is useful, at this point, to review the discussion of the dogmatic inconsistencies in acknowledging incorporeals as things.[81] It will be recalled that some scholars reject the idea that things may include incorporeals, while others acknowledge this idea only insofar as it is necessary to take heed of practical or policy considerations. Yet another view is to acknowledge incorporeals insofar as they amount to patrimonial rights that form the object of real rights. When things are **classified** based on corporeality or incorporeality, it is assumed that incorporeals are indeed acknowledged as capable of falling within the ambit of property law. It is inconsistent, therefore, to deny the existence of incorporeal things when defining the term, but then to acknowledge it once things have to be classified.[82]
>
> The fact that the classification of things acknowledges the distinction between corporeals and incorporeals underscores the argument that corporeality should not be a **prerequisite**, but should rather be recognised as a common characteristic of objects within the ambit of property law. Corporeality might, thus, serve as a **guideline**.

The distinction between corporeals and incorporeals is important since it affects the type of control that lies at the heart of many processes acknowledged in property law. So, e.g. land (a corporeal) may be acquired unilaterally if the acquirer is able to show that she has possessed the land openly as if she were the owner for a period of 30 years. An incorporeal, such as a **right** in land (e.g. a grazing right) may be acquired unilaterally if the acquirer can show that she has used the land **as if she were entitled to do so**, for a period of 30 years.[83]

2.4.2.2 Movable and immovable things

The classification of things as either corporeal or incorporeal is also important with regard to its role in the further classification of things as either movable or immovable. This latter distinction is crucial to determine how various things may be acquired. Different rules and procedures govern the two classes. Things are movable when they can be moved from one place to another without being damaged or losing their identity. Immovable things cannot be so moved.[84]

Typical examples of movables are furniture, vehicles, money, and clothing. Land is the most typical example of an immovable. Everything that permanently attaches to land is also regarded as immovable.[85] This includes buildings or other installations and things permanently attached thereto, and vegetation such as trees, and unharvested crops. These examples are all, simultaneously, examples of **corporeal** things.

---

80 *Ex parte Eloff* 1953 (1) SA 617 (T); ss 56(1), 60, 68(2), 69(4), 71(5)-(6) and 77(1)of the Deeds Registries Act. See *Wille's Principles* p 419 and pp 21-22 above.
81 See pp 21-22 above.
82 Van der Merwe *Sakereg* p 37.
83 See ch 7 below.
84 *Silberberg & Schoeman Property* p 34; *Wille's Principles* p 421; *LAWSA* Vol 27(1) at para 224.
85 See pp 167-175 below.

The attempt to classify incorporeals as either movable or immovable based on mobility seems illogical: incorporeal things cannot physically be moved. It is nevertheless necessary to classify incorporeals as either movable or immovable because this determines how such things may be alienated or acquired; what kind of real security rights may be established over them; whether they may be sold in execution and how this may be undertaken; which jurisdictional rules would be applicable if a dispute in respect of the thing has to be settled in terms of international law; and which rules of criminal law may be applicable.[86]

In Roman-Dutch law, the mobility of an incorporeal thing was established only when necessary,[87] the reference point being the nature of the object of the right concerned.[88] Essentially, this distinction still applies in modern South African law. Thus, all real rights over immovables are immovable (where they function as objects of further rights), while real rights over movables are movable under such circumstances.[89] Personal rights are always movable, regardless of whether the underlying asset could be classified as movable or immovable.[90] A usufruct over the contents of a home would thus be an incorporeal movable, while a usufruct over the house itself would be an incorporeal immovable. (Of course, the necessity of this classification only arises if the usufruct functions as the object of a further right, such as a real security right.)

Some incorporeals will always be immovable because their object is immovable.[91] Examples include rights of use or habitation of land (*usus* and *habitatio* respectively), praedial servitudes, and building restrictions. Incorporeals recognised as movable include shares in a company, a member's interest in a close corporation, the goodwill of a business, and immaterial property rights, such as patents, designs, and trademarks.

COUNTER POINT — **Distinguishing movable and immovable incorporeals**

The simplest method of distinction between movable and immovable incorporeals is to determine first whether the right pertains to an immovable. If it does, it would most likely be classified as an immovable incorporeal. If it does not, the likeliest classification would be as a movable incorporeal. In case law, the distinction between movable and immovable incorporeals has nevertheless proved problematic.

First, as regards mortgage bonds, for instance, various decisions demonstrate uncertainty as to the correct classification. The problem in the case of a mortgage bond is that it couples a personal obligation (the repayment of the debt) with real security (tendering an immovable thing to secure the personal obligation), and hence has a dual character. Early case law supported the classification of a mortgage as sometimes movable and sometimes immovable. The situation was clarified in *Lief NO v Dettmann*,[92] where the court held that the determining factor for such classification was the purpose for which the classification had to be undertaken. So, if the fact that the bond constitutes an acknowledgement of debt is paramount, then the classification of the bond would be as movable, while if the bond's importance in the particular circumstances relates to the fact that it proves title to the real security right, then the classification would be immovable.

---

86 Silberberg & Schoeman *Property* pp 35*ff*; *Wille's Principles* pp 421–422.
87 Silberberg & Schoeman *Property* p 35.
88 Silberberg & Schoeman *Property* pp 35*ff*; *Wille's Principles* pp 422*ff*.
89 *Wille's Principles* pp 421–422.
90 Silberberg & Schoeman *Property* p 35.
91 Silberberg & Schoeman *Property* p 34; *Wille's Principles* p 421.
92 1964 (2) SA 252 (A) at 266.

> Second, as regards rights in respect of land, the definitions under the Deeds Registries Act[93] of registered long leases, registered leaseholds, and initial ownership under the Development Facilitation Act[94] as immovable, implies that unregistered long leases and all short leases of land are movable.[95] This means that security rights over unregistered long leases and short leases should be constituted differently from security rights over registered long leases, leaseholds and initial ownership. Badenhorst et al. correctly point out that this is a deviation from the supposition that rights pertaining to immovables can function as immovable incorporeal things.[96]
>
> Third, trading rights, licences and quotas have also proved problematic to classify. On the one hand, a court has found a liquor licence to be not rateable for municipal purposes, and not subject to transfer duty upon sale of the land because the licence was not immovable property.[97] On the other hand, sales quotas seemingly follow the land to which they have been allotted for some purposes, as is demonstrated by a number of (somewhat inconsistent) cases concerning sugar quotas.[98] There is not enough clarity in case law to enable the formulation of a single rule in this regard.

2.4.2.3 Single and composite things

Things may further be categorised as single or composite. Single things are individual things that exist independently and comprise an entity that has use and value.[99] In some instances, single things have value only when they are dealt with in quantities, e.g. sand or bees. Each grain of sand and each bee are, technically, separate legal entities in law. But individual grains of sand and single bees do not usually have economic value. Conventionally, therefore, such items are dealt with by reference to their weight (e.g. cubic tons of sand) or quantity (e.g. 1 000 honeybees). The weight or quantity measure allows the entity to be dealt with more conveniently for purposes of transfer of ownership, and so on.[100]

Sometimes various single entities are grouped and dealt with as an economic unit:[101] a flock of sheep, a collection of baseball cards or paintings by a particular artist. Such a grouping is called a collection or an aggregate. The individual things in the aggregate exist independently, may be alienated or acquired independently, but may also be acquired, alienated, encumbered or protected as an aggregate. Note, however, that an aggregate or

---

93 Section 102 of the Deeds Registries Act 47 of 1937.
94 That is, the right created by s 62 of the Development Facilitation Act 67 of 1995, which must be recorded in and published by the Deeds Registry, and which enables someone to use and occupy land as if she were the registered owner thereof under normal circumstances, even though the land may not yet be capable of registration because the ordinary requirements of surveying cannot yet be met.
95 *Silberberg & Schoeman Property* p 36.
96 *Silberberg & Schoeman Property* p 37.
97 *Receiver of Revenue, Cape v Cavanagh* 1912 AD 459 at 463; *Pietermaritzburg Corporation v South African Breweries Ltd* 1911 AD 501.
98 See the discussion in *Silberberg & Schoeman Property* p 37 of *Samuel v Pagadia* 1963 (3) SA 45 (D); *Secretary for Inland Revenue v Sturrock Sugar Farms (Pty) Ltd* 1965 (1) SA 897 (A); *De Chazal De Chamarel's Estate v Tongaat Group Ltd* 1972 (1) SA 710 (D); and *Scheepers v Robbertse* 1973 (2) SA 508 (N).
99 *Silberberg & Schoeman Property* pp 41–43; *Wille's Principles* pp 420–434; *LAWSA* Vol 27(1) at para 220.
100 *Wille's Principles* p 420.
101 *Wille's Principles* p 420.

collection is not the same legal concept as a composite thing. Items in a collection may be single or composite things themselves. The collection or aggregate describes the grouping.

Composite things consist of different components joined together to form a single entity in law,[102] such as a sectional title unit, a house or a bicycle. The components that make up a composite thing are the principal thing and the accessory things. There may also be auxiliary things (appurtenances) that belong with the composite thing for some purpose. The principal thing is that part which gives the entity its identity or character,[103] such as the frame of a bicycle, or a chassis of a car. Accessories are things that have been physically attached to the principal thing so that they have lost their independent legal identities. Prior to attachment, they existed independently, each with its own legal identity. The law dictates the circumstances under which accessories attach permanently to the principal thing.[104] If the accessories can be detached, they resume their independent existence. A pearl that has been set in a pendant is an accessory. Likewise, a chandelier fitted to the living room ceiling is an accessory of the house.

Auxiliary things (appurtenances) are not usually physically attached to the principal thing, but they belong with the principal and thus are destined to follow it for some purpose.[105] However, unlike accessories, auxiliaries do not lose their legal independence. To identify an auxiliary, it must be evident that it is meant to be of permanent use to the principal thing, and, in fact, necessary for the effective use of the principal thing. In other words, the relationship between the principal thing and the thing thought to be an auxiliary must be scrutinised carefully. A typical example is the key to a house. The key is a separate thing, but is meant to serve the principal thing (house on the land) and is necessary for the effective use of the house, which classes it as an auxiliary. The house key, despite retaining its legal identity and independence would go with the house when it is transferred to a purchaser. Ordinary furniture in the house, however, would not be regarded as auxiliary to it. But, if the house contains a built-in bar, accompanied by customised bar stools, the latter may be regarded as forming an economic unit with the bar, and thus be juridically tied to the house.[106]

Consequent to some transactions, auxiliaries go with the principal thing automatically. Thus, when the principal thing is sold, or is made subject to a usufruct or mortgage, then the auxiliaries are destined to follow the principal thing. In all other transactions, it should never be assumed that auxiliaries are automatically included. This is because the things under consideration may, in fact, not be in an auxiliary relationship with the principal thing, but may rather be separate entities, such as the ordinary furniture described above. If this is the case, the items must be included expressly in the contract to ensure they can be acquired at the same time as the house.

---

102 *Wille's Principles* p 420; *Silberberg & Schoeman Property* p 41.
103 *Silberberg & Schoeman Property* p 41; and see further ch 6 below.
104 See further ch 7 below.
105 *Silberberg & Schoeman Property* pp 41–42; *Wille's Principles* p 420.
106 *Senekal v Roodt* 1983 (2) SA 602 (T).

> **PAUSE FOR REFLECTION**
>
> **Composite things**
>
> Consider the situation where one builds a house on land. The bricks and mortar, the window frames and window panes are physically attached to the building. Consequently, each item loses its independent existence in the eyes of the law. They become part of the composite entity that is the house, which is permanently attached to the land. The whole follows the destiny of the land. The separate bricks, mortar, frames and panes may of course be removed at a later stage, but this would mean that the house is demolished, either partially or completely, or that it changes substantially. While the house stands, the bricks, mortar, frames and panes have no separate legal identity. The law recognises the product as an entity, and treats the combination of things as a unit for purposes of protection, acquisition, encumbrance and alienation.
>
> Now consider the following example of a composite thing, which comprises both corporeal and incorporeal elements, namely a sectional title unit. This phrase refers to the object of apartment ownership. In South African law, the apartment owner (i.e. the sectional title unit owner) acquires (1) ownership of a particular apartment ('section') in a given block (i.e. the 'scheme'); (2) joint co-ownership of the common parts of the land and building (i.e. the 'common property'). In addition, each owner has obligatory membership of the 'body corporate', an entity comprising all the owners. These components are inextricably linked, cannot be alienated separately, and are referred to collectively as the sectional title 'unit'.[107]

Fruits are products of a principal thing, which may be a living creature, plant matter or even an incorporeal.[108] Fruits are destined to be separated from the principal thing and, through separation, to gain separate legal identity.[109] Fruits may be **natural**, such as the offspring of animals, or **civil**, such as the income produced by the investment (i.e. dividends, interest on capital, royalties or rental). The general principle is that the owner of the principal thing is also the owner of the fruits.[110] However, the owner may entitle another to draw the fruits. This is the case with, for example, a usufructuary or a lessee. A lessee is not automatically entitled to fruits; the terms of the lease agreement govern whether such entitlement exists.[111] The point at which someone other than the owner becomes owner of the fruits depends on whether the fruits are still attached to the principal thing or whether they have been separated or harvested already.

The decision in *Khan v Minister of Law and Order*[112] provides a good example of the application of the principles regarding the classification of things according to their nature, into principal, accessory and auxiliary things. Khan, the applicant, was dispossessed of his vehicle by the SA Police. The court proceedings emanated from his attempt to have the vehicle returned to him. The vehicle was built up from different wrecks, and the rear end was identified as part of a stolen vehicle. It was undisputed that the engine and inner front belonged to the applicant. There were other components, some of which may have been taken from the stolen vehicle and built into the vehicle of Mr Khan, while others seemed to have originated from a third source.

---

107 For more detail, see Van der Merwe, CG (1996) *Sectional Titles* Vol 1 in *Sectional Titles, Share Blocks and Time-sharing* pp 2–4.
108 *Wille's Principles* p 426; *Silberberg & Schoeman Property* pp 43–44.
109 *Silberberg & Schoeman Property* p 43.
110 *Silberberg & Schoeman Property* p 43.
111 *Silberberg & Schoeman Property* p 43.
112 1991 (3) SA 439 (T).

Accessories follow the principal thing. It was thus important for the court to establish which part of the built-up vehicle formed the principal thing, and which parts were merely accessory to it. The applicant could have the vehicle returned if his part was determined to be the principal part. The court reiterated the rule that 'where one movable is joined to another in a manner as to form an entity, the owner of the principal thing becomes the owner also of the thing joined to it'.[113] The court indicated that deciding which part is the principal and which the accessory is generally a matter of common sense. Guidelines, which may aid the decision, refer to the value, bulk or size of the thing. In this particular case, the court found that the thing that gave the composite whole its 'character, form and function' would decisively be the principal thing. The court said, 'One must view the thing that was ultimately formed, and decide what is the identity ... and the component that gives the ultimate thing its identity will be the principal thing, while the other will have acceded to it'.[114] Applying this reasoning to the facts at hand, the court found that the stolen rear end of the built-up vehicle gave it its character, form and function, which meant that Khan could not recover the vehicle because the part that belonged to him originally had acceded to the principal part, i.e. the stolen part.

Some of the issues that arise from this case are taken up in later chapters. For the moment, it is useful to note the manner in which the court distinguished between the principal and accessory things in this particular context, by enquiring into which of the combined things lent character or form to the ultimate object, and which determined its function. In this particular context, the consideration that weighed heavily on the decision was the fact that the vehicle looked more like that used to rebuild the rear end. The fact that the internal components (especially the engine and the inside front panels) were from the vehicle of the applicant, was not as weighty as the overall appearance of the vehicle.

2.4.2.4 Divisible and indivisible things

A thing is divisible when it can be separated into parts, each of which has the same nature and function as the whole before it was divided. The total value of the separated parts should not be significantly less than the value of the whole.[115] Indivisible things cannot be so divided.

Divisibility refers to **legal** divisibility rather than physical divisibility.[116] A car or bicycle may, for instance, be separated into its various parts, but these parts will not have the same nature or function as the car or bicycle when in its whole state. Such items are therefore not divisible things as the requirements mentioned cannot be met. By contrast, a barrel of wine may be divided into separate bottles. In such a case, the wine still has the same nature and function after being bottled as when it was still in the barrel. Similarly, land may be divisible, subject to certain statutory limitations.[117]

---

113 *Khan* at 442; see also *Wille's Principles* pp 425–426.
114 *Khan* at 443.
115 *Silberberg & Schoeman Property* p 39.
116 *Silberberg & Schoeman Property* p 39.
117 See e.g. the Subdivision of Agricultural Land Act 70 of 1970 (now repealed, although the repeal has not yet taken effect).

The distinction between divisible and indivisible things is important in the context of co-ownership.[118] In the event of termination of co-ownership, a division of things that are legally indivisible cannot be ordered even if they could be divided physically. In such a case, the court makes an order that the thing be sold by public auction and that the proceeds of the sale be divided among the co-owners. Alternatively, the court may award the thing to one of the co-owners and order that the other co-owners be compensated for their loss.[119]

2.4.2.5 Consumable and non-consumable things

Things are consumable when they are destined to be used up, i.e. consumed by use.[120] In the case of non-consumable things, use does not result in a substantial change to or reduction of the things. Typical examples of consumable things are food and fuel. Non-consumables are things such as land or artwork. When things can be partially (rather than fully) used up through use, the distinction becomes more problematic. So, for instance, it is contentious whether clothing, machinery or vehicles, which may become worn or less effective through use, are consumable or not. In modern South African law, it is suggested that such things should be classified as consumable or non-consumable based on a test of the reduction in value of the things. If there is a substantial reduction in the value over time, the thing should be classified as consumable.[121]

This distinction is important as regards loans for consumption and loans for use.[122] It is also relevant in respect of the kinds of things that may form the subject of a usufruct as the usufructuary is obliged to preserve the substance of the thing in usufruct.[123] Consumables may be the object of a quasi-usufruct, in which case the usufructuary may consume the thing, but has to restore the equivalent thereof when the usufruct expires.[124]

2.4.2.6 Fungible and non-fungible things

Fungible things are separate individual entities that are identical to one another, such as several 340 ml cans of Coca Cola. One resembles another so that they are not individually determined and can be interchangeable for some purposes. While it is possible to deal with them individually, in general trade they are usually dealt with by reference to their weight, number or size.[125] Non-fungibles, however, are individually determined. By this is meant that they are unique by nature, have distinctive individual qualities, or some specified characteristic that makes them different from other things. Interchangeability is either impossible or not permitted.

Some things are by nature non-fungible (e.g. the painting of Mona Lisa), while other things may be designated non-fungible (e.g. when the merchant wants a specific quality of potato and will not accept a substitute). If things are not by nature fungible or non-fungible, then they can be so designated by the intention of parties to a contract or by the intention of a testator in drawing up his will.

---

118 See ch 5 below.
119 *Bennett NO v Le Roux* 1984 (2) SA 134 (Z).
120 *Silberberg & Schoeman Property* p 40.
121 *Silberberg & Schoeman Property* p 40.
122 *LAWSA* Vol 27(1) at para 222; Sonnekus, JC & Neels, JL (1994) *Sakereg Vonnisbundel* (Durban, Butterworths) p 37.
123 *Silberberg & Schoeman Property* p 40.
124 *LAWSA* Vol 27(1) at para 425.
125 *Silberberg & Schoeman Property* p 40.

The distinction between fungible and non-fungible is more important in the law of succession and the law of contract than in the law of property. However, in the context of the *mandament van spolie*, the courts have dealt with whether restoring the *status quo ante* means that exactly the same things have to be restored to the spoliated possessors, or whether (fungible) material 'of similar size and quality' could be substituted.[126]

2.5 Concluding remarks

This chapter has focused on the qualities of the legal object that is protected in property law. We have commented on the use of the terms 'things' and 'property' to identify these legal objects; and on the distinction between 'rights' and 'things'; as well as on how both concepts are included in the term 'property'. We have discussed the various ways of classifying things, and have pointed out the importance thereof. In the next chapter, we look more closely at how this type of control constitutes relationships acknowledged by the law (i.e. rights), and how such rights are created and enforced.

---

126 See below at pp 81*ff*.

Chapter 3

Rights

'One has to look not so much to the right, but to the correlative obligation.'
Ex parte Geldenhuys 1926 OPD 155 at 164

3.1	Introduction	41
3.2	**Rights in respect of property**	42
3.2.1	Conventional categories of real rights	42
3.2.2	Real and personal rights	45
3.2.2.1	Why the distinction between real and personal rights is important	46
3.2.2.2	When the distinction is hard to draw	48
3.2.2.3	Courts' approach to the distinction between real and personal rights	50
3.3	**The principle of publicity and the doctrine of notice**	56
3.3.1	Publicity	56
3.3.2	Doctrine of notice	58
3.3.2.1	Successive sales	61
3.3.2.2	Unregistered servitudes	62
3.4	**Concluding remarks**	63

3.1 Introduction

The particular kind of relationship between a person and property depends on the consequences attached to it in law. In basic terms, one may distinguish between two types of relationships in respect of property, namely possession and rights. This chapter contains a basic discussion of the latter. The next contains a discussion of the former.

The distinction between proprietary relationships (i.e. relationships in respect of property) is depicted in the diagram below:

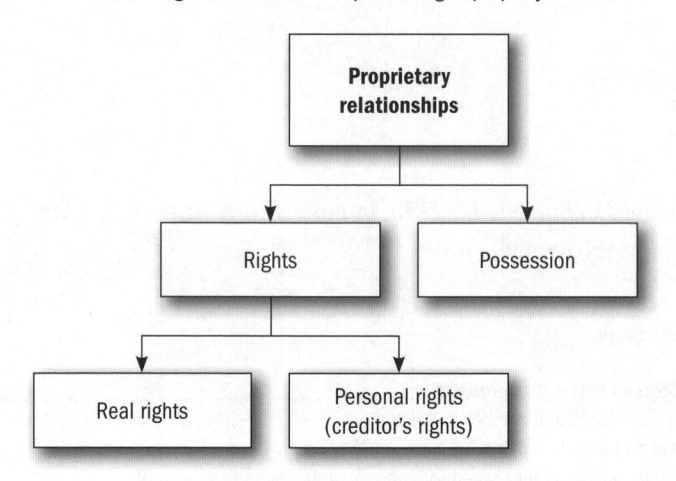

Figure 3.1: Relationships relating to property

```
                    Proprietary
                    relationships
                   /            \
              Rights            Possession
             /      \
       Real rights   Personal rights
                     (creditor's rights)
```

Rights in property refer to the claims of legal subjects as regards property, and as against other persons.[1] The law acknowledges different kinds of rights in respect of property. The main distinction is between real rights in property and personal (or creditor's) rights. One must be able to distinguish between the different kinds of rights because the manner in which they may be acquired, exercised and protected depends on this distinction. Some rights in respect of land, for instance, may be registrable in the Deeds Registry as real rights, while others may not be registrable. It is important to realise at the outset that not all rights in respect of property will automatically be typified as 'real' rights.

3.2 Rights in respect of property

South African law acknowledges a variety of rights in respect of property, the most prominent of which have been outlined above.[2] Real rights consist of either ownership or limited real rights. Ownership is the most complete real right and is the only real right held in one's own property *(ius in re propria)*. Chapters 5 to 8 below are dedicated to a discussion of ownership in particular. A limited real right is a real right held by a non-owner in the property owned by another *(ius in re aliena)*. A more detailed discussion of the various subcategories of limited real rights is contained in chapters 9 to 12 below. The current discussion concerns the nature of real rights generally and the distinction between real and personal rights.

3.2.1 Conventional categories of real rights

Conventionally, real rights are categorised according to their nature and the entitlement to hold them. The basic distinction is between ownership on the one hand, and limited real rights on the other, as the diagram below demonstrates.

---

[1] *Silberberg & Schoeman Property* p 44; *Wille's Principles* pp 406–408.
[2] For a complete list, see *Silberberg & Schoeman Property* p 47.

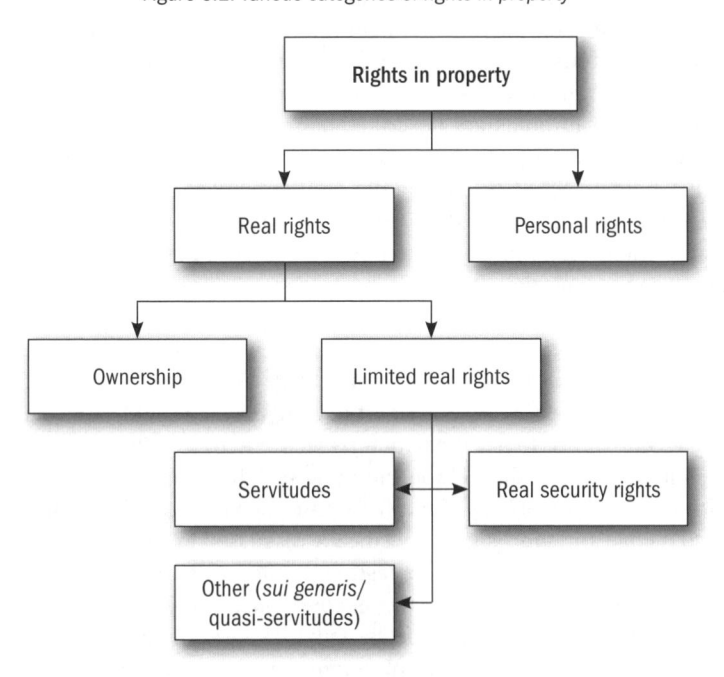

Figure 3.2: Various categories of rights in property

```
                    Rights in property
                    /              \
              Real rights      Personal rights
              /        \
        Ownership    Limited real rights
                     /            \
              Servitudes  ←→  Real security rights
                  ↓
          Other (sui generis/
            quasi-servitudes)
```

In the following paragraphs, the main distinction between the different types of rights is discussed briefly. More detailed discussions are found in the chapters dedicated to the different rights below.

Of all real rights, the right of ownership in its unrestricted form constitutes the most comprehensive relationship between a person and a thing.[3] Ownership is the only real right that one can hold in respect of one's own property (i.e. a *ius in re propria*).[4] The mainstream view on the legal nature of ownership distinguishes it from other forms of entitlement based on its characteristic independence.[5] By contrast, other rights to property are **derived from** ownership and have a more circumscribed content. If they are real by nature, and are held by someone **other** than the owner of the property, they are typified as limited real rights (i.e. *iura in re aliena*).[6] The content of ownership is dealt with in more detail in chapter 5 below.

Servitudes are limited real rights, usually in respect of land. These rights entitle the holder to specified uses of property belonging to another and consequently they restrict the exercise of ownership entitlements by the owner.[7] For instance, in his will, Jan may bequeath his farm to his son, Karel, subject to a provision that Jan's wife (and Karel's mother), Susan, is entitled to the use and fruits of the farm until her death or remarriage. Susan becomes the holder of a limited real right – a usufruct – in respect of the farm when Jan dies. Karel becomes the owner. Karel may not have much use and enjoyment of the farm

---

3   *Silberberg & Schoeman Property* p 47; *Wille's Principles* p 427.
4   *Silberberg & Schoeman Property* p 47.
5   Van der Merwe *Sakereg* p 176.
6   *Silberberg and Schoeman Property* pp 47–48.
7   *Wille's Principles* pp 407, 409, 419–422, 431–432, 592*ff*.

while Susan holds the usufruct as he must accept that Susan occupies the farm and draws its fruits. She may even run the farm as a commercial enterprise for her own benefit. By contrast, Susan has extensive rights of use and enjoyment, but she does not have the rights of an owner. She may, for instance, not alienate the farm. Hence, the limited real rights such as those that Susan holds are described as servitudes: they are rights restricted to particular kinds of use in respect of the property of someone else. In this way, they **serve** their particular holders, while restricting the entitlements of the owners of the property. Servitudes are discussed in greater detail in chapter 9 below.

Real security rights are created and enforced to ensure the performance of a specific obligation between two parties. They give the holder (creditor) an interest in the property of the debtor so that if the debtor fails to perform in terms of the contract, the creditor can realise her interest in the property to satisfy the debt. For instance, a real security right such as a pledge (in the case of movables) or mortgage (in the case of immovable property) provides the creditor with certainty that a particular debt will be paid. If the debtor is unable to raise the necessary funds to pay the debt thus secured, the creditor is entitled to demand that the specific property of the debtor, the thing which forms the object of the security right, be sold and that the proceeds of such a sale are used to satisfy the creditor's claim. The law relating to pledge and mortgage is specifically discussed in chapter 12 below.

South African law does not admit of a restricted category of real rights. It acknowledges the development of new forms of real rights beyond those known in Roman law.[8] Although the traditional classification deals specifically with various kinds of servitudes and different types of real security rights, it is important to remember that there may be rights in South African law that do not fit comfortably into either of these categories but, nevertheless, qualify as limited real rights. So, for instance, the position of mineral rights within the traditional classification was always contested. In early jurisprudence, the judicial approach to this particular type of right was that it amounted to a quasi-servitude.[9] Scholarly opinion, however, favoured a description of mineral rights as real rights *sui generis*.[10] This referred to the fact that these rights are not readily classifiable within traditional categories of rights. The controversy regarding mineral rights has dissipated with the adoption of a new legal regime relating to minerals and petroleum from 2004 onwards because the construction of mineral rights as it was known was replaced by statutory rights, which are classified either as limited real rights or not.[11] However, the historical notion of mineral rights provides a good example of the fact that not all rights can be classed as real in South African law. They resemble the traditionally known limited real rights in the Roman law classification. How rights are classed as real is discussed in greater depth below.

---

8   *Silberberg & Schoeman Property* p 48.
9   See especially *Lazarus and Jackson v Wessels, Oliver and the Coronation Freehold Estates, Town and Mines Ltd* 1903 TS 499 (T) at 510 where Innes CJ stated that '[mineral rights] seem at first sight to be very much of the nature of personal servitudes; but then they are freely assignable.' In some instances, mineral rights were described as personal quasi-servitudes *(Nolte v Johannesburg Consolidated Investment Co Ltd Respondent* 1943 AD 295 at 305) or mineral servitudes (*Van Vuren and Others v Registrar of Deeds* 1907 TS 289 at 295-297).
10 This view was followed in a minority of cases, see e.g. *Ex Parte Pierce* 1950 (3) SA 628 (O) at 634; but was strongly supported in scholarly writing: see e.g. Viljoen, HP & Bosman, PH (1979) *A Guide to Mining Rights in South Africa* (Johannesburg, Lex Patria Publishers) p 7; Van der Merwe *Sakereg* p 553.
11 See the discussion in ch 10 below.

3.2.2 Real and personal rights

As mentioned above, South African law knows no closed category *(numerus clausus)* of limited real rights.[12] This often renders the distinction between real and personal rights problematic, especially where no explicit statutory identification of the nature of such rights exists. Difficulties arise specifically in respect of rights pertaining to land which do not fall within the traditional Roman law categories of limited real rights (i.e. servitudes or real security rights).[13] The issue is compounded by the fact that the land registration system permits registration of real rights in land only, and precludes registration of personal rights except in strictly circumscribed circumstances.[14]

Various theories attempt to explain the difference between real and personal rights. These theories focus on different elements of the rights, and highlight particular elements as important. The South African courts have developed a special approach to distinguish between real and personal rights in circumstances where the distinction is particularly problematic. This is discussed in greater detail below.

To begin with a basic theoretical distinction, one can say that real rights establish a direct relationship between the person and the property, while personal rights establish a relationship between one person and another in respect of a delictual or contractual obligation, called a 'performance'.[15] The performance may entail that one person is obliged to do or not do something, or to give something to the other person in the relationship. Whereas the direct relationship in the case of real rights is between a person and a thing, the direct relationship in the case of personal rights is between one person and another. This kind of description amounts to a distinction based on classical Roman law theory because it focuses on the **objects** to which the particular rights relate.[16]

A complementary explanation is found in the personalist theory. This theoretical approach to the distinction between real and personal rights focuses on the **persons** against whom the particular rights operate. The holder of a real right can enforce his right to the property in principle against **all other persons**. This means that the right is enforceable against anyone who interferes with the relationship between the right holder and the property and who disregards the holder's entitlement over the property. By contrast, a personal right can be enforced only against **the person who is party to the agreement** creating the right. Because of this contrast, real rights are said to be absolute, while personal rights are said to be relative.[17]

---

12 *Silberberg and Schoeman Property* p 48.
13 *Silberberg & Schoeman Property* pp 48-49.
14 Sections 16 and 63(1) of the Deeds Registries Act 47 of 1937.
15 *Silberberg & Schoeman Property* p 51.
16 Detailed explanations in *Silberberg & Schoeman Property* pp 50-51; *Wille's Principles* p 429.
17 Detailed explanations in *Silberberg & Schoeman Property* pp 51-54; *Wille's Principles* pp 428-429.

> **PAUSE FOR REFLECTION**
>
> **Implications of the difference between real and personal rights**
>
> The theoretical distinctions between real and personal rights and their pitfalls are discussed in other authoritative sources on South African property law, and need not be discussed in detail here.[18] The treatment of this topic in such sources demonstrates, however, that it is not always easy to distinguish whether a particular relationship in respect of property amounts to a real right or a personal right. Often, the content of the right is such that it is possible to construe the right as either real or personal in a particular context.
>
> For example, Ayanda may agree with his neighbour, Bulelani, that Bulelani may use a part of Ayanda's land as pasture for Bulelani's cattle. In an example such as this, it will not be immediately obvious whether the right conferred on Bulelani relates directly to the land, or directly to the relationship between Ayanda and Bulelani. In other words, it is unclear whether only a contractual arrangement exists between Ayanda and Bulelani or whether a real right is intended. The significance is that if Bulelani's use of the pasture is contractual, then he has a personal right and therefore his successor in title will not automatically enjoy the same benefit. Similarly, a successor in title to Ayanda would not be obliged to permit Bulelani or his successor in title to graze the cattle on the land. If Ayanda and Bulelani intended a real right for Bulelani, then, assuming all the formalities have been completed, a successor in title to Ayanda would be bound automatically to permit Bulelani to graze his cattle. On the face of it, the content of the right would be similar whether the right is real or personal: Bulelani's cattle would graze on Ayanda's land. However, the period of time for which this activity may carry on is affected. If Ayanda and Bulelani have only a contractual arrangement, then the duration of the arrangement is for as long as Ayanda is owner of the land and Bulelani has cattle that can use the land for grazing (assuming that these are the terms of the agreement). To establish whether a real right is intended, the intention of the parties must be investigated, including whether they dealt with each other as owners rather than in their personal capacities. It is thus important to be able to make this distinction because if the right created between Ayanda and Bulelani by this agreement is real, the commitment would survive and bind Ayanda's successor in title. If not, the commitment would cease once Ayanda is no longer owner of the land.

There are other theoretical approaches to this distinction as well, but they are not dealt with here. Instead, the focus is on the practical manner in which the South African courts have approached this problem of distinguishing real rights from personal rights. The discussion below highlights the reasons why the distinction is important, and illustrates when the distinction can be particularly problematic.

3.2.2.1 Why the distinction between real and personal rights is important

Real rights and personal rights are acquired and transferred in different ways. They may be exercised in different ways and are protected differently. Hence, it is important to distinguish between real and personal rights for various reasons.

First, the different legal rules applicable to the various modes of transfer render it important to be able to distinguish between the types of rights that are transferred in these

---

18 See e.g. *Silberberg & Schoeman Property* pp 50*ff*, *Wille's Principles* pp 428*ff*; Van der Merwe *Sakereg* pp 60–63; *LAWSA* Vol 27(1) at para 233; and the sources discussed there.

different ways. As the personalist theory suggests, real rights may be exercised against 'the world at large',[19] whereas personal rights usually bind only a specific person or a defined group of persons. The type of right determines the extent to which (and the persons against whom) it can be exercised.

Second, real rights are dealt with in property law, whereas the law of obligations (i.e. contract and delict) governs personal rights. Hence, real rights are protected by proprietary remedies, while personal rights are protected by the availability of contractual and delictual remedies. To know which remedies may be invoked to protect rights in a specific setting, it is important to be able to distinguish between the kinds of rights.

Third, real rights are transferred either by way of registration (in the case of immovable property) or delivery (in the case of movables),[20] whereas personal rights are transferred by way of cession. For instance, the Registrar of Deeds is statutorily required to register servitudes and other real rights in land, but (with a few exceptions) is restrained from registering any personal right in respect of immovable property or any condition that does not restrict the exercise of a right of ownership.[21] A real right in land is thus adequately protected by its registration in the Deeds Registry. The Deeds Registries Act further provides for ownership in land to be conveyed by a process of publicising and recording the transfer at the Deeds Registry.[22] Limited real rights in land, which restrict the exercise of the entitlements of ownership by the landowner, are the only other kinds of rights (with a few exceptions) capable of being registered in terms of the existing registration system.

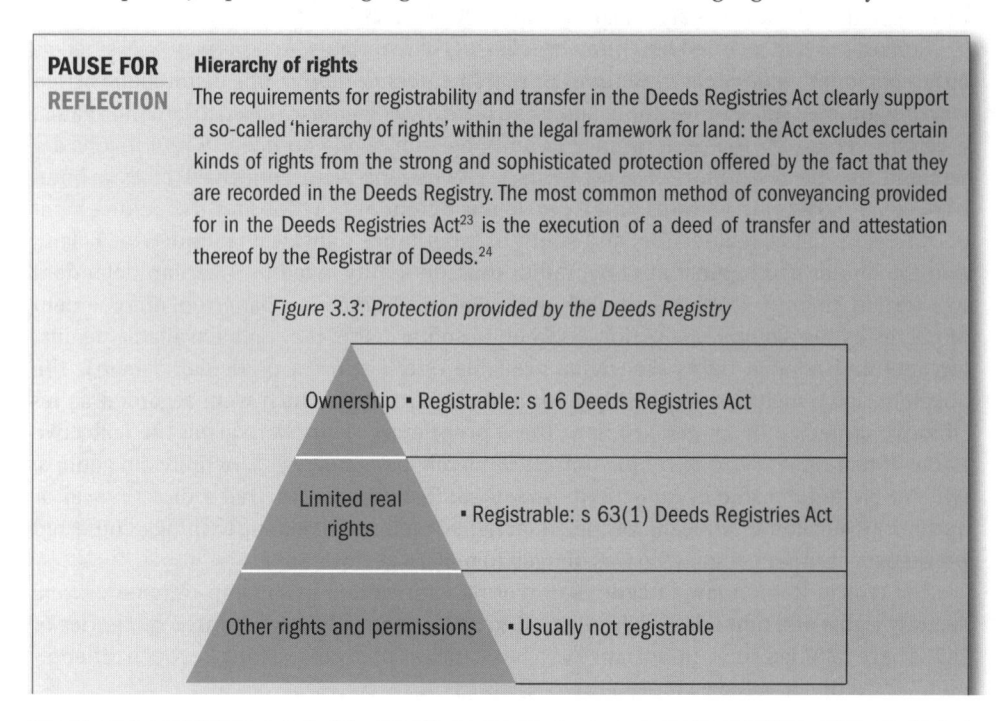

> **PAUSE FOR REFLECTION**
>
> **Hierarchy of rights**
>
> The requirements for registrability and transfer in the Deeds Registries Act clearly support a so-called 'hierarchy of rights' within the legal framework for land: the Act excludes certain kinds of rights from the strong and sophisticated protection offered by the fact that they are recorded in the Deeds Registry. The most common method of conveyancing provided for in the Deeds Registries Act[23] is the execution of a deed of transfer and attestation thereof by the Registrar of Deeds.[24]
>
> Figure 3.3: Protection provided by the Deeds Registry
>
> - Ownership • Registrable: s 16 Deeds Registries Act
> - Limited real rights • Registrable: s 63(1) Deeds Registries Act
> - Other rights and permissions • Usually not registrable

---

19 *Wille's Principles* p 428.
20 See ch 7 below.
21 Section 63(1) of the Deeds Registries Act 47 of 1937.
22 Section 16 of the Deeds Registries Act 47 of 1937.
23 Section 16 of the Deeds Registries Act 47 of 1937.
24 Jones, RJM & Nel, HS (1991) *Conveyancing in South Africa* 4 ed (Cape Town, Juta) p 91.

> Registration brings to fruition the principle of publicity underlying the law of property. When rights in land are registered, the holders thereof are afforded the necessary security of title to enable them to enforce and protect their rights against the public at large, and to use such rights as security to gain access to finance.[25] This system espoused by the Deeds Registries Act supports the idea that landownership is the pinnacle of (or the most important right within) the hierarchy of rights, with limited real rights following close at heel.[26] Other rights are understood as being in stages of inferiority to ownership. This hierarchical approach to landownership and other rights to land is supported in a large part of the land reform legislation,[27] although it is increasingly coming under scrutiny for failing to provide acceptable solutions to the increased pressure placed by the proliferation of land reform legislation on the existing registration and land control system in South Africa.

3.2.2.2 When the distinction is hard to draw

In the South African context, the difficulty with distinguishing between real and personal rights is compounded by the fact that any relationship that amounts to a real right will be acknowledged as such, regardless of its content. There is no *numerus clausus* of real rights in South African law. This means there is no checklist for easy recognition of real rights. On this point, the law deviates significantly from its Roman law roots.

Roman law had a closed list *(numerus clausus)* of real rights. Actions were classified as either personal *(actiones in personam)* or real *(actiones in rem)*.[28] This distinction carried with it significant substantive implications: an *actio in personam* involved a demand against a certain person for the performance of an obligation, while an *actio in rem* involved a demand for the restitution of a *res* (thing). Obligations were conceived of as a bond **between a particular plaintiff and a particular defendant**. Actions for the enforcement of ownership rights, real security and family or inheritance rights were founded on a claim that the holder had **against anyone**, rather than on a duty owed by a certain defendant to a certain plaintiff. Medieval scholars explained this Roman law pattern of enforcement of claims as involving a distinction between absolute rights (i.e. rights available against anyone) and relative rights (i.e. rights available only against a particular person). The absolute rights included ownership and limited real rights, which were regarded as *res* (things), protected by an *actio in rem*. These proprietary rights were given the collective name of real rights *(iura in re)* in contrast to merely personal rights, namely obligations, which were enforceable by an *actio in personam*. Real rights conferred a direct power or authority over a thing, while merely personal rights, even when relating to things, conferred power over another person who was obliged to make a performance.

The typical Roman law categories of real rights included ownership, servitudes, real security rights and a building right referred to as *superficies*.[29] The first three categories of rights have retained some importance as a basic means of distinguishing between different

---

25 Mostert, H *Modern Studies II* pp 3-4.
26 *Silberberg & Schoeman Property* p 65.
27 Mostert, H *Modern Studies II* pp 3-4.
28 *Wille's Principles* p 428 and the sources cited there.
29 Thomas, JAC (1976) *Textbook of Roman Law* (Oxford, New Holland) pp 195-210.

types of rights. One must keep in mind, though, that the demands of modern commerce and legal practice render it necessary sometimes to create rights that do not resemble the typical Roman law kinds of rights. Two reasons make this possible. First, South African law does not acknowledge a *numerus clausus* of real rights, which means that not all rights created and classified as real, easily fit into these traditional Roman law categories. Second, principles of freedom of contract and of testation (making a will) allow people to establish new, peculiar real rights in respect of their immovable property.

This can lead to difficulties in identifying accurately the nature of the rights thus created. It is especially rights in immovable property (land) that pose problems and, specifically (but not exclusively), where a monetary obligation is attached to the rights created in terms of an agreement or a bequest in a will. The following examples are taken from existing case law:

1. A testator bequeaths land to his son and links it to an obligation placed on the son to pay the surviving spouse of the testator an amount of money, either once-off, or at regular intervals.[30]
2. A testator bequeaths a farm to his children. The will contains detailed provisions as to how the farm should be divided, that is, by the drawing of lots. It further provides that the child who draws the part that includes the farmhouse has to pay an amount of money to his siblings.[31]
3. In an agreement to divide land, the co-owners of the land agree that if either part of the land is developed in future as a township, they and their descendants will share the profits.[32]
4. A contract of sale in respect of land contains a use restriction (e.g. it may only be used for industrial or conservation purposes). It also contains a clause that enables the seller to buy back the land from the purchaser if the land cannot be used in accordance with the limitation.[33]

In each case, the nature of the rights or obligations contained in the provision must be established as either real or personal. This is an important determination because only real rights in land are registrable[34] and hence automatically enforceable against successors in title. If the nature of the right or obligation is personal, then a successor in title cannot be automatically bound. This means that the full agreement or bequest might not be given effect, which would be contrary to the principles of freedom of contract and of testation. Registrability of the rights or obligations is thus an important mechanism by which rights may be enforced.

The above examples entail disputes about whether rights that were already created could or should be registered; or should have been registered and were not; or were registered, but erroneously. In one instance, the question was not registrability, but rather whether rights created gave rise to a particular kind of tax arising only from real rights. In the following section, the approach of the courts to distinguishing between real and personal rights to determine their registrability is discussed, with reference to the cases from which these examples were taken.

---

30 Compare *Nel NO v Commissioner for Inland Revenue* 1960 (1) SA 227 (A).
31 Compare *Ex parte Geldenhuys* 1926 OPD 155.
32 Compare *Lorentz v Melle* 1978 (3) SA 1044 (T).
33 Compare *Cape Explosive Works Ltd v Denel (Pty) Ltd* 2001 (3) SA 569 (SCA).
34 Section 63(1) of the Deeds Registries Act 47 of 1937.

3.2.2.3 Courts' approach to the distinction between real and personal rights

Section 63(1) of the Deeds Registries Act[35] provides that only real rights in land are registrable, and that personal rights may be registered only if, in the opinion of the Registrar, they are ancillary or otherwise complementary to registrable real rights. This provision often results in disputes about the registrability of unorthodox or unusual rights. Despite the theoretical explanations of the differences between real and personal rights,[36] a practical approach is necessary. The courts have developed a twofold test to deal with the registrability of rights: the right must be **intended to bind successors in title**, and it must also amount to a 'subtraction from *dominium*'; where ownership entitlements must be diminished by the granting of the right. These tests operate in tandem and are not mutually exclusive. Both aspects must be satisfied before it may be concluded that a real right has been created. However, the weighting afforded to each test varies in different court decisions. This means that case law is an important guide to determine the registrability of rights as different scenarios may give rise to particular interpretations.

The subtraction from dominium test. The subtraction from *dominium* test is articulated well in *Ex Parte Geldenhuys*,[37] which concerned a dispute about the registrability of rights created in a will. The will determined that the land in the estate would be divided in equal parts among the children of the deceased once the eldest came of age. When this happened, the portion to be allocated to each was to be determined by the children drawing lots. The will contained an additional provision to the effect that the child who drew the portion that included the homestead, would be obliged to pay an amount of money to the other children. The Registrar of Deeds refused to register these conditions, arguing that they did not establish real rights in land because no diminution of ownership entitlements resulted.

As regards the characterisation of rights as either real (being 'burdens upon the land') or personal (being binding only upon a particular individual), the court first indicated that:

> *when it is said that 'personal rights' cannot be registered against the title to land, the reference is not to rights created in favour of a 'person', for such rights may be real rights against the land. The reference is to rights, which are merely binding on the present owner of the land, and which thus do not bind the land, and do not constitute jura in re aliena over the land, and do not bind the successor in title of the present owner.*[38]

To determine whether rights are registrable, the court composed the following formula, indicating that:

> *[o]ne has to look not so much to the right, but to the correlative obligation. If that obligation is a burden upon the land, a subtraction from the dominium, the corresponding right is real and registrable; if it is not such an obligation, but merely an obligation binding on some person or other, the corresponding right is a personal right, or a right in personam, and it cannot as a rule be registered.*[39]

---

35 Act 47 of 1937.
36 See pp 45–46 above.
37 1926 OPD 155.
38 *Ex parte Geldenhuys* 1926 OPD 155 at 163–164.
39 *Ex parte Geldenhuys* 1926 OPD 155 at 164.

In applying the distinction to the case at hand, it was found that the provision dealing with **the time and manner** in which the land had to be divided indeed amounted to a subtraction from the *dominium*. The stipulation restricted the common law right of co-owners to claim division of the land held jointly at any time they chose and to divide it as they chose. This restriction, it was found, adhered to and affected so directly the entitlements of ownership of undivided co-ownership shares that, necessarily, they had to be regarded as a real burden upon that co-ownership. In response to a question as to why the division could not proceed immediately, the court found that the identity of the person who would be obliged to pay the money was unclear. There could be no certainty that the eldest child would reach majority first.

The other provision, relating to the **payment of a determined amount of money**, was found **not** to constitute a burden on the land because the obligation sounded in money, and because it was seen as being 'altogether uncertain and conditional'. In other words, the obligation to pay the money was on a specific person rather than on the land and once the obligation had been performed, it would be satisfied. No further payments would be required. These aspects gave the right the character of a personal right. Yet, even though this right did not amount to a real right, nevertheless, the court held that to give proper effect to the will, it had to be registered on the basis that the right was so 'intimately connected' with the other registrable real rights.[40]

The act of registering a personal obligation does not change its character. Registration permits the personal obligation to be publicised but does not make it automatically binding on third parties. In other words, despite registration, the doctrine of constructive notice does not apply to a personal right or obligation.

This case clearly demonstrates that the subtraction from *dominium* test entails an enquiry into whether the extent of ownership entitlements in respect of land is curtailed when rights in the land are granted to others. Such curtailment can occur when the right confers upon the holder some ownership entitlements, or prohibits the owner from exercising such entitlements for himself or herself. The case further demonstrates that personal rights may have to be registered when they are closely connected to a registrable real right that burdens the land. It also provides an example of the kind of right that may be regarded as ancillary to a registrable real right.

The subtraction from *dominium* test, as formulated in *Ex parte Geldenhuys*, was applied in subsequent case law, but in different ways and with varying results. In *Lorentz v Melle*,[41] a declaratory order was sought regarding the nature of the registered reciprocal rights of landowners to share the net profits from a township development on the neighbouring land. The applicant, a successor in title to one of the original landowners, argued that the rights should not have been registered because they did not create real burdens. The court held that the clause dealing with the potential township development in the agreement between the original co-owners, did not bind subsequent owners. The reason was that 'the conditional obligation to pay attaches of necessity not to the land (which is not burdened) but merely to the owner thereof'.[42] The obligation to share the profits was conditional because it was uncertain whether and when a township development might occur. This finding meant that the rights had been erroneously registered for some 50 years. Despite

---

40 *Ex parte Geldenhuys* 1926 OPD 155 at 165–166.
41 1978 (3) SA 1044 (T).
42 *Lorentz* at 1052E–F.

the 'sanctity of the registry', the matter had to be rectified by removal of the right from the register. The court, however, confirmed the position that upon permissible registration of a condition conferring only personal rights, such rights remained personal.[43]

> **PAUSE FOR REFLECTION**
>
> **Interpreting the subtraction from *dominium* test**
>
> The court in *Lorentz v Melle* interpreted the subtraction from *dominium* test as requiring that the burden upon land should amount to a curtailment of the 'enjoyment of the land **in the physical sense**'.[44] It is worthwhile considering carefully the implications of such an interpretation of the subtraction from *dominium* test.
>
> On the one hand, it may be seen as a restrictive interpretation of the test as formulated in the *Geldenhuys* decision.[45] It requires the imposition upon the land to be an **immediate and actual** interference with the owner's rights of use and enjoyment. On the other hand, the statement in the *Lorentz* decision, quoted above, may be interpreted to refer simply to the fact that the provision in the subdivision agreement did not give rise to a burden on the land at all, but only to an obligation on the person of the owner. A crucial element in analysing this decision is whether profits from the sale of the land could be seen as fruits of the land. If profits are regarded as fruits, then, arguably, ownership entitlements of the person who makes the profit in circumstances such as the *Lorentz* case would be diminished by the agreement to share the profits. However, the agreement in *Lorentz* amounts to no more than an ordinary monetary obligation, namely if a development occurs and it is successful, then the profits will be shared. This can happen only once. Consequently, one of the requirements for a servitude, viz that there be some ongoing benefit derived from the land that accrues to the *dominus*, is absent. This means that ownership entitlements are not directly diminished and hence that the obligation is not a real obligation.
>
> Given the decision in the classical case of *Geldenhuys*, the courts should be hesitant to classify such obligations as real. On this view, therefore, the interpretation afforded by *Lorentz* of the subtraction of *dominium* test is not as restrictive as it may seem at first glance.
>
> In evaluating the decision, further consideration should be given to policy considerations relating to the purpose of registering rights in land. These are discussed below.

The interpretation of the subtraction from *dominium* test in *Lorentz* may be contrasted with the similar exercise in *Pearly Beach Trust v Registrar of Deeds*.[46] Here a court order was sought, declaring a certain condition in a deed of sale registrable. The condition entitled a third party to receive from the transferee and its successors in title a third of the consideration received in return for an option or right to prospect for minerals on the property, as well as a third of the compensation if the property was expropriated or sold to an authority empowered to expropriate.

The Registrar of Deeds declined to register the condition, arguing that the condition did not restrict the right of ownership as contemplated by s 63(1) of the Deeds Registries Act since it did not amount to a subtraction from *dominium*. However, the court regarded the right to dispose of the property *(ius disponendi)* as restricted by the condition, in that the owner was precluded from obtaining the full benefit of the disposition.[47] Consequently, the

---
43 *Lorentz* at 1055E–F.
44 *Lorentz* at 1052F.
45 Van der Walt, AJ (2006) *Law of Property Casebook for Students* 6 ed (Cape Town, Juta) p 26.
46 1990 (4) SA 614 (C).
47 *Pearly Beach Trust* at 617I.

court found that the condition satisfied both tests: here was a subtraction from *dominium* and an intention to bind successive owners.[48]

This decision is not reconcilable with the decisions in *Lorentz v Melle* or *Ex parte Geldenhuys*. The condition in *Pearly Beach* required a sum of money to be paid to a third party in the event that either a prospecting licence was issued or an expropriation occurred. Should either of these trigger events take place, the money in terms of the obligation would come from the state's coffers, not the land, which indicates that no fruits of the land are implicated by the agreement. Consequently, there is no real burden on the land, but merely an agreement between persons that a sum of money would be paid if a particular event took place. The ownership entitlements were thus not restricted in any way. Similarly to both *Lorentz* and *Ex Parte Geldenhuys*, it was uncertain whether and when the events might take place. Furthermore, should the event occur, there would be a once-off payment only. This is characteristic of a personal right, which means that the right should not have been registered. Furthermore, unlike in *Ex parte Geldenhuys*, where it was decided that the personal right could be registered on the basis that there was an intimate connection between it and other registrable real rights, the *Pearly Beach* scenario did not include a limited real right to which the personal right could be seen as ancillary. Consequently, a finding that the personal rights could be registered because they were 'intimately connected' or complementary to other registrable real rights, was impossible.

> **COUNTER POINT**
>
> **Implications of varying interpretations**
>
> The dilemma created by these various interpretations of the subtraction from *dominium* test in different provincial divisions of the Supreme Court (as it then was), was that none indisputably constituted binding precedent. Accordingly, the outcome of the interpretation of the subtraction from *dominium* test could differ considerably, depending on the jurisdiction in which the test was to be applied. Academic opinion on which of the two approaches represented by the *Lorentz* and *Pearly Beach* cases was most appropriate, also varied. Van der Merwe preferred the interpretation of *Lorentz v Melle*, and criticised the outcome of the *Pearly Beach* case.[49] The basis for his criticism was that the negotiability of land should not be impaired by allowing too many restrictions on ownership. On the other hand, Van der Walt's approach is that rights such as those declared real in *Pearly Beach* should be recorded in the Deeds Registry for policy considerations and to ensure clarity.[50]

The interpretative uncertainties of the subtraction from *dominium* test have not yet been resolved, even though the Supreme Court of Appeal had an opportunity to apply the test in *Cape Explosive Works Ltd v Denel (Pty) Ltd*.[51] This case concerned a condition in a deed of sale that limited the use of the property and linked the impossibility of performance in terms of the use limitation to a right of repurchase in favour of the original seller. Although the rights had originally been registered, they were not brought forward into all title deeds in subsequent subdivisions, consolidations and transfers. The result was that the initially registered right remained registered only in respect of a very small portion of the original

---

48   *Pearly Beach Trust* at 617H–618A.
49   Van der Merwe *Sakereg* p 76.
50   Van der Walt, AJ (2006) *Law of Property Casebook for Students* 6 ed (Cape Town, Juta) pp 9, 27–28.
51   2001 (3) SA 569 (SCA).

land. The dispute centred on whether the omission of the right from subsequent title deeds terminated the right or not. It was argued before the Supreme Court of Appeal that the omission was erroneous and not fatal and that the rights remained as binding on successive owners as they had been originally, despite their omission from most of the currently registered title deeds. The Supreme Court of Appeal formulated the test for registrability as follows:

> *To determine whether a particular right or condition in respect of land is real, two requirements must be satisfied:*
>
> *(1) the intention of the person who creates the real right must be to bind not only the present owner of the land, but also his successors in title; and*
>
> *(2) the nature of the right or condition must be such that the registration of it results in a 'subtraction from dominium' of the land against which it is registered.*[52]

The court then considered the conditions in the original deed of sale, indicating that the right of repurchase was not an independent right, but part of the limitation on the use of the land, rendering it a subtraction from *dominium*. In terms of this approach, there was no need for either a restricted or generous interpretation of the subtraction from *dominium* test since the limitation on the use of the land so obviously constituted an inroad on the rights of the owners.

A considerable part of the court's analysis focused on the first test it mentioned, i.e. the intention to bind successive owners. This test is considered next.

The intention to bind successors in title test. The subtraction from *dominium* test goes a long way towards resolving issues about the registrability of rights in land created in wills or per agreement. It is not the only consideration taken into account to determine registrability, however. The intention with which rights are created is of equal importance in determining whether a particular right is real or not.

In *Nel NO v Commissioner for Inland Revenue*,[53] the registrability of a right to receive payment of money arose in the context of a determination of the dutiable value of an estate. A number of properties had been donated and transferred to the son of the donor, subject to certain conditions. Among others, the conditions stipulated that the properties were donated subject to a usufruct in favour of the donor, and that, after his death, his son would be obliged to pay a regular monthly sum of money to his mother (the testator's wife). This obligation was made a condition of transfer and accordingly registered against the title deeds of the properties. In determining the value of the donor's estate for purposes of estate duty later, it was argued that the registered right amounted to a 'usufructuary or other like interest' which should be deducted from the total value of the property in the estate. This argument was rejected in the court *a quo*.

On appeal, the then Appellate Division deliberately left open the question whether a burden imposing an obligation to pay money, that will bind a successor in title either for an ascertainable time or indefinitely, would be registrable against the title of the land. It was decided, however, that the obligation to pay the annuity was personal, binding only on

---

52 *Cape Explosive Works* at para 12. The court referred to *Erlax Properties (Pty) Ltd v Registrar of Deeds and Others* 1992 (1) SA 879 (A) at 885B.
53 1960 (1) SA 227 (A).

the son. An analysis of the intention with which the right was created in the will led to the decision:

> The donor knew that the son would be well provided for ... The donor wanted his widow to have the use of the residential land, and he wished his son to contribute something towards her maintenance. The donor knew that the son, as owner, would have to grant both the annuity and the usufruct, and he imposed upon him the obligation to do so. [54]

This case demonstrates the court's wariness of assuming the creation of real, registrable rights. The intention with which the rights were created was vital in determining whether they constituted rights binding upon successors in title. Evidence of the intention was sought in the documents that set out the testator's wishes.

In *Cape Explosive Works Ltd and Another v Denel (Pty) Ltd and Others*,[55] discussed in broad terms above,[56] the rights at stake were created upon the sale and transfer of particular pieces of land to the second respondent, Armscor. The sale was subject to certain restrictions upon the use of the land: the first restriction was that Armscor could use it only to manufacture armaments; the second restriction was that once the land was no longer required for this particular purpose, Armscor would advise Cape Explosive Works that the land was no longer to be used as envisaged, and that the latter would then have the first right to repurchase the land. The restrictive conditions in respect of the smaller of the two pieces of land were cancelled by notarial deed. In a transfer of the larger of the two pieces of land from Armscor to Denel, the conditions were brought forward into the new title deed. However, in a subsequent consolidation of the two pieces of land, the second restriction was omitted, and the first restriction was made applicable only to a small portion of the consolidated land, and not to the entire extent of the land. In the dispute that ensued between Cape Explosive Works and Denel, the latter argued that the land was unencumbered by the resale restriction. The former, on the other hand, sought an order to rectify the title deed to include both restrictions.

The court *a quo* held that the second restriction was not registrable in terms of s 63(1) of the Deeds Registries Act, whereupon Cape Explosive Works appealed. The Supreme Court of Appeal held that the two restrictions should have been carried forward into new title documentation. The court attached great importance to the intention with which the land was transferred. It referred to the requirement that any transfer of ownership should be accompanied by the intention to transfer and receive the property at stake. Reading the two clauses together (i.e. as creating one restriction), the court further held that the intention to bind successors in title of Armscor appeared clearly from the original agreement. Because the provisions restricted the use of the property by the owner, the court held that they amounted to a subtraction from *dominium*.

The court further indicated:

> A real right is adequately protected by its registration in the Deeds Office ... Once Capex's rights had been registered they were maintainable against the whole world. They were not extinguished by their erroneous omission from subsequent title deeds and the fact that Denel's title deed, registered in the Deeds Office, did not reflect those rights, does not assist Denel.[57]

---

54 *Nel NO v Commissioner for Inland Revenue* 1960 (1) SA 227 (A) at 234A-C.
55 2001 (3) SA 569 (SCA).
56 See p 53 above.
57 *Cape Explosive Works Ltd and Another v Denel (Pty) Ltd and Others* 2001 (3) SA 569 (SCA) at para 16.

This case demonstrates the important point that erroneous registration or omission to carry forward previously registered rights does not affect the nature of the right as being either real or personal. The determination of whether a right is real or personal hinges on whether the right is enforceable against someone in her personal capacity or in her capacity as the owner of a particular property, in which case successors in title are bound, and on whether the right subtracts from *dominium*, i.e. diminishes ownership entitlements.

3.3 The principle of publicity and the doctrine of notice

The discussion about the distinction between real and personal rights indicated that the holder of a real right may enforce that right against anyone, i.e. 'the world at large'.[58] Real rights are enforceable even against third parties who act in good faith and against parties who, in good faith, acquire such rights for value.[59] Because of the prejudice this may cause, it is desirable (even indispensable) that the existence of a real right as well as its content and the identity of its holder should be made known, i.e. publicised to the world at large. The next section shows how the principle of publicity is given effect to in South African law, and how the law deals with situations in which the publicity of specific real relations is impaired.

3.3.1 Publicity

For a real right in a thing to be transferred or newly created, the transferee must know the identity of the holder of the real right as well as the extent of that right.[60] To 'advertise' the existence of a real right in respect of land, its extent and scope, as well as the identity of its holder, these facts must be made known to the world at large. This process is in accordance with the publicity principle.[61] This principle entails that outsiders should be able to deduce from externally perceivable indications whether real rights in things exist, and when transfer of a real right from one person to another occurs. In other words, it requires 'consonance between the legal and the factual situations'.[62]

In the case of movables, publicity is served mainly by possession of the thing[63] and by delivery at transfer:[64] physical control of the thing suggests a particular kind of real relationship between the holder and the thing.[65] In the context of land rights, publicity is achieved primarily by registering rights in respect of land in a public office, the Deeds Registry. Since the registry is open to the public, anyone may access the records held in the Deeds Registry,[66] usually against payment of a small fee. Registration of title and limited real rights thus eases the burden on the owner to prove her title.

The publicity principle is served further by requirements that couple changes in physical control over things with changes in the legal relationships that underlie such control. For example, the requirements regarding the form of delivery for transfer of movables and registration formalities for transfer of land are designed to optimise publicity of the

---

58 *Silberberg & Schoeman Property* p 80.
59 *Silberberg & Schoeman Property* p 81.
60 *Silberberg & Schoeman Property* p 81.
61 Van der Merwe *Sakereg* p 13.
62 *Wille's Principles* p 410; Reid, KGC 'Obligations and Property: Exploring the Border' (1997) 225 *Acta Juridica* pp 236–237.
63 See ch 4 below.
64 See ch 7 below.
65 Van der Merwe *Sakereg* p 13.
66 Van der Merwe *Sakereg* p 13.

changed legal relationship regarding the property concerned. In turn, these requirements assist those persons who would rely on the outward manifestations of the changed legal position, by reference to where possession of the movable lies or to the records in the Deeds Registry. Further cumbersome research to establish the state of affairs in matters relating to title to land or movables is unnecessary.[67]

It should be noted, however, that the negative system of registration that prevails in South Africa makes complete reliance on the registry impossible. At any time, there may be real rights in existence or changes in ownership that have occurred but which have not yet been registered. Furthermore, the fact that a person is in physical control of movable property may not justify the conclusion that he is also the holder of a real right in it since the legal right to control its use may vest in someone else. Nevertheless, the rebuttable presumption that the person in physical control of movable property is the owner thereof, unless the contrary is proved, makes such a conclusion reasonable in many situations.[68]

Whereas the publicity value of physical control in the case of movables may often be dubious, publicity is of paramount importance in respect of land rights. Since real rights in respect of land are registered, every person is deemed to have knowledge of real rights so registered in the Deeds Registry.[69] This is referred to as the 'doctrine of constructive knowledge'.[70] This means that because the information is publicly available, one cannot use ignorance of the existence of a real right as an excuse to escape its implications: one is deemed to know of its existence. This doctrine protects both the registered owner as well as the general public. An owner's burden of proof in respect of proving her title to land is eased in that production of the title deed is prima facie proof of title. Also, because knowledge of the register is constructive, any member of the public is protected within certain limits if reliance is placed on the information in the register.[71]

Although it is said that the doctrine of constructive knowledge renders real rights 'enforceable against the world at large',[72] it is incorrect to use this doctrine to justify enforceability of real rights in this way. The converse is true: registration of real rights in land is one of the requirements of the creation and transfer of such rights and has the effect of advertising or announcing the existence of the real right. Thus, it is the fact that the real right exists that makes it enforceable against third parties. However, registration cannot change the nature of a right: it cannot convert a personal right into a real right.[73] In addition, erroneous omission of a previously registered real right from later title deeds does not extinguish it[74] nor change its status from real to personal.[75]

---

67 Van der Merwe *Sakereg* p 14.
68 *Silberberg & Schoeman Property* p 82.
69 *Frankel Pollak Vinderine v Stanton* 2000 (1) SA 425 (W) at 432H–438G.
70 Also sometimes called the doctrine of constructive notice. Note that this doctrine is not to be confused with the doctrine of notice.
71 Van der Merwe *Sakereg* p 340.
72 *Silberberg & Schoeman Property* p 81.
73 *Ex parte Geldenhuys* 1926 OPD 155.
74 *Cape Explosive Works Ltd v Denel (Pty) Ltd* 2001 (3) SA 569 (SCA).
75 See pp 207*ff* below.

3.3.2 Doctrine of notice

Although registration is usually[76] a necessary element in the creation of a new real right, a holder of an unregistered real right is also protected in certain circumstances.[77] Protection flows from the maxim that 'nobody may derive a benefit or advantage from his own bad faith' *(nemo ex suo delicto meliorem suam conditionem facere potest)*. In property law, this means that no one may defeat another person's potential real right for her own benefit if she knows of its existence.[78] This is also referred to as the 'doctrine of notice'. This doctrine is not to be confused with the doctrine of constructive knowledge.[79] It operates to force the acquirer of the real right to give effect to the earlier personal rights that would have given rise to the acquisition of a real right. By contrast, the doctrine of constructive knowledge operates to accord knowledge of certain real relationships to parties dealing with the rights arising therefrom.

There are many examples in case law where the doctrine of notice has been applied.[80] Such examples relate especially to instances where a purchaser acquires ownership of a thing sold with certain knowledge. One set of examples in case law relates to where the purchaser knows that the thing has been sold previously to someone else.[81] Another set relates to instances where the purchaser knows that a predecessor in title has undertaken to grant a servitude to the owner of a dominant tenement.[82] Yet another set of cases concerns the purchaser's knowledge that he is acquiring the thing contrary to an option[83] or right of pre-emption[84] of someone else, or contrary to a prohibition of alienation upon the seller.[85] A few other cases also relate to the purchaser knowing that a lessee has a right to occupy the thing sold.[86] The knowledge of the purchaser may also have to do with an earlier undertaking by a predecessor in title to create a real security right over the thing sold in favour of the predecessor's creditor.[87] Further examples of the application of the doctrine of notice relate to subsequent successors in title with knowledge of a prior personal right, even when the predecessor in title had no knowledge of that personal right.[88] The doctrine has further been applied also to the attachment of an asset of a judgment debtor with a view to execution of the judgment by a judgment creditor with knowledge of a prior personal right of a previous purchaser in respect thereof.[89]

Of all these examples, the two most prominent are discussed in greater detail below. These relate to successive sales and unregistered servitudes. It is worth noticing generally that in all the cases that concerned the application of the doctrine of notice, the prior personal right would lead to the creation of a real right. This is why the doctrine speaks of

---

76 The exception would be circumstances where acquisitive prescription occurs.
77 *Silberberg & Schoeman Property* p 81.
78 *Silberberg & Schoeman Property* p 83.
79 See above.
80 More detailed discussion in *Silberberg & Schoeman Property* p 84, where comprehensive lists of the example sets mentioned below are also provided; also *Wille's Principles* pp 429, 627. The following discussion relies primarily on the analysis in *Silberberg & Schoeman Property* pp 84*ff*.
81 E.g. *Cussons v Kroon* 2001 (4) SA 833 (SCA) at para 9.
82 E.g. *Grant v Stonestreet* 1968 (4) SA 1 (A) at 20A-D.
83 E.g. *Le Roux v Odendaal* 1954 (4) SA 432 (N) at 442E-F.
84 E.g. *Le Roux v Odendaal* 1954 (4) SA 432 (N) at 442D-G.
85 E.g. *Cussons v Kroon* 2001 (4) SA 833 (SCA) at para 9-10.
86 E.g. *Total South Africa (Pty) Ltd v Xypteras* 1970 (1) SA 592 (T) at 598A-B.
87 E.g. *Thienhaus v Metje & Ziegler Ltd* 1965 (3) SA 25 (A) at 43D-E.
88 *Grant v Stonestreet* 1968 (4) SA 1 (A) at 20B-C.
89 *Hassam v Shaboodien* 1996 (2) SA 720 (C) at 728E-F.

'potential real right'. It is important to grasp that ordinary personal rights, i.e. those that could never lead to the creation of a real right, do not fall under the doctrine of notice.

The doctrine of notice does not require proof of fraud, but merely knowledge of the prior personal right.[90] Fraud may, however, be construed from such knowledge,[91] but the rationale behind the doctrine is the protection of the personal right against the unlawful act of the acquirer of a real right.[92] The application of the doctrine of notice is triggered by the acquisition of the real right with the required knowledge.[93] Also, the doctrine may be applicable only in cases where the real right was acquired against payment of consideration. Where a real right is acquired gratuitously *(ex titulo lucrativo)*, the acquirer has to observe undertakings of her predecessor with regard to the thing, even in the absence of knowledge on her part.[94]

Three requirements must be met for the doctrine of notice to apply. First, a prior personal right must exist against the holder of a real right.[95] This does not mean that the doctrine of notice is applicable to all kinds of personal rights. It applies only to personal rights that would give rise to the acquisition of the thing *(iura in personam ad rem acquirendam)*.[96] The second requirement is that a subsequent acquirer of the real right, acquired after establishment of the personal right, must infringe upon the personal right. The infringement must amount to a wrongful action, which means that the rules of delict are applicable.[97] The third requirement is that the acquirer of the real right must know of the existence of the prior personal right.[98] 'Actual knowledge' of the prior personal right is required.[99] Constructive knowledge is not enough to activate the doctrine.[100] However, in circumstances where the acquirer wilfully closes his eyes to what is obvious, he might be deemed to have the knowledge even if he denies actual knowledge.

An important question is **when** the acquirer of the real right is expected to know of the prior personal right for the doctrine to find application.[101] There is some uncertainty on this point, in particular where there is a lapse of time between the contract and the transfer of the real right. However, the correct position is that the knowledge should exist at the time of acquisition of the real right, i.e. at the time of transfer. Before transfer, the acquirer has only a personal right (to claim transfer). A dispute between the two holders of personal rights would be solved by application of the *prior in tempore* rule (i.e. first in time, stronger in law).[102]

---

90 *Silberberg & Schoeman Property* p 86 (and cases cited in fn 120 & 121 there).
91 *Kazazis v Georghiades* 1979 (3) SA 886 (T) at 893G; *Associated South African Bakeries (Pty) Ltd v Oryx & Vereinigte Bäckereien (Pty) Ltd* 1982 (3) SA 893 (A) at 910E-F; *Cussons v Kroon* 2001 (4) SA 833 (SCA) at para 9.
92 *Silberberg & Schoeman Property* p 86; *Cussons v Kroon* 2001 (4) SA 833 (SCA) at 840E.
93 *Silberberg & Schoeman Property* p 87.
94 *Silberberg & Schoeman Property* p 88; *Wille's Principles* p 612.
95 This implies that the right must have been duly constituted; see *Silberberg & Schoeman Property* p 87. For example, an agreement of sale or a servitude agreement has to be contained in a deed of alienation and signed by the parties.
96 *Silberberg & Schoeman Property* p 87.
97 *Silberberg & Schoeman Property* p 87; Bobbert, MCJ 'Kennisleer' (1996) (21) 1 *TRW* 36 at 44.
98 *Silberberg & Schoeman Property* p 87; *Wille's Principles* pp 612-613; *Kazazis v Georghiades* 1979 (3) SA 886 (T) at 894B-C.
99 *Silberberg & Schoeman Property* p 88.
100 *Silberberg & Schoeman Property* p 86; *Contract Forwarding (Pty) Ltd v Chesterfin (Pty) Ltd* 2003 (2) SA 253 (SCA) at 258A.
101 *Silberberg & Schoeman Property* p 87; *Wille's Principles* pp 612-613.
102 See *Wahloo Sand Bpk v Trustees, Hambly Parker Trust* 2002 (2) SA 776 (SCA).

For example, Arnold purchases a farm from Bert. Typically, some time elapses between a purchase of land and the completion of the required registration procedures in the Deeds Registry. After the conclusion of the contract for the sale of the farm, but before registration is achieved, Arnold is informed by Cathy of the existence of an unregistered right of way in respect of the land, and is requested to co-operate in having the right registered. May Arnold refuse to co-operate because he was unaware of the unregistered servitude at the time of purchase? Or would Cathy be able to rely on the doctrine of notice to compel Arnold to co-operate in registering the servitude?

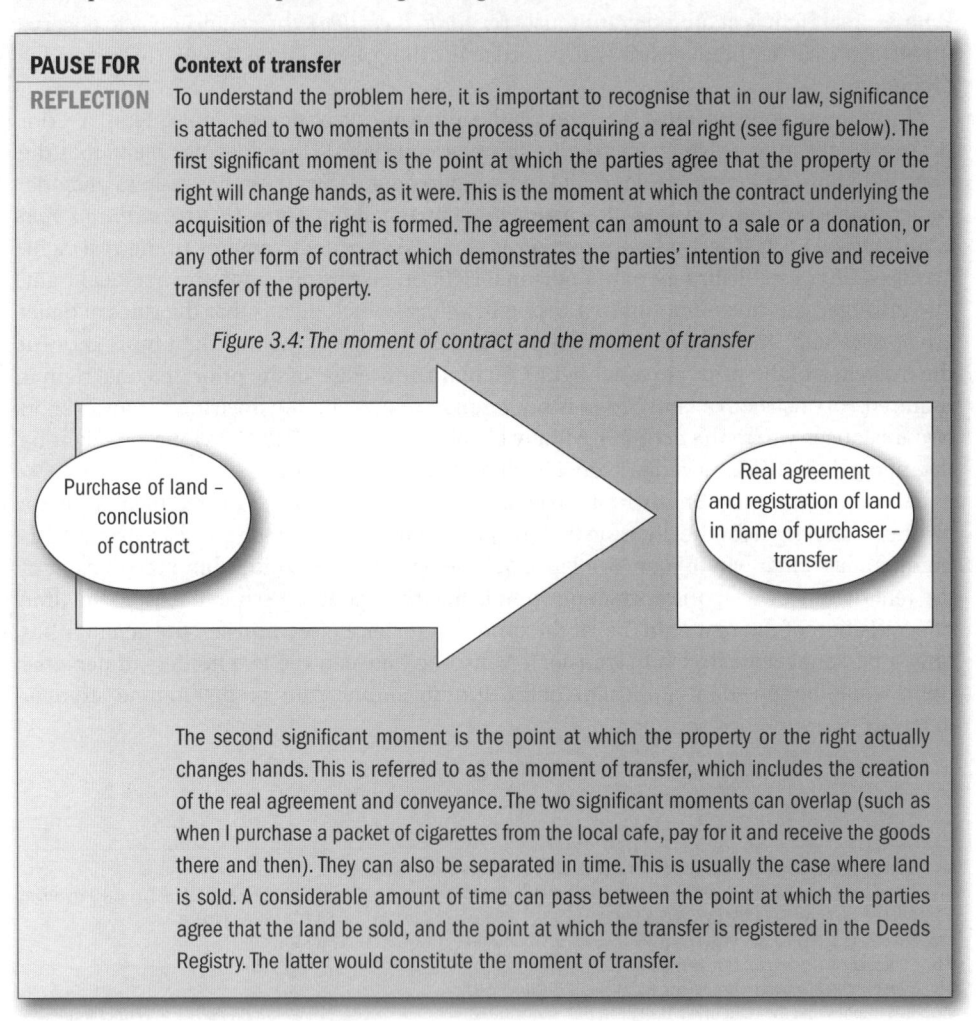

> **PAUSE FOR REFLECTION**
>
> **Context of transfer**
>
> To understand the problem here, it is important to recognise that in our law, significance is attached to two moments in the process of acquiring a real right (see figure below). The first significant moment is the point at which the parties agree that the property or the right will change hands, as it were. This is the moment at which the contract underlying the acquisition of the right is formed. The agreement can amount to a sale or a donation, or any other form of contract which demonstrates the parties' intention to give and receive transfer of the property.
>
> *Figure 3.4: The moment of contract and the moment of transfer*
>
> Purchase of land – conclusion of contract ⟶ Real agreement and registration of land in name of purchaser – transfer
>
> The second significant moment is the point at which the property or the right actually changes hands. This is referred to as the moment of transfer, which includes the creation of the real agreement and conveyance. The two significant moments can overlap (such as when I purchase a packet of cigarettes from the local cafe, pay for it and receive the goods there and then). They can also be separated in time. This is usually the case where land is sold. A considerable amount of time can pass between the point at which the parties agree that the land be sold, and the point at which the transfer is registered in the Deeds Registry. The latter would constitute the moment of transfer.

The issue set out in the example above arose (among others) in *Wahloo Sand Bpk v Trustees, Hambly Parker Trust*.[103] In this matter, the dispute arose because of the creation of reciprocal servitudes by owners of neighbouring properties, where one property was sold to another before the servitudes could be registered. The purchaser refused to consent to

---

103 2002 (2) SA 776 (SCA).

the registration of the servitudes, arguing that he had no knowledge of the agreement in terms of which the servitudes were created. The Supreme Court of Appeal held that lack of knowledge of a servitude created will only protect the subsequent purchaser after the property has already been registered in his name.[104] While the purchaser is not yet the registered owner of the land, the lack of knowledge of the servitude cannot be a defence against the claim by the owner of the dominant tenement for specific performance.

Where the purchaser of a thing acquires it with knowledge such as that described above, the doctrine of notice is applied to force the acquirer of the real right to give effect to the earlier personal rights. For current purposes, we demonstrate the application by referring to its effect in the case of successive sales and unregistered servitudes.

3.3.2.1 Successive sales

In the case of successive sales, the typical example would be where a seller, Amanda, sells a thing, either movable or immovable, first to Beth, and then subsequently sells the same thing to Carl.

Figure 3.5: Successive sales (example)

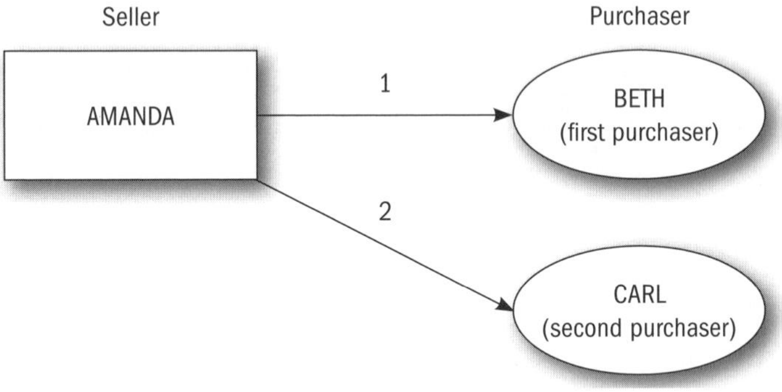

Ownership will be acquired by the purchaser who first obtains transfer of the thing sold. Transfer is effected either by delivery in the case of movables or, in the case of land, transfer is effected by registration. If the first purchaser (Beth) manages to obtain transfer first, her rights will be unassailable. But if the second purchaser (Carl) manages to obtain transfer first, his rights equally will be unassailable **if** Carl had purchased the thing without the knowledge of the prior sale to Beth. If Carl had prior knowledge, Beth could claim that the transfer to Carl be set aside, and ownership of the thing should be transferred to her instead.[105]

The doctrine of notice thus operates to enable the first purchaser who did not take transfer (Beth, in the example above) to claim that the second sale be cancelled, and to claim delivery or transfer of the property if it can be shown that the second purchaser (Carl, in the above example) had knowledge of the prior sale to the first purchaser.

---

104 *Wahloo Sand Bpk v Trustees, Hambly Parker Trust* 2002 (2) SA 776 (SCA) at para 11.
105 *Bowring v Vrededorp Properties CC* 2007 (5) SA 391 (SCA) at para 11.

Carl (the second purchaser) may well be acting in good faith. He may not know of the sale to Beth when he contracts with Amanda. He may acquire knowledge of the previous sale only later (e.g. when an attempt is made to deliver the thing). In such cases, the second purchaser's knowledge must be determined as at the time when he takes delivery or, in the case of immovables, at the time the land is registered in his name.[106]

3.3.2.2 Unregistered servitudes

In the case of unregistered servitudes, a typical example would be the case where the servitude is created by agreement between two parties, Adam and Brett. If, in terms of such an agreement, Adam becomes entitled to have a servitude registered over the land of Brett, Adam would have a personal right to claim that registration be effected. Once registration has been completed, any subsequent purchaser of the land will automatically be bound by the servitude as its object is the land itself and not merely a performance to be rendered by the original grantor (Brett).

Figure 3.6: The operation of the doctrine of notice in respect of unregistered servitudes (example)

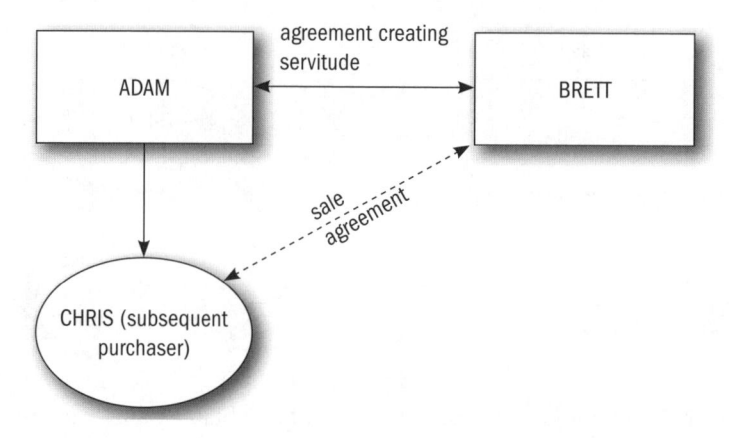

If, however, Brett should sell and transfer his land to Chris before registration of the servitude has occurred, Chris's knowledge or ignorance of Adam's potential real right would become relevant. The object of Adam's personal right, flowing from his agreement with Brett, is a performance to be rendered by Brett only, and not the land itself. Consequently, Chris would receive transfer of the land free from any servitude. If he had no knowledge of the unregistered servitude at the time of transfer, he would not be obliged to have a servitude registered over his land, and that would be the end of it. He would also not be expected to observe the unregistered servitude. However, if Chris had actual knowledge of Adam's unregistered servitude at the time of registration of transfer, he will be bound by it notwithstanding that the servitude is not registered. Chris would then be compelled to co-operate in having the servitude registered.

In *Bowring NO v Vrededorp Properties CC and Another*,[107] the dispute concerned a double sale of a parcel of land and registration of a servitude. It was not disputed that

---

106 *Wahloo Sand v Trustees, Hambly Parker Trust* 2002 (2) SA 776 (SCA) at para 11.
107 2007 (5) SA 391 (SCA).

the second purchaser had knowledge of the previous sale of a subdivided portion of the land concerned to Vrededorp. The appellant disputed whether Vrededorp could claim subdivision and transfer of the portion directly from the second purchaser (now the registered owner) rather than from the transferor. In other words, the issue was whether the contract between the transferor and Vrededorp (first purchaser) should in effect be enforceable against the second purchaser.

In considering whether registration of the servitude could be claimed from the second purchaser (now the registered owner), the court first had to determine the issue regarding the claim for transfer of the subdivided portion. This is because, unless that transfer could take place, the servitude would be a nullity on the basis that a servitude in respect of one's own property cannot exist.

Both issues required application of the doctrine of notice: first, in relation to the unregistered servitude and, second, in relation to the successive sales.

On the facts, the court found that on the basis of equity, Vrededorp could claim the subdivision and transfer of the portion directly from the second purchaser, and that the servitude must be registered with the co-operation of the second purchaser.[108]

3.4 Concluding remarks

A real right is sometimes said to be absolute in that it is generally enforceable against all other legal subjects. However, this feature should not be overemphasised. First, there are exceptional circumstances where real rights are not so enforceable. Second, personal rights also have to be respected by all persons in so far as an intentional infringement of a personal right constitutes an actionable wrong in our law.

---

108 *Bowring v Vrededorp Properties CC* 2007 (5) SA 391 (SCA) at para 18.

Chapter 4

Possession

'Although the minimum requirements of physical control and a specific mental attitude always need to be in place to constitute possession, the exact content of possession will depend on the context in which and the purpose for which it is used.'

PJ Badenhorst, JM Pienaar, H Mostert (2006) *Silberberg & Schoeman's Law of Property* p 273.

4.1	What is possession?	66
4.2	Nature of possessory rights	66
4.3	Elements of possession	70
4.4	**Protection of possession**	**73**
4.4.1	*Mandament van spolie*	75
4.4.1.1	Circumstances for applicability	75
4.4.1.2	Requirements	77
4.4.1.3	Application of remedy to incorporeals	78
4.4.1.4	Who can use the *mandament van spolie*?	80
4.4.1.5	Relief available	80
4.4.1.6	Defences	80
4.4.2	Possessory action	83
4.4.2.1	Circumstances for applicability	83
4.4.2.2	Requirements	83
4.4.2.3	Who can use the possessory action?	83
4.4.2.4	Relief available	83
4.4.2.5	Defences	83
4.4.3	Interdict	84
4.4.3.1	Circumstances for applicability	84
4.4.3.2	Requirements	84
4.4.3.3	Relief available	85
4.4.3.4	Defences	85
4.4.4	Delictual action	85
4.4.4.1	Circumstances for applicability	85
4.4.4.2	Requirements	85
4.4.4.3	Who can use the delictual action?	86
4.4.4.4	Relief available	86
4.4.4.5	Defences	86
4.5	**Concluding remarks**	**86**

4.1 What is possession?

Possession describes the situation where a person has physical control (*detentio*) of a thing together with the mental attitude *(animus possidendi)* that includes a consciousness of that control. Possession is thus relatively easy to understand because one can actually **see** that a person has physical control of a thing even if one cannot **know** for sure what the content of the mental attitude is. By contrast, it is not possible to see conclusively that a person is the owner of a thing merely by observing him or her in physical control.

Because possession includes physical control, one can say that possession in principle involves a corporeal or tangible thing. However, despite the impossibility of physical control of an incorporeal or intangible thing, the law recognises that some incorporeal property can be 'possessed'. By acknowledging such quasi-possession, the law attaches consequences to the control over (some) incorporeal things.

To understand the treatment of possession in the law, it is important to remember that the person who claims to possess must have legal capacity, conscious physical control, i.e. more than mere awareness, and a specific mental attitude appropriate to the factual context.[1]

4.2 Nature of possessory rights

Possession has two elements: the *corpus* or physical element (expressed as *detentio*) and the *animus* or mental element (expressed as *animus possidendi*). Both are necessary for factual or bare possession to exist. 'Bare possession' describes the factual situation where a person is in physical control and has the mental attitude that, at the very least, she intends to benefit from the physical control of the thing. In rights language, this factual situation is expressed as the right **of** possession, *ius possessionis*. When a person is in factual possession and is also entitled to be in possession, then two rights express the situation: the first right is *ius possessionis*, while the second is the right **to** possession, *ius possidendi*. For someone entitled to be in possession, the two rights exist simultaneously. More than one person simultaneously may have the right **to** possession *(ius possidendi)* of a particular thing. For example, two sisters are both entitled to be in possession of the computer that their parents have provided for their studies. Obviously, they must work out how the time in front of the computer is to be divided because it is difficult for both to use it at the same time. This means that the two sisters will not simultaneously have the right **of** possession *(ius possessionis)* because they will not easily have simultaneous *detentio*. The implication is that more than one simultaneous holder of the right of possession *(ius possessionis)* is a rare occurrence, but not impossible. The nature of the thing concerned may lend itself to such a possibility, for example two children simultaneously ride on the same see-saw. It follows, therefore, that the nature of the thing plays no role in determining whether more than one simultaneous holder of the right **to** possession is possible, but it plays an important role in determining whether more than one simultaneous holder of the right **of** possession is possible.

Not every person in factual possession of a thing is necessarily entitled to be in possession. For example, Ben finds a lost pen lying in the corridor and picks it up intending to use it. This puts Ben in bare possession of the pen, but the lost pen *(res deperditae)* belongs to someone else. With the pen in Ben's hand, he has the *ius possessionis*, which means that the owner of the pen has ceased to have the *ius possessionis* because he has lost physical

---

1   See *Wille's Principles* pp 445–453; *Silberberg & Schoeman Property* pp 273–286.

control over the pen. Nevertheless, the owner retains the *ius possidendi*, i.e. the right to possession, which entitles him to demand to be put (back) in possession, even though Ben has decided that he will keep the pen and continue to use it. It is thus possible in some circumstances for one or other element of factual possession to cease to exist temporarily without the entitled person losing the right to possession. In the example, the owner of the pen has lost physical control of the pen and thus the right of possession *(ius possessionis)* has ceased to exist, but the right to possession *(ius possidendi)* continues. As the person who picked up the pen, Ben's right of possession, flowing from his physical control of the pen combined with his intention to use it, cannot change its character: once he loses physical control, the right of possession is terminated. Ben cannot merely change his mental attitude to become entitled to possession.

It is important to grasp that the right of possession *(ius possessionis)* is not actually a right in the ordinary sense of a claim. That is, one cannot exercise the right of possession *(ius possessionis)* by claiming to have been put in possession of the thing, whereas the holder of the right to possession *(ius possidendi)* can. When the owner demands the pen from Ben, Ben has no entitlement with which to seek to defeat the owner's claim even though he may be finding the pen useful. He must therefore return the pen. The owner retains the right to possession *(ius possidendi)* which expresses the entitlement to be put in possession. If, however, the owner were to grab the pen from Ben in such a way as to disturb the peace, then, in principle, Ben would be able to ask the court to order the owner to restore the pen to him so that the matter can be sorted out in an orderly fashion. This is because Ben's right of possession *(ius possessionis)* entitles him to seek legal protection in his own right.

So, to return to the question: what is possession? It describes a factual situation that includes the right of possession or *ius possessionis*, on the one hand, and may also include a legal relationship between a person and a thing concerning the right to possession or *ius possidendi*, on the other. The right to possession, which entitles the holder to be in possession and to demand to be put in possession, is acquired from the owner of the thing, who has the full complement of entitlements possible in respect of a thing.

COUNTER POINT

Explaining possession

The position as set out above represents the basic point of departure in the overwhelming majority of case law and academic literature that deal with this aspect of property law. Van der Walt and Pienaar[2] choose, however, to explain the position differently. They focus on the type of physical control that is exercised in a particular case, and on the intention of control *(animus)* with which it is coupled. To simplify the comparison here, we refer to the position as explained with reference to the *ius possessionis* and *ius possidendi* above as the 'rights-based' approach, and to the exposition of Van der Walt and Pienaar as the 'control-based' approach.

Within the scheme of the control-based explanation, the term 'control' has a slightly more extended meaning than in the rights-based exposition above. 'Control' refers to a person's influence over things, and incorporates both a physical and a mental element. This term replaces the term 'possession' as used in the rights-based explanation. As explained below, possession in the control-based scheme has a more limited connotation. For corporeal things, **control** denotes a person's **actual physical power** over them, while for incorporeal things, it denotes the **ability** to exercise such control.

---

2   Notably, Van der Walt, AJ & Pienaar, GJ (2006) *Introduction to Property Law* (Cape Town, Juta) pp 169–176; 177–194.

Within the control-based exposition, the distinction between bare possession and possession as of right is dealt with on the basis of the lawfulness of the control. In other words, the point of departure foresees that the consequences of particular relationships with things vary depending on whether control is lawful or unlawful. Lawful control refers to those relationships with regard to things (i.e. real relationships) that are acknowledged by the law because the things are acquired and held in compliance with the specific legal rules applicable to the particular case. In such cases, the law protects the specific relationship and allows it to be enforced, regardless of whether the intention with which the specific thing is controlled is based on bona fides or *mala fides*. Unlawful control refers to those real relationships that are not acknowledged by the law because acquisition or holding of the relevant things is not in accordance with the applicable legal rules.

This control-based explanation avoids the rights-based terminology of *ius possessionis* and *ius possidendi*. Yet it fails to explain why some unlawful real relationships invoke proprietary protection in the form of the spoliation remedy (discussed below), other than by treating this as exceptional. The discussion of the possessory remedies below demonstrates that even relationships that, in terms of the control-based approach, could be typified as unlawful, nevertheless attract certain consequences. The unlawful occupant of land, for instance, enjoys specific protection under statutory law, and also has recourse to the spoliation remedy under common law.

The control-based approach proceeds to distinguish the consequences of unlawful instances of control by focusing on the bona fides or *mala fides* of the controller. A *mala fide* unlawful controller, on this description, is aware that his control is unlawful, but nevertheless continues to control the thing. A bona fide unlawful controller is unaware that her control is unlawful.

Although the control-based approach avoids the terminology of the rights-based explanation, it introduces criteria of lawfulness and *mala fides* or bona fides into the exercise of identifying certain real relationships so as to attach specific sets of consequences. In terms of the rights-based explanation, it is not necessary to build in separate enquiries as to the lawfulness or *mala fides* or bona fides of a particular real relationship since these elements are incorporated in the terms *ius possessionis* and *ius possidendi*. This is illustrated in the example below.

Imagine a scenario that involves a vehicle, for instance a brand new VW Golf. Suppose that the Golf is sold by First Motors (Pty) Ltd (a dealer), who is the first owner, to Chris on credit. A financing agreement is concluded with a financial institution, Wheels Bank (Pty) Ltd. In terms of the agreement, the bank acquires ownership from First Motors and sells the vehicle to Chris, reserving title until the last instalment is paid. The purchaser on credit (Chris) meanwhile has full use and enjoyment of the Golf. Then the Golf is stolen by Sydney, and later located by the police, who confiscate it from Sydney, acting in terms of statutory powers.

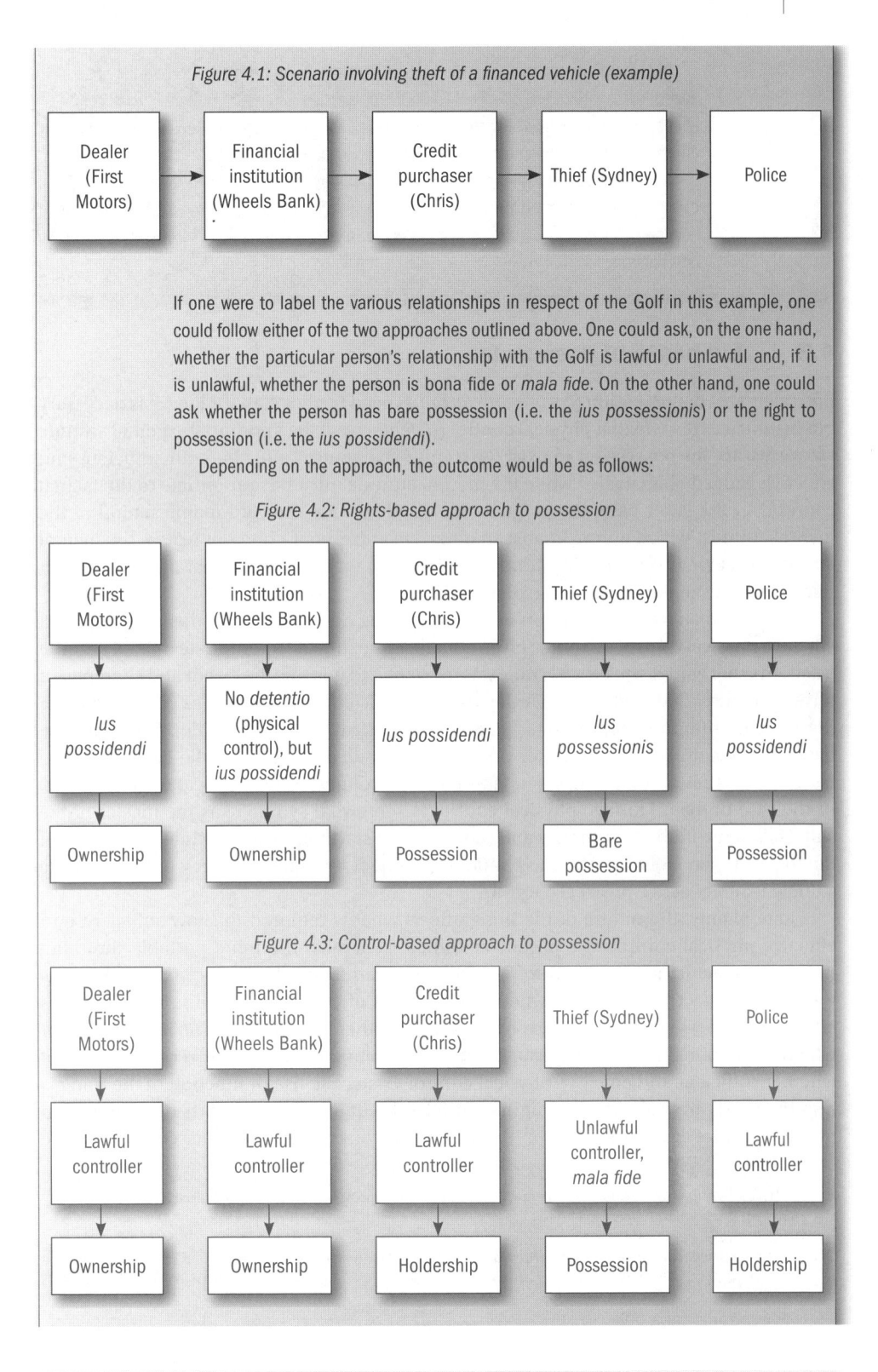

CHAPTER 4   POSSESSION   69

Figure 4.1: Scenario involving theft of a financed vehicle (example)

Dealer (First Motors) → Financial institution (Wheels Bank) → Credit purchaser (Chris) → Thief (Sydney) → Police

If one were to label the various relationships in respect of the Golf in this example, one could follow either of the two approaches outlined above. One could ask, on the one hand, whether the particular person's relationship with the Golf is lawful or unlawful and, if it is unlawful, whether the person is bona fide or *mala fide*. On the other hand, one could ask whether the person has bare possession (i.e. the *ius possessionis*) or the right to possession (i.e. the *ius possidendi*).

Depending on the approach, the outcome would be as follows:

Figure 4.2: Rights-based approach to possession

Dealer (First Motors)	Financial institution (Wheels Bank)	Credit purchaser (Chris)	Thief (Sydney)	Police
Ius possidendi	No *detentio* (physical control), but *ius possidendi*	*Ius possidendi*	*Ius possessionis*	*Ius possidendi*
Ownership	Ownership	Possession	Bare possession	Possession

Figure 4.3: Control-based approach to possession

Dealer (First Motors)	Financial institution (Wheels Bank)	Credit purchaser (Chris)	Thief (Sydney)	Police
Lawful controller	Lawful controller	Lawful controller	Unlawful controller, *mala fide*	Lawful controller
Ownership	Ownership	Holdership	Possession	Holdership

> This demonstrates that the outcomes of the rights-based explanation and the control-based explanation are the same. Both approaches attempt to explain why certain relationships in law invoke the consequences of the stronger proprietary remedies, while others invoke the consequences only of the possessory remedies.
>
> The label attached to each of the various relationships has less to do with the issue of control or possession (whichever terminology is preferred), and more to do with the intention *(animus)* that underpins a particular real relationship. This is discussed in the next section.

4.3 Elements of possession

Both elements of possession *(corpus* and *animus)* need further elaboration.[3] It is necessary but insufficient to state that physical control *(detentio)* and the appropriate mental attitude are necessary for possession to exist. First, physical control must be both sufficient and effective, judged objectively,[4] while the mental attitude must be appropriate to the factual context.[5] In the latter case, the judgement is made on the outward manifestation of the mental attitude, which approximates an objective judgement.[6] In other words, the mental attitude is taken as that which can be established by the outward appearance or conduct rather than by mere subjective personal testimony.

Second, one must pay attention to understanding how to establish that sufficient and effective physical control exists in a given situation and that the appropriate mental attitude exists. In other words, the factual context is relevant and informs the extent and character of physical control that would be regarded as both sufficient and effective as well as whether the mental attitude is appropriate.[7] Regarding physical control, consider the difference between the nature of an oil tanker that conveys crude oil from a Middle Eastern port to Durban and that of a fountain pen. How each is brought under physical control differs. In the case of the oil tanker, physical control is somewhat symbolic as the master of the ship is vested with both authority and the means to start the engines, while in the case of the fountain pen, holding it in one's hand or putting it into one's pocket would constitute sufficient and effective physical control.

Quite plainly, the nature of the thing affects what is required to show sufficient and effective physical control of a particular thing.[8] Generally, the more portable the thing is, the more actual physical control would be needed to satisfy the *corpus* element. It is a question of fact in each case whether the extent of physical control is sufficient and effective. Aspects such as the size of a thing, whether it is movable or immovable, or whether an animal is classed as game and so on will be relevant to the consideration of whether sufficient and effective physical control exists. The use or function of the thing is also relevant: physical control of agricultural land requires different sorts of actions from physical control of a domestic dwelling. One must consider also whether comprehensive

---

3   See *Wille's Principles* pp 449–452; *Silberberg & Schoeman Property* pp 275–284 for a detailed discussion.
4   *Silberberg & Schoeman Property* pp 276–277.
5   *Wille's Principles* pp 450–451.
6   See *Meyer v Glendinning* 1939 CPD 84; *De Beer v Zimbali Estate Management Association (Pty) Ltd* 2007 (3) SA 254 (N).
7   *Wille's Principles* p 450; *Silberberg & Schoeman Property* p 279; Van der Merwe *Sakereg* p 106; *LAWSA* Vol 27(1) at para 62.
8   *Silberberg & Schoeman* p 276.

control might be required: the physical control required for a 500 g packet of sugar would be different from that needed for a racehorse or for a high-rise building.

Physical control need not be exercised personally.[9] Consider the position where Gugu delivers her car to the garage for a service: she hands over physical control of the car to the mechanic. Does this mean that her possession is terminated because she no longer has physical control? The answer is no. In principle, another person can perform the physical control element on one's behalf, but careful attention should be paid to whether the other person acts wholly as an agent and derives no benefit from possession of the thing (e.g. the chauffeur who drives the car for the owner), or one who acts for the owner but derives personal benefit or gain from possession of the thing (e.g. a racehorse trainer who trains the horse of the owner). In the former situation, the mental attitude is insufficient to establish factual or bare possession, while in the latter, the trainer could have the mental attitude appropriate to establish bare possession and, therefore, to use the *mandament van spolie*.[10]

Similarly, physical control need not be exercised continuously.[11] However, the point at which the question about effective physical control is raised, influences the determination of exactly what constitutes effective control in the circumstances. If the question is asked to determine whether possession was **acquired**, then the requirements are more stringent than if the question is asked whether possession should be **retained**. The test for initial acquisition of physical control is stricter than for continuation thereof.[12] For example, Ayanda may come and go from a flat in a building without fearing that his physical control of the flat might be called into question during his absence. This is because, in principle, he is able to retake control of the flat without legal assistance since he has actual physical control of the necessary keys. Importantly, however, physical control must be more or less exclusively exercised. In *De Beer v Zimbali Estate Management Association (Pty) Ltd*,[13] the applicant, an estate agent, came and went from the Zimbali Estate, using an electronic key (access disc) that caused the boom at the access point to lift and lower itself. When her access disc was deactivated, she could no longer enter the estate. She launched an application for the *mandament van spolie*, seeking to have her access disc reactivated on the basis that she had been spoliated. The court held that she did not have an interest in the estate over and above that of an intermittent visitor and, as such, she could not establish sufficient and effective *detentio* (physical control).

On the other hand, a builder secures his lien against the owner by retaining the keys to the building under construction. Even though others come and go from the building site, they do so only with the builder's permission. In effect:

> *possession of the keys [is] equivalent to possession of the building and a temporary absence would not be taken as abandonment ... [T]he mere fact of making duplicate keys available to another ... does not always equate to the giving up of physical possession. Both the giving and receiving must be considered in context to answer the question.*[14]

---

9   *Strydom v De Lange* 1970 (2) SA 6 (T) at 11-12; *Mbuku v Mdinwa* 1982 (1) SA 219 (Tk). See further *Wille's Principles* p 450; *Silberberg & Schoeman Property* p 279.
10 See *Meyer v Glendinning* 1939 CPD 84 and *De Beer v Zimbali Estate Management Association (Pty) Ltd* 2007 (3) SA 254 (N); also *Wille's Principles* p 451; *Silberberg & Schoeman Property* pp 282-283.
11 *Welgemoed v Coetzer* 1946 TPD 701 at 720; *Silberberg & Schoeman Property* p 278.
12 *Underwater Construction and Salvage Co (Pty) Ltd v Bell* 1968 (4) SA 190 (C); and see *Silberberg & Schoeman Property* p 278.
13 2007 (3) SA 254 (N).
14 *Wightman t/a JW Construction v Headfour (Pty) Ltd and Another* 2008 (3) SA 371 (SCA) at 380-381.

> **COUNTER POINT** — **Physical possession?**
>
> Physical control *(detentio)* is but one of two elements of possession. Possession requires physical control and the appropriate mental attitude. The phrase 'physical possession' (as used in the *dictum* quoted above) is unfortunate because it is misleading to the extent that it suggests that possession does not require anything more than physical control.

To understand the required mental attitude *(animus possidendi)* and how to establish its appropriateness, a few insights are relevant. If one holds the thing solely for another person (the principal), then one cannot establish that the physical control is for one's own benefit because the mental attitude is inappropriate.[15] Also, one cannot change the nature of one's factual possession simply by changing one's mental attitude.[16] The example above of Ben who finds the lost pen and decides he would like to use it, illustrates an attempt to change his mental attitude. As was pointed out, this is not possible. Furthermore, even if one intends to gain benefit from one's physical control, sometimes that physical control is so diluted that it cannot be shown to be sufficient to support the existence of bare possession. A good example is provided by the estate agent in *De Beer v Zimbali Estate Management Association (Pty) Ltd*[17] who was classed as an intermittent visitor only, rather than someone with bare possession.

> **PAUSE FOR REFLECTION** — **Character of the mental attitude**
>
> It is helpful to consider the character of the mental attitude or *animus* element from the point of view of various persons, each of whom has the identical factual physical control over the thing in question, i.e. each person wears denim dungarees with a bib pocket in which lies a sterling silver charm.[18] It should be remembered that in addition to physical control and the appropriate mental attitude, the person must have legal capacity, i.e. the capacity to form the intention to benefit oneself.
>
> The first person is a one-year-old baby whose mother placed the charm in her pocket for luck. Does this baby have bare possession of the silver charm? In light of the criteria outlined above, the baby cannot have bare possession because the mental attitude is defective. Being an *infans* (less than seven years old), she is legally incapable of forming the appropriate mental attitude, notwithstanding that she might refuse to give the charm up when requested to do so!
>
> The second person is a 30-year-old man unaware of the silver charm in his pocket, put there by his companion for safekeeping. Does this person have bare possession? Without consciousness of physical control, bare possession cannot be established and thus this person too does not have the appropriate mental attitude.
>
> In third position is a 30-year-old woman who genuinely but mistakenly believes that she is the owner of the charm in her pocket. Would she have bare possession? In her case, the mental attitude is appropriate to support the conclusion that she has bare possession but not that she is owner.

---

15 *Meyer v Glendinning* 1939 CPD 84.
16 *Wille's Principles* p 451; *Marcus v Stamper and Zoutendijk* 1910 AD 58 at 62.
17 2007 (3) SA 254 (N).
18 See Van der Walt, AJ & Pienaar, GJ (2006) *Introduction to the Law of Property* 5 ed (Cape Town, Juta) pp 186–187 from whom this analysis is borrowed.

> The fourth person is a 30-year-old man who has accepted the silver charm from his friend as a pledge for a debt owed by the latter. In this instance, the mental attitude of the man is that he intends clearly to benefit from having physical control of the silver charm until his friend repays the money owed. Furthermore, he is conscious of the physical control and thus may be said to have bare possession.
>
> In the fifth instance, a 30-year-old woman holds the silver charm in her pocket for her friend whose pocket has a hole. Here the difference is that she holds for her friend, which means that she does not have any intention to benefit herself by the physical control – her physical control is solely on behalf of another and thus she does not have bare possession.

4.4 Protection of possession

There are a few remedies that protect possession, i.e. remedies that provide relief for a claim based on possession. They include the *mandament van spolie*, the possessory action, the prohibitory interdict and the delictual action. Which remedy is appropriate to the particular circumstances depends, in part, on who is to be protected, i.e. whether the person (natural or juristic) has an entitlement to possession or merely was in bare (factual) possession. The table below summarises the various aspects of these remedies by comparison. The details are discussed in the sections that follow.

Table 4.1: Remedies for protection of possession

Remedy	Circumstances	Applicability of remedies to protect possession			
		Requirements	Who can use?	Relief available	Defences
Mandament van spolie	Lost possession; respondent is spoliator; thing still in respondent's possession; requirements can be satisfied	Proof that applicant was in peaceful and undisturbed (bare) possession and that respondent unlawfully deprived her of that possession; no merits considered	Anyone who can prove requirements	Restore *status quo ante*; no damages	Challenge *facta probanda*; allege lack of *locus standi*; allege excessive delay; allege restoration is impossible
Possessory action	Possession lost; circumstances for *mandament van spolie* do not apply	Prima facie proof that plaintiff has entitlement to be in possession *(ius possidendi)*; that defendant was responsible for removing possession from plaintiff or is currently in control of the thing	Prove *ius possidendi* (entitlement to be in possession)	Recover possession of thing including ejectment (subject to statutory provisions governing eviction) and appropriate damages if thing no longer in same state	Challenge *facta probanda*
Prohibitory interdict	Possession disturbed or threatened with interference	Prima facie right (temporary interdict) or clear right (final interdict); harm committed or apprehended; irreparable damage; interdict is only suitable remedy	One who can prove prima facie right (temporary interdict) or clear right (final interdict)	Order to stop interference and to prevent further interference; no claim for damages but court has discretion to substitute award of damages for final interdict if would give sufficient protection	Challenge *facta probanda*
Delictual action	Claim for damages because thing cannot be recovered	All delictual elements	One who can prove delictual elements	Damages award	Challenge *facta probanda*

4.4.1 Mandament van spolie

The *mandament van spolie* is a true possessory remedy, originating in canon law.[19] The discussion below deals with the circumstances in which the remedy can be applied, its requirements and the relief available. It also addresses questions such as who is capable of instituting this remedy, and what defences exist against it.

4.4.1.1 Circumstances for applicability

The *mandament van spolie* is used to restore lost possession.[20] It does not apply in circumstances where possession is merely disturbed. This remedy is described as a true possessory remedy because it protects bare (factual) possession *(ius possessionis)* rather than the right to be in possession *(ius possidendi)*.[21] At the same time, it deters people from taking the law into their own hands.[22] Other remedies protect the *ius possidendi* but only someone who, on the face of it, is entitled to be in possession, i.e. can prove the *ius possidendi*, can make use of them.

> **PAUSE FOR REFLECTION**
>
> **Why should society protect bare possession?**
>
> Why, for example, should a thief be able to use a legal remedy to assist him when another person grabs the thing back? Is it fair to protect a thief? Consider this: what if the accuser is in error about the person being a thief? That is, the alleged thief is not actually a thief but the new owner? A fundamental principle of the rule of law is that one is not permitted to take the law into one's own hands. Another principle is *audi alteram partem*, i.e. hear the other side. It is thus rational and morally right to benefit society by protecting bare possession. This is expressed in the maxim, *spoliatus ante omnia restituendus est* – before all else restore unlawful dispossession. A successful application for the *mandament van spolie* has the consequence of halting one who takes the law into her own hands and also of creating an opportunity to hear the other side, albeit not immediately during those application proceedings. In this way, general societal welfare is improved even though, sometimes, individual wrongdoers might benefit from the delay in having to return the disputed thing to the entitled person.

The *corpus* element of possession is satisfied in similar fashion whether the person is a natural person or not, a thief or an owner, because whether *detentio* or physical control is satisfied depends on factual criteria: among others, the nature, size or function of the thing and what is required to establish sufficient and effective physical control, judged objectively, in the circumstances.[23] In other words, the focus is on the thing and an objective or neutral judgement is made about the existence of sufficient and effective physical control. For example, to determine whether sufficient and effective physical control of agricultural land exists, factual evidence of crop planting by the claimant or the presence of his grazing animals on the land would assist the assessment.

---

19 See *Meyer v Glendinning* 1939 CPD 84.
20 *Silberberg & Schoeman Property* p 288; *Wille's Principles* p 453.
21 *Nino Bonino v De Lange* 1906 TS 120 at 122.
22 See *Muller v Muller* 1915 TPD 28 at 30: 'The object of the law is to prevent people from taking the law into their own hands and so causing disturbance of the peace, and also to protect a person who has a possessory right ...'
23 See p 70 above.

Basic conditions for the *mandament van spolie* are set.[24] The person must have legal capacity. She must be conscious of the sufficient and effective physical control *(detentio)* of the thing and, at minimum,[25] must have the intention to benefit herself *(animus ex re commodum acquirendi)* from the factual possession of the thing.[26] She must be able to prove, on a balance of probabilities, that she was in peaceful and undisturbed possession when the respondent unlawfully deprived her of possession.

Apart from these requirements that must be proven (called *facta probanda*), there are several preconditions and points to note about choosing to use this remedy. It is available only against the spoliator, i.e. the person who carried out the unlawful deprivation.[27] So if the thing is in the hands of a bona fide third party, this remedy cannot be used against that party. It can be used in respect of both movable and immovable property[28] and, in principle, for both corporeal and incorporeal property. No damages may be claimed. If the requirements are satisfied, then the order can effect only a restoration of the *status quo ante* by the spoliator, i.e. matters are restored to their previous position.[29] Sometimes, to enable the restoration of the previously prevailing position, the court may order something be done in addition to mere restoration.[30] *Adminstrator, Cape v Ntshwaqela* states:

> [t]he accepted principle is that the mandament van spolie envisages not only the restitution of possession but also the performance of acts, such as repairs and rebuilding, which are necessary for the restoration of the status quo ante.[31]

In *Zinman v Miller*,[32] the main panel from an electricity meter chamber was removed and the electrical wiring was cut. In granting the spoliation order, the court included the restoration of the panel in addition to the reconnection of the wires to permit the flow of electrical current to the premises.

A successful application for the *mandament van spolie* leads to a court order, in terms of which the respondent is ordered to restore the *status quo ante*, i.e. to return matters to how they were before the deprivation.[33] The spoliation order does not take into account whether either the applicant or the respondent behaved badly or whether the applicant should be permitted to remain in possession because no merits may be considered. It is about remedying the breach of peace caused by someone taking the law into his own hands and unlawfully wresting possession from another.

The character of the remedy is robust and speedy.[34] The speediness of the remedy flows from the fact that proceedings usually take the form of special application proceedings, the successful outcome of which is to restore possession immediately, before all else. The application proceedings may be ex parte and even urgent in appropriate circumstances. The matter is dealt with generally on affidavits only, i.e. no oral evidence is heard.[35]

---

24 *Silberberg & Schoeman Property* pp 292ff; *Wille's Principles* pp 455-456; Van der Merwe *Sakereg* pp 129-137.
25 *LAWSA* Vol 27(1) at para 266.
26 *Meyer v Glendinning* 1939 CPD 84; *Yeko v Qana* 1973 (4) SA 735 (A).
27 *Silberberg & Schoeman Property* pp 294-295.
28 In the case of immovable property, the order sought would be an ejectment or eviction order. Note that eviction from a home is governed by legislation and only rarely does the common law still apply.
29 *Silberberg & Schoeman Property* p 289.
30 *Zinman v Miller* 1956 (3) SA 8 (T); *Administrator, Cape v Ntshwaqela* 1990 (1) SA 705 (A).
31 *Administrator, Cape v Ntshwaqela* 1990 (1) SA 705 (A) at 717.
32 1956 (3) SA 8 (T).
33 *Wille's Principles* p 463.
34 *Silberberg & Schoeman Property* pp 290-291.
35 Action proceedings and oral evidence are possible: see e.g. *Mpunga v Malaba* 1959 (1) SA 853 (W).

Its robustness stems from the fact that its requirements are few and relatively easy to establish, and the court's discretion is limited to consideration only of whether the requirements are met. In particular, the court may not consider the merits of the matter, i.e. which party has the better claim to be in possession of the thing.[36] The injustice of possession by the applicant is irrelevant.[37] This is because the purpose of the remedy is to give effect to the fundamental principles mentioned above, as well as to curtail the breach of peace occasioned by the respondent taking matters into her own hands. Hence, the maxim, before all else, restore unlawful dispossession *(spoliatus ante omnia restituendus est)*[38] underpins the remedy. Evaluation of the competing claims to be in possession must be dealt with in different proceedings, not in the course of the *mandament van spolie* proceedings. The relief afforded by this remedy is, at best, temporary.

> **PAUSE FOR REFLECTION**
>
> **Mandament van spolie a proprietary remedy?**
>
> Some legal scholars take the view that the *mandament van spolie* is not really a proprietary remedy but rather something *sui generis* (of its own nature – does not fit into a category), and designed only to prevent or rectify a breach of the peace.[39] However, no other circumstance of taking the law into one's own hands is remedied by the *mandament van spolie*. It is only in respect of loss of factual possession of property that this remedy is available, which seems to point to its connection with property and, specifically, bare possession, rather than with any other area of law.[40] However, in practical terms, it does not really matter how one classifies the remedy.

4.4.1.2 Requirements

The applicant must prove on a balance of probabilities that she was in peaceful and undisturbed possession. Both elements – *corpus* and *animus* – must be proved.[41] The applicant must further prove that the respondent unlawfully deprived[42] her of possession, i.e. committed a spoliation.[43]

In *Du Randt v Du Randt*,[44] the applicant could not prove bare possession of particular movable property because she had insufficient *animus* as an employee in the business. She had alleged that she was a partner but the factual evidence did not support the allegation. Thus, while she was clearly in physical control of the property concerned, the court stated that reliance could not be placed solely on the *corpus* element of possession. However, she used other movable property and benefited personally from the physical control thereof, and could successfully establish the requirements for the *mandament van spolie* in respect of that property. In *De Beer v Zimbali Estate Management Association (Pty) Ltd*,[45] the applicant, an estate agent, could not prove bare possession of the estate because she could not establish

---

36 *Nino Bonino v De Lange* 1906 TS 120 at 122.
37 See *Yeko v Qana* 1973 (4) SA 735 (A) at 739, citing Voet 41.2.16.
38 *Nino Bonino v De Lange* 1906 TS 120 at 122.
39 *Silberberg & Schoeman Property* pp 274-275; *Wille's Principles* p 446; De Vos, W ''n Bespreking van Sekere Aspekte van die Regsposisie van Besitters' (1959) *Acta Juridica* 184 at 191; see also Badenhorst, PJ & Coetser, PPJ 'Die Berging van Skeepswrakke – Enkele Aspekte – *Mills v Reck and Others* 1988 (3) SA 92 (K)' (1989) *TSAR* 137 at 138-140.
40 See also *dictum* from *Muller v Muller* 1915 TPD 28 at 30 (n 22 above).
41 *Meyer v Glendinning* 1939 CPD 84 ; *Du Randt v Du Randt* 1995 (1) SA 401 (O).
42 Deprivation requires actual loss of factual possession.
43 *Bon Quelle (Edms) Bpk v Munisipaliteit van Otavi* 1989 (1) SA 508 (A); *Yeko v Qana* 1973 (4) SA 735 (A); *Wightman t/a JW Construction v Headfour (Pty) Ltd and Another* 2008 (3) SA 371 (SCA).
44 1995 (1) SA 401 (O).
45 2007 (3) SA 254 (N).

sufficient and effective physical control, only that she was permitted to access the premises until such access was terminated. The *mandament van spolie* does not protect access.

4.4.1.3 Application of remedy to incorporeals

The *mandament van spolie* can be used when deprivation concerns incorporeal property in the form of a right of use.[46] Important to grasp is that rights in general and especially contractual rights are not protected by this remedy.[47] The conceptual difficulty with application of the *mandament van spolie* to incorporeal property is that factual evidence of physical control of an intangible is simply not possible. However, the law accommodates this difficulty by permitting recognition of quasi-possession, i.e. *detentio* or physical control is replaced by an approximation that is compatible with the right of use of something. The applicant must demonstrate that she made actual use of the content of the right of use in question.[48]

From case law, it is apparent that the nature of the right of use that may be protected generally takes one of two forms. Either the right of use has a servitutal nature[49] or it is incidental to factual possession of a corporeal thing.[50] One outlier case permitted the remedy to protect shareholder rights.[51]

Regarding a right of use with a servitutal nature, for example, use of water, the applicant must provide factual evidence to support the allegation that he actually used the water and did so undisturbed and peacefully until the respondent deprived him unlawfully of such use.[52] It would be erroneous to think that every use of water has a servitutal nature. One must thus think carefully about the factual context and ascertain whether, in principle, such facts might support the existence of a servitude, i.e. a limited real right. Note, however, that one is not required to prove the existence of a servitude.[53]

In *Le Riche v PSP Properties CC*,[54] the applicant used a supply of water for some 14 years in an undisturbed and peaceful manner until the respondent disconnected the pipe without notice. The disconnection of the pipe without notice constituted unlawful deprivation. In light of the requirements for the *mandament van spolie*, a question was whether the use of the water could constitute quasi-possession. In the circumstances, what was needed was for the applicant to show that he had conducted himself **as if** a water servitude existed. Factual evidence demonstrated that the applicant had actively accessed and used the supply of water **as if of right**. Note that the applicant was not called upon to prove the existence of a servitutal right. To do so would have been contrary to the requirements of the remedy, which does not consider the merits of the matter.

It is possible and perhaps more common that a contractual use of water is involved, in which case the *mandament van spolie* is not the appropriate remedy.[55] However, if the use of water is incidental to (flows from) the possession of a corporeal, then quasi-possession of the use of the water may be possible to establish.[56] For example, consider the position where a landlord cuts off the water supply to a garden cottage rented by Moosa. A successful

---

46 *Wille's Principles* p 453; *Silberberg & Schoeman Property* pp 296ff.
47 *Telkom SA Ltd v Xsinet (Pty) Ltd* 2003 (5) SA 309 (SCA).
48 *Wille's Principles* p 458; *Silberberg & Schoeman Property* p 297.
49 *Bon Quelle (Edms) Bpk v Munisipaliteit van Otavi* 1989 (1) SA 508 (A); *Le Riche v PSP Properties CC* 2005 (3) SA 189 (C).
50 See Rens, A *'Telkom SA Limited v Xsinet (Pty) Ltd'* (2004) 120 *SALJ* 749-756.
51 *Tigon Ltd v Bestyet Investments (Pty) Ltd* 2001 (4) SA 634 (N).
52 *Bon Quelle (Edms) Bpk v Munisipaliteit van Otavi* 1989 (1) SA 508 (A) at 514H-I; *Le Riche v PSP Properties CC* 2005 (3) SA 189 (C) at paras 14, 26.
53 *Wille's Principles* p 458; *Silberberg & Schoeman Property* p 297.
54 2005 (3) SA 189 (C).
55 *Zulu v Minister of Works, KwaZulu* 1992 (1) SA 181 (N) at 188.
56 *Plaatjie and Another v Olivier NO and Others* 1993 (2) SA 156 (O) at 159J-160E.

application for a spoliation order would have the water supply restored quickly. A question would be whether Moosa can demonstrate quasi-possession of the use of the water. In the circumstances, use of the water is incidental to his possession of the garden cottage. In other words, Moosa's use of the water flows from his occupation of the premises. It is easy to lead evidence of his occupation and to demonstrate the daily and ordinary use of the water as part of his occupation and hence to prove quasi-possession. The occupation of the premises extends to the use of installations for the supply of water and electricity. Examples in case law include *Zulu v Minister of Works, KwaZulu*[57] (use of water), and *Naidoo v Moodley*[58] (use of electricity).

Sometimes, however, the facts do not support such an inference. In *Plaatjie v Olivier NO*,[59] the use of the water was not incidental to the occupation of the dwellings in question. The taps were communal taps situated in the street, from where residents could draw water and carry it home for use in their dwellings. Furthermore, whether incidental installations include the supply of electronic communication services for telephone and internet is unclear. In *Du Randt v Du Randt*,[60] spoliation of telephone services was found to have occurred on the basis that the applicant was in occupation of the premises and in control of the use of the service through her occupation.[61] Similarly, in *Xsinet (Pty) Ltd v Telkom SA Ltd*,[62] both telephone and bandwidth (internet) services were held to have been spoliated following unlawful disconnection. But the Supreme Court of Appeal held in *Telkom SA Ltd v Xsinet (Pty) Ltd*,[63] that these services were provided only on a contractual basis and enforcement of contractual rights is not appropriate for the *mandament van spolie*.[64]

COUNTER POINT

Incidental use rights

While it is obvious that the Supreme Court of Appeal was correct in affirming that the *mandament van spolie* cannot be used to enforce contractual rights, it is less clear that it was correct in its interpretation of the facts of *Telkom SA Ltd v Xsinet (Pty) Ltd*. If one uses electronic or telephone services as part of one's occupation of premises, then it is difficult to see how this usage differs from that of electricity supplied to those same premises.

Whether a distinction is to be made between essential services and non-essential services and if so, whether this distinction is significant for purposes of the *mandament van spolie*, is unknown. Arguably, however, in modern South Africa, it is taken for granted that water, electricity and sanitation services are provided to premises. Indeed, many of the efforts to effect land reform and redistribution of resources are focused on bringing basic services to all citizens. However, it is not (yet) taken for granted that all premises have television signal receivers or internet bandwidth connections. Landline telephone services seem to fall somewhere in between. In *Du Randt*, such services were held to have been spoliated (thus qualifying for protection), but not so in *Telkom v Xsinet*. However, at a conceptual level, if the *mandament van spolie* can serve to protect the right of use of something incidental to physical control of corporeal premises, then it seems logical that use of electronic signals, whether they be used for the supply of telephone or internet services, ought to be included in the category of incidental use rights.

---

57 1992 (1) SA 181 (D).
58 1982 (4) SA 82 (T).
59 1993 (2) SA 156 (O).
60 1995 (1) SA 401 (O).
61 At 405.
62 2002 (3) SA 629 (C).
63 2003 (5) SA 309 (SCA).
64 See *Wille's Principles* pp 458–9 for a more detailed discussion.

4.4.1.4 Who can use the *mandament van spolie*?

As illustrated above, the content of the *animus* or mental attitude element varies according to the factual context. The minimum *animus* for the *mandament van spolie* is the intention to benefit oneself *(animus ex re commodum acquirendi)*.[65] Thus it follows that anyone who can establish the minimum *animus* together with sufficient and effective physical control (the components of the *ius possessionis*, i.e. factual or bare possession), can use this remedy. If one is unable to establish that minimum *animus*, then one is unable to use any legal remedy to protect one's factual possession in one's own right.

For example, Andrew asks Tanya to look after his briefcase while he attends a meeting. What is Tanya's relationship with Andrew's briefcase? Is Tanya in factual possession? Or is she a custodian of his briefcase? If she is the latter, then she would not be able to establish the minimum *animus* required to succeed with an application for the *mandament van spolie*.

A custodian is one who undertakes to look after someone else's thing: she has no interest in the thing over and above that which she has as a quasi-servant of the owner. She undertakes certain duties as a custodian: to take care of the thing, not to use it for personal benefit, and to return it to the entitled person when requested to do so. It ought to be clear from this that a custodian[66] cannot establish the minimum *animus* necessary for the *mandament van spolie*, and that if someone were to deprive the custodian of physical control of the briefcase unlawfully, then she would have to call upon the owner of the briefcase to pursue the matter rather than to do so herself as she would lack *locus standi*.

If, however, Tanya had borrowed the briefcase to carry her papers to a conference and someone unlawfully deprived her of physical control of the briefcase, then, in principle, she would be able to apply for the *mandament van spolie* herself. She would be able to demonstrate the appropriate mental attitude – she intended to benefit from the physical control of the briefcase – as well as sufficient and effective physical control.

4.4.1.5 Relief available

An order of restoration of the *status quo ante* requires the respondent to put the applicant in the position he was in prior to the spoliation. No damages may be claimed.[67]

4.4.1.6 Defences

The possible defences open to the respondent (spoliator) are to attack the *facta probanda*, i.e. the elements of the requirements, as well as to challenge the *locus standi* of the applicant. It is never a valid defence to allege that the respondent has a better right to be in possession; this allegation raises the merits of the matter, which is impermissible.[68] Thus, the respondent may assert that the applicant was not in possession because either of the elements was defective. In *Meyer v Glendinning*,[69] it was asserted that the applicant had mere custody, which is an allegation that there is insufficient *animus*. The respondent may also assert that the applicant was not in peaceful and undisturbed possession because there was constant repelling of others, especially the respondent.[70] Other defences are

---

65 See p 76 above.
66 A servant and an agent are in a similar position: both hold the thing solely on behalf of another.
67 See p 76 above.
68 *Nino Bonino v De Lange* 1906 TS 120 at 125.
69 1939 CPD 84.
70 *Meyer v Glendinning* 1939 CPD 84 at 86.

that the respondent was not the spoliator or that he did not effect a spoliation, i.e. the deprivation was not unlawful. For example, if the applicant voluntarily handed the property over or acquiesced in the taking thereof, invoking the *mandament van spolie* will not be successful.

A further defence is that there has been an unreasonable delay in bringing the application which ought to lead to an inference that the applicant was acquiescent in the termination of her possession. In *Le Riche v PSP Properties CC*,[71] the respondent argued that because there was a delay of nearly two years between the termination of the water supply and the launch of application proceedings, the applicant had delayed unreasonably or had acquiesced in the termination of the water supply. Under the circumstances of that particular case, this argument failed.

PAUSE FOR REFLECTION	What time period constitutes an unreasonable delay?
	In practice, there is no fixed time period after which a delay is unreasonable. Case law shows that a delay of a few hours might be too long or one of several months is still reasonable and acceptable, and even that a delay of two years might be acceptable.[72] The point is that the factual scenario informs what ought to be seen as reasonable or not. Generally, however, when the delay is for less than one year, the person alleging that this is unreasonably long (the respondent) must show persuasive reasons why the court should share her view. When the delay is for more than one year, then the applicant must show why this is not unreasonable. The assessment of the reasonableness of the delay in all cases is a question of fact. In *Le Riche* the time period between the dispossession and the launch of the application proceedings was nearly two years. However, the facts did not support an inference of undue delay on the part of the applicant as there had been unsuccessful mediation efforts, attempts to settle out of court as well as correspondence, all of which took up a considerable amount of time.

Another defence is that restoration is impossible because the thing no longer exists, is broken, or because it is in the hands of a third person.[73]

COUNTER POINT	What happens when restoration is impossible?
	Regarding the impossibility of restoration, an interesting series of cases reflects a policy-based stance by some courts in the pre-constitutional era when people's homes were demolished by the authorities acting under draconian anti-squatting legislation. Appalled by the heartlessness of the conduct of the authorities and notwithstanding that materials used in building the shacks were bent out of shape or even missing as a result of the demolition, the court in *Fredericks v Stellenbosch Divisional Council*[74] ordered the respondent to supply additional materials to restore the shacks. This clearly policy-based decision was followed in other cases involving similar facts. However, in many instances, the courts were unable to grant the spoliation order because the

---

71   2005 (3) SA 189 (C).
72   *Mans v Loxton Municipality* 1948 (1) SA 966 (C); *De Beer v Firs Investments Ltd* 1980 (3) SA 1087 (W); *Ness v Greeff* 1985 (4) SA 641 (C); *Le Riche v PSP Properties CC* 2005 (3) SA 189 (C) at para 48.
73   *Rikhotso v Northcliff Ceramics (Pty) Ltd* 1997 (1) SA 526 (W).
74   1997 (3) SA 113 (C).

> authorities had ensured that materials were actually destroyed either by burning or by complete destruction.[75]
>
> Van der Walt[76] has argued in support of replacement as part of the spoliation order on the basis that people who indulge in unlawful self-help ought not to get away with it. He explored whether a replacement order could be accommodated in the South African legal system, and concluded that such orders might be justified on the basis of the classification of things into fungible and non-fungible things. Shacks are generally built from what might be seen as fungible materials. Furthermore, precedent exists for a usufruct in respect of fungible property and, in his view, there was no obstacle to permitting a spoliation order to include replacement of fungible property when appropriate.
>
> However, Van der Merwe[77] has countered with the dogmatically correct view that the principle of specificity that underpins the notion of real rights in a thing would preclude such a justification. A real right is held in respect of a specific thing, for example a sheet of corrugated iron. If a substitute sheet is donated, for argument's sake, to the person, then a new real right is created; the previous real right was extinguished upon abandonment of the destroyed sheet.
>
> It seems that it would be in keeping with the spirit of ubuntu and the constitutional principles for policy to permit fungible materials to be replaced in a situation where deliberate destruction of materials occurs and the *mandament van spolie* is the appropriate remedy.[78]

Given that the lawfulness of the applicant's possession is not relevant to the proceedings, the question arises whether self-help by the respondent is a valid defence to the *mandament van spolie*. In other words, can the respondent allege that his action is lawful rather than unlawful self-help? Counterspoliation (self-help) is a valid defence and may succeed, provided the respondent has acted *instanter* (immediately) to recover possession.[79] A difficulty is that no clarity exists as to what time period would qualify as *instanter*. The rule of thumb is that the second dispossession must occur so that it can be seen as still part of the events surrounding the first dispossession. Precedent exists for a narrow interpretation (very short time period between the first and second dispossessions) and a broader interpretation (up to 11 days between the two dispossessions).[80]

In *De Beer v Firs Investments Ltd*,[81] the applicant had taken occupation of the respondent's premises against the respondent's will and had installed new locks, whereupon the respondent had these locks replaced to prevent the applicant from re-entering the premises. In an application for the *mandament van spolie*, the respondent asserted that its actions amounted to counterspoliation. In considering the factual circumstances, the court stated:

---

75 *Moleta v Fourie* 1975 (3) SA 999 (O).
76 Van der Walt, AJ 'Squatting, Spoliation Orders and the New Constitutional Order' (1997) 60 *THRHR* 522-528.
77 *Wille's Principles* p 460.
78 See e.g. *Tswelopele Non-Profit Organisation and Others v City of Tshwane Metropolitan Municipality and Others* 2007 (6) SA 511 (SCA); *Rikhotso v Northcliff Ceramics (Pty) Ltd and Others* 1997 (1) SA 526 (W).
79 *Silberberg & Schoeman Property* p 306.
80 *Mans v Loxton Municipality* 1948 (1) SA 966 (C) (narrow); *De Beer v Firs Investments Ltd* 1980 (3) SA 1087 (W) and *Ness v Greeff* 1985 (4) SA 641 (C) (broader). See *Wille's Principles* pp 465-466.
81 1980 (3) SA 1087 (W).

It is difficult to think what else the respondent should or could have done at the time when the first spoliation (that is installation of the locks) took place. The possession of space in respondent's building is involved and the only fact of possession is the control which is exercised through the locks and keys.[82]

The relevant insight is that the factual circumstances are important to the determination of whether the second dispossession occurs as part of the events surrounding the first dispossession and can thus be seen as *instanter*.

4.4.2 Possessory action

The possessory action is a remedy available under circumstances distinguishable from those in which the *mandament van spolie* would apply. These circumstances and the requirements for applicability are discussed below, together with the relief available to the claimant.

4.4.2.1 Circumstances for applicability

The possessory action is available to a possessor who has lost possession in circumstances where the *mandament van spolie* will not apply, such as where bare possession cannot be established or the spoliator has disposed of the thing to a third party.[83] Action proceedings require oral evidence.[84]

4.4.2.2 Requirements

The plaintiff must provide prima facie proof that she is entitled to be in possession, i.e. that she has the *ius possidendi*, and that this right is stronger than that of the defendant.[85] In other words, the merits of the matter will be considered by the court. The plaintiff must also prove that the defendant is currently in control of the thing concerned or that he was responsible for its removal from the plaintiff's control.

4.4.2.3 Who can use the possessory action?

The person who can prove she has the *ius possidendi* (entitlement to possession) and the other requirements may institute the possessory action.[86]

4.4.2.4 Relief available

The plaintiff may recover the thing, its value, or both (where the thing is damaged). If the property is immovable, recovery of the thing would take the form of an ejectment order (subject to the statutory requirements governing eviction from a home being satisfied). If the thing is not able to be recovered, and the plaintiff wants compensation instead, then a delictual action must be instituted, which means the elements for a delict must be proved.

4.4.2.5 Defences

The defendant can challenge on the basis that he has a stronger *ius possidendi*, i.e. that he should be awarded possession of the thing based on the better entitlement.[87]

---

82 At 1092.
83 *Wille's Principles* p 462.
84 *LAWSA* Vol 3(1) at para 28.
85 *LAWSA* Vol 27(1) at para 279.
86 *Silberberg & Schoeman Property* p 306; *Wille's Principles* p 467.
87 *LAWSA* Vol 27(1) at para 279.

4.4.3 Interdict

The *mandament van spolie* does not apply where possession is merely disturbed or where it is only anticipated that possession will be disturbed.[88] Under such circumstances, a prohibitory interdict may be the more appropriate remedy. The interdict is a remedy, obtainable on an urgent basis in appropriate circumstances, that can either prevent an encroachment from taking place, or stop interference when it is already occurring. It can also be instituted to order particular conduct on the part of the respondent. This remedy is available to owners and possessors with the *ius possidendi*. A prohibitory interdict is a judicial order that requires a person not to do something or to stop doing something that has already started.[89] It is available to owners and possessors when their rights are being infringed upon or are threatened by infringement.

4.4.3.1 Circumstances for applicability

The prohibitory interdict can be used where possession is merely disturbed or threatened with interference, i.e. the interference is currently happening or there is a threat that it will happen (again).[90] The effect of the interdict is to require the respondent to discontinue the interfering conduct or to refrain from doing it. The interference must be current. If it has passed and is unlikely to recur, then this is not the appropriate remedy. The applicant must be able to show that he is entitled to possession (*ius possidendi*).

4.4.3.2 Requirements

The interdict may be temporary or final. The requirements are largely similar.[91] For a temporary interdict, the applicant must prove a prima facie right. This means that he must prove that he, on the face of it, is entitled to undisturbed possession. For a final interdict, the requirements are similar but convincing proof of entitlement is required, i.e. a clear right must be proved.[92] For example, the plaintiff must show that he is the owner or possessor. The applicant must further prove (both for a temporary or a final interdict) that the respondent has committed a harm (by interfering with his possession) or is reasonably thought to intend to commit it, and that irreparable damage will result if the harm were to continue. Further, the interdict must be the only suitable remedy.

In *Victoria and Alfred Waterfront v Police Commissioner of the Western Cape*,[93] the application for an interdict barring specific homeless people permanently from entrance to the Waterfront was unsuccessful because of the last requirement as a similar result could have been achieved with less drastic measures. In considering the application for the interdict, the court considered specifically that the right to exclude others from entering one's property was also curtailed by the constitutional right to freedom of movement. Instead of barring access to the property, the court ordered that the people, who were causing annoyance by undesirable and aggressive conduct towards visitors and employees of the Waterfront, be interdicted from repeating the unlawful conduct.

---

88 *Silberberg & Schoeman Property* p 308.
89 *Silberberg & Schoeman Property* p 308.
90 *LAWSA* Vol 27(1) at para 278.
91 Compare *Setlolego v Setlolego* 1914 AD 221 at 227 with *Molteno Bros and Others v SAR and Others* 1936 AD 321 at 332; *Webster v Mitchell* 1948 (1) SA 1186 (W); *Ndauti v Kgami and Others* 1948 (3) SA 27 (W) at 35–37. See also Van der Merwe *Sakereg* pp 148–150.
92 *Silberberg & Schoeman Property* p 309.
93 2004 (5) BCLR 53(c).

Application proceedings are conducted based on affidavits only and, in general terms, no oral evidence is heard.[94] The matter is decided on the merits, i.e. who has the better claim. Thus, if there is a dispute of facts, the matter should go to trial unless the court is willing to hear limited oral evidence. The court has discretion to refuse to grant a final interdict if the applicant's interest and right can be effectively and sufficiently protected by an award of damages. Note that the applicant cannot apply for an award of damages using application proceedings; it is the court's discretion to make such an award.

4.4.3.3 Relief available

A successful application for a temporary interdict results in an order that requires the respondent to discontinue his (intended) conduct immediately.[95] It also sets a date upon which the parties must return to court to persuade the court as to whether the order should be made final. This is especially important if the application proceedings were ex parte because it gives the other party the chance to bring her side of the matter to court. This procedure gives effect to the *audi alteram* principle. In the case of a final interdict, the order prohibits the respondent from repeating the interfering conduct, at the risk of being found to be in contempt of court.

4.4.3.4 Defences

The respondent can challenge the *facta probanda*, and can also assert that he has a better claim, i.e. a *ius possidendi*.

4.4.4 Delictual action

Someone who wishes to protect a possessory relationship also has a delictual action at his disposal. The following paragraphs list the circumstances for applicability and requirements for this remedy, for whom the remedy is available, and the form of relief to be granted. Defences are also mentioned briefly.

4.4.4.1 Circumstances for applicability

When the thing is not available for recovery by the dispossessed person, a claim for compensation for patrimonial loss may be appropriate. The claim would be for the value of the thing and any subsequent damages suffered by the possessor because of the dispossession and loss of the thing. The claim is instituted by action proceedings under the *lex Aquilia*.[96]

4.4.4.2 Requirements

The plaintiff must prove all the delictual elements. This includes that she has a patrimonial interest in the thing or in its control, that this interest has been harmed as a result of the unlawful and culpable act of the defendant, which together caused the patrimonial loss for the plaintiff.

---

94 *LAWSA* Vol 3(1) at para 16.
95 *Silberberg & Schoeman Property* pp 308–309.
96 See *Wille's Principles* pp 1094*ff*.

4.4.4.3 Who can use the delictual action?

The person who can prove the delictual elements may institute the delictual action.

4.4.4.4 Relief available

An award of damages (compensation) may be made.

4.4.4.5 Defences

The defendant can challenge the *facta probanda*.

4.5 Concluding remarks

Possession may be regarded as the most fundamental concept of property law. It is from this notion of physical control with a particular intention that the other core concepts (rights and ownership) emanate. In the following chapters it will be demonstrated that the notion of possession is central to most aspects of property law. It is important in establishing the kind of remedies that are available if the relationship between a person and his property is breached. It largely determines whether the requirements for transfer have been met, or whether ownership has passed by means of an original mode of acquisition.

PART TWO

OWNERSHIP

CHAPTER 5 Content and forms of ownership 89

CHAPTER 6 Limitations on ownership 115

CHAPTER 7 Acquisition of ownership 159

CHAPTER 8 Protection of ownership 215

Chapter 5

Content and forms of ownership

'Like many other culturally loaded terms, property is at once a very dense idea, full of resonance in many fields, as well as one which is extraordinarily slippery.'

Margaret Davies (2007) *Property: Meanings, histories, theories* Oxford, Routledge-Cavendish p 9

5.1	Content of ownership	89
5.1.1	Definition of ownership	91
5.1.2	Content and entitlements of ownership	92
5.1.3	Limitations	95
5.2	**Forms of ownership**	**96**
5.2.1	Individual title	96
5.2.2	Co-ownership	96
5.2.2.1	General elements and classes of common law co-ownership	97
5.2.2.2	The undivided co-ownership share	98
5.2.2.3	The commonly owned property	99
5.2.2.4	Remedies	99
5.3	**Alternative forms of title**	**100**
5.3.1	Sectional title schemes	100
5.3.1.1	The nature of sectional ownership	101
5.3.1.2	Management of a sectional title scheme	102
5.3.2	Share block schemes	103
5.3.3	Modified uses of share blocks and sectional title	104
5.3.4	Communal property associations	105
5.3.5	Indigenous land rights	107
5.3.5.1	Pre-1991 tenure systems	110
5.3.5.2	The Communal Land Rights Act 11 of 2004	111
5.4	**Concluding remarks**	**113**

5.1 Content of ownership

Some form of ownership is important in all modern-day societies, especially those with a capitalist market economy. The centrality of the role of ownership is, however, intrinsically linked to the particular ideological, socio-political and economic foundation of the society in question.[1] This means, therefore, that ownership has different meanings in different

---

1   *Silberberg & Schoeman Property* p 1.

societies, and its content varies according to the role and function that ownership plays in the particular context.

A plausible explanation for the origin of the notion of ownership is that it emerged, with the expansion of general trade, from use rights.[2] In hunter-gatherer societies, even the simplest tools could be used only by one person at a time. It seems sensible, therefore, that use rights, including the right of exclusion, must have enjoyed some protection to avoid unnecessary conflicts between members of the group. As agrarian societies established themselves, the nature of herding and agriculture would have required that the use rights be protected for longer and longer periods. Scarcity of resources, including materials for tools, would have played a role too. Goods became important for their exchange value, relative to other goods in the market, which led to competition and trade. Ultimately, the need for legal regulation led to the notion of ownership, which in turn led to the creation of other legal institutions such as succession rules, methods of transacting in the marketplace (contract rules), as well as the concepts of legal subjects, legal objects and matters of capacity. As is quite apparent in the modern world, 'ownership, wills, contract, legal personality and property provide a conceptual framework that can be applied in diverse economic and social contexts'.[3]

In the South African context, the content of ownership, as well as the ability to exercise it, was affected by the race-based policies of the apartheid era.[4] Consequently, ownership, especially of land, has been and remains contentious. The origin of the South African ownership concept is essentially Roman-Dutch with some influence from the absolutist theories of the Pandectist movement of the latter part of the nineteenth century.[5]

The traditional conceptualisation of ownership may be encapsulated in the phrase, *plena in re potestas*, i.e. the owner has the power to do as she pleases with the property owned, within the limits imposed by law. This view expresses the idea that ownership is the name given to the most extensive legal relationship possible between a person and property; it also acknowledges, however, that, by definition, ownership is not limitless.

The concept of ownership has never been absolute, not even in Roman times.[6] The institution of ownership includes the knowledge that **anyone** (within the boundaries of the prevailing law) can own property. In turn, it follows that nobody's ownership can be absolute because each owner must accommodate the fact that others exercise similar entitlements in the same context.[7] Limitations have thus always been part and parcel of the common law concept of ownership. Nevertheless, the Pandectist influence led to considerable emphasis being placed on the absoluteness of ownership,[8] which became a useful interpretation of ownership, especially related to land, during the apartheid era. It is worth pointing out that this interpretation of the Pandectist view was, in fact, a misinterpretation because rather than emphasising the absoluteness of the concept of ownership, the Pandectists highlighted the absoluteness of the **enforceability** of ownership entitlements.[9]

---

2   For more detail see Bennett, TW (2004) *Customary Law in South Africa* (Cape Town, Juta) pp 374*ff*.
3   Bennett, TW (2004) *Customary Law in South Africa* (Cape Town, Juta) p 376.
4   Van der Walt, AJ 'Property Rights and Hierarchies of Power: A Critical Evaluation of Land-Reform Policy in South Africa' (1999) (64) 2 & 3 *Koers* 259 at 261-264.
5   See p 11 above.
6   Visser, DP 'The "Absoluteness" of Ownership: The South African Common Law in Perspective' (1985) *Acta Juridica* 39 at 39-40.
7   Van der Merwe *Sakereg* pp 171*ff*.
8   Van der Merwe *Sakereg* pp 171-172.
9   Visser, DP 'The "Absoluteness" of Ownership: The South African Common Law in Perspective' (1985) *Acta Juridica* 43 at 46-48; Van der Walt, AJ 'Unity and Pluralism in Property Theory – A Review of Property Theories and Debates in Recent Literature: Part I' (1995) 1 *TSAR* 15 at 23-24, 31; Van der Walt, AJ 'Dancing with Codes – Protecting, Developing and Reconstructing Property Rights in a Constitutional State' (2001) 118 *SALJ* 258 at 274-275.

More recently, the new constitutional dispensation has revived debate about the content of ownership. The property clause is underpinned by the continued existence of the notion of private ownership, but its provisions indicate clearly that arguments in favour of the absoluteness of ownership are no longer sustainable, if they ever were.[10] The property clause sets out a framework that regulates the context and manner in which deprivation and expropriation of property can take place,[11] thus indicating that private ownership continues to exist. However, the clause also provides explicitly for the reform of access to land, water and other natural resources,[12] which indicates that a more socially responsible form of ownership is envisaged for the future. This development has resulted in academic attempts to revise the modern-day role and function of ownership.[13] Special emphasis is placed on the role of ownership, and property law in general, in the efforts to create and promote political, constitutional and social transformation processes.[14]

These occurrences underline that the content of ownership is dependent not only on the socio-political basis of a society, but is also affected by the passage of time because the content may vary in different periods of historical development. In this chapter, we demonstrate that the precise content of ownership in Roman-Dutch law differs from the modern-day content, although the principles governing the concept remain intact. It is predictable that the precise content of ownership in South Africa will continue to develop and adjust to meet societal needs over the coming decades or centuries, while the principles may remain largely similar to those known in Roman law.

An understanding of the content of ownership is essential to distinguish it from, for instance possession and limited real rights in property. Consequently, the first part of this chapter focuses on the definition and entitlements of ownership, i.e. the content of ownership. Thereafter, the different forms of ownership available in South African law are examined, including some of the latest developments in the context of land reform.

5.1.1 Definition of ownership

No single useful legal definition of ownership can serve all communities in all circumstances at all times. As discussed above, the nature and content of ownership are determined by the society within which ownership functions. The nature and content of ownership depend on the demands and needs of that particular society, and are informed by the history of that particular society. This section deals with the common law definition of ownership that is accepted in the South African context.

The common law definition of ownership focuses on the theoretical completeness of the right by describing it as the most complete right a legal subject can have in relation to an object.[15] This means that only the owner has the most complete and absolute entitlements to his property. This understanding is linked to the principle of *nemo plus iuris in alium transferre potest quam ipse haberet* (no one can transfer more rights than he has).[16] In other words, no one has more rights in relation to a thing than the owner and, when the owner is dispossessed and the property is put in the hands of a third party, ownership remains

---

10 *Silberberg & Schoeman Property* pp 93–101.
11 See pp 118*ff* below.
12 Section 25(8) of the Constitution of the Republic South Africa, 1996.
13 *Silberberg & Schoeman Property* pp 4–5.
14 Van der Walt, AJ 'Property, social justice and citizenship: property law in post-apartheid South Africa' (2008) *Stell LR* 325 at 325–346.
15 *Gien v Gien* 1979 (2) SA 1113 (T).
16 *Silberberg & Schoeman Property* p 73; *Glatthaar v Hussan* 1912 TPD 322.

intact. The person who purports to transfer ownership rights to the third party is unable to do so without the co-operation of the owner.[17]

The description of ownership as the most complete real right does not, however, mean that ownership is absolute or has no limits at all.[18] Ownership has always been limited by objective law (e.g. legislation and neighbour law)[19] and by the subjective rights of other persons (e.g. limited real rights and personal rights).[20] Nevertheless, in comparison with other real rights, ownership is the most complete.[21]

The possibility of employing ownership as a vehicle for transformation in society is being explored increasingly within the South African property law paradigm. In this regard, Van der Walt argues that a context-sensitive and reform-friendly view on ownership is not necessarily or fundamentally contrary to the idea that individual ownership is something worthy of the law's protection.[22] Depending on the particular facts and circumstances of each case, the focus ought to be on seeking to balance sustainable economic development, including building supportive communities, on the one hand, with social justice, on the other.

5.1.2 Content and entitlements of ownership

The fact that South African property law has always been one of the 'strongholds of civilian jurisprudence'[23] implies a particular understanding of the relationship between ownership and other rights in respect of property. It also implies a particular understanding of the content of ownership and other rights to property. In terms of this understanding, ownership is described as the 'most complete real right' in property.[24] 'Complete' indicates, first, that the owner has all possible proprietary rights in relation to the property and, second, that ownership comprises a potentially limitless number of entitlements, each of which confers the power to do something in relation to the property concerned. Which entitlements of ownership exist at a particular point depends on the specific type of property as well as on the governing circumstances of each situation. Consequently, the exact content of ownership may differ from situation to situation, depending on the specific circumstances in each case. A further aspect of this understanding of ownership is that, in mainstream South African property law, a distinction is made between the right of ownership, and other limited rights in respect of property.[25]

---

17 See further ch 7 below.
18 *Silberberg & Schoeman Property* pp 93–94; *Wille's Principles* p 406.
19 See ch 6 below.
20 See ch 3 above.
21 Van der Merwe *Sakereg* p 13.
22 Van der Walt, AJ 'Property, social justice and citizenship: property law in post-apartheid South Africa' (2008) *Stell LR* 325 at 345.
23 Van der Walt, AJ 'Tradition on Trial: A Critical Analysis of the Civil-Law Tradition in South African Property Law' (1995) 11 *SAJHR* 169; Zimmermann, R & Visser, DP (1996) 'Introduction: South African Law as a Mixed legal System' in Zimmermann, R & Visser DP (eds) *Southern Cross: Civil Law and Common Law in South Africa* (Cape Town, Juta) p 28.
24 Van der Merwe *Sakereg* p 13.
25 See also ch 3 above.

> **PAUSE FOR REFLECTION**
>
> **Theories underlying the description of the content of ownership**
>
> Two distinct theories are generally used to explain the right of ownership. In terms of the one theory, ownership may be described metaphorically as a 'bundle of rights'. In the 'bundle' or collection of rights comprising ownership (i.e. the 'standard incidents of ownership'[26]), there may be, among others, the right to dispose of the property *(ius disponendi)*, the right to use the property *(ius utendi)*, the right to draw the fruits *(ius fruendi)*, and the right to neglect the property *(ius abutendi)*. However, the important point is that the bundle contains an infinite number of rights. Using flaky pastry as a metaphor to explain this understanding of ownership, the pastry must contain a limitless number of layers 'where the texture is visibly complex, the substance splittable and sharable, and the layers genuinely uncountable'.[27]
>
> Though this bundle of rights theory enjoys recognition in Anglo-American legal systems, it has not had similarly overwhelming support in South African property law doctrine.[28] Instead, ownership is regarded (in terms of the second theory) as a concept of unity, with the entitlements mentioned above forming part of the whole.[29] This was the result of the significant impact of the theories of Grotius, alongside Windscheid and the Pandectists, on South African property law.[30] In terms of this view, ownership is characterised by traits such as its elasticity, exclusivity, independence and unlimited duration,[31] and defined with reference to the relationships it creates between persons in respect of things.[32]
>
> This mainstream South African view on the legal nature of ownership distinguishes it from other rights in property that are derived from ownership.[33] Essentially, however, the difference between the two approaches hinges on the prominence and place afforded to the residual character of ownership.

As indicated above, ownership may include several entitlements, notably the power to use, possess, alienate, encumber, vindicate and (under some circumstances) even neglect or destroy the property. The continued existence of ownership is not dependent on the permanent presence of all entitlements simultaneously: some entitlements may be assigned to other persons by the owner, thereby diminishing the number of remaining entitlements.

So, for instance, Lindiwe may choose to let her apartment in Sea Point to a group of soccer tourists for the duration of the 2010 World Cup soccer tournament. By doing so, she surrenders her entitlement to occupy, use and enjoy the apartment and the accompanying amenities for a limited period, in exchange for payment of the rent as agreed between her and the tourists. This assignment of entitlements by no means diminishes the legal fact of ownership as such.

---

26 Honoré, AM 'Ownership' (1961) in Guest, AG (ed) *Oxford Essays in Jurisprudence* (Oxford, Oxford University Publishers) p 113; Lewis, C 'The Modern Concept of Ownership of Land' (1985) *Acta Juridica* 241 at 243*ff*.
27 Cooke, E (2003) *The New Law of Land Registration* (Oxford, Hart Publishing) pp 3-4.
28 Compare Honoré, AM 'Ownership' (1961) in Guest, AG (ed) *Oxford Essays in Jurisprudence* (Oxford, Oxford University Publishers) pp 124*ff* and Van der Merwe *Sakereg* p 174.
29 Van der Merwe *Sakereg* p 174.
30 Van der Walt, AJ 'Unity and Pluralism in Property Theory – A Review of Property Theories and Debates in Recent Literature: Part I' (1995) *TSAR* 15 at 22-24.
31 Van der Merwe *Sakereg* pp 175-176.
32 In the South African context, this is illustrated well by the decision in *Elektrisiteitsvoorsieningskommissie v Fourie en Andere* 1988 (2) SA 627 (T). See also Van der Vyver, JD 'Expropriation, Rights, Entitlements and Surface Support of Land Recent Cases' (1988) 105 *SALJ* 1-16.
33 Van der Merwe *Sakereg* p 176; Silberberg & Schoeman *Property* pp 47-48.

To illustrate further, Jan, a landowner, may grant a right of way to Stephan, his neighbour and the owner of the adjacent plot, thereby creating a servitude in favour of the neighbouring land. This means that Stephan acquires a limited real right in the property of Jan and that the latter gives up the entitlement to exclusive use of the road in question. Although the exclusivity of use of the property has been affected, ownership itself is not taken away: Jan is still the owner of his land, although the content of his ownership has been altered. The difference between the examples of Lindiwe and Jan is that in Lindiwe's case, the content of her right of ownership is altered temporarily, while in Jan's case, the fact that the right of way serves the adjacent land in perpetuity means that the content of his ownership has altered permanently.

Not all entitlements are afforded the same kind of prominence by all scholars. For instance, some may opine that the entitlement to destroy or consume the property is not an integral part of ownership because of legal prohibitions against the destruction or consumption of certain types of property. For example, with regard to land, the law strictly prohibits demolition of historically or architecturally important buildings. This means that the content of landownership may exclude the *ius abutendi* under certain circumstances.[34] Lately, moreover, government policy has veered towards a preference for the so-called 'use it or lose it principle' in the context of land and resource reform. For instance, a holder of old order mineral rights can be compelled to convert them into new order rights that must be actively exercised.[35] The fact that the *ius abutendi* is severely restricted under such circumstances does not detract from its relevance in other circumstances: Jeanette remains entitled to destroy her troublesome kettle if she so wishes, and she is not compelled to use her hairdryer just because she has one! Furthermore, she is free to demolish her house that has no particular historical significance.

The completeness of ownership in any context, thus, depends on whether all entitlements are available to the owner or whether some entitlements have been assigned to other persons or are limited by legislation. The point is that temporary assignment of some entitlements does not extinguish ownership. It does, however, have an effect on the content of ownership of a particular person in relation to a specific property at a specific time. The number of entitlements may thus fluctuate, which allows for a considerable degree of flexibility in a content-based definition of ownership. This is supplemented, further, by the particular form that ownership takes in any given scenario. In the final analysis, it would be fair to say that, for any given owner, in any given situation, the content of the right is almost as unique as her fingerprints!

In the following paragraphs, typically occurring entitlements are discussed briefly. These are the entitlement to use the property *(ius utendi)*; the entitlement to control the property physically *(ius possidendi)*; the entitlement to alienate or encumber the property *(ius disponendi)*; and the entitlement to vindicate the property *(ius vindicandi)*. After this discussion, different forms of ownership are considered.

An owner has the entitlement to use and enjoy her property, which may be the main reason for acquiring it in the first place.[36] Linked to use and enjoyment is the entitlement to take the fruits resulting from the property, both civil (interest or rental payments) and natural (crops and young of animals). This entitlement may be restricted voluntarily by the

---

34 See e.g. National Heritage Resources Act 25 of 1999 and the example discussed in ch 6 below, pp 117–118.
35 *AgriSouth Africa v Minister of Minerals and Energy; Van Rooyen v Minister of Minerals and Energy* Case No: 55896/2007; Case No: 102351/2008, Unreported; Reuters 'Use it or lose it, government warns farmers' (05-03-2009) *Cape Times* p 4.
36 Lewis, C 'The Modern Concept of Ownership of Land' (1985) *Acta Juridica* 241 at 260.

owner or it may be restricted involuntarily by legislation. On the one hand, for example, Sue, a landowner, may voluntarily limit her entitlements by assigning the entitlement of use to her daughter, Jesse, by granting the latter a servitude of usufruct, which allows Jesse to use and enjoy the property and to take its fruits. On the other hand, legislation restricts use of property for some categories of owners, i.e. the type of property triggers particular restrictions on use. For example, ownership of weapons, arms and ammunition is strictly controlled and regulated to the extent that there are age restrictions as well as competency requirements and a licensing process.[37] Similarly, the use of a motor vehicle is regulated by traffic rules.[38]

An owner is entitled to be in physical control of her property.[39] However, it should be noted that because physical control of property is visible to third parties, it underpins the presumption that the person in physical control of property is the owner thereof, unless the contrary is proven.[40] This entitlement can also be voluntarily assigned to another, such as when the owner delivers the property to a pledgee to be held as security for an outstanding debt.[41] Legislation may also restrict this entitlement, for instance some criminal offences may lead to confiscation of property used in the commission of the crime.[42] A claim based on ownership for the return of the property may have no effect if the confiscation provisions are absolute.[43]

An owner is entitled to dispose of her property by way of sale, donation or abandonment.[44] In each case, specific requirements govern the transfer or termination of ownership. Transfer of ownership can only be effected by the owner or a duly authorised agent.[45]

The owner may use the property to serve as security for debts or may encumber (burden) it by granting limited real rights in the property to third parties.[46] The granting of such limited real rights burdens ownership, and thus prevents full exercise of entitlements for as long as the limited real rights are intact. The nature and function of these limited real rights are discussed in more detail in chapter 3 above and chapter 9 below.

Vindication enables the owner to claim her property from whoever possesses it. This power may be exercised only by an owner. This means that this entitlement cannot be assigned to others in the form of a limited real right.[47]

5.1.3 Limitations

As demonstrated above, the sum total of entitlements inherent to ownership may differ, depending on the particular circumstances of each case. It is worth noting here that these entitlements may be limited by objective law (legislation and neighbour law),[48] or by subjective rights of other persons (limited real rights or personal rights).[49] In general terms, various sets of limitations on ownership can be distinguished, depending on the reason

---

37 See Chapter Six of the Firearms Control Act 60 of 2000.
38 Road Traffic Act 29 of 1989.
39 See the discussion on the *ius possidendi* in ch 4 above.
40 *Silberberg & Schoeman Property* p 286.
41 See ch 12.
42 Prevention of Organised Crime Act 121 of 1998.
43 See e.g. *Prophet v National Director of Public Prosecutions* 2007 (6) SA 169 (CC).
44 Lewis, C 'The Modern Concept of Ownership of Land' (1985) *Acta Juridica* 241 at 243.
45 See ch 7.
46 Pienaar, GJ 'Registration of Informal Land-use Rights in South Africa: Giving Teeth to (Toothless?) Paper Tigers' (2000) 3 *TSAR* 442 at 442.
47 See below for a more detailed discussion on the implementation of the right to vindicate, and ch 7 p 209 for further discussion of the inability to assign the right to vindicate.
48 See ch 6.
49 See ch 3 above.

for limitation. For example, it may be necessary to limit ownership to conserve nature or to preserve historical buildings. The limitations upon ownership are discussed in greater detail in chapter 6 below.

5.2 Forms of ownership

Two forms of common law ownership can be distinguished, namely individual title and co-ownership. Legislative developments in the past 30 years or so have created statutory forms of ownership that comprise interesting and useful amendments to core elements of each form of common law ownership. More recently, land reform measures have contributed further innovation, especially in relation to landownership. The following sections provide an overview of the available forms of ownership, as well as a discussion that contrasts them and emphasises their various uses.

5.2.1 Individual title

Individual title (also called freehold title) vests in one person only. The single owner has the sum total of entitlements in relation to the property, movable or immovable, subject to the particular relevant limitations.[50] Individual title is also affected by legislative measures, especially those dealing with land reform matters, in relation to immovable property. In this regard, reference may be made to land reform legislation that provides new mechanisms for vesting individual title that, nevertheless, retain the common law characteristics of ownership.

For example, the Land Reform (Labour Tenants) Act[51] regulates the acquisition of rights in land in particular circumstances. The rights include both ownership and limited real rights essential for the exercise of ownership. The Act provides the mechanism whereby persons who qualify as 'labour tenants' can become individual owners of the parcel of land that the particular individual has utilised for residential, cropping and grazing purposes for at least a generation.[52]

Similarly, an 'occupier',[53] for purposes of the Extension of Security of Tenure Act (ESTA), can apply for ownership of land either 'on the farm' or 'off the farm'.[54] In both examples, the mechanisms and procedures for acquisition of ownership are provided for and regulated by legislation, but, in essence, it is common law ownership that is exercised.

5.2.2 Co-ownership

In contrast to individual title, co-ownership (also called joint title or ownership in common) entails ownership in the same property by more than one person (or entity) simultaneously.[55] Co-ownership can be categorised into co-ownership derived from common law and statutory co-ownership.

Common law co-ownership is further divided into free and bound (or tied) co-ownership, both relating to movable and immovable property. These are discussed in

---

50 See ch 3 above and ch 9 below.
51 Chapter III of the Land Reform (Labour Tenants) Act 3 of 1996
52 Sections 16–28 of the Land Reform (Labour Tenants) Act 3 of 1996.
53 Act 62 of 1997.
54 Section 4 of ESTA.
55 *Wille's Principles* pp 557–558.

the following paragraphs. Statutory co-ownership, however, relates mainly to immovable property. This category includes sectional title schemes, share block schemes and time-sharing as forms of ownership. They are discussed below.[56]

5.2.2.1 General elements and classes of common law co-ownership

Joint ownership or co-ownership occurs where more than one person simultaneously has ownership rights in a property. Each owner acquires an undivided co-ownership share in the property concerned. Accordingly, co-ownership involves two elements:[57] an undivided share in the property, reflecting each co-owner's interest, which may be equal or not; and property which is movable or immovable. That co-ownership exists, has certain implications,[58] for instance the property cannot be divided as long as co-ownership endures and one co-owner cannot burden or alienate the property without the consent of the other co-owner(s).

The specific consequences of co-ownership depend on whether free or bound co-ownership is involved. The term 'bound co-ownership' (also called tied co-ownership) signifies an underlying relationship that binds the co-owners, separately from the fact that they are co-owners.[59] For example, the co-owners may be married in community of property or be partners in business. Marriage in community of property has the consequence of automatic co-ownership in the property brought to and accumulated during the marriage. In a partnership, the partners co-own the property of the partnership. These examples show that the underlying relationship of bound co-ownership determines how the co-ownership entitlements may be exercised. The main consequences of bound co-ownership are that the co-owners cannot alienate or burden their undivided co-ownership share as long as the underlying relationship is intact, and that the co-ownership cannot be terminated unilaterally.[60]

Free co-owners are not bound by such an underlying relationship. Co-ownership is the only relevant relationship between the parties in this instance.[61] Free co-ownership differs sharply, therefore, from bound co-ownership in that a free co-owner can alienate or burden his undivided co-ownership share in the property independently (i.e. unilaterally). Furthermore, free co-ownership can be terminated unilaterally and the content of co-ownership as well as how it may be exercised is not dependent on an underlying relationship. Say, for instance, that Bernard, Robbie and John pool funds to buy a holiday house at Plettenberg Bay. Each puts in one-third of the purchase price and, in terms of the agreement between them, each receives a one-third undivided share in the house, which translates into about 17 weeks of use and enjoyment of the house for each annually. Exactly how and when these entitlements can be exercised must be worked out by the three parties among themselves. They would be well advised to put their use agreement in writing. If, for instance, Bernard later decides that the holiday house does not suit his needs and wants to opt out of co-ownership, he can sell his one-third undivided share in the house to whoever offers to purchase it. If Robbie and John want to have control over who buys

---

56 See pp 100*ff* below.
57 Van der Merwe *Sakereg* pp 380–381.
58 *Wille's Principles* pp 559–561.
59 *Silberberg & Schoeman Property* p 133.
60 For more detailed discussion, see *Wille's Principles* pp 257–262; 557–563; 1004–1016; *Silberberg & Schoeman Property* pp 133–136.
61 Van der Merwe *Sakereg* p 379.

into the scheme, they should have negotiated that as part of their initial agreement. In the absence of any such limitations, Bernard would be free to alienate to the first person who comes along, or to the one who makes the highest offer.

5.2.2.2   The undivided co-ownership share

The undivided co-ownership share in the co-owned property is distinguishable from the property itself.[62] The undivided share reflects each co-owner's interest in the property. Where free co-ownership exists, the undivided share in the property may generally be dealt with as the particular co-owner wishes. As indicated above, the undivided share may be alienated or burdened independently, i.e. without the consent or collaboration of the other co-owner(s). When the undivided share is alienated to a third party, it vests in the third party, who replaces the previous co-owner, by stepping, as it were, into his shoes. This change in itself has no impact on the commonly owned property as it is the undivided share that has been alienated rather than the property. An undivided share may also be encumbered to the extent of the co-owner's share, for instance by granting a limited real right of security to a third party.[63]

If a co-owner can generally do as she pleases with her undivided share, a relevant question is whether this has any effect on the commonly owned property. What are the practical implications of an undivided share? As already mentioned, the undivided share embodies the co-owner's particular interest in the property. Co-owners may have equal undivided shares, e.g. each may have a 50 per cent undivided share in the property, or their shares may be unequal, e.g. one co-owner may have a 70 per cent share, while the other has only a 30 per cent share.

To illustrate the practical implications of an undivided share, let's return to the example of Bernard, Robbie and John, who each have a one-third undivided share in a parcel of land. This ratio of co-ownership shares entitles each co-owner to make reasonable use of the whole of the land, proportionate to the extent of the undivided share of each, as mentioned already. Robbie would not be able to claim 70 per cent of the use of the land when he has only a one-third interest in it (unless, of course, Bernard and John are willing to agree to such an arrangement, in which case contractual principles apply).

In addition, that the co-ownership shares are equal does not imply that the land or the house is divided into three separate parts and that each co-owner has access to and use of the land or house on that basis only. For practical reasons, however, it is possible (and advisable) to enter into an agreement that sets out day-to-day arrangements regarding use of the land. Such a use agreement may include provisions on the allocation of particular portions to each co-owner. The precise nature of such arrangements would depend on the nature of the property concerned as well as on whether it is divisible. If it is divisible, a section may be allocated to each of the co-owners. If it is not, the use may be organised on the basis of time. In other words, the co-owners can agree that each uses the property at particular times of the year, for instance Robbie over Easter, Bernard at Christmas, and John over New Year. It should be noted that such use agreements bind only the parties to the agreement because mere personal rights are created. It follows, thus, that a successor in title to a co-owner is not automatically bound by a use agreement. The agreement would have to compel the parties to bind successors in title to the use agreement by making it a condition of sale.

---

62   *Wille's Principles* p 558.
63   Van der Merwe *Sakereg* pp 384–386.

5.2.2.3 The commonly owned property

Whereas co-owners may deal with an undivided share as they please, the position regarding the commonly owned property is quite different. Any legal act relating to or affecting the commonly owned property must be performed by the co-owners jointly.[64] First, they must decide how and for which purposes the property may be used. This means the proportionate use linked to the undivided share must be reasonable. Unreasonable use includes a change to the use and enjoyment of the property by one co-owner; unilaterally granting use rights to third parties by one co-owner;[65] and exercising ownership entitlements to the prejudice of the other co-owners.

The purpose for which the property may be used depends on the use for which the property was destined and the use agreement entered into by the co-owners. The latter may be formal, constituting a written document, or informal, such as a verbal agreement. If the co-owners cannot agree on the use of the property, it is doubtful whether a majority of co-owners can bind the minority to the former's wishes.[66] Consequently, either co-ownership must be terminated by agreement, or a court may be approached to evaluate the reasonableness of co-owners' conduct and the feasibility of continued co-ownership.[67] Unreasonable conduct may lead to a claim for damages.[68]

The shared use and enjoyment of the commonly owned property have many implications for co-owners.[69] It is imperative that the property is maintained as required by its use. All co-owners must contribute to maintenance costs, proportionate to their undivided shares.[70] Correlative to this obligation is the right to enjoy any profits, fruits and income generated by the property on a pro rata basis (i.e. proportionately).[71] A claim may be instituted for division of fruits or profits, if necessary.

5.2.2.4 Remedies

The consequences and obligations of co-ownership sometimes lead to practical difficulties. Common law commentators encapsulated the reality of co-ownership in the phrase, *communio est mater rixarum*, meaning that co-ownership is the mother of disputes.[72] It is essential that when the rules regulating co-ownership are unsuccessful in maintaining harmonious relationships, remedies are available to bring relief.

Unreasonable conduct on the part of one co-owner may be halted or prevented by an interdict.[73] If harm has resulted from such unreasonable use, a claim for damages may be instituted.

Where the co-ownership relationship has deteriorated so that it cannot continue, then it should be terminated. The common law separation action, *actio communi dividundo*, provides the means to terminate co-ownership.[74] It permits the commonly owned property to be divided (if it is divisible); it requires a final calculation of expenses and losses; and

---

64 *Silberberg & Schoeman Property* p 134.
65 *Pretorius v Nefdt & Glas* 1908 TS 854.
66 *Silberberg & Schoeman Property* p 134.
67 Van der Merwe *Sakereg* p 388.
68 *Wille's Principles* p 559.
69 *Silberberg & Schoeman Property* p 134.
70 *Wille's Principles* p 560.
71 *Silberberg & Schoeman Property* p 134.
72 *Wille's Principles* p 558.
73 *Pretorius v Nefdt & Glas* 1908 TS 854.
74 *Wille's Principles* pp 561–562.

it formally ends the legal relationship of co-ownership. In practice, co-owners should attempt to reach agreement about how to divide the property and end their co-ownership. Failing this, a court may be approached for relief. However, the co-owners should suggest a plan for resolving the matter, including that one co-owner buys the undivided shares of the other co-owners. As a last resort, the court will order a division of the property if it is divisible. Alternatively, it can postpone division until a later date, or order the sale of the property and that the proceeds are distributed among the co-owners proportionately.[75] The new owner acquires ownership only when delivery or registration has taken place together with the other necessary formalities.

5.3 Alternative forms of title

Legislation makes various forms of title possible to serve the needs of new developments in housing and other land use. Some forms have been created pursuant to the constitutional provisions for land reform, which enjoin the state to undertake three separate, though interconnected, projects, namely to redistribute land, to facilitate more secure tenure, and to restore land and rights in land to those who were dispossessed in terms of racist apartheid legislation and policies. Examples include the Restitution of Land Rights Act,[76] the Land Reform (Labour Tenants) Act[77] and the Extension of Security of Tenure Act.[78] Other forms make densification in housing developments possible by modifying the common law rule that an owner of land owns both the land and the space above it. Examples include sectional title ownership, share block schemes, and time-share schemes.

This section discusses sectional title ownership, share block schemes, and time-share schemes. It also deals with an example of innovative land reform legislation in the form of a communal property association; and, finally, indigenous land tenure is examined. Since the topics are complex and detailed, only the bare conceptual essentials are described here, there being excellent discussions in other sources.[79]

5.3.1 Sectional title schemes

Sectional title provides the basis for apartment ownership, thus enabling densification of residential and commercial use of buildings. In other words, several persons can simultaneously own the land and individually own a part of the building. To permit such schemes, legislative intervention was necessary because, in terms of the common law, the principles of *superficies solo cedit* (buildings form part of the land) or *omne quod inaedificatur solo cedit* (everything built on the soil belongs to the soil), and *cuius est solum eius est caelum* (the owner of the soil is the owner of the sky above it) preclude separate ownership of parts of a building.[80] The notion of sectional title ownership thus varies these common law principles. First introduced in the early 1970s and modified since, this form of landownership is governed by the Sectional Titles Act.[81]

---

75 Van der Merwe *Sakereg* p 389; see e.g. *Drummond v Dreyer* 1954 (1) SA 306 (N).
76 Act 22 of 1994.
77 Act 3 of 1996.
78 Act 62 of 1997.
79 See *Silberberg & Schoeman Property* pp 441-492; *Wille's Principles* pp 564-585; Van der Merwe, CG & Sonnekus, JC (2008) *Sectional Titles, Share Blocks and Time-sharing* (Durban, LexisNexis Butterworths) Vol I and Vol II; Bennett, TW (2004) *Customary Law in South Africa* (Cape Town, Juta); Claassens, A & Cousins, B (eds) (2008) *Land, Power & Custom: Controversies generated by South Africa's Communal Land Rights Act* (Cape Town, UCT Press).
80 *Silberberg & Schoeman Property* p 441; *Wille's Principles* p 564; Van der Merwe, CG (2008) *Sectional Titles, Share Blocks and Time-sharing* (Durban, LexisNexis Butterworths) Vol I pp 1-7 to 1-8.
81 Act 95 of 1986.

5.3.1.1 The nature of sectional ownership

In terms of the Sectional Titles Act,[82] a new composite thing was created: a sectional title unit that consists of a section of the building and an undivided co-ownership share in the common parts of the building and the land.[83] The section is the principal component and the undivided share is the accessory. To this must be added that a central characteristic of sectional ownership is the compulsory membership of the juristic person responsible for the management of the sectional title scheme. The unit is thus a statutory form of immovable property and is treated similarly to a plot of land.

Sectional title is a form of ownership that combines individual ownership and joint ownership. In so doing, some of the ordinary entitlements of ownership are varied and restricted, e.g. the entitlement to exclusive use and enjoyment is restricted of necessity in relation to parts of the land. Communal living in a block of flats requires considerably more consciousness of the effects on close neighbours than living in a free-standing dwelling does. In addition, the co-ownership is of necessity tied co-ownership.

Consequently, a sectional owner acquires a unit, which comprises individual ownership of a section (i.e. the flat or commercial apartment) and tied co-ownership (joint ownership) of common areas, including the outer skin of the building, called the common property.[84] The co-ownership share is calculated according to a formula prescribed by the Act, called the participation quota, which is the total floor area of a section expressed as a percentage (in decimal form) of the total floor area of the scheme.[85] The body corporate is the sum of all unit owners (who are automatically members) and has separate juristic personality.[86]

Sectional ownership is also possible when separate buildings (such as townhouses) are built on a plot of land. In similar fashion, the owners own their townhouses individually and co-own the land and other common areas. In effect, sectional title ownership is ownership in a specific community with its own governing body corporate which manages the scheme by way of (statutory) management rules and (statutory) conduct rules. Quite plainly, the owner acquires a real right.[87]

To illustrate the nature of the composite thing, consider the following. Bill acquires ownership of a sectional title unit in Whispering Dolphins, a luxury apartment complex in Clifton, Cape Town. The complex is located on the ocean front and has easy access to the beaches below. A fully equipped gym and a heated indoor pool are included in the common areas. Bill, however, likes to swim only in the ocean. Can Bill alienate his undivided share in the common area to Bob who also owns a unit in the complex? The answer is no: Bill's undivided share is inextricably part of the unit he owns and is inalienable as a separate thing. This is why sectional title ownership includes tied co-ownership. Can Bill use his sectional ownership as collateral for a bank loan? In other words, does Bill acquire a real right? The answer is yes: sectional ownership is genuine ownership, albeit that it differs in scope and extent from ordinary individual title or free co-ownership.

---

82 Act 95 of 1986.
83 *Silberberg & Schoeman Property* p 445; *Wille's Principles* p 564; Van der Merwe, CG (2008) *Sectional Titles, Share Blocks and Time-sharing* (Durban, LexisNexis Butterworths) Vol I pp 2-4 to 2-8.
84 *Silberberg & Schoeman Property* p 443; *Wille's Principles* pp 566-568; Van der Merwe, CG (2008) *Sectional Titles, Share Blocks and Time-sharing* (Durban, LexisNexis Butterworths) Vol I p 2-8.
85 *Silberberg & Schoeman Property* pp 459-462; *Wille's Principles* pp 569-571.
86 Van der Merwe, CG (1996) *Sectional Titles, Share Blocks and Time-sharing* (Durban, LexisNexis Butterworths) Vol I ch 1-3.
87 *Silberberg & Schoeman Property* pp 442-443; *Wille's Principles* p 579; Van der Merwe, CG (2008) *Sectional Titles, Share Blocks and Time-sharing* (Durban, LexisNexis Butterworths) Vol I pp 2-12 to 2-15.

> **PAUSE FOR REFLECTION**
>
> **Dealings with designated areas on the common property**
>
> The Sectional Titles Act permits designated parts of the common property to be used exclusively,[88] and hence also leased under specific circumstances. For instance, if Bill has two garages, indicated as so-called 'exclusive use areas' registered in his favour, and he needs only one, under certain circumstances and with permission of his body corporate, he would be able to lease the other to a fellow sectional title owner in the scheme, and possibly also to an outsider, depending on the scheme's rules. He would not, however, be able to alienate the garage to someone from outside the scheme.[89]

5.3.1.2 Management of a sectional title scheme

The body corporate, consisting of all owners of units, meets annually to approve a financial budget that must provide for the payment of utility bills, rates and taxes, insurance premiums (for the building excluding the interiors of sections), general maintenance and repairs, and for special projects such as refurbishment of the building and upgrading of security measures.[90]

At this annual general meeting, the owners elect from among their number trustees who undertake the day-to-day management of the body corporate's affairs.[91] The trustees are required to act in the best interests of the body corporate and to manage both the financial and material health of the scheme. The trustees may appoint a managing agent to do most of the day-to-day work but must, nevertheless, meet regularly and keep a close eye on matters.[92]

The financial health of a sectional title scheme depends on each owner's monthly contribution, called a levy,[93] being paid punctually. The amount that each owner pays is calculated on the basis of the participation quota for his unit. The participation quota is established at the time the sectional title register is opened to establish the scheme. This calculation forms the basis for all financial contributions by individual owners, unless the body corporate resolves differently by special resolution.[94]

The material health of a sectional title scheme depends on each owner co-operating to keep his section in a state of good repair and in compliance with the Act, as well as on the trustees' diligence in regularly seeing to maintenance and repairs, including refurbishment. Failure to do so inevitably leads to physical deterioration of the building and grounds, which, in turn, leads to probable devaluation of the asset for individual owners.

Sectional title ownership is rule-dependent. The Act provides management and conduct rules.[95] The management rules guide the body corporate in financial matters and also in its relationship with the outside world. The conduct rules provide instruction on

---

88 Van der Merwe, CG (1996) *Sectional Titles, Share Blocks and Time-sharing* (Durban, LexisNexis Butterworths) Vol I pp 3-13 to 3-14; 11-34 to 11-35.
89 Mostert, H 'The Alienation and Transfer of Rights of Exclusive Use in Sectional Title Law' (2002) *Stell LR* 265 at 274–275.
90 *Silberberg & Schoeman Property* p 468; *Wille's Principles* p 583; Van der Merwe, CG (1996) *Sectional Titles, Share Blocks and Time-sharing* (Durban, LexisNexis Butterworths) Vol I pp 2-19 to 2-20.
91 *Silberberg & Schoeman Property* p 468; *Wille's Principles* p 584; Van der Merwe, CG (1996) *Sectional Titles, Share Blocks and Time-sharing* (Durban, LexisNexis Butterworths) Vol I pp 2-22 to 2-25.
92 Van der Merwe, CG (1996) *Sectional Titles, Share Blocks and Time-sharing* (Durban, LexisNexis Butterworths) Vol I pp 15-3 to 15-4.
93 *Silberberg & Schoeman Property* p 445; *Wille's Principles* pp 579–580.
94 Van der Merwe, CG (1996) *Sectional Titles, Share Blocks and Time-sharing* (Durban, LexisNexis Butterworths) Vol I pp 4-8.
95 See Annexures 8 and 9 of the Sectional Titles Act 95 of 1986; also *Silberberg & Schoeman Property* pp 462*ff*; *Wille's Principles* pp 581–583.

what may or may not take place within the scheme. While the rules may be altered by resolution, they are not easy to change, especially the management rules.

5.3.2 Share block schemes

A share block scheme is one where a juristic person, the share block company, owns or leases a building, and the members of that juristic person (i.e. the block shareholders) acquire a right of use in relation to a part of the building (a flat, office or shop) on the basis of their shareholding.[96] Share block title consists of a combination of common law possession and company law rules, governed by the Share Blocks Control Act,[97] which provides measures for consumer protection and the management of the company among other matters.

Three elements of the share block construction are highlighted here. First, in this kind of scheme, a share block company, which has holding and control of immovable property as its primary purpose, owns or leases the building.[98] If the company owns the building, it has a real right of ownership. If it leases the building, and the lease is for 10 years or more, the lease may be registrable, giving rise to a limited real right for the company. A lease for fewer than 10 years would give rise to personal rights only for the company.

Second, a person acquires a block of shares in the company, which block is linked inextricably with exclusive use of part of the building.[99] In other words, the shareholder acquires a contractual right to the exclusive use of a part of the building. The use right can be full time or intermittent (i.e. on a time-share basis). Each participant concludes a use agreement with the company, which sets out the scope of the right to use the particular part of the building, the obligations of both parties and so on.[100]

The nature of the right of use is personal rather than real. However, the content of the use right is such that it affords the holder virtual ownership insofar as the exercise of entitlements is concerned.[101] Because a real right is not acquired, the share block cannot be used as collateral for a bank loan. This is seen by many to be a disadvantage of share block schemes in comparison with sectional title schemes, although some commentators indicate the existence of ample possibility for collateral security in terms of the share block use agreement, the shares and the rights to the paid-up portion of the loan allocated to the company.[102]

Third, the share block construction is a flexible mechanism which may be useful in situations where the strict regulatory context of the Sectional Titles Act restricts possibilities. For instance, since the company may lease the building, more flexibility of location is possible than with sectional title schemes where the developer is required to own the land. Furthermore, a share block scheme is not restricted to buildings like a sectional title scheme is. This means that large movable property, such as an ocean-going yacht, can become the object of shared use via a share block scheme. Because of the flexibility this scheme offers, it has been suggested that share blocks could be used effectively in the land reform context to ensure sufficient tenure security without complying with constraining rules regarding land

---

96   *Silberberg & Schoeman Property* p 494; *Wille's Principles* p 586.
97   Act 59 of 1980.
98   Sonnekus, JC (2003) *Sectional Titles, Share Blocks and Time-sharing* (Durban, LexisNexis Butterworths) Vol 2 p 1–7f p 1–3.
99   Sonnekus, JC (2003) *Sectional Titles, Share Blocks and Time-sharing* (Durban, LexisNexis Butterworths) Vol 2 p 1–7f p 2–13.
100 Sonnekus, JC (2003) *Sectional Titles, Share Blocks and Time-sharing* (Durban, LexisNexis Butterworths) Vol 2 p 1–7f pp 2–20 to 2–26.
101 See Sonnekus, JC (2003) *Sectional Titles, Share Blocks and Time-sharing* (Durban, LexisNexis Butterworths) Vol 2 p 1–7f for a discussion on the theoretical difficulties.
102 See *Silberberg & Schoeman Property* pp 508–509 for a more detailed discussion of the different views.

registration.[103] However, the Share Blocks Control Act[104] excludes the use of share blocks in relation to agricultural land unless the Minister consents thereto. This limits possibilities in the land reform context to some extent.

The scheme is run and managed by the participants in the scheme when the company owns the building or land. They hold general meetings and elect a board of directors, who carry out the day-to-day running of the scheme. The articles of association of the company set out the procedures and parameters of the company's business, the powers of the directors and the content of the use agreements.

5.3.3 Modified uses of share blocks and sectional title

Conventional (freehold) title coupled with contractual obligations towards a homeowners' association, co-ownership, sectional title and block shareholding represent four basic alternatives for organising communal living. Many forms of communal living arrangements exist in South Africa. In this section, we demonstrate how some of the basic arrangements may be modified to cater for specific needs, such as time-share and retirement schemes.

Time-share schemes are associated mostly with recreational use of property, e.g. holiday resorts in different parts of the country. A time-share interest is 'any right to or interest in the exclusive use or occupation, during determined or determinable periods during any year.'[105] In other words, a time-share interest allows different people to use the property at different times of the year, for instance for accommodation purposes, on an annual basis.[106]

The Property Time-sharing Control Act[107] permits a variety of legal bases for such a scheme, including sectional title ownership, use rights in a share block scheme and membership of a club that includes use rights.[108] If sectional title forms the basis of the time-share scheme, the existing procedures must be supplemented with an exclusive use agreement which provides the sectional title joint owners with the exclusive right to occupy the unit recurrently and periodically, and which suspends the co-owners' right to demand partition for the duration of the scheme. If co-ownership is used as the basis of the time-share scheme, the size of the co-owner's undivided share determines the period of occupation. Again, the co-owners are contractually precluded from claiming partition before the scheme terminates. The principle that the co-owners cannot appropriate any particular piece of the property for occupation would have to be circumvented contractually in some instances. If the share block construction is used, the size of the share block determines the length of occupation. If the time-share is organised on the basis of a club, its members purchase the right to participate in the activities or functions of the club. They are also compelled to join a management association.

Retirement schemes address the specific interests of people (usually from the middle or upper income classes) who are retired or about to retire.[109] The need for security of tenure is accompanied by the need for additional amenities such as frail care and on-premises medical care; heightened physical security measures, maintenance and garden services; opportunities to socialise and enjoy on-premises dining facilities; and limited administrative

---

103 Pienaar, JM 'Wisselwerking tussen die Wet op die Beheer van Aandeleblokke 59 van 1980 en die Wet op Uitbreiding van Sekerheid van Verblyfreg 62 van 1997' (2001) *TSAR* 134 at 144–146.
104 Section 1 of Act 59 of 1980.
105 Section 1 (definition of 'time-sharing interest') of the Property Time-sharing Control Act 75 of 1983.
106 *Silberberg & Schoeman Property* pp 513–514; *Wille's Principles* p 587.
107 Act 75 of 1983.
108 See the more detailed discussion in *Silberberg & Schoeman Property* pp 514–515.
109 See the more detailed discussion in *Silberberg & Schoeman Property* pp 516*ff*.

responsibilities. Investors are usually required to pay a lump sum up front to obtain a 'housing interest' in a scheme, and then to make further regular contributions to a levy fund for the purpose of maintenance and administrative costs. The Housing Development Schemes for Retired Persons Act[110] governs the alienation of housing interests, but does not exhaustively regulate the establishment or operation of retirement schemes.

A retirement scheme may be based on sectional title, block shareholding, club membership or any other construction, but it cannot operate as a time-share venture.[111] The three most frequent methods of establishment rely on sectional title, block shareholding and 'life rights'.[112] The latter enables the holder of such a life right to occupy a unit in the scheme for as long as she lives, usually against payment of an interest-free loan. When she dies, the unit reverts to the developer, and the lump sum minus a share of the profit is paid to her estate. The share in the profit realised from the sale of the life right to another person goes to the scheme. The Act renders the life right a statutory real right (in respect of schemes established after 1989) in the nature of registered leases.[113]

5.3.4 Communal property associations

Since 1994, a variety of land reform statutes and policy documents have been aimed at achieving redistribution of land, more secure tenure and also restitution of land rights lost as a result of dispossession.[114] These measures, among others, introduced a new juristic person in the form of a communal property association, which has the express purpose of owning, managing and controlling property, both movable and immovable.[115] The discussion here is limited to the new form of ownership that flows from this innovative juristic entity.

The communal property association (CPA) was developed to promote two of the above aims, namely access to land and tenure security. The Communal Property Associations Act[116] provides an institutional framework for disadvantaged communities to form juristic entities to acquire, hold and manage property on a basis agreed to by the members in terms of a written constitution. Theoretically, this juristic entity is a useful vehicle for acquisition of ownership in the context of restitution and redistribution of land because any number of people may be members of a CPA and thus gain access to the land in question as a whole. This is especially useful in situations where the land is not viable for subdivision into smaller units. In addition, the mechanism of a CPA makes it possible for members of communities who traditionally would not have had access to or control over land as individuals, to be included formally as members of a CPA, thus broadening the spectrum of beneficiaries dramatically.

In terms of the Act,[117] an association may acquire or dispose of immovable property and real rights, and it may encumber the immovable property or real rights by mortgage,

---

110 Act 65 of 1988.
111 Section 1 (definition of 'housing development scheme') of the Housing Development Schemes for Retired Persons Act 65 of 1988.
112 *Silberberg & Schoeman Property* p 517.
113 Butler, DW 'The statutory protection of investors in retirement schemes' (1992) *TSAR* 12 at 23; *Boland Bank Bpk v Engelbrecht* 1996 (3) SA 537 (A) at 546E-G, 547B-D.
114 Department of Land Affairs (1997) White Paper on SA Land Policy; Restitution of Land Rights Act 22 of 1994; Extension of Security of Tenure Act 62 of 1997; Land Reform (Labour Tenants) Act 3 of 1996; Provision of Land and Assistance Act 123 of 1993; Transformation of Certain Rural Areas Act 94 of 1998; Interim Protection of Informal Land Rights Act 31 of 1996; Communal Property Associations Act 28 of 1996; Communal Land Rights Act 11 of 2004; Prevention of Illegal Eviction from and Unlawful Occupation of Land Act 19 of 1998; Development Facilitation Act 67 of 1995.
115 In terms of the Communal Property Associations Act 28 of 1996.
116 Act 28 of 1996.
117 Section 8(6)(*c*).

servitude, or lease and so on. This enables the community to access finance via the CPA to develop the land or a specific commercial undertaking, albeit on a small scale.

The essential statutory elements of a CPA include the requirement that decision making be democratic, based on the fundamental principles of justice, equity and fairness, especially as regards gender equality. A second requirement is that the constitution of the CPA must be drawn up by the prospective members themselves in accordance with the statutory guidelines so that it is significant and relevant for the particular members, but also complies with the values of the Constitution. A CPA constitution must demonstrate fair and inclusive decision-making processes; equality in membership and powers of members; fair access to property; and mechanisms to ensure accountability and transparency. In addition, the Act requires that the constitution must deal with specified matters, including whether membership of the CPA is based on an individual or family basis; the grounds and procedures for terminating membership and the fate of rights and property of the member concerned; whether members may sell their rights and, if so, to whom; and the fate of a member's rights upon her death.

The statutory directions for drawing up a constitution seek to ensure that administrative and substantive matters are deliberated on before the CPA is formally established.[118] This approach should have the effect that matters run smoothly in the lifetime of the CPA. The constitution is a 'legally binding agreement between the [CPA] and its members and [is] deemed to be a matter of public knowledge'.[119]

Membership of the CPA must be determined prior to the formal establishment and registration thereof. However, the Act permits persons who are currently not specifically identified also to be listed as prospective members.[120] This radical departure from the usual rule that landowners must be specifically identified accommodates the fact that dispossession under the apartheid policies of forced removal led to the displacement and dispersal of many communities. Especially in the context of a successful land restitution claim, community members or their descendants whose whereabouts are currently unknown, may nevertheless reappear and wish to be members.

The character of the powers granted in terms of the Act may thus be described as a combination of theoretical aspects of traditional communal land tenure with aspects of common law ownership principles, and principles that govern commercial juristic persons added to the mix. Hence, there are requirements for ensuring that decision making is democratic but also systematic and structured, and that accountability mechanisms are included in the constitution as well as specific requirements for ensuring that the fundamental principles of justice, equity and fairness are heeded. The specific requirement for gender equity provides a significant departure from traditional land tenure principles among black people.[121]

The nature of ownership in this context is that the CPA owns the land and any movable property acquired by it. The members of the CPA have use rights as determined by the constitution. In other words, the individual has a personal right against the CPA in terms of which he may use property or portions thereof. In addition, members are free to acquire private assets that are not the property of the CPA. However, the constitution ought to address this specifically to avoid unnecessary conflict. For example, William, a member

---

118 See ss 5, 6 and 7 of the Act. See also Carey Miller, DL & Pope, A (2000) *Land Title in South Africa* (Cape Town, Juta) pp 469*ff*.
119 Section 8(6)*(e)*.
120 Section 8(6)*(e)* of the Communal Property Associations Act 28 of 1996.
121 Section 9(1)*(b)*(i); Cousins, T & Hornby, D (2003) 'Communal property institutions: Adrift in the sea of land reform' in Greenberg, S (ed) *Piecemeal Reforms and Calls for Action* Vol 44 *Development Update* 127 at 138.

of the CPA, may acquire a lawnmower using his private funds and may then legitimately refuse to let others use it on the basis that it belongs only to him. Almost inevitably, however, this kind of situation could lead to conflict and ultimately to bad relations which would be counterproductive in the context of a CPA.

Specific provision is made for dispute resolution[122] and dissolution of the CPA.[123] The Act also envisages a close relationship between the Department of Land Affairs, through the office of the Director-General, and a CPA. The idea is that support for emerging farmers and other new landowners is necessary. Consequently, several provisions refer to the need for monitoring and inspection,[124] to the assistance owed by the Director-General in the event that a member complains that the constitution of a particular CPA is not being adhered to, etc.[125]

In theory, thus, this innovative mechanism and the legislatively mandated support ought to have provided a solid basis for recipients of restitution or redistribution awards of land to make significant developmental and economic progress. In practice, however, CPAs have not proven to be very successful. Some of the difficulties have stemmed from the communities themselves who find it difficult to decide on who could be a member,[126] or to accept the constitutional requirement of gender equality[127] and thus permit women to have equal say in the de facto management of a CPA, and so on. Other more serious difficulties flow from the fact that establishing a CPA and effecting legal transfer of the land in question can be a slow process. This creates a state of uncertainty as to whether and when the community has control of the land, and thus are entitled to a say in how it is to be managed and protected; also regarding whether there is legitimate community leadership that will act to protect the land from squatters, for instance.[128] Furthermore, state support has been slow, often without continuity or the requisite competence. Consequently, many CPAs have foundered, leaving disillusionment and increasing poverty in their wake.[129]

5.3.5 Indigenous land rights

Presently, vast tracts of land in South Africa are under communal tenure. This type of land holding is particularly prevalent in areas designated as 'national states' and 'self-governing territories' during the apartheid era. Pursuant to the introduction of a new constitutional order after the first democratic elections in 1994, the South African territory was reorganised and the erstwhile 'national states' of Transkei, Venda, Bophuthatswana and Ciskei were reincorporated into the Republic, while the 'self-governing territories'[130] lost their status and were re-assimilated. This means that all provinces, except the Western and Northern Cape, contain areas held under traditional communal tenure.[131]

---

122 Section 11(6).
123 Section 13.
124 Section 11.
125 Section 12.
126 E.g. see *In re Elandskloof Vereniging* 1999 (1) SA 176 (LCC); Mayson, D, Michael, B & Cronwright, R (1998) 'Elandskloof Land Restitution: Establishing Membership of a Communal Property Association' in Barry, M (ed) *Proceedings of the International Conference on Land Tenure in the Developing World,* (University of Cape Town) pp 444–456.
127 Section 9 of the Constitution of the Republic of South Africa, 1996.
128 James, D (2007) *Gaining Ground? 'Rights' and 'Property' in South African Land Reform* (Oxford, Routledge-Cavendish) p 160.
129 Cousins, T & Hornby, D (2003) 'Communal property institutions: Adrift in the sea of land reform' in Greenberg, S (ed) *Piecemeal Reforms and Calls for Action* Vol 44 *Development Update* 127–148.
130 E.g. Lebowa, GaZankulu, KwaZulu, QwaQwa and KaNgwane.
131 For more detail, see Van der Merwe, CG & Pienaar, JM (1997) 'Land reform in South Africa' in Jackson, P & Wilde, DC (eds) *The Reform of Property Law* (Dartmouth, Ashgate) pp 334*ff*.

As commonly understood in South Africa, communal land is 'owned' and controlled by the community concerned. The communal land can be used for residential and agricultural purposes, with the remaining land – the commonage – being reserved for grazing or for extending the existing residential or agricultural areas.[132] The term 'communal tenure' is used usually to describe the situation where, in terms of indigenous African law, entitlements to property, especially land, are allocated by the head of the group to individuals who belong to a particular political or ethnic group. In other words, the property is regarded as belonging to the group and individuals are entitled to use (parts of) the property on the basis of their group membership.[133] However, to use conventional common law property terminology does not do justice to the actual meaning of communal tenure in the customary law context.[134]

> **PAUSE FOR REFLECTION**
>
> **On the largely misunderstood meaning of communal tenure**
>
> As the term 'communal tenure' is generally described in property law terms, it implies collective ownership and access to use of all land and natural resources based on allocation patterns for the particular group.[135] The reason for this understanding of communal tenure originates from the encounters between colonialism and customary systems of tenure. The colonial authorities assumed, erroneously, that the language of ownership was universally understood and applicable. Academic writers contributed to the misunderstanding by equating **customary** tenure that includes the right to exclude others, with **communal** tenure, in the sense that land was owned and worked collectively.[136]
>
> This notion of collective ownership is not accurate because the members of the group do not have equal rights, in the common law sense, in respect of the land and other resources. The traditional leader also does not have a claim, based on ownership, to personal benefit from being in control of allocating the use of the land.[137]

Instead, understanding of indigenous land rights requires one to seek the meaning of 'property in land in the African social order.'[138] What this social order creates is not 'property rights over land per se'. Instead, it establishes a 'set of reciprocal rights and obligations that bind together and vest power over land in community members.'[139] To know who has access to or exercises control over the land and associated resources that the specific communities occupy, one must look at how and by whom the rights are performed. Furthermore, cross-cutting horizontal and vertical lines of reciprocal

---

132 Pienaar, GJ 'The Land Titling Debate in South Africa' (2006) 3 *TSAR* 435 at 441–442.
133 Bennett, TW (2004) *Customary Law in South Africa* (Cape Town, Juta) pp 376–379.
134 Bennett, TW (2004) *Customary Law in South Africa* (Cape Town, Juta) pp 376–381; Claassens, A & Cousins, B (eds) (2008) *Land, Power & Custom: Controversies generated by South Africa's Communal Land Rights Act* (Cape Town, UCT Press) pp 5–8.
135 Claassens, A & Cousins, B (eds) (2008) *Land, Power & Custom: Controversies generated by South Africa's Communal Land Rights Act* (Cape Town, UCT Press) p 5.
136 Bennett, TW (2004) *Customary Law in South Africa* (Cape Town, Juta) pp 376–379.
137 Cross, C 'An Alternate Legality: The Property Rights Question In Relation To South African Land Reform' (1992) *SAJHR* 305 at 311.
138 Okoth-Ogendo, HWO (2008) 'Nature of land rights under indigenous law in Africa' in Claassens, A & Cousins, B (eds) *Land, Power & Custom: Controversies generated by South Africa's Communal Land Rights Act* (Cape Town, UCT Press) pp 95*ff* at 100.
139 Okoth-Ogendo, HWO (2008) 'Nature of land rights under indigenous law in Africa' in Claassens, A & Cousins, B (eds) *Land, Power & Custom: Controversies generated by South Africa's Communal Land Rights Act* (Cape Town, UCT Press) pp 95*ff* at 100.

social and family obligations are part of indigenous land rights systems.[140] Importantly, moreover, the content of indigenous land rights varies widely, both across and within language groups. In addition, customary or indigenous practices are not static, but evolve and change over time.[141]

Within this context, traditional leaders have the power to allot land, to regulate use of common resources and to require individuals, or even the group, to give up their allotted land in the interests of the group as a whole.[142] Bennett explains that the term 'trustee' probably comes closest to describing the position of traditional leaders, 'but even this term cannot do full justice to the sense of responsibility inherent in their office.'[143] The traditional leader is regarded as the authoritative head of the community. He (traditional leaders are rarely female) allocates land to family heads (most of whom are male), who in turn allocate it to houses within the family. In polygynous societies, each wife has her own house and allotment of land for cultivation. As soon as the land is allocated to a particular family or household, it is regarded as belonging to that family or household.[144]

Most indigenous property systems include clearly defined individual and family rights to some types of land, although there are generally no formalised boundaries dividing these portions of land or dividing those portions allocated to different members of the community. Naturally occurring topographical features (such as streams, particular trees, hills or rivers) are often used to define boundaries broadly, which means that there is a fair degree of imprecision and uncertainty as regards such boundaries. Nevertheless, it is accepted that all members of the community have access to the commonage and may use its resources. This explains why vesting of specific limited real rights, similar to servitudes, is not necessary in these communities: access and use rights already exist as a matter of entitlement based on membership. This differs from common law where any person, in principle, can acquire ownership or real rights in relation to land, and where such rights are circumscribed in different ways.

PAUSE FOR REFLECTION	The basis of indigenous land use rights and obvious similarities with common law landholding
	Access to indigenous land use rights depends on the person or family being a member of the political or ethnic unit.[145] This requirement is unknown in the South African common law notion of ownership. In principle, anyone can acquire ownership or a real right in land in terms of common law. There may be or have been exclusionary provisions, most notoriously those of the apartheid era when black people were not allowed to own land, but, conceptually, any adult person of sound mind is permitted to own land outright. This concept is not part of customary land tenure, which is about membership of a group, reciprocal obligations and access to land.

---

140 Bennett, TW (2004) *Customary Law in South Africa* (Cape Town, Juta) p 382.
141 Claassens, A & Cousins, B (eds) (2008) *Land, Power & Custom: Controversies generated by South Africa's Communal Land Rights Act* (Cape Town, UCT Press) p 10.
142 Bennett, TW (2004) *Customary Law in South Africa* (Cape Town, Juta) pp 382–390.
143 Bennett, TW (2008) '"Official" vs "Living" customary law: dilemmas of description and recognition' in Claassens, A & Cousins, B (eds) *Land, Power & Custom: Controversies generated by South Africa's Communal Land Rights Act* (Cape Town, UCT Press) p 149.
144 Bennett, TW (2004) *Customary Law in South Africa* (Cape Town, Juta) pp 382–384.
145 Claassens, A & Cousins, B (eds) (2008) *Land, Power & Custom: Controversies generated by South Africa's Communal Land Rights Act* (Cape Town, UCT Press) p 8.

> Control of property is traditionally less important than the duty to provide for dependants, which fact gives rise to a complex web of obligations, including control of property. Some similarity with the common law duty to maintain children is evident: in terms of the common law, a person's entitlement to alienate property may be restricted if not to do so would result in a breach of the duty to maintain his children. However, under common law social systems, material security 'owes less to belonging to a family and more to a series of impersonal relationships in the labour market'.[146] In contrast, in the indigenous law context, the web of obligations referred to above arises from membership of the political or ethnic grouping.
>
> Common law property rights can be discussed without reference to other areas of the law, whereas customary property law can best be understood within the context of marriage, family and succession, and the relationships prevalent there. Again, these relationships and contexts are not static; instead they may change and adapt to new challenges. The social context is nevertheless of primary importance because the status and role of the person in control of property as a member of a specific social group, family or tribe is the determining factor.[147] Traditional indigenous patterns of property systems are changing[148] due, among other things, to increasing urbanisation, changing occupations and the ability to earn money in the labour market.

These differences between common law and indigenous law have to be borne in mind when land reform programmes are considered.[149] Issues such as belonging to a group and changes wrought by urbanisation compound the question whether land reform initiatives can fit into the prevailing cadastral, conveyancing and registration systems that govern land administration.[150] In promoting land and tenure reform, the 'dilemma for law-makers in relation to all group-based tenure systems is where to vest rights to land and the associated powers of decision-making.'[151] To cast light on this problem, and the manner in which it is being handled, the following discussion provides a brief overview of the situation before the reforms of the past two decades were initiated, and then focuses specifically on the new order for communal tenure proposed by the Communal Land Rights Act[152] (CLRA).

5.3.5.1   Pre-1991 tenure systems

Like other rights in land in South Africa, indigenous land rights were also regulated by government in the pre-constitutional era. This resulted in a diverse land control system that differed from area to area, depending on the applicable legislation and whether the area was a national state or a self-governing territory. The result was a complicated, tangled web of legislative measures.[153]

---

146 Bennett, TW (2004) *Customary Law in South Africa* (Cape Town, Juta) p 323.
147 Cross, C 'An Alternate Legality: The Property Rights Question In Relation to South African Land Reform' (1992) *SAJHR* 305 at 311.
148 See e.g. *Bhe v Magistrate, Khayalitsha* 2005 (1) SA 580 (CC).
149 See ch 13 below.
150 See Kingwill, R (2008) 'Custom-building freehold title: the impact of family values of historical ownership in the Eastern Cape' in Claassens, A & Cousins, B (eds) *Land, Power & Custom: Controversies generated by South Africa's Communal Land Rights Act* (Cape Town, UCT Press) pp 184*ff*.
151 Claassens, A & Cousins, B (eds) (2008) *Land, Power & Custom: Controversies generated by South Africa's Communal Land Rights Act* (Cape Town, UCT Press) p 10.
152 Act 11 of 2004.
153 *Silberberg & Schoeman Property* p 585.

Communal tenure entailed a landholding system on behalf of the community for their benefit and in their interest, but the land belonged to the state. A system of permits controlled access to land. 'Permission to occupy' permitted occupation of unsurveyed communal land against payment of rental. Individualisation of tenure was permitted by the quit-rent system which entailed surveying plots and registering titles in the Deeds Registry.[154] Traditional indigenous land tenure was thus altered by legislation.[155]

Accordingly, land located in the various communal tenure areas is held under diverse forms of tenure. Depending on its location and the applicable legislation, either traditional communal, individual or trust tenure exists. These tenure forms are undesirable in the constitutional era because the tenure is insecure as a result of racially discriminatory laws or practices, does not adequately reflect gender equality, and cannot serve as collateral for access to financial support because it does not qualify as a real right.[156] Over the past 15 years, much legislation has been created in the land reform initiative, including efforts to address the shortcomings of communal tenure. The most recent is the Communal Land Rights Act, which is discussed next.

5.3.5.2 The Communal Land Rights Act 11 of 2004

Drafted as a response to the constitutional imperative in s 25(6), the Communal Land Rights Act is meant to secure tenure for millions of people who live on communal land. Not yet in operation, the Act aims to formalise the traditional system of communal land tenure, to bring it in line with constitutional principles, and to promote certainty by creating a uniform national registration system. It aims, furthermore, to provide for systematic and democratic administration of communal rights through statutorily instituted community rules and bodies.[157]

The Act is intended to apply to all communal tenure land in the country, as well as to 'beneficiaries of communal land or land tenure rights in terms of other land reform laws'.[158] The Act seeks to address shortcomings in previous land control forms. 'Current land rights of each individual on ... communal land, called "old order rights", are to be secured, converted or cancelled.'[159] Converted rights become new order rights which are registrable. The process of substituting old order rights in favour of new order rights is set out in the Act. Apart from the long, complicated conversion process, the Act also introduces new role players, quite foreign to communal land tenure communities, such as a land administration committee and a land rights board. The land administration committee is burdened with the day-to-day management of land matters in the community, whereas the land rights board has an advisory role to play, and functions as a link between the community and the Minister.

---

154 See e.g. Elton Mills, ME & Wilson, M (1952) *Land Tenure* (Keiskammahoek Rural Survey Vol IV) (Pietermaritzburg, Shuter and Shooter) pp 69*ff*, pp 147*ff*; also Bennett, TW (1996) 'African Land – A History of Dispossession' in Zimmerman, R & Visser DP *Southern Cross: Civil Law and Common Law in South Africa* (Cape Town, Juta) pp 73–75.
155 E.g. by Proclamation R188 of 1969.
156 Mostert, H (2003) 'The Diversification of Land Rights and its Implications for a New Land Law in South Africa' in Cooke, EJ (ed) *Modern Studies in Property Law,* (Oxford, Hart Publishing) pp 4–6.
157 Mostert, H & Pienaar, JM (2005) 'Formalization of South African Communal Land Title and its Impact on Development' in Cooke EJ (ed) *Modern Studies in Property Law* III (Oxford, Hart Publishing) pp 317–340.
158 Section 39 of the Communal Land Rights Act 11 of 2004.
159 Smith, H (2008) 'An Overview of the Communal Land Rights Act 11 of 2004' in Claassens, A & Cousins, B (eds) *Land, Power & Custom: Controversies generated by South Africa's Communal Land Rights Act* (Cape Town, UCT Press) p 39.

COUNTER POINT

The Communal Land Rights Act critiqued

The Communal Land Rights Act's passage through Parliament was hotly contested. Many activists and scholars[160] believe it will do more harm than good because of its institutionalisation of bureaucratic processes unknown to customary law settings, and the elevated and unchallengeable position of traditional leaders permitted by the Traditional Leadership Governance and Framework Act.[161] By combining 'elements of both land titling [ownership] and recognition of customary land tenure',[162] the Act does not actually achieve its goal of providing secure tenure for individuals, according to some commentators. They point out that individual community members will hold 'only a secondary and poorly defined right to land,' while ownership vests in the group living under the jurisdiction of a traditional council, represented by the land administration committee that will exercise ownership on behalf of the group.[163] Furthermore, there is no mechanism by which to hold the committees accountable to community members.

Claassens and Cousins et al. provide an extensive critique of the Act,[164] outlining and discussing the policy and technical difficulties that are seen to be inevitable when the Act comes into effect. Among these difficulties are how to choose whether private ownership or customary land rights should prevail; how to describe the nature and content of customary land rights; how to transform in practical ways the gender inequalities that seem to be endemic in customary tenure systems; and, especially, how to honour traditional political structures but also, at the same time, ensure accountability, and avoid abuse of authority and corruption. In addition, the important distinction between official and living customary law must be taken into account when consonance with constitutional principles is sought. The procedure adopted for the enactment of the Communal Land Rights Act does not appear to have included specific deliberation on all these matters.

Consequently, there is a danger that the very people who should benefit from more secure tenure and increased access to land may find themselves as insecure as they currently are, and are also subject to rules that are alien. In the past it was thought that communal land tenure prevented destitution in difficult economic times via the reciprocal family and social obligations. However, if land is privatised and used as security for bank loans, it is possible that land may be lost (if loans cannot be repaid) which would be detrimental to the particular household and the community as land will not fall back to the commonage. If a right less than ownership is created, then using that right as collateral for a loan may not be possible, which means that access to land will not have led to a means to wealth creation and consequent economic development. Other matters such as boundary disputes and restrictive access to commonage would also arise if ownership is the prevailing right.[165]

---

160 Ntsebeza L (2008) 'Chiefs and the ANC in South Africa: The Reconstruction of Tradition?' in Claassens, A & Cousins, B (eds) *Land, Power & Custom: Controversies generated by South Africa's Communal Land Rights Act* (Cape Town, UCT Press) p 255.
161 Act 41 of 2003.
162 Cousins, B (2008) 'Contextualising the Controversies: Dilemmas of Communal Tenure Reform in Post-Apartheid South Africa' in Claassens, A & Cousins, B (eds) *Land, Power & Custom: Controversies generated by South Africa's Communal Land Rights Act* (Cape Town, UCT Press) p 15.
163 Cousins, B (2008) 'Contextualising the Controversies: Dilemmas of Communal Tenure Reform in Post-Apartheid South Africa' in Claassens, A & Cousins, B (eds) *Land, Power & Custom: Controversies generated by South Africa's Communal Land Rights Act* (Cape Town, UCT Press) p 15.
164 Claassens, A & Cousins, B (eds) (2008) *Land, Power & Custom: Controversies generated by South Africa's Communal Land Rights Act* (Cape Town, UCT Press) p 15.
165 Cousins, B (2008) 'Contextualising the Controversies: Dilemmas of Communal Tenure Reform in Post-Apartheid South Africa' in Claassens, A & Cousins, B (eds) *Land, Power & Custom: Controversies generated by South Africa's Communal Land Rights Act* (Cape Town, UCT Press) p 15.

5.4 Concluding remarks

Both the common law and statutory forms of title are important in South Africa. Ownership or aspects thereof remains a central organising concept in day-to-day dealings with property as well as in regard to the quest to provide access to secure tenure and to adequate housing for the millions of South Africans who still wait for better living and accommodation conditions.

The statutory forms of title are designed particularly to serve the needs of new developments in housing and other land use. Some forms lend themselves to projects where abundant suitable land is scarce, resulting in the need for densification, i.e. increasing the number of dwellings that are permitted on a particular erf size. For example, sectional title ownership, share block schemes, and time-share schemes all permit multi-storey buildings to be used and permit secure title in one form or another. Some forms, such as sectional title schemes, share block schemes and communal property associations are especially appropriate when subdivision into smaller units of land is not viable.

The choice of statutory title may be guided by the intended purpose of the development. In the case of a communal property association (CPA), application is limited to disadvantaged communities, which implies that economically mixed communities cannot make use of this form. For example, an enlightened wine farmer on a farm that has been in his family for 200 years, may wish to facilitate independent economic development and acquisition of secure tenure for the farm workers and their families on a particular part of the land. It will be surveyed and subdivided so that this part is legally separate from the rest of the farm. However, he wishes to retain an interest in this land for himself and to ensure that his descendants will retain the interest. An obvious choice for ownership would be a CPA because not only does this form of title go hand in hand with mandatory state support and guidance, which would clearly benefit emerging farmers, but it also does not assume a high level of sophisticated knowledge of commercial entities. But, in accordance with the Act, the farmer would not qualify to be a member because he is not a disadvantaged person. A share block company which would allocate block shares to the farm workers may be conceptually attractive, but is problematic because the Act excludes agricultural land from its ambit unless consented to by the relevant Minister.[166] Furthermore, share block schemes assume a certain level of sophistication and do not include any state support or guidance. In the case of sectional title schemes, a large managing agent industry has grown out of the fact that sectional title owners find it difficult to comply with the Act on a day-to-day basis without assistance, including professional assistance with financial matters. This points to the unsuitability of this vehicle for large-scale land reform purposes.

This chapter has attempted to illustrate the role of ownership and its parts, as well as the different forms of title currently available in South Africa. The intrinsic link of title to the particular ideological, socio-political and economic context has been highlighted, as well as the need to consider carefully the practical effects of proposed changes to forms of title.

The next chapter focuses on the limitations that may exist or be imposed upon all such forms of ownership.

---

166 See s 5(a) of the Share Blocks Control Act 59 of 1980.

Chapter 6

Limitations on ownership

'The principle of "give and take, live and let live", ... forms the basis of our law.'
Allaclas Investments (Pty) Ltd and Another v Milnerton Golf Club and Others 2008 (3) SA 134 (SCA) at para 21

6.1	Introduction	116
6.2	Types of limitations	117
6.3	**Constitutional limitations: Section 25 of the Constitution**	**118**
6.3.1	Constitutionality of interference with property	119
6.3.1.1	Non-arbitrariness	123
6.3.1.2	Law of general application	125
6.3.1.3	Public purpose or public interest	126
6.3.1.4	Compensation	127
6.3.2	Proportionality of interferences	129
6.3.3	Interferences that 'go too far'	130
6.4	**Private law limitations: Neighbour law**	**132**
6.4.1	Nuisance	134
6.4.1.1	Nuisance in the narrow sense	134
6.4.1.2	Nuisance in the wide sense	137
6.4.2	Traditional rules of neighbour law	139
6.4.2.1	Encroachment	139
6.4.2.2	Lateral support	143
6.4.2.3	Party walls and fences	144
6.4.2.4	Surface water	144
6.4.2.5	Elimination of dangers, including collapsing buildings	145
6.5	**Public law limitations: Planning law**	**145**
6.5.1	Structure of planning law	147
6.5.2	The scope of planning law	148
6.5.3	Content of planning law	149
6.5.3.1	Land use planning	149
6.5.3.2	Land use management	153
6.5.4	Enforcement of planning measures	156
6.6	**Concluding remarks**	**156**

6.1 Introduction

In chapter 5 it was indicated that ownership is usually described as autonomous, unrestricted and individualistic. Conventionally, it is understood as providing the most extensive entitlements that a person can have over property and as conferring the most complete or comprehensive control over a thing. This understanding is summarised by the principle of *plena in re potestas*. As indicated, ownership comprises numerous entitlements that, in principle, entitle the owner to deal with her property as she pleases, within the limits of the law.[1]

The previous chapter also demonstrated, however, that this understanding of ownership was never realistic or literally accurate.[2] Instead, it is accepted fairly generally that ownership is subject to limitations.[3] In the neighbour law context, this is well expressed by the courts in their references to the 'live and let live' principle underlying the law.[4] This implies that owners must accept the inevitable limitations associated with ownership. Ownership is not only about rights, but also about responsibilities.[5]

> **PAUSE FOR REFLECTION**
>
> **The limits of ownership are its responsibilities**
>
> It is important to understand the tensions created by choosing a particular definition of ownership because the understanding attributed to ownership in the law affords great power, politically, economically and otherwise. Keeping in mind that the conventional definition of ownership focuses on the rights and entitlements it comprises and that political power has been associated with ownership (and thus control of land) for a very long time in South Africa, it is easy to understand why, since the early 1990s, a clearer articulation of the limits and responsibilities of ownership has become increasingly desirable. In addition, the increasing public awareness of different attitudes towards the concept of ownership makes it important to grapple with the concept and to describe its boundaries, its associated responsibilities as well as the legitimate expectations that owners may have of the state.
>
> On the one hand, ownership can be viewed as so eroded by legislation serving social, economic and political purposes, that it has become something 'less than' ownership. In other words, that it is no longer *plena in re potestas* because an owner can no longer do as she pleases with her property.[6] On the other hand, all the legislative developments do not impose new limitations because the inherent nature of ownership includes limitations to accommodate social, economic and political purposes.

As regards the difficulties with defining the concept of ownership, it has been remarked that the scope of ownership can really only be determined by reference to the limitations imposed by law.[7] This chapter deals with limitations on ownership. It discusses the kinds of

---

1 See ch 5 above.
2 See ch 5 above.
3 Van der Merwe, CG (1989) *Sakereg* 2 ed (Durban, Butterworths) pp 176-178; *Silberberg & Schoeman Property* p 95; *Wille's Principles* pp 471-476.
4 *Lombard v Fischer* [2003] 1 All SA 698 (O) at 701; *Kirsh v Pincus* 1927 TPD 199 at 203-205; *Regal v African Superslate (Pty) Ltd* 1963 (1) SA 102 (A) at 111, 112, 114D and 114E.
5 Alexander, G 'Critical Land Law' in Bright, S and Dewar, J (1998) *Land Law - Themes and Perspectives* (Oxford, Oxford University Press) p 77.
6 See Lewis, C 'The Modern Concept of Ownership of Land' (1985) *Acta Juridica* 241 at 242, 244.
7 *Silberberg & Schoeman Property* p 95, with reference to *Gien v Gien* 1979 (2) SA 1113 (T) at 1120D-H.

limitations that may be imposed on ownership by selecting examples from different fields that illustrate particularly well the dichotomy between the rights and responsibilities that underlie ownership.

6.2 Types of limitations

The limitations imposed on ownership by the law are so comprehensive that it is impossible even to give a superficially complete overview here. The chapter therefore highlights only a few kinds of limitations from different established categories to demonstrate the extent to which ownership is restricted. Restrictions may be categorised based on the sphere of the law from which they emanate. Thus, there are restrictions stemming from the constitutional context, from private law and from public law. The main categories are depicted, coupled with examples, in the figure below.

Figure 6.1: Categories and examples of restrictions on ownership

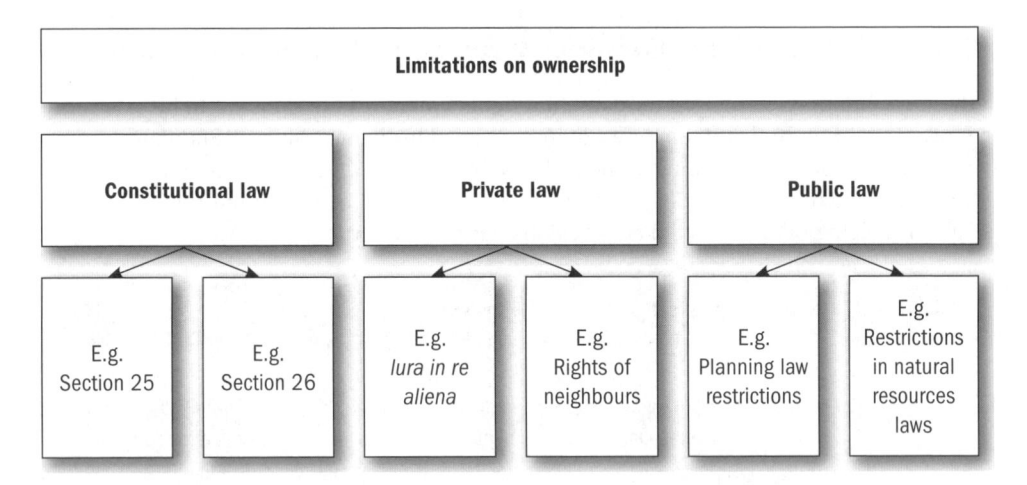

```
                        Limitations on ownership
        ┌───────────────────┬───────────────────┬───────────────────┐
        Constitutional law      Private law           Public law
        ┌─────┬─────┐       ┌─────┬─────┐       ┌─────┬─────┐
        E.g.   E.g.         E.g.   E.g.         E.g.   E.g.
        Section Section     Iura   Rights of    Planning Restrictions
        25      26          in re  neighbours   law      in natural
                            aliena              restrictions resources laws
```

The most obvious limitations on ownership are those brought about by the rights of others, as discussed above in chapter 3. The very existence of limited real rights *(iura in re aliena)* demonstrates that ownership is not unrestricted. The owner herself, the courts or the legislature can, in appropriate circumstances, grant rights in the property to someone else. Because the impact of individual real rights on ownership has been dealt with elsewhere,[8] this chapter excludes that aspect but deals with restrictions resulting from the rights of neighbours.

The vast majority of limitations on ownership originate from public law. The element of responsibility inherent in ownership is determined largely by these types of limitations. They are justified by the constitutional provisions on the limitation of property,[9] and are imposed for the benefit of society as a whole or in the interests of certain sections of society.[10]

---

[8] See ch 3 above.
[9] Section 25 of the Constitution.
[10] *Silberberg & Schoeman Property* p 95; *Colonial Development (Pty) Ltd v Outer West Local Council* 2002 (2) SA 589 (N) at 611A–B.

So, for instance, the recently promulgated legislation governing water law and mineral and petroleum law has a significant regulatory impact on common law property rights to these resources.[11] Also, the law regulating land use has always been subject to considerable legislative regulation. Before 1991, the race-based land law system 'was regulated by a profusion of legislative measures.'[12] More recent statutory law that deals with reform of the racially-based system is as abundant.[13]

Importantly, limitations on ownership also result directly from the constitutional context in which property law functions.[14] Background to the constitutional paradigm has already been provided.[15] Here some of the constitutional provisions that affect ownership receive more detailed attention. The focus is, first, on the limitations on ownership imposed by the Constitution. Thereafter, the limitations that form part of neighbour law are discussed in greater detail. Aspects of planning law are discussed as an example of public law limitations on ownership, which also intersects with neighbour law. The restrictive regulatory context of ownership of natural resources is covered in chapters 10 and 11 below, in a different setting.

6.3 Constitutional limitations: Section 25 of the Constitution

The Constitution's chapter on fundamental rights[16] includes the right not to be arbitrarily deprived of property[17] and the right not to be evicted from one's home.[18] Standards are set in the event that these guarantees are infringed by the state. Other fundamental rights may also impact on the property right, but for present purposes the focus is only on the property right. The right not to be evicted is treated in chapter 8 below.

> **PAUSE FOR REFLECTION**
>
> **Horizontal application of human rights in property law**
>
> The primary purpose of fundamental (human) rights is to protect individuals against abuse of state power. These rights thus have so-called vertical operation between the individual and the state. Where applicable, however, the South African fundamental rights provisions also apply to infringements by individuals or non-state entities.[19] This is referred to as the horizontal applicability of fundamental rights. It means that the constitutional provisions do not only protect individuals from the state (vertical application), but also protect private persons from each other in particular circumstances (horizontal application). The extent to which fundamental rights are horizontally applicable varies depending on the nature of the rights at stake, as well as the predisposition of a particular constitutional

---

11 See ch 10 and 11 below.
12 *Silberberg & Schoeman Property* p 95.
13 *Silberberg & Schoeman Property* pp 585–665.
14 See ch 1 above.
15 See pp 15–16 above.
16 Chapter 2 of the Constitution.
17 Section 25(1) of the Constitution.
18 Section 26(3) of the Constitution.
19 Section 8(2) of the Constitution; Van der Walt *Constitutional Property Law* pp 43–50; Van der Walt, JWG 'Perspectives on horizontal application: *Du Plessis v De Klerk* revisited' (1997) 12 *SA Public Law* 1–31; Woolman, SL (2000) 'Application' in Woolman, SL & Chaskalson, M (eds) *Constitutional Law of South Africa* 2nd ed (Cape Town, Juta); *Khumalo and Others v Holomisa* 2002 (5) SA 401 (CC) (2005) at para 33.

> dispensation for horizontal applicability of such rights. In South Africa, it is accepted that fundamental rights apply horizontally, directly or indirectly.[20] This is of limited relevance to issues arising from the property clause,[21] mainly because the most severe form of deprivation, expropriation, can be imposed only by a state organ, and because the requirements in s 25 presuppose state involvement.[22] However, the issue of horizontal applicability may arise in the context of the right not to be evicted from one's home[23] (s 26(3) of the Constitution).

While some of the provisions in s 25 have a protective purpose, others have a reform purpose. Section 25(1) to (3) provides for the circumstances in which property rights may be infringed, and the conditions that must be fulfilled. The rest of the provisions in the property clause, s 25(5) to (9), deal with land and resource reform to 'promote transition of the prevalent system of property holdings and property law.'[24] Section 25(4) defines property, indicating that, for purposes of the Constitution, it denotes more than land. It also confirms that public interest includes the nation's commitment to land and resource reform. The discussion here is concerned mainly with the relationship between infringement of property rights and their constitutional protection.

6.3.1 Constitutionality of interference with property

The constitutional property clause (s 25) prescribes the conditions under which infringements of property rights are constitutionally justifiable. It sets the parameters for interference (by the state) with property rights. Protection is envisaged as a 'two-pronged mechanism' that protects private property against impermissible impositions, but also achieves transformation of existing patterns of private property.[25] The clause contains provisions that deal with protection of property, justifiable infringements of property and compensation for expropriation.

The constitutional provisions guarantee the continued existence of the institution of private property, but also permit the state to interfere in circumscribed circumstances. Interference may take the form of deprivation in terms of s 25(1), or expropriation in terms of s 25(2). Deprivation amounts to the exercise of the state's 'police power', i.e. its ability to regulate use of private property by restricting owners' entitlements.[26] In South Africa, the results of the state's capacity to regulate property are referred to as deprivations of property, due to the wording of s 25(1), which stipulates that no one may be arbitrarily 'deprived' of property unless certain conditions are fulfilled.

---

20 Section 39 of the Constitution; Roederer, CJ 'Post-matrix legal reasoning: horizontality and the rule of values in South African law' (2003) 19 (1) *SAJHR* 57–81.
21 *Phoebus Apollo Aviation CC v Minister of Safety and Security* 2003 (2) SA 34 (CC) at para 4.
22 Roux, T (2002) in Woolman, SL et al. *Constitutional Law* at 46-6 to 46-7; De Waal, J Currie, I & Erasmus, G (2001) *Bill of Rights Handbook* 4 ed (Cape Town, Juta) p 412; Currie, I & De Waal, J (2005) *Bill of Rights Handbook* 5 ed (Cape Town, Juta) pp 534–535; Van der Walt *Constitutional Property Law* p 48.
23 *Modderklip Boerdery (Edms) Bpk v President van die Republiek van Suid-Afrika* 2003 (6) BCLR 638 (T) at 693–694, accepted in *Modderfontein Squatters, Greater Benoni City Council v Modderklip Boerdery (Pty) Ltd; (AgriSA and Legal Resources Centre, Amici Curiae); President of the Republic of South Africa and Others v Modderklip Boerdery (Pty) Ltd (AgriSA and Legal Resources Centre, Amici Curiae)* 2004 (6) SA 40 (SCA) at para 31; Van der Walt *Constitutional Property Law* p 47.
24 Silberberg & Schoeman *Property* p 521; Van der Walt *Constitutional Property Law* pp 12*ff*.
25 Silberberg & Schoeman *Property* p 521.
26 Silberberg & Schoeman *Property* p 96; Van der Walt *Constitutional Property Law* p 13.

Expropriation amounts to exercise of the state's power of eminent domain. This phrase refers to the state's ability to 'take' private property without the consent of the owner, for a public purpose or in the public interest, against payment of compensation. Section 25(2) empowers the state to 'terminate unilaterally, under constitutionally prescribed circumstances, all the entitlements of particular property right holders for public use or public purposes.'[27] Section 25(3) must be read with s 25(2) and prescribes how and to what extent owners must be compensated for infringements amounting to expropriation.

The state's regulatory powers differ markedly from its powers of expropriation.[28] First, the state is compelled to compensate owners when their property is expropriated, while no compensation is due when the state's actions amount to regulation only of owners' entitlements. Second, expropriation amounts to withdrawal of owners' entitlements, either completely or partially, while exercise of the state's police powers does not (usually) have that effect. Third, South African common law assumes that expropriation gives rise to an appropriation by the state. No such requirement exists for deprivations. There are further distinctions enumerated in legal literature, such as those based on whether the infringement is temporary or permanent, how extensive the infringement is, and so on. Literature also points out that there are difficulties with almost all the tenets of distinction between deprivation and expropriation.[29] Because of these difficulties, it is necessary to discuss the permitted types of interference with property in South African law in more detail below.

The framework within which the constitutionality of deprivation and expropriation of property is tested was set out by the Constitutional Court in the directional decision of *First National Bank of SA Ltd t/a Wesbank v Commissioner, South African Revenue Service; First National Bank of SA Ltd t/a Wesbank v Minister of Finance*.[30] The case dealt with the constitutionality of a law that permitted SARS to confiscate property owned by one party to settle a tax debt owed by another party. In this matter, SARS confiscated motor vehicles that belonged to First National Bank to settle the tax debt of some of the bank's debtors (Lauray Manufacturers CC and Airpark Halaal Cold Storage CC), who were purchasing the property by way of instalments.[31] The court found the law to be unconstitutional. The reasoning of the court clarifies the judicial understanding of the relationship between deprivation and expropriation of property.

The court confirmed that s 25 foresees a broad range of limitations on property rights generally designated as deprivations. Expropriation is the most severe form of deprivation and is treated as a **special subcategory** that requires the payment of compensation.[32] In terms of this understanding of s 25(1), read with the general limitations clause, s 36(1), all deprivations (including expropriations) must be imposed in terms of a law of general application; they may not be arbitrary; and they must be reasonable and justifiable in an open and democratic society based on human dignity, equality and freedom. Additionally,

---

27 Silberberg & Schoeman *Property* p 540; Van der Walt *Constitutional Property Law* p 220.
28 See generally Silberberg & Schoeman *Property* pp 541*ff*; Van der Walt *Constitutional Property Law* pp 123–128.
29 Silberberg & Schoeman *Property* pp 541–544.
30 *First National Bank of SA Ltd t/a Wesbank v Commissioner for the South African Revenue Service; First National Bank of SA Ltd t/a Wesbank v Minister of Finance* 2002 (4) SA 768 (CC) (also referred to below as the *FNB* case).
31 Section 114 of the Customs and Excise Act 91 of 1964. See Van der Walt, AJ 'Negating Grotius – The constitutional validity of statutory security rights in favour of the state: *First National Bank t/a Wesbank v Commissioner of the South African Revenue Services* 2001 (7) BCLR 715 (C)' (2001) 18 *SAJHR* 86–113.
32 *First National Bank of SA Ltd t/a Wesbank v Commissioner for the South African Revenue Service; First National Bank of SA Ltd t/a Wesbank v Minister of Finance* 2002 (4) SA 768 (CC) at paras 59*ff*.

s 25(2) expressly requires expropriations to be for a public purpose or in the public interest. Furthermore, a constitutionally valid expropriation invariably requires payment of compensation in accordance with s 25(3).

There are further decisions by the Constitutional Court that reinforce the precedent[33] that expropriation is a particular 'subspecies' of deprivation. Diagrammatically, this view may be depicted as follows:

Figure 6.2: Relationship between expropriation and deprivation

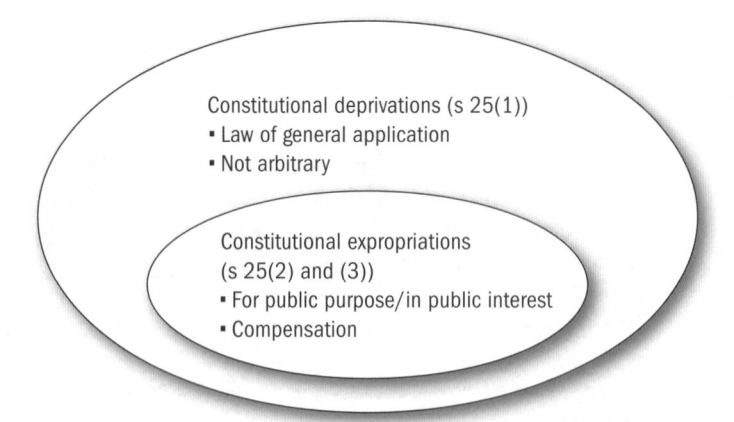

Constitutional deprivations (s 25(1))
- Law of general application
- Not arbitrary

Constitutional expropriations (s 25(2) and (3))
- For public purpose/in public interest
- Compensation

In line with this approach, **all** infringements of property (i.e. police power and eminent domain interferences) must comply, in the first place, with the requirements for deprivation as set out in s 25(1). Where it is averred that an infringement amounts to an expropriation, this must be tested against the additional requirements in s 25(2) and (3).[34] Furthermore, all enquiries are subject to the general limitations clause, s 36, which provides that fundamental rights may be limited insofar as this is reasonable and justifiable in an open and democratic society based on human dignity, equality and freedom.

PAUSE FOR REFLECTION	**Distinguishing deprivation from expropriation**
	The manner in which the court in *FNB* linked the deprivation provision with the expropriation provision achieved a flexible approach to testing the constitutionality of an infringement of property.[35] However, this approach may also create the impression that no clear distinction exists between deprivation and expropriation, and that it is simply a matter of degree as to whether the requirements of s 25(2) and (3) must be met in addition to the requirements of s 25(1). This impression is false.

---

33   *FNB* at para 57; *Mkontwana v Nelson Mandela Metropolitan Municipality; Bissett v Buffalo City Municipality; Transfer Rights Action Campaign v Member of the Executive Council for Local Government and Housing, Gauteng* 2005 (1) SA 530 (CC) at paras 34*ff*; Van der Walt *Constitutional Property Law* p 181.
34   Silberberg & Schoeman *Property* p 541.
35   Mostert, H 'The Distinction between Deprivations and Expropriations and the Future of the "Doctrine" of Constructive Expropriation in South Africa' (2003) 19(4) *SAJHR* 567 at 589.

> Still, it is not always easy to distinguish between an 'ordinary' deprivation (i.e. an exercise of the state's regulatory power) and an expropriation. For example,[36] consider that, hypothetically, a law prohibits unauthorised demolition of buildings with particular historical significance. Furthermore, authorisation is not possible for buildings older than 100 years. In other words, no permit may be issued to demolish such buildings. Thabo owns a building that is 130 years old. He wishes to demolish it to make way for a new industrial development. No viable commercial or residential use is possible in the building's current state. It is poorly situated for residential purposes and the cost of maintaining such an old building is exorbitant. In accordance with the law, Thabo finds himself in the unenviable position of not being able to obtain a demolition permit nor to use the property for any other purpose. Reasonably, he wishes to contest the constitutionality of the law that prohibits absolutely demolition of buildings older than 100 years.
>
> For this purpose, it may be important to ask whether the infringement created by this law amounts to an expropriation. If it does, compensation is payable to Thabo. If the law makes no provision for compensation, then the relevant provisions must be struck down as unconstitutional. If the law amounts merely to ordinary deprivation, it would be permissible and constitutional if it is of general application and not arbitrary, as s 25(1) provides. Accordingly, the outcome of the enquiry may vary, depending on the point of departure.
>
> In the abovementioned example, the purpose of the law is to protect cultural, architectural heritage. The law applies generally and evenly throughout society. It does not intend to expropriate anyone specifically. Hence, the law most likely was intended to be an ordinary deprivation of property (i.e. regulation in terms of police power), rather than to constitute an extreme inroad or complete withdrawal of entitlements. However, in Thabo's case the impact is particularly severe and detrimental because of the peculiarities of his situation. Though the law was intended to regulate use of property, it denies Thabo the opportunity to engage in profitable activity with his property. Does this mean that the infringement amounts to an expropriation? To answer this question, an understanding of how the requirements of s 25(1) and (2) and s 36 are interpreted and applied is required. These requirements for constitutionality are discussed below.

Because of the *FNB* decision, it is now clear that the structure of an enquiry into the constitutionality of an infringement of property is that, first, the court asks whether the affected interest qualifies as property under s 25. If so, it must be determined whether a deprivation of that property interest has occurred. If it has, the next question is whether the deprivation is in conflict with s 25(1), in particular the requirement of non-arbitrariness. If not, it must be determined whether the deprivation is justifiable in terms of the general limitations clause (s 36(1)). Thereafter, it must be determined whether the deprivation amounts to an expropriation in terms of s 25(2) and, if so, whether it complies with the requirements of both s 25(2)*(a)* and *(b)*. If it does not, the final question is whether the expropriation is nevertheless justifiable in terms of s 36.

As per the structure developed by the *FNB* decision, the requirements of non-arbitrariness and law of general application are applicable to all infringements. So is the requirement of proportionality, which stems from the provisions of s 36.

---

36 Adapted from the German 'monument protection' case, BVerfGE 100, 226 *(Denkmalschutz)*. Section 34 of the South African National Heritage Resources Act 25 of 1999 provides that a permit is required for the demolition of buildings older than 60 years. See also discussion of the Act below p 153.

6.3.1.1 Non-arbitrariness

Section 25(1) prohibits arbitrary deprivation of property. This means that the law causing the deprivation should demonstrate a rational connection between a legitimate governmental purpose and the manner in which it should be achieved. There must, furthermore, be adequate cause for the deprivation.[37] The non-arbitrariness requirement is flexible and all-encompassing. It may in some instances amount to a procedural safeguard, while in others, it may amount to a more substantive safeguard, requiring a proportionate balance between the purpose of the deprivation and the extent of the infringement.[38]

In the *FNB* decision, the court relied on the s 25(1) prohibition against arbitrary deprivation to develop a flexible test by which to determine whether sufficient reason exists for an infringement of property rights.[39] To determine this, various relationships must be considered, such as the purpose of the infringement in relation to the law imposing it; the purpose of the infringement in relation to the affected property or its owner; and the nature of the affected property in relation to the extent and purpose of the deprivation.[40]

Figure 6.3: Relationships determining sufficient reason for infringement according to the FNB case

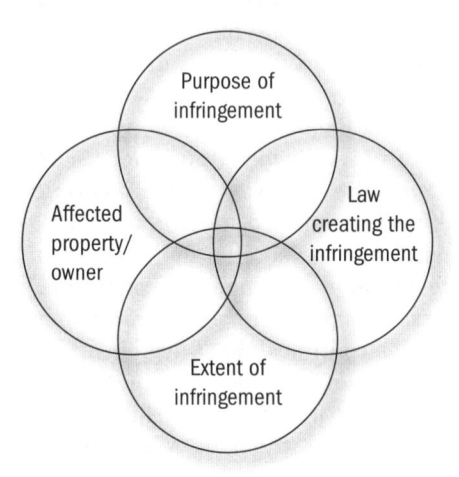

The court outlined broadly the purposes that would justify infringement of property rights. Where ownership of land or corporeal movable property was affected by a restriction, the purpose of the restriction would have to be more compelling than in the case of lesser property rights. Similarly, for an all-encompassing restriction that affects all the incidents of ownership, there would have to be a more compelling purpose than where only some of the incidents of ownership are affected.[41] The court stressed that sufficient reason would sometimes be established by 'no more than a mere rational relationship between means

---

37 *Silberberg & Schoeman Property* p 545.
38 Van der Walt *Constitutional Property Law* pp 145–156.
39 *First National Bank of SA Ltd t/a Wesbank v Commissioner for the South African Revenue Service; First National Bank of SA Ltd t/a Wesbank v Minister of Finance* 2002 (4) SA 768 (CC) at paras 100*ff*.
40 *FNB* at para 100.
41 *FNB* at para 100(e)-(f).

and ends,' while, in other cases, a full-blown proportionality enquiry would be necessary.[42] In the event of the latter, the non-arbitrariness requirement overlaps with the requirement of proportionality envisaged by s 36(1).[43]

Section 36(1) forms part of the general limitations provision, which stipulates the conditions under which the rights entrenched in the chapter on fundamental rights may be restricted. Generally, fundamental rights may be restricted only if this is:

> *reasonable and justifiable in an open and democratic society based on human dignity, equality and freedom, taking into account all relevant factors, including the nature of the right; the importance of the purpose of the limitation; the nature and extent of the limitation; the relation between the limitation and its purpose, and less restrictive means to achieve the purpose.*[44]

In this way, s 36 imposes a proportionality test, which tests whether a particular interference with a fundamental right is necessary, appropriate and moderate.[45]

In *FNB*, the court found that the law enabling SARS to confiscate the movable property of one person to settle the tax debt of another 'cast [the net] far too wide'.[46] The contested provision was struck down for being unconstitutional. The test as applied in *FNB* was all-encompassing, resembling the proportionality test as described above more closely than the rationality test. But the court did not fix the level of scrutiny for all subsequent cases.

In the subsequent decision of *Mkontwana v Nelson Mandela Metropolitan Municipality; Bissett and Others v Buffalo City Municipality; Transfer Rights Action Campaign and Others v Member of the Executive Council for Local Government and Housing, Gauteng and Others*,[47] the standard of scrutiny differed in respect of the non-arbitrariness requirement. According to the Constitutional Court's interpretation of the test in this case, where deprivations are minimal, a simple identification of the rational connection between means and ends would be adequate. The reason for the infringement must be more compelling where the deprivations are extensive. The court held that a 'legitimate and compelling' government purpose would be sufficient reason for a deprivation if the owner could reasonably be expected to bear the risk at stake.[48] In this case, the infringement arose from deficiencies in the municipal debtor management structures. A number of laws[49] establishing security interests for municipalities in the payment of water and electricity charges were disputed. These laws embargoed the sale of land where such charges were outstanding. They placed

---

42   More detailed analysis in Mostert, H 'The Distinction between Deprivations and Expropriations and the Future of the "Doctrine" of Constructive Expropriation in South Africa' (2003) 19 *SAJHR* 567–592.
43   *Silberberg & Schoeman Property* p 546.
44   Section 36 (1) of the Constitution.
45   Mostert, H (2002) *The Constitutional Protection and Regulation of Property and its Influence on the Reform of Private Law and Landownership in South Africa and Germany – A Comparative Analysis* (Heidelberg, Springer) p 89; Woolman SL (2000) 'Limitations' in Woolman, SL & Chaskalson, M (eds) *Constitutional Law of South Africa* 2 ed (Cape Town, Juta).
46   *FNB* at para 108.
47   2005 (1) SA 530 (CC).
48   *Mkontwana* at para 51.
49   Section 118 of the Local Government: Municipal Systems Act 32 of 2000; ss 49 and 50(1)(*a*) of the Gauteng Local Government Ordinance 17 of 1939, which have more or less the same effect.

the responsibility for ensuring payment on the landowners,[50] even where the landowners did not incur the debts because the land was occupied either unlawfully or by tenants who were responsible contractually for paying their consumption charges.[51] In some instances, the owners were not even aware that the debts were escalating,[52] due to the poor administrative practices of the municipalities involved.[53] The Constitutional Court nevertheless found that the relevant legislation did not result in arbitrary deprivation of property,[54] based on the level of scrutiny it attached to the non-arbitrariness requirement.

6.3.1.2   Law of general application

The requirement that only a law of general application may limit property rights appears twice in the property clause itself (in s 25(1) and (2)), and in the general limitations clause (s 36(1)). The phrase means that infringements can arise from statutes and accompanying legislative regulations, or from the rules of common law or customary law. The limitation must be 'authorised by the democratically elected legislature, acting within the constitutional parameters.'[55] The limitation must furthermore be generally applicable. A law will fall foul of this requirement if it singles out particular persons for unfairly discriminatory treatment.[56]

> **PAUSE FOR REFLECTION**
>
> **Applying the law of general application and non-arbitrariness**
>
> Applying the requirements to the example above, Thabo's difficulty with the hypothetical law protecting architectural heritage seems, indeed, to amount to an infringement that needs to be tested against the constitutional property provisions. It may be assumed that the law applies generally. Whether it complies with the non-arbitrariness requirement depends on how strictly this requirement is applied. If a *Mkontwana*-type application is preferred, one may assume that a court would find that protection of cultural heritage is a legitimate and compelling reason, justifying the infringement of property. The full *FNB* sufficient reason test would make it harder to justify the infringement, judging by its effect and extent.

---

50   The case before the Constitutional Court involved a number of appeals from lower courts in various separate matters, which resulted in conflicting decisions by different provincial divisions of the High Court. All matters involved legislative restrictions on alienation of land due to outstanding debts to municipalities. In *Geyser and Another v Msundizi Municipality and Others* 2003 (5) SA 18 (N), the High Court of KwaZulu-Natal held that the provisions did not result in unconstitutional arbitrary deprivation of property. The South Eastern Cape Local Division of the High Court, however, held in two instances (*Mkontwana v Nelson Mandela Municipality* unreported Case No 1238/02 and *Bissett v Buffalo City Municipality* unreported Case No 903/02) that an arbitrary deprivation was indeed caused by the relevant provisions, and that it was in conflict with s 25 of the Constitution.
51   In most of the cases joined for hearing, there were either tenants or unlawful occupants on the properties concerned.
52   *Mkontwana* at paras 18–21.
53   The municipalities were in a predicament because they were simply not able to collect outstanding charges through other means. The debts were bad already, and the ultimate municipal weapon – the disconnection of services – was ineffective because services were simply reconnected unlawfully. Whether the predicament was due to the lack of effort on the part of the municipalities, or to the lack of reasonable and responsible conduct on the part of the owners, was something about which the parties could not agree. *Mkontwana* at para 22.
54   *Mkontwana* at paras 31, 33*ff*.
55   *Silberberg & Schoeman Property* p 545.
56   *Silberberg & Schoeman Property* p 545.

6.3.1.3 Public purpose or public interest

In addition to complying with the abovementioned two requirements, expropriations must be for a public purpose or in the public interest. This is to ensure that the state's power of eminent domain is not abused.[57] In general, the prerogative of deciding what is in the public interest is with the legislature.[58] Yet, the courts must ensure that the constitutional standards are met.[59]

The Constitution does not give a comprehensive definition of what the terms 'public interest' or 'public purpose' require. Section 25(4)*(a)* simply specifies that public interest includes the 'nation's commitment to land reform and to reforms to bring about equitable access to all South Africa's natural resources.' This means that expropriation of land for purposes of land reform is permitted, which 'places a specific reformative spin on the provisions protecting existing property relations.'[60]

Prevailing understanding of these terms, derived from precedent, could assist in interpreting these terms. The term 'public purpose' is used in the Expropriation Act,[61] which is pre-constitutional legislation still applicable. South African courts have had many opportunities to interpret the term 'public purpose' as it appears in the Expropriation Act and other legislation.[62] Although the continued value of such precedents may be doubtful under the new constitutional dispensation, the precedents do make clear that the term 'public purpose' has various meanings depending on the context and on the particular authorising statute being considered.[63] For instance, public purpose could refer to all purposes which pertain to or benefit the general public rather than private individuals.[64] This is a broad interpretation. The same term has also been understood in a much narrower sense, referring to governmental purposes.[65] And between these extremes, other possible interpretations also exist.[66]

In the context of expropriation, public purpose was normally afforded a generous interpretation.[67] Because of this, it is assumed that the terms 'public purpose' and 'public interest' can be used interchangeably with reference to expropriation in terms of s 25(2).[68] Further, it is accepted that the public purpose requirement may be met even if the measure undertaken benefits private parties, rather than the general public, as long as the purpose is legitimate.[69] Given the text of s 25(4), the objectives of the land reform programme would be a typical example of a legitimate purpose resulting in benefit

---

57 Van der Walt *Constitutional Property Law* p 242; *Silberberg & Schoeman Property* p 566.
58 *Lebowa Mineral Trust Beneficiaries Forum v President of the Republic of South Africa* 2002 (1) BCLR 23 (T) at 31B–C; Gildenhuys, A (2001) *Onteieningsreg* 2 ed (Durban, LexisNexis Butterworths) pp 98–99.
59 Van der Walt *Constitutional Property Law* p 269.
60 *Silberberg & Schoeman Property* p 523.
61 Act 63 of 1975.
62 Mostert, H (2002) *The Constitutional Protection and Regulation of Property and its Influence on the Reform of Private Law and Landownership in South Africa and Germany – A Comparative Analysis* (Heidelberg, Springer) pp 330–331.
63 Mostert, H (2002) *The Constitutional Protection and Regulation of Property and its Influence on the Reform of Private Law and Landownership in South Africa and Germany – A Comparative Analysis* (Heidelberg, Springer) p 330.
64 *Slabbert v Minister van Lande* 1963 (3) SA 620 (T) at 621H; *Silberberg & Schoeman Property* p 567.
65 *Rondebosch Municipal Council v Trustee of Western Province Agricultural Society* 1911 AD 271 at 283; *Slabbert v Minister van Lande* 1963 (3) SA 620 (T) at 621F.
66 *Silberberg & Schoeman Property* p 567.
67 *African Farms and Townships Ltd v Cape Town Municipality* 1961 (3) SA 392 (C) at 397C–E; *Slabbert v Minister van Lande* 1963 (3) SA 620 (T) at 622G–H.
68 *Silberberg & Schoeman Property* p 567.
69 Van der Walt *Constitutional Property Law* p 269.

for private parties. Formal expropriations of rights in land for purposes of land reform, or expropriations of mineral rights or water rights for redistribution of mineral rights or water rights, would, thus, meet the requirement of public interest.[70] Section 25(8) of the Constitution provides that no provision of the property clause may impede the state from taking legislative and other measures to achieve land, water and related reform, to redress the results of past racial discrimination. Hence, legislation or measures to achieve land, water and related reform may also be regarded as in the public interest. This includes the Mineral and Petroleum Resources Development Act,[71] the National Water Act[72] and others.

6.3.1.4 Compensation

According to the requirements of s 25(2) and (3) of the Constitution, expropriation is valid only if the law of general application that causes the infringement, provides for compensation for the affected owner. The law must provide for the amount, time and manner of compensation, either by agreement between the expropriator and expropriatee (and other affected persons), and approval of such an agreement by a court, or a court must decide these matters.

To be constitutional, compensation must be just and equitable as regards the **amount**, the **time** and **manner** of payment.[73] The compensation amount must, furthermore, reflect an equitable balance between the public interest and the individual interests of the expropriatee and other affected parties.[74] This means that all relevant circumstances will be considered to determine whether the constitutional norm is met. So the current use of the property; the history of acquisition and use thereof; its market value; the extent of direct state investment and subsidy in the acquisition and beneficial capital improvement of the property; and the purpose of the expropriation will be taken into account, among others.[75]

PAUSE FOR REFLECTION	The Expropriation Act, the Constitution and the place of market value as standard for compensation
	Section 12 of the Expropriation Act[76] still controls the calculation and payment of compensation for expropriation, even though it dates from the pre-constitutional era. The notion of market value as a measure for compensation is the point of departure. Market value is the amount which the expropriated property would have realised if sold, on the date of notice of expropriation, in the open market by a (hypothetical) willing and well-informed seller to a (hypothetical) willing and well-informed buyer.[77] The comparable

---

70 *Silberberg & Schoeman Property* p 567.
71 Act 28 of 2002.
72 Act 36 of 1998.
73 Section 25(2) of the Constitution; Gildenhuys, A (2001) *Onteieningsreg* 2 ed (Durban, LexisNexis Butterworths) p 99.
74 *Silberberg & Schoeman Property* p 568.
75 Section 25(3) of the Constitution, and see Gildenhuys, A (2001) *Onteieningsreg* 2 ed (Durban, LexisNexis Butterworths) pp 170–179 for more detail on how these factors are interpreted and understood.
76 Act 63 of 1975.
77 Section 12(1)(*a*)(i); *Opera House (Grand Parade) Restaurant (Pty) Ltd v Cape Town Municipality* 1989 (2) SA 670 (C) at 675I–J; Gildenhuys, A (2001) *Onteieningsreg* 2 ed (Durban, LexisNexis Butterworths) pp 175; 275–297. See also *Kangra Holdings (Pty) Ltd v Minister of Water Affairs* 1998 (4) SA 330 (SCA) at 336G–H.

sales method[78] is taken by the courts as the most acceptable method to determine the market value of property.[79]

In terms of the Constitution, however, relevant circumstances (some of which are listed) influence the determination of the compensation amount. It may seem, therefore, that a discrepancy exists between the provisions of the Expropriation Act and those of the Constitution regarding the basis for calculation of compensation. Recent judgments concerning expropriation, decided in the new constitutional era, show that the courts are aware that the basis for calculating compensation has shifted.[80] Hence, in theory, market value remains a relevant factor, but, in view of the objectives of the property clause, it cannot be the only, or even the most important, factor in determining the just and equitable amount of compensation.[81] Yet, in fact, market value will probably remain the starting point[82] because it is more readily quantifiable than other relevant factors mentioned.

In *Khumalo v Potgieter*,[83] the Land Claims Court adopted a two-tiered approach. First, it established the market value of the property concerned.[84] Thereafter, it considered the influence on the determined value of the constitutional indications for valuation of property to be expropriated.[85] The *Khumalo* approach has since been applied in more recent case law.[86] The outcomes of this approach outside the land reform context have been criticised,[87] for fear that it may eventually affect reform initiatives negatively.[88] However, no alternative approach has received court endorsement yet.

The **current use of the property** is a consideration that provides justification for expropriation of scarce resources, such as land and minerals. Examples include where these resources are not being used productively and they are needed for reformative purposes, such as access to housing or access to the mining industry for historically disadvantaged parties, or to support emerging farmers.[89] The **history of the use of the property** may indicate the extent

---

78 For a discussion of this technique of valuation, see Gildenhuys, A (2001) *Onteieningsreg* 2 ed (Durban, LexisNexis Butterworths) pp 213*ff*; Southwood, MD (2000) *The Compulsory Acquisition of Rights* (Cape Town, Juta) pp 81–83.
79 *Pietermaritzburg Corporation v South African Breweries Ltd* 1911 501 (AD) at 506; *Minister of Water Affairs v Mostert* 1966 (4) SA 690 (A) at 723F; *Estate Marks v Pretoria City Council* 1969 (3) SA 227 (A) at 253H–254B; *Hargovan v Minister of Agriculture* 1971 (1) SA 858 (A) at 871; *Bouwer v Stadsraad van Johannesburg* 1978 (1) SA 624 (W) at 627H.
80 *Kerksay Investments (Pty) Ltd v Randburg Town Council* 1997 (1) SA 511 (T) at 522E-G; *Du Toit v Minister of Transport* 2003 (1) SA 586 (C) at paras 14, 27.
81 *Kerksay Investments (Pty) Ltd v Randburg Town Council* 1997 (1) SA 511 (T) at 522E-G. See also Claassens, A 'Compensation for Expropriation: The Political and Economic Parameters of Market Value Compensation' (1993) 9 *SAJHR* 422 at 422*ff*; Eisenberg, A 'Different constitutional formulations of compensation clauses' (1993) 9 *SAJHR* 412 at 416*ff*.
82 *Ex parte Former Highland Residents: In re Ash v Department of Land Affairs* 2000 (2) All SA 26 (LCC) at 40D; *Khumalo v Potgieter* 2000 (2) All SA 456 (LCC) at para 23; Gildenhuys, A (2001) *Onteieningsreg* 2 ed (Durban, LexisNexis Butterworths) p 167.
83 *Khumalo v Potgieter* 2000 (2) All SA 456 (LCC).
84 *Khumalo* at paras 72–92.
85 *Khumalo* at paras 93*ff*.
86 E.g. *Du Toit v Minister of Transport* 2003 (1) SA 586 (C).
87 See the comments of Van der Walt *Constitutional Property Law* pp 277*ff*.
88 Van der Walt, AJ 'Reconciling the State's Duties to Promote Land Reform and to Pay "Just and Equitable" Compensation for Expropriation' (2006) 123 *SALJ* 23 at 24, relying on a minority judgment in *Du Toit v Minister of Transport* 2003 (1) SA 586 (C) at para 84.
89 Budlender, G (1998) 'Constitutional Protection of Property Rights' in Budlender, G, Latsky, V & Roux, T (eds) *Juta's New Land Law* (Cape Town, Juta) pp 1–56*ff*.

to which it has been developed. The **history of the acquisition of the property** is relevant, for instance, where expropriatory compensation must be determined in respect of land to be expropriated in the present but which was acquired as a result of forced removals and made available to white farmers at low prices, accompanied by generous state subsidies and low interest loans.[90] **Direct state investment and subsidy** is similarly relevant.[91] The **purpose of expropriation** is mentioned explicitly in the Constitution because it offers justification for expropriations that are aimed at alleviating pressing social needs.[92] Downward adjustment of the amount of compensation may be justified on this basis too.

In addition to the factors mentioned explicitly in the Constitution, **other** factors may be relevant. For instance, in terms of the Mineral and Petroleum Resources Development Act,[93] a relevant consideration is the state's obligation to redress the results of past racial discrimination in the allocation of and access to mineral and petroleum resources; the state's obligation to bring about reforms to promote equitable access to all South Africa's natural resources; the provisions of s 25(8) of the Constitution; and whether the person concerned will continue to benefit from the use of the property in question or not. These considerations must be viewed in the light of and complementary to the constitutional provisions.

6.3.2 Proportionality of interferences

Section 36(1) of the Constitution sets out the circumstances when a fundamental right may be restricted. With regard to the relationship between ss 25 and 36, the implication is that infringements that do not meet the requirements of s 25 could be validated nevertheless in terms of the limitations clause because they are necessary, appropriate and moderate.[94] Whether this is possible would depend on the level of scrutiny applied when the requirement of non-arbitrariness[95] was considered.

As indicated above,[96] the *FNB* decision resulted in a flexible test for non-arbitrariness. This implies that the levels at which an infringement of property is scrutinised will vary from case to case, according to the circumstances. Where a low level of scrutiny is applied (i.e. where the test is 'thin'[97]), the court will ask simply whether the criteria and procedural safeguards for the infringement were heeded. So, for instance, when the court considers the non-arbitrariness requirement and applies a 'thin' test, it asks whether the infringement is rationally connected to some legitimate state purpose.

Where a strict level of scrutiny is applied (i.e. where the test is 'thick'[98]), the courts ask whether the infringement is justifiable for striking a proportionate balance between the purpose of the infringement and the manner in which it is imposed. In undertaking this balancing exercise, the court must take into account the benefit of the infringement for

---

90 Gildenhuys, A (2001) *Onteieningsreg* 2 ed (Durban, LexisNexis Butterworths) p 172; Chaskalson, M & Lewis, C (1996) 'Property' in Chaskalson, M, Kentridge, J, Klaaren, J, Marcus, G, Spitz, G & Woolman, SL (eds) *Constitutional Law of South Africa* (Cape Town, Juta) Vol 2 pp 31-19.
91 Gildenhuys, A 'Editorial' (1996) 1 *Human Rights and Constitutional Law Journal of South Africa* p 22.
92 Budlender, G (1998) 'Constitutional Protection of Property Rights' in Budlender, G, Latsky, V, & Roux, T (eds) *Juta's New Land Law* (Cape Town, Juta) pp 1-66; Van der Walt *Constitutional Property Law* p 276.
93 Act 28 of 2002, item 12 of Schedule II.
94 See pp 121-122 above.
95 See pp 123-125 above.
96 See p 120-122 above.
97 Van der Walt *Constitutional Property Law* p 145.
98 Van der Walt *Constitutional Property Law* p 145.

the public and the harm it may cause to an individual or a small group of people.[99] This is typically what is required by the proportionality test espoused by s 36(1). This kind of test inevitably requires a court to make value judgments.[100]

Because of the reasoning in the *FNB* case, which created the flexible sufficient reason test,[101] the point at which proportionality is considered with reference to a s 25 dispute may vary. The proportionality question may be asked early in the enquiry, for instance when the court considers the non-arbitrariness of the infringement, as occurred in the *FNB* decision. To do so does not mean that the court in *FNB* equated the non-arbitrariness test with the proportionality test. Depending on the circumstances of a particular case and the court's treatment thereof, however, it is to be expected that the non-arbitrariness test and the proportionality test may sometimes overlap significantly.[102]

> **PAUSE FOR REFLECTION**
>
> **Applying the proportionality test**
>
> Returning to the example of Thabo as set out above, it was indicated that the hypothetical law protecting cultural heritage most probably did not intend to be expropriatory, but that it nevertheless had a particularly severe effect on Thabo. This means that it does not have to comply with the requirements for expropriation, but it must nevertheless be proportional if it is to be valid.
>
> Applying a 'thin' test would probably result in the law passing the constitutionality standard. A 'thick' test would likely make it more problematic to find that the law is constitutional because this would require the court to consider 'substantive issues of justifiability'.[103] However, the possibility of a finding that the law is constitutional even on a 'thick' scrutiny, cannot be excluded completely. If the proportionality of the infringement is tested in Thabo's case, it will be noted that Thabo is particularly severely affected by the law, even though the state purpose of the law may be perfectly legitimate, and even though the law does not have the same kind of effect on other property holders. The question that arises is how this particularly severe infringement should be treated.

6.3.3 Interferences that 'go too far'

In those instances where expropriation was not intended, but where the deprivation of property is so severe that it denudes the owner of most of his entitlements, the consequences must be considered. In theory, such interferences may not amount to expropriation, but in practical terms, they amount to nothing less. Accordingly, they are dubbed 'de facto expropriations' or 'constructive expropriations' or 'inverse condemnations' depending on their effects.[104] The very fact that an interference may technically stop short of being classifiable as an expropriation but to all intents and purposes has the effect of an expropriation, demonstrates the need for a protective mechanism for affected individuals. Even though the state acts to regulate property for the sake of the public good, when such action is excessive in its effect, protection is necessary.[105]

---

99 *Silberberg & Schoeman Property* p 550.
100 *Silberberg & Schoeman Property* p 551; Van der Walt *Constitutional Property Law* p 147.
101 See p 120–122 above.
102 *Silberberg & Schoeman Property* p 553.
103 *Silberberg & Schoeman Property* p 552.
104 Van der Walt *Constitutional Property Law* p 125.
105 *Silberberg & Schoeman Property* p 553.

Of course, the particular interference could simply be struck down for being unconstitutional. This is the approach taken in *FNB* where the court found that the particular law 'cast the net far too wide'.[106] However, this might not always be appropriate because the merits of other legislation that leads to an infringement may be beyond reproach. Consequently, infringements that 'go too far' may occasionally merit an award of compensation[107] in some jurisdictions.[108] In other jurisdictions, this approach is rejected.[109]

Because expropriation is seen as a subset of deprivation in South African law, the possibility of treating particularly severe deprivations as expropriations exists in theory.[110] Yet, early cases in which the courts experimented with whether a doctrine of constructive expropriation might be feasible in South Africa, demonstrated that this kind of reasoning may become problematic.[111] It is unclear whether deprivation not intended to be expropriation should **always** lead to compensation. It may be that a particular individual owner is required to bear the burden of diminished entitlements in the public interest. Another aspect is that if excessive deprivation should lead to alternative protective mechanisms, then the discretion that the judiciary would need to exercise may be far-reaching. Pursuant to the *FNB* decision, it seems unlikely that the courts will be prepared to order payment of expropriatory compensation for an infringement which does not intend to be an expropriation, but nevertheless is particularly severe.[112]

This does not mean that the aggrieved owner's only recourse is to have the law struck down as unconstitutional. Faced with the dilemma of striking down a legislative measure that has merit, but nevertheless requires excessive sacrifice from a particular individual, the court could utilise equalisation measures.

Equalisation is a mechanism employed to temper the harsh effects of a particular infringement on an individual's interests in instances where it is not sensible to invalidate the legislative measure as unconstitutional.[113] For instance, transitional measures could be imposed to ease the immediate burden on individuals particularly affected by a specific exercise of the state's police power. Also, the legislature may be urged to deliberate on cases of severity and to develop conditions for exceptional treatment. Where neither of these interventions would assist a particular individual, the possibility of financial equalisation may be considered.[114]

---

106 *First National Bank of SA Ltd t/a Wesbank v Commissioner for the South African Revenue Service; First National Bank of SA Ltd t/a Wesbank v Minister of Finance* 2002 (4) SA 768 (CC) at para 23.
107 Allen, T (2000) *The Right to Property in Commonwealth Constitutions* (Cambridge, Cambridge University Press) pp 162*ff*; Van der Walt, AJ 'Compensation for excessive or unfair regulation: A comparative overview of constitutional practice relating to regulatory takings' (1999) 14 *SAPR/PL* 273-331.
108 This solution has featured, for instance, in the US case of *Lucas v South Carolina Coastal Council* 505 US 1003 (1992), and see *Pennsylvania Coal Co v Mahon* 260 US 393 (1922).
109 E.g. in the German 'wet gravel extraction' case: BVerfGE 58 300 (Nassauskiesing).
110 More detail in Van der Walt, AJ 'Moving towards Recognition of Constructive Expropriation? *Steinberg v South Peninsula Municipality* 2001 (4) SA 1243 (SCA)' (2002) *THRHR* 459-473; Mostert, H 'The Distinction between Deprivations and Expropriations and the Future of the "Doctrine" of Constructive Expropriation in South Africa' (2003) 19(4) *SAJHR* 567-592.
111 See the more detailed discussion of *Harksen v Lane NO* 1998 (1) SA 300 (CC) and *Steinberg v South Peninsula Municipality* 2001 (4) SA 1243 (SCA) in *Silberberg & Schoeman Property* p 555.
112 Mostert, H 'The Distinction between Deprivations and Expropriations and the Future of the "Doctrine" of Constructive Expropriation in South Africa' (2003) 19(4) *SAJHR* 591-592.
113 See e.g. Van der Walt, AJ 'Regulation of building under the Constitution' (2009) 49 *De Jure* 32-47.
114 See e.g. in relation to German law: BVerfGE 100, 226 at 245-246.

Although the idea of equalisation is not yet fully developed in South Africa, at least one example of an imposition of equalisation measures exists. The case of *President of the RSA and Another v Modderklip Boerdery (Pty) Ltd and Others*[115] arose from the inability of the state to assist landowners to execute a legitimate eviction order,[116] or to control massive, incessant influx of unlawful occupiers onto their land. A vast informal settlement had established itself by the time the matter came before the Constitutional Court, which had to decide the kind of relief due to the landowners by the state.[117] The court ordered that the occupants should be allowed to stay on the land, but that the landowners had to be compensated. Although the compensation amount had to be determined by the same standards as for expropriatory compensation, the court did not indicate that an expropriation had occurred. Instead, it is generally accepted that the order was for an equalisation payment, or constitutional damages.[118]

> **PAUSE FOR REFLECTION** **Applying equalisation**
>
> Returning to Thabo's case, as set out above, equalisation seems to offer a solution to the problem. The court could be approached for an order in terms of the Constitution that the law must be revised to provide for transitional measures or exceptions to the rule, in lieu of which financial equalisation would become payable.[119]

6.4 Private law limitations: Neighbour law

When considering an example of private law limitations on ownership, one must keep in mind the description of ownership as comprising entitlements or powers.[120] These entitlements include the entitlements of use, enjoyment, control, encumbrance and vindication, among others. Each owner has these same entitlements. Therefore, when an owner exercises his entitlements, it can negatively affect his neighbour in her enjoyment of similar entitlements. The entitlements of an owner of land to use and enjoy that land are restricted by the fact that neighbours have similar entitlements in respect of their own land. This situation can lead to conflicts between neighbours.

Neighbour law regulates the way in which conflicts between neighbours are resolved. A general principle of neighbour law is that each owner is entitled to the use and enjoyment of her property, exercised in a reasonable manner to avoid unreasonable infringement of the neighbour's similar entitlement.[121]

---

115 2005 (5) SA 3 (CC) at para 34.
116 Obtained in terms of the Prevention of Illegal Eviction from and Unlawful Occupation of Land Act 19 of 1998, in *Modderklip Boerdery (Pty) Ltd v Modder East Squatters* 2001 (4) SA 385 (W). Subsequent attempts to have the order enforced went to the Supreme Court of Appeal in *Modderfontein Squatters, Greater Benoni City Council v Modderklip Boerdery (Pty) Ltd (AgriSA and Legal Resources Centre, Amici Curiae); President of the Republic of South Africa v Modderklip Boerdery (Pty) Ltd (AgriSA and Legal Resources Centre, Amici Curiae)* 2004 (6) SA 40 (SCA) at para 9.
117 *President of the Republic of South Africa v Modderklip Boerdery (Pty) Ltd (AgriSA and Legal Resources Centre, Amici Curiae)* 2005 (5) SA 3 (CC) at para 42.
118 Van der Walt, AJ 'The State's Duty to Protect Property Owners v The State's Duty to Provide Housing: Thoughts on the Modderklip Case' (2005) *SAJHR* 144–161; Van der Walt *Constitutional Property Law* p 333; *Silberberg & Schoeman Property* p 558.
119 This was the solution to the problem in the German 'monument protection' case BVerfGE 100, 226, from which this example was taken and adapted for the South African context.
120 See ch 5 above.
121 *Silberberg & Schoeman Property* pp 111–112.

Neighbour law derives its rules from a mixture of Roman and Roman-Dutch law, on the one hand, and English law, on the other.[122] Roman and Roman-Dutch law provided a limited number of real remedies. In English law, the treatment of neighbour conflicts is dealt with as a tort of nuisance. There are historical reasons for the mix of rules in South Africa, and the result is that South African neighbour law does not rest on a single principle, but rather provides a set of general principles and several sets of particular rules associated only with particular factual circumstances. Thus, the overarching criteria of reasonableness and fairness govern neighbour relations in property law, but matters concerning encroachments, surface water, party walls and lateral support are dealt with by application of the specific rules received into South African law from Roman and Roman-Dutch law.[123] For the sake of convenience, these aspects are often depicted as aspects or subdivisions of neighbour law, as in the diagram below.

Neighbour law involves both the law of property, which provides the remedy for an infringement of the neighbour's use and enjoyment, and the law of delict, which deals with intentionally or negligently caused damage (patrimonial loss).

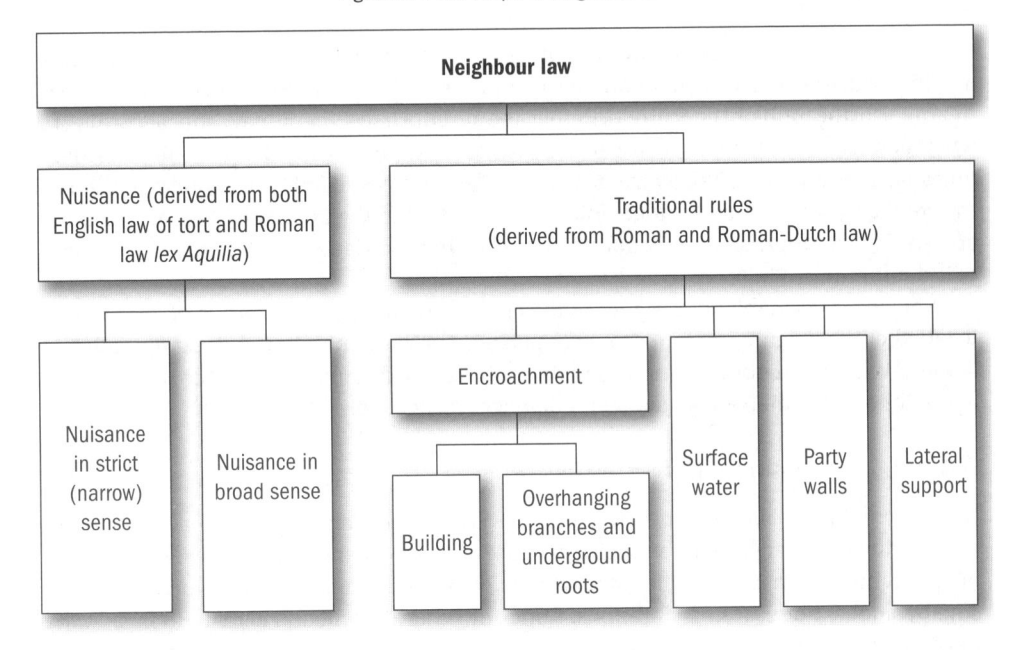

Figure 6.4: The scope of neighbour law

```
                          Neighbour law
                   ┌───────────┴───────────┐
      Nuisance (derived from both     Traditional rules
      English law of tort and Roman   (derived from Roman and Roman-Dutch law)
           law lex Aquilia)
      ┌───────┴───────┐        ┌──────┬──────────┬──────┬──────┬──────┐
   Nuisance      Nuisance in   Encroachment   Surface  Party  Lateral
   in strict     broad sense   ┌────┴────┐    water    walls  support
   (narrow)                 Building  Overhanging
   sense                              branches and
                                      underground
                                      roots
```

---

122 *Wille's Principles* pp 476–477.
123 For more detail, see *Wille's Principles* pp 476–482; *Silberberg & Schoeman Property* pp 119–132.

> **PAUSE FOR REFLECTION**
>
> **Property or delict?**
>
> The law of property provides the rules that regulate the relationship between a person and a thing. Where that relationship is disturbed, a proprietary remedy is used to restore the relationship, e.g. where the thing is taken from the owner unlawfully, its return can be claimed with the *rei vindicatio*.[124]
>
> In certain circumstances, the thing may be damaged. The owner of the damaged thing may wish to be compensated for the damage. This is the field of the law of delict, which provides the rules that determine when and the extent to which a person will be held liable for having committed a delict, i.e. a civil wrong in terms of which a person causes harm to another person or his property. The remedy available to a person who has suffered patrimonial loss is an action for damages, the *actio legis Aquiliae*.

In the discussion below, the focus is on the dual foundations of South African neighbour law. First, the general principle of nuisance is discussed. Thereafter, focus is placed on some of the traditional rules of neighbour law.

6.4.1 Nuisance

The term 'nuisance' is derived from English law.[125] Its ambit can be viewed in a narrow and in a wide sense. The distinction between these two senses does not lead to a different treatment of the problem concerned. Rather, the appropriate remedy may differ according to whether nuisance in the strict sense or the wide sense is under consideration. To determine nuisance in each case, an objective reasonableness test is applied. The enquiry is whether the conduct complained of is to be tolerated, i.e. whether the activity is proper, becoming and socially appropriate *(secundum bonos mores)* in accordance with the prevailing views of the community.[126]

Note that reasonableness applies to the conduct or activity complained of, rather than to whether the neighbour is a reasonable person. This latter notion is the test for delictual liability. Where the conduct is unreasonable or has caused actual damage, the remedies are a prohibitory interdict and an action for damages respectively.

6.4.1.1 Nuisance in the narrow sense

Nuisance[127] in the narrow or strict sense – also termed an annoyance – denotes an infringement of a neighbour's entitlement of use and enjoyment so that it affects her quality of life, i.e. ordinary health, comfort and convenience, by an ongoing wrong, such as causing smells, smoke, noise, water, vibrations, fumes or other detrimental activity to invade the neighbour's property. Noisy activities are frequently contentious. Case law provides many examples, including the use of an apparatus to scare away baboons,[128] the keeping of chickens,[129] the holding of religious activities,[130] and the keeping of seals in a residential

---

124 See ch 8 below.
125 *LAWSA* Vol 19 (2) at para 164; *Silberberg & Schoeman Property* p 111.
126 See *Wille's Principles* p 478.
127 'Nuisance' comes from the Latin word *nocere*, meaning 'to harm'. See *Wille's Principles* p 477 n 56.
128 *Gien v Gien* 1984 (3) SA 54 (T).
129 *De Charmoy v Day Star Hatchery* 1967 (4) SA 188 (D).
130 *Prinsloo v Shaw* 1938 AD 570.

area.[131] Other examples include smells emanating from a brick kiln[132] or an animal skin store,[133] smoke[134] and game farming operations causing disease to cattle.[135]

Whether the effects of an activity complained of are sufficiently serious to constitute an actionable wrong, is a question of fact and a matter of degree.[136] The test is whether, based on an objective assessment, the conduct complained of is reasonable and thus to be tolerated.[137] The enquiry is whether an ordinary person, who finds herself in the position of the plaintiff, would have tolerated the relevant interference. The objective assessment is guided by various factors that the court considers and then decides, on a balance of probabilities, whether the conduct complained of is reasonable and therefore to be tolerated. It should be noted that a court does not necessarily consider every factor in each matter. In other words, the factual scenario determines which factors, discussed below, are actually considered in each matter.

The gravity of harm caused to the neighbour is considered because if the complaint is based on only a trivial inconvenience, then it is unlikely to be reasonable.[138] In addition, the time, duration and nature of the interference are examined. The locality where the complaint arises is relevant. Usage of land for residential, commercial, industrial or agricultural purposes gives rise to different expectations regarding the activities that would be considered acceptable in a particular locality.[139]

Whether the landowner benefits from the activity and, if so, to what degree, are also to be considered and weighed against the extent of harm caused to the neighbour.[140] If the harm to the ordinary quality of life of the neighbour could have been avoided or diminished by the owner taking different measures which were available, then it is likely that the conduct would be unreasonable.[141]

The personality of the plaintiff may be relevant because the ordinary person is taken to be someone of sound and liberal tastes rather than someone who is perverse, fastidious or overly scrupulous.[142] Thus, if the plaintiff is someone who is sensitive and is affected particularly by an activity that would not unduly disturb others, then the plaintiff cannot be considered to be an ordinary person.[143] Consequently, it is likely that the activity would not be considered unreasonable.

The utility of the activity to the general public[144] is assessed because sometimes individual neighbours are required to put up with inconvenience when the general public derives an interest from the particular activity.[145] Where the activity is carried out solely because the owner's motive is to annoy the neighbour *(animo vicino nocendi)*, it is likely that the activity would be considered unreasonable.[146]

---

131 *Leith v Port Elizabeth Museum Trustees* 1934 EDL 211.
132 *Winshaw v Miller* 1916 CPD 439.
133 *Windhoek Municipality v Lurie & Co (SWA) (Pty) Ltd* 1957 (1) SA 164 (SWA).
134 *Turkstra Ltd v Richards* 1926 TPD 276.
135 *Wright v Cockin* 2004 (4) SA 207 (E).
136 *Silberberg & Schoeman Property* p 112.
137 Originally formulated in *Holland v Scott* 1882 EDC 307 at 322. See also *Vogel v Crewe* [2004] 1 All SA 587 (T).
138 *Die Vereniging van Advokate (TPA) v Moskeeplein (Edms) Bpk* 1982 (3) SA 159 (T) at 163.
139 *Du Toit v De Bot, Du Toit v Zuidmeer* (1883) 2 SC 213; *Gien v Gien* 1979 (2) SA 1113 (T).
140 *Malherbe v Ceres Municipality* 1951 (4) SA 510 (A) at 517-518.
141 *Gien v Gien* 1979 (2) SA 1113 (T).
142 *Prinsloo v Shaw* 1938 AD 570 at 575; *De Charmoy v Day Star Hatchery (Pty) Ltd* 1967 (4) SA 188 (D) at 192D-193A.
143 *Du Toit v De Bot, Du Toit v Zuidmeer* (1883) 2 SC 213.
144 See *Wille's Principles* p 479; *Silberberg & Schoeman Property* p 112.
145 *Gibbons v SAR&H* 1933 CPD 521 at 531.
146 *Kirsh v Pincus* 1927 TPD 199; *Gien v Gien* 1979 (2) SA 1113 (T) 1121.

The remedy for a neighbour whose health, comfort or convenience has been infringed by an ongoing annoyance, is a prohibitory interdict. Such an order requires the owner to cease or to diminish (abate) the interference caused by the activity.[147] Where the harm has been deliberately caused, a claim for sentimental damages also might lie under the *actio iniuriarum*.[148]

In *Laskey and Another v Showzone CC and Others*,[149] the applicants complained of the noise that emanated from a theatre-restaurant situated in the same building as their apartments. They alleged that the noise was excessive; it occurred regularly and at night during hours when ordinary people would expect quieter conditions conducive to sleep; that they had suffered material discomfort; and that there were measures that the respondent could have taken to diminish the effect of their activities.

Noise can be measured objectively (in decibels) with the use of technical instruments. The extent of noise permitted is regulated by various pieces of legislation, including municipal by-laws. Acceptable levels of noise are laid down to ensure human comfort and well-being, even in busy urban areas. In the *Laskey* matter, the Environment Conservation Act[150] and the Noise Control Regulations (Western Cape)[151] were involved. While some level of noise is inevitable in modern settlements, especially in urban areas, the difficulty is to determine the level at which 'a disturbance ... ceases to be a "to-be-expected-in-the-circumstances" interference ... and becomes an unwarranted and actionable interference.' This is largely a question of fact, and of judgement and opinion.[152]

Where noise is complained of, the material factors to be considered in the determination of whether the interference is actionable are 'the type of noise, the degree of its persistence, the locality involved and the times when the noise is heard.'[153] It may be noted that while these factors are similar to those outlined above, there is an added nuance that permits the examination of the particular disturbance (in this case noise) under consideration. In other words, the factors are utilised in a way that allows the reasonableness and fairness of the particular conduct complained of to be examined as objectively as possible.

In *Laskey*, an actionable nuisance was found to exist because the 'extent of the increase in the noise levels' as a result of the productions at the theatre-restaurant was significant; the noise occurred regularly and during late hours of the evening; and there were 'obvious steps that [could] be taken ... to ameliorate the situation.'[154] It was revealed in the course of the hearing that soundproofing measures installed for the respondent had been completely unsuitable and ineffective. Its efforts did show, however, that it had tried to improve the situation. The court granted an interdict that prohibited the respondent from conducting its theatre-restaurant business until effective measures had been taken to abate the nuisance. However, in the interest of fairness to the respondent, the interdict was suspended for four months to give it the opportunity to institute effective soundproofing measures.

---

147 *Silberberg & Schoeman Property* p 117; *LAWSA* Vol 27 (1) at para 314.
148 Scott, S 'Recent developments in case law regarding neighbour law and its influence on the concept of ownership' (2005) *Stell LR* 351 at 353.
149 2007 (2) SA 48 (CPD).
150 Act 73 of 1989.
151 Published under PN 627 of 1998 (*PG* 5309 of 20 November 1998) in terms of s 25 of the Environment Conservation Act 73 of 1989.
152 *Laskey and Another v Showzone CC and Others* 2007 (2) SA 48 (CPD) at para 22.
153 *Laskey* at para 22.
154 *Laskey* at para 37.

In *Allaclas Investments (Pty) Ltd and Another v Milnerton Golf Club and Others*,[155] a home situated alongside the fairway of the sixth hole of a golf course was plagued by showers of misdirected golf balls hit from the tee-off position. In the period between December 2003 and March 2006, some 875 golf balls landed in the property of the appellants. The unpredictability with which golf balls were hit onto the premises, and the concomitant danger posed to people, animals and property, made the garden unusable in the ordinary way. In August 2003, a 4,7 m high net had been erected on the western and southern aspects of the property, but this had failed to prevent balls from being hit into the garden 'in circumstances where they were likely to cause damage to any property they came into contact with or any person who was in their path of travel'.[156]

The court found that the number of golf balls entering the property was 'excessive and unreasonable in all circumstances'. It also found that the respondent was not making unusual use of its land but that while it was reasonable that a neighbour should tolerate some badly hit golf balls, what was being experienced was substantially more than 'what a neighbour is obliged to put up with on the application of the principle of "give and take, live and let live", which forms the basis of our law on this point'.[157]

Even though the golf course had been in use since 1925 and the appellant knew when it purchased the property that it was adjacent to the golf course and it would be vulnerable to stray golf balls, it could not have known that the sixth hole of the course was badly designed and would give rise to the safety concerns experienced. Consequently, the court ordered an interdict prohibiting use of the sixth hole until measures were implemented to cure the problem.

6.4.1.2 Nuisance in the wide sense

This type of nuisance results from conduct by a landowner involving abnormal or unusual use of land that infringes the exercise of ownership entitlements, or that results in actual damage to the neighbour's property. South African courts accept that such improper use may be interdicted as a nuisance if it continues or is likely to be repeated. If it is accompanied by *culpa* and loss, it may form the basis for an action in damages.[158]

The use of the land must be assessed objectively to determine whether it is reasonable and may continue, or whether it should be stopped or changed to prevent further infringement of the neighbour's exercise of entitlements. The main factor taken into account is natural use, i.e. whether the land is being used in the expected and ordinary manner for the location and circumstances.[159] Not every case where damage is inflicted is necessarily because of unreasonable use of the land. The neighbour's use of land is also examined because if the cause of complaint arises because the neighbour's activities are unusually sensitive, then it would be unreasonable and unfair to penalise the owner who uses his land in a reasonable manner.[160] The point is that the matter is examined from both sides to determine whether the use of land is reasonable.

---

155 2008 (3) SA 134 (SCA).
156 *Allaclas Investments* at para 19.
157 *Allaclas Investments* at para 21.
158 *Dorland and Another v Smits* 2002 (5) SA 374 (CPD).
159 *Wille's Principles* p 479; *Prinsloo v Shaw* 1938 AD 570 at 575.
160 *Silberberg & Schoeman Property* p 113.

The circumstances of the particular case are decisive in determining how the factors relevant to the reasonableness criterion should be considered. This is illustrated by a number of examples from case law.

In *Regal v African Superslate (Pty) Ltd*,[161] large quantities of slate waste from an upstream slate quarry had been washed downstream and deposited on the neighbour's land. This obviously constituted an infringement of the neighbour's entitlements. Although the original events occurred before the current owner obtained ownership of the land on which the quarry was situated, there was a possibility that this would happen again. While it was clear that liability accrued to the current owner on the basis that the harm originated on its property, the court refused to impose on the current landowner the major expenses entailed to prevent further harm. In the court's view, the omission by the landowner to take the costly preventative measures was reasonable in the circumstances since the harm suffered by the neighbour was not great. However, it was pointed out that the previous owner, under whose ownership the harm originated, would have been compelled to ensure that the slate waste no longer washed downstream.

Two insights from this case are important. First, a subsequent owner who inherits a harm-causing state of affairs may be liable to the neighbour if the activity is found to be unreasonable. In other words, that a previous owner permitted the state of affairs to develop cannot excuse the subsequent owner from liability. Second, whether such liability leads to the imposition of the duty to rectify the problem and the consequent expense for the subsequent owner, depends on the factual scenario, including the measures available and the cost involved to rectify the problem.

In *Malherbe v Ceres Municipality*,[162] oak trees were planted along the streets of the town and, seasonally, their leaves would fall into and block the gutters of a house, causing inconvenience and some damage. Roots from the trees also allegedly damaged the foundations. Here the question was whether this harm constituted an actionable nuisance. The court rejected the claims, holding that the planting of oak trees along the road in that part of the country was regarded as putting trees to their natural and ordinary use, which must be tolerated by neighbours.[163] In *Kirsh v Pincus*,[164] however, willow trees were planted next to the boundary of a malt manufacturer, causing the willow leaves to fall on to the wheat which was being dried on cement floors, thus adulterating the malt ingredients. The evidence showed that the willow trees were planted primarily to annoy the neighbour, which led to the conclusion that this use of land was not reasonable in the circumstances.

Where the abnormal or unusual use of land is unreasonable, the infringement can be prohibited by means of an interdict if the conduct is ongoing. If actual damage has occurred, a claim for compensation for patrimonial loss can be instituted using a delictual action.[165]

Whether aesthetic considerations play a role in neighbour law was considered in *Dorland and Another v Smits*,[166] where the court expressed the view that '[t]he trouble with aesthetics, visual or other, is that they are notoriously subjective and personal,'[167] and that 'as a matter of judicial policy' the courts should avoid such considerations. The finding was thus that 'purely aesthetic considerations are irrelevant in the common law relating

---

161 1963 (1) SA 102 (A).
162 1951 (4) SA 510 (A).
163 See also *Vogel v Crewe* [2004] 1 All SA 587 (T).
164 1927 TPD 199.
165 *Silberberg & Schoeman Property* p 114.
166 2002 (5) 374 (CPD).
167 *Dorland* at 383G.

to nuisance and neighbours'.[168] In the same matter, attention was given to the relationship between nuisance and danger. The court pointed out that danger or a threat of danger could constitute a nuisance, but whether it in fact did, was a matter of degree. 'The enquiry is whether the offending owner is acting unreasonably in all the circumstances.'[169] The matter concerned an electrified fence erected on a boundary wall (not a party wall) that the neighbour complained was ugly and constituted a danger. On a balance of probabilities, the court found that it was reasonable to add security measures such as an electrified fence in an area where housebreaking was a known threat and, consequently, the conduct was not unreasonable in the circumstances.

6.4.2 Traditional rules of neighbour law

As indicated, the general reasonableness test is complemented by special traditional rules of neighbour law. These relate specifically to encroachments, lateral support, party walls and fences, surface water and elimination of danger, all of which are discussed below.

6.4.2.1 Encroachment

Encroachment results in an interference with the possession entitlement of the neighbour who, in principle, is entitled to removal of the encroachment. Encroachment takes two forms, namely encroachment by building and encroachment by overhanging branches and underground roots of trees.

Encroachment by building. Building on land is regulated mainly by statutes, which determine issues such as zoning, height of buildings, densities, and building lines.[170] Encroachment occurs where an owner, without consent, builds over the boundary line between his property and that of the neighbour. Encroachment by building occurs also when foundations, eaves of a roof or balconies go over the boundary line.

The affected neighbour is entitled to demand removal of the encroachment.[171] The court's role is to consider whether to support the demand for removal or not. In some circumstances, it may choose to exercise its discretion and order a different solution. It is within the court's discretion to grant an award of damages instead of an order for removal.[172] Such a substitution may be desirable in situations where an order for removal may result in disproportionate harm to the offending owner when compared with the harm suffered by the aggrieved neighbour. If the court supports the demand for removal, then the bona fide encroacher is entitled, generally, to compensation on the basis of unjustified enrichment. A *mala fide* encroacher is unlikely to be compensated,[173] but may remove his materials and restore the land to its previous state.

---

168 *Dorland* at 383I.
169 *Dorland* at 384A.
170 E.g. the National Building Regulations and Building Standards Act 103 of 1977. Van der Walt, AJ & Pienaar, GJ (2006) *Introduction to the Law of Property* 5 ed (Cape Town, Juta) p 86; Van der Walt, AJ 'Regulation of building under the Constitution' (2009) *De Jure* 32-47. See also below pp 145*ff.*
171 *Silberberg & Schoeman Property* p 122.
172 *Rand Water Board v Bothma* 1997 (3) SA 120 (C) at 130F; *Naude v Bredenkamp* 1956 (2) SA 448 (O); Scott, S 'Recent developments in case law regarding neighbour law and its influence on the concept of ownership' (2005) *Stell LR* 351 at 360-362; *LAWSA* Vol 27 (1) at para 127; *Silberberg & Schoeman Property* p 123.
173 Van der Walt, AJ 'Replacing property rules with liability rules: encroachment by building' (2008) *SALJ* 592-626.

> **PAUSE FOR REFLECTION**
>
> **Does the court's discretion include an order for transfer?**
>
> Several current textbooks[174] state that the court's discretion includes the power to order a transfer of the land on which the encroachment is built to the encroacher. The encroached-upon owner would be compensated for the loss of her land. The authority for this statement is given as *Christie v Haarhof* and *Van Boom v Visser*.[175] However, analysis of these two cases reveals that the encroached-upon owners were willing to divest themselves of ownership in the land on which the encroachments were situated. This means that they co-operated in the transfer of title in those portions, i.e. a bilateral transaction took place. In turn, this indicates that the court did not order a transfer of title, i.e. the court did not order a forced sale or a unilateral taking of ownership. There does not seem to be any basis, especially under the Constitution, on which such an order would be proper. Section 25 of the Constitution prohibits an arbitrary deprivation of property and, if there is to be an expropriation, then full compliance with s 25(2) and (3), as well as with the Expropriation Act,[176] is required.[177] In the situation where an owner is unwilling to co-operate in the subdivision and transfer of a portion of her land, there would need to be careful analysis and justification before it can be assumed that a court has the power to order a forced sale. Therefore, the only basis for saying that transfer of the neighbour's land is a possible solution is to indicate clearly that this solution depends upon agreement between the owners, i.e. derivative acquisition of ownership.[178]

Reasonableness and fairness are important criteria in the assessment and balancing of interests that take place. In *Lombard v Fischer*,[179] the court expressed the view that neighbour law seeks to harmonise relationships. Reasonableness and fairness dictate that the exercise of ownership has to be restricted to the extent that it causes prejudice to neighbours. The courts have a discretion to intervene and provide just and equitable solutions.

In *Lombard v Fischer*, a road providing access to Fischer's garage was partly on Lombard's property. Neither of the parties was aware of this, thinking that the road was on Fischer's property. On becoming aware of the true situation, Lombard erected a wall in the middle of the access road, thus preventing clear access to the garage. Furthermore, Lombard applied for an order to restrain Fischer from encroaching on his (Lombard's) property. Fischer's response was that Lombard was motivated by malice and was acting unreasonably and unfairly. The court found that Lombard's conduct was most unreasonable and unfair, and was calculated to cause grave prejudice. It dismissed the application and ordered that if the parties did not agree to an alternative solution, Lombard was free to erect a wall along the disputed road on their side, leaving a 2,5 m space between the wall and Fischer's house, so that the latter could access his garage. In other words, the court exercised its discretion in favour of the encroaching owner, Fischer, on the basis that it was reasonable and fair in the circumstances.

---

174 See e.g. *LAWSA* Vol 27 (1) at para 127; *Silberberg & Schoeman Property* p 123.
175 *Christie v Haarhof* (1886) 4 HCG 349 and *Van Boom v Visser* (1904) 21 SC 360, cited in Milton, JRL 'The law of neighbours in South Africa' (1969) *Acta Juridica* 123 at 234.
176 Act 63 of 1975.
177 See ch 7 below.
178 See Pope, A 'Encroachment or Accession?' (2007) 124 *SALJ* 537 at 547.
179 [2003] 1 All SA 698 (O).

> **PAUSE FOR REFLECTION**
>
> **What kind of right does the approved encroacher acquire?**
>
> In *Lombard v Fischer*,[180] the court exercised its discretion to find an acceptable solution to the dispute between the neighbours. The order gave the parties some latitude to find their own solution but, failing this, the encroaching owner (Fischer) was given permission, in effect, to continue to encroach on the property of the neighbour so as to be able to reach his garage.
>
> The court did not indicate what sort of right, if any, was acquired by Fischer as a result of this order. This omission, it is suggested, is material for future owners of the properties concerned. In effect, a court-imposed servitude was created and, therefore, the order should have included a provision requiring registration of the servitude.[181] Application of the subtraction from *dominium* test and the intention to bind successors in title test would show that Fischer's property benefits from use of Lombard's property.[182]
>
> Between the parties, the arrangement per the court order is binding, but what happens when one or other alienates his property? What would the position be when either Lombard or Fischer decides to transfer ownership in his home to a third party? Would that person be bound by the court order to permit use of the road, notwithstanding that this is an encroachment?
>
> From an objective viewpoint, were a wall to be erected, the impression that the access road to Fischer's garage lies on Fischer's property would be even greater than it currently is. This means that anyone interested in acquiring Fischer's property would assume, quite reasonably, that access to the garage is guaranteed. Similarly, a prospective purchaser of Lombard's land might assume that the boundary of that property is the wall.
>
> For future owners, a claim based on acquisitive prescription of the portion of land would be impossible because, quite clearly, these proceedings result in an acknowledgment of Lombard's superior title, which fatally contaminates the necessary *animus* element. A claim based on acquisitive prescription was not possible at the time of these proceedings because only 28 years of possession of use of the road could be accounted for. This prolonged use of the road by Fischer led, however, to a successful claim based on the *mandament van spolie* prior to these proceedings.
>
> In view of the probability that in the foreseeable future, a third party will acquire ownership of either property, the only sensible interpretation of the court order in this matter is that, in effect, a court-imposed servitude has been created in favour of Fischer's property. In other words, Fischer's property is the dominant tenement and Lombard's is the servient tenement.
>
> It would, of course, still be open to the current owners to enter into an agreement whereby the portion of land concerned may be acquired by Fischer and consolidated into his erf, against appropriate compensation for Lombard who would have to co-operate in the transfer. However, the possibility of this arrangement seems remote, given that the previous offer by Fischer to purchase the portion was rejected by Lombard.
>
> If, indeed, a court-imposed servitude has been created, then it should be registered because a failure to do so will lead to even greater confusion and potential for further disputes in the future.

---

180 [2003] 1 All SA 698 (O).
181 See ch 9 below.
182 See ch 3 above.

In *Trustees of the Brian Lackey Trust v Annandale*,[183] the encroacher applied for an order declaring the defendant owner disentitled to removal of the encroachment on his land. The encroachment consisted of half a luxury house that covered 80 per cent of the neighbour's land. Following the pattern of earlier cases, the extent of the encroachment did not affect the assessment of whether removal should be ordered or not. If removal were to be ordered, the potential economic loss to the encroacher would be considerable. This fact seemed to be influential on the court's decision that through exercise of its wide and general discretion, it could award damages to the encroached-upon owner. It thus declared that the defendant owner was 'not entitled to the removal ... of the encroachment'.[184]

> **PAUSE FOR REFLECTION**
>
> **Overlap between encroachment and accession**
>
> The treatment of encroachment in *Trustees of the Brian Lackey Trust v Annandale* is problematic for a couple of reasons. The facts of this case present an unusually stark picture of the fact that more than one set of rules is applicable when encroachment by building occurs. Usually when building on land takes place, the structure that is built on the land accedes to the land; in other words, the rules of accession, specifically *inaedificatio*, govern the situation.[185] By operation of law, ownership rights in the movable things are reallocated to the owner of the land on the basis of the maxim that declares the owner to be owner of all that is attached to the land.
>
> The question that arises thus is how to determine whether and when an encroachment should be treated as an instance of accession or as an encroachment, i.e. an interference with the entitlement of possession.
>
> This judgment follows the usual pattern of earlier South African encroachment cases by assuming that the encroachment rules apply. However, all these cases seem to deal with encroachments that are trivial in extent.
>
> A further problem is that these cases fail to distinguish clearly between unjustified enrichment issues and interferences with proprietary rights. This blurring of issues creates the potential for an arbitrary deprivation of the neighbour's property.
>
> Because of the extent of the encroachment in this case, the omission to recognise the other applicable rules revealed itself. The implications of the omission are significant. Why did the part of the house built on the defendant owner's land not accede to the land? What made it possible for the rules of accession to be overridden by mere exercise of the court's discretion? How are the defendant owner's constitutional rights given due consideration when the only question considered is whether to order removal or whether to compensate the defendant owner?
>
> It is clear that some guidance is needed to determine when the encroachment rules should override the accession rules and vice versa. Current case law provides no guidance on the point. It has been suggested that the extent of the encroachment is integral to a constitutionally sound consideration of the situation where building occurs partly on another's land.[186]

---

183 2004 (3) SA 281 (C).
184 At para 4.
185 See ch 7 below.
186 See Pope, A 'Encroachment or Accession?' (2007) 124 *SALJ* 537–556. See also *Wille's Principles* pp 483–485.

> The extent of the encroachment must guide the court in its decision to regard the interference with possession as an encroachment rather than as an instance of accession. If indeed encroachment rules should apply, then the extent of encroachment must inform the decision whether to support the demand for removal. If the decision is to compensate the encroached-upon owner, then the extent of encroachment informs the measure of compensation to be awarded in light of the requirements of s 25(3) of the Constitution. This approach would maintain the integrity of the principle-based structure of property law. It is further suggested that application of the encroachment rules should be limited to instances where the extent of encroachment is insignificant.

Encroachment by overhanging branches and underground roots. The branches, leaves and roots of trees may encroach on a neighbour's property when the branches overhang the boundary or the roots grow underground across the boundary line. It is the responsibility of the owner of the trees to ensure that they do not interfere with the neighbour's use and enjoyment of her property. The neighbour may acquiesce in the encroachment, e.g. because she benefits from the shade provided, but may not later demand removal of the leaves or fruits that fall onto her property.

If the neighbour objects to the encroachment, then there are various options available depending on the source of the problem. The neighbour can request the owner of the trees to remove the encroaching leaves and branches. Should this not be done within a reasonable time, the neighbour may remove them herself.[187] The cost for removal may be claimed from the owner of the trees. The neighbour may, however, not keep the branches unless the owner of the branches fails to remove them or does not remove them within a reasonable time after demanding their removal.[188] The owner of the trees may be compelled by an interdict to remove the encroaching branches.[189] Furthermore, a prohibitory interdict may prevent future encroachments.

In the case of encroaching roots, a neighbour may remove them herself,[190] but ought also to be entitled to an order compelling the owner of the trees to remove them. In cases where roots encroach perennially and cause damage to structures on the neighbour's land, it may even be possible to obtain an order for removal of the tree(s) concerned.[191]

6.4.2.2 Lateral support

An owner of land is entitled to the lateral support supplied by the land of a neighbour.[192] Although an owner is entitled to make excavations on his land for building or mining purposes, this entitlement is limited by the duty not to excavate to an extent that causes the neighbour's land to subside. Should subsidence occur, the owner who made the excavations is liable for the damage caused to the neighbour's land. It should be noted

---

187 *Malherbe v Ceres Municipality* 1951 (4) SA 510 (A).
188 *Silberberg & Schoeman Property* p 126.
189 *Malherbe v Ceres Municipality* 1951 (4) SA 510 (A).
190 *Bingham v City Council of Johannesburg* 1934 WLD 180; *Smith v Basson* 1979 (1) SA 559 (W).
191 See *Wille's Principles* p 486; *Silberberg & Schoeman Property* pp 120-122.
192 *LAWSA* Vol 27 (1) at para 316.

that this principle is applicable only to land in its natural state.[193] In built-up areas, town planning and building regulations regulate the position.

In alleging a failure to observe the duty of lateral support, the aggrieved neighbour only has to prove that the owner disturbed the lateral support.[194] It is not necessary to prove culpability or wrongfulness. In other words, the owner is subject to strict liability for actual loss, excluding future loss. The neighbour could also apply for an interdict to prevent future non-compliance with the duty of lateral support, i.e. future disturbance of the natural state of the land.

6.4.2.3 Party walls and fences

A party wall is a wall built on the boundary between two properties. The law allocates the ownership rights in the wall to both owners, despite the fact that the wall may have been built by only one of them.[195]

Each owner owns the wall to its midpoint. Shared ownership of the wall has the consequence that both owners share similar rights and duties in respect of the wall.[196] Each may use his part of the wall, up to its midpoint, as he chooses, provided that no unilateral change is effected that may affect the neighbour's half of the wall. However, neither owner may do anything that will damage the wall or affect its stability. Neither owner may demolish the wall, except with the consent of the other.

Fences are regulated by the Fencing Act.[197] This Act is applicable in municipal areas only where the erf is more than three morgen (2,57 hectares) in extent and is one of a number, contiguous to each other, on which farming operations are carried on.

6.4.2.4 Surface water

In principle, a lower-lying property has the duty to receive the natural flow of water.[198] However, an owner may not interfere with the natural flow of water by artificial means or in a manner which may prejudice the lower-lying property. Prejudice would include causing an increased volume or rate of water to flow.

This principle applies largely to rural land, rather than to urban land where the natural topography has been altered considerably by building. An owner of rural land is obliged to show more tolerance for water flowing over her land from higher-lying land. An urban owner has the duty to let rainwater flow into the street, as far as possible.[199]

To determine whether one is dealing with a rural or urban tenement, *Redelinghuys v Bazzoni*[200] set out the following criteria: the extent of the land; the extent of the building development in the catchment and drainage area; and the identifiability of the original topographical qualities of the land.

---

193 See *Wille's Principles* pp 482–483; *Silberberg & Schoeman Property* pp 119–121 for more detail.
194 *Wille's Principles* p 482.
195 *Silberberg & Schoeman Property* pp 129–131.
196 *Silberberg & Schoeman Property* pp 129–131; Van der Merwe *Sakereg* pp 390–394.
197 Act 31 of 1963.
198 See *Wille's Principles* pp 486–487; *Silberberg & Schoeman Property* pp 122–123. See also Van der Merwe, CG (1996) 'Neighbour Law' in Zimmermann, R & Visser, DP *Southern Cross* (Cape Town, Juta) pp 765–773.
199 Van der Walt, AJ & Pienaar, GJ (2006) *Introduction to the Law of Property* 5 ed (Cape Town, Juta) p 109.
200 1976 (1) SA 110 (T).

6.4.2.5 Elimination of dangers, including collapsing buildings

An owner of land has the duty to prevent damage to a neighbour's land, resulting from the omission to exercise proper control within reasonable limits.[201] Examples include the keeping of wild or dangerous animals, or poisonous plants. An owner also has the duty to take reasonable steps to prevent a fire or a plague of locusts from spreading onto the land of a neighbour.[202] If a neighbour is concerned about possible damage to her property because of buildings that might collapse on the adjacent property, the neighbour must protest against the imminent danger before instituting a claim for compensation.[203]

> **COUNTER POINT** **A right to a view?**
>
> A right to a view is not an entitlement or natural attribute of ownership. However, an owner may be prohibited by a servitude, a restrictive condition or a town planning scheme from erecting a building that obstructs the view of the neighbour.[204]
>
> The case of *Paola v Jeeva NO*[205] created the popular but incorrect impression that a right to a view is an entitlement of ownership. This case dealt, rather, with the procedure for approval of building plans, which is discussed under planning law limitations below.

6.5 Public law limitations: Planning law

In chapter 5 and in the course of this chapter, it was demonstrated that the conventional understanding of ownership as extensive, complete and comprehensive (*plena in re potestas*)[206] is neither realistic nor accurate. Yet, it creates perceptions of power that are ingrained in our society. This dichotomy between reality and perception is one of the fundamental contradictions of ownership.

Scholars who have grappled with this contradiction offer varying explanations. According to one view, restrictions on ownership are merely exceptional.[207] According to another, ownership is regarded as so eroded by legislation serving social, economic and political purposes, that it is no longer *plena in re potestas* – an owner can no longer do what she pleases with her property.[208] According to yet another view, all the legislative developments do not impose new limitations because the inherent nature of landownership includes limitations to accommodate social, economic and political purposes.[209]

In the planning law context, this latter view is clearly illustrated. For example, Jane owns a double-storey house in the residential neighbourhood of Parkhume, situated near the university. She wants to convert the house into a commune with twenty rooms for students. She plans to do this by adding a third storey and by converting the garage into four bedrooms.

---

201 *Silberberg & Schoeman Property* pp 131-132.
202 Quathlamba (Pty) Ltd v Ministry of Forestry 1972 (2) SA 783 (N). See also *Silberberg & Schoeman Property* pp 131-132.
203 *Wille's Principles* p 487; *LAWSA* Vol 27(1) at para 320.
204 *Silberberg & Schoeman Property* p 127.
205 2004 (1) SA 396 (SCA). See also Scott, S 'Recent developments in case law regarding neighbour law and its influence on the concept of ownership' (2005) *Stell LR* 351 at 373-376.
206 See ch 5.
207 Van der Merwe *Sakereg* p 172.
208 Lewis, C 'The modern concept of ownership of land' (1985) *Acta Juridica* 241 at 262.
209 Milton, JRL 'Planning and property' (1985) *Acta Juridica* 267-288 at 275-276; Van Wyk, J (1999) *Planning Law – Principles and Procedures of Land-use Management* (Cape Town, Juta) pp 74-75 (hereafter referred to as Van Wyk *Planning Law* in this chapter).

However, her property is subject to the municipality's zoning restrictions regarding height, density, and floor area ratio in terms of the applicable town planning (or zoning) scheme. Moreover, she cannot begin building without first submitting building plans to the local authority, which must approve the planned development. She also has to ascertain whether the envisaged development would have a negative impact on the environment, including her immediate neighbours, in which case she must obtain authorisation from the relevant environmental authority. The neighbours' views must also be canvassed by the local authority.

Planning law and related aspects of environmental law give rise to numerous, and often serious, limitations on ownership. These limitations are imposed mainly by statute, but restrictive conditions[210] also limit what a person can do with her property.

Planning law deals with two fundamentally opposed concepts, namely the sanctity of individual ownership, on the one hand, and the necessity of regulation in the public interest, which may be imposed without regard to ownership, on the other. Regulation includes the goal of sustainable development,[211] as the definition of planning law indicates:

> *Planning law can be defined as that area of the law which provides for the creation of a sustainable spatial planning framework as well as for the management of land use and land development with the purpose of ensuring the health, safety and welfare of society as a whole and taking into account environmental factors.*[212]

In similar vein, the purpose of planning law may be described as:

> *the orderly, harmonious and effective (economically and otherwise) development of the area, 'to promote the health, safety, good order, amenity, convenience and general welfare of such area'.*[213]

Since the early 1990s, the interpretation and understanding of ownership has been required to recognise the social context.[214] This is apparent from legislation[215] and court decisions[216] which look at the larger social policy structure. A good example is *Minister of Public Works and Others v Kyalami Ridge Environmental Association and Others*.[217] This case concerned a clash between the exercise of private rights of ownership and the state's obligation to provide shelter and housing for people who were victims of flooding. Another example, *Boiler Efficiency Services CC v Coalcor (Cape) (Pty) Ltd*,[218] shows that an owner of premises cannot do as it pleases, for instance operate a coal yard on the premises, unless the area is specifically zoned for that type of activity. The zoning requirement is imposed in

---

210 See ch 9.
211 *Director, Mineral Development, Gauteng v Save the Vaal Environment* 1999 (2) SA 709 (SCA) at para 19.
212 Van Wyk *Planning Law* p 5.
213 *Knop v Johannesburg City Council* 1995 (2) SA 1 (A) at 30E-F. See also *BEF (Pty) Ltd v Cape Town Municipality* 1983 (2) SA 387 (C); *Malan v Ardconnel Investments (Pty) Ltd* 1988 (2) SA 12 (A); *Vereeniging City Council v Rhema Bible Church* 1989 (2) SA 142 (T); *Esterhuyse v Jan Jooste Family Trust* 1998 (4) SA 241 (C); *Pick 'n Pay Stores and Others v Teazers Comedy and Revue CC and Others* 2000 (3) SA 645 (WLD); *Hayes and Another v Minister of Finance and Development, Planning and Administration, Western Cape* 2003 (4) SA 598 (C).
214 Van der Walt, AJ 'Developments that may change the institution of private ownership so as to meet the needs of a non-racial society in South Africa' (1990) *Stell LR* 26–48.
215 E.g. the Development Facilitation Act 67 of 1995; Prevention of Illegal Eviction from and Unlawful Occupation of Land Act 19 of 1998; Extension of Security of Tenure Act 62 of 1997.
216 See *Diepsloot Residents' and Landowners' Association v Administrator, Transvaal* 1993 (1) SA 577 (T); *Diepsloot Residents' and Landowners' Association v Administrator, Transvaal* 1993 (3) SA 49 (T); *Diepsloot Residents' and Landowners' Association v Administrator, Transvaal* 1994 (3) SA 336 (A).
217 2001 (3) SA 1151 (CC).
218 1989 (3) SA 460 (C).

the interests of the public because of the risk of, for instance, air pollution that emanates from activities in a coal yard. Similarly, in a third example, a medical doctor was not permitted to use residential property for the sole use as consulting rooms because this would detrimentally affect the residential character of the neighbourhood.[219] Fourth, the Subdivision of Agricultural Land Act[220] protects agriculture as an important economic activity in the national interest by preventing the fragmentation of agricultural land into small non-viable, uneconomic units, and by preventing uncontrolled urban sprawl which would serve to decrease the extent of available agricultural land. This purpose is served by preventing subdivision without the consent of the Minister.[221] In a fifth example, protection of the natural environment in the interests of sustainable nature conservation leads to restrictions on establishment of townships.[222]

A discussion of planning law limitations can only take place in the context of its structure and content, which is the topic of the next section.

6.5.1 Structure of planning law

Planning law functions in a triangular relationship structure. The three angles denote the state authorities, the individual owner of land and third parties in the form of neighbours, the community or society, respectively.

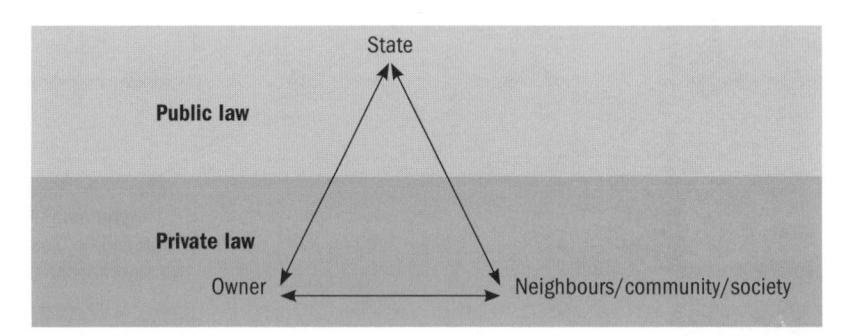

Figure 6.5: Relationship structure for planning law

The court decision in *Knop v Johannesburg City Council*[223] was the first to identify this structure by indicating that there are potentially conflicting interests at stake, namely those of the owner who wants 'to use his property to his own best advantage'; those of neighbouring owners in the area 'who may be adversely affected by the subdivision'; and those of the local authority.[224] The case arose because a developer applied to the Johannesburg City Council (the municipality) for permission to subdivide an erf in terms of the Johannesburg Town Planning Scheme. The Council approved the subdivision into erven with a minimum size of 200 m². Consequently, the developer procured finance, entered into sales of the erven and proceeded with building operations. Some months later, the Council notified the

---

219 *Stadsraad van Vanderbijlpark v Uys* 1989 (3) SA 528 (A).
220 Act 70 of 1970.
221 *Tuckers Land and Development Corporation (Pty) Ltd v Truter* 1984 (2) SA 150 (SWA); *Geue v Van der Lith* 2004 (3) SA 333 (SCA); *Kotzé v Minister van Landbou* 2003 (1) SA 445 (T); *Van der Bijl v Louw* 1974 (2) SA 493 (C); *Sentraalwes Personeel Ondernemings (Edms) Bpk v Wallis* 1978 (3) SA 80 (T); see also *Silberberg & Schoeman Property* pp 107–109.
222 *Corium (Pty) Ltd v Myburgh Park Langebaan (Pty) Ltd* 1995 (3) SA 51 (C).
223 1995 (2) SA 1 (A).
224 Knop at 30 E–F.

developer that approval had been granted in error; the applicable town planning scheme laid down a minimum size of erven of 250 m². This meant that the development as currently planned could not go ahead because the plans would have to be redrawn so that erven were the required size. Consequently, the building process was delayed by 10 months which led to financial loss for the developer.

This case clearly demonstrates that an owner or a developer cannot unilaterally subdivide and develop the property concerned. An application must be made to the relevant municipality, which must decide in accordance with the applicable town planning scheme[225] whether the development can go ahead. It also shows that state authorities as well as private individuals are involved in matters of planning law. This indicates that the scope of planning law requires some discussion.

6.5.2 The scope of planning law

The diagram below demonstrates that planning law contains elements of both public law and private law.

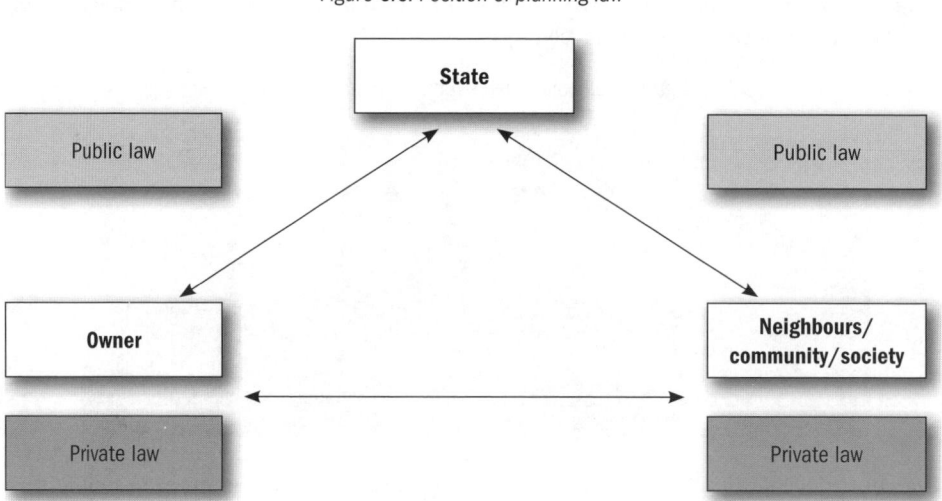

Figure 6.6: Position of planning law

The Constitution provides the overarching legislative framework in terms of which regional planning and development is a concurrent national and provincial legislative competence.[226] Provincial planning is the exclusive legislative domain of the provinces,[227] while municipalities have specific legislative planning functions at local authority level.[228] The public law relationship between the state and the individual includes interpretation of the relevant legislation as well as administrative decision making by state officials, both being central to planning law. In general terms, an individual seeks the assistance of the state to gain permission to do what she wishes with her property.

---

225 A town planning scheme is classified as legislation.
226 In terms of Schedule 4 to the Constitution.
227 In terms of Schedule 5 to the Constitution.
228 Part B of Schedule 4 and Part B of Schedule 5 to the Constitution.

Private law is involved, too, because in planning law, owners of property and developers must take the rights and interests of neighbours and other third parties into account. This is because each owner has similar entitlements and because limitations ought to be evenly distributed so that fairness and reasonableness govern the imposition of further limitations.

6.5.3 Content of planning law

Planning law is concerned, on the one hand, with the determination of land use by means of plans (or forward planning) and, on the other, with management of changes in the use of land (or development control). Essentially, a plan for an area is drawn up. This sets out certain uses for land for a certain period of time, and is also called **forward planning** or **plan creation**. Provision must also be made for changes or alterations to that plan to allow for flexibility. This process must be regulated and is known as **development control** or **land use management**.

The distinction between **land use planning** and **land use management** is important as they form two subdisciplines of planning law. The diagram below depicts the distinction, which is discussed in the subsequent sections.

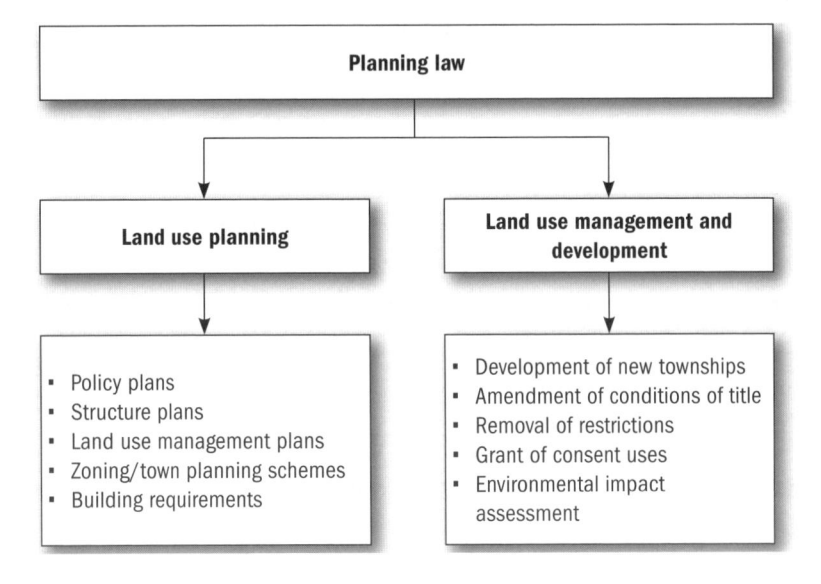

Figure 6.7: Subdisciplines of planning law

```
                        ┌─────────────────┐
                        │  Planning law   │
                        └────────┬────────┘
                    ┌────────────┴────────────┐
                    ▼                         ▼
        ┌───────────────────┐    ┌──────────────────────────┐
        │ Land use planning │    │ Land use management and  │
        │                   │    │       development        │
        └─────────┬─────────┘    └─────────────┬────────────┘
                  ▼                            ▼
    ┌──────────────────────────┐   ┌──────────────────────────────┐
    │ • Policy plans           │   │ • Development of new townships│
    │ • Structure plans        │   │ • Amendment of conditions of title│
    │ • Land use management    │   │ • Removal of restrictions    │
    │   plans                  │   │ • Grant of consent uses      │
    │ • Zoning/town planning   │   │ • Environmental impact       │
    │   schemes                │   │   assessment                 │
    │ • Building requirements  │   │                              │
    └──────────────────────────┘   └──────────────────────────────┘
```

6.5.3.1 Land use planning

Land use planning (i.e. forward planning or plan creation) is the creation of a blueprint for future land use which will support sustainable development. This is done, first, by means of policy plans that contain statements of policy and include land development objectives (LDOs); integrated development plans (IDPs); and spatial development frameworks (SDFs). Second, land use planning is done by means of instruments that indicate specific land uses, such as town planning, zoning or land use schemes.

6.5.3.1.1 Zoning

Policy plans, structure plans, land use management plans and zoning or town planning schemes all determine, identify and allocate specific land uses to specific properties. The principle of zoning underlies these plans. Zoning may be described as the creation of districts within a city where different building regulations are applied (affecting the height, bulk and coverage of buildings), and within which different use activities are permitted or prohibited.[229] A person's exclusive use of her land is compromised by its zoning. In *Pick 'n Pay Stores Ltd v Teazers Comedy and Revue CC*,[230] zoning is described as an aspect of town planning which is primarily concerned with certain restrictions or limitations on ownership and use of land. For this reason, zoning is a limitation or condition restricting the exercise of ownership.[231]

In the constitutional context, zoning is a legitimate deprivation of property.[232] It occurs in terms of law of general application and is justifiable on the basis that it is in the public interest to facilitate good land use planning and management.

Zoning determines whether land can be used for residential, commercial or industrial purposes. Restrictive conditions in deeds of transfer play a similar role since these also determine how the land designated in the title deed may be used, for instance the title deed may contain a clause that states 'the erf shall not be subdivided'.[233]

This determination of the uses to which land may be put is contained in all land use plans, but, most specifically, it refers to the use of individual erven in a town planning or zoning scheme. Such schemes typically contain a schedule that has four columns or sections.

Figure 6.8: Aspects of a town planning scheme

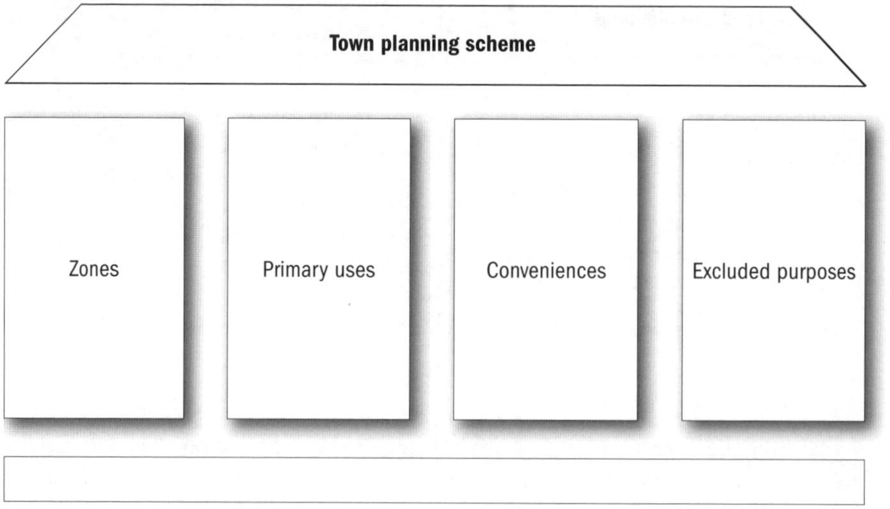

Town planning scheme

| Zones | Primary uses | Conveniences | Excluded purposes |

---

229 Milton, JRL 'Planning and property' (1985) *Acta Juridica* 267-288 at 269. See also the description in *Boiler Efficiency Services CC v Coalcor (Cape) Pty (Ltd)* 1989 (3) SA 460 (C) at 467.
230 2000 (3) SA 645 (WLD).
231 *Pick 'n Pay Stores Ltd v Teazers Comedy and Revue CC* at 656.
232 In terms of s 25(1) of the Constitution.
233 See ch 9.

The first column indicates the various use zones, namely residential, business, etc. The second column indicates the purposes for which buildings may be erected or used. These are the primary uses for each use zone, for instance dwelling houses in the case of a residential use zone and factories in the case of an industrial use zone. The third column contains a list of purposes for which buildings may be erected or used only with consent of the local authority. These are the uses belonging to a specific use zone that are not primary uses, but that are necessary in a specific area because they provide certain conveniences. In the case of a residential use zone, these uses would include places of worship, social halls and sports facilities. Since these uses could cause inconvenience, loss of amenity and possibly economic damage if not regulated carefully, special consent is required from the local authority for their construction. The fourth column indicates the purposes for which buildings may not be erected and used. In a residential use zone, for example, the erection and use of noxious industrial buildings is prohibited.[234]

A zoning scheme also contains provisions that regulate matters such as boundary lines, height restrictions, floor area ratios (FAR), sometimes referred to as bulk and coverage. Boundary lines or building lines are areas at the front, rear and sides of buildings which may not be built upon.[235] They are imposed primarily for privacy between neighbours and safety in the event of fire. They also sometimes provide servitudes of access for service providers regarding storm water disposal, water services, electricity supply lines and so on. It is possible to obtain permission from the local authority to reduce these.

The height of buildings varies from use zone to use zone. In lower density areas, the height will normally be two storeys, whereas in higher density areas, blocks of flats can be up to twenty storeys high. The floor area ratio is the maximum size (bulk) of building permitted on the plot of land. It is expressed as a percentage, in decimal form, of the total size of the plot. Coverage describes the extent of the erf covered by a building expressed as a percentage.

These limitations on the planning of land use are contained in legislation, which is enacted at the various levels of government. The next section provides an outline and brief discussion of the legislation.

National legislation. The Local Government: Municipal Systems Act[236] provides that a municipality must under-take developmentally orientated planning to ensure that the objects and developmental duties of local government are achieved and given effect to, and that, together with other organs of state, the individual rights as set out in the Constitution can be realised over time.[237] The developmental duties of local government specifically include the promotion of social and economic development of the community.

All municipalities must adopt an integrated development plan (IDP),[238] which is the principal strategic planning instrument that guides and informs all planning and development as well as all decisions regarding planning, management and development in

---

234 See *Pretoria City Council v South African Organ Builders (Pty) Ltd* 1953 (3) SA 400 (T) for an indication of how the Schedule sets out these uses.
235 See *Paola v Jeeva* 2004 (1) SA 396 (SCA).
236 Act 32 of 2000.
237 Section 23(1) of the Local Government: Municipal Systems Act, referring to the Constitution: s 152 (objects of local government); s 153 (developmental duties); s 24 (environmental clause); s 25 (property clause); s 26 (housing clause); s 27 (children's rights clause) and s 29 (education clause).
238 Section 25(1) of the Local Government: Municipal Systems Act.

the municipal area.²³⁹ One of the components of an IDP is a spatial development framework (SDF) that must include provision of basic guidelines for a land use management system for a municipality.

A proposed Land Use Management Act²⁴⁰ will repeal older planning legislation. This will include the Development Facilitation Act,²⁴¹ which sets out general principles for land development and land development objectives²⁴² and the Physical Planning Act,²⁴³ which provides for a hierarchy of plans, namely, national development plans, regional development plans, regional structure plans and urban structure plans.

The National Environmental Management Act²⁴⁴ lays down national environmental management principles. A central principle is that 'development must be socially, environmentally and economically sustainable'.²⁴⁵ This Act also provides for the compilation of environmental implementation plans and environmental management plans.²⁴⁶

The Advertising on Roads and Ribbon Development Act²⁴⁷ provides for general plans to regulate the display of advertisements outside certain urban areas at places visible from public roads²⁴⁸ and prohibits the erection of certain structures.²⁴⁹

Provincial legislation. Provincial planning legislation contains procedures to create town planning, zoning or land use schemes. The Ordinances of the erstwhile provinces of the 'old' South Africa²⁵⁰ are still applicable and contain detailed provisions regarding the creation of town planning schemes.²⁵¹ These Ordinances will be repealed as soon as the proposed new provincial legislation is in place. The Northern Cape Planning and Development Act²⁵² is one of the more recent provincial planning statutes. It provides for a Provincial Development and Resource Management Plan as well as for district council plans and land development plans. In areas that were situated outside the so-called 'white areas' of apartheid South Africa, the old town planning legislation is still applicable.²⁵³

6.5.3.2   Land use management

Land use management or land development (also known as development control or changes in the use of land) is the part of planning law that provides flexibility in planning because it deals with the accommodation of changes to land use as set out in the original

---

239 Section 35(1) of the Local Government: Municipal Systems Act.
240 Land Use Management Bill [B27-2008].
241 Act 67 of 1995.
242 In terms of s 3 of Act 67 of 1995. See *Municipality City of Port Elizabeth v Rudman* 1999 (1) SA 665 (SE).
243 Act 125 of 1991.
244 Act 107 of 1998.
245 In terms of s 2(3) of Act 107 of 1998.
246 In Chapter 3 of Act 107 of 1998. See *Director, Mineral Development, Gauteng v Save the Vaal Environment* 1999 (2) SA 709 (SCA); *Minister of Public Works and Others v Kyalami Ridge Environmental Association and Others* 2001 (3) SA 1151 (CC) for the application of these principles.
247 Act 21 of 1940.
248 In terms of s 2. See further *Silberberg & Schoeman Property* pp 109–111.
249 In terms of s 9. See further *Silberberg & Schoeman Property* pp 109–111.
250 Namely, the Town Planning Ordinance 27 of 1949 of Natal; the Townships Ordinance 9 of 1969 of the Orange Free State; the Land Use Planning Ordinance 15 of 1985 of the Cape; and the Town-planning and Townships Ordinance 15 of 1986 of the Transvaal.
251 See Van Wyk *Planning law* pp 173–174.
252 Act 7 of 1998.
253 GN R1888 of 1990, entitled *Land Use and Planning Regulations,* provides for the town planning schemes and structure plans.

plan. However, any change in the use of land must take place in terms of specific procedures, and certain requirements must be met. A variety of procedures is envisaged here, including rezoning (amendment of town planning schemes), the grant of so-called consent uses, and subdivision of land.

The most important procedure is township establishment (also known as subdivision of land or the establishment of land development areas). Many developments may have a detrimental impact on the environment, which means that authorisation must be obtained to undertake such developments. Authorisation is dependent on the outcome of a type of environmental impact assessment. Both national and provincial legislation impose limitations on ownership in particular situations where changes in land use are proposed. Examples are provided below.

National legislation. Sometimes, legislation provides a shortened procedure, for instance for the establishment of a less formal township. This makes it possible for the authorities to meet the urgent need for people to obtain land to settle in a less formal manner. The Less Formal Township Establishment Act[254] provides for a shortened procedure, which is quicker and cheaper than the procedures in the provincial Ordinances.

The National Heritage Resources Act[255] introduces an integrated and interactive system for management of the national heritage. In the land use planning context, this Act protects old buildings by prohibiting demolition of a structure or part of a structure that is older than 60 years without a permit.[256] It also provides that a person who wishes to undertake a certain type of development that will affect a heritage resource, must include an assessment of the impact of the development on the heritage resource in question in his application.[257]

The Removal of Restrictions Act[258] contains procedures whereby certain restrictions and obligations in respect of land can be altered, suspended or removed. Should an owner wish to amend the zoning to change the use of his property, he must follow the prescribed procedures and submit an application to the municipality. The premier of a province must be satisfied that the removal or amendment of a restriction is in the interests of the establishment or development of any township, or in the interests of any area, or in the public interest.[259] The general public has the opportunity to raise objections because notice of the application for rezoning must be published in daily newspapers in the area. Needless to say, the general public must accept the responsibility of being alert to these processes if it wishes to be heard.

---

254 Act 113 of 1991.
255 Act 25 of 1999.
256 Section 34(1)-(2) of the National Heritage Resources Act. See *Provincial Heritage Resources Authority, Eastern Cape v Gordon* 2005 (2) SA 283 (EC). Also *Qualidental Laboratories (Pty) Ltd v Heritage Western Cape and Another* 2008 (3) SA 160 (SCA).
257 Section 38 of the National Heritage Resources Act.
258 Act 84 of 1967. This Act is due to be repealed by the proposed Land Use Management Bill [B27-2008]. Gauteng has its own Removal of Restrictions Act 3 of 1996.
259 Section 2(1)*(a)*. See *Camps Bay Ratepayers and Residents' Association and Others v Minister of Planning, Culture and Administration, Western Cape, and Others* 2001 (4) SA 294 (C). See also in connection with restrictive conditions ch 9.

The Subdivision of Agricultural Land Act[260] restricts the subdivision of agricultural land except with the permission of the relevant Minister.[261] The Act was scheduled to have been repealed in terms of the Subdivision of Agricultural Land Act Repeal Act,[262] which was never put into operation. This led to confusion about whether the former Act was repealed or applicable. These issues were the subject of court applications to the Supreme Court of Appeal and the Constitutional Court. In *Stalwo (Pty) Ltd v Wary Holdings (Pty) Ltd*,[263] the Supreme Court of Appeal declared the Act invalid and permitted subdivision of agricultural land without consent from the Minister for the first time in almost forty years. This decision led to an appeal to the Constitutional Court in *Wary Holdings (Pty) Ltd v Stalwo (Pty) Ltd*,[264] which held that, in the context of the current structure of municipalities in South Africa, the Act is still applicable.

In terms of the Environmental Impact Assessment Regulations, 2006[265] (regulations in terms of the National Environmental Management Act),[266] authorisation to develop is possible after consideration of a type of environmental impact assessment in circumstances where development might have a detrimental impact on the environment.[267]

The National Building Regulations and Building Standards Act[268] promotes uniformity in the law relating to erection of buildings and prescribes building standards. One of its most important provisions is that prior approval of the local authority concerned is required for any building in respect of which plans and specifications are to be drawn in terms of the Act.[269] Whether approval will be granted depends on various considerations, including whether the building to be erected will derogate from the value of the adjoining or neighbouring properties.[270]

In *Paola v Jeeva*,[271] the respondents were trustees of a trust which sought approval of building plans for alterations to a property, situated lower down and in front of the appellant's property. The alterations envisaged would have substantially impaired the appellant's current 180 degree view over Durban and its surroundings. An estate agent and a valuer testified that the building to be erected on the trust property would significantly diminish the market value of the appellant's property. The court held that once it was clear that the execution of building plans would significantly diminish the value of the adjoining property, then the relevant section of the National Building Regulations and Building Standards Act precluded approval of the building plans.

Provincial legislation. The procedures regulating establishment of townships (in the Western Cape, this is known as subdivision of land) are still as set out in the Ordinances of

---

260 Act 70 of 1970.
261 Section 3 of the Act prohibits subdivision of agricultural land or the acquisition of an undivided share in agricultural land without consent from the Minister of Agriculture and Land Affairs. See also West, A 'Consent or no consent? The Subdivision of the Agricultural Land Act 70 of 1970' (Feb 2003) *De Rebus* 59.
262 Act 64 of 1998.
263 2008 (1) SA 654 (SCA).
264 2009 (1) SA 337 (CC).
265 The procedure is set out in Government Notice No R385, Government Notice No R386 and Government Notice No R387, published on 21 April 2006 in *Government Gazette* 28753.
266 Act 107 of 1998.
267 See e.g. *Silvermine Valley Coalition v Sybrand van der Spuy Boerderye and Others* 2002 (1) SA 478 (C).
268 Act 103 of 1977.
269 Section 4 of the National Building Regulations and Building Standards Act.
270 Section 7(1)*(b)*(ii)(aa)(ccc) of the National Building Regulations and Building Standards Act.
271 2004 (1) SA 396 (SCA).

the erstwhile four provinces of pre-1994 South Africa.[272] An exception is the Northern Cape where the Northern Cape Planning and Development Act[273] is applicable. In areas that were situated outside the so-called 'white areas' of apartheid South Africa, specific old township establishment legislation is still applicable.[274]

Rezoning (otherwise known as the amendment of a town planning scheme or a departure) is also regulated by the Ordinances.[275] The procedure is similar to that set out in the Removal of Restrictions Act.[276] A decision to rezone land from, for instance a lower density residential to a higher density residential use, requires an examination of the factual need and desirability of the required density amendment. In *Hayes and Another v Minister of Finance and Development Planning, Western Cape, and Others*,[277] the test for desirability was described as a positive advantage which will be served by granting the application.

> **PAUSE FOR REFLECTION**
>
> **Overlap effect of simultaneous applications for rezoning and environmental clearance**
>
> It often happens that simultaneous applications are made to rezone property as well as to obtain authorisation in terms of environmental legislation to develop the property concerned. This can lead to conflicting decisions by the different authorities.
>
> A leading decision on this point is *Fuel Retailers Association of Southern Africa v Director-General Environmental Management, Department of Agriculture, Conservation and Environment, Mpumalanga Province and Others*.[278] At issue in this case was the nature and scope of the obligations of environmental authorities regarding decisions that may have a substantial detrimental impact on the environment. The applicant was an organisation representing the interests of fuel retailers. The respondents were the various environmental authorities involved in granting authorisation to build a petrol filling station, the Mbombela local municipality (which granted the rezoning application), Lowveld Motors (Pty) Ltd and the trustees of a trust, which had been granted the rezoning application and authorisation to build the filling station. The applicant applied for a decision to authorise the construction of a petrol station to be reviewed and set aside. The Constitutional Court found that the authorities had failed to apply their minds[279] to the socio-economic impact of the filling station and ordered that the decision be set aside. An environmental authority, therefore, considers whether a development is environmentally justified. When considering whether to grant a rezoning application for the same development, a local authority would consider the need and desirability of the development from a town planning perspective.

---

272 Town Planning Ordinance 27 of 1949 (N); the Townships Ordinance 9 of 1969 (OFS); the Land Use Planning Ordinance 15 of 1985 (C); and the Town-planning and Townships Ordinance 15 of 1986 (T).
273 Act 7 of 1998.
274 Proclamation R293 of 1962 entitled *Regulations for the Administration and Control of Townships in Black Areas* contains township establishment measures; Proc R1897 of 1986 entitled *Regulations Relating to Township Establishment and Land Use* provides for the establishment of townships; GN R1886 of 1990, promulgated in terms of the Black Administration Act 38 of 1927, entitled *Township Development Regulations for Towns* provides for procedures pertaining to township establishment.
275 Van Wyk *Planning Law* pp 203-205.
276 Act 84 of 1967. See above p 153.
277 2003 (4) SA 598 (C).
278 2007 (6) SA 4 (CC).
279 Section 24 of the Constitution and the National Environmental Management Act 107 of 1998 provide that the need for development must be determined by its impact on the environment, sustainable development as well as social and economic interests.

6.5.4 Enforcement of planning measures

All parties in a planning law relationship – owners, neighbours (or other third parties) and the state – must abide by the planning provisions applicable to them. Failure to do so has consequences. This was illustrated in *Hayes and Another v Minister of Finance and Development, Planning and Administration, Western Cape and Others*.[280] A developer wanted to build a four-storey block of flats in a residential area of Stellenbosch. In terms of the Stellenbosch Zoning Scheme Regulations, the area is zoned as 'general residential', which permits only single-storey residential buildings. The developer nevertheless began to build the four-storey block of flats, contrary to the provisions of the zoning scheme.

To prevent continuation of a development, such as in the example above, the owner of a neighbouring erf (or another third party) affected by the development has two possible remedies. The owner can apply for an interdict[281] to prevent the developer from proceeding. This remedy falls within the private law sphere of planning law because the action is between an owner and a neighbour or third party. Alternatively, the owner can apply for a *mandamus*[282] against the municipality to compel it to enforce the zoning scheme. This remedy falls within the public law sphere (administrative law) of planning law because the owner wants to force the municipality to act in a certain way in accordance with its statutory obligations. In other words, the municipality must apply the zoning scheme rules to prevent the developer from continuing with the unlawful building.

Most planning legislation imposes on the authority concerned the duty to enforce the planning provisions it contains. For example, the Local Government: Municipal Systems Act[283] provides that an integrated development plan binds both the municipality and all other persons.[284] The Ordinances of the erstwhile provinces provide that the municipality must observe and enforce the town planning scheme.[285] It is an offence to contravene the provisions of a town planning scheme.

6.6 Concluding remarks

This chapter has demonstrated by way of a few examples, the extent to which the notion of ownership is restricted in the law. The idea that ownership entails rights as well as responsibilities is one ever more frequently articulated in scholarship and by the judiciary. The implications of this view in the South African setting are only beginning to emerge now, as cases such as *Modderklip* and *Mkontwana* illustrate.[286] As the constitutional jurisprudence on property protection and regulation grows, this idea is likely to be developed further.

---

280 2003 (4) SA 598 (C).
281 The requirements for an interdict are set out in ch 4.
282 A *mandamus* is a mandatory interdict against the state.
283 Act 32 of 2000.
284 Section 35(1)*(b)–(c)* of the Local Government: Municipal Systems Act.
285 E.g. Town Planning Ordinance 27 of 1949 (N) s 31(2); the Land Use Planning Ordinance 15 of 1985 (C) s 39(1)–(2); and the Town-planning and Townships Ordinance 15 of 1986 (T) s 40(1). See also *City of Tshwane Metropolitan Municipality v Grobler* 2005 (6) SA 61 (T).
286 See pp 120–128 above.

This does not mean, however, that the notion of ownership as a collection of rights and **responsibilities** is novel. It has been evident in many other jurisdictions for quite some time. Even in South African law, the idea is embedded, although it might be worded differently in different contexts. For instance, this chapter demonstrated that in the context of neighbour law, ownership denotes and requires reciprocal respect for rights. In the context of planning law, the sanctity of individual ownership is constantly challenged by the need to regulate property in the public interest. These ideas find resonance in the constitutional approach to the entrenchment of property, which confirms that when it comes to property, the basic principle of 'live and let live' is indeed about the acceptance of restrictions on basic freedoms.

This does not mean, however, that an owner's responsibility towards society leaves him without recourse to protect his ownership entitlements. In fact, the owner has strong protection in the law, even if this protection cannot confirm that ownership generally conveys absolute powers of exclusion under all circumstances.

Chapter 7

Acquisition of ownership

'... the law likes [the creation and transfer of interests in property] to be done unambiguously, deliberately and publicly.'
Elizabeth Cooke (2006) *Land Law* p 63

7.1	**Introduction**	**160**
7.2	**Original acquisition of ownership**	**161**
7.2.1	Appropriation *(occupatio)*	163
7.2.2	Accession *(accessio)*	164
7.2.2.1	General requirements	165
7.2.2.2	Accession of movable property to other movable property	165
7.2.2.3	Accession of movables to immovable property	167
7.2.2.4	Accession of immovable property to immovable property	175
7.2.3	Acquisition of fruits *(separatio* and *perceptio)*	175
7.2.4	Manufacture *(specificatio)*	176
7.2.5	Mingling and mixing *(confusio et commixtio)*	178
7.2.6	Acquisitive prescription	179
7.2.6.1	The requirement of possession	181
7.2.6.2	The temporal requirement: Uninterrupted 30-year period	182
7.2.7	Expropriation	188
7.3	**Derivative acquisition of ownership**	**188**
7.3.1	Transfer of ownership as an abstract juristic act	190
7.3.2	Requirements for a valid transfer of ownership	191
7.3.2.1	The real agreement (subjective mental element)	192
7.3.2.2	Sale of movables and transfer of ownership	194
7.3.2.3	Delivery or registration (objective physical element)	197
7.3.3	Delivery	197
7.3.3.1	*Clavium traditio* (symbolic delivery)	201
7.3.3.2	*Traditio longa manu* (delivery with the long hand)	201
7.3.3.3	*Constitutum possessorium*	203
7.3.3.4	*Traditio brevi manu* (delivery with the short hand)	204
7.3.3.5	Attornment	206
7.3.4	Transfer of immovable property – registration	210
7.3.4.1	Publicity and certainty	210
7.3.4.2	Effect of registration	211
7.4	**Concluding remarks**	**213**

7.1 Introduction

When and how ownership is acquired depends, in the first instance, on whether the property concerned is movable or immovable. This is because different rules govern acquisition of ownership of movable and immovable property. Second, it must be established whether ownership is being **transferred** from one person to another (by far the more common occurrence) or not because derivative acquisition of ownership is treated differently from original acquisition of ownership. In this chapter, both transfer of ownership and original acquisition of ownership are discussed.

The identifying characteristic for **transfer** of ownership is that one person derives ownership from another person.[1] This implies that a bilateral transaction must occur, i.e. at least two persons are involved when **derivative** acquisition of property is at stake. Furthermore, the *nemo plus iuris* rule[2] as well as the existence of registered real rights[3] play an important role in determining whether ownership can be transferred and, if so, whether ownership entitlements are limited for the successor in title.

Under the rules of **original** acquisition of ownership, there is no derivation of ownership.[4] The acquirer gains ownership by operation of law; at the same time, any previously existing ownership rights are terminated. By acknowledging original acquisition of ownership, the law achieves consonance between the factual and legal situations.

It is possible also to acquire a limited real right by original acquisition. For instance, Nelson has allowed his cattle to graze on the land of his neighbour, Werner, for 30 years, as if by right (i.e. without permission from Werner). By operation of law, Nelson's use of the pasture could become an **entitlement** to use the pasture, i.e. a right of grazing. The mechanism that turns Nelson's long usage of the pasture into an entitlement is acquisitive prescription, one of the modes of original acquisition. Whether his use of Werner's land has become an entitlement depends on an objective and careful assessment of the factual scenario in light of the requirements for acquisitive prescription.

The mechanisms or modes of original acquisition of ownership comprise factors that permit objective assessment of the specific factual situation to determine whether the requirements are fulfilled and whether a reallocation of rights has thus occurred. The will or intention of the previous owner of the property concerned is not relevant, unlike the situation when transfer of ownership occurs. This is the important and fundamental distinction between original and derivative acquisition of ownership.[5]

PAUSE FOR REFLECTION	Essential for acquisition of ownership
	For both derivative and original acquisition of ownership, there must always be a particular point in time when one can say, **Now** I am owner of the property', or when others can ascertain that from **this** point forward, for instance, Xolisa is the owner of the property. This underlying principle supports the **principle of publicity** which is fundamental to the

---

1 *Silberberg & Schoeman Property* p 137; *Wille's Principles* p 519; Carey Miller, DL & Pope, A '(2004) Acquisition of ownership' in Zimmermann, R, Visser, D & Reid, K (eds) *Mixed Legal Systems in Comparative Perspective: Property and Obligations in Scotland and South Africa* (Cape Town, Juta) p 675.
2 See ch 5 above.
3 See chs 3 above and 9 below.
4 *Silberberg & Schoeman Property* p 137; *Wille's Principles* p 488.
5 *Wille's Principles* p 488; *Silberberg & Schoeman Property* pp 71-73 .

law of property.⁶ The necessary requirements must coincide to allow a particular point in time to serve as the beginning point of Xolisa's ownership. This creates certainty both in law and in the social context.

In addition, determining whether acquisition of ownership has been achieved requires an objective determination of the factual evidence in light of the requirements for the particular mode. Each mode is applicable in particular circumstances only, depending on the nature of the property as well as what happens to it at the time. The modes are not interchangeable. A particular set of facts may appear to indicate the possibility of more than one mode. Careful analysis of the facts in light of the legal framework should reveal, however, that only one mode of acquisition of ownership is actually applicable.

7.2 Original acquisition of ownership

The rules for original acquisition of ownership utilise elements of possession, i.e. physical control *(corpus)* and the appropriate mental attitude *(animus)*, as important indicators of whether original acquisition of ownership has occurred.[7] In each case, the acquirer gains ownership by operation of law; at the same time, any previously existing ownership rights are terminated. In other words, a unilateral act occurs[8] when specific, objectively determined factors concur (at a particular point in time) and, upon which, by operation of law, ownership rights are reallocated. Importantly, the will or intention of the previous owner is not relevant to the determination of whether reallocation has occurred.

These rules respond to one of the underlying tensions of property law: that between the interests of the individual, on the one hand, and those of third parties (the public), on the other. The tension is expressed by the principle of publicity. The rules work to limit the effect of the subjective intention of the individual by ensuring sufficient publicity at the time of reallocation of ownership rights.[9]

Another tension relevant to original acquisition of ownership is that between principle and policy. Sometimes, for policy reasons, principles may be overridden to achieve a pragmatic outcome. However, the choice to override principle in favour of a pragmatic outcome should be exercised cautiously and only with a well-reasoned justification. A failure to provide a well-reasoned justification can lead to unruly and ad hoc variations of principle which, in turn, could result in disorder and uncertainty for property and ownership. This would not be good for an economy in which property and ownership are mainstays.

Over time, the various rules of original acquisition of ownership have distilled into specific legally recognised categories or modes. From a practical point of view, the most important modes are appropriation *(occupatio)*, accession *(accessio)*, manufacture *(specificatio)*, mingling or mixing *(confusio* or *commixtio)* and acquisitive prescription (long possession).[10] Which mode applies in the particular circumstances depends on the prevailing factual circumstances, the nature of the things concerned and what has happened to them, e.g. whether they have been joined, mingled or mixed. The various modes are discussed below, with reference to the elements flagged.

---

6 Van der Merwe *Sakereg* p 216.
7 See ch 4 above for a detailed discussion of the elements of *corpus* and *animus*.
8 *Wille's Principles* p 488; Silberberg & Schoeman *Property* p 137.
9 Carey Miller, DL & Pope, A (2004) 'Acquisition of ownership' in Zimmermann, R, Visser, D & Reid, K (eds) *Mixed Legal Systems in Comparative Perspective: Property and Obligations in Scotland and South Africa* (Cape Town, Juta) p 675.
10 For discussion of other modes such as treasure trove, see *Wille's Principles* p 492.

Table 7.1: Recognised modes of original acquisition

	Circumstances	Requirements: Corpus	Requirements: Animus	Additional considerations	Consequences: Ownership	Consequences: Remedies (if any)
Occupatio	Currently unowned corporeal thing (not lost)	Nature of thing significant	Animus domini	Applicable legislation?	Appropriator acquires ownership	
Accessio	Join between corporeal things belonging to different owners	Sufficient join indicating permanence	Indefinite join intended – inferred	Identify principal and accessory	Owner of principal owns whole; accessory loses legal identity	Previous owner of accessory might have claim against owner of principal
Accession of movables	Join between corporeal movable things	Sufficient join indicating permanence	Indefinite join intended – inferred	Identify principal using guidelines from *Khan*	Owner of principal owns whole	Previous owner of accessory might have claim against owner of principal
Accession of movable to immovable	Join between corporeal movable and immovable things	Sufficient join indicating permanence; guidelines from *Macdonald*	Indefinite join intended – inferred or subjective?	Land always principal	Landowner owns whole	Previous owner of accessory might have claim against landowner
Accession of immovables	Addition to immovable by action of water	Sudden increase or slow imperceptible increase	Inferred from settled state of increased land	Fixed land is principal	Owner of fixed land owns increase	Previous owner of (especially suddenly) lost land may have claim against landowner
Specificatio	Use of things to produce new thing; no consent; things owned by different people	Use irretrievably changes form, nature, chemistry etc. of things	New product intended	Role of good faith?	Maker acquires ownership	Previous owner has claim against maker
Confusio/ Commixtio	Things of more or less equal value combined; usually fungible things	Liquids inseparable; solids indeterminable	Inferred		Owners of mingled liquids = co-owners; owners of mixed solids remain individual owners	Co-owners must obtain legal separation order before claiming portion; owners of solids may vindicate equivalent pro rata share of mix
Prescription	Long use of movable or immovable property as if owner	Possession for 30 years	Animus domini	Prescription Act	Possessor acquires ownership	Previous owner may have claim against prescriptive owner

7.2.1 Appropriation *(occupatio)*

The mode of appropriation applies to currently unowned property that is capable of private ownership (i.e. *res nullius*).[11] Two categories of property fall under this classification heading, namely *res nullius* proper,[12] which is property that has never been owned and includes wild animals,[13] products of the sea and seashore;[14] and *res derelictae*, which is property that was **previously** owned but subsequently abandoned. Both categories are open to appropriation. The important distinction between *res derelictae* and *res deperditae* (lost things) should be noted: the latter category is not *res nullius* and is not open to appropriation.[15] A finder of lost property can acquire ownership only by acquisitive prescription.[16]

Whether particular property is lost or abandoned must be determined from factual evidence. Abandonment might be inferred from factual circumstances that support the inference that the owner has given up physical control with the intention to relinquish ownership. In some cases, it is presumed that there is no abandonment until proof of the contrary exists, such as a wreck, or flotsam and jetsam.[17] Wreck includes property from foundered ships and downed aircraft.[18]

The requirements for appropriation include both a *corpus* and an *animus* element. Appropriation occurs when there is a unilateral taking of possession by the acquirer.[19] Both elements of possession must be satisfied, i.e. there must be sufficient and effective physical control and the appropriate mental attitude, which in this case is the intention to be owner *(animus domini)*. Note that it is insufficient to intend to **become** owner. The required intention is that of the owner.

The nature of the property affects the extent of the required physical control element. For example, to bring a fish under physical control would be different from what is required when dealing with an antelope. The relevant legal question in each case would be whether there is **sufficient and effective** physical control.[20] The wild creature or animal must be captured and not just wounded. In other words, it must be brought under the control of the person with the *animus domini*. As was indicated above, satisfaction of the requirements must coincide so that the acquirer can reasonably be inferred to be the owner at a particular point in time.

Who owns the catch when the capture is unlawful? Application of the above principles raises the issue of unlawful capture and its effect on acquisition of ownership. For example, if fish or lobsters are caught out of season (i.e. unlawfully), do they nevertheless become the property of the capturer? Under the common law, ownership was not acquired by the unlawful capturer,[21] but *S v Frost, S v Noah*[22] held that the construction of the applicable legislation may affect whether ownership is acquired. In other words, if specific legislation

---

11 See *Wille's Principles* pp 489–492; *Silberberg & Schoeman Property* pp 137–147 for detailed discussion.
12 For more detail, see ch 2 above.
13 Subject to the Game Theft Act 105 of 1991.
14 Subject to the Marine Living Resources Act 18 of 1998; Sea-shore Act 21 of 1935; Cape Town Foreshore Act 26 of 1950.
15 See ch 2 above.
16 See pp 179*ff* below.
17 *Wille's Principles* p 491.
18 The Wreck and Salvage Act 94 of 1996 is the governing legislation. The National Heritage Resources Act 25 of 1999 is relevant also where property (including wreck) is more than 60 years old.
19 *Wille's Principles* p 489; *Silberberg & Schoeman Property* p 137.
20 Van der Merwe *Sakereg* p 219.
21 *Dunn v Bowyer* 1926 NPD 516.
22 1974 (3) SA 466 (C).

applies to the situation, the legislation has to be interpreted to ascertain what the intention of the legislature was regarding acquisition of ownership. This implies that applicable legislation can have a significant impact on the manner in which the legal principles are applied to particular kinds of property.

The Game Theft Act[23] governs ownership of game, defined broadly in the Act to include animals (and their parts) that are held for commercial or hunting purposes. Wild animals or creatures not listed in the Act are not game for purposes of the Act. Importantly, the Act alters the common law rule that wild animals regain *res nullius* status when they escape from captivity.[24] The Act stipulates that ownership of game that escapes from captivity (as described in the Act), is retained and the owner can vindicate the escaped animals. This means that the finder-capturer of an escaped animal classed as game in terms of the Act, cannot acquire ownership by appropriation. The Act also prohibits the acquisition of ownership of game by anyone who takes possession of the game in contravention of the Act or without permission of the owner or person in control.

Whether land is open to acquisition by appropriation would depend on whether the land is *res nullius* by becoming *res derelictae*. It would be most unusual in modern South Africa for this to occur because all unallocated land within the territorial border vests in the state. Furthermore, the prevailing view is that land cannot be *res nullius*; rather, upon abandonment by the owner, it accrues to the state.[25]

7.2.2 Accession *(accessio)*

Accession concerns the joining of items of property that belong to different people.[26] Literally, the term means an addition to or an increase of a thing. Accession occurs when two or more separate entities (things) are joined by natural or artificial means, and form another composite thing or entity. The legal consequence is that the owner of the principal component of the composite entity automatically becomes owner of the accessory (joined thing) by operation of law. This is because the accessory loses its **legal** identity upon accession, which implies that ownership of this thing as a separate entity is terminated. The (previous) owner of the accessory hence loses ownership, but may claim compensation.[27]

It is important to understand that the **factual** identity of the joined thing may survive, but this has little bearing on whether the join has caused accession. For example, a toilet bowl installed in a bathroom is quite plainly still a toilet bowl: its factual identity survives. Yet, it forms part of the fabric of the building: its separate legal identity is lost.

Accession depends on objectivity because (subjective) agreement between parties should not easily be permitted to contradict reality,[28] i.e. what is obvious to a third party observer. For example, an agreement to reserve ownership in bags of cement that have already been mixed and sandwiched between bricks to build a house, cannot reverse the changed legal status of the cement, namely that it has acceded to the land.[29] To the observer, the outward appearance of the cement ought to match its legal status.

---

23 Act 105 of 1991.
24 Van der Merwe *Sakereg* p 218.
25 *Wille's Principles* p 492; *Silberberg & Schoeman Property* p 141.
26 See *Wille's Principles* pp 493–505; *Silberberg & Schoeman Property* pp 141–156 for more detailed discussion.
27 *Wille's Principles* p 493; *Silberberg & Schoeman Property* p 154.
28 *Unimark Distributors (Pty) Ltd v Erf 94 Silvertondale (Pty) Ltd* 1999 (2) SA 986 (T) at 1001H.
29 *Melcorp SA v Joint Municipal Pension Fund (Transvaal)* 1980 (2) SA 214 (W) at 223 D-E; *Silberberg & Schoeman Property* p 147.

Different sets of rules govern accession between two or more movable things or between movable and immovable property. Moreover, where movables join immovable property, the **kind** of movable involved triggers different sets of rules: accession of plants or seeds to land is treated differently from accession of built structures to land. It is also possible that immovable property may be joined to other immovable property, which triggers yet other rules. It is worth remembering that these 'specific context' rules all derive from the general principles outlined above. In each case, the rules have crystallised over time and have come to be regarded as specific to the particular circumstances.

7.2.2.1 General requirements

The first point to note is whether the joined things are movable, immovable or a combination because this difference triggers use of the crystallised rules. Generally, accession applies only to corporeal things, but some incorporeals can increase naturally, such as interest earned on an investment account. It is necessary to distinguish between cases that involve a join between two or more movables, between movables and land, and between different immovables. The discussion below is structured according to this distinction.

Second, the focus is on whether there is an increase in, an addition to or a join between two or more things to form a composite thing. The join may be natural or artificial (industrial), but must be permanent and by sufficient means. It must be obvious that the two things have not been brought together temporarily. For example, storing a bicycle frame by hanging it on a hook in the garage does not lead to the inference that the bicycle is part of the fabric of the house. However, a bicycle frame welded into a sculptured work of art is quite obviously part of the sculpture.[30] The issue of permanence is particularly well indicated by the cases involving attachment of built structures to land, discussed in more detail below.[31]

It must be possible to identify a principal thing and an accessory thing. If this is not possible, then accession is not the appropriate mode. When accession involves immovable property, land is always the principal thing.[32] When two or more items of movable property are united, then determining which part is the principal may present difficulties. A factual investigation is needed, guided by the principles as outlined in *Khan v Minister of Law and Order*.[33]

7.2.2.2 Accession of movable property to other movable property

The circumstances for this form of accession always involve industrial or human intervention to bring about the join. The challenge is to determine which of the things can be labelled the principal thing, and which the accessory. As indicated above, this question is crucial in the determination of whether accession has occurred: the owner of the principal thing becomes owner of the joined thing.

Pragmatic special rules have evolved to deal with specific instances such as writing on paper, painting on canvas or other surface, as well as welding of two metals.[34] Beyond these instances, the courts rely on judicially sanctioned tests or criteria to guide the decision as to which of the movables must be seen as the principal thing.

---

30 See below regarding legal consequence of welding.
31 See pp 138*ff* below.
32 *Wille's Principles* p 498; *Silberberg & Schoeman Property* p 147.
33 1991 (3) SA 439 (T). See p 37 above.
34 *Wille's Principles* p 493; *Silberberg & Schoeman Property* pp 154–155.

As regards the pragmatic rules, first, the author of the writing acquires ownership of the written-upon paper but owes paper of the same type and quality to the previous owner. Second, welding involves joining two pieces of metal by forging, fusing or application of pressure. A legally permanent bond is created. Soldering, however, is achieved by the application of an alloy of easily fusible metals to join two pieces of metal. The join is easily separable and does not lead to a legally permanent bond.[35] An artist who paints on another's surface may acquire ownership of that surface, depending on the nature of the surface, its value and also the value of the painting.

> **PAUSE FOR REFLECTION**
>
> **Art and accession**
>
> Consider the following examples: When Rory, who is artistic, paints a work of art on Joe's canvas, it is probable that Rory acquires ownership of that canvas, especially if it is fungible by nature. If Rory is not artistic and merely makes paint scribbles on Joe's canvas, then perhaps the value of the canvas outweighs the value of the painting, allocating ownership of the combination of paint and canvas to Joe. However, when Rory paints on the wall of Joe's house, Joe acquires ownership of the painting because land is always the principal thing. When Rory paints on Joe's car, common sense indicates that Joe owns the combination of paint and car. But what if Rory is the new Picasso?[36] Then, in the absence of an agreement between the parties, an argument for manufacture *(specificatio)*[37] would be strengthened on the basis that the decorated car has become a (new) work of art. The point is that while the value of the various components can guide the determination of whether ownership rights should be reallocated, there is no hard and fast rule, especially where works of art are concerned.

Beyond these clearly delineated instances of accession, a reallocation of ownership rights must be determined with reference to the requirements set for attachment of two or more movables. First, the join or attachment must not give rise to manufacture *(specificatio)*.[38] A principal and accessory must be identifiable, failing which the appropriate mode might be mingling or mixing.[39] Further, the join must be permanent, i.e. not easily separable.

If the join is easily separable without great cost or effort, and without decreasing the value of either component, then it cannot be regarded as permanent, which means that the join does not effect accession. In this instance, the inference must be that the joined things remain separate entities and that no composite thing is formed. However, the modern tendency to renovate and the availability of enhanced technologies may lead to the erroneous inference that merely because a separation *can* be effected, accession did not occur. The central issue may be described as whether the join leads to the termination of legal identity of one of

---

35 Solder: low-melting alloy, especially one based on lead and tin or (for higher temperatures) on brass or silver, used for joining less fusible metals (p 1893). Weld: join together (metal parts) by heating surfaces to point of melting with blowpipe, electric arc or other means, and uniting them by pressing, hammering etc. (p 1998) *Oxford Dictionary of English* 2 ed Rev 2005 (Oxford, Oxford University Press).
36 Picasso was known for his habit of drawing on walls of restaurants etc. Failure to recognise the artist led to many instances of Picasso's work being cleaned off the walls and thus the destruction of what came to be recognised as artistic genius.
37 See pp 176*ff* below.
38 See pp 176*ff* below.
39 See pp 178*ff* below.

the joined components and hence a reallocation of ownership rights.[40] Whether its factual identity survives and whether in fact it can be removed are only part of the investigation.

Employing different criteria to determine which of the movables in the join is the principal thing may sometimes lead to significantly different results. For instance, Julie, a goldsmith, takes a diamond from her grandmother without permission, and sets it on one of her (Julie's) existing gold rings. Does this mean the ring has acceded to the diamond (on the basis that the stone is the more valuable of the two things)? Or has the diamond acceded to the ring (on the basis that the identity of the thing is a ring, even if adorned with an expensive stone)? Or does it mean that no accession has occurred, but that a completely new thing has been manufactured?

There are no easy answers to these questions. In part, this is because there is no single judicially approved test by which to determine the principal part. One test looks at the value of the things involved on the basis that the more valuable thing should be the principal thing. Alternatively, the bulk or mass of the joined things could be the decisive consideration if it is argued that the bigger or heavier thing should be the principal thing. Or the purpose of the respective things could be decisive; for instance, if one of the things is there merely for the purpose of adornment, it could be assumed that such a thing is accessory. Another way of testing is to ascertain the final identity of the thing: which of the movables in the join gives the final composite thing its identity, its character, form, and function?

The criteria for determining which of the movables in a joinder is the principal thing were considered in *Khan v Minister of Law and Order*.[41] Although the judgment took note of tests based on value, and bulk or mass, it applied the test based on which of the models gave the resultant composite thing (the built-up vehicle) its character, form and function.[42] Although the *Khan* decision does not exclude the other tests to determine the status of the different components of a composite thing, it indicates that a consideration of the final identity of the composite thing must weigh heavily on the decision as to which component is the principal.

7.2.2.3 Accession of movables to immovable property

Human effort is nearly always involved in joining movable things to immovable property. The principle is that what is attached to the land becomes part of the soil as accessory.[43] Two forms of this accession exist, namely planting and sowing, and building.

Planting and sowing. Planting and sowing involve a combination of human effort and natural processes. The maxim, *omne quod implantatur solo cedit,* states that all that is planted in the soil accedes to the soil.[44] This means that the owner of the soil (land) owns the plants. The point in time that accession occurs is when the seeds or plants have taken root and draw nourishment from the soil.[45]

---

40 *Wille's Principles* p 496.
41 1991 (3) SA 439 (T). See p 37 above.
42 *Khan v Minister of Law and Order* 1991 (3) SA 439 (T) at 443.
43 *Wille's Principles* p 496; *Silberberg & Schoeman Property* p 147.
44 *Wille's Principles* pp 496–497; *Silberberg & Schoeman Property* p 146.
45 *Secretary for Lands v Jerome* 1922 AD 103.

Plants, whether newly planted or well established, are sometimes destined to be removed from the soil, such as in the case of a plant nursery.[46] In other words, at the time of attachment, the intention is **not** that they should remain in place indefinitely. In this instance, the plants remain movable; in other words, accession does not occur, notwithstanding that the plants have taken root. By its very nature, the business of a plant nursery requires the plants to be movable. In other cases, such as when land is leased, the terms of the lease may indicate that the lessee who has planted is permitted to remove the rooted plants at the termination of the lease, provided the land is returned to the owner in a restored state.[47]

Where planting takes place in ignorance of the fact that the land belongs to another, the planter can claim compensation for the plants that have acceded as well as for the costs of labour. However, where deliberate planting takes place on another's land in the absence of an agreement, no compensation would be due.[48]

The difference in outcome between planting deliberately or in ignorance has led some commentators[49] to infer a requirement of good faith. But good faith is irrelevant for original acquisition of ownership. The question is always whether the specified factors, assessed objectively, indicate that a reallocation of rights must be confirmed or denied. Good faith is, however, relevant for determining matters of compensation. For example, a justification for not compensating a *mala fide* planter might be that she is in effect deliberately trespassing.

One can thus infer that the general rule is that rooted plants are part of the soil and belong automatically to the owner of the land, but that a different outcome is possible in accordance with the factual circumstances and legal tradition. The factual circumstances would include whether a special legal relationship, such as a lease, exists between the owner of the land and the owner of the (unrooted) plants.[50]

Building (inaedificatio). The legal consequences of building *(inaedificatio)* flow from the application of the Roman maxims, *superficies solo cedit* and *omne quod inaedificatio solo cedit,* which indicate that everything built on or attached to the land forms part of the land as accessory, the principal being the land.[51] The owner of the land therefore owns also that which is attached to the land, or to a building on the land. Whether building has led to accession is a question of fact.[52] In other words, the facts must be scrutinised in terms of the legal framework to decide whether accession has occurred.

Underlying principles are publicity and protection of ownership. The publicity principle is served by the requirement of an objective assessment of the reasonable expectation of an outsider who views the building works. Protection of ownership is visible in the reluctance to assume the occurrence of accession: the decision to confirm or deny accession is a question of fact in the circumstances.[53]

---

46   *Gore NO v Parvatas (Pty) Ltd* 1992 (3) SA 363 (C) at 367.
47   *Wille's Principles* p 497; *Silberberg & Schoeman Property* p 146.
48   *Wille's Principles* pp 496–497; *Silberberg & Schoeman Property* pp 146–147 for more detailed discussion.
49   *Wille's Principles* p 497.
50   *Gore NO v Parvatas (Pty) Ltd* 1992 (3) SA 363 (C) at 367.
51   *Wille's Principles* p 498; *Silberberg & Schoeman Property* p 147.
52   *Macdonald Ltd v Radin NO and the Potchefstroom Dairies and Industries Co Ltd* 1915 AD 454; see also *Wille's Principles* pp 498–505; *Silberberg & Schoeman Property* pp 147–154 for more detailed discussion.
53   *Macdonald Ltd v Radin NO and the Potchefstroom Dairies and Industries Co Ltd* 1915 AD 454 at 466.

For accession to occur, the attachment must indicate permanency. Hence the join cannot merely be for temporary use. For a finding of permanency, the facts must show, on a balance of probabilities, that specified objectively determined factors are satisfied and coincide at a particular time. In the case of building, these factors are the nature and purpose of the movable, the manner and degree of its attachment and the intention at the time of the attachment.[54]

Understanding the scope and interplay of the factors is crucial for a well-reasoned decision as to the occurrence of accession or not. Thus, the movable, by its nature and purpose, must be capable of attachment and destined to serve the land. Building materials such as bricks and mortar have this nature and purpose, but a spade does not, even though it is used to mix the mortar.

In similar vein, the consideration of the manner and degree of attachment entails that one asks whether the movable thing can be removed without damage or a feat of engineering.[55] Here the bricks and mortar example used above is equally illustrative: the manner and degree in which the joining occurs results in the formation of a unity. Moreover, unlike in the case of accession of movable to movable, the join need not be artificial, but may result from the mere weight of the movable pressing down on the soil.[56]

The intention with which the attachment is made is a relevant but problematic factor. The intention at the time of attachment logically should be inferred from the combination of the other two factors. This approach would be in keeping with the nature of original acquisition of ownership, which, in principle, does not take account of subjectivity. However, the cases show that either an objectively inferred intention or a subjective intention is considered.[57] Furthermore, *inaedificatio* case law reveals an inconsistent approach to the weighting of the factors. Some courts have relied on an objective assessment of the join brought about between the movable and the land to infer an intention that the movable should serve the immovable indefinitely or not. In other words, if an objective assessment of the nature and purpose of the movable as well as the manner and degree of its attachment leads to a clear outcome, then the interpretation is that the movable was meant to be joined indefinitely. The consequence is that the occurrence of accession must be confirmed. This has been called the 'traditional approach', as set out in *Macdonald Ltd v Radin NO and the Potchefstroom Dairies and Industries Co Ltd*.[58]

Other courts have looked to the owner of the movable to ascertain her subjective intention regarding the attachment. The other two factors are used as indications of an inferred intention, which is weighed against the stated subjective intention *(ipse dixit)* to arrive at the 'real' intention on a balance of probabilities. This is the so-called 'new' approach, adopted in *Theatre Investments (Pty) Ltd v Butcher Brothers Ltd*.[59]

In both leading cases, the facts included contracts that governed the circumstances under which the movable property was attached. In *Macdonald*, the attachment was done by a third party, whereas in *Theatre Investments*, it was done by a party to the contract.

---

54 See *Wille's Principles* p 498 n 266 for authorities.
55 *Standard-Vacuum Refining Co of SA (Pty) Ltd v Durban City Council* 1961(2) SA 669 (A).
56 *Standard-Vacuum Refining Co of SA (Pty) Ltd v Durban City Council* 1961(2) SA 669 (A).
57 See e.g. *Theatre Investments (Pty) Ltd v Butcher Brothers Ltd* 1978 (3) SA 682 (A).
58 1915 AD 454.
59 1978 (3) SA 682 (A).

The presence of the contracts permitted the introduction of subjectivity in the otherwise objective assessment of the factors for *inaedificatio*. That this is so, may be seen in *Macdonald* itself where the court states:

> *The annexation could only operate to transfer the dominium of the plant, if, when it was put up, the plaintiff intended that it should remain there permanently or authorised Jacobson [the annexor] to affix it with that intention. And the evidence does not show that. The attitude of Macdonald, the managing director, who controlled this transaction throughout, was perfectly consistent. He had no idea of parting with the right to remove his machinery if default was made in payment, and he intended that its attachment to the building should be subject to that right, which was quite inconsistent with placing it there permanently. Any other state of mind would have involved a renunciation of the benefits of his contract, which it is clear he never contemplated.*[60]

PAUSE FOR REFLECTION — **Use of terminology**

The use of legal terminology as well as ordinary language has a profound effect on how others, especially long after the event, interpret that language or terminology. At first reading, especially for modern readers, the dictum above seems to deal with derivative acquisition of ownership. However, it becomes clear from careful reading of *Macdonald*, that Innes CJ was confining himself to discussion of accession, notwithstanding that he often used the phrase 'transfer of *dominium*'. Original acquisition of ownership does not involve transfer of title, but rather acquisition of title by operation of law.

Inaedificatio case law uses various phrases to describe the intention factor. The 'inferred' or 'imputed' intention is that which is taken to be indicated by the outcome of an objective examination of the nature and purpose of the movable together with the manner and degree of its attachment. In *Standard-Vacuum Refining Co of SA (Pty) Ltd v Durban City Council*,[61] the fact that the tanks could be moved only following considerable engineering interventions, led to the inference that the installation was meant to be permanent.

The 'expressed' or 'professed' intention – also called the *ipse dixit* – is subjective and is gleaned from the person herself or from other evidence. For example, in *Theatre Investments*,[62] the lease contract provided evidence of the intention at the time of attachment, alongside the customised nature of the movables installed in the theatre.

The introduction of subjectivity has been unfortunate and has led to decisions in subsequent cases that are counterintuitive and confusing. For example, in *Simmer and Jack Mines Ltd v GF Industrial Property Co (Pty) Ltd*,[63] a mine dump was held to remain movable despite its size and weight, while *Melcorp SA v Joint Municipal Pension Fund (Transvaal)*[64] permitted subjectivity to lead to the finding that the lift in a high-rise building did not form part of that building. More recently, in *De Beers Consolidated Mines Ltd v Ataqua Mining (Pty) Ltd*,[65]

---

60 *Macdonald Ltd v Radin NO* 1915 AD 454 at 469.
61 1961 (2) SA 669 (A).
62 *Theatre Investments (Pty) Ltd v Butcher Brothers Ltd* 1978 (3) SA 682 (A).
63 1975 (2) SA 654 (W).
64 1980 (2) SA 214 (W).
65 (O) Case No: 3215/06 13 December 2007, unreported.

the then Orange Free State High Court found a tailings dump to be movable on the basis that the owner of the ore deposited in the tailings dump did not intend it to accede to the land.

In *Macdonald*, the question was whether certain refrigerating machinery had acceded to the factory (immovable property). The then Appellate Division found that the intention of the owner of the movable was important in circumstances where the attachment was such that removal was neither difficult nor very expensive. On the facts, it was clear that there was no intention to part with ownership if there was default in payment.[66] The majority stated that:

> ... the intention required (in conjunction with annexation) to destroy the identity, to merge the title, or to transfer the *dominium* of movable property, must surely be the intention of the owner. It is difficult to see by what principle of law the mental attitude of any third party could operate to effect so vital a change.[67]

What troubled the majority is the proposition that 'A may take the property of B, and give it to C, by annexing it to the building of the latter, even though the annexation be of such a character that it may be severed without injury either to the premises or to the thing attached'.[68] Especially controversial are circumstances where the factual identity of the movable is clearly preserved **and** removal is neither difficult nor expensive. Consequently, the court required evidence that attachment was meant to be permanent, i.e. that it was intended to be attached indefinitely or for permanent use. That evidence, in the court's view, could only be subjective in the circumstances.

The minority in *Macdonald* took the view that:

> the intention, which has to be regarded in determining whether machinery which has been annexed to buildings has become portion of the immovable property, is whether it was annexed by the owner of the premises for permanent and not merely for temporary use. And I find it somewhat difficult to see how that intention is affected by the fact that the plant was not bought out and out, but under a hire-purchase agreement. For a purchaser under such a contract has the same intention as any other purchaser, namely to acquire the property as his own, and when he erects the plant, as in this instance, in buildings set apart for a special business, he does so intending presumably to use it for the purposes of that business for so long as he continues to carry it on.[69]

The difference of opinion between the majority and minority judgments lies in whether the existence of a hire-purchase agreement (evidencing subjectivity) should alter the objective assessment of the factors for accession by building. One view is that business transactions depend upon agreements being honoured and that general harm would flow from mechanistic application of property law rules in the face of breach of such agreements.[70] Another view is exemplified by Solomon JA's comment in *Macdonald* that 'the ... company must, in my opinion, accept the consequences which legally flow from

---

66 *Macdonald Ltd v Radin NO and the Potchefstroom Dairies and Industries Co Ltd* 1915 AD 454 at 469.
67 *Macdonald* at 466.
68 *Macdonald* at 466.
69 *Macdonald* at 479.
70 *Melcorp SA v Joint Municipal Pension Fund (Transvaal)* 1980 (2) SA 214 (W) at 224: 'clause 14 of the contract ... embodies the very basis upon which the plaintiff was prepared to install the lifts in the building without prior payment therefor ...'

its own act',[71] namely, to permit the installation of its property into immovable property, contrary to the terms of its reservation of ownership. That the decision of the *Macdonald* court was not unanimous, but rather on the basis of a 3:2 split, points to the difficulty of clearly articulating the boundaries of accession by building as a mode of original acquisition of ownership.

In *Theatre Investments (Pty) Ltd v Butcher Brothers Ltd,*[72] a building was leased for the express purpose of establishing a theatre. Movables installed in the building included customised theatre seats, an emergency lighting plant and a projection dimmer board. The lease contract stipulated that upon termination of the lease, all fixtures would accrue to the owner of the building, thus varying the lessee's common law right of removal at termination of the lease. Nevertheless, at the termination of the lease, the lessee disputed that these items accrued to the owner of the building on the basis that no permanent join had been effected and hence accession had not occurred.

The analysis of the facts in light of the factors showed that each of the items had been specially designed for the theatre or were essential theatre equipment. As to their removability, removal of some would cause damage to the fabric of the building but not others. Again, therefore, the outcome of the examination of the first two factors was equivocal, resulting in the need to scrutinise the intention at the time of attachment. The contract provided evidence of the cause for, and the circumstances that led to, the attachment of the movables. In the circumstances, the contract indicated what was anticipated by both parties at the end of the lease (which could have lasted for 99 years), namely that the fixtures accrued to the owner of the building. The claim to reinstate the common law right of removal was thus not persuasive. In other words, the occurrence of accession was confirmed.

In *Melcorp SA (Pty) Ltd v Joint Municipal Pension Fund (Transvaal),*[73] it was argued that the nature of the movable (a lift) and the manner of its attachment necessarily led to the imputed intention of permanent attachment. The lift was integral to the building and essential for it to function properly. The court agreed, stating that if the facts supporting this inference stood alone, the imputed intention would be the proper and necessary inference. However, a remaining question was whether the imputed intention should override the expressed intention. The contract expressly reserved ownership in the lift until fully paid for. In *Theatre Investments* in 1978, the then Appellate Division stated that the role of the contract was to provide a context for assessing the intention at the time of the attachment. Yet, some two years later, *Melcorp* demonstrates the view that the contract served as the *ipse dixit* and that the expressed intention must prevail. This approach led to the strange conclusion that the lift remained movable.

Konstanz Properties (Pty) Ltd v Wm Spilhaus en Kie (WP) Bpk[74] involved a dispute over ownership of goods supplied and installed by a third party on land. The wholesaler (Spilhaus) supplied components for an irrigation system to a retailer, subject to a reservation of ownership. In turn, the retailer installed them on Konstanz Properties' land to form the irrigation system. The retailer failed to pay for the components and the wholesaler consequently wished to vindicate what it regarded as its property from Konstanz Properties. Whether the components remained movable or had acceded to the land had to be established.

---

71 *Macdonald* at 475.
72 *Theatre Investments (Pty) Ltd v Butcher Brothers Ltd* 1978 (3) SA 682 (A).
73 1980 (2) SA 214 (W).
74 1996 (3) SA 273 (A).

In analysing the facts in light of the factors, the court pointed out that unlike in *Macdonald's* case, Spilhaus did not sell a completed system, but rather a number of components, each separately priced and invoiced. This made it difficult to view the components as an economic or functional unit, as was alleged by Konstanz Properties.

Regarding the legal framework for *inaedificatio*, the court suggested that perhaps it was time to revisit which is the appropriate approach and whose intention is relevant. However, this dogmatic aspect was not argued and therefore a decision could not be made on the points. Given that the components were not impossible to remove and that Spilhaus had expressly reserved ownership, the court concluded that the intention of the owner of the movable prevailed and therefore accession was denied.

> **COUNTER POINT**
>
> **Analysis of approaches to determination of *inaedificatio***
>
> Is there a material difference between the so-called traditional and new approaches? Careful analysis of *Macdonald* and *Theatre Investments* reveals there is no difference in principle between the two cases. Both cases approach their respective facts with some subjectivity. The labelling by legal scholars[75] and other courts[76] of a traditional and a new approach seems to flow from confusion between the application of the legal framework and the factual analysis in each case.
>
> In *Macdonald*, the join between the movable and the immovable was not plausibly permanent, even though it was quite clear that, had the bills been paid, the machinery would have remained in place indefinitely. The majority's interpretation of the factual analysis was that the (unpaid) owner of the movable did not intend to give up ownership and thus that accession was to be denied. As was pointed out above, the minority (by one judge) took the opposite view.
>
> In *Theatre Investments*, the lease indicated that the improvements became the property of the owner of the land. Here the unanimous court considered the terms of the lease as evidence of the intention at the time of attachment, the customised construction of the seating and other equipment, and concluded that, notwithstanding the fact that the various bolts could be undone, the seating and other equipment had been incorporated into the fabric of the theatre building. Accession thus was confirmed.
>
> In both cases, therefore, the same approach was adopted in coming to a finding on the facts: failing a clear outcome on the objective assessment, resort was had to subjective evidence of intention. The conclusion must be that the difference between the traditional and new approaches as a legal framework does not exist; rather the facts differ and must be interpreted accordingly. That this must be so may be seen in the decision in *Melcorp*, which chooses to give paramountcy to the contract. Unfortunately, in the absence of a clear theoretical justification, this choice introduced the requirements for derivative acquisition of ownership rather than remaining true to those for original acquisition of ownership, which served to add to the confusion.
>
> The approach to accession by building, we suggest, may be described as follows: where the objective assessment of the facts shows that the movable has been attached firmly

---

75 See e.g. Lewis, C 'Superficies solo cedit – sed quid est superficies' (1979) 96 *SALJ* 94 at 98-99, 105-107; Van der Merwe *Sakereg* pp 253-258.

76 See the discussion and cases cited in *Unimark Distributors (Pty) Ltd v Erf 94 Silvertondale (Pty) Ltd* 1999 (2) SA 986 (T) at 998-999.

and is meant for permanent use, then introducing a contrary and subjective viewpoint is not acceptable. Accession should be confirmed. If, however, the attachment is ambiguous, then the court has a choice. As a matter of **policy**, it can choose either *to* **preserve** the **new composite whole** (i.e. by confirming the occurrence of accession) or **to protect ownership of the movable** (by denying the occurrence of accession). The choice to preserve the new composite whole would serve the publicity principle. The basis on which the choice is made is not clearly articulated in the cases.

Arguably, if it is not clear that the join is for permanent use and, consequently, that the intention at the time of attachment was for the joined thing to serve the principal indefinitely, then the choice ought to be to invoke the policy to protect ownership, leading the court to deny accession. Only in special circumstances, clearly justified, should the policy to preserve the whole be invoked when attachment is ambiguous. This approach to policy choice is compatible with the constitutional prohibition against arbitrary deprivation of property.[77] It should not be necessary to resort to the subjective intention of the owner of the movable.

Frequently, the more subjective approach has been invoked when a third party has attached the movable or when the property has been sold on credit terms, subject to a reservation of ownership.[78] In such matters, the courts have tended not to consider whether the attachment took place because the movable property was destined to serve the land or building indefinitely (in which case the reallocation of rights must be confirmed). Instead, the question has been whether the owner of the movable property intended to part with ownership. Invariably, the outcome has favoured the owner of the movable or the hire-purchase seller rather than confirmed the reallocation of ownership rights on the basis of accession. The rationale has been that attachment was not intended to be permanent because ownership should not be lost unwillingly. However, as was pointed out earlier, the intention of the owner of the movable is irrelevant to original acquisition of ownership, which makes this rationale dubious. Furthermore, the logic of the rationale is questionable: 'the movable accedes now if in the future the debt is paid, but does not accede if, in the event, the debt is unpaid'. In other words, a 'present matter of accession is determined by reference to an unknown future event'.[79] In addition, the publicity principle is poorly served when subjectivity is permitted to override objectivity without sound justification. This makes no sense in the context of property law. It has to be that subjective intention is not relevant to the determination of permanency of attachment. The 'invisible' reservation of ownership should be trumped by the 'visible' impression created for third parties.[80]

---

77 Section 25 of the Constitution.
78 *Macdonald Ltd v Radin NO and the Potchefstroom Dairies and Industries Co Ltd* 1915 AD 454; *Melcorp SA v Joint Municipal Pension Fund (Transvaal)* 1980 (2) SA 214 (W); *Konstanz Properties (Pty) Ltd v Wm Spilhaus en Kie (WP) (Bpk)* 1996 (3) SA 273 (A).
79 Carey Miller, DL & Pope, A (2004) 'Acquisition of ownership' in Zimmermann, R, Visser, D & Reid, K (eds) *Mixed Legal Systems in Comparative Perspective: Property and Obligations in Scotland and South Africa* (Cape Town, Juta) p 681.
80 Carey Miller, DL & Pope, A (2004) 'Acquisition of ownership' in Zimmermann, R, Visser, D & Reid, K (eds) *Mixed Legal Systems in Comparative Perspective: Property and Obligations in Scotland and South Africa* (Cape Town, Juta) p 681.

> Careful thinking about the concepts and the legal framework, together with rigorous analysis of the facts, are irreplaceable. It is argued here that South African law does not have two approaches to accession by building but rather that it has a policy-driven approach when objective assessment of the facts does not give a clear answer. The choice is to preserve the new composite whole or to protect ownership of the movable. These choices are theoretically sound insofar as each is underpinned either by the fundamental publicity principle or by the constitutional prohibition against arbitrary deprivation of property.

7.2.2.4 Accession of immovable property to immovable property

This form of accession occurs naturally, i.e. without human or industrial intervention. It involves either a sudden or an imperceptible increase in the size or volume of land caused by the action of water.[81] When the increase is sudden, it is known as avulsion; when imperceptible, it is called alluvion. In both cases, at least one boundary of the land must be determined by a natural phenomenon, for instance a river. Such erven (plots of land) are called *agri non limitati*.[82] Few such erven survive in modern South Africa because of the cadastral system upon which the deeds registration system is based. Consequently, few examples of this form of accession occur and its practical application is limited.

7.2.3 Acquisition of fruits (*separatio* and *perceptio*)

Fruits, natural and civil, are produced by the principal thing by means of separation of the accessory from the principal. A form of reverse accession underpins the rules for acquisition of ownership of fruits. That is, separation rather than joinder is required. Upon separation, the accessory (i.e. the fruit) gains separate legal identity. The legal consequence of the separation is that the owner of the principal is owner also of the separated fruit with its own legal identity. For example, a pregnant sheep delivers a live lamb: the owner of the sheep is owner also of the lamb, which acquires separate legal identity at birth. Similarly, the apple tree produces an apple, which, upon separation from the tree, acquires separate legal identity. The owner of the land upon which the apple tree grows is owner also of the separated apple.

The legal consequence of separation of fruit from its principal is that the owner of the principal is owner also of the new legal entity (the fruit) upon separation *(separatio)*. Entitlement to the fruit can be reserved to a different person if the owner of the principal so wishes, as is the case with the personal servitude of usufruct. However, when someone other than the owner is entitled, then mere separation is insufficient to create ownership rights in the fruits. Gathering or collecting *(perceptio)* is required for a usufructuary, as is explained below.[83] Similarly, if a lease agreement gives entitlements to fruits to a lessee, then the lessee must gather the fruits before ownership entitlements accrue. Mere separation is insufficient. For example, assume that Frank is entitled, in terms of his lease agreement, to the lemons off the tree in the garden of the house he rents. A strong wind blows the lemons

---

81 *Wille's Principles* pp 494–495; *Silberberg & Schoeman Property* p 144.
82 *Wille's Principles* p 494.
83 See ch 9 below.

off the tree. While passing the garden, Sarah notices the lemons on the ground, hops over the low wall, collects as many as she can carry, and goes on her way. Can Frank pursue the lemons using the *rei vindicatio*? Only if he is the owner of the lemons, which he will not be because he had not yet gathered them when Sarah took them. He would have to look to the owner of the house to pursue the lemons because, for the period between separation from the tree and gathering, the owner of the house owns the lemons.

7.2.4 Manufacture *(specificatio)*

This mode of acquisition of ownership occurs when one person makes a new product *(nova species)* from materials that belong wholly or in part to another person.[84] Literally, 'manufacture' means to make, originally by hand, now usually by machinery and on a large scale. The process of manufacture involves the use or combination of things to form a new product *(nova species)*.

If all the materials belong to the maker, then, obviously, the maker owns the new product. If materials belonging to another are used with permission, then, equally obviously, that agreement may be assumed to govern the ownership of the new product. But where another person's materials are used without permission, then the rules of manufacture *(specificatio)* indicate who acquires the property interests in the new product.[85] In other words, in the absence of an agreement regarding the use of the materials to manufacture a new product, the rules of *specificatio* provide a solution.

The mere fact of combining things to form another entity is insufficient to trigger the rules of manufacture *(specificatio)*. The manufacturing process must irretrievably alter the form, nature, chemistry, etc. of the thing for these rules to be applicable.[86] For example, if Carl combines his table top with Jean's table legs, is this an example of *specificatio*? No, because there is no irretrievable alteration of either the table top or the table legs.[87] In law, this combination would be an example of *accessio*. What if Jean combines her sugar and eggs with Carl's flour, milk and baking powder, and then puts the mixture into a hot oven? Is the resulting product an example of *specificatio*? Would it be possible to undo the combination of the ingredients that is now known as a cake? The answer to the latter question is no, which in turn means that this is indeed an example of *specificatio*. In other words, in the absence of an agreement, ownership of the ingredients combined to produce a cake must be resolved using the rules of *specificatio*. *Aldine Timber Co v Hlatwayo*[88] reminds us of the examples of *specificatio* provided in the old authorities:

> *The circumstances of the case show that the work done on the old material was not in the nature of specification, because no new species has been created and the original article has not ceased to exist as such. The illustrations given of turning grapes into wine and corn into bread show clearly what specification means and ... there can be no doubt that on the facts of this case the material does not fall into this category.*

---

84 See *Wille's Principles* pp 505–507; *Silberberg & Schoeman Property* pp 157–159 for more detailed discussion.
85 *Wille's Principles* p 505; *Silberberg & Schoeman Property* p 157.
86 *Wille's Principles* p 505; *Silberberg & Schoeman Property* p 158.
87 Compare *S v Riekert* 1977 (3) SA 181 (T).
88 1932 TPD 337.

Specificatio does not necessarily require a 'mix' of the property of various owners, although this may occur. If Gert takes fabric from Designer Fabrics (Pty) Ltd and, without its permission, fashions a wedding dress from the fabric, this would amount to *specificatio* in the same way as when Jamie takes eggs from Peter and milk and flour from Paul to make a cake without their permission. The crucial issue is whether a new product was created: one that cannot be reduced to the original form of its ingredients or components.

The distinguishing characteristics of *specificatio* are thus that the manufacturing process must irretrievably alter the things that are used or combined; the combination must give rise to a new product; the materials used in the manufacturing process must not belong to the maker; and there must be no agreement governing the use of the materials.[89]

Some writers indicate that good faith is a requirement.[90] Why does it matter whether the maker used materials in good faith? It appears that some commentators use the presence or absence of good faith (bona fides) to assess the moral blameworthiness of the maker. However, these considerations are irrelevant in the assessment of whether ownership rights have been reallocated by operation of law. That the maker acted in good faith may affect the determination of compensation owed to the (previous) owner of the materials.

If the new thing created cannot be restored to its previous form or state, then it belongs to the maker; if it can be restored to its original form or state, then ownership remains as it was.[91] In other words, *specificatio* does not apply to the latter instance. Importantly, by implication, if *specificatio* does apply, then the act of combining things to form the new thing extinguishes the legal identity of the individual materials and creates a new legal entity with its own legal identity. Simultaneously, ownership in the materials is terminated and created in the new entity.

PAUSE FOR REFLECTION

Controversies and anomalies

The rules of manufacture *(specificatio)* seem simple at first glance, but there are several points of controversy or debate.

First, while the illustrative examples of the old authorities of turning grapes into wine and corn into bread give one a clear sense of the nature of the process and outcome that are envisaged for these rules, it is not clear exactly what a new species should look like. Some guidance may be found in whether the new product is known by a different name, e.g. cake or pizza, or whether there is a complete loss of the previous form of the materials, and so on.

Second, the principle of reducibility, i.e. whether the form or state is irretrievably altered, gives rise to some anomalies in South African law. Compare the sculptor who uses wood or stone belonging to another to sculpt a likeness of a person with one who uses metal to do the same. According to the principle of reducibility, ownership of the sculpture made from wood or stone lies with the maker because the previous form and state of the wood and stone are not retrievable. In the case of the metal sculpture, however, the position is different because the nature of metal is to be reducible at least to a melted state; hence, ownership would remain with the owner of the metal. In other jurisdictions, this contradictory state of affairs has been resolved by legislation which awards ownership of the new product to the maker when the value thereof far exceeds the value of the material used.[92]

---

89 *Wille's Principles* p 506; *Silberberg & Schoeman Property* p 157.
90 See authorities cited in *Wille's Principles* p 507; *Silberberg & Schoeman Property* p 158.
91 *Wille's Principles* p 505; *Silberberg & Schoeman Property* p 157.
92 *Wille's Principles* p 506 at n 343.

> Third, opinions remain divided about whether the maker must display good faith in her actions.[93] Many South African scholars[94] formerly opined, and some[95] still do, that bona fide conduct is indeed required. There are also obiter suggestions to this effect in case law.[96] Most of the more recent scholarly texts[97] opine that good faith is not required. They base their opinions on different reasons. Van der Merwe's[98] argument is that the rationale for the change in ownership is to reward the manufacturer for his labour, regardless of his bona fides or *mala fides*. He continues that bona fides is not required for any of the other forms of original acquisition, and hence it is anomalous to require it for *specificatio*. He also points out that it is problematic to vindicate something which has been irreducibly changed into something else. Van der Walt and Pienaar's[99] argument focuses on the practical considerations that dictate that bona fides should not be required, whereas Badenhorst et al.[100] object to the requirement on a principled basis, indicating that it is inconsistent with the basic principles of original acquisition to protect a previous owner since his co-operation is irrelevant in the context of original acquisition. Our view on this topic has been discussed above.[101]
>
> Lastly, manufacture *(specificatio)* does not apply to the natural development and maturation of live creatures.[102] For example, if Bongani takes the eggs of Thabo's hens and hatches them on his premises, using his incubator equipment, the resulting live chicks do not belong to Bongani by *specificatio*. Bongani's acts of husbanding the eggs and chicks by keeping the environmental conditions optimal are insufficient to trigger the use of the rules of manufacture.

7.2.5 Mingling and mixing *(confusio et commixtio)*

Mingling and mixing are modes of acquisition of ownership used when 'similar things of more or less equal value belonging to different owners are mingled or mixed without consent and become inseparable (liquids) or indeterminable (solids)'.[103] Things that can be mingled or mixed are usually fungible things either in liquid or solid form. Examples of liquids that mingle include oil and vinegar, bunker oil, and wines of different vintages. Metals are treated as liquids because, generally, it is in this state that mingling can occur, e.g. bronze is an alloy (mixture) of tin and copper, achievable only when both tin and

---

93 *Wille's Principles* p 507; *Silberberg & Schoeman Property* pp 158–159.
94 *Wille's Principles* p 176; Scholtens, JE (1960) in Hahlo, HR & Kahn, E *The Union of South Africa: The Development of its Laws and Constitution* (Cape Town, Juta) p 587.
95 Sonnekus, JC & Neels, JL (1994) *Sakereg Vonnisbundel* (Durban, Butterworths) pp 306–307.
96 *S v Riekert* 1977 (3) SA 181 (T).
97 *Wille's Principles* p 507; *Silberberg & Schoeman Property* p 158; Van der Merwe *Sakereg* pp 261–262; Carey Miller, DL & Pope, A (2004) 'Acquisition of ownership' in Zimmermann, R, Visser, D & Reid, K (eds) *Mixed Legal Systems in Comparative Perspective: Property and Obligations in Scotland and South Africa* (Cape Town, Juta) p 683.
98 Van der Merwe *Sakereg* p 262 (following Maasdorp); also *Wille's Principles* p 505.
99 Van der Walt, AJ & Pienaar, GJ (2006) *Introduction to the Law of Property* (Cape Town, Juta) p 110.
100 *Silberberg & Schoeman Property* p 159.
101 See pp 176–177 above.
102 Carey Miller, DL & Pope, A (2004) 'Acquisition of ownership' in Zimmermann, R, Visser, D & Reid, K (eds) *Mixed Legal Systems in Comparative Perspective: Property and Obligations in Scotland and South Africa*. (Cape Town, Juta) p 683 with reference to a Scottish case concerning whether smolt (baby salmon) turning into adult salmon involved *specificatio*. The Court of Session held that it did not.
103 *Wille's Principles* p 507.

copper are melted.[104] Examples of solids include ostrich feathers,[105] sheep, cars, and coins. Note that liquids must be mingled in containers but mixing of solids does not require containerisation.

The rules for *confusio et commixtio* are triggered when mingling or mixing occurs without consent, and the mixture cannot readily be restored to its previous state or individually identified.[106] The consequence of mingling is that the mingled liquids are co-owned in undivided shares. Each owner's portion must be legally separated (using the *actio communi dividundo*) before it can be vindicated. In the case of mixing, the consequence is that ownership does not change; each owner can vindicate her proportionate share. Money forms the exception to the rule for mixed solids: coins and notes (currency) may not be vindicated. Ownership vests in the possessor who is liable for the equivalent sum.[107]

The characteristics of mingling and mixing, contrasted with accession and manufacture, are that the mingled or mixed things are of more or less equal value, and the mixture is not readily separable or determinable. In the case of mingled liquids, inseparability leads to termination of legal identity of the original liquids and creation of legal identity for the combined liquids. This explains why co-ownership is acquired in the combination of liquids. In the case of mixed solids, no loss of legal identity occurs, which is why there is no change of ownership.

7.2.6 Acquisitive prescription

Open and uninterrupted possession of property for a long time can lead to the acquisition of ownership by acquisitive prescription.[108] Sometimes the nature of the possession is not compatible with full ownership but may still lead to the acquisition of a limited real right, e.g. a servitude, by acquisitive prescription. The nature of the required possession varies according to the nature of the property. Both elements of possession must be satisfied: physical control must be sufficient and effective, and the mental attitude must be *animus domini*, i.e. commensurate with being owner.

As with the other modes of original acquisition of ownership, the effect is to make the legal situation accord with the factual scenario. Thus, at a point in time when the acquirer has possessed the movable or immovable property openly as if owner for an uninterrupted 30 years, he acquires ownership by operation of law.[109] In the case of land, this legal fact (change of ownership) will contradict the entry in the Deeds Registry and it is, therefore, open to the prescriptive owner to apply to court for the title deed and the Deeds Registry to be amended. For this reason, and given the status and value attached to land, most, if not all, the case law deals with acquisitive prescription of land. But it is as well to remember that the rules apply to both movable and immovable property.

Acquisitive prescription is governed by statute while the common law remains a residual source of law because the legislation is not codifying.[110] The Prescription Act of 1969[111] is current and applies to prescriptive periods beginning 1 December 1970. It is not retrospective.

---

104 Note that when a new product, e.g. a recognised useful alloy, is produced, the relevant mode would be *specificatio* rather than *confusio*.
105 *Andrews v Rosenbaum & Co* 1908 EDC 419.
106 *Wille's Principles* p 507; *Silberberg & Schoeman Property* pp 159-160.
107 *Wille's Principles* p 508.
108 See in general *Wille's Principles* pp 510-517; *Silberberg & Schoeman Property* pp 160-173.
109 *Wille's Principles* pp 510-511; *Silberberg & Schoeman Property* p 160.
110 *Wille's Principles* p 511; *Silberberg & Schoeman Property* p 161.
111 Act 68 of 1969.

Prior to this date, the Prescription Act of 1943[112] applies, although it is only in isolated instances that this earlier Act is still relevant. For purposes of studying the requirements for prescription, however, the provisions of the 1943 Prescription Act are useful. They demonstrate continuity between the statutory rules and the principles of common law as regards prescription. They also provide a point of comparison with the requirements in the subsequent 1969 Act, which aids understanding of the provisions of the latter.

Acquisitive prescription is statutorily defined in the 1943 Act as:

the acquisition of ownership by the possession of another person's movable or immovable property ... continuously for thirty years nec vi, nec clam, nec precario.[113]

In the 1969 Act, the requirements for acquisitive prescription are set out as follows:

... a person shall by prescription become the owner of a thing which he has possessed openly and as if he were the owner thereof for an uninterrupted period of thirty years or for a period which, together with any periods for which such thing was so possessed by his predecessors in title, constitutes an uninterrupted period of thirty years.

It is apparent from these broadly similar definitions that acquisitive prescription has two major elements: possession and an uninterrupted period of time.

> **PAUSE FOR REFLECTION**
>
> **Comparison of the 1943 and 1969 Acts**
>
> There are several similarities in the two Acts, which serve to highlight their main points of difference. First, both Acts confirm the common law requirements of prescription relating to (1) **possession**, (2) for a **continuous period**. Both Acts confirm that this period, in South African law, is 30 years. Second, in terms of both Acts, the possession of predecessors in title may be taken into account when determining continuous possession. This is referred to in common law as the *coniunctio temporum*: the accumulation of holding periods of predecessors in title. Third, as regards the requirement of possession, although the wording of the two Acts differs, essentially, *possessio civilis* is required, i.e. possession with the intention to be owner. In this context, of course, possession is always without entitlement (i.e. the acquirer has the *ius possessionis*, not the *ius possidendi*).[114] Fourth, as regards the temporal requirement,[115] both Acts confirm that, in specific circumstances, prescription may be either terminated (interrupted) or suspended (temporarily stalled).
>
> The two main differences between the Acts relate to the possession requirement and the temporal requirement. First, as regards possession, the definitions used in the two Acts differ. In the 1943 Act, acquisitive prescription was defined as: acquisition of ownership by the possession of another person's movable or immovable property ... *nec vi, nec clam, nec precario*. In terms of the 1969 Act, the possessor must act **openly as if he were the owner**. The 1969 Prescription Act thus eliminates the *nec vi* element and replaces the *nec precario* element with the requirement that the possessor must hold 'as if he were the owner'.
>
> Second, as regards the temporal requirement, both Acts provide for circumstances under which prescription may be interrupted or suspended. However, there are significant differences between them. In essence, the 1969 Act has softened some of the previous strict requirements about continuity of possession by providing more rigorous rules to determine the onset of suspension or the occurrence of interruption.

---

112 Act 18 of 1943.
113 '*Nec vi, nec clam, nec precario*' translates as 'without force, without secrecy, without revocable permission'.
114 See ch 4 above
115 i.e. the time period.

7.2.6.1 The requirement of possession

The type of possession required is civil possession, i.e. the combination of sufficient and effective physical control with the intention of an owner *(animus domini)*. Note that, by definition, possession for purposes of acquisitive prescription is **unlawful** in the sense that there is **no entitlement** to possession. Note further, however, that were possession also to be **illegal**, in the sense that a statutory prohibition is violated, then neither ownership nor any other right can be acquired by acquisitive prescription.[116]

The two Acts use different terminology to describe the statutory requirements for acquisitive prescription, but analysis reveals that both intend civil possession as the possession element.[117] The 1943 Act's '*nec vi, nec clam, nec precario*' (without force, without secrecy, without revocable permission) are commensurate with the 1969 Act's 'openly, as if owner'.

The presence of sufficient and effective physical control is determined objectively in light of the particular circumstances, and must be consistent with the intention of an owner.[118] The manner by which the possessor came to be in possession of the property is not as important as the manner by which she has remained in possession for 30 years. The *nec vi* requirement of the 1943 Act means that the possessor should not have **retained** possession by force; it does not mean that possession may not have been **acquired** by force.[119] For example, a robber who acquires possession of someone's wallet by force but then uses it in the ordinary way becomes owner after 30 years. This 'without force' requirement is not explicit in the 1969 Act because it has no real practical purpose. If property is possessed 'openly, as if owner', then, impliedly, it is also possessed without force.

Consider a cattle farmer who grazes his cattle for 30 years on land belonging to another. The act of sending his cattle to graze on this land for 30 years is compatible with the intention of an owner, but does grazing constitute sufficient and effective physical control for purposes of ownership? The character of the land would be an important consideration: if it is open veld, used primarily for grazing, then it might be sufficient;[120] if it is a wooded area, not generally used for grazing, then it might not be sufficient.[121] In other words, the conduct that constitutes physical control must satisfy the statutory requirements: openly, as if owner (1969 Act); *nec vi, nec clam, nec precario* (1943 Act). Sometimes, if the requirements for acquiring ownership are not met, those for acquiring a limited real right, e.g. a grazing servitude, might be.

Consider also a man who for 30 years pays rates (municipal taxes) on a plot of land adjacent to his own, believing that, after 30 years, he can acquire ownership. Payment of taxes is conduct that an owner would perform, but does it constitute sufficient and effective physical control? In *Hayes v Harding Town Board*,[122] it was said that:

although the payment of rates may well demonstrate an intention to claim ownership of land, or an intention to possess it, it does not ... amount in itself to a physical holding or detention of the land and, in the absence of such a detention, the conditions necessary for prescription do not exist.[123]

---

116 See the discussion in *Silberberg & Schoeman Property* pp 165–166.
117 See p 180 above.
118 *Wille's Principles* p 514; *Silberberg & Schoeman Property* p 162.
119 *Wille's Principles* p 512.
120 *Van Wyk v Louw* 1958 (2) SA 154 (C).
121 *Wilderness (1921) Ltd v Union Government* 1927 CPD 455; *Minister van Lande v Swart* 1957 (3) SA 508 (C).
122 1958 (2) SA 297 (N).
123 *Hayes v Harding Town Board* 1958 (2) SA 297 (N) at 299E–F.

The acquirer need not exercise physical control personally but, importantly, whoever exercises it on his behalf, must clearly do so at the will of the acquirer.[124] This is vital to keep the 'chain of evidence' of physical control alive. The will of the acquirer must be to mandate the third party to take and be in physical control on his behalf. This ensures that the intention to be owner (with the acquirer) is not separated from the physical control (held by the agent of the acquirer).[125]

The openness requirement is also determined objectively. This means that the true owner of the property cannot defend by denying personal knowledge of the possession by the acquirer.[126] If, from the point of view of the ordinary owner, the possession was 'so patent that the owner, with the exercise of reasonable care, would have observed it',[127] then the fact that he personally did not observe it, cannot prevent acquisitive prescription.

The requirements that the possessor must act 'as if he is the owner' and '*nec precario*' describe the fact that the acquirer must possess as if by right, without acknowledging a better title or power to dispossess him.[128] An understanding of the common law notion of *precarium* helps to clarify this requirement:

> ... [P]recarium is the legal relationship which exists between parties when one party has the use or occupation of property belonging to the other on sufferance, by the leave and licence of the other. Its essential characteristic is that the permission to use or occupy is revocable at the will of the person granting it.[129]

For example, Julia's neighbour, Alexandra, permits Julia to use her garage while Alexandra is without a car. Six months later, Alexandra acquires a car and tells Julia she must vacate the garage. Julia has no basis to claim continued use because her use was based on *precarium*. For acquisitive prescription, the relationship between the property and the acquirer must not resemble *precarium*.

The *animus* element is also determined objectively, i.e. the state of mind of the acquirer is what the reasonable person would infer from the acquirer's physical control in the circumstances.[130] Evidence that the physical control is contrary to the true owner's interests can serve to establish the necessary *animus domini*. On the other hand, evidence that the acquirer has made public statements indicating an awareness of a better title could serve to negate the presence of *animus domini*.[131]

7.2.6.2 The temporal requirement: Uninterrupted 30-year period

As was indicated above,[132] the acquirer does not have to be in possession personally for the entire period. The 1969 Act is explicit on this point: '... a period which, together with any periods for which such thing was so possessed by his predecessors in title ...' . This means that the acquirer can add to his own period of possession time that the predecessor

---

124 *Wille's Principles* p 514; *Silberberg & Schoeman Property* p 169.
125 *Silberberg & Schoeman Property* p 163.
126 *Wille's Principles* p 512; *Silberberg & Schoeman Property* p 165.
127 *Smith v Martin's Executor* (1899) 16 SC 148 at 151, adopted by the then Appellate Division in *Bisschop v Stafford* 1974 (3) SA 1 (A) at 8.
128 *Wille's Principles* pp 512–513; *Silberberg & Schoeman Property* pp 168–169.
129 *Malan v Nabygelegen Estates* 1946 AD 562 at 573.
130 See ch 4 above.
131 *Morkels Transport (Pty) Ltd v Melrose Foods (Pty) Ltd* 1972 (2) A 464 (W); *Minister van Landbou v Sonnendecker* 1979 (2) SA 944 (A).
132 See p 180 above.

was in possession, provided that the character of possession, including the mental element, is compatible with acquisitive prescription.

The acquirer need not be present continuously.[133] It is normal for an owner to take a holiday or to go on a business trip. So too for the prescriptive acquirer: he may leave the property from time to time, but not indefinitely. The important point is that the objective impression must be that the acquirer possesses **as if owner** for the requisite period of time.

Sometimes, however, events occur which may serve to disturb the acquirer's possession. There are two kinds of events which have a material effect on acquisitive prescription: interruption and suspension. The 1943 Act is silent on disturbance of possession, which means that the common law rules (as residual law) must apply. The 1969 Act makes specific provision for both kinds of disturbance, adapting the common law position to ease the possibility of acquisition of title by prescription.

Interruption. The prescriptive period may be interrupted when an event caused by external forces persuades the acquirer to give up possession.[134] A distinction is made between natural interruption and civil interruption, depending on the type of event that caused the loss of possession.

Natural interruption occurs when the acquirer voluntarily or involuntarily gives up possession,[135] e.g. because the land is flooded *(vis maior)*, or because the true owner or a third party demands return of the property. Actual loss of physical control must occur. However, not every surrender of physical control equates with natural interruption. For example, if the prescriptive acquirer leases the property to a third party, thereby giving up possession, then this is not natural interruption because the lessee acquires physical control under rights derived from the prescriptive acquirer. By permitting the lessee to lease and occupy the property, the acquirer is, in fact, displaying *animus domini*.

Second, if the true owner demands the return of the property, then natural interruption occurs only if the prescriptive acquirer actually gives up physical control.[136] Mere demand for return is insufficient to interrupt the running of the prescriptive period.

The consequence of natural interruption is that, under the common law, the running of prescription stops and, if the acquirer were to regain possession again, the required 30-year period would begin afresh *(de novo)*.[137] The common law position is, of course, also that of the 1943 Act since this Act is silent on the point of disturbance of the 30-year period. Under the 1969 Act, however, the position is different. The harsh consequence of the common law is ameliorated by s 2 of the Act, which provides that if there is **involuntary** loss of possession, then prescription will not be interrupted if the acquirer regains possession either through legal proceedings within six months of the dispossession or by other lawful means within one year of the dispossession. This means that the prescriptive acquirer could institute the *mandament van spolie* to regain possession within six months from one who dispossessed her. Assuming that the remedy successfully restores possession, then prescription would continue to run without interruption. Similarly, if a natural disaster

---

133 See ch 4 above.
134 *Wille's Principles* pp 514–516; *Silberberg & Schoeman Property* pp 169–172.
135 *Wille's Principles* p 514; *Silberberg & Schoeman Property* p 170.
136 *Wille's Principles* p 514; *Silberberg & Schoeman Property* p 170.
137 *Wille's Principles* p 514; *Silberberg & Schoeman Property* p 170.

forced the acquirer to leave the property, but the acquirer is able to regain control within one year, then prescription would not have been interrupted.

Civil interruption (also called judicial interruption) occurs when legal proceedings are initiated by the true owner against the prescriptive acquirer.[138] The true owner's claim must be based on ownership, rather than on a claim for compensation for unlawful possession. This means that ownership rights must be asserted. A claim for compensation would not be sufficient for interruption.

Service of process on the acquirer, in terms of which ownership rights are asserted, constitutes a civil interruption.[139] 'Process' means any document initiating legal proceedings. This common law rule is confirmed by the 1969 Act. Under the 1943 Act, the effect of service of process is to halt the running of prescription. Under the 1969 Act, the service of process halts the running of prescription **pending the outcome of the legal proceedings**. If the true owner's claim is unsuccessful, or if he withdraws the claim, or abandons a successful judgment, then the consequence is that no interruption of prescription occurs. If the judgment is successful and acted upon, the date of the final judgment is the date on which prescription is interrupted.[140]

7.2.6.2.2 Suspension

Suspension describes the consequence of the change to the true owner's personal circumstances that affects the ability to form or maintain the *animus domini*, which is a necessary element of ownership. For example, due to illness, the true owner may lose the mental capacity to form or maintain the *animus domini*. Such loss of capacity is an impediment (obstacle) to the running of prescription because prescription is not permitted to run against a person who is unable to assert her rights.[141] Sometimes the impediment is legal rather than due to changed personal circumstances, e.g. when the true owner is a minor or a fideicommissary. The rationale for the rule nevertheless applies.

The consequence of a lack of mental or legal capacity is that the prescriptive period must stop running temporarily until the impediment ends, e.g. until the true owner regains the necessary mental capacity or becomes a major. Under the common law, the running of prescription stopped for the duration of the existence of the impediment and continued when the impediment fell away.[142] The 1969 Act makes specific provision for suspension: the common law is altered to the extent that the running of prescription is not stopped. Instead the 1969 Act postpones the completion of prescription in circumstances where the true owner is incapacitated. The focus of attention is on the final few years of the prescriptive period only. Suspension (postponement) occurs only if the 30 years would have been completed on, before or within three years after the date on which the impediment ended.[143] Suspension serves to extend the prescriptive period by three years after the date on which the impediment falls away.[144]

---

138 *Wille's Principles* p 515; *Silberberg & Schoeman Property* p 171.
139 *Wille's Principles* p 515; *Silberberg & Schoeman Property* p 171.
140 *Wille's Principles* p 515; *Silberberg & Schoeman Property* p 171.
141 *Wille's Principles* p 515; *Silberberg & Schoeman Property* p 171.
142 *Wille's Principles* p 515; *Silberberg & Schoeman Property* p 171.
143 *Wille's Principles* pp 515–516; *Silberberg & Schoeman Property* pp 171-172.
144 In effect, the normal extinctive prescriptive period for the assertion of civil claims is added to the acquisitive prescriptive period.

Section 3 of the 1969 Prescription Act[145] reads as follows:

3. *Completion of prescription postponed in certain circumstances*
   (1) If–

   (a) the person against whom the prescription is running is a minor or insane, or is a person under curatorship, or is prevented by superior force from interrupting the running of prescription as contemplated in section 4; or
   (b) the person in favour of whom the prescription is running is outside the Republic, or is married to the person against whom the prescription is running, or is a member of the governing body of a juristic person against whom the prescription is running; and
   (c) the period of prescription would, but for the provisions of this subsection, be completed before or on, or within three years after, the day on which the relevant impediment referred to in paragraph (a) or (b) has ceased to exist,

   the period of prescription shall not be completed before the expiration of a period of three years after the day referred to in paragraph (c).

   (2) Subject to the provisions of subsection (1), the period of prescription in relation to fideicommissary property shall not be completed against a fideicommissary before the expiration of a period of three years after the date on which the right of that fideicommissary to that property vested in him.

The effect of the 1969 Act's change to the common law is to focus the attention on the practicality and importance of the completion period: it is at this stage that it is necessary for the true owner to have the capacity to protect his or her ownership rights. Impediments that fall away well before the completion period are not relevant to the issue of the acquirer becoming owner at a particular point in time.

---

145 Act 68 of 1969.

PAUSE FOR REFLECTION

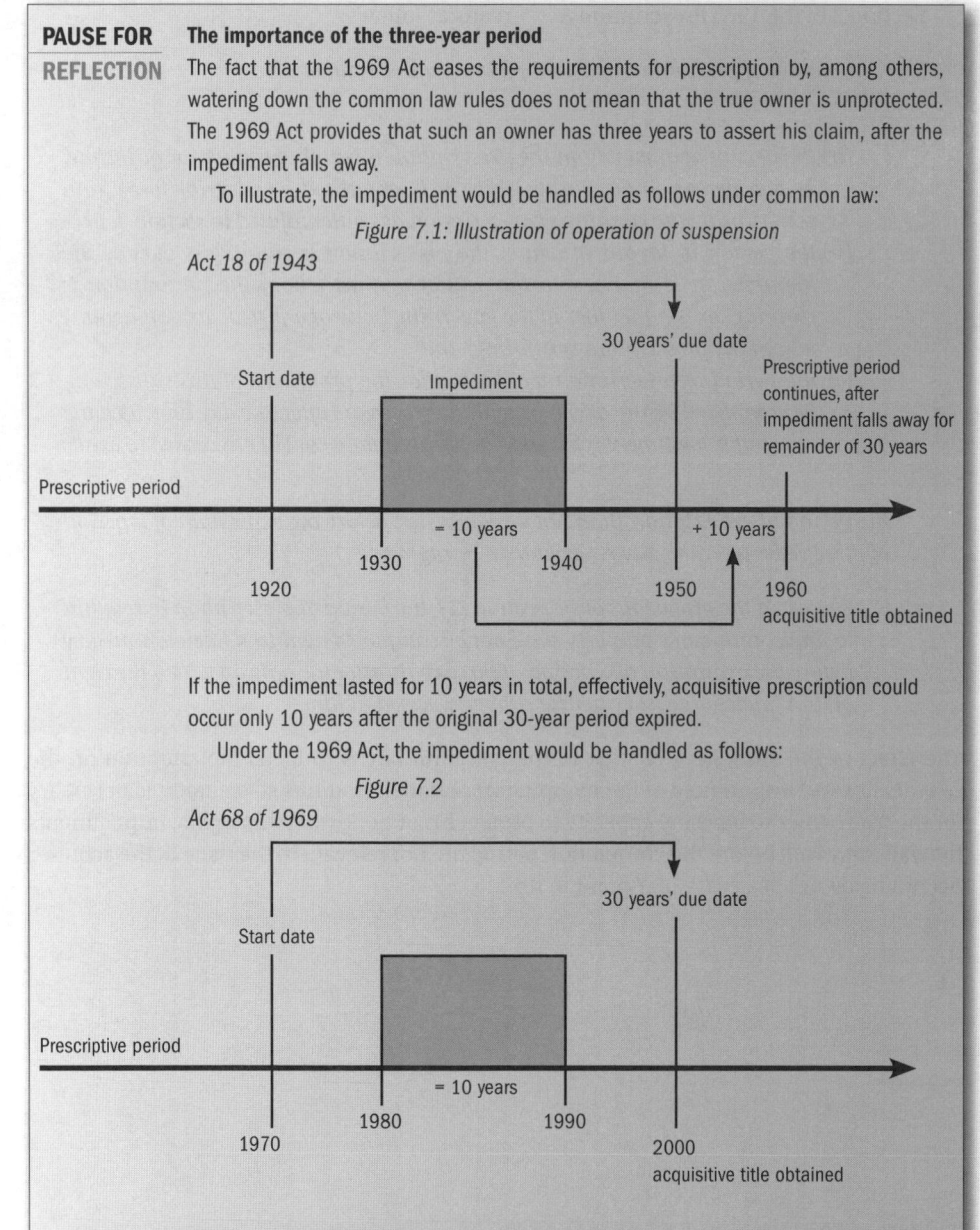

The importance of the three-year period

The fact that the 1969 Act eases the requirements for prescription by, among others, watering down the common law rules does not mean that the true owner is unprotected. The 1969 Act provides that such an owner has three years to assert his claim, after the impediment falls away.

To illustrate, the impediment would be handled as follows under common law:

Figure 7.1: Illustration of operation of suspension

If the impediment lasted for 10 years in total, effectively, acquisitive prescription could occur only 10 years after the original 30-year period expired.

Under the 1969 Act, the impediment would be handled as follows:

Figure 7.2

If the impediment terminated at any point other than during the three years before or after the original due date, it would have no effect on the date on which rights are reallocated: the original due date would still be the relevant date on which title is acquired.

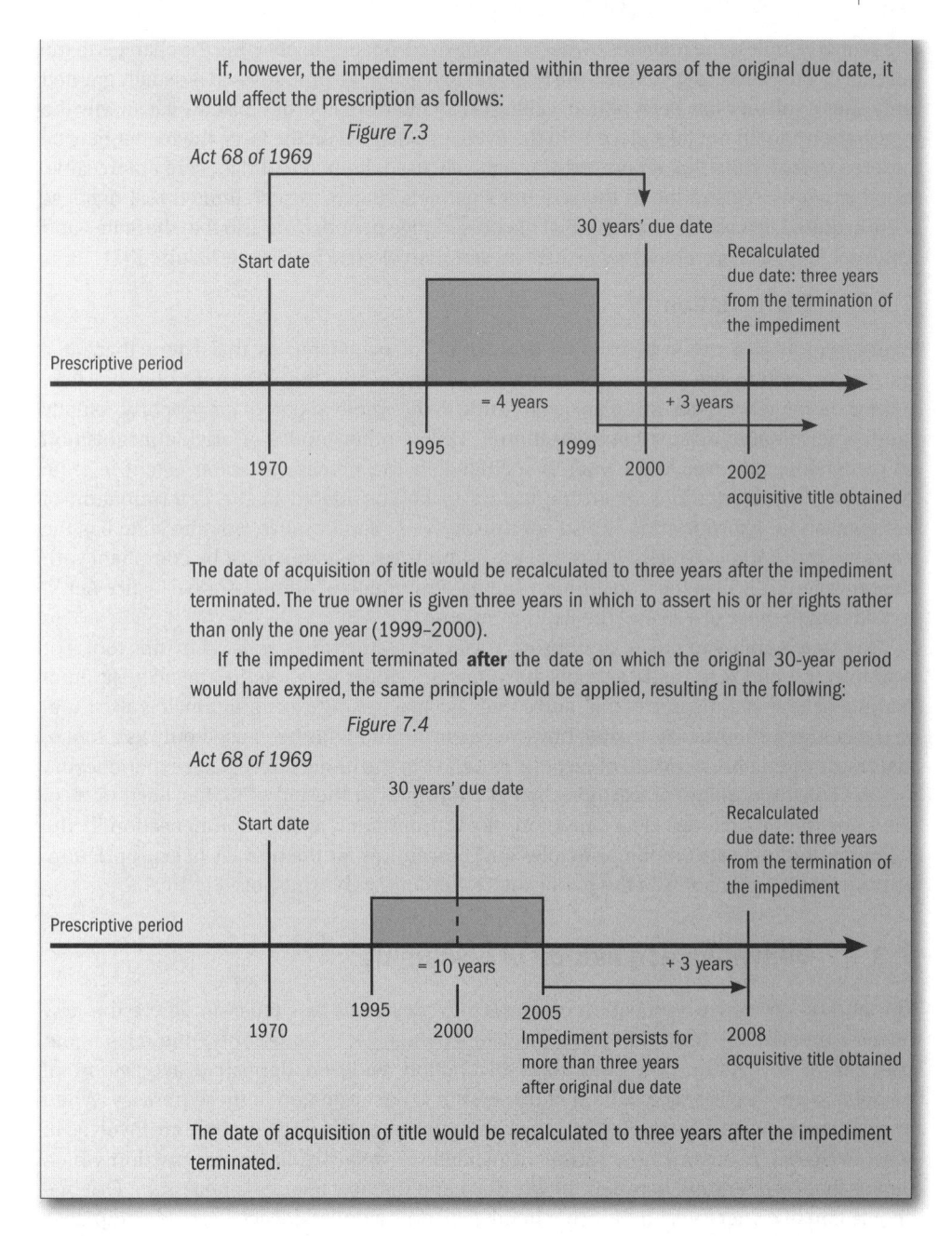

If, however, the impediment terminated within three years of the original due date, it would affect the prescription as follows:

Figure 7.3

```
Act 68 of 1969
                                        30 years' due date
         Start date                                          Recalculated
                                                             due date: three years
                                                             from the termination of
                                                             the impediment
Prescriptive period
                            = 4 years        + 3 years
                       1995            1999
               1970              2000       2002
                                            acquisitive title obtained
```

The date of acquisition of title would be recalculated to three years after the impediment terminated. The true owner is given three years in which to assert his or her rights rather than only the one year (1999–2000).

If the impediment terminated **after** the date on which the original 30-year period would have expired, the same principle would be applied, resulting in the following:

Figure 7.4

```
Act 68 of 1969
                      30 years' due date
         Start date                                          Recalculated
                                                             due date: three years
                                                             from the termination of
                                                             the impediment
Prescriptive period
                          = 10 years              + 3 years
                     1995            2005
               1970         2000     Impediment persists for   2008
                                     more than three years     acquisitive title obtained
                                     after original due date
```

The date of acquisition of title would be recalculated to three years after the impediment terminated.

Until the necessary elements for acquisitive prescription coincide, the acquirer does not become owner. It is thus only in the last few years of the 30-year period that the true owner's interests are really threatened by the fact that the law could reallocate the ownership rights.

The legal effect of acquisitive prescription is that, by operation of law, the acquirer becomes the owner of the property and is entitled to demand registration of the land so acquired in her name. A court order is necessary before the Registrar of Deeds may register the property, unless the previous owner is willing to co-operate in effecting the changes to the title deed. The court order compels the Registrar to register the property and is usually granted only after a rule *nisi* has been issued, calling on all interested parties to show cause why the registration should not take place.[146] In the event of a dispute on the facts, the matter may be ordered to trial. Note that all pre-existing, actively used, limited real rights are enforceable. In other words, registration in the acquirer's name is subject to such limited real rights as were acquired before the completion of the prescriptive period. Note also that the State Land Disposal Act[147] has prohibited acquisitive prescription of state land since 28 June 1971.

7.2.7 Expropriation

Expropriation is a mode of original acquisition of ownership to the extent that, at a particular point in the process, by operation of law, ownership is acquired by the state. Expropriation takes place when an owner's title in the whole or part of his property, usually land, is terminated against compensation.[148] Unlike other modes of original acquisition of ownership, however, the owner is included in the process to some extent, e.g. he may make representations regarding factors to be considered in the determination of compensation. Expropriation is also administrative action because only the state has the power to expropriate, which means that the administrative action must be compliant with the provisions of s 33 of the Constitution and the Promotion of Administrative Justice Act,[149] in addition to those of s 25 and the Expropriation Act.[150]

The state's ability to create or improve social infrastructure is assisted by this tool. For example, to build new roads, schools, hospitals or bridges may require the acquisition of additional land. Acquisition of this land could take place using expropriation. It is also a tool in the land reform process; to date however, expropriation has been used only as a tool of last resort when unreasonable objections or delays to the project have been experienced.

The constitutionality of expropriation is confirmed in the Bill of Rights. Section 25 of the Constitution includes clear provisions for expropriation against compensation.[151] The Expropriation Act sets out the principles and procedures for the process of expropriation. In principle, it occurs only in the public interest or for a public purpose.

7.3 Derivative acquisition of ownership

The phrase 'derivative acquisition of ownership' describes the situation where the new owner's title derives from that of the previous owner. More commonly, one talks about **transfer** of ownership. The important distinction between derivative acquisition of ownership and original acquisition of ownership is encapsulated in these phrases. When one derives ownership from another person, by definition, at least two people are involved in the transaction. In other words, transfer of ownership involves a bilateral transaction, which means that co-operation between the previous and the new owners is necessary. Original acquisition of ownership, on the other hand, concerns a unilateral act, i.e. ownership does not derive from the previous owner but rather is created anew or originally.

---

146 *Wille's Principles* p 517; *Silberberg & Schoeman Property* pp 172–173.
147 Section 3 of Act 48 of 1961.
148 *Wille's Principles* p 517; *Silberberg & Schoeman Property* pp 173–174.
149 Act 3 of 2000.
150 Act 63 of 1975.
151 See ch 6 above.

Transfer of ownership is commonly accompanied by a contract of sale and purchase, but such a contract is not a necessary element. Ownership can be transferred for reasons other than sale and purchase, e.g. when a donation is made. That a contract of sale and purchase commonly accompanies transfer of ownership leads to confusion about the nature of the transaction that transfers ownership. It is important to grasp that the topic here is the law governing transfer of ownership, not the law of contract. The focus is on **what is required to achieve transfer** of ownership rather than **why** it might be transferred. Failure to grasp this important point leads to failure to understand that unless there is proper compliance with the requirements, transfer of ownership will not be achieved, notwithstanding the existence of the contract that explains the reason for the (desired) transfer.

> **PAUSE FOR REFLECTION**
>
> **Separation of transfer from underlying contract**
>
> In some other legal systems, e.g. in England or France, ownership passes upon agreement and delivery between the parties.[152] However, in South Africa, the agreement between the parties that ownership is to transfer because of sale and purchase, gives rise to personal rights and obligations. A separate transaction – the real agreement together with conveyance (delivery) – is needed to transfer ownership and thus give the new owner the real right.
>
> Figure 7.5: The relationship between the underlying contract and the transfer 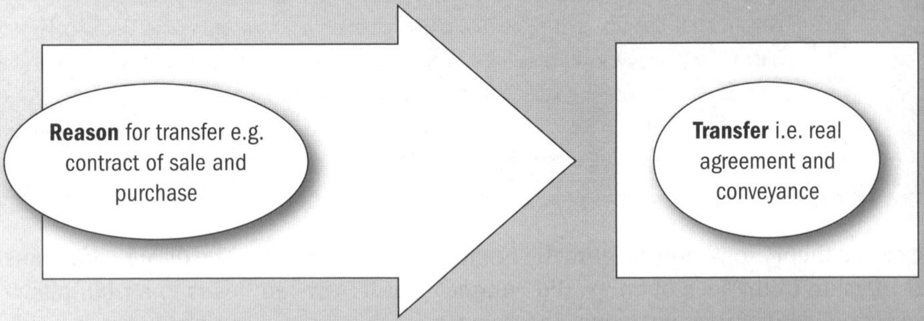
>
> **Reason** for transfer e.g. contract of sale and purchase ⟹ **Transfer** i.e. real agreement and conveyance
>
> It ought to be clear from this that there are actually two transactions involved in, for instance, making the T-shirt at the craft market one's own. On the one hand, there is a contract of sale and purchase and, on the other, the transaction that transfers ownership. To illustrate further: it is necessary but insufficient that Devin and the stallholder agree that Devin wishes to buy the T-shirt and that the stallholder wishes to sell it. If Devin is to become the owner of the T-shirt, it is also necessary that he intends to acquire ownership of the T-shirt, that the stallholder intends to give up ownership thereof, that Devin hands over his cash (the purchase price), that the stallholder hands him (delivers) the T-shirt, and that both have legal capacity. In other words, both must satisfy the requirements of the real agreement and must effect delivery.
>
> A failure to distinguish clearly between the requirements for transfer of ownership and those for a valid contract leads to considerable confusion. It is particularly important to grasp that payment of the purchase price and delivery, on their own, are insufficient to transfer ownership.

---

152 See *Wille's Principles* p 520.

7.3.1 Transfer of ownership as an abstract juristic act

Two systems are possible for transfer of ownership, namely the causal system and the abstract system. South Africa follows the abstract theory.[153] The causal theory requires a *iusta causa* (i.e. a valid cause or basis, usually manifested by a contract) to underpin the transfer of ownership, while the abstract theory separates the underlying cause or basis from the transaction that effects transfer of ownership.[154] In other words, the real agreement and delivery are abstracted from the underlying cause for transfer.

> **PAUSE FOR REFLECTION**
>
> **Where the underlying cause is invalid**
>
> Where the cause underlying the transfer is invalid, the outcome differs according to which theory of transfer is followed. For example, Anele and Busi agree to transfer ownership in a textbook from one to the other. The underlying cause for the transfer is problematic: Anele thinks she is selling the book, while Busi thinks Anele is giving her (donating) the book. In other words, Anele thinks there is a contract of sale and purchase, while Busi thinks there is a contract of donation. It should be quite clear that there is no valid contract here: the parties are not *ad idem*, i.e. they are not of the same mind.
>
> Under a causal system, ownership will not transfer between Anele and Busi. The lack of a valid underlying *iusta causa* invalidates the transfer transaction. However, under the abstract system, the issue is not whether there is a valid underlying contract, but rather whether the parties are *ad idem* (of the same mind) about transferring ownership. Whether the book is sold or donated, the intention is to transfer ownership. Anele and Busi clearly intend ownership to transfer and, because under the abstract system the transfer transaction is abstracted from the underlying cause, ownership would transfer from Anele to Busi when Anele hands the book to Busi. They would then have to sort out their differences using a contractual remedy.

The causal theory impliedly favours the original owner (transferor) by disallowing transfer of ownership in the face of an invalid contract. But this system leads to a multiplicity of legal actions when things go wrong. The transferor is entitled to pursue his property with an action *in rem*, while each subsequent acquirer must revert to her specific contracting party using an action *in personam*, leading inevitably to a multiplicity of legal claims.

The abstract theory, on the other hand, tends to favour the acquirer (transferee and subsequent acquirers) by permitting transfer of ownership, in principle, on the basis of a valid real agreement and conveyance, notwithstanding the existence of an invalid contract.[155] The transferor loses ownership but pursues her claim against the transferee (action *in personam*) to rectify whatever the problem was. It ought to be obvious that the abstract system promotes legal certainty by protecting third parties who rely on the transferor's apparent ownership. One should not be misled, however, into thinking that the abstract system abandons the original owner. There are stringent requirements for transfer of ownership.

---

153 *Air-Kel h/a Merkel Motors v Bodenstein* 1980 (3) SA 912 (A).
154 See *Wille's Principles* p 522; *Silberberg & Schoeman Property* pp 74–76.
155 See *Wille's Principles* pp 522–523; *Silberberg & Schoeman Property* p 76.

Policy determines the choice of system. Early case law shows that the causal system was used in South Africa, probably following the English pattern.[156] Later cases were less specific about which system was used, but used *iusta causa* as evidence for the intention to transfer ownership.[157] In *Commissioner of Customs & Excise v Randles, Brothers & Hudson Ltd*,[158] the Court stated:

> *Ownership of movable property does not in our law pass by the making of a contract. It passes when delivery of possession is given accompanied by an intention on the part of the transferor to transfer ownership and on the part of the transferee to receive it. If it is delivered in pursuance of a contract of sale, the ownership may pass at the time of delivery or it may not. The form of the contract between the parties does not therefore determine whether a delivery in pursuance of it passes ownership ... Whether or not an intention to transfer ownership by delivery exists is a question of fact, not of law.*

Finally, in *Air-Kel h/a Merkel Motors v Bodenstein*,[159] the then Appellate Division explicitly acknowledged that South Africa follows the abstract system of transfer of ownership. This position was confirmed in *Dreyer and Another NNO v AXZS Industries (Pty) Ltd*.[160] However, some lack of clarity persisted as to whether the abstract theory of transfer of ownership applied also to immovable property. In the High Courts, several judgments indicated that transfer of ownership in both movable and immovable property was governed by the abstract theory of transfer.[161] Recently, in *Legator McKenna Inc and Others v Shea and Others*,[162] the Supreme Court of Appeal confirmed that the abstract theory of transfer applies also to immovable property.

7.3.2 Requirements for a valid transfer of ownership

Transfer of ownership depends on a valid real agreement together with a form of conveyance. It is possible to discern a subjective mental element and an objective physical element in the transfer of ownership. The mental element – the intention to transfer ownership – is part of the real agreement. The physical element is the conveyance: delivery or *traditio* for movables and registration for immovable property. This configuration accords with the publicity principle which requires that transfer of ownership be a public act and that the parties intend to transfer ownership.[163]

---

156 *Beyers v McKenzie* 1880 Foord 125 at 127.
157 *Wille's Principles* p 523; *Silberberg & Schoeman Property* p 75.
158 1941 AD 369 at 398.
159 1980 (3) SA 917 (A).
160 2006 (5) SA 548 (SCA) at para 17.
161 See e.g. *Brits v Eaton NO* 1984 (4) SA 728 (T) at 735E; *Klerck NO v Van Zyl and Maritz NNO and Related Cases* 1989 (4) SA 263 (SE) at 273D–274C; *Kriel v Terblanche NO* 2002 (6) SA 132 (NC) at paras 28–40 as cited in *Legator McKenna Inc and Others v Shea and Others* [2008] JOL 22819 (SCA).
162 [2008] JOL 22819 (SCA).
163 *Wille's Principles* p 520; *Silberberg & Schoeman Property* p 73.

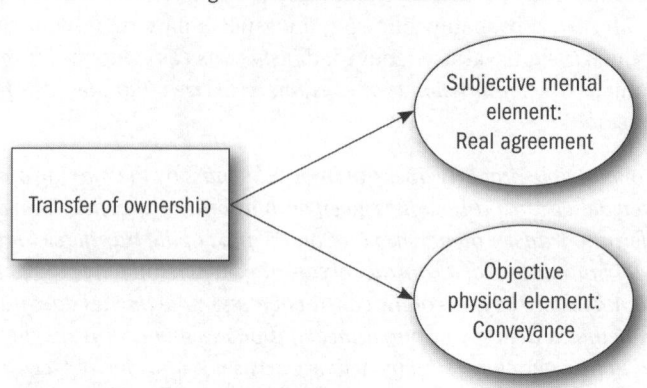

Figure 7.6: Elements of transfer

```
                          ┌─────────────────────┐
                          │ Subjective mental   │
                       ┌──│ element:            │
┌──────────────────┐   │  │ Real agreement      │
│ Transfer of      │───┤  └─────────────────────┘
│ ownership        │   │  ┌─────────────────────┐
└──────────────────┘   │  │ Objective           │
                       └──│ physical element:   │
                          │ Conveyance          │
                          └─────────────────────┘
```

The rule thus is: transfer of ownership happens only when delivery or registration occurs **and** a valid real agreement exists simultaneously. Like most rules, however, this one also has exceptions: marriage in community of property has the consequence that each spouse **automatically** acquires ownership of half of the joint estate (see *Ex parte Menzies et uxor*).[164] Similarly, when a person is declared insolvent (bankrupt), **automatically** ownership of his remaining assets is transferred to the trustee of the insolvent estate.[165]

7.3.2.1   The real agreement (subjective mental element)

Several preconditions are needed before a valid real agreement can be concluded.[166] First, the property (movable or immovable) must be capable of private ownership; in other words, it must be *res in commercio*.

Second, both the transferor (the person who will transfer ownership) and the transferee (the person who will receive ownership upon transfer) must be capable of effecting the transfer. They must have legal capacity to transfer ownership, and the transfer must be undertaken by the owner or a properly authorised agent.

Third, both parties must intend the transfer of ownership. The appropriate *animus* (mental attitude) for the transferor is that he must intend to transfer ownership, while the transferee (acquirer) must intend to acquire ownership. This combination of mental attitudes must be present at the moment the transfer is effected, not at the time the agreement was entered into. For example, Anashri may offer her property for sale, intending to give up ownership. Khirya may go so far as to enter into an agreement with Anashri to purchase the property but, until transfer takes place, Anashri could change her mind about giving up ownership of the property. Khirya may be upset and seek to force Anashri to transfer the property. She will be unsuccessful, but may instead have a claim based on contract.

It could, of course, happen that Khirya changes **her** mind about acquiring ownership. A similar outcome will follow: Anashri will be unable to force Khirya to continue with the transaction but Khirya may be liable in contract to Anashri.

---

164   1993 (3) SA 799 (C) at 807.
165   *Wille's Principles* p 521; *Silberberg & Schoeman Property* pp 177–178.
166   *Wille's Principles* p 521; *Silberberg & Schoeman Property* p 176.

Figure 7.7: Process of transfer

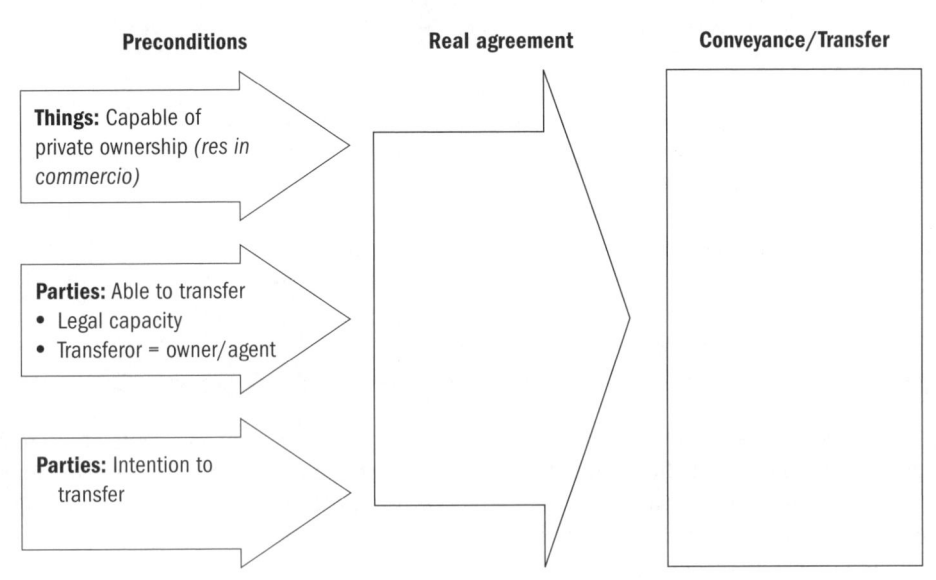

Preconditions → **Real agreement** → **Conveyance/Transfer**

- **Things:** Capable of private ownership *(res in commercio)*
- **Parties:** Able to transfer
  - Legal capacity
  - Transferor = owner/agent
- **Parties:** Intention to transfer

Concor Construction (Cape) (Pty) Ltd v Santambank Ltd[167] involved a dispute as to whether Santambank had acquired ownership of a certain road grader. This equipment was damaged by Concor's employee's negligence and Santambank wished to claim compensation as owner of the property. However, its ownership was disputed on the basis that the requirements for acquisition of ownership were not satisfied. The court reiterated the requirements for transfer of ownership, emphasising that the:

> ... transferor must be capable of transferring ownership ... delivery must be effected ... with the intention of transferring ownership and taken ... with the intention of accepting ownership.[168]

On the facts, it could not be established that delivery had been effected properly with the requisite intention to give and receive ownership.

PAUSE FOR REFLECTION

Importance of *nemo plus iuris* maxim

A fundamental principle in property law is *nemo dat quod non habet* (nobody can give what he does not have). This principle stems from the Roman maxim, *nemo plus iuris transfere potest quam ipse habet* (nobody can transfer more rights than he has). The importance of this maxim cannot be overstated. Several insights should be noted here.

First, a non-owner may contract to transfer ownership but will be unable to effect the transfer without the co-operation of the owner. Thus it is possible to **sell** anything, even if it does not belong to one, but it is not possible to give the buyer ownership unless one is the owner of the property (or a properly authorised agent) at the time of dealing with the buyer.

---

167 1993 (3) SA 930 (A).
168 *Concor Construction* at 933B.

> A further point is that even if the buyer has given the seller the money (purchase price), and the seller has handed the property to him, he cannot become owner without the co-operation of the owner, who must intend to transfer ownership and comply with the other requirements of the real agreement.
>
> Lastly, if the current owner's rights are limited in some way, then ownership as currently limited (not unlimited ownership) is what can be transferred. Because the transferee derives her title from that of the predecessor, her title 'will be subject to any infirmities in the predecessor's title'.[169] For example, ownership may be limited by a servitude, a mortgage bond or a use restriction. The new owner cannot acquire unencumbered ownership. This latter point should permit one to see more clearly the important practical effect of registered limited real rights and other restrictions on ownership, including personal rights with real effect, at the time of transfer.[170]

In *Dreyer & Another NNO v AXZS Industries (Pty) Ltd*,[171] whether the elements of the real agreement had been satisfied and thus whether ownership had transferred were in dispute. The matter involved the sale of particular goods at a post-liquidation auction sale. The purchaser (respondent) understood the goods concerned to be included in the sale. They were not reflected, however, in the written conditions of sale approved by the liquidators. Consequently, the appellants contended that the agent of the sellers did not have authority to sell assets not included in the conditions of sale. The Supreme Court of Appeal found that two elements of the real agreement were not satisfied: the person who purported to transfer ownership was not authorised to transfer ownership and, furthermore, by his own account, he did not intend to transfer ownership to the respondent, thus sounding 'the death knell of the real agreement'.[172] The real agreement requires a meeting of minds: the parties must be *ad idem* on the giving and receiving of ownership.[173]

7.3.2.2 Sale of movables and transfer of ownership

Special common law rules[174] govern transfer of ownership following the sale of movables. These rules evolved in response to the vagaries of the commercial world where goods move extremely swiftly from one person to another, while the wheels of justice grind slowly. The rules are that if the sale is for **cash**, then ownership transfers upon **payment with delivery**, the real agreement being valid. If the sale is for **credit**, i.e. later payment is permitted, then ownership transfers upon **delivery alone**.[175] In each situation, a valid real agreement remains a necessary element.

For example, Abel owns a bicycle; he sells it to Barney and accepts a cheque in payment. Barney then sells the bicycle to Chris who pays cash and rides away on it. Then Abel discovers that Barney's cheque has been returned. Barney has no money in his account and so no payment has been made for the bicycle. This means that ownership did not transfer from Abel

---

169 *Silberberg & Schoeman Property* p 72.
170 See ch 3 above.
171 2006 (5) SA 548 (SCA).
172 *Dreyer* at 555-556.
173 *Air-Kel h/a Merkel Motors v Bodenstein* 1980 (3) SA 917 (A) at 922.
174 Note the National Credit Act 34 of 2005 is not under consideration here.
175 *Wille's Principles* pp 521-522; *Silberberg & Schoeman Property* pp 176-177.

to Barney and in turn, therefore, that Barney was unable to transfer ownership to Chris. The requirements for transfer of ownership are payment and delivery, and a valid real agreement. No payment occurred and therefore no transfer of ownership to Barney was possible. Application of the *nemo plus iuris* rule results in Barney being unable to transfer ownership to Chris.

Since Abel is still the owner, he is entitled to recover his property, and may do so wherever that property is currently to be found (action *in rem*). Chris, on the other hand, is entitled to claim breach of contract against Barney (action *in personam*).[176]

While Abel is entitled to recover his bicycle, it may be impractical to find Chris. He would have to rely on Barney for details as to the identity of Chris. It could take months to find Chris, let alone institute action against him. And would Chris not be surprised to lose the bicycle? What did he do wrong? He fulfilled his side of the transaction and had no obvious way to know that Barney was not in a position to transfer ownership. But the rules are clear: where a sale of movables underlies the transfer of ownership, the general rule is that if the real agreement is valid and the sale is for **cash**, then ownership transfers upon **payment with delivery**; if the sale is for **credit**, i.e. later payment is permitted, then ownership transfers upon **delivery alone**. That Abel did not receive payment means that, despite delivery and the intention to transfer ownership, Abel could not transfer ownership to Barney.

Is it possible that by accepting a cheque, Abel intended to allow Barney credit terms of payment, i.e. to permit him to pay later or by instalment? Is payment by cheque a cash or credit transaction? Payment by cheque is a cash transaction, provided the cheque is honoured on presentation.[177] That is, the account upon which the cheque is drawn must have sufficient funds to make the payment. The delay between the time that Barney hands Abel the cheque and the time that Abel deposits the cheque is of no consequence.[178] In the example above, Abel accepted the cheque but when he presented it, there were insufficient funds in Barney's account. The rule for a cash transaction requires payment and delivery concurrently for ownership to pass.

But, what if Abel and Barney had done business regularly over several years? For example, Abel acquires bicycles specifically for reselling and Barney regularly sells on the bicycles. In other words, there is a business relationship between them, in terms of which Abel usually accepts a cheque from Barney and the cheque is usually honoured. Both parties are thus usually happy with the way things work. Ownership of the bicycles moves swiftly from Abel to Barney to the third person. One day, though, Barney is short of cash and his cheque is not honoured, which means that ownership cannot transfer from Abel.[179]

However, what did Abel actually intend at the time of dealing with Barney? Did Abel intend to transfer ownership in the bicycle? Yes, but of course only if Barney paid for it. But, if Abel really intended ownership to pass and, for technical reasons, he can hide behind the law because the cheque unexpectedly was dishonoured, is this fair for someone like Chris? The courts did not think so. In *Eriksen Motors Ltd v Protea Motors Warrenton and Another*,[180] where the facts were comparable to the scenario sketched above, the then Appellate Division stated:

---

176 *Wille's Principles* p 522.
177 *Wille's Principles* p 522; *Silberberg & Schoeman Property* p 178.
178 *Wille's Principles* p 522; *Silberberg & Schoeman Property* pp 177–178. Note that a post-dated cheque points to a credit transaction.
179 *Grosvenor Motors (Potchefstroom) v Douglas* 1956 (3) SA 420 (A).
180 1973 (3) SA 685 (A).

> *It depends whether the totality of circumstances shows, by inference or otherwise, that the parties intended ownership to pass or not to pass as the case may be ... It follows that, in the circumstances of the present case, the question whether the sale was for cash or credit is relevant but not conclusive.*

In other words, in general, when a sale of movables underlies a transfer of ownership, whether the transaction is for cash or credit guides the determination of whether transfer of ownership took place. But in some circumstances, the factual context must be scrutinised more carefully to ascertain from 'the totality of circumstances' whether the parties intended ownership to pass on delivery. If so, then something such as a dishonoured cheque should not prejudice a bona fide third party's acquisition of ownership. This is in keeping with the spirit of the abstract system of transfer of ownership.

PAUSE FOR REFLECTION

Reserving ownership

Can a transferor in a common law credit transaction protect her ownership rights? In other words, can she deliver the property, expecting payment at a later time, but also prevent ownership from transferring at the time of delivery? One method that can achieve this is to reserve ownership, i.e. to permit credit terms of payment but to state explicitly that ownership will not transfer until payment is completed, and to require the transferee to agree to these terms. This reservation of ownership preserves the use of the *rei vindicatio* for the transferor as owner.

But what happens to the reservation of ownership when the movable thing does not remain movable because it is attached to immovable property? In other words, what happens when the rules of original acquisition of ownership[181] enter the picture? When dealing with a problem that requires the application of the rules of original acquisition of ownership and also the rules of derivative acquisition of ownership, there are various considerations to take into account.

Whether one set of rules takes precedence over the other is not really clear. However, arguably, the nature of original acquisition of ownership seems to dictate that a reservation of ownership may be nullified in circumstances where accession was foreseeable. That is, the law is clear that upon the simultaneous satisfaction of stipulated objectively determined factors, ownership rights are reallocated by operation of law. In other words, where the owner of the movable goods reserves ownership despite knowing at the time of the sale that the purchaser intends to affix the movable to immovable property, and nevertheless allows the purchaser to take the goods without paying for them in full, it is likely that accession would override the reservation of ownership.[182]

But, given the inconsistent approach by the courts to the weighting of the factors used to determine the occurrence of *inaedificatio*, it is also possible that, in particular circumstances, the reservation of ownership might be upheld notwithstanding the occurrence of accession.

---

181 See pp 161*ff* above.
182 See pp 168*ff* above.

7.3.2.3 Delivery or registration (objective physical element)

The basic requirements as discussed above regarding the real agreement apply to both movable and immovable property. However, the requirements as regards the physical element are adapted to the circumstances of the two classes of property. The objective physical element of transfer is satisfied by way of delivery *(traditio)* in the case of movables, and registration in the case of immovable property (i.e. land).

To transfer ownership in land, a real agreement and registration at the relevant Deeds Office are required. In other words, the basic requirements are the same as for movables except that the form of conveyance is registration.[183] There is only one form for immovable property. In addition to these requirements, there are also statutory requirements,[184] e.g. that the agreement to alienate the land must be in writing. Registration is discussed in more detail below.

Delivery may take one of two forms: actual delivery where possession and thus physical control are handed over to the transferee, or constructive delivery where no physical handing over occurs but other substitute elements must be present.

7.3.3 Delivery

Delivery itself also has mental and physical elements, which must be satisfied to effect a valid delivery, whether actual or constructive. This is illustrated by the diagram below.

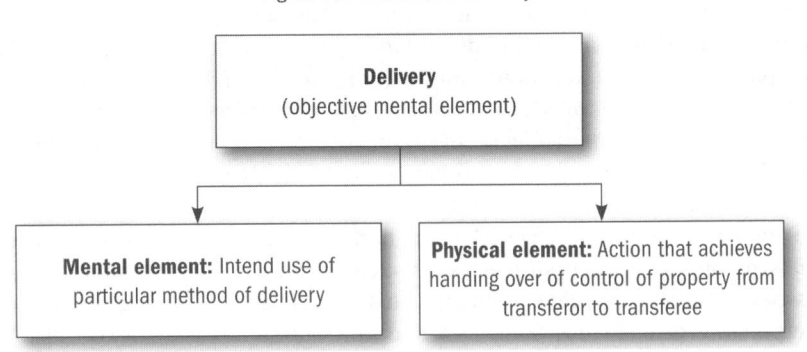

Figure 7.8: Elements of delivery

```
                    ┌─────────────────────────┐
                    │         Delivery        │
                    │ (objective mental element) │
                    └─────────────────────────┘
                        │                │
          ┌─────────────┘                └─────────────┐
          ▼                                            ▼
┌──────────────────────────┐          ┌──────────────────────────────┐
│ Mental element: Intend   │          │ Physical element: Action that │
│ use of particular method │          │ achieves handing over of      │
│ of delivery              │          │ control of property from      │
│                          │          │ transferor to transferee      │
└──────────────────────────┘          └──────────────────────────────┘
```

Apart from the physical element of delivery, which involves that the parties hand over and receive control of the property, they must also **intend** to deliver in a specific way. This is what is meant by the mental aspect of delivery.

---

183 *Cape Explosive Works Ltd v Denel (Pty) Ltd* 2001 (3) SA 569 (SCA) at 577 para 10.
184 The Alienation of Land Act 68 of 1981, the Deeds Registries Act 47 of 1937, and the Land Survey Act 8 of 1997 are key statutes. Significant new legislation, introduced since the early 1990s, aims to facilitate implementation of land reform goals, including to facilitate acquisition of ownership of land, e.g. the Restitution of Land Rights Act 22 of 1994, the Development Facilitation Act 67 of 1995, the Land Reform (Labour Tenants) Act 3 of 1996, and the Extension of Security of Tenure Act 62 of 1997.

Essentially, the transferor must hand over possession of the thing to the transferee, who must be able to exercise physical control over it. This is referred to as **actual delivery**: the thing is actually, physically, handed over and received. An agent can effect such delivery for either party.

Sometimes the nature of the thing or entity makes handing over in the literal sense impractical or even impossible. For example, Kumi wishes to deliver a flock of goats to Jivan. Both parties are present at the scene, so actual delivery would be appropriate, but should Kumi literally pick up and hand over each goat of the flock to Jivan to comply with the requirements? It would be silly for the law to require such literalism. Instead, it should be remembered that a flock of goats can be regarded as a legal entity for some purposes,[185] notwithstanding that the real right of ownership subsists in each goat rather than in respect of the flock. One such purpose is delivery. Thus Kumi may herd the goats into Jivan's vehicle or goat-pens and complete delivery in this way. Similarly, a load of wood can be delivered by offloading it in the transferee's yard; the transferor does not have to hand each plank or stick of wood to the transferee. The mental element of delivery is satisfied by establishing that the parties both intend this method of delivery to be how delivery is to be effected, while the physical element is obvious: the flock of goats moves physically from Kumi's control to that of Jivan's.

Constructive delivery is used in such circumstances where the nature of the thing makes actual delivery difficult or even impossible, or the circumstances are such that actual delivery is inappropriate.[186] Although there is no physical handing over of the property concerned, the required physical element is present. The mental element involves the parties being *ad idem* about the method to be used to effect delivery. Does this mean that the parties can agree to choose any method they like? No, the legally acceptable methods are finite (i.e. there is a *numerus clausus* of constructive delivery forms),[187] and each is suitable only for a particular set of circumstances. In other words, only the methods endorsed by the law are acceptable and they are not interchangeable. Each is appropriate only to a particular set of circumstances.

The *numerus clausus* of acceptable methods of constructive delivery are *clavium traditio* (symbolic delivery), *traditio longa manu* (delivery with the long hand), *constitutum possessorium, traditio brevi manu* (delivery with the short hand), and attornment. Because of the interpretation given to the principles of attornment in some cases, the so-called 'cession of the right of vindication' *(cessio iuris vindicationis)* is sometimes added to this list. The first four methods stem from Roman law, the fifth comes from English law, while the last – if one chooses to think that this represents an independent mode of delivery – has been developed by the South African courts.

---

185 See ch 2 above.
186 *Wille's Principles* p 525; *Silberberg & Schoeman Property* p 181.
187 *Wille's Principles* p 525; *Silberberg & Schoeman Property* p 181 expresses doubt as to the existence of a *numerus clausus*.

The diagram below summarises the different modes of delivery.

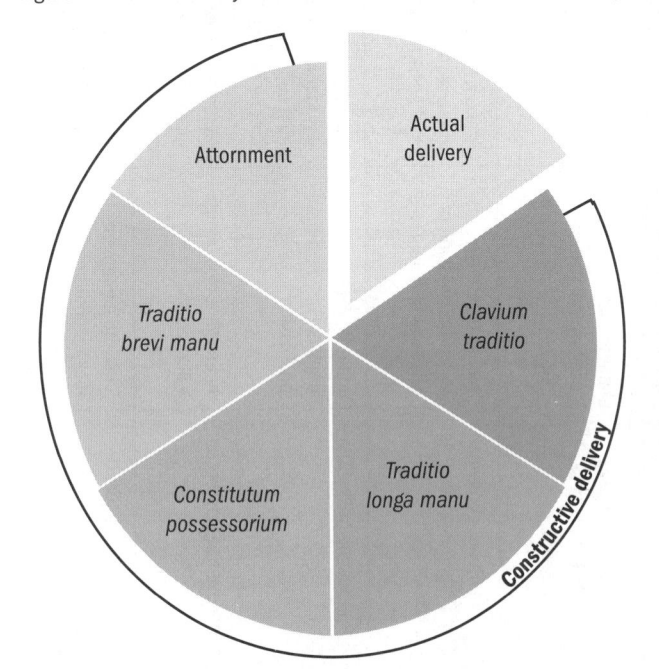

Figure 7.9: Actual delivery and different modes of constructive delivery

- Actual delivery
- Attornment
- Traditio brevi manu
- Clavium traditio
- Constitutum possessorium
- Traditio longa manu

(Constructive delivery)

Most transactions to transfer ownership in movables make use of actual delivery. In most cases, meeting the physical requirement for transfer is unproblematic. Difficulties arise more readily where the physical requirement cannot be met simply by actually handing over the property, and where delivery has to be constructive. The table below summarises the triggers for and the elements of the various modes of constructive delivery, followed by discussion of the requirements for the various modes of constructive delivery.

Table 7:2: Triggers for and the elements of the various modes of constructive delivery

Mode	Modes of constructive delivery			
	Trigger circumstances	Physical element	Mental element	Special applications or considerations
Clavium traditio	Goods contained in warehouse or other container	Symbol of exclusive means to take physical control	Intend that handing over symbol delivers goods	CIF contracts
Traditio longa manu	Goods bulky/large or external factors prevent actual delivery	Pointing out in presence of T^{ee}; goods at disposal of T^{ee}	Intend that T^{or} remains in bare possession of goods until T^{ee} removes them	T^{ee} must be able to take possession without legal assistance
Constitutum possessorium	Goods to be used in terms of contract by T^{or} after transfer of ownership	Pre-existing possession by T^{or}	Intend ownership will transfer; T^{ee} not to have possession	*Causa detentionis* is key; factual evidence must support inference of bona fide conduct
Traditio brevi manu	T^{ee} in possession before transfer	Pre-existing possession by T^{ee}	Intend that ownership will transfer	Factual evidence must support inference of bona fide conduct
Attornment	Third party in possession of goods when ownership must transfer	Tripartite agreement; third party must at minimum have right to control goods	Tripartite agreement includes third party to achieve concurrence of mind	Notification to third party of change of ownership not sufficient

7.3.3.1 *Clavium traditio* (symbolic delivery)

Clavium traditio is a method of constructive delivery used when property, e.g. bags of grain, is held in a warehouse or other container that is accessed by key. Rather than physically hand over each bag of grain to the transferee, the transferor hands the key of the warehouse to the transferee.[188]

The key (the physical element) symbolises the **means by which the transferee can gain access to and take physical control** of the property. It is vital that the transferee is able to deal **exclusively** with the property.[189] This means that the transferor should not retain a spare key for use in the period prior to the transferee taking actual physical control of the property. To do so would dilute the ability of the transferee to exercise exclusive physical control. In other words, the key must be handed over with the intention that this act will deliver the contents of the warehouse rather than afford the transferee an opportunity to inspect the goods. This satisfies the required mental element. Symbols other than a key include documents of title, bills of lading or warehouse receipts.[190]

A common application of symbolic delivery is in respect of Carriage, Insurance & Freight (CIF) contracts, which are used when goods must travel by sea between the transferor and the transferee, and thus actual delivery is unsuitable.[191] For example, Max grows apples near Ceres for the export market, specifically the fresh produce market in London. It would be impractical for Max to travel with his apples to hand them over to the transferee in London. Instead, he delivers the apples to a carrier (Springs Shipping (Pty) Ltd) who is contracted to deliver them physically to the transferee, Tesco (Pty) Ltd.

A mercantile practice has developed whereby Max can transfer ownership of the apples to Tesco long before the apples reach London. Transfer of ownership is effected by handing over the shipping documents, including the bill of lading, to Tesco.[192] Delivery can be by electronic transmission.[193] The bill of lading is the principal document among the shipping documents, which include an insurance policy and the invoice. The bill of lading is a written acknowledgement by the master of the ship that the goods have been delivered on board and it evidences an undertaking to carry the goods to the stated destination.

7.3.3.2 *Traditio longa manu* (delivery with the long hand)

As the name suggests, this method of constructive delivery requires a pointing out of the property to be delivered.[194] It is used when the property is bulky and not easy to move, or where special arrangements for its removal must be made because of external imperatives. For example, public health regulations may require a permit to be obtained before removing the property. Again, for the sake of efficiency, it may be desirable to effect transfer of ownership sooner rather than later. However, the consequence of this method is that the transferor may remain in possession of the property for a period of time while the

---

188 *Wille's Principles* p 525; *Silberberg & Schoeman Property* pp 181–182.
189 *Wille's Principles* p 526; *Silberberg & Schoeman Property* p 182.
190 *Wille's Principles* p 526; *Silberberg & Schoeman Property* p 182.
191 *Wille's Principles* p 526; *Silberberg & Schoeman Property* p 182.
192 See *Lendalease Finance (Pty) Ltd v Corporacion de Merçadeo Agricola* 1975 (4) SA 397 (C) for a discussion about the nature of CIF contracts; also *Hochmetals Africa (Pty) Ltd v Otavi Mining Co (Pty) Ltd* 1968 (1) SA 571 (A) at 579: '[A bill of lading] is a key which in the hand of the rightful owner is intended to unlock the door of the warehouse floating or fixed, in which the goods may chance to be.'
193 In terms of s 3(1)(*b*) of Sea Transport Documents Act 65 of 2000.
194 *Wille's Principles* p 526; *Silberberg & Schoeman Property* p 183.

transferee becomes the new owner with immediate effect. In other words, the transferor has possession on behalf of the new owner. His role may be likened to that of a custodian.[195]

Because of the obvious ambiguity that results from the transferor remaining in possession where goods are easily portable, the choice to use this method of constructive delivery will be carefully scrutinised by the courts in the event of a dispute. Such scrutiny would seek to protect the interests of third parties, especially creditors. 'A resort to [*traditio longa manu*] in respect of "portable" movables would need some very special explanation.'[196]

It is required that the transferor must point out the property in the presence of the transferee and must place the property at the disposal of the transferee so that the latter can exercise physical control without legal assistance.[197] It follows that exclusive physical control is not necessary. The property must furthermore be clearly identified or easily ascertainable.

The mental element requires that the parties intend that, following delivery, the transferor (now in a custodial role) will remain in possession while the transferee is the owner and makes the arrangements to remove the property concerned from the transferor's premises.[198] In *Groenewald v Van der Merwe*,[199] a threshing machine with engine was sold to Groenewald who inspected it but left it with the seller until further notice. Some eighteen months later, the seller sold it again to Van der Merwe. When Groenewald heard of the second sale, he removed the threshing machine to his own property, but Van der Merwe objected and sued for delivery of the machine. The question was whether 'valid delivery was made to either, and if so, to which one'.[200] Note that it would have been impossible for ownership to transfer to both. If, on the facts, a valid delivery took place between the seller and Groenewald, then the seller could not transfer ownership to Van der Merwe because of the *nemo plus iuris* rule.

In the circumstances, the court found that the mental attitude of Groenewald:

> *when the parties discussed the matter was not shown to be such as was requisite for the transfer of possession ... He did not intend there and then to acquire and exercise control over the thing as his own, for his mind was not directed to that point.*[201]

This meant that there was not a valid delivery *longa manu* between the seller and Groenewald, and hence Groenewald did not acquire ownership of the machine. Van der Merwe, on the other hand, under the guidance of an astute candidate attorney, had explicitly walked around the machine in the presence of the transferor and stated that the machine was henceforth his, thus evidencing very clearly the requisite mental attitude. The consequence was that a valid delivery *longa manu* had been made to Van der Merwe, not to Groenewald, and thus ownership had transferred to Van der Merwe. The pointing out and inspection of the property to be transferred by *traditio longa manu*, therefore, is of the utmost importance.

---

195 *Wille's Principles* p 529.
196 *Groenewald v Van der Merwe* 1917 AD 233 at 239.
197 *Eskom v Rollomatic Engineering (Edms) Bpk* 1992 (2) SA 725 (A).
198 See *Wille's Principles* pp 526–527 and *Silberberg & Schoeman Property* pp182–184 for more detailed discussion.
199 1917 AD 233.
200 *Groenewald* at 238.
201 *Groenewald* at 240.

7.3.3.3 Constitutum possessorium

Constitutum possessorium can be used when the parties agree that the transferor will retain possession following transfer, but on the basis of a **contractual arrangement** between them.[202] In other words, the transferor continues to possess the property, but does so with permission of the transferee (who is now the owner) and in terms of the newly established contractual relationship between them. For instance, Sandra purchases her wedding dress from Mayers (Pty) Ltd, but has to leave it at the shop so that the waist can be taken in: Mayers is no longer the owner of the dress, but has entered into a contract with Sandra to effect alterations to the dress. Once again, ownership is transferred on the basis of a changed relationship between the parties. Note that the basis for Mayers remaining in possession of the dress is the **contract of service**.

The pre-existing possession by the transferor serves as the physical element. Similarly to *traditio longa manu*, the possibility for fraud exists. Hence the focus of attention is on the mental element.

The mental element entails that the parties must intend that, at a given moment, the current possessor (i.e. the transferor) will cease to be the owner and will be merely the possessor; and that the transferee will become the owner, but will not take possession. In other words, the intention must be that there will be a change of legal status for both parties vis-à-vis the property concerned.[203] Since it is difficult to know without personal testimony what a person's intentions are, the courts' attitude to this method of delivery is one of extreme caution.[204] *Constitutum possessorium* is never presumed, but must be proven.

Strict requirements have been laid down in case law.[205] The party who relies on *constitutum possessorium* as the method of delivery, must provide clear factual evidence from which such an inference necessarily follows. The transferor must be the owner and must be in possession at the time of transfer. The transferor must cease to possess for himself and begin to possess for the transferee, who must agree that the transferor retains possession.

The key is to demonstrate clearly the existence of a distinct *causa detentionis*, i.e. a genuine new contractual relationship between the parties on the basis of which the transferor retains possession.[206] In other words, the factual evidence must demonstrate clearly that the arrangement between the parties is bona fide, and that it explains and underpins why the transferor continues to have possession of the property. Note that this contractual arrangement does not refer to why the transfer of ownership has occurred, but to why the transferor continues to be in possession.

The reason the courts take such a strict approach to this method of delivery is because sometimes parties do not really want to transfer ownership, but rather wish to create a real right of security.[207] In the case of movable property, creating a real security right of pledge requires that possession of the property must be delivered to the pledgee (creditor) who retains possession until the debt is repaid.[208]

The difficulty with this requirement is that usually the debtor needs to retain possession of the property to generate revenue to repay his debts to the creditor. So the parties resort to

---

202 *Wille's Principles* p 528; *Silberberg & Schoeman Property* p 188.
203 *Wille's Principles* p 529; *Silberberg & Schoeman Property* p 188.
204 *Wille's Principles* pp 529–530; *Silberberg & Schoeman Property* p 189.
205 See cases cited in *Wille's Principles* p 529; *Silberberg & Schoeman Property* pp 189-193 .
206 *Wille's Principles* p 529; *Silberberg & Schoeman Property* pp 188–189.
207 *Wille's Principles* p 529; *Silberberg & Schoeman Property* p 190.
208 See ch 12 below.

subterfuge: they pretend that they intend to transfer ownership in terms of a sale and lease-back arrangement, or a sale and immediate resale, using *constitutum possessorium* as the method of delivery. Here the transferor retains possession, but there is no genuine *causa detentionis*. This may be evidenced by an unrealistic purchase price (*Vasco Dry Cleaners v Twycross*),[209] or a lack of plausible connection between the parties to explain the contractual relationship.[210]

It should be remembered that it is quite possible to enter into a **genuine** sale and lease-back or sale and immediate resale agreement, and to use *constitutum possessorium* as the appropriate method of delivery. The line between a genuine and a fraudulent transaction is fine and thus caution should be exercised when contemplating an alleged delivery by *constitutum possessorium*.

> **PAUSE FOR REFLECTION**
>
> **Revisiting *Groenewald v Van der Merwe***
>
> In *Groenewald v Van der Merwe*,[211] it was contended in argument that delivery to Groenewald might have occurred on the basis of *constitutum possessorium*. The necessary *causa detentionis* would be fulfilled by the arrangement that Du Toit would keep and use the threshing machine for his own account, provided he effected the necessary repairs to the machine. On the face of it, this kind of arrangement might support the necessary inference that *constitutum possessorium* was the intended method of constructive delivery. However, the absence of sufficient factual evidence to support the conclusion that Groenewald intended to acquire ownership at the time of the transaction did not allow the argument to succeed.

7.3.3.4 *Traditio brevi manu* (delivery with the short hand)

Traditio brevi manu can be used in circumstances where the transferee is already in possession of the property of which he will acquire ownership,[212] e.g. he leases the property but has agreed to purchase it and take transfer of ownership from the owner. His status thus changes from that of possessor (via the lease agreement) to owner (via the transfer). Ownership transfers on the basis of the real agreement and the agreement that, at a particular point in time, the transferee will henceforth be the owner and that this method of delivery will transfer ownership.

No actual handing over takes place; the physical element is satisfied by the pre-existing possession on the part of the transferee.[213] The content of mental attitude changes for both parties: the transferor intends to give up ownership to the transferee, while the transferee intends to acquire ownership, and to continue to possess the property, but now as owner. The parties must intend that, at an agreed moment, the current possessor (transferee) will cease to be the possessor and will be the owner. In the absence of any physical handing over, factual evidence to support the inference that a change in mental attitude has occurred and is bona fide is vital. The scope for fraud against creditors of the transferor ought to be obvious. However, given the presumption that the possessor is the owner unless the

---

209 1979 (1) SA 603 (A).
210 See *Wille's Principles* pp 528–529 and *Silberberg & Schoeman Property* pp 188–198 for more detailed discussion and examples.
211 1917 AD 233 at 240.
212 *Wille's Principles* p 527; *Silberberg & Schoeman Property* p 184.
213 *Wille's Principles* pp 527–528; *Silberberg & Schoeman Property* p 184.

contrary is established, this method of delivery does not seem to excite as much doubt as *constitutum possessorium*[214] because the publicity principle is served by the fact that the transferee is already in possession of the movable.

An example would be where Hermes, a watchmaker, purchases a watch from Rijk that the latter left with Hermes for repairs. *Traditio brevi manu* occurs when the parties' intention that Hermes should henceforth continue to hold the watch as owner is clear.

Another example may be taken from *Meintjies v Wilson*,[215] in which a company settled a director's claim for salary arrears by transferring ownership in his office furniture and equipment to the director, using *traditio brevi manu* (i.e. by agreeing with the director that such furniture and equipment already in his possession should become his personal property). Subsequently, a creditor was unable to attach that furniture and equipment in execution of a judgment for a debt owed by the company.

> **PAUSE FOR REFLECTION**
>
> **Should the postponed transfer of ownership in case of credit sale agreements be regarded as delivery *brevi manu*?**
>
> Whether hire-purchase agreements give rise to transfer of ownership by *traditio brevi manu* has always been a matter of some uncertainty. Some authors[216] and case law[217] contend that this is indeed a case in which *traditio brevi manu* occurs. Another view[218] is that *traditio brevi manu* can only occur when the hire purchaser still possesses the thing at the time the last payment is made. A further view[219] is that postponed transfer does not use *traditio brevi manu* as ownership passes immediately with delivery of possession, and only the consequences are suspended.[220] It ought to be obvious that the uncertainty is caused by a confusion of two different scenarios, i.e. where the transferee is in possession when the last payment is made, and where he is not.[221]
>
> Generally, a hire purchaser already has physical control of the thing at the moment when the last instalment is paid. If this is the case, then indeed delivery can certainly take place by means of *traditio brevi manu* when the final payment is made.[222] But if the hire purchaser has on-sold the item, or has given up physical control by way of pledge, then the requirements for *traditio brevi manu* cannot be fulfilled upon payment of the last instalment. This is because the transferee is not in physical control of the property at the moment when the *animus* to transfer and receive ownership is present.
>
> *Info Plus v Scheelke*[223] suggested that requiring possession at the moment when the last payment is made is a pointless interpretation of the law. Thus, transfer should occur upon payment of the last instalment, regardless of whether the thing is still in the transferee's possession. If this is the case, however, then it is not *traditio brevi manu* that conveys ownership: the physical requirement is not met where the transferee is no

---

214 See *Wille's Principles* pp 527–528 and *Silberberg & Schoeman Property* pp 184–188 for more detailed discussion.
215 1927 OPD 183 at 188–189.
216 Van der Walt, AJ & Pienaar, GJ (2006) *Introduction to Property Law* (Cape Town, Juta) p 132.
217 *Info Plus v Scheelke and Another* 1998 (3) SA 184 (SCA) at 189G–191A.
218 Van der Merwe *Sakereg* p 321.
219 Cronje, DSP 'Die Verkryging van Eiendomsreg deur 'n Huurkoopkoper' (1979) *TSAR* 16 at 50.
220 This view is based on an interpretation of the decision in *Pennefather v Gokul* 1960 (4) SA 42 (N) at 44B.
221 *Silberberg & Schoeman Property* pp 186–187.
222 See e.g. *Forsdick Motors v Lauritzen and Another* 1967 (3) SA 249 (N).
223 1998 (3) SA 184 (SCA) at 192C.

longer in possession. This must mean that the rules pertaining to hire purchase may have resulted in a new form of conveyance resembling *traditio brevi manu*, but without the physical element.

The new National Credit Act,[224] which was phased in between 2006 and 2007, distinguishes between seven types of credit agreements, i.e. (1) pawn transactions; (2) discount transactions; (3) incidental credit agreements; (4) instalment agreements; (5) mortgage agreements; (6) secured loans; (7) leases. It also acknowledges an eighth, open category of credit agreements, namely (8) any other. Of these, the two categories most significantly affected by the debate about *traditio brevi manu* and hire-purchase agreements are (4) instalment agreements and (7) leases.

Instalment agreements concern movables, where the price is paid in instalments. Possession and use of the property is delivered, but ownership is reserved until the last payment, or ownership is transferred immediately, coupled with a right to repossession. Leases pertain to movables leased to a consumer. Rent is payable in instalments and can be deferred in whole or in part. The lessee pays a fee, charge, or interest. The contract provides that ownership passes at the end of the agreement, either absolutely or upon satisfaction of specified conditions.[225]

As far as can be gleaned at this point, the common law principles regarding *traditio brevi manu* are not adapted by the Act. Instead, the different categories of credit agreements confirm that it is possible that one may be dealing here with an additional form of transfer not provided for in common law.

7.3.3.5 Attornment

When neither the transferor nor the transferee is in possession of the property to be delivered, but rather a third party has possession in terms of some arrangement with the current owner, then attornment can be used.[226] Adopted from English law,[227] attornment involves a tripartite agreement: the transferor, the transferee and a third party who has possession of the property are the parties to the agreement.

Figure 7.10: Attornment – parties to the tripartite agreement

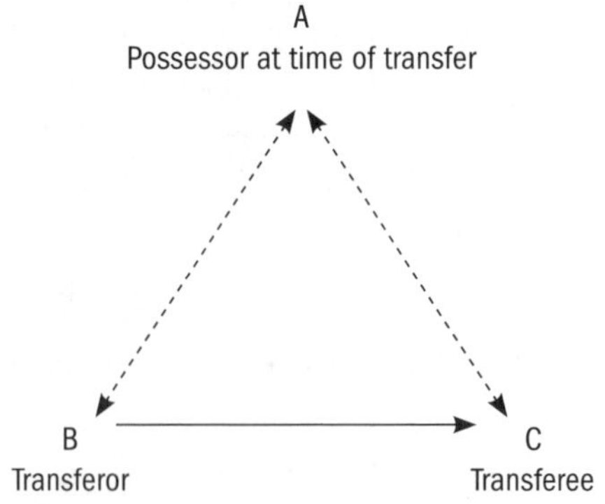

A
Possessor at time of transfer

B
Transferor

C
Transferee

---

224 Act 34 of 2005.
225 See definition of instalment agreement in s 1(*c*)(ii) of the National Credit Act 34 of 2005.
226 See *Wille's Principles* pp 530–533; *Silberberg & Schoeman Property* pp 194–198.
227 In *Standard Bank v O'Connor* (1888) 6 SC 32 at 44.

As concerns the physical element, the third party's possession of the property derives from the owner, which means that, first, he derives possession from the transferor and then, at transfer, his possession changes to derive from the new owner (transferee). The tripartite agreement includes a provision that the possessor ceases to hold for the transferor and begins to hold for the transferee at a particular point in time. It is important to note that the third party must be in possession[228] or at least retain the right to control[229] at the time of the transfer.

As concerns the mental element, the importance of the provision in the tripartite agreement lies in keeping the mental elements 'alive' to achieve concurrence of minds. For the real agreement, the transferor must intend to transfer ownership of specified property, the transferee must intend to receive ownership of that same specified property, and each must be able to 'connect' to the property itself to satisfy the mental element of the delivery method. This is achieved by keeping the possessor-third party in the circle. Importantly, notification to the third party by the transferee is not sufficient; the transferor must instruct the third party who must agree henceforth to hold for the transferee.[230] In other words, all three parties must be aware of what is to happen and that this intention is what will effect delivery by attornment.

To illustrate, suppose Xolani owns a car which he sells to Nyoko on a hire-purchase agreement, reserving ownership until the last instalment has been paid. As a hire-purchase acquirer, Nyoko is not owner until she has completed payment but she possesses the car. Then Xolani decides he wishes to transfer ownership immediately to John, who will step into Xolani's shoes and, in so doing, will continue to receive the instalment payments from Nyoko. In other words, the idea is that Xolani will transfer (the real right of) ownership to John **and** will cede his (personal) rights in terms of the hire-purchase agreement to John. The only way in which this transfer of ownership can be achieved is to effect delivery by attornment.

---

228 *Hearne & Co (Pty) Ltd v Bleiman* 1950 (3) SA 617 (C); *Southern Tankers (Pty) Ltd t/a Unilog v Pescana D'Oro Ltd (Velmar Ltd Intervening)* 2003 (4) SA 566 (C).
229 *Barclays Western Bank Ltd v Ernst* 1988 (1) SA 243 (A) at 253.
230 See *Air-Kel (Edms) Bpk h/a Merkel Motors v Bodenstein* 1980 (3) SA 917 (A).

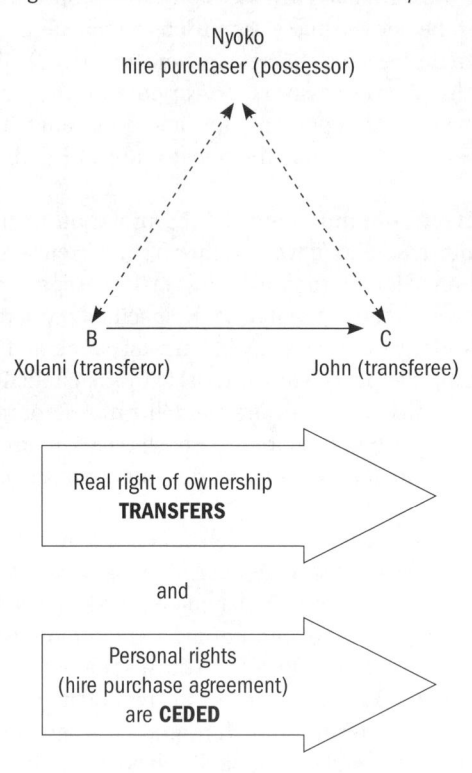

Figure 7.11: Attornment – transfer of ownership and cession of personal rights

Nyoko
hire purchaser (possessor)

B — Xolani (transferor)
C — John (transferee)

Real right of ownership **TRANSFERS**

and

Personal rights (hire purchase agreement) are **CEDED**

To require Nyoko to bring the car back so it can be handed over to John by Xolani and then handed back to her by John would be wasteful. However, it is vitally important that Nyoko knows that, at a particular point, her possession will cease to derive from Xolani's ownership of the car and begin to derive from John's ownership of the car. Hence, there must be an instruction (the tripartite agreement) from the transferor, Xolani, to her as possessor and to the transferee, John, which sets out the particulars.[231] Nyoko's role is not to give permission to the transfer, but rather to be informed and to agree that, from the stated date, she derives her possession from the new owner.

If, for some reason, at the stated time, Nyoko is not in physical control of the car (her cousin has borrowed it to go to a nearby town on business), does this mean delivery by attornment is ineffective? Case law[232] indicates that, at the least, the possessor must be able to retake physical control without legal assistance, but preferably must be in direct physical control of the property. In the case of Nyoko and her cousin, arguably, she retains the right to control the car and thus is able without more ado to demand its return, which may qualify her to be a possessor for the purposes of attornment. However, each factual scenario must be carefully scrutinised to see what the parties' intentions were because the courts will not assume that attornment has taken place, unless convincing factual evidence supports such an inference.

---

231 *Air-Kel (Edms) Bpk h/a Merkel Motors v Bodenstein* 1980 (3) SA 917 (A) at 924; *Southern Tankers (Pty) Ltd t/a Unilog v Pescana D'Oro Ltd (Velmar Ltd Intervening)* 2003 (4) SA 566 (C) at 573.
232 *Air-Kel (Edms) Bpk h/a Merkel Motors v Bodenstein* 1980 (3) SA 917 (A) at 924; *Southern Tankers (Pty) Ltd t/a Unilog v Pescana D'Oro Ltd (Velmar Ltd Intervening)* 2003 (4) SA 566 (C) at 573.

Thus in *Hearn & Co (Pty) Ltd v Bleiman*,[233] the third party was not in physical control of the property at the time of the tripartite agreement, yet it agreed henceforth to hold on behalf of the new owner. This was patently impossible to do because it had given up physical control of the property to another in pledge. The court found that delivery by attornment had not occurred and hence that transfer of ownership was not effective.

On the other hand, in *Southern Tankers (Pty) Ltd t/a Unilog v Pescana D'Oro Ltd (Velmar Ltd Intervening)*,[234] the court was asked to examine whether storage could satisfy the possession requirement for attornment. A catch of fish was in cold storage with an agent, Atlantic Cold Storage, for Dockmaster's account. Unilog wished to attach the catch for purposes of establishing jurisdiction in South Africa to pursue its claim against Pescana. Velmar Ltd intervened, on the basis that it had acquired ownership of the catch from Pescana, delivery by attornment with Atlantic Cold Storage as the possessor. Unilog questioned whether Atlantic Cold Storage could properly be the possessor when the fish was stored for Dockmaster. The fish had never left the physical control of Atlantic Cold Storage, which persuaded the court that Atlantic Cold Storage was the possessor for the purposes of attornment. But analysis of the facts revealed that Atlantic Cold Storage had not been instructed by Pescana to cease holding for Pescana and to begin holding for Velmar. Also, Atlantic Cold Storage had not agreed to begin holding for Velmar and therefore delivery to Velmar had not been effective. In other words, notification of the third party by the transferee is not sufficient to establish the tripartite agreement.

> **PAUSE FOR REFLECTION**
>
> **Cession in the context of attornment**
>
> Some cases, such as *Caledon & Suid-Westelike Distrikte Eksekuteurskamer Bpk v Wentzel*,[235] refer to cession in relation to attornment, stating that the transferor cedes the right of ownership to the transferee. It is not possible to cede ownership, nor is it possible to cede the right to use a proprietary remedy (see below). Cession pertains to transfer of **personal rights**. An agreement that purports to 'cede' ownership can, at best, serve as evidence of the intention to transfer ownership, i.e. evidence of the real agreement. This should be borne in mind when this terminology is encountered in connection with attornment. It is likely that more than one transaction is involved and that this has been overlooked. In the example above, transfer of ownership and cession of rights under the hire-purchase agreement were involved; it is easy to conflate the transactions (i.e. to fail to keep them separate) and thus to slip into using less than accurate terminology. Correctly speaking, the ownership rights are transferred, while the personal rights under the hire-purchase agreement may be ceded. The need for precision and accuracy in property law is high, both in relation to the description and measurement of property, and regarding the terminology for the various transactions that transfer or limit real rights.

---

233   1950 (3) SA 617 (C).
234   2003 (4) SA 566 (C).
235   1972 (1) SA 270 (A).

> **COUNTER POINT**
>
> **Cessio iuris vindicationis**
>
> Cession of the right of vindication *(cessio iuris vindicationis)* is sometimes mentioned as a possible new method of constructive delivery.[236] However, the idea that one can transfer ownership or cede the right to use a proprietary remedy, using this method of delivery, presents conceptual difficulties.
>
> The notion of using cession to transfer ownership flows from an obiter dictum in *Caledon & Suid-Westelike Distrikte Eksekuteurskamer Bpk v Wentzel*.[237] The discussion concerned whether the goal of the transferor and the transferee could not be achieved without the conscious involvement of the third party, i.e. whether mere notification to the third party would be sufficient. However, if the mental element for both the real agreement and the delivery method must, as it were, pass through the mind of the third party to transfer the real right, then it is difficult to see how mere notification can suffice. It would mean that the third party would be ignorant of the transfer. This runs counter to the principle of publicity, which demands that transfer of ownership be transparent and certain. How would the third party be in a position to respond accurately to a stranger who enquires about the ownership of the property? The notification may never reach him. The tripartite agreement of attornment ensures that all three parties at a particular time share the 'same mind' so that the transfer of ownership using attornment as delivery method occurs properly. In the absence of such an agreement, there can be no transfer.
>
> One case[238] involving transfer of ownership of shares in a company took the view that cession of an incorporeal, such as a share, could effect transfer of ownership even when the shares were pledged and thus the certificates were in the possession of a third party. The pledgee could be notified of the change in ownership without suffering any detriment. The conceptual difficulty with this is that shares can only be 'transferred' by cession: first, they are inherently unable to be delivered in the way that is usually envisaged because of their incorporeal nature. Additionally (and even more importantly), shares are bundles of **personal** rights that the 'owner' has against the company concerned. 'Ownership' of shares is a loose description because dogmatically it is inaccurate. Furthermore, at the time of the case, corporeal evidence of the shares in the form of share certificates was routinely available. Today, however, shares are dematerialised via STRATE and dealt with electronically. The evidence for their existence is also electronic. All these considerations indicate that what was found to be acceptable in *Etkind* is not generalisable and that cession of the right of vindication is simply not possible.
>
> A further point to note is that while the *ius vindicandi* (the owner's entitlement to vindicate his property where he finds it) is a legitimate ownership entitlement, conceptually, it cannot form the content of a limited real right to be held by a non-owner. In other words, at a conceptual level, it cannot stand alone like the entitlement to use and enjoy the property can, which points to the conclusion that the entitlement to vindicate property is inseparable from ownership. Although one can understand the assumptions behind the view that it is possible to cede the *ius vindicandi* and hence transfer ownership, closer analysis confirms that this thinking does not stand up to scrutiny. It should be accepted that cession of the right of vindication is not an acceptable delivery method.

---

236 See *Wille's Principles* pp 533–534; *Silberberg & Schoeman Property* pp 198–200 for more detailed discussion and examples.
237 *Caledon & Suid-Westelike Eksekuteurskamer Bpk v Wentzel* 1972 (1) SA 270 (A) at 275.
238 *Etkind v Hicor Trading Ltd* 1999 (1) SA 111 (W) at 125.

7.3.4 Transfer of immovable property – registration

When transfer of ownership is to be registered, it must occur at the Deeds Registry situated within the jurisdiction of the court of the place where the property is situated.

> **PAUSE FOR REFLECTION**
>
> **Coram judice rei sitae**
>
> The principle that governs conveyance of immovable property is *coram judice rei sitae*, i.e. transfer should occur before the court of the place where the property is situated. In South Africa, the forum for such registrations is the Deeds Registry, where the Registrar of Deeds fulfils the function originally attributed to a judge.[239] The *lex rei sitae* (the law of the place where the property is situated) governs immovable property. This is why the Deeds Registry at which the transfer is to be registered must be in the same jurisdiction as the land concerned.

7.3.4.1 Publicity and certainty

The objective of the registration system is to 'compile a complete register of real rights in all land, showing ownership of every parcel and any limitation or restriction to which the ownership of each parcel may be subject'.[240] This registration system forms the backbone of the current system of transfer of immovable property in South Africa. It is also central to the implementation of the very idea that land can be carved up into individual parcels and made subject to private ownership.[241]

Publicity and certainty are two of the most important goals of the registration system. To this end, each Deeds Registry has a register of all the agricultural, other rural and urban plots within its jurisdiction. Each deed of transfer is carefully scrutinised and then executed by a conveyancer in the presence of the Registrar and which is attested to by the latter.[242] These measures ensure sufficient publicity of the transfer. The Deeds Registry itself is open to the public, so it is possible for anyone to ascertain who the owner is of a particular parcel of land. In pursuit of certainty, '[e]ach plot is clearly identified with reference to maps and diagrams drawn up by the surveyor-general'.[243] The division of land into precise units that are surveyed and represented on diagrams or a general plan is called the cadastral system. Surveying means to measure, describe and to locate geographically with exacting precision. The diagrams serve as decisive proof of boundaries between the plots of land. Precision and excellence are the hallmarks of the South African cadastral and registration systems, but the inevitable slowness that results from being so precise provides a considerable challenge in respect of providing a speedy, reliable and cost-effective demarcation system for the rapid release of land, especially in urban areas, for the building of housing.

---

239 *Silberberg & Schoeman Property* pp 204, 215; *Wille's Principles* pp 534–535.
240 *Wille's Principles* p 535; *Silberberg & Schoeman Property* pp 206–208.
241 See ch 2 above.
242 Section 16 of the Deeds Registries Act 47 of 1937.
243 *Wille's Principles* p 535.

7.3.4.2 Effect of registration

The effect of registration is that it creates the (new) real right and it protects a real right by providing prima facie evidence of its existence.[244] Registration thus has a dual function: it indicates the act of delivery in the transfer of real rights, and it provides a public record of all real rights in land:[245]

> *The owner of a registered [right] is protected not because every person in the world must be deemed to have knowledge of the [right] but because registration has by law the same effect as the express notification to all the world would have.*[246]

It is important to understand that registration by itself is insufficient to transfer ownership, even though registration is a necessary element of transfer of ownership of immovable property. Also, the fact that registration has occurred does not necessarily mean that ownership has **transferred**. Registration **can** occur erroneously[247] in which case it may be invalidated by an order of court.[248] That said, the examination procedures in the South African registration process are sufficiently meticulous to avoid frequent erroneous registrations.[249]

Furthermore, original acquisition of landownership by means, for instance, of acquisitive prescription is also possible.[250] Registration of the prescriptive owner's title does not indicate a **transfer of ownership**, it merely confirms the *de lege* position, and enables the prescriptive owner to undertake further dealings with the land. Moreover, the creation of limited real rights requires registration as part of the creation process but registration does not signify a transfer of ownership, merely the transfer of some of the owner's entitlements.

From the point of view of a third party, can one in good faith rely on the information in the Deeds Registry? In other words, if someone in good faith relies on the information in the Deeds Registry, is she protected if the information turns out to be inaccurate? For example, Joan carefully checks the Deeds Registry to see whether Kevin is indeed the registered owner of the stand at Port Owen before she agrees to lend him money. She wants to be sure that in the event of Kevin failing to repay the debt, there is property that could be sold to raise money to satisfy a claim for repayment of the debt. The search reveals that Kevin is the registered owner. Later, however, it is revealed that Kevin is married in community of property (and the title deed has never been endorsed to reflect this fact), which of course means that Kevin's spouse owns 50 per cent of the property. This in turn reduces the amount that could be realised from a sale in execution, which could prejudice Joan's interests. The question here is whether Joan's interests can be protected in the light of the fact that the information in the Deeds Registry does not reflect the true state of affairs.

The answer is that it depends on whether the registration system in place is a positive or negative system of registration. A positive system of registration guarantees the accuracy of information.[251] This means that a third party, who in good faith acquires property, having relied on the information, will be protected. In other words, a bona fide acquirer of what turns

---

244 *Frye's (Pty) Ltd v Ries* 1957 (3) SA 574 (A) at 584.
245 *Silberberg & Schoeman Property* p 237.
246 *Frye's (Pty) Ltd v Ries* 1957 (3) SA 574 (A) at 584.
247 See e.g. *Barclays Nasionale Bank Bpk v Registrateur van Aktes, Transvaal* 1975 (4) SA 936 (T); *Standard Bank van SA Bpk v Breitenbach* 1977 (1) SA 151 (T).
248 See e.g. *Knysna Hotel CC v Coetzee NO* 1998 (2) SA 743 (A) at 753C-754C.
249 *Silberberg & Schoeman Property* p 235.
250 See pp 179*ff* above.
251 *Silberberg & Schoeman Property* pp 232*ff*; *Wille's Principles* pp 536-538 for more detail.

out to be a deficient or flawed 'real right' that has been registered, can enforce his registered claim against the actual entitled person. This is sometimes referred to as 'indefeasibility of title'. The state underwrites a fund that may compensate a person who suffers loss as a result of information that turns out to be inaccurate. Under a positive system, therefore, third parties have greater legal certainty, while the position of original holders of real rights is less certain.

A negative system of registration does not provide a guarantee of accuracy.[252] Someone who relies on the information which turns out to be inaccurate will not be protected against the actual entitled person. In addition, a third party who suffers loss as a result of relying on the information will not have a claim against the state, unless it can be proved that Deeds Registry officials were grossly negligent. If a conveyancing attorney in private practice was at fault, a delictual claim may lie against the firm. Under a negative system of registration, the position of original holders of real rights is more certain than that of third parties who rely on information in the registry.

South Africa uses a modified negative system of registration,[253] i.e. the information is not guaranteed to be accurate, but there is high degree of accuracy and active involvement of registry officials. However, the Deeds Registries Act expressly excludes liability of registry officials unless there was gross negligence or bad faith. Does this mean that the information in the Deeds Registry should be regarded with suspicion? On the contrary: despite the lack of a guarantee of accuracy, South Africa's registration system together with its cadastral system is highly regarded. A high standard of accuracy is maintained and the Deeds Registry is a good and reliable source of information about real rights in land. Most of the responsibility for ensuring the accuracy of information rests on the conveyancing attorney. He must check all documents meticulously, including that a previously registered mortgage bond has been cancelled, or that a servitude is registered or cancelled (as the case may be) before the new transfer is registered.

In addition, it should be remembered that a positive system of registration would be in conflict with various modes of acquisition of ownership that are part of South African property law. For example, acquisitive prescription, marriage in community of property, and insolvency provide the possibility that, at any time, ownership of land might change and, consequently, that the true state of affairs will not be reflected in the Deeds Registry. Similarly, modes of termination of ownership such as abandonment, merger or extinction of the principal debt secured by a mortgage bond are not immediately reflected in the Deeds Registry.

But what happens when a previously registered limited real right is erroneously omitted in a subsequent deed of transfer? Does the omission mean that the limited real right has ceased to exist and that the successor in title acquires with clean title? The Supreme Court of Appeal had to decide this question in *Cape Explosive Works (Pty) Ltd v Denel (Pty) Ltd*.[254] Drawing on established principles governing transfer of ownership and the acquisition of limited real rights, the court reiterated that:

> it is the intention with which transfer was given and received which had to be determined in so far as a causa was required for the transfer of the properties subject to conditions 1 and 2.[255]

---

252 *Silberberg & Schoeman Property* pp 230ff; *Wille's Principles* pp 536–538 for more detail.
253 See *Wille's Principles* pp 536–537; *Silberberg & Schoeman Property* pp 229–238 for more detailed discussion.
254 2001 (3) SA 569 (SCA).
255 *Cape Explosive Works* at 577 para 10. Note that the *causa* referred to in the dictum is that which is required by the Deeds Registries Act and is not the same as the term used in the discussion on the systems of transfer of ownership.

In this case, these two conditions had been omitted erroneously from subsequent title deeds. When the error was discovered, the new owner disputed that its title was limited by the conditions. However, the court found that transfer had been intended to be subject to the conditions and that the factual evidence pointed to the transferee's intention to receive transfer subject to the conditions. Furthermore:

> *a real right is adequately protected by its registration in the Deeds Office. Once Capex's rights had been registered they were maintainable against the whole world. They were not extinguished by their erroneous omission from subsequent title deeds and the fact that Denel's title deed, registered in the Deeds Office, did not reflect those rights does not assist Denel. We have a negative system of registration where the deeds registry does not necessarily reflect the true state of affairs and third parties cannot place absolute reliance thereon.*[256]

It ought to be clear, thus, that once a limited real right is properly registered, an administrative error cannot terminate it. Whether it is properly registered, i.e. actually eligible for registration, is a different question.

7.4 Concluding remarks

In this chapter, the focus has been on the various methods of acquiring ownership in South African law. It was demonstrated that ownership can be acquired either with or without the co-operation of the previous title holder (if there is one), i.e. either bilaterally or unilaterally. Although each of the modes has its own requirements, the basic objectives of the law in regulating such acquisition are common to all the modes. This fact is summarised eloquently by the quote that opens this chapter: the law wants the creation and transfer of property interests to be done 'unambiguously, deliberately and publicly'. In essence, as we have tried to show, the various requirements of the different modes of acquisition of ownership serve certainty and publicity. This explains the focus on both the mental and physical elements in each of the modes of acquisition. Variations between the different modes are accounted for by the circumstances that determine the need for a specific mode of acquisition as well as the type of property involved.

The ability to prove conclusively the existence of title is crucial for any attempt to assert ownership rights. So, where a claimant wishes to enforce a proprietary entitlement, a preliminary question is whether she, in fact or in law, has such an entitlement. Determining the answer to the question frequently precedes the enquiry into the availability of specific remedies. In the next chapter, the remedies available to the owner are discussed in more detail.

---

256 *Cape Explosive Works* at 579 para 16, footnotes omitted.

Chapter 8

Protection of ownership

'Our law jealously protects the right of ownership and the correlative right of the owner in regard to his property, unless, of course, the possessor has some enforceable right against the owner.'

Oakland Nominees (Pty) Ltd v Gelria Mining and Investment Co (Pty) Ltd **1976 (1) SA 441 (A) at 452A**

8.1	Introduction	215
8.2	**Real remedies**	216
8.2.1	*Rei vindicatio*	217
8.2.1.1	Requirements	218
8.2.1.2	Defences against the *rei vindicatio*	219
8.2.1.3	Limitations on the use of *rei vindicatio*	219
8.2.2	*Actio negatoria*	226
8.3	**Delictual remedies**	227
8.3.1	*Condictio furtiva*	227
8.3.2	*Actio ad exhibendum*	228
8.3.3	*Actio legis Aquiliae*	229
8.4	**Unjustified enrichment**	229
8.5	**Concluding remarks: How to choose a remedy**	230

8.1 Introduction

Various remedies protect ownership. Depending on the particular circumstances and facts of each case, three categories of remedies are available, namely real remedies, delictual remedies and unjustified enrichment remedies.[1] **Real remedies** restore physical control of the property, or confirm the ability of an owner to exclude others from access, use or enjoyment of the property, e.g. by preventing infringement of entitlements. **Delictual remedies**, however, are relevant when the owner has suffered financial loss either because the property itself has been alienated, damaged or destroyed, or because he could not exercise his ownership entitlements. These remedies provide a claim for payment of compensation or damages. **Unjustified enrichment** remedies provide

---

1   In general, see *Silberberg & Schoeman Property* p 242; *Wille's Principles* p 538; *LAWSA* Vol 27(1) at para 380.

payment of compensation for unjustified enrichment. This occurs when someone other than the owner is unjustifiably enriched at the expense of the owner. The classification of remedies may be depicted diagrammatically as follows:

Figure 8.1: Classification of the owner's remedies

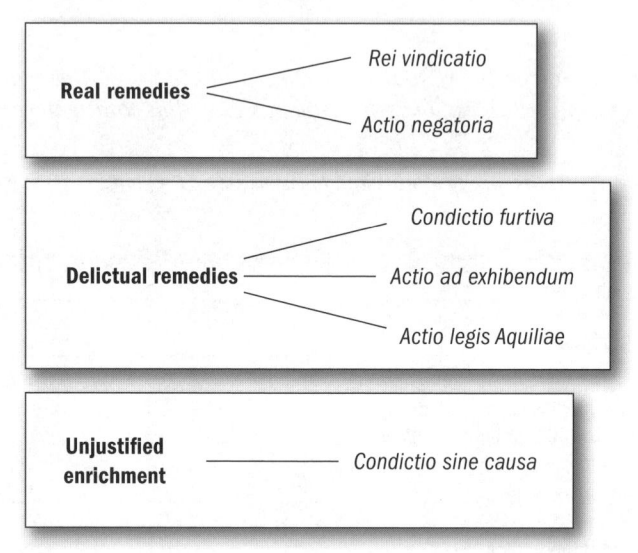

- **Real remedies**
  - Rei vindicatio
  - Actio negatoria

- **Delictual remedies**
  - Condictio furtiva
  - Actio ad exhibendum
  - Actio legis Aquiliae

- **Unjustified enrichment**
  - Condictio sine causa

Each category includes distinctive remedies or actions, which have different requirements and apply only to particular situations. It is therefore important to establish when to use each remedy. Although all the categories are discussed here because all are relevant to protection of ownership, the delictual remedies and those based on unjustified enrichment are not discussed in great detail. These remedies are covered in more detail in law of delict[2] and unjustified enrichment[3] publications.

8.2　Real remedies

Generally, real remedies restore physical control of property to the owner, or they prevent infringement of the owner's entitlements.[4] Each remedy has distinctive requirements which must be met to ensure a successful outcome for the owner. The real remedies discussed below are the *rei vindicatio*, and the *actio negatoria*. In addition to these real remedies, an interdict and a declaratory order are also available to owners and possessors alike.[5] The interdict is discussed in chapter 4 above. A declaratory order sets out the rights and responsibilities of parties involved in a particular dispute, and is usually employed before an actual infringement of rights occurs. It will not be discussed in further detail here.

2　*Wille's Principles* pp 1091–1231; Neethling, J et al. (2006) *Law of Delict* (Durban, LexisNexis Butterworths) pp 235*ff*.
3　*Wille's Principles* pp 1041–1088; Visser, D (2008) *Unjustified Enrichment* (Cape Town, Juta).
4　*Chetty v Naidoo* 1974 (3) SA 13 (A).
5　See ch 4 above.

8.2.1 *Rei vindicatio*

The *rei vindicatio* is a real remedy which can be instituted by the owner to reclaim his property from anyone who is unlawfully in physical control thereof.[6] The maxim, *ubi rem meam invenio, ibi vindico,* captures the gist of the *rei vindicatio* well: where my property is found, there I vindicate it. This means that, in general, an owner can claim back his property wherever he finds it and from whosoever has it.

As indicated in previous chapters,[7] recent analyses of the notion of ownership are generally critical about the claim that ownership is absolute or even all-exclusive. Yet, ownership still permits pursuit of the property. In *Chetty v Naidoo,* the court stated that ownership includes the entitlement of 'exclusive possession of the *res,* with the necessary corollary that the owner may claim his property wherever found, from whosoever holding it'.[8] This links with the premise that, apart from situations where original acquisition of ownership has occurred,[9] an owner cannot lose ownership without consent.[10] This premise is founded on the *nemo plus iuris* rule, the basic principle of transfer of ownership,[11] i.e. a person cannot transfer more rights than he has. Consequently, when a non-owner purports to transfer 'rights' to a bona fide party, who believes she will acquire ownership and may even have paid for that benefit, the true owner remains owner and can thus claim his property from the bona fide purchaser. Good faith is thus no defence against the *rei vindicatio.*[12]

Only an owner can use the *rei vindicatio*. It may be instituted in relation to both movable and immovable property. In the latter instance, it takes the form of an eviction order. As concerns eviction from land, however, the applicability of the *rei vindicatio* is restricted because of the operation of s 26(3) of the Constitution, which provides that 'no one may be evicted from their home without a court order and only after all relevant circumstances have been considered.' The procedure which must be followed in the case of such evictions is further set out in the Prevention of Illegal Eviction from and Unlawful Occupation of Land Act[13] (PIE), and the courts have worked out the application of these rules in cases such as *Ndlovu v Ngcobo, Bekker v Jika*.[14] The implication is that the *rei vindicatio* applies to eviction from land or property **only** when it is being used for business, trade or industrial purposes,[15] or when the defendant does not fit the definition of 'unlawful occupier' or 'occupier' under PIE or ESTA respectively.[16] The provisions of PIE (as interpreted by the courts) apply to an eviction from one's home. In addition, the Supreme Court of Appeal judgment spelled out the requirements for eviction from a home.[17] The requirements for the *rei vindicatio* and its limitations are set out in the sections below.

---

6   See *Wille's Principles* pp 539-541; *Silberberg & Schoeman Property* pp 242-246 for more detailed discussion.
7   See ch 5 and ch 6 above.
8   *Chetty v Naidoo* 1974 (3) SA 13 (A) at 20B.
9   See ch 7 above.
10 *Grosvenor Motors (Potchefstroom) Ltd v Douglas* 1956 (3) SA 420 (A) at 427A.
11 See *Wille's Principles* p 521; *Silberberg & Schoeman Property* pp 72-73. See ch 7 above.
12 *Mngadi NO v Ntuli* 1981 (3) SA 378 (D&C) at 485A.
13 Act 19 of 1998.
14 2003 (1) SA 113 (SCA).
15 *Ndlovu v Ngcobo, Bekker v Jika* 2003 (1) SA 113 (SCA).
16 See e.g. *Ellis v Viljoen* 2001 (5) BCLR 487 (C). See also Pope, A 'Eviction and the protection of property rights: a case study of *Ellis v Viljoen*' (2002) 119 *SALJ* 709-720.
17 See *Wille's Principles* pp 548-552; *Silberberg & Schoeman Property* pp 247-255 for more detailed discussion.

8.2.1.1 Requirements

Three requirements must be met for a claim based on the *rei vindicatio* to be successful. First, the person who institutes the action (the owner) must prove that she is owner of the property claimed. Second, the property must exist and be identifiable; and third, at the time that the action is instituted, the property claimed must be in the defendant's physical control.[18]

As ownership forms the basis of the claim, it is essential that the person who institutes the *rei vindicatio*, proves, on a balance of probabilities, that she is indeed owner.[19] The nature of proof depends on the kind of property being claimed. For example, if the property is immovable, the title deed may be produced to indicate ownership. A title deed serves as prima facie evidence of proof of ownership in land. If the property is movable, various methods may be used to prove ownership. For example, the registration papers of a vehicle or an invoice can evidence proof of purchase and a consequent inference of continued ownership. The presumption that the person in possession or detention of movable property is the owner thereof, may make it difficult to prove ownership in the absence of documentary evidence. The claimant can also prove ownership by means of an original form of acquisition.[20]

The objective of the *rei vindicatio* is to restore physical control of the property to the owner. This can occur only if the property is in existence and can be identified clearly.[21] If the property no longer exists, then the *rei vindicatio* is not the appropriate remedy. Rather, a delictual remedy may compensate the owner for his patrimonial loss. Furthermore, if the property is not in its original form, e.g. because it has become part of another entity by way of accession, then ownership is lost at the moment of accession, which consequently excludes the *rei vindicatio*.[22] The nature of the property concerned influences what the claimant needs to demonstrate to prove its existence and identification. For example, an artwork destroyed in a fire no longer exists, thus excluding the *rei vindicatio*. If poachers kill game on a game farm and remove the carcasses, in principle, the owner may still reclaim the carcasses with the *rei vindicatio* (because carcasses belong to the owner under the Game Theft Act[23]). Paint that has been applied to a wall belonging to someone else cannot be reclaimed by the owner of the paint because it has acceded to the wall.

The objective of the *rei vindicatio* can be achieved only if the person against whom the action is instituted, is actually in physical control of the property being claimed. In other words, the defendant must be in a position to carry out an order to return possession of the property to the owner. If the defendant has lost physical control, then a different remedy has to be used against him.[24] For example, if Tess, the owner of a stolen vehicle, can prove that Nazeem (the defendant) was responsible for taking the property, and that this led to patrimonial loss for Tess, then a delictual claim for such patrimonial loss could lie against Nazeem. If Nazeem has already disposed of the vehicle, the *rei vindicatio* would in principle not be available.

---

18 See *Wille's Principles* pp 539–540; *Silberberg & Schoeman Property* pp 243–246.
19 *Chetty v Naidoo* 1974 (3) SA 13 (A) at 20A.
20 See ch 7 above.
21 See *Wille's Principles* p 539.
22 On the basis that the object must exist and be identifiable – see *Leal & Co v Williams* 1906 TS 554.
23 Act 105 of 1991. See p 164.
24 See discussion of delictual remedies at pp 227*ff*.

> **COUNTER POINT**
>
> **_Rei vindicatio_ and damages**
>
> The true application of the *rei vindicatio* is aimed at restoring lost possession to the owner. It does not include the possibility of damages. However, in *Mlombo v Fourie*,[25] where an owner instituted the *rei vindicatio* against a defendant who had fraudulently ceased to possess the property, the court ordered the defendant to make good the value of the lost thing. This blurring of the distinction between the *rei vindicatio* and the *actio ad exhibendum* has been justifiably criticised by legal commentators.[26] The *rei vindicatio* is a restorative proprietary remedy, while the *actio ad exhibendum* is a delictual remedy.

8.2.1.2 Defences against the *rei vindicatio*

To defend against the *rei vindicatio*, the *facta probanda* can be challenged,[27] i.e. the essential elements of the requirements may be contested. Thus, the defendant may allege that the person who instituted the *rei vindicatio* is not the owner of the property claimed. Clearly, the defendant would have to produce documentary evidence to support his allegation.

It is open to the defendant to prove that the property is no longer identifiable or has been destroyed. Furthermore, the defendant may allege that he is not in physical control of the property claimed. Or the defendant may allege that the possession is not unlawful, e.g. that it is based on consent or another legal basis such as lien, lease or a real security right enforceable against the owner.

Note that the claimant need not aver that the defendant is in unlawful possession, but the defendant can defend by proving that his possession is lawful.[28] Once the claimant proves ownership and that the defendant has possession of the property, the onus shifts to allow the defendant to prove that possession is indeed lawful. This can be done, e.g. by proving that his possession flows from consent or that a lease agreement exists. Thereafter, if necessary, the onus may shift again to the claimant, who may lead evidence to prove that the consent or lease has lapsed, thereby rendering the continued possession unlawful.[29] If, however, the claimant does allege initially that the possession is unlawful, e.g. because the lease has expired, then the claimant must lead evidence to prove this allegation.[30] In other words, the onus of proof rests on the claimant in this situation.

8.2.1.3 Limitations on the use of *rei vindicatio*

The rule that an owner can pursue his property and vindicate it can be countered by the defences discussed in the preceding section. In addition, there are limitations imposed by the law that either prevent the use of the *rei vindicatio* altogether or have an immediate neutralising effect, following institution of the action.[31] These limitations occur in the form of statutory limitations (of which those regarding immovable property are so important that the topic warrants separate discussion here), as well as estoppel and other common law limitations.[32]

---

25 1964 (3) SA 350 (T).
26 See Van der Merwe *Sakereg* p 349; *Silberberg & Schoeman Property* p 246.
27 See *Wille's Principles* p 540; *Silberberg & Schoeman Property* p 245.
28 *Ruskin NO v Thiergen* 1962 (3) SA 737 (A) at 745F.
29 To see how this works in practice, see *Chetty v Naidoo* 1974 (3) SA 13 (A). Note, however, that developments have occurred regarding unlawful occupation of land – see pp 220*ff*.
30 *Chetty v Naidoo* 1974 (3) SA 13 (A).
31 See *Wille's Principles* pp 546–555; *Silberberg & Schoeman Property* pp 255–262.
32 See *Wille's Principles* p 547; *Silberberg & Schoeman Property* pp 260–262.

Statutory and common law limitations generally prevent institution of the *rei vindicatio*. The result is that no real or other statutory remedy is available. In effect, therefore, the owner is prevented from vindicating his property. Estoppel, on the other hand, may be raised in certain circumstances as a defence to the *rei vindicatio*, and, if successful, may limit the effect of the *rei vindicatio*. These limitations are discussed in more detail below.

Statutory limitations. Some statutory provisions explicitly exclude the *rei vindicatio*. An example of statutory exclusion of the *rei vindicatio* is s 36(5) of the Insolvency Act,[33] which provides that after an insolvency auction, the property sold and transferred or registered may not be vindicated by way of a *rei vindicatio*.

As a further illustration, s 70 of the Magistrates' Courts Act[34] similarly provides that a sale in execution of property is not liable to impeachment against a purchaser in good faith and without notice of any defect. In other words, the previous owner cannot attack the sale in execution and subsequent transfer of ownership. In the case of movables, this limitation applies after delivery, while in the case of immovable property, it applies after registration. Note, however, that when the sale in execution involves a home, the warrant of execution must be issued under judicial supervision, in accordance with *Jaftha v Schoeman and Others; Van Rooyen v Stoltz and Others*.[35]

In *Menqa and Another v Markom and Others*,[36] a warrant of execution was issued by the clerk of the magistrates' court without judicial supervision. Despite the warrant being issued prior to the *Jaftha* decision, the sale in execution was found to be null and void, and not subject to s 70 of the Magistrates' Court Act. This is because the ruling in *Jaftha* is retrospective to the inception of the Constitution[37] and because s 70 applies only to a **valid** sale in execution.[38] The Constitutional Court held in *Jaftha* that s 66(1)(*a*)[39] of the Magistrates' Courts Act was unconstitutional to the extent that it permitted an infringement of the judgment debtor's right of access to housing in terms of s 26 of the Constitution.

Where a purported sale in execution is a nullity, it cannot serve to pass title to the purchaser or any successor in title. The judgment debtor would thus be able to recover the property with a *rei vindicatio*. This kind of situation provides an exception to the scope of s 70 of the Magistrates' Court Act.

Immovable property, eviction and the rei vindicatio. The commencement of ss 25 and 26 of the Constitution had major consequences for the protection of immovable property, on the one hand, and the promotion of access to land and housing, on the other.[40] In this regard, s 26(3) of the Constitution provides that persons may be evicted from their homes only by court order and only after the court has considered all relevant circumstances. Subsections 25(5) and (6), respectively, mandate a broadening of access to land and the promotion of more secure tenure.

These provisions have led to two broad categories of legislative measures that deal with eviction, among other matters, namely legislative measures that regulate eviction in

---

33 Act 24 of 1936.
34 Act 32 of 1944.
35 2005 (2) SA 140 (CC); 2005 (1) BCLR 78.
36 2008 (2) SA 120 (SCA).
37 *Menqa and Another v Markom and Others* 2008 (2) SA 120 (SCA) at paras 18, 21.
38 *Menqa* at para 21.
39 Which permits execution against immovable property.
40 See *Wille's Principles* pp 548–552; *Silberberg & Schoeman Property* pp 247–255.

response to unlawful occupation of land and buildings; and legislative measures that deal with redistribution of land and tenure issues. The latter measures also affect eviction of specific categories of occupiers. These are the topics of this section.

First, as regards regulation of unlawful occupation of land, the Prevention of Illegal Eviction and Unlawful Occupation of Land Act[41] (PIE) embodies the essence of both ss 25(1) and 26(3) of the Constitution. It provides new procedural and substantive requirements with regard to eviction of 'unlawful occupiers' from a home. These requirements are aimed at balancing the interests of both the 'unlawful occupiers' and the owners in the particular situation.[42] Furthermore, s 4(1) explicitly excludes use of the common law *(rei vindicatio)* when eviction of 'unlawful occupiers' is at stake. Initially, there was some doubt as to whether PIE applies only to invasions of vacant land without any consent, or whether it applies to all kinds of unlawful occupation, including occupation that was lawful to begin with but unlawful at a later stage.[43] Whereas the former may be conveniently dubbed 'classical squatting', the latter is now generally referred to as 'holding over'. The matter was clarified in 2003 in *Ndlovu v Ngcobo and Bekker v Jika*,[44] where the Supreme Court of Appeal held that PIE applies to all unlawful occupation for residential purposes. Thus, when someone is evicted from land, a house, or a building used as a home and fits the definition of 'unlawful occupier', PIE's procedures must be followed.

Depending on whether the property is privately owned, and whether urgency is an issue, three different procedural options are provided for in PIE. Section 4 is the usual eviction application used by private owners or persons in charge of the land concerned. Section 6 sets out the procedures applicable to state organs instituting eviction proceedings in relation to property situated within their jurisdictional areas. In both instances, written and effective notice has to be given to identified respondents, not less than 14 days prior to the hearing, setting out the grounds for eviction. Urgent eviction proceedings are provided for in s 5, but this procedure may be used only in particular circumstances, e.g. when actual harm to persons or property is imminent. The main benefit of the urgent eviction procedure is that the prescribed time period is dispensed with, making matters move more quickly than they do with the usual procedure.[45]

Eviction orders are granted only if it is just and equitable to do so, taking all relevant circumstances into account.[46] A list of considerations (which is not exhaustive), is provided in ss 4(7) and 6(7) respectively. Courts must take these considerations into account when deciding whether an eviction order would be just and equitable. This deliberation process presupposes a balancing and assessment of relevant considerations for both unlawful occupiers and landowners. Recent trends in case law indicate that local authorities are usually joined as parties in eviction applications because the local authority is responsible

---

41 Act 19 of 1998.
42 *President of the Republic of South Africa v Modderklip Boerdery (Pty) Ltd* 2005 (5) SA 3 (CC) at para 55.
43 For example, in so-called 'holding over' cases, where a tenant breaches a lease agreement but refuses to vacate the premises; or where a former landowner remains on the property, refusing to vacate it after the land has been transferred to a new owner, following a sale in execution.
44 2003 (1) SA 113 (SCA).
45 Section 5(2); see *Groengras Eiendomme (Pty) Ltd v Elandsfontein Unlawful Occupants* 2002 (1) SA 125 (T) at para 31.
46 Sections 4(7) and 6(1); see also *Port Elizabeth Municipality v Various Occupiers* 2005 (1) SA 217 (CC).

for assisting in the alleviation of the housing need.[47] Whether an eviction order may be issued in the absence of suitable alternative accommodation is still contentious.[48]

The second category of legislation dealing with eviction entails the land reform laws on tenure security and redistribution. Two Acts of Parliament were promulgated to promote tenure security and to broaden access to land for particular categories of rural dwellers: the Extension of Security of Tenure Act[49] (ESTA) and the Land Reform (Labour Tenants) Act[50] (Labour Tenants Act). Although neither Act is aimed primarily at regulating eviction, both have specific provisions regarding eviction of 'occupiers' and 'labour tenants' respectively. These procedures result in the exclusion of the *rei vindicatio*.[51]

ESTA[52] applies to rural areas only and relates to 'occupiers'. These are persons with tacit or implied consent to reside on the land; who do not use the land for commercial purposes; and who do not have an income exceeding R5 000 per month.[53] Depending on whether the person was an 'occupier' before or after February 1997, s 10 or s 11 regulates eviction proceedings. Occupation may be terminated on any lawful ground, after which the formal procedure set out in s 9 has to be followed. This includes, among others, that written notice must be given to the 'occupier' two months before the eviction hearing, and that the grounds for eviction must be provided in the notice.

An eviction order may be granted only after all formalities have been satisfied, and only if the eviction is just and equitable in the particular circumstances.[54] All eviction orders granted by magistrates' courts are reviewed automatically by the Land Claims Court before they are executed. In some instances, an eviction order will not be granted. For example, if Jacob meets the requirements to be an 'occupier' in terms of ESTA, and he is older than 60 years, and has lived on the land for at least 10 years, then he cannot be evicted. Being a 'long term occupier', he may live out his life on the land. In exceptional circumstances, e.g. if Jacob is a threat to other occupiers, to the landowner or to property, he may be evicted.

The Labour Tenants Act[55] focuses on 'labour tenants'. They are persons who reside on land; and who have or had cropping or grazing rights on that land; and whose parents or grandparents also had such rights.[56] The term 'labour tenancy' is, therefore, a technical term that has certain requirements.

The main thrust of this Act is to regulate acquisition of rights in land by 'labour tenants', thereby eliminating the former labour tenancy relationship, and establishing the labour tenants as landowners in their own right instead. Eviction is possible in terms of this Act and various sections deal with the requirements,[57] which include that an eviction must be just

---

47 *Blue Moonlight Properties 39 (Pty) Ltd v Occupiers of Saratoga Avenue and the City of Johannesburg* 2009 (1) SA 470 (W); *Lingwood and Schon v The Unlawful Occupiers of Erf 9, Highlands* (Case No: 2006/16243, 16 October 2007, unreported).
48 The Constitutional Court recently granted an eviction order on condition that alternative accommodation be provided for the occupants – see *Residents of Joe Slovo Community, Western Cape v Thubelisha Homes* 2009 JDR 0580 (CC) (decided on 10 June 2009). See also *Port Elizabeth Municipality v Various Occupiers* 2004 (12) BCLR 1268 (CC); *President of the Republic of South Africa and Another v Modderklip Boerdery (Pty) Ltd (AgriSA and Others, Amici Curiae)* 2005 (5) SA 3 (CC).
49 Act 62 of 1997.
50 Act 3 of 1996.
51 Section 9(1) in relation to ESTA and ss 5 and 15A(1) in relation to the Labour Tenants Act.
52 Act 62 of 1997.
53 Section 1(1)*(x)*(c).
54 Section 11(3). A just and equitable date for eviction must also be determined: s 12(1) and (2).
55 Act 3 of 1996.
56 Section 1.
57 Section 7 for ordinary eviction proceedings and s 15 for urgent eviction proceedings.

and equitable in the circumstances.[58] The procedures set out in s 7 (ordinary proceedings) or s 15 (urgent proceedings) must be followed.

> **PAUSE FOR REFLECTION**
>
> **Eviction instruments**
>
> As must be apparent from the preceding discussion, South African law acknowledges different kinds of eviction procedures for different situations. Different legal instruments must be used to achieve eviction in each of the following instances:
>
> First, the group of unlawful occupiers who live in shacks they put up on vacant land that belongs to the local authority: s 6 of PIE applies.
>
> Second, Jonas, a farm worker, employed in 1995, is in breach of his employment contract; he lives in a house on the private farm where he is employed: s 10 of ESTA applies.
>
> Third, MT Consult CC, a small communication consultancy that continues to occupy business premises, despite the lease having been cancelled: the *rei vindicatio* should be employed.
>
> Fourth, Vusi lives on the same land on which his father lived; he provides services in return for the right to reside on and use the land for cropping and grazing; he is in breach of his agreement with the landowner: s 7 of the Labour Tenants Act applies.
>
> Fifth, Sarel moved into the vacant beach house of Piet without permission, and has been in occupation for eight months; Piet wants to evict him: s 4 of PIE applies.

Estoppel. Estoppel may be raised as a defence against the *rei vindicatio* in some circumstances.[59] As a limitation on the use of the *rei vindicatio*, estoppel acts to bar its vindicatory function. Ownership of the person instituting the *rei vindicatio* is not disputed and essentially remains in place, but the owner is unable to regain possession of the property for the duration of estoppel. This is because a successful defence of estoppel suspends the owner's entitlement to vindicate the property. Necessarily, this suspension also affects other entitlements, such as the entitlement to the use and enjoyment of the property.

Initially, estoppel cases dealt almost exclusively with movable property, especially motor vehicles. But in *AGS van Suid-Afrika (Maitland) v Capes*,[60] it was confirmed that estoppel can apply also to immovable property. Estoppel hence operates as a defence against the *rei vindicatio* in circumstances where the owner placed his movable or immovable property in the physical control of someone else, so that third parties were led to believe, through the negligence of the owner, that the person in physical control was owner of the property or had the power to dispose of it. If all these requirements are met, the owner is 'estopped' (i.e. precluded) from utilising his *rei vindicatio*. These requirements are set out in the diagram below:

---

58 Section 7(2)*(a)* and *(b)*.
59 See *Wille's Principles* pp 552–555; *Silberberg & Schoeman Property* pp 255–259.
60 1978 (4) SA 48 (C).

Figure 8.2: Requirements of estoppel

- Negligently/Culpably (i.e. with fault)
- Content of misrepresentation
- Party acted upon misrepresentation
- Owner misrepresents
- **Requirements of estoppel**
- To detriment

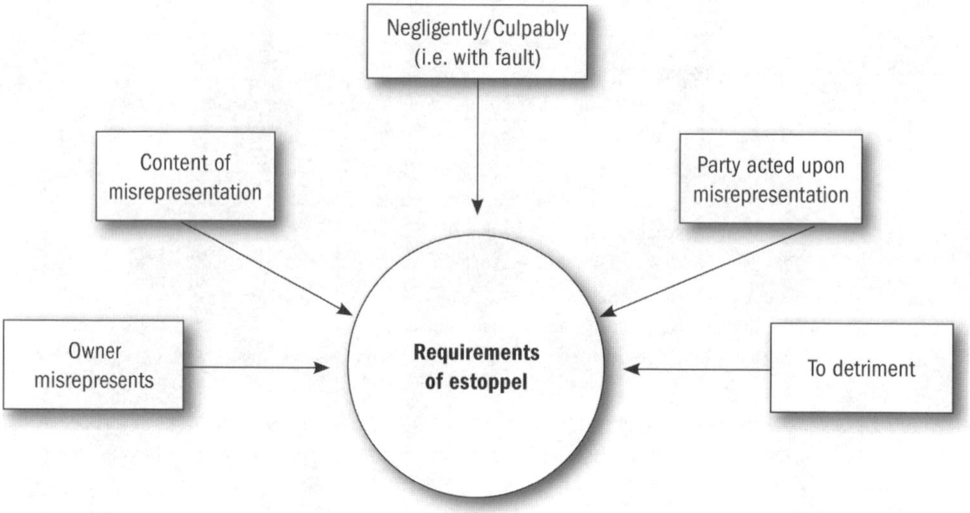

As the diagram illustrates, the owner of the property in question must have negligently (culpably) created the impression, through conduct or otherwise, that the person in control of the property is the owner or is entitled to dispose of the property.[61] The person who raises estoppel must have relied on the misrepresentation made by the owner and such reliance must have led the person to act to his detriment.[62]

The first requirement is that the **owner** must create the impression or misrepresentation. If someone else, such as the person in physical control of the property, creates the impression, then estoppel will not be successful as the owner cannot be held accountable for someone else's conduct.[63] Second, the content of the misrepresentation is important. Third parties must have the impression that the person in control of the property is the owner or at least has the power to dispose of it. Third parties thus should be convinced that when dealing with the person in control, they are dealing with the owner or a person authorised to act on behalf of the owner.[64]

> **PAUSE FOR REFLECTION**
>
> **When can an outsider be misled?**
>
> South African law accepts that merely placing one's property in the possession of someone else does not, by itself, constitute a misrepresentation.[65] Something more than merely handing over possession is required. The *indicia* of ownership or of the *ius disponendi*, should accompany possession. For example, placing Mary Anne in possession of Ben's car by itself does not create the impression that she owns it. However, if Ben gives her the car and the registration papers together with a signed transfer of registration form, then a third party

---

61 *Oakland Nominees (Pty) Ltd v Gelria Mining and Investment Co (Pty) Ltd* 1976 (1) SA 441 (A); *Electrolux (Pty) Ltd v Khota* 1961 (4) SA 244 (W).
62 *Quenty's Motors (Pty) Ltd v Standard Credit Corporation Ltd* 1994 (3) SA 188 (A).
63 *Morum Bros Ltd v Nepgen* 1916 CPD 392.
64 *Quenty's Motors (Pty) Ltd v Standard Credit Corporation Ltd* 1994 (3) SA 188 (A).
65 *Electrolux (Pty) Ltd v Khota* 1961 (4) SA 244 (W).

> would be reasonable in thinking that Mary Anne is the owner or is at least authorised to alienate it on Ben's behalf. Other means might also create the misrepresentation, such as words, written or oral, conduct, or remaining quiet when the owner could have exposed the wrong impression when the opportunity to do so arose.[66]
>
> In *Grosvenor Motors (Potchefstroom) Ltd v Douglas*,[67] the possessor of a particular vehicle had a letter that stated merely that the vehicle had been sold to him. The court's view was that this letter could not have created a misrepresentation that the possessor actually had ownership or the authorisation to dispose of the vehicle. Something more than this letter was required. In this instance, the possessor rather than the owner created the misrepresentation for the third party who relied on the possessor's conduct. Consequently, the defence of estoppel could not succeed.

Third, fault is required on the part of the owner.[68] This means that the misrepresentation must have been created culpably, i.e. negligently. *Johaadien v Stanley Porter (Paarl) (Pty) Ltd*[69] confirmed that intention is not necessary for a successful defence of estoppel. In *Quenty's Motors (Pty) Ltd v Standard Credit Corporation Ltd*,[70] the owner placed his vehicle in the possession of the dealer, with signs attached indicating that it was for sale. The latter displayed this vehicle among the other stock-in-trade. The court's view was that the owner should have foreseen that ordinary members of the public would be misled into thinking that the dealer was authorised to sell the vehicle. Consequently, the owner acted negligently by not taking steps to prevent the misrepresentation.

The fourth requirement is that the person raising estoppel must have relied on the misrepresentation.[71] The person raising the defence must prove that, but for the misrepresentation, she would not have entered into the relevant transaction. In other words, the impression created must have led to the consequent transaction. It must be clear to the courts that it was the misrepresentation, and not something or someone else, that persuaded the person to deal with the person in possession of the property. In *Absa Bank Ltd t/a Bankfin v Jordasche Auto CC*,[72] the defence of estoppel was unsuccessful because the defendant could not provide sufficient evidence that it relied on the misrepresentation.

The fifth requirement is that the defendant must have acted upon the misrepresentation to his detriment.[73] In other words, the defendant must show that reliance on the misrepresentation was the cause of his decision to transact, which led to the negative consequences that followed. Reliance on the misrepresentation must inevitably have resulted in the defendant acting to his detriment.

---

66   *Kia Motors (SA) (Edms) Bpk v Van Zyl* 1999 (3) SA 640 (O).
67   1956 (3) SA 420 (A).
68   *Johaadien v Stanley Porter (Paarl) (Pty) Ltd* 1970 (1) SA 394 (A).
69   1970 (1) SA 394 (A).
70   1994 (3) SA 188 (A).
71   *Standard Bank of SA Ltd v Stama (Pty) Ltd* 1975 (1) SA 730 (A) at 743B–D.
72   2003 (1) SA 401 (SCA).
73   *Quenty's Motors (Pty) Ltd v Standard Credit Corporation Ltd* 1994 (3) SA 188 (A).

> **PAUSE FOR REFLECTION**
>
> **What happens when the defendant is successful?**
>
> If the defendant can successfully prove all the above requirements, he is immune to the *rei vindicatio* of the owner. This means that the owner cannot claim back the property from that particular defendant. The question that arises is what status the defendant has after his victory. Did he acquire ownership of the property? *AGS van Suid-Afrika (Maitland) v Capes*[74] raised the question whether a successful defence of estoppel results in acquisition of ownership by the defendant. Although the issue was not canvassed in detail, the court held that the effect of estoppel was to suspend some entitlements of ownership, rather than to vest ownership in the other person. In other words, a successful defence of estoppel does not lead to transfer of ownership; rather it bars the owner from exercising all his entitlements for as long as the property remains in the possession of the person who raised the defence successfully.[75] This decision thus confirms that bona fide acquisition of property is not an acknowledged mode of acquisition of ownership in South African law.

8.2.2 Actio negatoria

As a real remedy, the *actio negatoria* permits an owner to deny the existence of an alleged servitude or other right for the defendant to cause physical disturbance of the land. In other words, the *actio negatoria* restricts physical disturbance of land.[76] Thus, Aron, the landowner, can institute the *actio negatoria* against Lillith if she claims to have a servitude on his land or against Rebecca, who does have a limited real right, but exceeds the limits of the right. In both instances, the infringement of ownership entitlements is addressed.

The *actio negatoria* can also be used when movable property has been alienated without the owner's consent and delivered notwithstanding the absence of consent, pending the institution of the *rei vindicatio*.[77] In addition, it is used in situations where a person has interfered with the owner's enjoyment, to compel that person to restore the *status quo ante*.[78]

With the *actio negatoria*, the owner may claim that any structures which have been placed on the land unlawfully must be removed. The owner can also institute the action to obtain a declaration of rights, to claim damages, or to obtain security against any future disturbance of his right.[79]

To be successful with the *actio negatoria*, the owner (claimant) must show the following.[80] First, he must prove ownership. Second, he must show that the property exists and is identifiable. Third, he must show that the defendant's conduct infringes upon his rights, either because it amounts to an excessive exercise of an acknowledged limited real right, or because the defendant is assuming a limited real right where it does not exist.

---

74 1978 (4) SA 48 (C).
75 See also *Wille's Principles* p 554; *Silberberg & Schoeman Property* p 259.
76 *Wille's Principles* p 541.
77 *Wille's Principles* p 541.
78 See *Wille's Principles* pp 541–542.
79 *Silberberg & Schoeman Property* p 262.
80 In general, see *Silberberg & Schoeman Property* p 262.

8.3 Delictual remedies

Whereas real remedies are employed to restore possession of property to the owner, or to restore or prevent infringement of ownership entitlements, delictual remedies are appropriate when physical restoration is not possible.[81] For example, the property may have been destroyed, lost, or damaged so that it cannot be identified or cannot be used for its destined purpose. In these instances, the owner must be compensated for her patrimonial loss. Three remedies are relevant here: the *condictio furtiva*, the *actio ad exhibendum*, and the general action for damages, namely the *actio legis Aquiliae*. These are all personal remedies, not real remedies.

8.3.1 Condictio furtiva

The *condictio furtiva* is used in cases where property was stolen, to recover patrimonial loss caused by the theft.[82] It is a delictual remedy, originating in Roman law, available to owners or anyone with an interest in the stolen thing.[83] It is a personal action instituted against the thief. Depending on the circumstances, it is possible to use this remedy in the alternative to the *rei vindicatio*,[84] as is explained below.

The person instituting the *condictio furtiva* must prove either ownership of the property claimed, or a lawful interest in it. *Clifford v Farinha*[85] confirmed that a person with a lawful interest in the stolen property, e.g. the lessor, also has *locus standi* to institute this remedy. This renders the *condictio furtiva* the only ownership remedy extended to include a non-owner with a lawful interest in the property.

It is essential that the claimant is the owner or has a lawful interest in the property **at all relevant times**.[86] In other words, the interest must exist at the time of the theft and must still endure at the time that action is instituted. In *Minister van Verdediging v Van Wyk*,[87] the *condictio furtiva* was unsuccessful because the owner, the Defence Force, had sold the property at stake (wreckage) before the *condictio furtiva* was instituted. As the Defence Force was not owner at the time the remedy was instituted (and no longer had an interest in the property), it was disqualified from using the *condictio furtiva*.

The *condictio furtiva* is available only against the thief or, in the case of death, his heirs. It cannot be instituted against bona fide or *mala fide* acquirers of the stolen property.[88] For purposes of the *condictio furtiva*, theft is defined more widely than in criminal law. What is important for present purposes is that the person removed the thing without the necessary consent, with fraudulent motives.[89] The claim is for the property and its fruits, or its highest value since the theft.

---

81 *Wille's Principles* p 541.
82 *LAWSA* Vol 27(1) at para 387.
83 *Clifford v Farinha* 1988 (4) SA 315 (W) at 323F–324. See also *Wille's Principles* pp 544–545; *Silberberg & Schoeman Property* pp 265–266.
84 *Minister van Verdediging v Van Wyk* 1976 (1) SA 397 (T).
85 1988 (4) SA 315 (W).
86 *Minister van Verdediging v Van Wyk* 1976 (1) SA 397 (T).
87 1976 (1) SA 397 (T).
88 *LAWSA* Vol 27(1) at para 387.
89 *Clifford v Farinha* 1988 (4) SA 315 (W).

8.3.2 Actio ad exhibendum

In Roman law, the *actio ad exhibendum* was instituted alongside the *rei vindicatio* to compel the possessor of the property at stake to bring it to the proceedings. If the possessor failed to do so, he had to compensate the owner for the value of the property.[90] The action thus originally had a real aim, not a delictual one. However, this function of the *actio ad exhibendum* has not been confirmed in South African law. Currently, the *actio ad exhibendum* serves as a general personal action with a delictual function: it is instituted by the owner against the person who wrongfully and deliberately disposed of the property. As the property cannot be recovered, the claim is for the value of the property. Since the basis of liability is bad faith (*mala fides*), this must be alleged and proved by the claimant.[91]

There is some overlap evident in case law between the *actio ad exhibendum* and the *rei vindicatio* in the situation where the property itself cannot be recovered.[92] However, the better view is that the *rei vindicatio* is appropriate only when the property still exists.[93]

The following is required for successful reliance on the *actio ad exhibendum*.[94] The remedy can be instituted only by the owner of the property. The defendant must have wrongfully and intentionally disposed of it. In other words, the defendant must have acted in bad faith when disposing of the property. The owner must have suffered patrimonial loss as a result of the disposal of the property. As the thing in question cannot be claimed because it has been disposed of, its market value at the time of disposal is claimed instead.

Some of these requirements need to be elucidated. First, as concerns the person instituting the action, he must prove that he was the owner of the property at the time that the defendant wrongfully disposed of it. In *RMS Transport v Psicon Holdings (Pty)*,[95] the action was instituted by a person who claimed to have an interest in the property, being copper cables. The court confirmed that the function of the action had changed over centuries and that, initially, it had a real rather than a delictual application. However, the action had not evolved to the extent that it was available also to a person with a lawful interest in the thing disposed of, as is the case with the *condictio furtiva* (discussed above). So, despite having been developed, the *actio ad exhibendum* is still only available to owners. Accordingly, ownership in the consumed, destroyed, alienated or disposed of property must be proven.

Second, as concerns the defendant, two elements are important. On the one hand, it must clearly have been the defendant who disposed of, destroyed, consumed or alienated the thing.[96] On the other, the defendant must have acted in bad faith at the time of disposal.[97] *Frankel Pollak Vinderene Inc v Stanton NO*[98] confirmed that the action lies only if the defendant disposed of the property with (constructive) knowledge of the plaintiff's title or claim. Destruction or damage of property without fault on the defendant's part does not lead to liability under the action.

---

90 *Wille's Principles* p 542.
91 *Alderson & Flitton (Tzaneen) (Pty) Ltd v EG Duffeys Spares (Pty) Ltd* 1975 (3) SA 41 (T).
92 See *Wille's Principles* p 543 where it is explained that the confusion originates with Voet who permitted the *rei vindicatio* instead of the *actio ad exhibendum* when the property had been disposed of fraudulently in knowledge of the owner's title. See also p 214.
93 See the discussion above.
94 *RMS Transport v Psicon Holdings (Pty) Ltd* 1996 (2) SA 176 (T).
95 1996 (2) SA 176 (T).
96 *Philip Robinson Motors (Pty) Ltd v NM Dada (Pty) Ltd* 1975 (2) SA 420 (A).
97 *Alderson & Flitton (Tzaneen) (Pty) Ltd v EG Duffeys Spares (Pty) Ltd* 1975 (3) SA 41 (T).
98 2000 (2) SA 425 (W) at 429–430.

8.3.3 Actio legis Aquiliae

The two delictual remedies discussed above have particular application: the *condictio furtiva* is employed only in the case of theft, whereas the *actio ad exhibendum* is utilised when the possessor wrongfully disposed of the property in bad faith. The *actio legis Aquiliae*, however, is a general action to claim compensation in all cases where property has been destroyed or damaged by the defendant in an unlawful and culpable manner.

Since this action is a general delictual action, the usual requirements for delictual claims must be proved. In brief, there must have been conduct or an omission by the defendant, who acted wrongfully with culpability, causing the owner of the property in question to suffer patrimonial loss, which could include pure economic loss. The scope of this book does not permit a detailed discussion of the *actio legis Aquiliae*, which is discussed at length in all the standard works on delict in South African law.[99]

8.4 Unjustified enrichment

It is possible for an owner to institute an enrichment action (*condictio sine causa*) against a person who was unjustifiably enriched, without cause, by deriving a benefit from possession of the thing, which benefit ought to have accrued to the owner. The benefit could derive from consumption or alienation of the property.[100] The availability of the enrichment claim depends on whether the person against whom action is instituted, received the thing for consideration (*ex causa onerosa*) or without consideration (*ex causa lucrativa*). In other words, it depends on whether money exchanged hands. The action is available only in the situation where no consideration was given (*ex causa lucrativa*).[101]

Depending on the circumstances, the enrichment claim in the form of the *condictio sine causa* may be the only remedy available to the owner, especially in relation to bona fide possessors who consumed or alienated property. Say, for instance, Busi purchases paint on credit from Handiman trading as The Handiman's Store (Pty) Ltd, which he uses to paint the exterior of Malena's house. Just as he is about to complete the paintwork, he falls from a ladder and dies, leaving behind an insolvent estate. Under such circumstances, Malena may be vulnerable to a claim of unjustified enrichment by Handiman, over and above any claims that Busi's deceased estate may have against her for the provision of services. For Handiman, none of the other remedies would be available: the *rei vindicatio* would not lie because the property no longer exists as a separate entity (the paint has acceded to the walls); the *actio ad exhibendum* would not lie because there was no *mala fide* conduct on Malena's part; the *condictio furtiva* would not lie because there was no theft involved; and the *actio legis Aquiliae* would not lie because there was no fault.

To be successful with an enrichment claim, the owner must show that he was impoverished (in the sense that what should have accrued to the owner, has not). The defendant, moreover, must have been enriched at the expense of the owner. This financial shift must have been without a legal basis (*sine causa*) and the defendant must have acted bona fide.[102]

---

99 See e.g. Neethling, J et al. (2006) *Law of Delict* (Durban, Lexisnexis Butterworths) pp 7-11, 238, 253-295.
100 For detailed exposition on this topic, see Visser, D (2008) *Unjustified Enrichment* (Cape Town, Juta).
101 *Morobane v Bateman* 1918 AD 460.
102 See *Silberberg & Schoeman Property* p 267.

8.5 Concluding remarks: How to choose a remedy

The interrelationship between a successful enforcement of ownership rights and the palette of remedies available is important. The table below provides an overview of the various remedies available and the circumstances in which they are applicable.

The *rei vindicatio* is the best remedy if the property still exists and is identifiable. If, however, the property cannot be traced, the facts have to be considered carefully to decide which remedy would give the best result in the particular circumstances. For example, if a thief lost or destroyed the property intentionally to avoid the *rei vindicatio*, then the *actio ad exhibendum* and the *condictio furtiva* are both available to the owner. Because the highest value of the property since the theft may be claimed with the *condictio*, it would be the better remedy in these circumstances. However, if the thing was lost or destroyed through no fault of the thief's, then neither the *actio ad exhibendum* nor the *rei vindicatio* would be available, leaving the *condictio furtiva* to remedy the situation. Of course, a delictual action would be possible too, but if a choice can be made between an ordinary Aquilian action and the *condictio furtiva*, the latter has the advantage of enabling the owner to claim double the value of the property. Whether this would be the appropriate remedy would depend on whether the patrimonial loss that can be proven under the Aquilian action exceeds double the value of the property.

> **PAUSE FOR REFLECTION**
>
> **Consider the following hypothetical case**
>
> Karel entered into a three-year lease agreement with BATA Motors Ltd relating to a new Volkswagen Jetta. In terms of this agreement, Karel has use and enjoyment of the Jetta, and must pay a monthly instalment. According to the terms of the agreement, Karel bears the risk if anything should happen to the car. Before leaving for Johannesburg on a business trip, Karel specifically ordered his house mate, Pieter, not to touch his car in his absence. However, the moment Karel departed, Pieter and his girlfriend, Marie, took the car from the locked garage and went out for a night on the town.
>
> If, under such circumstances, the vehicle was stolen from the parking area while Pieter and Marie were at the movies, Karel's best recourse would be to institute the *condictio furtiva* against Pieter and Marie. The *rei vindicatio* would be out of the question because the whereabouts of the car is uncertain. The *actio ad exhibendum* would be a possibility, but does not enable as large a claim for damages as the *condictio furtiva* does. On the facts, it is clear that Pieter and Marie's conduct fits the broad definition of theft as it is used in the context of the *condictio furtiva*.
>
> If, under the circumstances outlined above, the car was not stolen, but was destroyed beyond repair in an accident when Pieter negligently lost control of the car, Karel's best recourse would still be the *condictio furtiva*. The *actio ad exhibendum* would not be the appropriate remedy here, for two reasons. First, Karel is not the owner and as explained, this remedy may only be employed by the owner; and second, *mala fides* on the part of Pieter when the car was destroyed is absent.

Table 8.1: Remedies for the protection of ownership

REAL REMEDIES

MAIN AIM(S) OR FOCUS
- Restore physical control
- Restore or prevent encroachment on entitlements

Forms	Rei vindicatio	Actio negatoria	Interdict	Declaratory order
WHO can institute remedy?	• Owner	• Owner	• Owner • Person in lawful possession	• Owner • Possessor
WHAT is claimed?	• Thing • Eviction from immovable property	• Prevent encroachment on entitlements of owner • Prevent exceeding bounds of servitude	• Prevent or cease certain conduct (prohibitory) • Order certain conduct (mandatory)	• Declaration of relevant rights and obligations of parties
AGAINST WHOM can it be instituted?	• Any person in control of property	• Person or party encroaching	• Infringer or invader	• Opposing party in dispute

DELICTUAL REMEDIES

MAIN AIM(S) OR FOCUS
- Compensation
- Damages

Forms	Condictio furtiva	Actio ad exhibendum	Actio legis aquiliae
WHO can institute remedy?	• Owner • Person with lawful interest	• Owner	• Owner • Bona fide possessor
WHAT is claimed?	• Stolen property or • Highest value since theft	• Market value of thing	• Damages
AGAINST WHOM can it be instituted?	• Thief or • Heirs of thief if deceased	• Possessor who lost, destroyed, disposed of, or alienated property	• Person or party who caused patrimonial loss

PART THREE

SPECIFIC FORMS OF RIGHTS IN PROPERTY

CHAPTER 9 Servitudes and restrictive conditions 235

CHAPTER 10 Minerals 265

CHAPTER 11 Water 283

CHAPTER 12 Real security 295

Chapter 9

Servitudes and restrictive conditions

'Servitudes are by their nature often the creation of preceding generations devised in another time to serve ends which must now be satisfied in a different environment.'
Linvestment CC v Hammersley and Another 2008 (3) SA 283 (SCA) at 292–293

9.1	Introduction	235
9.2	Definition and classification	236
9.2.1	Praedial servitudes	240
9.2.1.1	Requirements	240
9.2.1.2	Rights and duties	245
9.2.1.3	Types of servitudes	246
9.2.2	Personal servitudes	248
9.3	Creation, termination and enforcement of servitudes	251
9.3.1	Creation	251
9.3.2	Extinction or termination	253
9.3.3	Enforcement	254
9.4	Restrictive conditions	254
9.4.1	Definition and examples	255
9.4.2	Nature, character and status of restrictive conditions	256
9.4.3	Enforcement and defences	259
9.4.3.1	Judicial remedies	259
9.4.3.2	Statutory remedies	261
9.4.3.3	Defences	261
9.4.4	Removal or amendment of restrictive conditions	261
9.4.4.1	Removal by court application	262
9.4.4.2	Statutory procedures for removal	262
9.5	Concluding remarks	263

9.1 Introduction

Chapter 3 indicates that the law acknowledges different kinds of rights in respect of property. This chapter is concerned with limited real rights (i.e. *iura in re aliena* or rights in the property of another). The main distinction between real rights in property and personal (or creditor's) rights as well as much of the theory regarding the establishment and enforcement of real rights are covered in chapter 3. This chapter focuses firstly on an established category of real rights, namely servitudes, and deals in greater depth with the particular requirements and means of acquiring servitudes. It also pays attention to restrictive conditions as a type of servitude, which plays an important role in planning law.[1]

9.2 Definition and classification

The term 'servitudes' refers to the real rights that are 'carved out of the full *dominium* of the owner' and exercised by another person.[2] The content of a particular servitude is whatever entitlements of ownership are assigned to the other person by the owner. This is why a servitude is a *ius in re aliena*, i.e. a limited real right in the property of another. By definition, therefore, one cannot have a servitude in one's own property. In other words, it is not possible for an owner to assign some entitlements of ownership to himself. Essentially, therefore, a servitude confers a real right to benefit from the property of another,[3] either because it affords powers of use and enjoyment to someone other than the owner, or because it requires the owner to refrain from exercising one or more of his entitlements of ownership. Conversely, the notion of servitude implies that the property serves either another property or another person,[4] and that the *dominium* of the owner of the servient (burdened) property is diminished by the servitude.

There is a rebuttable presumption that ownership is unencumbered and free from servitudes. This means that the person who alleges the existence of a servitude, must prove it on a balance of probabilities.[5] Chapter 3 indicates that the content of both a real right and a personal right may be identical. The important implication is that servitudes cannot be distinguished from other types of rights merely by reference to their content. Servitudes are distinguishable from mere personal rights in respect of property in that they entail a direct relationship between the holder of the servitude and the property to which it relates.[6] Hence, they invariably amount to burdens on the property.

In general terms, movable property is seldom the object of a servitude. Usually, only the personal servitude of usufruct might have movable property as its object, e.g. a usufruct may exist over a herd of cattle. In the majority of cases, the notion of servitude is encountered in the context of land law, i.e. in respect of immovable property. Accordingly, all further references to and examples of servitudes are with regard to immovable property.

It is useful at the outset to note some points regarding the relationship between the holder of a servitude and the owner of the servient property (i.e. the servient owner). First, the holder of the servitude has priority, in principle, as regards the exercise of the particular entitlement covered by the servitude. This means that the servient owner may exercise all the usual rights of ownership, but may not impair the rights of the servitude holder, and hence may not exercise those rights that are inconsistent with the servitude, or grant further servitudes where these would infringe on the existing servitude. The implications of this rule were particularly onerous, historically, in the context of mineral rights.[7] In common law, the mineral right holder's entitlements to enter the land, search

---

1   See further ch 6 above, for more on planning law.
2   *Consistory of Steytlerville v Bosman* (1893) 10 SC 67 at 69.
3   *Lorentz v Melle* 1978 (3) SA 1044 (T) at 1049C.
4   *Wille's Principles* p 592; *Lorentz v Melle* 1978 (3) SA 1044 (T) at 1049C.
5   *Ley v Ley's Executors* 1951 (3) SA 186 (A); *Northview Properties (Pty) Ltd v Lurie* 1951 (3) SA 688 (A) at 696.
6   Silberberg & Schoeman *Property* p 321.
7   Van der Merwe *Sakereg* pp 562–563; *Trojan Exploration Co (Pty) Ltd and Another v Rustenburg Platinum Mines Ltd and Others* 1996 (4) SA 499 (A) at 509I.

for minerals and to extract them when they were found, often rendered other commercial or agricultural activity on the land impossible for the owner. Second, the servitude holder is entitled to perform all acts necessary for the proper exercise of the servitude. The holder must, however, exercise the servitude *civiliter modo*, i.e. so that as little inconvenience as possible is caused to the servient owner, and that the burden on the servient property is not increased beyond the express or implied terms of the servitude.[8]

In Roman law, only a strictly limited number *(numerus clausus)* of limited real rights *(iura in re aliena)* was acknowledged. These included the category of servitudes that incorporated various kinds of rights of way, grazing rights, rights in respect of water use, and rights that related to the extraction of resources such as lime and clay.[9] It also included the right of *ususfructus* (usufruct – the right to use and enjoy, and to take the fruits of property) and *superficies* (the right to build upon another's land). The strict limitations on the kinds of servitudes permissible have been relaxed significantly since then, so much so that South African law knows no *numerus clausus* of real rights in respect of land. However, new types are permitted only with great caution, in accordance with the view that land should not be unnecessarily burdened.[10]

In conventional terms, servitudes may be divided into two distinct categories, depending on whether the servitude benefits successive owners or not. In terms of this classification, the two basic categories are praedial servitudes and personal servitudes.[11] Praedial servitudes are limited real rights that vest in successive owners of one piece of land (the dominant tenement), which derives a benefit from another piece of land (the servient tenement) that belongs to someone other than the owner of the dominant tenement. Personal servitudes are limited real rights in movable or immovable property of another, which vest in a particular person only.

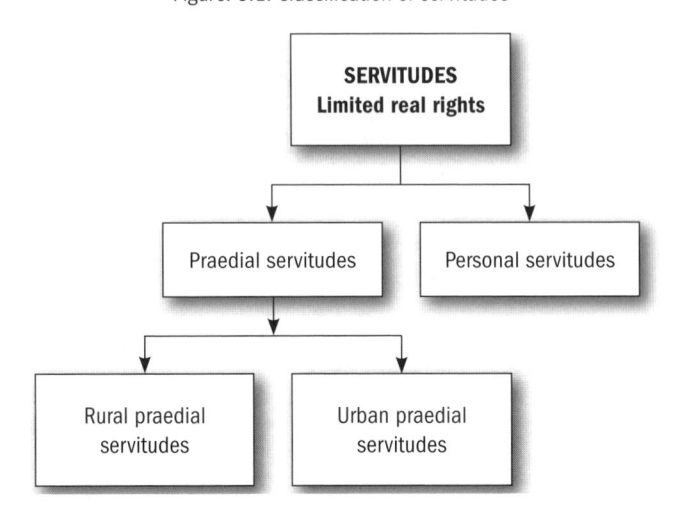

Figure: 9.1: Classification of servitudes

```
                    ┌─────────────────────┐
                    │     SERVITUDES      │
                    │ Limited real rights │
                    └──────────┬──────────┘
                               │
                ┌──────────────┴──────────────┐
                │                             │
    ┌───────────────────────┐     ┌───────────────────────┐
    │  Praedial servitudes  │     │  Personal servitudes  │
    └───────────┬───────────┘     └───────────────────────┘
                │
        ┌───────┴────────┐
        │                │
┌───────────────┐ ┌───────────────┐
│ Rural praedial│ │ Urban praedial│
│  servitudes   │ │  servitudes   │
└───────────────┘ └───────────────┘
```

---

8 *Silberberg & Schoeman Property* p 331; *Wille's Principles* p 593.
9 *Silberberg & Schoeman Property* p 326; *Wille's Principles* p 604, and see for examples, Borkowski, A & Du Plessis, P (2005) *Textbook on Roman Law* 3 ed (Oxford, Oxford University Press) pp 171*ff*.
10 See ch 3 for more detail.
11 *Silberberg & Schoeman Property* pp 321–322; *Wille's Principles* p 592.

> **PAUSE FOR REFLECTION**
>
> **Praedial and personal servitudes**
>
> Because it is a limited real right in immovable property, by definition, a servitude leads to a burden on the servient property and a benefit for the dominant property (or person). This means that the servitude automatically binds successive owners of the property that it burdens. This is where the diminution of the owner's entitlements may be seen, when (in the words of *Ex parte Geldenhuys*) one looks 'not at the right but at the correlative obligation'.[12] In other words, the owner of the burdened property is unable to exercise the full complement of entitlements because of the existence of the servitude. On the benefit side of the equation, whether the benefit automatically favours successive owners depends on whether the servitude benefits a particular piece of land or a particular individual. If the benefit favours land, then, regardless of the identity of the owner at any given point, successive owners will benefit from the interest in the servient land. If the benefit favours a particular person, then, at best, the benefit exists for the lifetime of that person. It is important to keep in mind that all servitudes are limited real rights, regardless of whether they are personal or praedial servitudes.

Figure 9.2: Main distinctions between praedial and personal servitudes

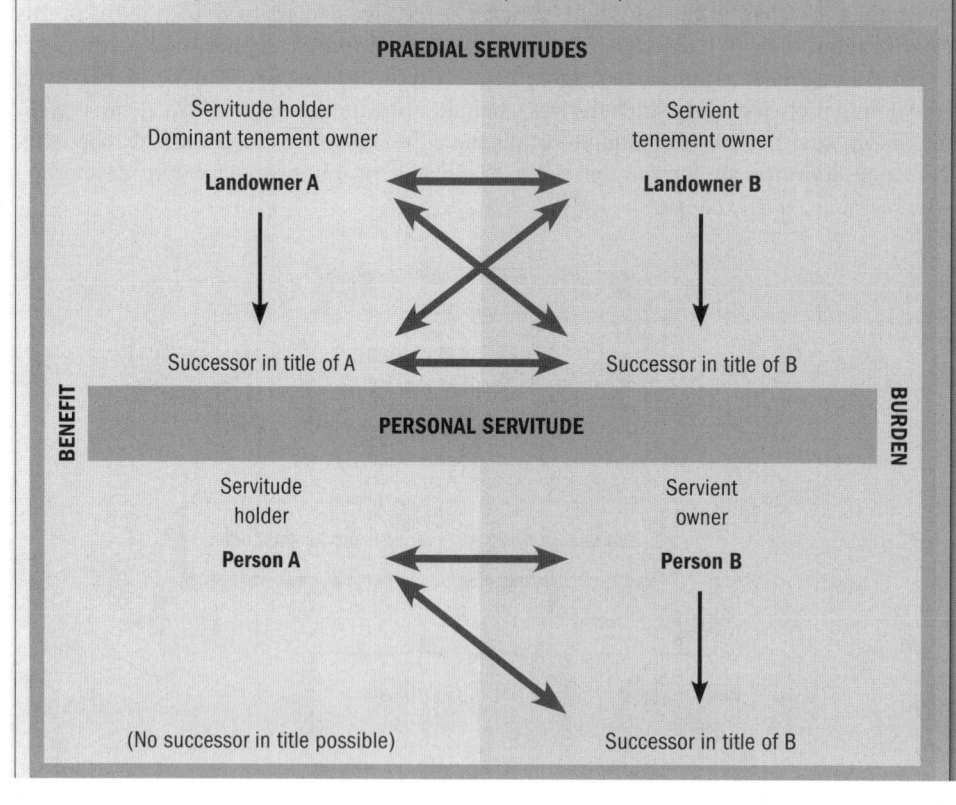

PRAEDIAL SERVITUDES

Servitude holder / Dominant tenement owner — **Landowner A** ↓ Successor in title of A

Servient tenement owner — **Landowner B** ↓ Successor in title of B

BENEFIT ← → BURDEN

PERSONAL SERVITUDE

Servitude holder — **Person A** — (No successor in title possible)

Servient owner — **Person B** ↓ Successor in title of B

---

12 *Ex parte Geldenhuys* 1926 OPD 155 at 164.

> The description of servitudes as either praedial or personal has nothing to do with the nature of the rights as either real or personal: all servitudes are real rights because they burden ownership. The description is significant because it denotes whether the particular servitude benefits a person in his capacity as the owner of specific property or in his personal capacity. So, the adjectives 'praedial' and 'personal' used to describe different servitudes, serve to identify who benefits from the servitude, and not the extent to which the rights are absolute or relative. It is important to grasp that a personal servitude is, undeniably, a limited real right and conceptually distinctive from a personal (creditor's) right. Note in the diagram above that, inevitably, the **burden** passes automatically to the successor in title in both instances, but that the **benefit** passes automatically to the successor in title only when the servitude is praedial. In other words, the benefit of a personal servitude is not transferable from one person to another.

Praedial and personal servitudes may be distinguished in the following ways.[13] First, a praedial servitude can exist only in respect of land, and always involves at least two pieces of land. A personal servitude can exist over both land and movable property. Second, a praedial servitude is constituted in favour of a particular plot of land, successive owners of which will benefit from the right. Put differently, the owner of the land benefits from the servitude in the capacity as landowner. A personal servitude is constituted in favour of a particular person, i.e. the person holds the servitude and benefits from it in his personal capacity, and not as landowner. Third, because of its effect, a praedial servitude is inseparably bound to the land that it benefits. When the land is alienated, the new owner becomes the holder of the praedial servitude because it follows the destiny of the land with which it is associated. A personal servitude cannot be transferred by its holder. Fourth, where both the benefit and the burden necessarily transfer to successive owners respectively, as in the case of praedial servitudes, the servitude is said to 'run with the land', in principle, perpetually.[14] Personal servitudes are extinguished when the period for which they are granted lapses, or when the holder of the personal servitude dies. Where the holder is a juristic person, the servitude lapses after 100 years. Finally, praedial servitudes are indivisible, while personal servitudes (e.g. a usufruct) are divisible. This means that the personal servitude, in principle, can exist over a part of the property (depending on the nature of the property), while a praedial servitude, in principle, exists over the whole of the affected land.[15]

Praedial and personal servitudes have many aspects in common. Importantly, both categories deal with real rights (as explained above). Moreover, the rule that no one can hold a servitude in respect of his own property *(nemini res sua servit)* applies to both categories.[16] So does the maxim that no further servitude may be imposed on an existing servitude *(servitus servitutus esse non potest)*.[17] Both categories of servitudes are created

---

13 *Silberberg & Schoeman Property* pp 322–342; *Wille's Principles* pp 593–611; *LAWSA* Vol 24 at para 388.
14 Section 75(1) of the Deeds Registries Act 47 of 1937 provides, however, that praedial servitudes may be registered for limited periods.
15 See, however, the discussion below on indivisibility and subdivision of tenements.
16 *Silberberg & Schoeman Property* p 323; *Wille's Principles* p 592; *LAWSA* Vol 24 at para 389.
17 *Silberberg & Schoeman Property* p 323; *Wille's Principles* p 592; *LAWSA* Vol 24 at para 389.

and terminated in similar ways,[18] and both categories accommodate either positive or negative servitudes.[19] A servitude is positive when it entitles the holder to do something on or with the servient property, while a negative servitude entitles the holder to claim that the owner refrains from exercising one or more ownership entitlements.

9.2.1 Praedial servitudes

The discussion below deals firstly with the requirements for praedial servitudes. Then the rights and duties of the servitude holder and the servient owner are discussed. The typical forms of praedial servitudes encountered in practice follow. And, finally, a more detailed discussion of restrictive conditions as a specialised type of praedial servitude is provided.

9.2.1.1 Requirements

Praedial servitudes require at least two pieces of land (also called erven or tenements) owned by different persons. Since a praedial servitude always constitutes a burden imposed on one piece of land (servient tenement) in favour of another piece of land (dominant tenement), there can be no praedial servitude unless there are two tenements.[20] This is in line with the rule of praedial servitudes that 'one piece of land serves another'.[21] It also corresponds with the rule that nobody can hold a servitude over his own property *(nemini res sua servit).*[22] Moreover, servitutal benefits cannot be severed from the land to which they are attached.[23] Consequently, there cannot be a servitude imposed on a servitude *(servitus servitutis esse non potest).*[24] The owner of the dominant tenement cannot assign her servitude or allow it to be used for the benefit of a tenement other than the dominant tenement.[25]

Furthermore, a praedial servitude must benefit the owner of the dominant tenement in her capacity as owner of the land.[26] In other words, the owner may not benefit only in her personal capacity. This is referred to as the requirement of utility *(utilitas).* Essentially, the question is whether the value derived from the dominant tenement is enhanced by the praedial servitude. For example, the servitude may enhance any aspect of the agricultural, economic, industrial or professional potential of the dominant tenement.[27]

To determine utility, it is necessary to consider the following factors. First, in line with the rule of vicinity *(vicinitas),* the two tenements must be close enough to each other so that the servient tenement can reasonably enhance the use and enjoyment of the dominant tenement.[28] The tenements need not be contiguous (adjacent). Typically, if the tenements are not adjacent, it is necessary to establish servitudes over intervening tenements as well to ensure access.[29]

---

18 *Silberberg & Schoeman Property* pp 336–338 and 342; *Wille's Principles* p 592; *LAWSA* Vol 24 at paras 450–462.
19 *Silberberg & Schoeman Property* p 322; *Wille's Principles* p 593–611; *LAWSA* Vol 24 at para 402.
20 *Silberberg & Schoeman Property* p 322.
21 *Silberberg & Schoeman Property* p 322.
22 *Silberberg & Schoeman Property* p 323; *Wille's Principles* p 592; *LAWSA* Vol 24 at para 389.
23 *Silberberg & Schoeman Property* p 322; *Berdur Properties (Pty) Ltd v 76 Commercial Road (Pty) Ltd* 1998 (4) SA 62 (D) at 70B–C.
24 *LAWSA* Vol 24 at para 389.
25 *Silberberg & Schoeman Property* pp 323–324.
26 *Silberberg & Schoeman Property* p 323; *Wille's Principles* p 594; *LAWSA* Vol 24 at para 396.
27 *Wille's Principles* pp 594–595.
28 *Briers v Wilson* 1952 (3) SA 423 (C) at 433; *Bisschop v Stafford* 1974 (3) SA 1 (A); *Wille's Principles* p 594.
29 *Hawkins v Munnik* (1830) 1 Menz 465; *Briers v Wilson* 1952 (3) SA 423 (C) at 433.

Second, the benefit created by the praedial servitude must not satisfy merely the pleasure or caprice of the person who happens to be the landowner at a particular point, but must benefit the dominant tenement itself.[30] It must promote the use and enjoyment of the dominant tenement on a permanent basis *(servitutes perpetua causas habere dabent)*. The use made of the servient land must be based on some permanent feature or attribute of the servient land.[31] For example, the right to picnic on a neighbour's land may constitute a personal servitude, but would probably not meet the criteria of the *utilitas* requirement for a praedial servitude. Similarly, a right to sail on the dam on the neighbouring land can only amount to a praedial servitude if (among other things) the dam is permanent.

> **COUNTER POINT**
>
> **Role of utility**
>
> In *De Kock v Hänel & Others*,[32] it was stated that utility is required only for the creation of a praedial servitude, and not for its continued existence.[33] This is clearly mistaken. If a servitude is no longer of permanent use to the dominant tenement, there is no further reason for its existence. While a grazing servitude cannot exist where the servient tenement never has sufficient pasture, a praedial servitude may exist despite the fact that pasture is insufficient for a particular period, e.g. because of drought.[34]

Third, servitudes are passive in character, which means that, traditionally, a servitude cannot impose an active or positive duty (i.e. a duty to do something) on the owner of servient land.[35] This is the gist of the passivity principle, summarised by the maxim, *servitus in faciendo consistere nequit*, i.e. a servitude does not oblige the servient owner to render a performance. Instead, it requires the servient owner either to allow the holder of the servitude to do something with or on the servient tenement, or to refrain from doing something with the land himself. The obligation to render a performance is characteristic of a personal right. There are only two exceptions to this rule of passivity, namely the servitude to compel the owner of the servient property to construct a building of a certain height *(servitus altius tollendi)*, and the servitude that imposes a duty on the owner of servient land to keep the adjoining wall in a good state of repair *(servitus oneris ferendi)*.[36]

In *Schwedhelm v Hauman*,[37] this approach to the rule of passivity was upheld. A registered servitude entitled the plaintiff to draw water from a dam on the defendant's land. It also compelled the defendant (the servient owner) to provide and suitably maintain any windmill, pipes, etc., necessary to convey the water over the two properties to points determined by the plaintiff. Although the court found the right to draw water to amount to a valid servitude, it was not willing to regard the obligation on the defendant to perform positive duties in respect of that servitude also as a servitude.[38] The positive obligation was personal in nature.

---

30   *Silberberg & Schoeman Property* p 323; *Wille's Principles* p 594; *LAWSA* Vol 24 at para 396.
31   *Wille's Principles* p 594; *Lorentz v Melle* 1978 (3) SA 1044 (T) at 1049; *Venter v Minister of Railways* 1949 (2) SA 178 (E) at 185.
32   1999 (1) SA 994 (C).
33   See *Wille's Principles* p 595.
34   *Silberberg & Schoeman Property* p 323 n 17; *Wille's Principles* p 595.
35   *Silberberg & Schoeman Property* p 324; *Wille's Principles* p 595.
36   *Silberberg & Schoeman Property* p 324; *Wille's Principles* p 595.
37   1947 (1) SA 127 (E).
38   *Schwedhelm* at 233.

> **COUNTER POINT**
>
> **Rule of passivity: A different interpretation**
>
> The opposite stance was taken in *Van der Merwe v Wiese*.[39] On facts similar to those in *Schwedhelm v Hauman*,[40] the court here held that the passivity principle is merely a useful guideline for the interpretation of rights to determine whether they amount to servitudes. The incorporation of a positive obligation into a servitude, according to this decision, does not necessarily mean that the right binding successive owners is invalid. The decision has been widely criticised, however, for the manner in which it misinterpreted Roman-Dutch sources, and for engaging in dubious comparative research.[41]
>
> Since both conflicting decisions in *Schwedhelm v Hauman*[42] and *Van der Merwe v Wiese*[43] were handed down at provincial level, confirmation of the more appropriate approach must come from statute or the Supreme Court of Appeal. Generally, however, it is uncontroversial that the approach followed in *Schwedhelm* is regarded as more acceptable.[44] This approach was followed also in *Low Water Properties (Pty) Ltd v Wahloo Sand CC*.[45] The dilemma is to balance the needs of practice, which obviously were considered in the case of *Van der Merwe v Wiese*,[46] with an historically more correct interpretation of the law, as is found in *Schwedhelm v Hauman*.[47] To date, the Supreme Court of Appeal has not found it necessary to 'deal with the question as to whether or not the rule relied upon in *Schwedhelm* is absolute'.[48]
>
> In *Cape Explosive Works Ltd v Denel (Pty) Ltd*,[49] the dispute concerned whether a right to repurchase the land in question survived being omitted in error from subsequent title deeds. This right was part of the conditions of transfer, which included a use restriction in relation to the land. Part of the argument was that the right to repurchase should not have been registered in the first place because it did not give rise to a real right. The court found it unnecessary to consider the right of repurchase separately and thus to re-examine the *Schwedhelm* approach. Instead, it held that the use restriction and the complementary mechanism that would provide a way for Capex to repurchase the land with its use restriction or for the use restriction to be terminated were inseparable. Together, as a 'composite whole', they specifically burdened the land. In other words, in this situation, the right to repurchase was not a clearly separate right, but rather was part of a complex condition of transfer.[50]

---

39 1948 (4) SA 8 (C).
40 1947 (1) SA 127 (E).
41 *Wille's Principles* p 596 and the sources mentioned there.
42 1947 (1) SA 127 (E).
43 1948 (4) SA 8 (C).
44 *Wille's Principles* p 596.
45 1999 (1) SA 655 (SE) at 661D.
46 1948 (4) SA 8 (C).
47 1947 (1) SA 127 (E).
48 *Cape Explosive Works Ltd v Denel (Pty) Ltd* 2001 (3) SA 569 (SCA) at 579A–B.
49 2001 (3) SA 569 (SCA).
50 See *Cape Explosive Works Ltd v Denel (Pty) Ltd* 2001 (3) SA 569 (SCA) at 578H–579D.

> In our opinion, it is counterproductive to permit conditions that burden landowners with positive duties to be registered as real rights against the title deed. To do so would inhibit the negotiability of land. The passivity principle is more than merely a guide for the determination of whether a specific agreement creates servitutal rights.[51] It is a 'negative requirement' for the establishment of praedial servitudes, in that it 'prescribes what may or may not be the content of a praedial servitude'.[52] It presents a means to protect the commercial viability of land.[53]

In terms of s 63 of the Deeds Registries Act,[54] the Registrar of Deeds can allow registration of rights or conditions that impose a positive duty on the owner of a servient tenement if, in the opinion of the Registrar, such right or condition is complementary or ancillary to a registrable condition or right contained in the deed. Although this proviso to the rule addresses the difficulties created by the discrepancy between the decisions of *Ex parte Geldenhuys*[55] and *Schwedhelm*,[56] on the one hand, and *Van der Merwe*,[57] on the other, registration does not convert a provision that obliges the servient owner to act positively into a real obligation.[58] In other words, the character of the obligation remains personal. Even though the conditions may be registered, the positive obligation does not devolve automatically on successive owners of the servient land. Subsequent owners may be bound by personal obligations only when they expressly commit to these obligations, and acquire the land with full knowledge of the contents of the servitude including the ancillary obligations.[59] Knowledge is required to validate the express consent.

Fourth, praedial servitudes are indivisible.[60] This means that a praedial servitude is imposed on the whole of the servient tenement. The rule regarding indivisibility is particularly important where the land is later subdivided.[61] For example, if the dominant tenement that benefits from a general right of grazing on the servient tenement is subdivided, the rule regarding indivisibility entails that both parts of the original dominant tenement (i.e. both new dominant tenements) are entitled to exercise the servitude, provided the burden on the servient tenement is not increased.[62] Similarly, if the servient tenement is subdivided, both subdivisions continue to serve the dominant tenement.

This rule is affected by the manner in which the servitude is defined in the title deed,[63] i.e. whether the servitude is generally or specifically created. If there are specific indications as to where or how a particular servitude is to be exercised, and the servient land is subsequently subdivided, then the specificity of the servitude might entail that it continues to exist over a part of the land only. On the other hand, if the servitude is

---

51   Contra *Van der Merwe v Wiese* 1948 (4) SA 8 (C).
52   *Wille's Principles* p 596.
53   De Waal, MJ (1996) 'Servitudes' in Zimmermann, R & Visser, DP *Southern Cross* (Cape Town, Juta) p 803.
54   Act 47 of 1937.
55   1926 OPD 155.
56   1947 (1) SA 127 (E).
57   1948 (4) SA 8 (C).
58   *Low Water Properties (Pty) Ltd v Wahloo Sand CC* 1999 (1) SA 655 (SE) at 662.
59   *Wille's Principles* p 596; De Waal, MJ (1996) 'Servitudes' in Zimmermann, R & Visser, DP *Southern Cross* (Cape Town, Juta) p 803 n 149.
60   *Silberberg & Schoeman Property* pp 325-326; *Wille's Principles* p 597; *LAWSA* Vol 24 at para 398.
61   *Silberberg & Schoeman Property* p 325.
62   *Silberberg & Schoeman Property* p 326.
63   *Wille's Principles* p 597.

general, i.e. if no specific indications exist as to exactly where or how the servitude is to be exercised, then the whole of the original servient tenement remains bound after subsequent subdivisions.

Example
Dominant tenement A is served by a right of way over servient tenement B.

Figure 9.3: Right of way

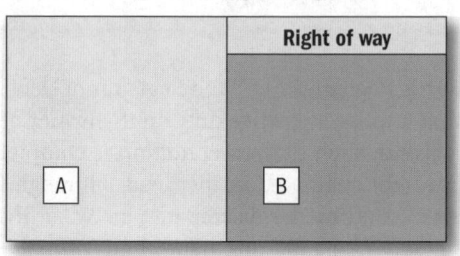

The right of way may be specifically defined, for instance 'a right of way 15 m wide along the northern boundary of tenement B'; or it may be a general right of way, in which case no specifications appear in the constituting document as to where the servitude is to be exercised. Commonly, the original servient owner may have indicated verbally where the right could be exercised most conveniently.

If the servient tenement is subdivided later, both the manner of subdivision as well as the nature of the servitude (i.e. as either general or specific) would play a role in determining the extent to which the various parts of the subdivided servient tenement would continue to be bound by the servitude.

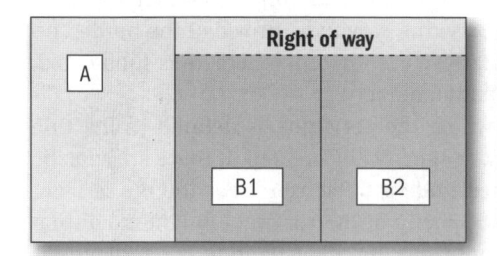

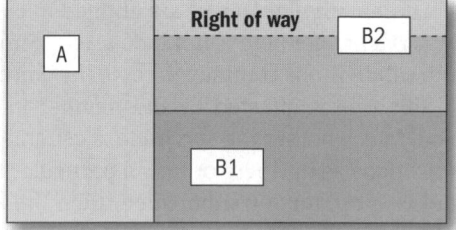

Figure 9.4: Right of way after subdivision

The same would apply *mutatis mutandis* to the subsequent subdivision of the dominant tenement.

PAUSE FOR REFLECTION	Praedial servitudes and flexibility
	Praedial servitudes are, by nature, designed to survive generations of landowners. They are, after all, destined to serve the land (or, conversely, the landowner in her capacity as landowner), and not any particular person in a personal capacity. They are usually created without considering the possibility of future changed circumstances.

> In the context of general servitudes of right of way, some measure of flexibility is provided for in the law. The servitude exists over 'every inch of the servient tenement'.[64] The owner of the dominant tenement may select the line of the servitude,[65] but, even after a specific route has been fixed, the general nature of the servitude remains. The servient owner may retract the use of the place over which the servitude was delimited, and allocate a different but equally convenient route.[66]
>
> Traditionally, the same flexibility did not exist for servitudes of right of way specifically defined. In such cases, the course of the route could be changed only by mutual consent of the dominant and servient owners.[67] However, in the recent decision of *Linvestment CC v Hammersley and Another*,[68] this principle was overturned. It was held to be indefensible to enforce a servitude rigidly where 'sanctity of the contract or the strict terms of the grant benefit[ted] neither party, but on the contrary, operate[d] prejudicially on one of them'.[69] Instead, it was held that a right of way, delimited specifically, should be capable of amendment if the circumstances change in a way that justifies amendment of the route.
>
> To fortify the decision, Heher JA relied on a reinterpretation of the historical sources that distinguished between servitudes created generally and specifically. In setting the original precedent governing amendment of specifically delimited servitudes, the courts overlooked important principles. Heher JA further relied on a brief comparative analysis of the position in other jurisdictions to conclude that South African law should allow more flexibility on this point.[70]
>
> Finally, the court's inherent capacity to develop the common law was seen as further justification for overturning existing precedent. The implication of this decision is that the position regarding the relocation of a servitutal road on a servient tenement is now governed by the principles that previously applied only to relocation of servitutal roads created under general servitude (i.e. *simpliciter*).

9.2.1.2 Rights and duties

The rights and duties of the dominant and servient owners depend primarily on the terms of the agreement that constitute the servitude.[71] Generally, the agreement is interpreted strictly and its terms are construed in the least burdensome way for the servient owner, whose freedom to use the land is necessarily impaired by the existence of the servitude.[72] Accordingly, the dominant owner must exercise the servitutal rights in a civilised manner, with due regard to the rights of the servient owner *(civiliter modo)*. This entails that the servitude must be exercised properly and carefully to cause as little inconvenience as

---

64 *Linvestment CC v Hammersley and Another* 2008 (3) SA 283 (SCA) at 289; see also *Nach Investments (Pty) Ltd v Yaldayi Investments (Pty) Ltd and Another* 1987 (2) SA 820 (A) at 831D.
65 *Willoughby's Consolidated Co Ltd v Copthall Stores Ltd* 1918 AD 1 at 16; *Hollmann and Another v Estate Latre* 1970 (3) SA 638 (A) at 645D.
66 *Rubidge v McCabe & Sons and Others; McCabe & Sons and Others v Rubidge* 1913 AD 433.
67 *Gardens Estate Ltd v Lewis* 1920 AD 144.
68 2008 (3) SA 283 (SCA).
69 *Linvestment* at 292.
70 *Linvestment* at 292.
71 *Glaffer Investments (Pty) Ltd v Minister of Water Affairs and Forestry* 2000 (4) SA 822 (T) at 828E–829D.
72 *Silberberg & Schoeman Property* p 331.

possible to the servient owner.[73] This does not mean that the dominant owner is restricted in exercising the servitutal rights merely because to do so would detrimentally affect the servient owner.[74] By definition, a servitude burdens the servient land.

Either party may approach a court for a declaration of rights.[75] Specific duties may be enforced by way of interdict.[76] Damages may be awarded where either party exceeds the terms of the servitude, and where patrimonial loss has been suffered.[77]

9.2.1.3 Types of servitudes

There are several conventional types of servitude, which are categorised according to the benefit attaching to the dominant land. These types are discussed below, where the existence of special types of servitudes, most notably ways of necessity and restrictive conditions, are also highlighted. Because of the manner in which they are created and because of their special functions, these latter types of servitude have specific requirements, which are outlined below.

Rural and urban praedial servitudes. Praedial servitudes are usually classified as either rural or urban, depending on the use of the land affected.[78] Where the dominant land is used mainly for agricultural purposes, servitudes that enhance its value are classed as rural. On the other hand, where the use is mainly for purposes of habitation, trade or industry, the servitudes are classed as urban.[79] Although this distinction also existed in Roman law, in modern law it appears that little reason for the distinction remains. There is, for instance, no longer a reason to distinguish between rural and urban servitudes for purposes of acquisitive prescription. There is also no justification for requiring a stricter application of the requirement of vicinity (*vicinitas*)[80] in the case of rural servitudes.[81]

As regards rural praedial servitudes, three main categories are usually identified, namely, rights of way, water servitudes, and grazing servitudes.[82] Praedial rural servitudes created in the South African context further included trekpath and outspan. Both have lost their importance to a significant extent due to industrialisation and advances in transport modes. Another example is commonage.[83]

Urban servitudes traditionally incorporated rights of support, rights to encroach on neighbouring land and negative servitudes to preserve a view or source of light.[84] In the modern context, the most important category of such servitudes is restrictive conditions. These serve to regulate and order township development.[85] This area of law has become so specialised and is so important that it warrants separate discussion below.

---

73 *Silberberg & Schoeman Property* pp 330–331; *Wille's Principles* p 593; *LAWSA* Vol 24 at para 391.
74 *Fourie v Marandellas Town Council* 1972 (2) SA 699 (R); *Van Rensburg v Taute* 1975 (1) SA 279 (A) at 301H.
75 *Silberberg & Schoeman Property* p 331.
76 *Silberberg & Schoeman Property* p 331.
77 *Silberberg & Schoeman Property* p 331.
78 Any of the standard texts can be consulted for an exposition of the various conventional rural and urban servitudes. See e.g. Silberberg & Schoeman Property pp 326*ff*; *Wille's Principles* p 597.
79 *Wille's Principles* p 597.
80 See p 240 above.
81 *Wille's Principles* p 597.
82 *Silberberg & Schoeman Property* pp 326–327; *Wille's Principles* pp 598–600; *LAWSA* Vol 24 at para 404.
83 For further detail, see *Wille's Principles* p 600; see also ch 5 above.
84 *Silberberg & Schoeman Property* p 327.
85 *Wille's Principles* p 601.

Ways of necessity. A way of necessity *(via necessitatis)* is a peculiar praedial servitude with special requirements.[86] This servitude of way may take any of the conventional forms for a right of way, i.e. a right of footpath, a right to drive cattle or vehicles across land and so on. However, it is different from the conventional forms because a way of necessity does not require the consent of the servient owner. A court imposes this servitude.[87] Ways of necessity serve landlocked tenements, i.e. those encircled by other land to the extent that they have no direct or reasonably sufficient access to a public road. Accordingly, a servitutal right of way is necessary for access to the public road.

The owner of a landlocked tenement may claim reasonable and sufficient access to a public road.[88] Where the only access to a public road would be a long journey over difficult terrain, for instance, a way of necessity can be granted to ease access, even where the land might not be completely cut off from the public road.[89] However, a way of necessity cannot be claimed simply based on convenience, e.g. to shorten the distance to the public road, even though it could be reached without crossing the adjacent land. The guiding principle is that the route allocated must be that which causes least damage to the servient tenement, and that enables the shortest route over the servient tenement (*'ter naaste lage en minste schade'*).[90] Where the terrain is rugged, or where the servient owner is likely to be unduly prejudiced, the court may deviate from this principle.[91] Generally, the attempt is made to balance the interests of the respective parties.[92] So, for instance, ways of necessity tend to be created along the boundary of the servient land, but even this rule is not applied rigidly.[93]

A court-imposed way of necessity is open for use by anyone wishing to gain access to the landlocked tenement.[94] The way of necessity may be granted either as a permanent right of way *(ius viae plenum),* or as a precarious right of way to be used only in emergencies *(ius viae precario).*[95] In the former instance, reasonable compensation would be payable, whereas the latter type of right would not attract payment of compensation.[96] *Van Rensburg v Coetzee*[97] indicates, however, that the distinction between permanent and precarious ways of necessity has become less pronounced with the advent of modern agricultural activity, which requires constant use of vehicles.

The original need for a way of necessity may determine the creation thereof, but such needs might not remain static. Where the way of necessity is the only access to the land, and the needs of the dominant landowner have changed, this should be recognised as far as reasonableness dictates.[98]

---

86 For more detail, see *Silberberg & Schoeman Property* pp 328-330; *Wille's Principles* pp 598-599; *LAWSA* Vol 24 at para 407.
87 *Silberberg & Schoeman Property* p 328.
88 *Van Rensburg v Coetzee* 1979 (4) SA 655 (A) at 671E.
89 *Illing v Woodhouse* 1923 NPD 166 at 168.
90 *Wille's Principles* p 599.
91 *Van Rensburg v Coetzee* 1979 (4) SA 655 (A) at 672H-673A.
92 *Van Rensburg v Coetzee* 1979 (4) SA 655 (A) at 675E; *Jackson NO and Others v Aventura Ltd and Others* [2005] 2 All SA 518 (C) at 530d-e.
93 *Silberberg & Schoeman Property* p 329.
94 *Silberberg & Schoeman Property* p 328.
95 *Van Rensburg v Coetzee* 1979 (4) SA 655 (A) at 671-672.
96 *Silberberg & Schoeman Property* p 329; *Wille's Principles* p 599.
97 1979 (4) SA 655 (A) at 672C.
98 *Silberberg & Schoeman Property* p 330; *Naudé v Ecoman Investments* 1994 (2) SA 95 (T) at 99C.

9.2.2 Personal servitudes

A personal servitude is a limited real right.[99] It may have either movable or immovable property as its object. The personal servitude is inextricably tied to the holder thereof since the benefit accrues to the holder in a personal capacity. Hence, a personal servitude cannot extend beyond the lifetime of the holder (100 years in the case of a juristic person), and cannot be transferred to a third party.[100]

There is no *numerus clausus* of personal servitudes, but the most common and conventional forms still in use in South Africa are the usufruct *(ususfructus)*, the right of use *(usus)* and the right to occupy a house *(habitatio)*.

A usufruct is a personal servitude that entitles a specific person to use and enjoy another's property, and to draw its fruits,[101] without impairing the substance of the property.[102] The personal servitude of *usus* (right of use) is more restricted than usufruct, in that it entitles the holder to use the property, but not to draw its fruits.[103] *Habitatio* entitles the holder of the servitude to live in a house without detriment to the substance of the property.[104]

Other newly developed categories of personal servitudes include so-called 'irregular servitudes' (i.e. servitudes that have content usually associated with praedial servitudes, but constituted in favour of an individual);[105] restrictive conditions in favour of certain lot-holders in a township;[106] and typically South African personal servitudes such as trading rights;[107] and the right of a developer to extend the sectional title scheme in terms of s 25 of the Sectional Titles Act.[108]

> **PAUSE FOR REFLECTION**
>
> **Irregular servitudes**
>
> Irregular servitudes, i.e. those that have content similar to that of praedial servitudes, but which benefit a particular person in his personal capacity only, may give rise to uncertainty in determining whether a particular servitude is praedial or personal. Where such servitudes are encountered, the intention with which the right was created must be decisive. Generally, the intention appears from the constituting documents, i.e. the agreement between the parties, the deed of grant or the will. If the intention to benefit the holder in a personal capacity is not clear from the constituting documents, the court considers the surrounding circumstances to ascertain the intention. Under these conditions, the presumption is for the lesser burden, i.e. that the condition amounts to a personal servitude rather than a praedial servitude.[109] This is in line with the general principle that servitudes must be interpreted restrictively, and that the landowner must not be burdened more than is necessary.[110]

---

99 *Lorentz v Melle* 1978 (3) SA 1044 (T) at 1049–1050.
100 Silberberg & Schoeman *Property* p 339; *Wille's Principles* p 604; *LAWSA* Vol 24 at para 420.
101 Silberberg & Schoeman *Property* p 339; *Wille's Principles* pp 604–605; *LAWSA* Vol 24 at para 422.
102 Silberberg & Schoeman *Property* p 339; *Wille's Principles* pp 604–605; *LAWSA* Vol 24 at para 422.
103 Silberberg & Schoeman *Property* p 341; *Wille's Principles* p 610; *LAWSA* Vol 24 at para 441.
104 Silberberg & Schoeman *Property* p 341; *Wille's Principles* pp 610–611; *LAWSA* Vol 24 at para 446.
105 Silberberg & Schoeman *Property* p 341.
106 *Alexander v Johns* 1912 AD 431; see *Wille's Principles* pp 604 n 111.
107 *Wille's Principles* p 604; *LAWSA* Vol 24 at para 421.
108 Act 95 of 1986.
109 Silberberg & Schoeman *Property* p 342.
110 *Jonordan Investment (Pty) Ltd v De Aar Drankwinkel (Edms) Bpk* 1969 (2) SA 117 (C) at 125–126; Silberberg & Schoeman *Property* p 342 n 277.

The treatment here of usufruct is representative of the characteristics of personal servitudes, as well as the rights and duties invoked by a personal servitude. *Usus* and *habitatio* differ only as far as the scope and content of the respective rights are concerned,[111] and, consequently, are not discussed in detail.

As mentioned, the content of a usufruct is that the usufructuary may use and enjoy the servient property, which can be movable or immovable, and corporeal or incorporeal. The usufructuary may draw fruits from the property and acquires ownership of such fruits.[112] The usufruct is typically employed when a testator wants to provide for surviving family members after his death, but wants the property itself to go to someone other than the usufructuary (i.e. the beneficiary in terms of the usufruct). Being highly personal, a usufruct cannot extend beyond the lifetime of the usufructuary.[113]

Even though the usufructuary's right is quite extensive – more so than is the case with *usus* and *habitatio* – a usufruct remains a limited real right, which creates a right in another's property. On the face of it, however, the usufructuary's ability to use and enjoy the property closely resembles what an owner would be able to do with the property. Nevertheless, the usufructuary is not an owner and does not have *dominium* over the property. Importantly, this means that the usufructuary may not alienate the property, may not consume it or destroy it. Moreover, the usufructuary may not alienate his right in the property. However, the usufructuary interest may be alienated, pledged, mortgaged or sold in execution.[114]

PAUSE FOR REFLECTION

Usufructuary interest

Note that it is not the usufruct itself that may be alienated, but only the interest(s) flowing from the usufruct, such as the ability to use and enjoy the property, or the ability to draw fruits. Once the usufruct terminates, either because the right holder dies or the condition sets in which leads to its termination, the rights in respect of the servitude terminate as well.

For example, a testator, Allan, bequeaths his farm to his only son, Cas, subject to a usufruct in favour of the testator's surviving spouse, also the son's mother, Bella. A condition stipulates that the usufruct continues until her remarriage or death. The usufruct, thus, foresees that Bella will be able to use and enjoy the land, and draw its fruits, for as long as she lives or at least until she remarries. If Bella were to decide not to live on the farm, but to lease it to Dirk who would farm the land actively, then Bella can do so. This is because she is permitted to alienate her usufructuary interest. Dirk would be able to use and enjoy the land, and draw its fruits, depending on the terms of the lease, for as long as Bella holds the right of usufruct. If she remarries or when she dies, Dirk's rights in respect of the lease agreement will terminate immediately because the usufruct itself will terminate.

In *Durban City Council v Woodhaven Ltd*,[115] the court questioned the fine distinction drawn between the usufruct itself and the right of enjoyment comprised by the usufructuary interest. The implication of this decision is that the nature and purpose of a particular personal servitude should determine whether the rights under the servitude are alienable.

---

111 See *Silberberg & Schoeman Property* p 341.
112 See p 175.
113 *Wille's Principles* p 605.
114 *Silberberg & Schoeman Property* pp 340–341.
115 1987 (3) SA 555 (A).

A usufructuary's rights include possession, administration, use, and enjoyment of the property as well as its civil and natural fruits. Civil fruits (such as interest on a capital investment or rental income) are acquired as soon as they become due. Natural fruits are acquired by the usufructuary when they are gathered, not just separated from the fruit-producing thing. Ungathered fruits remain the property of the owner of the property subject to the usufruct.[116]

Consumable property cannot be the object of a usufruct since the usufructuary must be able to give the property back to the owner *salva rei substantia* (essentially intact) at the end of the usufructuary period.[117] Quasi-usufructs may be established over consumables, however. A usufruct over money, for instance, means that the money becomes the property of the quasi-usufructuary, and that the quasi-usufructuary can use and enjoy it, and the income derived from it. The quasi-usufructuary is obliged, however, to restore the equivalent of the capital amount to the owner upon expiry of the usufruct.[118] The quasi-usufruct was an important construction in the context of mineral law, but this importance has waned significantly since the introduction of the Mineral and Petroleum Resources Development Act.[119]

> **PAUSE FOR REFLECTION**
>
> *Salva rei substantia*
>
> Returning the property *salva rei substantia* implies that the usufructuary may not destroy or consume the property, impair its value, or change its character.[120] The obligation is to return the property in the same condition as it was received, fair wear and tear excepted. It means, therefore, that the usufructuary must look after the property.[121] What this entails exactly, is not treated consistently in modern scholarly sources. Most authors seem to agree that the usufructuary is responsible for ordinary repairs and maintenance expenses, as well as payment of rates and taxes.[122] For example, the usufructuary of a homestead on a farm should, accordingly, replace defunct light bulbs in the house at own cost, call the plumber when sanitation works need attention, etc. The usufructuary is not responsible for ordinary depreciation of the property.[123] The standard seems to be that the usufructuary must keep the property in good condition, fair wear and tear excepted.[124] Since the expectation is that a usufructuary's conduct will be that of a sensible person, if the property requires maintenance work to keep it in good order, then that maintenance work should be carried out. However, extraordinary repairs must be borne by the owner.[125] For example, if a tornado rips off the roof, then the owner is responsible for seeing to repairs. This is part of the duty on an owner to facilitate a servitude holder's ability to exercise his rights. However, the prevalence of insurance sometimes makes it difficult to understand clearly where the obligations lie. Thus, in the event of storm damage, insurance policy underwriters would usually be called upon to see to storm damage repairs.

---

116 More detail in ch 2 and ch 3 above.
117 *Silberberg & Schoeman Property* p 340; *Wille's Principles* p 605.
118 *Wille's Principles* p 605.
119 Act 28 of 2002. See ch 10 below.
120 *Silberberg & Schoeman Property* p 340; *Wille's Principles* p 608.
121 *Silberberg & Schoeman Property* p 340; *Wille's Principles* p 609; *LAWSA* Vol 24 at para 434.
122 *Silberberg & Schoeman Property* p 340; *Wille's Principles* p 609; *LAWSA* Vol 24 at para 436.
123 *Wille's Principles* p 609; *Silberberg & Schoeman Property* p 340; and the sources cited in both texts.
124 *Wille's Principles* p 609; *Silberberg & Schoeman Property* p 340.
125 *Silberberg & Schoeman Property* p 340; *Wille's Principles* p 609.

> On the other hand, if property has been allowed to deteriorate over time, there is no clear obligation on either the owner or the usufructuary to restore the property: 'neither the usufructuary nor the owner is liable to replace buildings that have fallen into disrepair through age or which have been accidentally destroyed'.[126] In other words, the usufructuary cannot look to the owner to bring about repairs if he receives the property in a state of disrepair. He is free to refuse the usufruct. In accordance with his entitlements, on the other hand, the owner is free to permit his property to disintegrate, subject to statutory obligations, e.g. regarding slum prevention. However, once the usufruct exists, the owner is obliged to permit the usufructuary to exercise his rights, which means, e.g. that structural repairs required to keep the house habitable may have to be undertaken by the owner.

The usufructuary must use the property reasonably, i.e. for the purpose for which it was intended.[127] In some circumstances, the owner may require the usufructuary to draw up an inventory of the property under the usufruct and to furnish security for the proper use and eventual return of the property.[128] Usually a usufructuary is not entitled to compensation for improvements made to the property, but may claim compensation for expenses necessarily incurred for the preservation of the property.[129]

The owner of the property retains all rights of ownership, subject to the usufruct.[130] The owner may thus alienate or mortgage the property, subject to the usufruct. The owner may not prejudice or interfere with the usufructuary's rights. The owner may further burden the property with a praedial servitude only if the usufructuary consents. The owner may claim damages from the usufructuary where the latter has intentionally or negligently caused damage to the property.[131]

9.3 Creation, termination and enforcement of servitudes

Generally, personal and praedial servitudes can be created in similar ways. These methods are discussed first in the following paragraphs, after which focus shifts to the distinctive ways in which praedial and personal servitudes terminate.

9.3.1 Creation

An agreement between the owner of the dominant tenement and the owner of the servient tenement[132] commonly establishes a praedial servitude over private land. Typically, the terms of the agreement include provisions as to the nature, scope and extent of the servitutal right; the price payable by the owner of the dominant tenement as a consideration for the grant of the servitude; and the duration of the servitude.[133] Praedial servitudes may

---

126 *Wille's Principles* p 609.
127 *Wille's Principles* p 608.
128 *Wille's Principles* p 609; *Silberberg & Schoeman Property* p 340.
129 *Wille's Principles* p 609–610; *Silberberg & Schoeman Property* p 340.
130 *Wille's Principles* p 608; *LAWSA* Vol 24 at para 433.
131 *LAWSA* Vol 24 at paras 435 and 439.
132 *Willoughby's Consolidated Co Ltd v Copthall Stores Ltd* 1918 AD; *Felix v Nortier* [1996] 3 All SA 143 (SE) 150e-f.
133 *Silberberg & Schoeman Property* p 332.

be granted in perpetuity, in line with the principles outlined above;[134] but they may also exist for a specified period, or until a specific condition is fulfilled.[135] The agreement gives rise to a personal right, in terms of the contract, to claim registration of the servitude. Registration[136] of the servitude creates its real nature.[137] A personal servitude may also be created by agreement between the servitude holder and the servient owner. However, it is far more common for a personal servitude – especially a usufruct – to be created in a will, as explained above.[138]

A servitude may be created by state grant. This is the case where the state grants a servitude over state land or grants land but reserves a servitude over or in favour of the land granted.[139] This mode of creation pertains mainly to praedial servitudes, but does not exclude personal servitudes.

Both kinds of servitudes may also be created by statute. In the Sectional Titles Act,[140] for instance, s 28 creates implied servitudes of subjacent and lateral support, and of passage and provision of water and electricity over each of the sections in a sectional title scheme. These servitudes are deemed to be incorporated in the title deeds of all sectional owners. They amount to praedial servitudes. The right of extension of the developer (to develop the scheme in phases)[141] was interpreted to be a personal servitude.[142] Some scholars, however, take the view that the right of extension in s 25 of the later Sectional Titles Act,[143] is a *sui generis* right.[144]

Acquisition of a servitude may also occur by acquisitive prescription. Section 6 of the Prescription Act[145] provides that:

acquisitive prescription of a servitude occurs if the acquirer has openly and as though he were entitled to do so, exercised the rights and powers which a person who has a right to such servitude is entitled to exercise. This action must have taken place for an uninterrupted period of thirty years in the case of both praedial and personal servitudes. In the case of praedial servitudes any periods for which such rights and powers were exercised in the required way by the predecessors in title of the acquirer could be taken into account to constitute jointly an uninterrupted period of thirty years.

The principles applicable to the acquisition of prescriptive title are applicable in this context too. Chapter 7 deals with this in more detail.

---

134 See pp 241*ff* above.
135 See ss 75(1) and 76(1) of the Deeds Registries Act 47 of 1937.
136 Either through reservation in a deed of transfer as envisaged by s 76 of the Deeds Registries Act 47 of 1937 or by the registration of a notarial deed, accompanied by an appropriate endorsement against the title deeds of the dominant and servient tenements, respectively (s 75 of the Deeds Registries Act).
137 *Silberberg & Schoeman Property* p 332.
138 See p 248 above.
139 *Silberberg & Schoeman Property* p 332; *LAWSA* Vol 24 at para 453.
140 Act 95 of 1986.
141 Comprising s 18(1) read with s 23(6) of the first generation Sectional Titles Act 66 of 1971.
142 *Erlax Properties (Pty) Ltd v Registrar of Deeds* 1992 (1) SA 879 (A) (decided in terms of the first Sectional Titles Act 66 of 1971).
143 Act 95 of 1986.
144 See *Silberberg & Schoeman Property* p 458.
145 Act 68 of 1969.

Servitudes may also result from a court order, e.g. a servitutal way of necessity *(via necessitatis)*[146] originates most frequently from an order of court.[147] Furthermore, when a court decides to permit an encroachment, the result may be the creation of a servitude.[148]

9.3.2 Extinction or termination

Although praedial and personal servitudes often terminate in similar ways, some modes of termination apply only to praedial servitudes, while others apply only to personal servitudes. In the same way that servitudes may be constituted by agreement, they may also be terminated by agreement. An agreement to cancel binds the parties immediately, but becomes binding on third parties only once the cancellation is registered or if they have knowledge of the cancellation.[149] Lack of consent from the servitude holder to terminate (or amend the terms of) the servitude can veto an attempt to terminate or amend a servitude.[150]

Servitudes may be abandoned.[151] Proof of the intention to abandon the servitude is necessary. The conduct of the servitude holder may be decisive here. Leading scholars indicate that a praedial servitude cannot be abandoned if it would mean serious injury to the servient tenement.[152]

Whether a servitude may be extinguished by the effluxion of time (i.e. expire because of non-use) depends on its content. Statutory law[153] distinguishes between positive and negative servitudes in this regard. A positive servitude (i.e. a right that permits the holder to do something actively with the servient owner's property) expires if its holder fails to exercise the right for an uninterrupted period of 30 years. A negative servitude (i.e. a right that prohibits the servient owner from particular activities on his property) does not expire simply because of non-use. A holder of a negative servitude is deemed to exercise the right as long as nothing is done to the property that would impair the enjoyment of the servitude by the holder.[154] This means that for a negative servitude to expire through non-use, the **servient owner must act so as to hinder or prevent exercise of the servitude, while the servitude holder acquiesces in the conduct.**

As a matter of course, a servitude terminates if the property to which it relates is destroyed. It can revive, however, if the property is restored.[155] For instance, a right of *habitatio* cannot survive if the house is destroyed in a fire. If the owner decides, however, to rebuild the house, the right of *habitatio* is restored. If the property is changed to the extent that exercise of the servitude becomes permanently impossible, then there is no chance of revival.[156] For instance, if a fountain that forms the basis of a servitude of leading water dries up permanently, then the servitude expires.[157]

---

146 See p 247.
147 *Silberberg & Schoeman Property* p 334.
148 For more on encroachments in South African law, see p 139 above and Pope, A 'Encroachment or accession? The importance of the extent of encroachment in light of South African constitutional principles' (2007) 124 *SALJ* 537-556.
149 *Silberberg & Schoeman Property* p 336 and see the criticism levelled there against the proposition that the purchaser should know both of the registered servitude and of its cancellation. See also *Hall & Kellaway Servitudes* pp 140-141.
150 *Ex parte Uvongo Borough Council* 1966 (1) SA 788 (N).
151 *Silberberg & Schoeman Property* p 336.
152 *Hall & Kellaway Servitudes* p 144.
153 Section 7(1) and (2) of the Prescription Act 68 of 1969.
154 *Silberberg & Schoeman Property* p 337.
155 *Silberberg & Schoeman Property* p 338.
156 *Du Toit v Visser* 1950 (2) SA 93 (C) at 102; *Eichelgruen v Two Nine Eight South Ridge Road (Pty) Ltd* 1976 (2) SA 678 (D).
157 *Wille's Principles* p 615.

Naturally, a servitude constituted for a limited period, or under specific conditions, expires at the end of the stipulated period, or when the conditions are fulfilled and a court order confirms the termination.[158] A servitude may also expire in terms of a statute.[159]

In the case of praedial servitudes, merger of the dominant and servient tenements results in permanent termination of servitudes, i.e. when the same person owns both properties.[160] It can revive automatically only if the merger was not intended to be permanent.[161] If the merger was intended to be permanent, but the properties are separated again later, both registered and unregistered servitudes need to be reconstituted again. It is not sufficient simply to refer to the notarial deed that originally constituted the servitude.[162]

Praedial servitudes terminate, furthermore, when the requirements for their constitution can no longer be fulfilled. Here, the requirement of utility is of particular relevance.[163]

A personal servitude, by definition, cleaves to the *persona* of its holder, and hence will expire at the death of the holder. It may expire earlier upon fulfilment of a resolutive condition (such as the remarriage of the servitude holder), as explained above.[164] The Deeds Registries Act provides for registration of the expiry of a personal servitude.[165]

9.3.3 Enforcement

Most of the remedies available to an owner are also available, *mutatis mutandis*, to a servitude holder. Thus, a servitude holder may approach a court for a declaration of rights if his servitutal rights have been infringed or there is a risk of interference.[166] With a mandatory interdict, the wrongdoer may be compelled to restore the *status quo ante*. A prohibitory interdict may be employed to prohibit future wrongdoing.[167] The servitude holder may also invoke the *mandament van spolie*[168] to restore lost actual use (quasi-possession) of a servitutal right.[169] Finally, an action for damages would lie where the requirements for a delictual action are met.[170]

9.4 Restrictive conditions

Restrictive conditions are a unique set of limited real rights that operate in specific circumstances, namely planning and management of land use. Classified as praedial servitudes,[171] restrictive conditions deserve special discussion here because of their specialised function. They consist of a wide range of restrictions on the use of land and are usually contained in a deed of transfer.[172] Frequently, the courts have found that the

---

158 *Silberberg & Schoeman Property* p 338.
159 *Silberberg & Schoeman Property* p 338, referring to s 133 of the National Water Act 36 of 1998; *Glaffer Investments (Pty) Ltd v Minister of Water Affairs and Forestry* 2000 (4) SA 822 (T).
160 *Mocke v Beaufort West Municipality* 1939 CPD 135.
161 *Wille's Principles* p 615.
162 *Du Toit v Visser* 1950 (2) SA 93 (C) at 102-103.
163 See p 240 above.
164 See p 248 above.
165 Section 68(1) of the Deeds Registries Act 47 of 1937; *Silberberg & Schoeman Property* p 342.
166 *Saunders v Executrix of Hunt* (1828-1849) 2 Menz 313.
167 *LAWSA* Vol 24 at para 463.
168 *Bon Quelle (Edms) Bpk v Munisipaliteit van Otavi* 1989 (1) SA 508 (A).
169 See above.
170 *LAWSA* Vol 24 at para 463.
171 See p 256 below.
172 See *Wille's Principles* pp 601-603; *Silberberg & Schoeman Property* pp 343-356.

purpose of restrictive conditions is to create a co-ordinated and harmonious layout for a township development in the interest of all erf holders, as well as to preserve the character of a neighbourhood.[173] This purpose would be negated and frustrated if contrary use were to be allowed or to continue.[174] For example, the view that restrictive conditions serve to maintain the character of an area is relevant in a case where removal of a restrictive condition is sought. A person may wish to remove a restrictive condition that prohibits property from being used for business purposes. A neighbour who objects could argue that the character of the area would be compromised by removal of the restriction, which would lead to an increase in noise, traffic, and pollution.

In the following sections, restrictive conditions are discussed with reference to the manner in which they are defined, their nature, and how they may be enforced.

9.4.1 Definition and examples

The law governing restrictive conditions lacks clarity regarding the terminology that pertains to this field. Restrictive conditions can be described in a broad or a narrow sense. In the broad sense, a restrictive condition includes a registered restrictive condition of title, which is a restriction registered in the deed of transfer. It also includes any restriction in 'any other deed or other instrument in terms of which a right in land is held'.[175] Such 'deed or other instrument' would include the provisions of a town planning scheme because the latter may be described as an instrument in terms of which a right in land is held that restricts the use of land.[176] In practice, restrictive conditions work hand-in-hand with town planning, zoning or land use schemes. For example, a particular erf may be zoned for residential use and carry a density restriction on the number of dwellings that may be erected. The deed of transfer for that erf would similarly restrict the use thereof to a single residential dwelling. When the use of the particular erf is changed, the zoning category must be amended and the restrictive condition removed.

Restrictive conditions in the narrow sense[177] are those registered restrictions on the use of land. They originate from the English law of restrictive covenants. Restrictive conditions include those conditions inserted into a deed of transfer during the process of township development. They are therefore statutory successors to restrictive covenants. This category of restrictive conditions is distinct from the provisions of town planning or land use schemes.

The discussion here is confined to restrictive conditions in the narrow sense as described above. In short, therefore, the term 'restrictive conditions', as used in this section, refers to conditions that restrict the use of land and that are registered in the title deeds and other registered instruments in terms of which a right in land is held.

---

173 *Ex parte Vinkati Investments (Pty) Ltd* 1965 (4) SA 421 (W); *Malan v Ardconnel Investments (Pty) Ltd* 1988 (2) SA 12 (A) at 38G; *Van Rensburg v Nelson Mandela Metropolitan Municipality* 2008 (2) SA 8 (SECLD) at 11; *Hayes v Minister of Finance and Development Planning, Western Cape* 2003 (4) SA 598 (C). See also Van der Westhuizen, JM 'Locus standi in judicio van persone wat nakoming van beperkende voorwaardes eis' (1990) 53 *THRHR* 130-136 at 132; *Silberberg & Schoeman Property* pp 344-345; Van Wyk, J *Planning Law* pp 36-37; Van Wyk, J 'Removing restrictive conditions and preserving the residential character of the neighbourhood' (1992) 55 *THRHR* 369-385; Van Wyk, J 'Preserving the character of the neighbourhood – a German perspective' (1995) 28 *De Jure* 396-404.
174 *Stadsraad van Vanderbijlpark v Uys* 1989 (3) SA 528 (A).
175 Section 1 (definition of 'restrictive condition') of the Land Use Management Bill [B 27-2008].
176 *Silberberg & Schoeman Property* p 343; Van Wyk, J 'The historical development of restrictive conditions' (1992) *TSAR* 280-297.
177 *Silberberg & Schoeman Property* p 343.

> **PAUSE FOR REFLECTION**
>
> **Terminology**
>
> Accurate use of terminology is important to avoid ambiguity and confusion. The terms 'restrictive condition',[178] 'condition of title',[179] 'restrictive title condition',[180] 'restrictive title deed condition',[181] 'title deed restriction',[182] and 'title deed condition'[183] are used interchangeably by the courts and legal commentators as well as by practitioners.
>
> All these terms refer more or less to the same thing. For present purposes, the preferred term is 'restrictive conditions', to indicate those conditions that are registered in title deeds and other registered instruments, in terms of which rights in land are held, and that place restrictions on the use of land other than restrictions of town planning or land use schemes. Since the term 'restrictive conditions' is used in both a wide and a narrow sense, it is important to clarify the terminology to avoid subsequent uncertainty. Note that the preferred term excludes restrictions of town planning and land use schemes.

The following are examples of restrictive conditions found in title deeds:
(1) The erf shall not be subdivided ...
(2) ... the erf [shall] be used for residential purposes only, that only one single dwelling house for use by a single family and ordinary outbuildings required for such use be built on the erf, and that no garage other than for ordinary use for persons residing on the erf may be erected on the erf.[184]
(3) Such building must ... be a dwelling house and no two or more dwelling houses shall be erected under one roof, nor shall more than one dwelling house be erected on any one lot, and such dwelling houses shall not be used as a flat or flats ...[185]
(4) ... the erf [shall] be used for trade or business purposes only; provided that it shall not be used for a warehouse, or a place of amusement or assembly, garage, industrial premises or a hotel ...[186]

9.4.2 Nature, character and status of restrictive conditions

Restrictive conditions are a unique instrument employed to regulate land use. The elements of their unique nature include that they are classified as urban praedial servitudes; they are regarded as constitutional property; and they have both a public and a private law character. These elements are discussed below, followed by some comment on the status of restrictive conditions as compared to other town planning measures.

---

178 See e.g. *Ex parte Rovian Trust (Pty) Ltd* 1983 (3) SA 209 (D); *Camps Bay Ratepayers Association v Minister of Planning, Western Cape* 2001 (4) SA 194 (C); *Van Rensburg v Nelson Mandela Metropolitan Municipality* 2008 (2) SA 8 (SECLD); *Warren v MEC of Housing, Local Government and Traditional Affairs* EL220/07; ECD 520/07, unreported.
179 See e.g. *Camps Bay Ratepayers Association* 2001 (4) SA 194 (C). See also Van Wyk, J 'Revaluation of conditions of title' (2002) 65 *THRHR* 642-649; Van Wyk, J 'Contravening a condition of title can lead to a demolition order' (2007) 70 *THRHR* 658-662.
180 See e.g. *Malan v Ardconnel Investments (Pty) Ltd* 1988 (2) SA 12 (A); *Camps Bay Ratepayers Association v Minister of Planning, Western Cape* 2001 (4) SA 194 (C); *Van Rensburg v Nelson Mandela Metropolitan Municipality* 2008 (2) SA 8 (SECLD).
181 See e.g. *Camps Bay Ratepayers Association v Minister of Planning, Western Cape* 2001 (4) SA 194 (C); *PS Booksellers (Pty) Ltd v Harrison* 2008 (3) SA 633 (C).
182 In *Ex parte Optimal Property Solutions CC* 2003 (2) SA 136 (C); *PS Booksellers (Pty) Ltd v Harrison* 2008 (3) SA 633 (C).
183 *Camps Bay Ratepayers Association v Minister of Planning, Western Cape* 2001 (4) SA 194 (C); *PS Booksellers (Pty) Ltd v Harrison* 2008 (3) SA 633 (C); *Ex parte Optimal Property Solutions* 2003 (2) SA 136 (C).
184 *Van Rensburg v Nelson Mandela Metropolitan Municipality* 2008 (2) SA 8 (SECLD) at para 7.
185 *Camps Bay Ratepayers Association v Minister of Planning, Western Cape* 2001 (4) SA 194 (C).
186 *Ex parte Vinkati Investments (Pty) Ltd* 1965 (4) SA 421 (W).

First, as regards their classification, several court decisions, such as *Ex parte Rovian Trust (Pty) Ltd*[187] and *Malan v Ardconnel Investments (Pty) Ltd*,[188] *Van Rensburg v Nelson Mandela Metropolitan Municipality*[189] and *Ex parte Optimal Property Solutions CC*,[190] characterise restrictive conditions as praedial servitudes in favour of other erfholders. A slightly different approach was taken, however, in *Camps Bay Ratepayers Association v Minister of Planning, Western Cape*.[191] The court indicated that:

> *where restrictive title conditions are registered in favour of all the other properties in a particular township, they have the same status and legal effect as praedial servitudes, which can be enforced by any owner of property in that township against any other owner who may be acting in breach of those conditions.*

Whether one accepts that a restrictive condition is actually a praedial servitude, or has the same effect as or is akin to a praedial servitude, the end result is the same. All parties concerned are mutually and reciprocally bound to one another to adhere to the provisions of the restrictive conditions. Should anyone contravene any condition, the others have the right to enforce the provisions of the conditions. Similarly, should a person wish to have the restrictive condition removed or amended, any of the other parties bound by the condition are entitled to object to such removal or amendment.

PAUSE FOR REFLECTION

Restrictive condition as praedial servitude

As indicated above, a praedial servitude is a limited real right that grants the holder of the servitude, in his capacity as owner of land (the dominant tenement), certain entitlements over the land of someone else (the servient tenement).[192] A restrictive condition is classified as a praedial servitude, which means that operation of the servitude is extended to all persons in whose favour the restrictive condition is registered. Because restrictive conditions are registered in the title deeds of all the owners of erven in a particular neighbourhood, the restrictive condition is deemed to operate mutually and reciprocally among all these owners. This classification as a praedial servitude is thus problematic because restrictive conditions differ in many respects from traditional praedial servitudes.[193] The proposition here is that a restrictive condition is a *sui generis* limited real right.[194]

---

[187] 1983 (3) SA 209 (D).
[188] 1988 (2) SA 12 (A) at 36J–38A. See also Van Wyk, J 'Revaluation of conditions of title' (2002) 65 *THRHR* 642 at 643; Van Wyk *Planning Law* pp 18–20; Silberberg & Schoeman *Property* pp 343–356; Van Wyk, J 'The nature and classification of restrictive covenants and conditions of title' (1992) *De Jure* 270–288; Pienaar, J 'Die regsaard van beperkende voorwaardes' (1992) 55 *THRHR* 50 at 52–55.
[189] 2008 (2) SA 8 (SECLD) at para 8.
[190] 2003 (2) SA 136 (C) at 139C–D.
[191] 2001 (4) SA 194 (C) at 324J–325A. See also Van Wyk, J 'Revaluation of conditions of title' (2002) 65 *THRHR* 642 at 643.
[192] See pp 236*ff* above.
[193] See *Wille's Principles* p 602; Silberberg & Schoeman *Property* pp 345–346 for more detailed discussion.
[194] Van Wyk, J 'The nature and classification of restrictive covenants and conditions of title' (1992) *De Jure* 270–288 at 281–287.

Second, restrictive conditions have a public law character.[195] This is clear from the fact that restrictive conditions have their origin in township establishment legislation.[196] *Van Rensburg v Nelson Mandela Metropolitan Municipality*[197] emphasises the public law character of restrictive conditions: a restrictive condition reciprocally binds all owners of the erven in the township, and also imposes the duty on the municipality concerned to be aware of the restrictive conditions and to act in accordance with them. In other words, restrictive conditions operate mainly between individuals in a private law sense, but they have a public law character because the state also has a duty to be aware of them and to act in accordance with them. A municipality's failure to act in accordance with the provisions of restrictive conditions gives rise to a public law remedy.[198]

Third, restrictive conditions are classified as property in the context of s 25 of the Constitution.[199] This was reiterated in *Ex parte Optimal Property Solutions CC*[200] where the court held that registered praedial servitutal rights are incorporated in the concept of property under s 25(1). Accordingly, 'any removal or deletion of such rights is *pro tanto* a deprivation of property'.[201]

Finally, as regards the status of restrictive conditions, the following remarks may be made. In certain situations, a conflict can arise between the provisions of a restrictive condition and a town planning or land use scheme. To resolve the conflict, it is necessary to determine which restriction takes precedence. Several court decisions have indicated that restrictive conditions take precedence over the provisions of a town planning scheme.[202] In other words, where there is an inconsistency between the provisions of a restrictive condition and a town planning or land use scheme, the restrictive condition prevails.

The reasons for elevating restrictive conditions include the consideration that restrictive conditions are classified as praedial servitutes.[203] In addition, town planning or land use schemes sometimes contain provisions that state that the restrictive conditions take precedence.[204] Furthermore, restrictive conditions often come into existence before the town planning scheme, which flows from legislation that is not retroactive.[205]

Because restrictive conditions take precedence over a town planning scheme, restrictive conditions cannot be removed automatically.[206] Before an owner can implement or take advantage of the terms of a town planning scheme, he must remove any existing legal

---

195 Van Wyk, J 'The historical development of restrictive conditions' (1992) *TSAR* 280-297; Van Wyk *Planning Law* p 79; Van der Merwe *Sakereg* p 501.
196 Van der Merwe *Sakereg* p 333; Van Wyk *Planning Law* p 20.
197 2008 (2) SA 8 (SECLD) at para 8. This case dealt with an application brought by neighbours for the demolition of a building built in contravention of restrictive conditions – see Van Wyk, J 'Contravening a condition of title can lead to a demolition order' (2007) 70 *THRHR* 658-662.
198 *Van Rensburg v Nelson Mandela Metropolitan Municipality* 2008 (2) SA 8 (SECLD) at para 1.
199 Van der Walt *Constitutional Property Law* 2005 pp 82-88; Du Plessis, W, Olivier, N & Pienaar, J 'Expropriation, restitution and land redistribution: An answer to land problems in South Africa?' (2003) *SA Public Law* pp 491-514, 505; Currie, I & De Waal, J (2005) *The Bill of Rights Handbook* 5 ed p 538.
200 2003 (2) SA 136 (C) at para 19. See also *Silberberg & Schoeman Property* p 355.
201 2003 (2) SA 136 (C) at para 19. See also *Silberberg & Schoeman Property* p 355.
202 *Malan v Ardconnel Investments (Pty) Ltd* 1988 (2) SA 12 (A); *Camps Bay Ratepayers Association v Minister of Planning Western Cape* 2001 (4) SA 194 (C); *Kleyn v Theron* 1966 (3) SA 264 (T); *Shell South Africa (Pty) Ltd v Alexene Investments (Pty) Ltd* 1980 (1) SA 683 (W); *Van Rensburg v Nelson Mandela Metropolitan Municipality* 2008 (2) SA 8 (SECLD).
203 *Van Rensburg v Nelson Mandela Metropolitan Municipality* 2008 (2) SA 8 (SECLD) at para 8.
204 Van Wyk, J 'Restrictive conditions – why fiddle with a recipe that works?' (2008) *SA Public Law* 38-58 at 49.
205 Van Wyk, J 'Restrictive conditions – why fiddle with a recipe that works?' (2008) *SA Public Law* 38-58 at 49.
206 *Ex parte Nader Tuis (Edms) Bpk* 1962 (1) SA 751 (T); *Kleyn v Theron* 1966 (3) SA 264 (T) at 272A-C.

impediment.²⁰⁷ Where a local authority (municipality) gives consent in conflict with a restrictive condition, the consent is of no force and effect. Furthermore, a local authority is compelled to refuse a building plan that is in conflict with a restrictive condition.²⁰⁸

9.4.3 Enforcement and defences

This part explains enforcement of restrictive conditions and the remedies available to a person or entity whose rights are infringed by the use of property contrary to the provisions of restrictive conditions. For example, Shabeeha uses her property contrary to the provisions of a restrictive condition that prohibits use for business purposes. She uses the property to sell clothes that she and other seamstresses make on the premises. In pursuing these activities, she acts contrary to the provisions of the restrictive condition. In the process, the entitlements of her neighbour, Ahmed, are infringed.

As the figure below demonstrates, the remedies available to a person affected by the use of property contrary to the terms of a restrictive condition include judicial remedies, such as an application for a prohibitory interdict, a mandatory interdict, a declaratory order, an action for damages, a constitutional remedy, and statutory remedies (i.e. relief in terms of the governing legislation). These are discussed briefly below.

9.4.3.1 Judicial remedies

A prohibitory interdict **prevents** a person from carrying out a certain activity, whereas a mandatory interdict **requires** a person to carry out a certain activity (a positive act).²⁰⁹ Where the activity must be performed by a public official and not a private person, the order is known as a *mandamus*. A prohibitory interdict can be temporary (interim) or final. A temporary interdict is a preliminary decision regarding the rights of the parties, while further legal process is pending.

A declaratory order (or a declaration of rights) may be resorted to where there is a dispute regarding a point of law or an administrative act.²¹⁰ The court determines the rights and duties of the contesting parties. The remedy has no direct effect on the merits of the matter; it sets out the rights of the parties but does not resolve the dispute. A declaratory order can be used to determine how a legal issue might be resolved even where there are other remedies available. An action for damages is a delictual remedy that awards compensation where private persons or public authorities breach their contractual or delictual duties.²¹¹

In addition to the above, there are further judicial remedies envisaged by the Constitution. The constitutional remedies include a declaration of invalidity, a declaration of rights, an interdict, or constitutional damages. The Constitution does not state specifically what relief can be granted by the courts, only that it must be appropriate relief.²¹² The courts can follow a flexible approach, therefore, in granting relief in constitutional matters. Constitutional remedies are needed to enforce human rights in society. It might not be sufficient only to declare a law or conduct invalid when it infringes on a right in the Constitution. It may be necessary to grant a remedy such as an interdict or damages to eradicate inconsistencies between the infringing law or conduct and the Constitution. This could occur, for instance,

---

207 *Enslin v Vereeniging Town Council* 1976 (3) SA 443 (T) at 447C-D.
208 *Shell South Africa (Pty) Ltd v Alexene Investments* 1980 (1) SA 683 (W) at 689H.
209 Van Wyk *Planning Law* pp 214–216.
210 Van Wyk *Planning Law* pp 220–221.
211 Van Wyk *Planning Law* p 217.
212 Section 8(3) of the Constitution.

where a municipality makes a wrong decision to remove restrictive conditions and a developer, acting on that decision, suffers serious financial losses.

To illustrate: Based on a plan for a cluster housing scheme, a municipal planning committee decides to approve an application to remove certain restrictive conditions. The provincial planning authority also approves the same application, but bases it on a plan for a five-storey block of flats. The developer is informed that the application has been approved and it commences building the flats. On becoming aware that the building of flats is underway, neighbours, who were under the impression that a cluster housing scheme would be built, object. The court grants an interdict to halt the building operations. In an application to review the decision, the court finds that the provincial authority failed to apply its mind to the matter. Construction is delayed until the restrictive conditions can be removed to permit the building of flats. The 30-month delay in the construction results in wasted costs, additional building costs, legal fees, interest and an escalation in building costs of more than R1 million for the developer.[213] Under such circumstances, the developer may be entitled to constitutional damages if it is found that the right to just administrative action under s 33 of the Constitution has been infringed.

Figure 9.5: Remedies for the enforcement of restrictive conditions

```
                    ┌─────────────────────┐
                    │  Judicial remedies  │
                    └──────────┬──────────┘
                               │
            ┌──────────────────┤
            │                  │
            ▶  Prohibitory interdict
            │
            ▶  Mandatory interdict
            │
            ▶  Declaratory order
            │
            ▶  Action for damages
            │
            ▶  Constitutional remedies
```

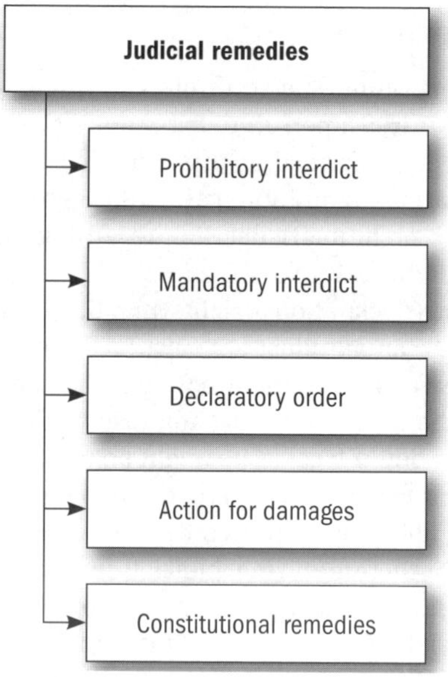

213 Based on the facts in *Beck v Premier, Western Cape* 1998 (3) SA 487 (C); *Faircape Property Developers (Pty) Ltd v Premier, Western Cape* 2000 (2) SA 67 (C); *Faircape Property Developers (Pty) Ltd v Premier, Western Cape* 2002 (6) SA 180 (C); *Premier of the Western Cape v Faircape Property Developers (Pty) Ltd* 2003 (6) SA 13 (SCA); See also Van Wyk, J 'Developers, municipalities, wrong decisions, liability and the Constitution' (2004) 19 *SA Public Law* 422–432.

9.4.3.2 Statutory remedies

Statutes and ordinances that govern restrictive conditions usually include provisions to the effect that a contravention of a restrictive condition constitutes an offence and carries stipulated penalties.[214] Other legislation provides for restoration of the land, the revocation of a permit and the removal of certain structures.[215]

9.4.3.3 Defences

Where action has been instituted to enforce the provisions of a restrictive condition, a possible defence is that the character of the area has changed so much that the original restrictive condition is no longer applicable, has become valueless and need not be enforced.[216] This means that the area must have changed radically. Factual evidence must support these allegations. To establish the character of a neighbourhood, the state of the township as a whole must be considered, not only the state of the immediate vicinity where the complaint arises.[217]

9.4.4 Removal or amendment of restrictive conditions

Removal of a restrictive condition usually benefits the person who applies for its removal. However, removal can lead to detrimental effects for the person in whose favour the restrictive condition operates. Because the nature of a restrictive condition is similar to that of a praedial servitude, it is important that removals and changes are dealt with equitably and fairly. Failure to do so could result in an arbitrary deprivation of property in terms of s 25 of the Constitution.

Removal of and amendments to restrictive conditions can occur in a number of different ways, as the figure below illustrates.[218]

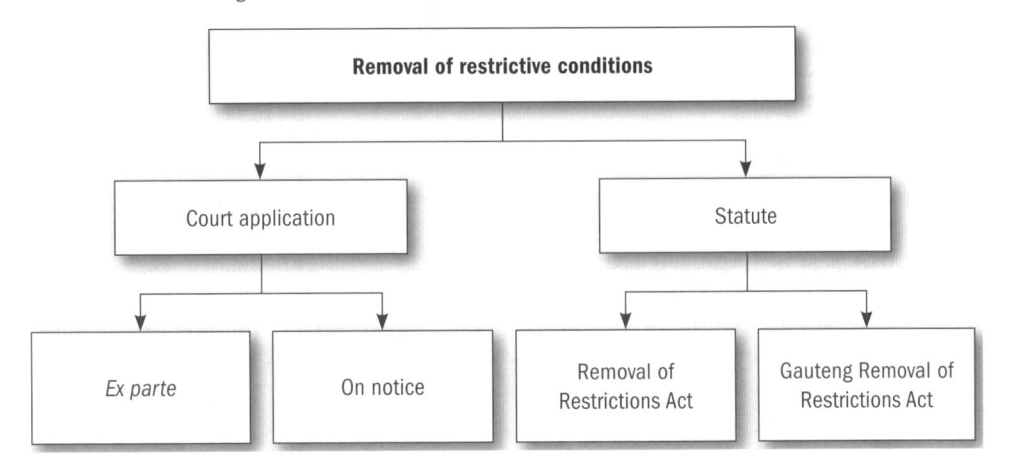

Figure 9.6: Overview of methods to remove restrictive conditions

```
                    Removal of restrictive conditions
                    ┌──────────────┴──────────────┐
              Court application                Statute
              ┌───────┴───────┐          ┌────────┴────────┐
           Ex parte        On notice   Removal of      Gauteng Removal of
                                      Restrictions Act  Restrictions Act
```

---

214 Van Wyk *Planning Law* pp 221–224.
215 Van Wyk *Planning Law* p 221.
216 Van Wyk *Planning Law* pp 227–228.
217 Van Wyk *Planning Law* pp 227–228.
218 Silberberg & Schoeman *Property* pp 354–356; Van Wyk *Planning Law* pp 190–211; *LAWSA* Vol 28 at para 541.

9.4.4.1 Removal by court application

Restrictive conditions may be removed subsequent to an ex parte application or an application on notice.[219] An application on notice informs interested parties that an application for the removal of a restrictive condition is being made,[220] whereas an ex parte application is an application brought by the person who wants the restrictive condition removed. Any possible objectors are not represented. If the court finds in favour of the applicant, a rule nisi is issued. This is a temporary interdict, which includes a call to interested persons to come to court on the return date to show cause why the order should not be confirmed (made final) on that date. *Ex parte Optimal Property Solutions CC*[221] recently confirmed the procedure for an ex parte application for removal of a restrictive condition.

> **PAUSE FOR REFLECTION**
>
> **An ex parte application is not ideal from the point of view of publicity**
>
> A negative aspect that people must be aware of the temporary interdict to raise any objections. Given that restrictive conditions serve to benefit more than one person, it is unfortunate when an ex parte application goes unnoticed by those who will be affected by the removal of the restrictive condition. Few guidelines exist for making the process fairer, but *Ex parte Saiga Properties (Pty) Ltd*[222] laid down solid guidelines for this type of application. A temporary interdict regarding the removal of a restrictive condition can be made final when sufficient justification is made out on the papers. In addition, the applicant must show that she has met reasonable expectations regarding obtaining consent for removal of the restrictive condition from other affected parties, and that notice was given to those parties who are clearly interested and readily available. Otherwise, the applicant must show that it is impossible or not reasonably practical to obtain the consent of other interested parties or to serve notice of the application on them.

9.4.4.2 Statutory procedures for removal

Legislation provides a more satisfactory process for removal of a restrictive condition. Examples include the Removal of Restrictions Act[223] and the Gauteng Removal of Restrictions Act.[224] These Acts contain procedures whereby certain restrictions and obligations in respect of land, including restrictive conditions, can be altered, suspended or removed. The procedure requires that the application in the prescribed form and accompanied by the required documents and particulars, be lodged with the local authority or with the Director-General of the provincial department concerned.[225] The applicant must deposit an amount of money sufficient to cover the expenses that will be incurred by the local authority or provincial administration, as the case may be, in connection with the application. If the land is encumbered by a mortgage bond and the application is made by the owner of the land, the bondholder's consent to the application must accompany the application.[226]

---

219 Van Wyk *Planning Law* pp 191-196.
220 Van Wyk *Planning Law* p 192.
221 2003 (2) SA 136 (C); Van Wyk *Planning Law* pp 192-193.
222 1997 (4) SA 716 (E) at 720G-I.
223 Act 84 of 1967.
224 Act 3 of 1996.
225 Section 3(1)-(3) of the Removal of Restrictions Act 84 of 1967; s 35(1) of the Gauteng Removal of Restrictions Act 3 of 1996.
226 Section 3(4) of the Removal of Restrictions Act 84 of 1967; s 5(2) of the Gauteng Removal of Restrictions Act 3 of 1996.

The Director-General of the department concerned must ensure that a notice is published in the *Provincial Gazette* and in a newspaper circulating in the area in which the land is situated. The notice must indicate that an application for removal of a restrictive condition has been made, that the application is open for inspection at the office of the Director-General and any other place mentioned in the notice, and that objections against the application may be lodged with the Director-General on or before a specified date, which must not be less than 21 days after the last publication of the notice.[227] The Director-General must also see ensure that, where possible, a copy of the notice is served on every owner of land, who, in his opinion, is directly affected by the application. Such service is to be effected by registered mail addressed to the owner at his last known address. A copy of every objection must be sent to the applicant by registered mail.[228]

Once the period within which objections may be lodged has expired, the Director-General must refer the application together with all objections and relevant documents to the townships board for investigation and recommendation. After consideration of the application, the recommendation of the townships board, the objections, and other relevant documents and particulars, the premier or the local authority may grant or refuse the application.[229]

Compared to the ex parte application procedure outlined above,[230] the statutory procedures provide the better process as far as serving the principle of publicity is concerned. Ordinary members of the public have a good chance of seeing the notice, and those persons who are thought to be directly affected are contacted personally in accordance with the procedures laid down.

9.5 Concluding remarks

The notion of servitude is one of the oldest constructions of rights in South African law in respect of property belonging to another. By its nature, a servitude is intended to endure for generations, often beyond the lifetime of the parties who created it. It is, therefore, conceivable that a particular servitude no longer benefits the dominant tenement in the way intended at its creation. As the decision in *Linvestment CC v Hammersley and Another*[231] so aptly illustrates, the court may be required to reinterpret such servitudes in a different setting to render them continuously useful for modern society.

This eventuality does not detract from the practical application of the servitude construction, which will continue to inform the development of land law for generations to come. The manner in which the principles that underlie the notion of servitude have been used and adapted in the context of restrictive conditions is illustrative of the usefulness of the concept. In similar vein, the principles relating to servitudes are relevant to the new law developing around resources such as minerals, petroleum and water. The following chapters deal with these aspects in greater detail.

---

227 Section 3(7) of the Removal of Restrictions Act 84 of 1967; s 5(8) of the Gauteng Removal of Restrictions Act 3 of 1996.
228 Section 3(7) of the Removal of Restrictions Act 84 of 1967; s 5(8) of the Gauteng Removal of Restrictions Act 3 of 1996.
229 Section 4(1)-(3) of the Removal of Restrictions Act 84 of 1967; s 6(8) of the Gauteng Removal of Restrictions Act 3 of 1996.
230 See p 262 above.
231 2008 (3) SA 283 (SCA) at 292–293.

Chapter 10

Minerals

'One cannot look at property, including mineral rights, in a simplistic manner. In view of the history of this country, it is not simplistic.'
De Beers Consolidated Mines Ltd v Ataqua Mining (Pty) Ltd and Others 13.12.2007 (Case No: 3215/06) unreported (OPD) at para 30

10.1	Introduction	265
10.2	History of mineral law	266
10.3	Ownership of minerals and petroleum under the MPRDA	269
10.4	Important concepts used in the MPRDA	273
10.5	Rights to minerals or petroleum	274
10.5.1	Nature of rights to minerals or petroleum	276
10.5.2	Content of rights to minerals or petroleum	276
10.5.2.1	Content of rights granted under the MPRDA	277
10.5.2.2	Activities and requirements	278
10.5.2.3	Competing rights of the surface owner	278
10.5.3	Transfer and encumbrance of rights to minerals or petroleum	279
10.5.4	Termination of rights to minerals or petroleum	279
10.6	Social and environmental responsibility and liability of the mineral and petroleum industry	280
10.6.1	Environmental provisions of the MPRDA	280
10.6.2	Black economic empowerment and access to mining	281
10.7	Mineral law as part of property law	281
10.8	Concluding remarks	282

10.1 Introduction

This chapter deals with the nature, content, acquisition, transfer and termination of mineral rights or petroleum rights. These features are governed by the provisions of the Mineral and Petroleum Resources Development Act[1] (MPRDA), which came into effect on 1 May 2004, introducing a new mineral law order in South Africa.

---

1 Act 28 of 2002 (MPRDA).

South African mineral law has always been based in property law.[2] At the core of mineral law was the concept of 'mineral rights', a term defined by property law concepts and governed largely by property law.[3] Yet, by means of the MPRDA, the legislature has done away with the traditional concept of 'mineral rights' which existed for more than a century in South Africa.[4] The prevalence of state power of control over the mineral and petroleum resources of the country is an important feature of the MPRDA.[5]

> **COUNTER POINT**
>
> **Mineral law as part of property law?**
>
> The treatment of rights in respect of minerals in the MPRDA once again draws attention to a question that has been asked already in respect of past dispensations of mineral law, namely[6] whether mineral law should be regarded as part of property law, or whether it is more appropriate to deal with it under administrative law. Entitlement to minerals and access to the mining industry in South Africa has been subject to significantly rigorous and rigid regulation over many years. This means that, necessarily, significant aspects of the law relating to minerals and mining will be subject to the rules of administrative law. The MPRDA introduced a dispensation that differs in some respects from preceding statutory dispensations regarding minerals, but the proprietary concepts that underpin mineral rights have not disappeared. Hence, we deal with those aspects of the new order mineral and petroleum rights that demonstrate the continued relevance of (some) principles of property law for the specialised field of mineral and petroleum law.

This chapter discusses the features of mineral and petroleum rights, the environmental and social responsibility of the mineral and petroleum industry, and how this influenced the provisions in the MPRDA. It refers briefly to the manner in which the transitional provisions in the MPRDA managed the shift from the previous dispensation as regards mineral rights, to the current dispensation of mining and prospecting rights relating to minerals and petroleum.

10.2 History of mineral law

Historically, the right to minerals fell within the ambit of property law.[7] Mineral rights were explained with reference to acknowledged categories of property rights. What made them peculiar was that mineral rights could be severed from the title to the land. Severance of the mineral rights from the surface rights enabled third parties to become holders of the mineral rights.[8] In contrast to other *iura in re aliena* (such as servitudes), the right to minerals thus could exist separately from ownership of the land once the right had been severed.

---

2   *Lazarus and Jackson v Wessels, Oliver and the Coronation Freehold Estates, Town and Mines Ltd* 1903 TS 499 (T) at 510.
3   Badenhorst, PJ & Mostert, H (2004) *Mineral and Petroleum Law of South Africa* (Cape Town, Juta) Revision Service 3 (2007) pp 1–9; 1–14*ff.*
4   *Meepo v Kotze* 2008 (1) SA 104 (NC) at 110G.
5   Section 3(1) of the MPRDA; *Meepo v Kotze* 2008 (1) SA 104 (NC) at 110I-J; 113I-J.
6   It was raised previously in a completely different statutory context, for instance, by Viljoen, HP & Bosman, PH (1979) *A Guide to Mining Rights in South Africa* (Johannesburg, Lex Patria Publishers) p 7.
7   Badenhorst, PJ & Mostert, H (2004) *Mineral and Petroleum Law of South Africa* (Cape Town, Juta) Revision Service 3 (2007) pp 1–9.
8   *AgriSouth Africa v The Minister of Minerals and Energy; Van Rooyen v The Minister of Minerals and Energy* 06.03.2009 (Case No: 55896/2007, 10235/2008) unreported (N&S Gauteng) at para 7.

To determine the nature and content of mineral rights, the courts relied on the established property law principles of servitudes.[9] In its conventional, common law sense, a mineral right comprised the entitlements to enter land,[10] to prospect[11] and to mine[12] upon it, and to remove the minerals, along with all ancillary rights[13] that enable extraction of the minerals. These particular entitlements have been subject to such considerable statutory regulation in South African law that, typically, a distinction is drawn between the right to mine or prospect, and the underlying mineral right.

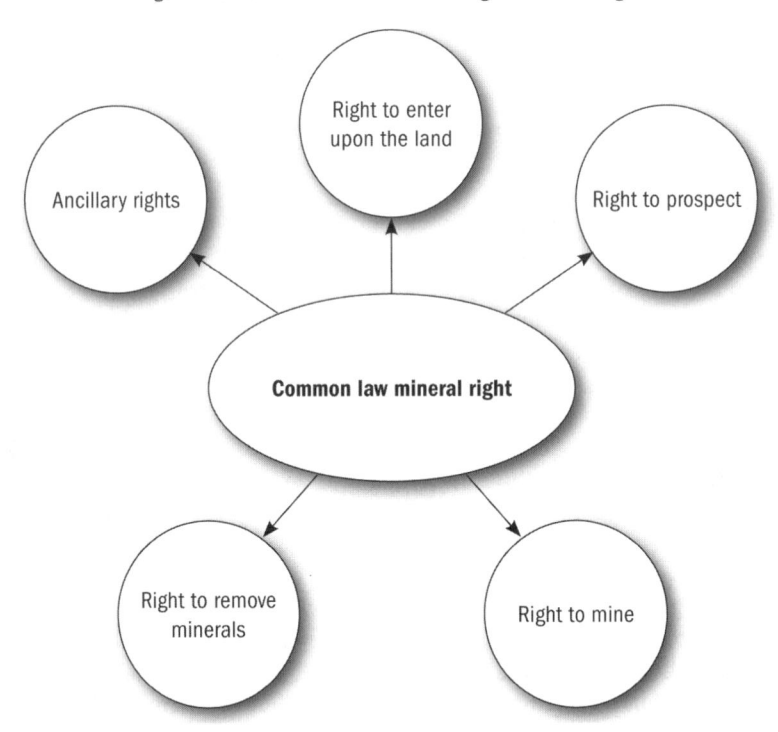

Figure 10.1: Common law understanding of a mineral right

Mineral rights were valuable assets.[14] Ownership of minerals passed from the landowner to the mineral rights holder (or the nominee) upon separation.[15] Under common law, the

---

9   Badenhorst, PJ & Mostert, H (2004) *Mineral and Petroleum Law of South Africa* (Cape Town, Juta) Revision Service 3 (2007) at pp 1–9; 1–14*ff.*
10 *Van Vuren and Others v Registrar of Deeds* 1907 TS 289 at 294; *Rocher v Registrar of Deeds* 1911 TPD 311 at 316; *Ex Parte Pierce* 1950 (3) SA 628 (O) at 634; *Aussenkjer Diamante (Pty) Ltd v Namex (Pty) Ltd* 1983 (1) SA 263 (A) at 274.
11 Section 5(1) of the Minerals Act 50 of 1991; *Rocher v Registrar of Deeds* 1911 TPD 311 at 316; Badenhorst, PJ & Mostert, H (2004) *Mineral and Petroleum Law of South Africa* (Cape Town, Juta) Revision Service 3 (2007) pp 3–12.
12 *Le Roux and Others v Loewenthal* 1905 TS 742 at 745; *Van Vuren and Others v Registrar of Deeds* 1907 TS 289 at 295 and 316; *Nolte v Johannesburg Consolidated Investment Co Ltd* 1943 AD 295 at 315; *Ex Parte Pierce* 1950 (3) SA 628 (O) at 634; *South African Railways and Harbours v Transvaal Consolidated Land and Exploration Co Ltd* 1961 (2) SA 467 (A) at 481.
13 *Trojan Exploration Co (Pty) Ltd and Another v Rustenburg Platinum Mines Ltd and Others* 1996 (4) SA 499 (A) at 520C.
14 *AgriSouth Africa v The Minister of Minerals and Energy; Van Rooyen v The Minister of Minerals and Energy* 06.03.2009 (Case No: 55896/2007, 10235/2008) unreported (N&S Gauteng) at para 7.
15 Van der Merwe *Sakereg* p 562.

mineral rights holder was under no obligation to exploit the rights.[16] He could let them lie fallow, or dispose of them by bequest or sale.

The rights to prospect and mine minerals were aspects of the common law mineral right. These rights to prospect and mine depended on statutory regulation from early in the history of South African mineral law. The criteria for obtaining and holding the right to extract the minerals (i.e. the right to mine) varied over time, along with the policies underlying regulation of the mining sector, as well as legislative attempts to translate the policies into statutory provisions.

At one time, the right to prospect for and mine natural oil and the right to mine precious stones and precious metals vested in the state.[17] Private stakeholders could acquire subordinate rights in respect of extraction of these minerals from the state. Later, the right to extract minerals could be accessed only by obtaining authorisation to mine or prospect for minerals, coupled with the consent of the common law mineral right holder.[18] In terms of the most recent legislation, the MPRDA, access to the industry is regulated through state-granted rights to prospect or mine.

This chapter focuses on the most recent round of mineral law statutes, i.e. the MPRDA and its companion, the Mining Titles Registration Act (MTRA).[19] This legislation has changed the practice of mineral law significantly over the past few years and has had a profound effect on issues pertaining to minerals that, conventionally, belonged in the domain of private law. The new mineral law dispensation introduced a system of state custodianship as the basis for regulatory control over minerals and mining. It also made it clear that 'the only way to acquire new rights is to obtain them from the state'.[20]

These features are analysed in the rest of the chapter. At this point, it should be noted that the MPRDA provided for the transition from the previous regime to the current.[21] These transitional provisions caused prospecting and mining rights, and authorisations acknowledged under the previous dispensation to cease to exist, and to be deregistered gradually over a period of approximately five years after commencement of the Act. Cessation of the rights could be coupled with conversion thereof to substitutes under the new dispensation. The process of controlled conversion rendered it possible to check compliance with the objectives of the Act, in particular those relating to broadening access to resources within, and importing empowerment goals into, the mining industry. Moreover, the transitional provisions acted as an important buffer against possible detriment arising from the overhaul of South African mineral law. In the recent decision of *AgriSouth Africa v The Minister of Minerals and Energy*, this point was underscored with the remark that:

> [b]ut for the ... provisions ... [of] ... schedule II to the act that gives certain rights to the holders of 'old order rights' ... the effect would have been to extinguish all [pre-existing] rights.[22]

---

16 *AgriSouth Africa* at para 9.
17 Section 2(1)*(a)* of the Mining Rights Act 20 of 1967 and s 2 of the Precious Stones Act 73 of 1964.
18 In terms of ss 6 and 9 of the Minerals Act 50 of 1991.
19 Act 16 of 1967, extensively revised in 2003 by the Mining Titles Registration Amendment Act 24 of 2003, read with the MPRDA.
20 *AgriSouth Africa* at para 11.
21 In Schedule II to the Act.
22 *AgriSouth Africa v The Minister of Minerals and Energy; Van Rooyen v The Minister of Minerals and Energy* 06.03.2009 (Case No: 55896/2007, 10235/2008) unreported (N&S Gauteng) at para 11. This case dealt only with the question of whether holders of so-called 'unused old order rights' could claim compensation for the possible expropriation of their rights, and the exception to this claim by the Minister of Mineral and Energy Affairs.

The transitional provisions hence fulfilled an important role in constructing the shift between the previous order of mineral law and the current one as espoused by the MPRDA. Since the transitional period has now lapsed, this chapter does not include a detailed discussion of this period. It is useful, however, to take note of the role of the transitional provisions.

10.3 Ownership of minerals and petroleum under the MPRDA

In terms of the South African common law maxim, *cuius est solum eius est usque ad coelum et ad inferos*, the owner of land is owner not only of the surface, but also of everything above and below the surface.[23] This implied that for as long as the minerals remain unsevered (in situ) from the land, ownership of the minerals vested in the owner of the land.[24]

> **PAUSE FOR REFLECTION**
>
> **Terminology**
>
> Note that the term 'unsevered' can be ambiguous. On the one hand, severance refers to the splitting of mineral title from the ownership of the land, as explained above. On the other hand, the term is also used with reference to the extraction of the minerals themselves from the land. In this context, it is less confusing to refer to minerals in situ, where reference is being made to unextracted (i.e. unsevered) minerals.

Legislation did away with the principle of *cuius est solum* quite soon. For instance, even before South Africa became a Republic and consolidated all existing mineral laws, British colonial law applicable in the Cape Colony required that 'royal minerals' (i.e. precious stones, gold and silver) were reserved as property of the Crown, even if the land in which these minerals were situated was in private hands.[25] It was always possible for the Crown to exclude minerals from the scope of a conveyance, either by express grant or by reservation of minerals, and English common law always recognised the possibility of separate ownership of the subsoil and minerals lying beneath the surface.[26]

Section 3(1) of the MPRDA provides that mineral and petroleum resources are the common heritage of all people of South Africa. The state is the custodian thereof for the benefit of all South Africans. The section does not, however, expressly reserve ownership of unsevered (in situ) minerals or petroleum to the state, as is the case in many other jurisdictions,[27] and as was the case for quite some time previously in parts of South Africa.

---

23 *Anglo Operations Ltd v Sandhurst Estates (Pty) Ltd* 2007 (2) SA 363 (SCA) at 371D; Franklin, BLS & Kaplan, M (1982) *The Mining and Minerals Laws of South Africa* (Durban, Butterworths) p 4.
24 *Trojan Exploration Co v Rustenburg Platinum Mines Ltd* 1996 (4) SA 499 (AD) at 537C.
25 Section 4 of Sir John Cradock's Proclamation on Conversion of Loan Place to Quitrent Tenure, dated 6 August 1813, provides an example of the preservation of the English law concept of the Crown prerogative in the former Cape Colony. See further Dale, MO (1979) *An Historical and Comparative Study of the Concept of Acquistion of Mineral Rights* LLD thesis (Pretoria, Unisa) p 217; *Benade v Minister van Mineraal- en Energiesake* 2002 JDR 0769 (NC) at 8. Sir John Cradock's Proclamation was repealed by the Pre-Union Statutes Law Revision Act 44 of 1968.
26 Bradbrook, AJ, MacCullum, SV & Moore, AP (2007) *Australian Real Property Law* (Rozelle NSW, Thomson Lawbook Co) pp 651–652. See *Anglo Operations Ltd v Sandhurst Estates (Pty) Ltd* 2007 (2) SA 363 (SCA) at 371E.
27 E.g. Butt, P (2006) *Land Law* 5 ed (Sydney, Thomson Lawbook Co) p 16; Bradbrook, AJ, MacCullum, SV & Moore, AP (2007) *Australian Real Property Law* (Rozelle NSW, Thomson Lawbook Co) p 653; Chambers, R (2008) *An Introduction to Property Law in Australia* 2 ed (Rozelle NSW, Thomson Lawbook Co) p 176.

The provisions of the MPRDA should be interpreted with due regard to the constitutional rights, norms and values that the legislature sought to encapsulate, protect and advance in the Act.[28] Most prominently, in the MPRDA, the state is given a custodial role over the mineral and petroleum resources of the nation.[29] This has given rise to a number of different interpretations of the new order created by the MPRDA. In particular, the absence of an express reservation of minerals and petroleum in favour of the state in the MPRDA makes it unclear where ownership of unsevered (in situ) minerals lies.

> **COUNTER POINT**
>
> **Who is owner of the minerals (and petroleum)?**
>
> Different interpretations exist as to where ownership of unextracted *(in situ)* minerals (and petroleum) lies. According to one view, ownership of minerals and petroleum not yet extracted from the land vests in the state.[30] According to this view, the *cuius est solum* rule of the common law, which implies that a landowner is the owner of the minerals in the land, has been abrogated by s 3(1) of the MPRDA. Section 4(2) states that in so far as the common law is inconsistent with the MPRDA, the latter prevails.[31] This rule of interpretation is said to support the view that unextracted minerals vest in the state.
>
> According to this view, too, the use of the term 'custodianship' with reference to the state's power over the mineral resources is a misnomer as the view propagates the idea that the MPRDA proposes actual vesting of the minerals in the state.[32] The difficulty with the term is that a custodian or curator does not hold property for himself, but on behalf of beneficiaries.[33] The problem with this view is that it disregards a specific policy choice made by the state. There is ample historical justification in South African law, as well as in comparative law, for vesting rights to minerals (and petroleum) in the state. It is, therefore, reasonable to assume that the legislature did not refer to the custodial duties of the state in metaphorical terms. What the literal meaning of the state custodianship is in the context of the law pertaining to natural resources continues, however, to be a contested question.
>
> Another view seeks to distinguish mineral and petroleum **resources** from minerals and petroleum **as such**. According to this view, it is the collective wealth of mineral and petroleum resources that 'belong' to the nation, while ownership of unsevered minerals still vests in the owner of the land, even though the owner may not be able to exploit such minerals.[34] This view relies on the fact that the MPRDA contains no specific provision whereby unextracted (in situ) minerals or petroleum on individual properties vest in anyone

---

28 *Meepo v Kotze* 2008 (1) SA 104 (NC) at 113I; see also 114B–C.
29 *Meepo* at 113I-J.
30 Badenhorst, PJ & Mostert, H 'Artikel 3(1) en (2) van die Mineral and Petroleum Resources Development Act 28 van 2002: 'n Herbeskouing' (2007) *TSAR* 469 at 476; Dale, MO 'Mining Law' (2002) *AS* 573 at 574, however, points out that such vesting in the state is not clear in so far as the Act does not expressly refer to ownership of minerals.
31 Badenhorst, PJ & Mostert, H (2004) *Mineral and Petroleum Law of South Africa* (Cape Town, Juta) p 13-3. See, however, Dale, MO, Bekker, L, Bashall, FJ, Chaskalson, M, Dixon, C, Grobler, GL & Loxton, CDA (2005) *South African Mineral and Petroleum Law* (Durban, LexisNexis Butterworths) pp MPRDA–4, MPRDA–10 and MPRDA–121, where it is argued that the provisions of the MPRDA do not warrant such departure from the common law. For a clarification of their view, see Badenhorst, PJ & Mostert, H 'Artikel (3)(1) en (2) van die *Mineral and Petroleum Resources Development Act* 28 of 2002: 'n Herbeskouing' (2007) *TSAR* 469 at 476.
32 Chamber of Mines *Memorandum to the Director-General: Mineral and Energy Affairs* (1989) Part 3 ch 2 para 2.2.2.1.
33 Dale, MO et al. (2005) *South African Mineral and Petroleum Law* (Durban, LexisNexis Butterworths) p MPRDA–115.
34 Dale, MO et al. (2005) *South African Mineral and Petroleum Law* (Durban, LexisNexis Butterworths) p MPRDA–122.

in particular. It is argued that since no provision of the MPRDA actually vests ownership of unextracted minerals in the state[35] or in the public,[36] it cannot vest in anyone but the landowner. The general public is certainly not endowed with private law rights to use the country's mineral resources.[37] This view is supported by the definitions of 'land' and 'owner' in the MPRDA.[38] According to this standpoint, the *cuius est solum* rule has not been abrogated.[39] The problem with this view is that while it acknowledges that ownership of minerals vests in the owner of land, it does not deal with the fact that the MPRDA excludes the ability of the owner to exploit the minerals beyond the legislative parameters. Ownership of the minerals in situ is thus denuded of all possible entitlements, save (possibly) the ability to counter unlawful extraction of the minerals or petroleum. However, the MPRDA does not clarify this issue either.

A third view engages with the notion of state custodianship. It is argued that custodianship does not amount to ownership of unsevered minerals and petroleum. According to this view, the landowner remains the owner of unextracted minerals and petroleum, subject to the public trust doctrine.[40] This doctrine forms part of Anglo-American law.[41] Because the phrase 'public trust' is used explicitly in the National Environmental Management Act[42] (NEMA) and the National Water Act,[43] some scholars assume that the doctrine has become part of South African law.[44] Furthermore, they are willing to extend the ambit of this doctrine to include mineral law. South African courts have referred to 'public trust' to mean that where property is held in public trust, the sovereign takes on the role of custodian.[45] The problem with this view is that the public trust doctrine finds application only when the resource in question vests 'sovereign ownership' in the state. Whether this can be derived from the MPRDA is contested.[46] In international law, the state is assumed to have sovereignty over its natural resources. However, there are further doubts as to whether the public trust doctrine, which originates from Anglo-American law, is suitable for import here. This is because South African law has the mechanisms of both

---

35   Dale, MO et al. (2005) *South African Mineral and Petroleum Law* (Durban, LexisNexis Butterworths) p MPRDA-10.
36   Dale, MO et al. (2005) *South African Mineral and Petroleum Law* (Durban, LexisNexis Butterworths) p MPRDA-12; see, however, Badenhorst, PJ & Mostert, H 'Artikel 3(1) en (2) van die Mineral and Petroleum Resources Development Act 28 van 2002: 'n Herbeskouing' (2007) *TSAR* 469 at 478–479.
37   Dale, MO et al. (2005) *South African Mineral and Petroleum Law* (Durban, LexisNexis Butterworths) pp MPRDA-121 and MPRDA-123.
38   See pp 273–274 below.
39   Dale, MO et al. (2005) *South African Mineral and Petroleum Law* (Durban, LexisNexis Butterworths) p MPRDA-121.
40   Glazewski, J (2000) *Environmental Law in South Africa* (Durban, LexisNexis Butterworths) pp 464, 468; Van der Schyff, E 'Who "owns" the country's mineral resources? The possible incorporation of the public trust doctrine through the Mineral and Petroleum Resources Development Act' (2008) *TSAR* 757 at 765–767.
41   Van der Schyff, E (2006) *The Constitutionality of the Mineral and Petroleum Resources Development Act 28 of 2002* (LLD thesis Potchefstroom University of the the North-West) p 106; Dale, MO et al. (2005) *South African Mineral and Petroleum Law* (Durban, LexisNexis Butterworths) p MPRDA-124.
42   Sections 2(4)(*o*), 28(5)(*e*) and 30(6)(*d*) of the National Environmental Management Act 107 of 1998.
43   Section 3(1) of the National Water Act 36 of 1998.
44   Glazewski, J (2000) *Environmental Law in South Africa* (Durban, LexisNexis Butterworths) pp 464, 468; Van der Schyff, E 'Who "owns" the country's mineral resources? The possible incorporation of the public trust doctrine through the Mineral and Petroleum Resources Development Act' (2008) *TSAR* 757 at 765–767.
45   See e.g. *Hichange Investments (Pty) Ltd v Cape Produce Co (Pty) Ltd t/a Pelts Products and Others* 2004 (2) SA 393 (E) at 418; *South African Shore Angling Association and Another v Minister of Environmental Affairs* 2002 (5) SA 511 (SE) at 525.
46   Dale, MO et al. (2005) *South African Mineral and Petroleum Law* (Durban, LexisNexis Butterworths) p MPRDA-115.

constitutionally entrenched environmental rights, as well as the concept of *res publicae* to deal with the issue.[47] Furthermore, the public trust doctrine is contentious even in the American setting.

A fourth view is that it is irrelevant where ownership of minerals and petroleum in the soil lies. According to this view, minerals in situ have value only once they can be and are extracted. The Minister of Minerals and Energy is empowered to grant rights in respect of minerals or petroleum and the land to applicants,[48] thereby activating these rights. However, it is not merely an academic issue where the ownership of unextracted minerals lies. The recent case of *AgriSA v Minister of Minerals and Energy; Van Rooyen v The Minister of Minerals and Energy*,[49] demonstrates that unextracted minerals can be valuable **because** they are not extracted. In this way, the holders of such rights can secure monopolies over a specific resource, or protect the land surface for agricultural use.

A fifth point of view is that because of the wording of s 3(1) of the MPRDA, mineral and petroleum resources in South Africa have become a (new) type of *res publicae*.[50] There is no historical justification in South African common law for treating mineral and petroleum resources as *res publicae*. However, that new categories of *res publicae* have been acknowledged in modern South African law, and that rights to minerals were reserved to the state in the past raise this possibility. Thus far, the judiciary has not supported this interpretation.[51] However, in our opinion, the *res publicae* argument is the most plausible explanation of the ownership regime introduced by the MPRDA.

For current purposes, this discussion assumes that the MPRDA creates a new type of *res publicae* by placing the mineral and petroleum resources under custodianship of the state. According to this view, the underlying property rights of the landowner in unextracted minerals have not been destroyed in theory, but such rights can no longer be of much practical use to the landowner. The state, in its custodial role, is endowed with the capacity to regulate access to the resources and is obliged to ensure optimal exploitation of the resources. In this capacity, it may react against unlawful mining of any mineral (or petroleum). Since the MPRDA's provisions are not exhaustive, the common law applies residually. Therefore, the owners' remedies continue to exist. A landowner confronted with unlawful mining activities on his land may, for instance, obtain an eviction order, or may have delictual claims if the necessary conditions apply.

47 See further Dale, MO et al. (2005) *South African Mineral and Petroleum Law* (Durban, LexisNexis Butterworths) p MPRDA-124; Badenhorst, PJ & Mostert, H 'Artikel 3(1) en (2) van die Mineral en Petroleum Resources Development Act 28 van 2002: 'n Herbeskouing' (2007) *TSAR* 469 at 478.
48 Section 3(2)*(a)* of the MPRDA. See further Badenhorst, PJ & Mostert, H 'Artikel 3(1) en (2) van die Mineral en Petroleum Resources Development Act 28 van 2002: 'n Herbeskouing' (2007) *TSAR* 469 at 479.
49 06.03.2009 (Case No: 55896/2007, 10235/2008) unreported (N&S Gauteng) at para 17.
50 Badenhorst, PJ & Mostert, H (2004) *Mineral and Petroleum Law of South Africa* (Cape Town, Juta) Revision Service 3 (2007) 13-4; 'Artikel 3(1) en (2) van die Mineral en Petroleum Resources Development Act 28 van 2002: 'n Herbeskouing' (2007) *TSAR* 469 at 476. See, however, Dale, MO et al. (2005) *South African Mineral and Petroleum Law* (Durban, LexisNexis Butterworths) pp MPRDA-115; MPRDA-120 to MPRDA-121, where it is argued, inter alia, that minerals were not regarded as *res publicae* in Roman law. For a clarification of their view, see Badenhorst, PJ & Mostert, H 'Artikel 3(1) en (2) van die Mineral en Petroleum Resources Development Act 28 van 2002: 'n Herbeskouing' (2007) *TSAR* 469 at 477-78; Van der Schyff, E (2006) *The Constitutionality of the Mineral and Petroleum Resources Development Act 28 of 2002* (LLD thesis Potchefstroom University of the the North-West) 237 n 237. The notion of *res publicae* is possible in terms of property theory only if individuality as a characteristic of a thing is also disregarded in respect of unsevered minerals.
51 See *De Beers Consolidated Mines Ltd v Ataqua Mining (Pty) Ltd and Others* 18.12.2007 (Case No: 3215/06) unreported (OPD).

The MPRDA is silent about ownership of minerals (and petroleum) once these are extracted (severed), whether lawfully or not. It would have been appropriate for the MPRDA to determine, for instance, that property rights in minerals vest in the prospector or miner from the moment that the minerals are separated from the land in accordance with the right to prospect or to mine, and that property rights in the minerals vest in the state if the minerals are extracted otherwise than in accordance with the right to prospect or mine.[52] Under common law, the holder of the right to minerals acquires ownership of the extracted minerals, which are classed as movables when they are extracted.[53] As the MPRDA states nothing to the contrary, it is assumed that the common law position prevails, and that holders of prospecting rights, mining permits, mining rights, exploration rights or production rights who are entitled to remove and dispose of the minerals or petroleum acquire ownership of the minerals or petroleum upon extraction.[54]

10.4 Important concepts used in the MPRDA

Three basic concepts are important in understanding the law dealing with minerals and petroleum: 'land', 'minerals' and 'petroleum'. In the conventional common law sense, 'land' refers to a parcel of land as indicated on a diagram in the Deeds Registry.[55] It includes the geological components of the land, for instance, the soil and minerals below the surface.[56] The MPRDA's definition goes beyond this, to include also the sea.[57] From this and other definitions[58] in the MPRDA, it is clear that South African authority and jurisdiction must prevail to enable control over the area under consideration. Moreover, the definition of 'land' read with the definition of 'owner' in the MPRDA suggests that the owner of the land is regarded as the owner of the minerals in the land, thus casting light on the ownership question raised above as regards minerals in situ.[59] Ownership of 'dry' land (i.e. land that is not sea) lies with the person in whose name the land is registered, and so the minerals in situ also belong to him. If the land is owned by the state, the state together with the occupant of the land is regarded as the owner,[60] by implication also of the in situ minerals. In relation to the sea, the state is the owner of the sea,[61] and as a result also the minerals in it.

From the definition of 'mineral',[62] one may deduce that to qualify as a mineral, a substance must be in solid, liquid or gaseous form, and must occur naturally in or on the earth, or water. Further, it must have been formed by, or subjected to, a geological process,

---

52 An example of such provisions are found in Australian mineral law, e.g. s 11 of the Mineral Resources (Sustainable Development) Act 1990 (Vic); s 11 of the Mining Act 1992 (NSW); s 310 of the Mineral Resources Act 1989 (Qld); s 18 of the Mining Right Act (SA); and s 85 of the Mining Act 1978 (WA).
53 *Van Vuren v Registrar of Deeds* 1907 TS 289 at 295; *Trojan Exploration Co v Rustenburg Platinum Mines Ltd* 1996 (4) SA 499 (AD) at 509I/J–510A.
54 Dale, MO et al. (2005) *South African Mineral and Petroleum Law* (Durban, LexisNexis Butterworths) p MPRDA-122.
55 *LAWSA* Vol 27(1) at para 226.
56 *LAWSA* vol 27(1) at para 226.
57 Section 1.
58 E.g. definition of 'sea' in s 1.
59 See p 269*ff* above.
60 Definition of 'owner' in s 1.
61 Definition of 'owner' in s 1.
62 See in general Badenhorst, PJ & Shone, RW '"Minerals", "petroleum" and "operations" in the Mineral and Petroleum Resources Development Act 28 of 2002: a geologist as devil's advocate for a change?' (2008) *Obiter* at 33–52; *LAWSA* Vol 18(2) at para 13.

or it must occur in residue stockpiles or residue deposits.[63] Substances such as sand, stone, rock, gravel, clay and soil, which had contested status as minerals in the past, are expressly recognised as minerals. Substances such as water as a carrier of minerals, petroleum or peat are excluded from the concept of a mineral.

To qualify as 'petroleum', a substance can be any liquid or solid hydrocarbon or combustible gas existing in a natural condition in the earth's crust, including that which has returned to a natural condition in the earth's crust. The substance may not, however, be coal, bituminous shale or other stratified deposits from which oil can be obtained by destructive distillation. It may also not be gas arising from a marsh or surface deposit.[64] The latter substances are generally treated as minerals, rather than as petroleum.

10.5   Rights to minerals or petroleum

In its capacity as custodian of the nation's mineral and petroleum resources, the state[65] may grant or refuse[66] different kinds of rights in respect of the mineral or petroleum and the land to which the rights relate.[67] The rights in respect of minerals are reconnaissance permissions, prospecting rights, permissions to remove minerals during prospecting, retention permits, mining permits and mining rights. The rights in respect of petroleum are reconnaissance permits, technical co-operation permits, exploration rights and production rights. As explained above,[68] the granting of prospecting rights or mining rights **as such** does not confer ownership of unsevered minerals.[69] This is in line with the common law position that the holder of rights to minerals or petroleum who is entitled to remove and dispose of the mineral or petroleum becomes the owner of the mineral once it is extracted.[70]

> **PAUSE FOR REFLECTION**
>
> **Expropriation of mineral rights?**
>
> The uncertainty surrounding ownership of extracted and unextracted minerals[71] has further repercussions. In *AgriSA v Minister of Minerals and Energy*, it was remarked that inactive common law mineral rights seem to have 'disappeared in thin air'.[72] This is indicative of the problem with determining what has become of the conventional, common law mineral rights.
>
> Some scholars have argued that incidents of ownership in relation to the exploitation of minerals have been destroyed by the MPRDA through 'institutional expropriation'.[73] This refers to the eradication of the concept of mineral rights as they were known in South

---

63   Residue deposits and residue stockpiles are defined in s 1 of the MPRDA.
64   *LAWSA* Vol 18 (2 ed) at para 14.
65   The Minister's power to grant certain rights has been delegated to designated officials. See *Meepo v Kotze* 2008 (1) SA 104 (NC) at 126C–127I as regards the ultra vires exercise of such delegated authority, which renders the right granted void.
66   The Minister is also empowered to control, administer and manage these rights.
67   Section 3(2)(a) read with s 5(1) of the MPRDA.
68   See counterpoint box on pp 270*ff*.
69   Dale, MO et al. (2005) *South African Mineral and Petroleum Law* (Durban, LexisNexis Butterworths) p MPRDA-11.
70   Dale, MO et al. (2005) *South African Mineral and Petroleum Law* (Durban, LexisNexis Butterworths) p MPRDA-122.
71   See counterpoint box on pp 270*ff*.
72   *AgriSouth Africa v The Minister of Minerals and Energy; Van Rooyen v The Minister of Minerals and Energy* 06.03.2009 Case No: 55896/2007, 10235/2008 unreported (N&S Gauteng) at para 11.
73   Dale, MO et al. (2005) *South African Mineral and Petroleum Law* (Durban, LexisNexis Butterworths) p MPRDA-122; *De Beers Consolidated Mines Ltd v Ataqua Mining (Pty) Ltd* 13.12.2007 Case No: at 3215/06 unreported (OPD) at para 39.

Africa prior to the MPRDA. Other scholars prefer to focus on a case-by-case analysis to determine how the conventional common law rights were substituted by new rights under the MPRDA.[74] Yet others hold the opinion that the MPRDA constitutes no more than a legitimate exercise of the state's regulatory powers over property, even if, in this case, they are so extensive as to denude the conventional common law concept of mineral rights completely.[75]

These different views have different consequences as regards expropriation under the Constitution. According to the first view, the MPRDA stands to be declared unconstitutional. With the second, the constitutionality of the MPRDA might not be at stake, although the state may be expected to compensate holders of rights who suffered loss because of the introduction of the MPRDA. According to the third view, the MPRDA is neither unconstitutional nor is compensation payable.

Where an expropriation is averred, the claimant has to prove the extent and nature of actual loss and damage suffered. The current use of the property must be indicated. The claimant has to submit proof of ownership of the property, and provide an account of the history of acquisition of the property and the purchase price. Details of the nature of the property must be provided. The claimant has to prove the market value of the property and how the value was determined. Lastly, the claimant has to indicate the extent of any state assistance and benefits received in respect of such property.[76] In determining 'just and equitable compensation' all relevant factors must be taken into account, including those specifically listed in the Constitution and the MPRDA, namely: (1) the current use of the property; (2) the history of the acquisition and use of the property; (3) the market value of the property; (4) the extent of direct state investment and subsidy in the acquisition and beneficial capital improvement of the property; (5) the purpose of expropriation;[77] (6) the state's obligation to redress the results of past racial discrimination in the allocation of and access to mineral resources;[78] (7) the state's obligation to bring about reforms to promote equitable access to all South Africa's natural resources; [79] (8) the constitutional commitment to ensure that legislative and other measures are taken to achieve land, water and related reform to redress the results of past racial discrimination within the parameters set by the constitutional property clause and the general limitations clause;[80] and (9) whether the person concerned will continue to benefit from the use of the property in question or not.[81]

The compensation claim must be lodged with the Director-General in the manner[82] 'prescribed by regulation 82A'.[83] Regulation 82A prescribes how a claim will be dealt with by the Department of Minerals and Energy once it has been instituted.[84]

---

74 Badenhorst, PJ & Mostert, H 'Revisiting the Transitional Arrangements of the Mineral and Petroleum Resources Development Act 28 of 2002 and the Constitutional Property Clause (Part Two)' (2004) 15 *Stell LR* 22 at 36.
75 Van der Walt *Constitutional Property Law* pp 378-383.
76 Item 12(2) of Schedule II to the MPRDA.
77 Section 25(3)*(e)* of the Constitution read with item 12(3) of Schedule II to the MPRDA.
78 Item 12(3)*(a)* of Schedule II to the MPRDA.
79 Item 12(3)*(b)* of Schedule II to the MPRDA read with s 25(8) of the Constitution.
80 Item 12(3)*(c)* of Schedule II to the MPRDA.
81 Item 12(3)*(d)* of Schedule II to the MPRDA.
82 Item 12(4) of Schedule II to the MPRDA.
83 Definition of 'prescribed' in s 1 of the MPRDA.
84 See further Badenhorst, PJ & Mostert, H (2004) *Mineral and Petroleum Law of South Africa* (Cape Town, Juta) Revision Service 3 (2007) at 25-29 to 25-31.

10.5.1 Nature of rights to minerals or petroleum

As in conventional property law, the registrability of mineral and petroleum rights goes hand in hand with their classification as either real or personal in character. The MPRDA classifies a prospecting right, mining right, exploration right, or production right granted by the Minister[85] as 'a limited real right in respect of the mineral or petroleum and the land to which such right relates'.[86] This classification of prospecting rights, mining rights, exploration rights, and production rights may be taken to mean the same as the common law phrase 'limited real right'. These rights must[87] be lodged for registration in the Mineral and Petroleum Titles Registration Office within 30 days after the right has become effective[88] or has been renewed.[89] A contract of prospecting, mining, exploration or production must be in notarial form to be registered.[90]

The MPRDA is silent about the nature of the other rights to minerals or petroleum recognised by the Act. These may only be recorded and filed.[91] Accordingly, it has been suggested that these rights are personal in nature.[92] The provisions concerning registration in the Mining Titles Registration Act, however, are not clear on this point.[93] For current purposes, it is assumed that because the MPRDA treats prospecting rights, mining rights, exploration and production rights differently from the other rights to minerals or petroleum, a distinction does indeed exist between those rights that can be classified as limited real rights and those that amount to personal rights.

The rights granted by the Minister are personal in all instances.[94] In *Meepo v Kotze*, the court indicated that the rights come into existence once the Minister, representing the state as custodian of the mineral resources, agrees to grant the applicant a right[95] to prospect for minerals on specified land for a specified period.[96] Upon registration of the prospecting rights, mining rights, exploration rights, or production rights in the Mineral and Petroleum Titles Office, the personal rights are terminated and limited real rights are created.[97] Other rights that can be recorded remain only personal in nature.[98]

10.5.2 Content of rights to minerals or petroleum

The MPRDA provides descriptions of the scope of the rights that may be created, among others, prospecting rights, mining rights, production rights and exploration rights.

---

85 Or the delegated person in the case of a prospecting right.
86 Section 5(1) of the MPRDA; *Meepo v Kotze* 2008 (1) SA 104 (NC) at 110I.
87 Section 5(1)(d) read with ss 19(2)(a), 25(2)(a), 82(2)(a), 86(2)(a) of the MPRDA.
88 I.e. approval of the environmental management programme or environmental management plan. This is not explicitly stated in the case of exploration rights and production rights. In *Meepo* at 125H, it was, however, decided that a prospecting right becomes effective upon the grant thereof and not the approval of the environmental management plan.
89 Section 3 of the Mining Titles Registration Act 16 of 1967 (MTRA); *Meepo* at 110I.
90 Section 15(2) of the MTRA.
91 Section 5(1)(v) of the MTRA.
92 Badenhorst, PJ 'Nature of New Order Rights to Minerals: a Rubikian exercise since passing the Mayday Rubicon with a cubic zirconium' (2005) 26 *Obiter* 505 at 520.
93 See s 5(1)(c) of the MTRA which incorrectly makes provision for registration in addition to recordal.
94 Badenhorst, PJ 'Nature of new order rights to minerals: a Rubikian exercise since passing the Mayday Rubicon with a cubic zirconium' (2005) 26 *Obiter* 505 at 520; *Meepo v Kotze* 2008 (1) SA 104 (NC) at 125D.
95 The court actually referred to a limited real right to prospect.
96 *Meepo v Kotze* 2008 (1) SA 104 (NC) at 125E.
97 Badenhorst, PJ 'Nature of new order rights to minerals: a Rubikian exercise since passing the Mayday Rubicon with a cubic zirconium' (2005) 26 *Obiter* 505 at 520.
98 See *Denel (Pty) Ltd v Cape Explosive Works Ltd* 1999 (2) SA 419 (T) at 435B–C.

Superficially, these rights are similar, but the specific activity connected to each shapes the precise content of each.

10.5.2.1 Content of rights granted under the MPRDA

A holder of **reconnaissance permission** to minerals is entitled to enter the land after consultation with the landowner for the purposes of conducting reconnaissance operations.[99] A **reconnaissance permit** enables the holder to undertake reconnaissance operations in respect of petroleum.[100] Reconnaissance operations involve searching for a mineral or petroleum by geological, geophysical, or photo-geological surveys and remote sensing techniques.[101] The holder may not conduct any prospecting or mining operations,[102] and does not acquire any exclusive right to a prospecting or mining right.[103]

A **prospecting right** or a **mining right** permits the holder to enter the land for prospecting and/or mining purposes.[104] The holder may prospect or mine[105] for the mineral, and remove and dispose of any mineral found. The right also permits use of water, subject to the provisions of the National Water Act.[106] A **retention permit** permits the suspension of a prospecting right.[107] In addition, it gives the holder an exclusive claim to a mining right in respect of the retention area and mineral in question.[108] As regards petroleum, the equivalents of a prospecting right and mining right to minerals are the **exploration right** and **production right** respectively.[109] The content of these rights is comparable to the content of prospecting rights and mining rights.

A holder of a **mining permit** may enter the land and build infrastructure for purpose of mining;[110] use water[111] subject to provisions of the National Water Act or sink a well or borehole required for use relating to prospecting or mining, on such land;[112] and to mine, for his own account, on or under that mining area for the mineral to which the mining permit relates.[113]

A **technical co-operation permit** to petroleum entitles the holder to apply exclusively for, and be granted, an exploration right in respect of the area to which the permit relates.[114]

---

99 Section 15(1) of the MPRDA.
100 See the definition of 'reconnaissance permit' in s 1 of the MPRDA.
101 Definition of 'reconnaissance operation' in s 1 of the MPRDA.
102 Section 15 (2)*(a)*; definition of 'reconnaissance operation' in s 1 of the MPRDA .
103 Section 15(2)*(b)* of the MPRDA.
104 Section 5(3) of the MPRDA. Entry includes bringing employees, plant, machinery, or equipment onto the land, as well as putting in infrastructure that may be required for the purposes of prospecting or mining.
105 The concepts of 'prospecting' and 'mine' have a technical meaning and are defined in s 1 of the MPRDA. In terms of the common law, the holder of a prospecting right is entitled to prospect only, whereas the holder of a mining right is entitled to prospect and mine.
106 Act 36 of 1998. The water used by a prospector or miner may be from a natural spring, lake, river, or stream situated on or flowing through the land. The water used may also be from any excavation made previously, and used for prospecting or mining purposes.
107 Section 32(2) of the MPRDA.
108 Secton 35(1) of the MPRDA.
109 Section 5(3) of the MPRDA.
110 Section 27(7)*(a)* of the MPRDA.
111 Water from any natural spring, lake, river, or stream situated on, or flowing through such land, or from any excavation previously made and used for prospecting or mining purposes.
112 Section 27(7)*(b)* of the MPRDA.
113 Section 27(7)*(d)* of the MPRDA.
114 Section 78(1) of the MPRDA.

The most prominent duty of the right holders is the payment of levies, fees or other consideration to the state.[115] This duty falls on holders of prospecting rights, mining rights and mining permits, as well as production rights. These moneys can take the form of prospecting or exploration fees, on the one hand, or a state royalty, on the other. The levying of royalties takes place in terms of the Mineral and Petroleum Resources Royalty Act (MPRRA).[116]

10.5.2.2 Activities and requirements

Prospecting for minerals entails intentional searching for a mineral to establish its existence, and to determine its extent and economic value. Any method that disturbs the surface or subsurface of the earth or a portion of the earth covered by sea or water may be used.

Mining of minerals takes place by any operation or activity (for instance, underground or opencast) for the purposes of winning (i.e. extracting) a mineral on or from the earth, water or any residue deposit. Lawful use of sand, stone, rock, gravel, or clay for farming, or effecting improvements on the land, or other community development purpose, is exempt from a prospecting right, permission to remove and dispose of a mineral, mining right or mining permit.[117] It hence does not qualify as mining.

Exploration of petroleum entails acquisition and/or processing of seismic data to identify a trap for testing. It also includes extended testing of a well with the intention of locating a discovery.[118] Production of petroleum is the equivalent of mining for minerals.

A prospective prospector or miner must apply for the right to prospect and mine, following the procedure and form provided by the MPRDA. Rights to minerals or petroleum become effective upon the grant of the rights to an applicant, prior to the approval of the environmental management programme or plan.[119] Nevertheless, these rights can be exercised only if three requirements are met.[120] First, the necessary authorisation must be acquired.[121] Second, the relevant environmental management arrangements must be made.[122] Third, the landowner or lawful occupier of the land must be notified and consulted.[123]

10.5.2.3 Competing rights of the surface owner

Constitutional values should govern resolution of conflicts that might arise between holders of rights to minerals or petroleum and owners of land, or in regard to threats to protection of the environment.[124] A rational balance between the interests of holders of prospecting or mining rights and the landowner must be sought.[125] Under past legal dispensations pertaining to minerals, the rights to mineral exploitation were given precedence in the event of irreconcilable conflict between a landowner and the holder of a mineral right.[126] This approach was continued after commencement of the MPRDA, as is apparent from the

---

115 Section 3(2)(b) of the MPRDA.
116 Act 28 of 2008.
117 Section 106(3) of the MPRDA.
118 See the definition of 'exploration operation' in s 1 of the MPRDA.
119 *Meepo v Kotze* 2008 (1) SA 104 (NC) at 125H.
120 *Meepo* at 125H-I.
121 Section 5(4)(b) of the MPRDA.
122 Section 5(4)(a) and 93(2) read with 69(2) of the MPRDA.
123 Section 5(4)(c) of the MPRDA.
124 *Meepo* at 114B-C.
125 *Meepo* at 111C.
126 *Hudson v Mann* 1950 (4) SA 485 (T) at 488E-G.

decision in *Anglo Operations Ltd v Sandhurst Estates (Pty) Ltd.*[127] The hierarchy created in common law has, therefore, survived the shift to the new order of mineral law.

Where rights are infringed, the possibility of compensation for expropriation arises. The Minister is expressly empowered by s 55(1) of the MPRDA to expropriate property for purposes of prospecting or mining if it is necessary to achieve the objectives of the MPRDA. This would be a formal expropriation incorporating provisions of the Expropriation Act.[128]

Surface use of an owner's land for the purposes of seeking or extracting minerals or petroleum will, however, not necessarily be subject to compensation, except in cases of formal expropriation, or where the measures in terms of s 54 of the MPRDA are relevant.[129] Section 54 provides for compensation under certain circumstances to be paid by the holder of the prospecting right or mining right.[130]

The decision in *Meepo v Kotze* suggests that compensation may further be claimed under item 12 of Schedule II to the MPRDA for expropriations above and beyond those occurring during the conversion of old order rights to prospecting and mining rights.[131] Although item 12(1) pertains to the transitional arrangements, it is cast in such wide terms that:

> [*a*]*ny person who can prove that his or her property has been expropriated in terms of any provision of [the MPRDA] may claim compensation from the State.*[132]

A landowner who loses her surface use because of the granting of a prospecting right or mining right, may hence claim compensation for expropriation[133] invoking this provision.

10.5.3 Transfer and encumbrance of rights to minerals or petroleum

As is common with registered limited real rights, registered mineral or petroleum rights can be alienated. Where a different right holder is envisaged, the written consent of the Director-General of the Department of Minerals and Energy is required.[134] Where the right is to be used as collateral, e.g. to secure a mortgage, then consent is not required if certain conditions are met.[135] Mineral or petroleum rights that are not registered may not be transferred, leased or encumbered by mortgage.

10.5.4 Termination of rights to minerals or petroleum

Rights to minerals or petroleum are not infinite. When the period for which they were granted expires, the rights lapse.[136] They also lapse when the holder dies or, in the case of a juristic person, when it is deregistered without a successor in title. Liquidation or sequestration

---

127 2007 (2) SA 363 (SCA) at 327J, 373A-B and 373E-F.
128 Section 55(2) of the MPRDA.
129 *Meepo* at 110H.
130 Badenhorst, PJ & Mostert, H 'Duelling prospecting rights: a non-custodial second?' (2008) *TSAR* 819 at 824.
131 Badenhorst, PJ & Mostert, H 'Duelling prospecting rights: a non-custodial second? (2008) *TSAR* 820 at 824; *Meepo v Kotze* 2008 (1) SA 104 (NC).
132 Own italics.
133 Dale, MO et al. (2005) *South African Mineral and Petroleum Law* (Durban, LexisNexis Butterworths) p MPRDA-129 also mention this possibility.
134 See s 11(1) of the MPRDA read with s 69(2); Item 1 of the Ministerial delegation of 12 May 2004.
135 Section 11(3) of the MPRDA.
136 Section 56*(a)* of the MPRDA.

also lead to the rights lapsing,[137] as does cancellation[138] or abandonment of the rights.[139] When the rights lapse, the holder must apply for a closure certificate.[140] Deregistration of lapsed rights is necessary.[141]

10.6 Social and environmental responsibility and liability of the mineral and petroleum industry

The MPRDA was enacted to achieve the necessary regulatory control to manage broadening of access to mineral resources, to ensure socially responsible extraction of minerals, alongside the measures facilitating environmentally responsible procedures. To these ends, the legislature opted to replace the previous dispensation of mineral law, rooted in private law, with a system of public law rights. The state has the capacity to dispose of rights in minerals, even though it cannot be regarded as having ownership in the private law sense over such minerals. The following paragraphs deal briefly with two important objectives of the MPRDA, namely to ensure socially and environmentally responsible mining. These objectives place certain expectations upon the applicants for, and holders of, rights granted in terms of the MPRDA.

10.6.1 Environmental provisions of the MPRDA

When applying for mineral or petroleum rights, an applicant must comply with requirements designed to manage the effect of extraction of minerals or petroleum on the environment. Included in these requirements is the need to make financial provision for the rehabilitation or management of negative environmental impacts.[142] Responsibility for environmental damage, pollution or ecological degradation arises whether it occurs inside or outside the boundaries of the area to which the permission, permit or right relates.[143]

The holder of a mineral or petroleum right remains responsible for any environmental liability,[144] pollution or ecological degradation, and its management, until a closure certificate has been issued.[145] Being responsible for 'environmental damage' implies delictual liability for non-compliance with the requirements of the MPRDA.[146]

---

137 Section 56*(d)* of the MPRDA.
138 Section 56*(e)* of the MPRDA.
139 Section 56*(f)* of the MPRDA.
140 Section 43(3)*(a)* of the MPRDA.
141 Section 5(1)*(d)* of the MTRA.
142 Section 41(1) of the MPRDA.
143 Sections 38(1)*(e)* and 69(2) of the MPRDA.
144 Dale, MO et al. (2005) *South African Mineral and Petroleum Law* (Durban, LexisNexis Butterworths) p MPRD-374 submit that the object of s 43(1) of the MPRDA is not to impose environmental liability but to emphasise that environmental responsibility remains until a closure certificate is issued.
145 Sections 43(1) and 69(2); item 18 of the Ministerial Delegation of 12 May 2004. Dale, MO et al. (2005) *South African Mineral and Petroleum Law* (Durban, LexisNexis Butterworths) pp MPRD-374 to MPRDA-378 indicate that the extent of exoneration is ambiguous.
146 Section 38(1) of the MPRDA.

10.6.2 Black economic empowerment and access to mining

One of the objectives of the MPRDA is to expand substantially and meaningfully opportunities for historically disadvantaged persons[147] (including women) to enter the mineral and petroleum industries, and to benefit from exploitation of the nation's mineral and petroleum resources. This objective is reflected in several aspects of the Act, including the requirements for conversion of old order mining rights,[148] and the requirements for applications for new mining rights.[149] Holders of mineral and petroleum rights are required to demonstrate compliance with black economic empowerment on an annual basis. Black economic empowerment refers to the social or economic strategy aimed at redressing the results of past or present discrimination based on race, gender or other disability or historical disadvantage.

A mining industry empowerment charter was developed, which provides for a scorecard approach to facilitate processing of licence conversions.[150] The mining charter is not legally relevant to conversion of pre-existing or old order rights to new order rights.[151] Yet, certain elements of the charter have found their way into the regulations made under the Act, where the content of the social and labour plan that must be filed with lodgement of an old order mining right[152] is at stake. However, both the charter and scorecard are policy documents, which at best may act as guidelines in the lodgement for conversions or in applications for new rights.[153]

10.7 Mineral law as part of property law

The MPRDA represents an overhaul of South African mineral law. It was necessitated by discrimination, inequality and injustice, which pervaded South African society throughout the preceding century. In particular, its laws on land and minerals were affected. The goals of broadening access to the mineral resources of South Africa, and of ensuring socially and environmentally responsible approaches to the extraction of minerals are pursued in a consistent (albeit occasionally clumsy) manner by this Act.

As this chapter demonstrated, legislature opted to replace the existing system of mineral law, which was rooted in the principles of private law, with a system of public law rights to achieve the regulatory control that is necessary to manage the processes of ensuring socially and environmentally responsible use of the country's mineral and petroleum resources. These rights retain a strong proprietary character, but cannot be theorised in terms of existing private law categorisation of property rights. As such, the new system of mineral rights is theoretically not comparable with previous generations of mineral law. Where a comparison must be undertaken, the only conclusion can be that rights conferred

---

147 Historically disadvantaged persons are defined as '(a) any person, category of persons or community, disadvantaged by unfair discrimination before the Constitution took effect; (b) any association, a majority of whose members are persons contemplated in paragraph (a); (c) any juristic person other than an association, in which persons contemplated in paragraph (a) own and control a majority of the issued capital or members' interest and are able to control a majority of the members' votes.' Section 1 of the MPRDA.
148 Item 7 of Schedule II to the MPRDA.
149 Section 123(1)(h) of the MPRDA.
150 Para 4.11, Broad-Based Socio-Economic Empowerment Charter for the South African Mining Industry GN 1639, 2004 *Government Gazette* 26661 (13.08.2004).
151 Dale, MO et al. *South African Mineral and Petroleum Law* (2005) (Durban, LexisNexis Butterworths) p App-2.
152 Item 7, of Schedule II, to the MPRDA.
153 Dale, MO et al. *South African Mineral and Petroleum Law* (2005) (Durban, LexisNexis Butterworths) p App-2.

in the current generation of mineral law, differ **conceptually** from those of the previous generations, but **functionally** they convey the same or similar abilities. Control over the vesting and duration of such rights, and the alienability and value thereof lies primarily with the state, and not (any more) with a private mineral rights holder or landowner, as the case may be.

To demonstrate: application of the *nemo plus iuris* rule presupposes that the state has the ability to dispose of the rights to minerals and petroleum. However, this need not mean[154] that the state must be the owner in the private law sense of all minerals and petroleum. It does require that the state be vested with the capacity to dispose of the rights. The latter was achieved statutorily by affording the state exclusive capacity to decide about granting of such rights, and by affording the state control over the process of awards.

10.8 Concluding remarks

Although the new mineral law defies a private law approach to minerals,[155] it does not deny the proprietary overlay of rights granted in terms of the MPRDA. This is confirmed by the explicit typification of several of the new order rights as 'limited real rights', and the provision for security of tenure through compulsory registration requirements. The perpetuation of a proprietary characterisation of rights, alongside provisions for registration thereof in the names of the holders of such rights, suggests that the new generation of mineral law goes beyond being merely regulatory. Indeed, one could venture to say that the new mineral law remains connected to property law, but that it has a much more prominent public character than it had in the past.

---

154 *Silberberg & Schoeman Property* p 674.
155 Dale, MO et al. (2005) *South African Mineral and Petroleum Law* (Durban, LexisNexis Butterworths) p MPRDA-114.

Chapter 11

Water

'Water is life, sanitation is dignity.'
Department of Water Affairs *'Strategic Framework for Water Services'* **September 2003**

11.1	Introduction	283
11.2	Brief historical background	285
11.3	The Water Act 54 of 1965	286
11.4	New water paradigm	286
11.5	The Water Services Act 108 of 1997	287
11.6	The National Water Act 36 of 1998: A new approach	288
11.6.1	State acts as trustee	288
11.6.2	Access to and use of water	288
11.6.3	Servitudes	289
11.6.3.1	Servitudes in respect of water	289
11.6.3.2	Creation of servitudes	290
11.6.3.3	Rights and duties of relevant parties	291
11.6.3.4	Cancellation of servitudes	291
11.7	Implications of the new water dispensation	292
11.7.1	Structural implications	292
11.7.2	Implications for the general public	293
11.8	Concluding remarks	294

11.1 Introduction

As the quote above indicates, the South African government is extremely aware of the basic needs fulfilled and constitutional values realised by access to water. Millions of people are affected on a daily basis by the fact that potable water and sanitation services are not provided to optimal standards. To realise the above-mentioned ideal in practice, water as a natural resource has been placed under the custodianship and responsibility of the South African government.[1]

---

1 See, in general, *Silberberg & Schoeman Property* ch 24; Van der Walt *Constitutional Property Law* (Cape Town, Juta) pp 370–378.

Although water always has been a scarce commodity in South Africa, it has not always been the property of government. Instead, according to common law, water fell within both the public and private domains. There was, however, a clear understanding that categories of private and public water existed and that private rights in water (ownership) formed an integral part of landownership.[2]

The National Water Act[3] terminated the distinction between private and public water in 1998. The need to regulate a scarce commodity more effectively was not the only motivation for promulgating new legislation. Access to and control of water was intrinsically linked with landownership. As landownership was skewed on the basis of race, access to and control of water was similarly distorted. Accordingly, the legal notion of water had to be 'opened up' or 'liberated' so that more persons could, in principle, have access to or control of it. All water is now regarded as public water. Furthermore, automatic private rights in water have been abolished and replaced by use rights or licences. Rights in water, therefore, no longer form part of the content of ownership. These changes explain why a discussion of water rights must now be dealt with under limited real rights in property, rather than under ownership and its entitlements.[4]

Water law straddles both property law and human rights law. On the one hand, there is the technical proprietary nature of possible limited real rights in water that must be considered. On the other, water as a scarce commodity has a human rights dimension. Access to water is a fundamental human right in the constitutional paradigm.[5] Although a discussion of this dimension of water rights may perhaps be seen by some as more suited to human rights jurisprudence, this aspect can no longer be severed from the other aspects of water rights that must be treated according to the rules of property law. This discussion of water rights takes account of the human rights aspect of water as well as its proprietary aspects.

This section explains how integral ownership entitlements relating to water developed into limited real rights or use rights (licences); why the change was desirable; and how these rights are being managed presently in the property law context. To begin with, a brief discussion of common law and the pre-1997 approach to water is helpful. This enables an appreciation of the dramatic change to the legal framework for water in South Africa. Whereas ownership entitlements were formerly the point of departure, the focus now is on access to water as a basic human right linked with dignity. A brief historical background introduces the common law approach, after which a discussion of the previous Water Act of 1965[6] follows. Thereafter, the new water paradigm and possible implications are discussed. Particular aspects that affect the study of property law are also considered.

11.2   Brief historical background

The common law approach was that a landowner was owner of all water arising on his land.[7] This meant that a landowner owned surface and underground water and, in general, could utilise the water as he wished within the limits of the law. Included was the power

---

2   *Silberberg & Schoeman Property* pp 717–718.
3   Act 36 of 1998.
4   See ch 5 above.
5   See s 27 of the Constitution.
6   Act 54 of 1965.
7   *Silberberg & Schoeman Property* p 658.

to grant water servitudes to non-owners where appropriate.[8] Accordingly, water could be owned privately or a limited real right in water could vest in another person, e.g. where neighbouring landowners did not have sufficient water on their own properties.

These rules stemmed from Roman-Dutch law, which forms the basis of South African common law.[9] Significantly, the development of seventeenth century Roman-Dutch law in the Netherlands occurred in a location with an abundance of water. It is understandable, therefore, that these common law rules were not necessarily best suited to the South African context where water is generally scarcer.

The principle of 'riparian ownership' dominated the South African water dispensation until 1998. Riparian ownership means ownership of water that is based on being an owner of land bordered by a river or stream. The principle of riparian ownership entails that every riparian owner is entitled to use a reasonable share of the water in the stream or river concerned. The concept of riparian ownership in relation to perennial rivers did not originate in the Netherlands, but developed with reference to English law.[10] Because of its colonial past, South African law adopted this concept along with the Roman-Dutch principles.[11]

Because perennial[12] streams also contained non-perennial water[13] that, to be useful, required storage, the water in a river was divided into 'normal flow' and 'surplus' water.[14] A reasonable share of the normal flow was available to all riparian owners. Any riparian owner of an original farm was entitled to store as much of the surplus water as he could reasonably use. When the original farm was subdivided and there was more than one riparian owner, each was entitled to a reasonable share of that to which the whole farm was entitled.[15] This approach made it almost impossible to divide and allocate water on a long river. This difficulty led to the development of the principle of 'prior appropriation' whereby secondary users were entitled to take only water left over after the first user. Further users similarly had to respect earlier users.

The two-fold legal foundations of South African water law, namely Roman-Dutch and, to a lesser extent, English law, clearly were not best suited to South African conditions. Nevertheless, the main common law principles, as set out above, were incorporated into the first Water Act[16] to apply nationally as discussed below.

11.3 The Water Act 54 of 1965

The distinction between public and private water was embodied in this Act. Although its main focus was to regulate access to and use of water, the point of departure was that private claims of riparian landowners regarding public water, as well as all claims of landowners in relation to private water, were acknowledged.

---

8   Thompson, H (2006) *Water law: a practical approach to resource management and the provision of services* (Cape Town, Juta) p 27 (hereafter cited as Thompson *Water Law*).
9   See ch 1 above.
10 *Silberberg & Schoeman Property* p 718 and the sources mentioned there.
11 Thompson *Water Law* pp 17–32.
12 'Perennial' means 'enduring' or 'continual'; thus, the river or stream does not run dry.
13 E.g. when there is a seasonal increase in rainfall.
14 Thompson *Water Law* p 56.
15 See for an excellent exposition of the Roman and Roman-Dutch water law as incorporated in South Africa, Burger A, 'Roman water Law (Part 1)' (2007) *TSAR* at 72–95.
16 Act 54 of 1965.

Although public water was defined generally as the water flowing or found in or derived from the bed of a public stream, whether visible or not,[17] various requirements determined whether a stream was deemed to be a public stream. However, the following sources all constituted private water: spring water; rainwater; surface water and drainage water before it joined a public stream; water flowing or found in or derived from a stream that was not a public stream; groundwater which was not flowing or found in or derived from the bed of a public stream after it had been abstracted; and public water that left a public stream naturally, for example after a flood.

Apart from these specific definitions, water was difficult to classify, invariably resulting in the Water Court having to adjudicate the matter. Classification was essential since it determined whether landowners could use the water as they pleased. Landowners had exclusive use and enjoyment of water on the surface of or under the ground of their properties. When authorised by a permit issued by the then Minister of Water Affairs, the landowner, furthermore, was free to alienate or otherwise dispose of water to any other person or user.[18] The notion of riparian owners, including use by up- and downstream landowners, was also formulated and regulated in detail in the Act.

Private ownership over public water could not exist,[19] although control over, use and enjoyment of such water was regulated in detail in the Act.

11.4 New water paradigm

Before the new water paradigm was introduced in the 1990s, water rights in South Africa were exercised mainly as follows.[20] Landowners were owners of all water on or under the surface of their land. Riparian owners did not own public water in rivers or streams, but could make use of the water by way of a permit system in accordance with the riparian principle as regulated by the Water Act. Downstream landowners also had a 'reasonable share' in surplus water, regulated by a permit system or a water division scheme entered into by the landowners concerned. Servitude holders could acquire a right to use water on or from servient land. These constituted limited real rights in relation to someone else's property.

Although there was a tendency to increase state control over water resources with each legislative measure passed since 1912,[21] the new water dispensation introduced in 1997 and 1998 wholly dispensed with private control in favour of firm state control. This shift coincided with the commencement of a new constitutional dispensation for South Africa. Concepts that, traditionally, were viewed through a private law lens, suddenly required a new approach as the Constitution specifically provided for reform measures relating to access to water, food, land, housing, minerals and all natural resources in general.

With regard to water, the following sections of the Constitution are relevant: s 27(1)(b) provides that everyone has the right to have access to sufficient food and water; while s 27(2) requires the state to take reasonable legislative and other measures, within its available resources, to achieve the progressive realisation of each of these rights. Section 25(8) provides that land reform may not impede the state from undertaking legislative and other

---

17 Section 1 of the Water Act 54 of 1965.
18 In terms of s 5(2) of the Water Act 54 of 1965.
19 Section 6(1) of the Water Act 54 of 1965.
20 *Silberberg & Schoeman Property* pp 717–718.
21 Irrigation and Conservation of Water Act 8 of 1912; see also Thompson *Water Law* p 59.

measures to achieve reform to redress the results of past racial discrimination. In addition, s 25(4) makes it clear that property is not limited to land. Section 24 is also relevant, because it provides for a safe environment, thereby including ecologically sustainable development and use of natural resources. When all the reform provisions are read together, as they should be,[22] it is clear that reform of all natural resources – including water – is provided for, either directly or indirectly.

The advent of the constitutional provisions resulted in various policy documents (e.g. the Free Basic Water Strategy) and two main legislative measures, namely the Water Services Act[23] and the National Water Act [24] preceded by the White Paper on a National Water Policy for South Africa in 1997. The 1997 Act sets out who has responsibility for realising access to water in practice, as well as how it is to be done. Accordingly, the 1997 Act provides the practical steps to be taken in this regard.

The departure from the common law approach to private and public water and the corresponding private rights in relation to water is to be found in the 1998 Act. This Act drastically affects the exposition of common law water rights as set out above. 'Authorisation to use water' as opposed to ownership of water is now the point of departure.

The discussion that follows sets out the most important measures of both Acts in an attempt to explain the new approach to water rights. First, the provisions of the Water Services Act[25] relevant to a property law analysis are outlined in brief. Then, the National Water Act[26] is discussed in more detail.

11.5 The Water Services Act 108 of 1997

Generally, the Water Services Act aims to facilitate access to water. Specifically, it sets the standards and norms relevant to the provision of water; water services development plans; a regulatory framework for water services institutions and intermediaries; as well as for financial assistance and monitoring of services. Essentially, this Act provides the regulatory framework for all role players responsible for realising access to water in practice.

The Act deals with household as well as industrial access to water. 'Basic water supply' is the prescribed minimum standard of water supply services necessary for a reliable supply of a sufficient quantity and quality of water to households (including informal households), to support life and personal hygiene.[27]

'Water services' entails the provision of water supply and sanitation services. A water services authority is a municipality, including a district or rural council, as defined in the Local Government Transition Act.[28] The municipality or local authority is the entity responsible for ensuring access to water services. The Act includes an entity called a water board, which is an organ of state established to provide water services to other water services institutions within its service area.

---

22 Van der Walt *Constitutional Property Law* pp 284, 369.
23 Act 108 of 1997.
24 Act 36 of 1998.
25 Act 108 of 1997.
26 Act 36 of 1998.
27 Section 1(ii) and (iii). A 'basic water supply' was determined initially at 25 *l* per person per day or 6 kl per month per household.
28 Act 209 of 1993.

An essential component of successful water services provision is monitoring and intervention. Where necessary, intervention at different levels and at different stages of the process is possible. Provision is also made for financial assistance to water services institutions.

The Water Services Act thus provides the technical and practical framework within which the water services providers operate at various levels. At the same time, it prescribes norms and standards, and a monitoring system.

11.6 The National Water Act 36 of 1998: A new approach

Fundamental reform of the prevailing water law is the main focus of the Act, which commenced on 1 October 1998 and repealed all former legislation dealing with water.[29] The point of departure is that water is a scarce natural resource to which everyone is entitled to have equitable access; but, due to the past racially discriminatory and fragmentary approach, access has been skewed. Accordingly, it is now government's responsibility to regulate and preserve this scarce natural resource, taking into account environmental and sustainable development considerations. The Act dismantles the common law approach to access, control over and use of water rights and effectively 'opens up' the notion of water in South Africa to be accessed more equitably. The new premise is that a person is entitled to use water only if that use is permissible under the Act.

11.6.1 State acts as trustee

As trustee of water sources in the country, the state has various duties and responsibilities.[30] Accordingly, the state is empowered to regulate the use, flow and control of all water within the Republic of South Africa.[31] The Minister of Water and Environmental Affairs is responsible for the realisation of the ideals and objectives of the Act.[32] The practical aspects of carrying out these responsibilities, in terms of the Water Services Act,[33] have been discussed above.[34]

11.6.2 Access to and use of water

As mentioned above, the distinction between private and public water no longer exists. Private ownership of water has been abolished. Since the state is custodian of and the entity responsible for regulating access to water, any person (including a juristic person) who wants access to and use of water can do so only in accordance with the Act. Generally, this means that an existing lawful use of water does not require a licence, e.g. water for reasonable domestic use, domestic gardens, animals, firefighting and recreation.[35]

Existing lawful water use may continue under certain conditions, for instance to the extent that it is not limited, restricted or prohibited by the Act. Any use of water is conditional in that it may not be wasted, and is subject to any restrictions and limitations under the Act.

---

29 See also the aims set out in s 2 of the Act, namely, the development of water, the effective use thereof, and equitable access to water. Sustainability and equity form the foundations of the current water paradigm.
30 In terms of s 3(1)-(3) of the National Water Act 36 of 1998.
31 In terms of s 3(3) of the National Water Act 36 of 1998.
32 In terms of s 3(2) of the National Water Act 36 of 1998.
33 Act 108 of 1997.
34 See pp 287-288 above.
35 As set out in Schedule 1 to the Act; see also s 4(1).

For other purposes, a licence is needed to gain access to and make use of water. There are some exceptions to this rule, e.g. where the relevant authorising authority[36] has abandoned this requirement,[37] or where the use of water is in accordance with a general authorisation to that effect.[38]

11.6.3 Servitudes

The main points of the Act have been set out above, namely that private ownership of water has been abolished, and that licences to use water are now required. A relevant question, however, is whether servitudes (limited real rights to make use of water belonging to another landowner) fit within the new paradigm. Below, this question is considered with reference to the types of servitudes that may exist in respect of water, the creation of such servitudes and their termination.

11.6.3.1 Servitudes in respect of water

Common law servitudes of water were usually praedial servitudes in that two parcels of land were identified: the servient land provided the water and the dominant land enjoyed the benefit thereof. Registration of the servitude resulted in a permanent burden on the servient land.[39]

The National Water Act makes provision for servitudes where there is a need to take water from one property to another where the water is needed. Persons authorised to use water may acquire personal or praedial servitudes for abutment, the abstraction and leading of water, and for submersion (of land by water), as is necessary to meet the requirements of the particular authorisation.[40]

A servitude of abutment is the right to occupy, by means of a waterworks, the bed or banks of a stream or adjacent land belonging to another. A servitude of *aquaeductus* is the right to occupy land belonging to another by means of a waterworks for abstracting and/or leading water *(aquaehaustus)*. A servitude of submersion entails a right to occupy land belonging to another by submerging it, i.e. covering it with water. These statutory servitudes may be personal or praedial.

The holder of a statutory personal servitude need not utilise the water itself and need not own the land where the water is used. It would seem that these servitudes will generally be utilised by water regulators to provide water services. Unusually, the statutory personal servitude is transferable from one water regulator to another in the case of water mismanagement.[41] It should be noted, therefore, that these statutory personal servitudes of water differ from common law water servitudes, not only in regard to content and transferability, but also in regard to their overall aim and purpose.

If the servitude is praedial, the claimant must own the property on which the water is to be used.[42] In the usual way, the successor in title to the owner becomes the holder of the servitude, which generally does not lapse.

---

36 As defined in the Act.
37 In terms of s 22(1)*(c)*.
38 In terms of ss 4(3), 22(1)*(a)*(iii).
39 See for more detail *Silberberg & Schoeman Property* pp 322-336.
40 In terms of s 127(1)-(2).
41 In terms of s 136(1)*(a)-(b)*.
42 In terms of s 127.

11.6.3.2 Creation of servitudes

In this section, the creation of servitudes is discussed. Generally, the procedure to create servitudes in respect of water is statutory, but the possibility of alternative ways of creation has not been completely abandoned.

Statutory procedure. A water servitude is created by registering a notarial deed in terms of the Deeds Registries Act[43] or by a court order.[44] The process of creating a servitude under the Act starts with written notice to the relevant landowner setting out the application for the servitude. The particular content of the notice is prescribed.[45] Essentially, an applicant must indicate what he aims to do with the servitude, why it is needed and how it is going to be utilised. A plan depicting the location of the proposed waterworks has to accompany the application. Any person who has an interest in the land, for instance a lessee, also needs to receive a copy of the notice.

Within the prescribed time after the notices have been served, an application claiming the servitude must be made to a high court. The court must consider various factors before the servitude can be granted.[46]

The acquisition, amendment or cancellation of a servitude by court order takes effect only when the order is noted in the Deeds Registry.[47] Where payment of compensation is appropriate, the requirements of just and equitable compensation and the considerations listed in s 25(3) of the Constitution also need to be taken into account.[48]

> **PAUSE FOR REFLECTION**
>
> **Alternative to statutory procedure**
>
> Relying on s 132(2) of the National Water Act, which states that nothing in that section[49] prevents a person from choosing to register the acquisition, amendment or cancellation of a servitude in accordance with the Deeds Registries Act,[50] Thompson[51] explains that the claimant of the servitude and the landowner may accordingly enter into an agreement on the matter. Such agreement may be registered as a servitude as contemplated in the Water Act without approaching a high court beforehand.
>
> Furthermore, the possibility of creating a servitude in terms of common law and registering it accordingly also exists.[52] The provisions of the National Water Act would not be applicable to these types of servitudes. Although no case law has focused on this issue as such, it would seem as if two sets of servitudes in relation to water would co-exist in practice.

---

43 Act 47 of 1937.
44 In terms of s 129(1)*(a)-(b)*.
45 Item 8 of Schedule 2 to the National Water Act 36 of 1998.
46 In terms of s 130.
47 In terms of s 132 of the Deeds Registries Act 47 of 1937.
48 See pp 118*ff* above.
49 But providing for the noting of servitudes.
50 Act 47 of 1937.
51 Thompson *Water Law* p 572.
52 Section 132(2); See Thompson *Water Law* p 572.

11.6.3.3 Rights and duties of relevant parties

Where a water servitude is created in accordance with the National Water Act, both the holder and the landowner have various rights and duties.[53] These are similar to the landowner's common law rights and duties, and include a right of reasonable access to the land subject to the servitude to enable effective use and enjoyment of the servitude. The passivity requirement, namely that a positive duty may not be placed on the servient landholder,[54] is essentially maintained with regard to these statutory servitudes. When the owner of land subject to the servitude is of the opinion that the servitude area, the waterworks and access roads are in need of repair and maintenance, the servitude holder has to be informed in writing to effect the necessary repairs. If the servitude holder fails to carry out the repairs, the landowner may arrange for the work to be done and may recover any reasonable costs from the servitude holder.[55]

11.6.3.4 Cancellation of servitudes

An application for cancellation of a servitude may be lodged with the high court when the authorisation associated with the servitude has lapsed; if the rights and obligations in respect of the servitudes have not been exercised for a period of three years; or for any other lawful reason.[56]

The acquisition of servitudes under the National Water Act is not prescriptive. Section 129, read with s 132(2) of the Act provides that a servitude contemplated under the Act *may* be acquired or an amendment or cancellation *may* be obtained under that secti that a person may still elect to register the acquisition, amendment or cancellation under the Deeds Registries Act. Accordingly, two sets of servitudes relating to water may operate in parallel, although the actual complications and consequences of such co-existence are difficult to contemplate as yet.

---

53 In terms of s 128.
54 See pp 241–243 above.
55 Section 128(3)–(4).
56 Section 133; Thompson *Water Law* p 573.

Basic distinctions between these two sets of servitudes may be set out as follows:

Table 11.1: Distinctions between common law and statutory water servitudes

	Common law water servitudes	**National Water Act servitudes**
Requirements	Common law requirements[57]	Statutory requirements – ss 127, 129
Mechanism	Chiefly praedial servitudes relating to a dominant and a servient land parcel	Personal and praedial servitudes equally employed
Aim(s)	Main aim: address need of dominant land parcel due to lack of water	Diverse aims: • address lack of water • provide access to water • enable water services institutions to provide water for water users, thus water distribution
Exercise of rights and duties	Rights and duties exercised on the basis of *civiliter modo*	Rights and duties essentially *civiliter modo* point of departure, but may include particular, unique and additional rights and duties depending on the particular characteristics and purposes of said servitude
Termination	Common law lapse and cancellation of servitudes[58]	Cancellation of servitude linked with termination of water authorisation; non-exercise of rights for a continuous period of three years; or cancellation on any lawful ground

11.7 Implications of the new water dispensation

In this section, the implications of the new water dispensation are outlined. That access to water is regulated by statute has several important implications, both as far as the structure of the law is concerned, as well as for the general interest of the public.

11.7.1 Structural implications

The new statutory paradigm for water law means that it is imperative, in the first place, that the relevant legislation is implemented effectively and monitored regularly.

Second, legislative measures that affect the provision of water should be sensibly aligned. Although the National Water Act has 'opened up' access to water, stringent procedures incorporated in the Local Government: Municipal Structures Act[59] require strict compliance. Ironically, therefore, a more 'open' approach to water has resulted in an intricate, complicated regulatory system.

Third, all role players' responsibilities and duties must be clear, while, at the same time, these parties must be empowered to contribute effectively and in line with constitutional imperatives. Presently, no legislative measure regulates the role of traditional leaders in relation to water resources management despite the fact that traditional leaders are already

---

57 Compare ch 9 above.
58 Compare ch 9 above.
59 Act 117 of 1998.

involved, on a daily basis, in regulating and providing access to land and natural resources such as water. Traditional leaders have representation in local government structures and, as such, are involved in the provision of water services. Incorporation of traditional leaders in the water management structures in the relevant areas in South Africa would formalise their role in this regard more clearly.

Lastly, the practicality of placing responsibility for the cost-effectiveness of water delivery in the hands of local authorities already struggling with budgeting and capacity shortfalls is problematic. One of the underlying motivations for introducing wall-to-wall municipalities was that the resulting tax bases would enable local authorities to provide services at a sustainable level. Unfortunately this has not proven to be successful, especially in relation to rural municipalities. In this regard, more emphasis may be placed on public-private partnerships to improve provision of services. Greater subsidisation from provincial government to municipalities struggling with cost recovery may furthermore improve the situation.[60]

11.7.2 Implications for the general public

Since the advent of the Water Services Act[61] and the National Water Act,[62] government is clearly more involved in broadening provision of water services to the general public. Its involvement takes place at various levels and through different roles. But whether the new water law paradigm affects the general public may be questioned.

For the general public who live in urban areas, or in towns and settlements in rural areas, the rights relating to use of water have not altered much in practice: normal everyday use of water continues as before. In other words, additional authorisations or licences are unnecessary for the usual daily consumption of water.

However, the general position has improved greatly for some people in that a certain amount of free water per person per day is now guaranteed. In March 2009, in *City of Johannesburg and Others v Mazibuko and Others*,[63] the Supreme Court of Appeal confirmed that the City of Johannesburg had to increase the free basic water supply from 25 l to 42 l per person per day for each Phiri resident who could not afford to pay for water. The provision of free water would continue to the extent that it is reasonable to do so, having regard to available resources and other relevant considerations. The City of Johannesburg was also ordered to reconsider and reformulate its free water policy in light of the finding that the prepaid water meters used in the Phiri settlement were unlawfully installed. It should be noted that the increased free basic supply of water is available only to persons resident in Phiri registered as indigents with the City.

The matter went to the Constitutional Court, which held on 8 October 2009 that it is inappropriate for a court to decide on the amount of water that is sufficient (in terms of s 27(1)(*b*) of the Constitution), and that this is a matter for the executive arm of the state. Second, the court held that the Free Basic Water policy and the introduction of pre-paid water meters in Phiri as a result of Operation Gcin'amanzi did not violate s 27, and were not unfair or discriminatory.[64]

---

60 De Vissier J, Cottle E & Mettler J 'Realizing the right of access to water: pipe dream or watershed?' (2003) 1 *Law, Democracy & Development* at 27–54.
61 Act 108 of 1997.
62 Act 36 of 1998.
63 2009 (3) SA 592 (SCA).
64 *Lindiwe Mazibuko and Others v City of Johannesburg and Others* CCT 39/09 [2009] ZACC 28.

11.8 Concluding remarks

The water paradigm has changed dramatically. However, the use of common law water servitudes is still an option. The viability and suitability of two sets of water servitudes remain to be seen, especially in light of the general tenor and aims of the Act. Hence it is envisaged that common law water servitudes will eventually be replaced by statutory servitudes, and that the process of replacement will require the responsible authorities to regulate entitlements, to accept the surrender of entitlements to water, to issue new licences, to amend existing licences, and generally to regulate water use. This will bring about significant changes to the ambit and content of property law, which will be elaborated upon more generally in the final chapter.

Chapter 12

Real security

'Few people can buy a home immediately: by providing security for a loan, a mortgage bond enables them to do so.'
Standard Bank of Southern Africa Ltd v Saunderson 2006 (2) SA 264 (SCA) at para 1

12.1	Introduction	296
12.2	Personal and real security	297
12.3	Real security	298
12.3.1	Categories of real security rights	298
12.3.2	Functions of real security rights	299
12.3.3	Nature of real security rights	299
12.3.4	The security object	301
12.3.5	The security parties	301
12.3.6	The legal transactions	301
12.4	Express real security rights: created by agreement	303
12.4.1	Special mortgage in immovable property	303
12.4.1.1	Definition	303
12.4.1.2	Constituting the mortgage	304
12.4.1.3	Form and content of a mortgage bond	307
12.4.1.4	Operation of a mortgage bond	309
12.4.1.5	Types of mortgages	313
12.4.1.6	Termination of the mortgage	314
12.4.2	Pledge	314
12.4.2.1	Definition	314
12.4.2.2	Constituting a pledge	315
12.4.2.3	Form and content	316
12.4.2.4	Delivery	317
12.4.2.5	Operation	319
12.4.2.6	Termination of the pledge	320
12.4.3	Notarial bonds	321
12.4.3.1	General notarial bonds	322
12.4.3.2	Special notarial bonds	322
12.5	Tacit real security rights: created by operation of law	325
12.5.1	Tacit hypothecs	325
12.5.1.1	Lessor's tacit hypothec	325
12.5.1.2	Tacit hypothec of a seller under an instalment sale agreement	328

12.5.2	Right of retention or lien	328
12.5.2.1	Requirements	329
12.5.2.2	Operation	330
12.5.2.3	Types of liens	330
12.5.3	Termination	331
12.6	**Judicial real security rights: created by court order**	**332**
12.7	**Concluding remarks**	**333**

12.1 Introduction

In a country such as South Africa, which has a modern, industrialised economy alongside a developing economy, it is common for a person to incur monetary debts and obligations as he goes about his everyday life. Most of these debts are for relatively small sums of money, e.g. when someone borrows money from a friend to buy a book or to pay for a meal. Some of these debts, however, are for large sums of money, e.g. when someone borrows money from a bank or financial institution to buy a house or a motor car.

Whenever a bank, a financial institution or a friend (in each case called the creditor) lends money to a person (the debtor), the creditor risks that the debtor may not repay the loan. To reduce this risk, the law has created a process that provides some protection for the creditor. It allows the creditor to take steps to recover the money still owed in the event that the debtor does not meet his obligation to repay the debt. The process distinguishes between cases where a debtor is **unwilling** and those where a debtor is **unable** to repay the loan.

Where a debtor is unwilling to repay a loan, the creditor may apply for a court order that instructs the debtor to repay the loan. Failure to comply permits the creditor to enforce the court order by issuing a writ of execution. The writ instructs the sheriff to attach the debtor's assets to the value of the debt owed, to sell them at a public auction, and to use the proceeds to repay the debt.

Where the debtor is unable to repay the loan, the creditor may apply for a court order that declares the debtor insolvent. Upon the declaration of insolvency, ownership in the debtor's remaining assets is transferred to the court-appointed trustee of the insolvent estate. The trustee collects the debtor's assets, sells them in accordance with the creditors' instructions, and uses the proceeds to repay the debtor's debts.

Although these processes make it possible for a creditor to be repaid, at least in part, they do not cure the problem. Several disadvantages ensure that the creditor's risk remains quite high. For example, the debtor may have disposed of all his assets. This has the result that the debt-recovery process has no practical value for the creditor because there are no assets to sell.[1]

Second, the debtor's liabilities may exceed his assets. This means that the sale of assets cannot cover the amount of the debt. The consequence is that only limited practical value

---

[1] Clarke, A & Kohler, P (2005) *Property Law Commentary and Materials* (Cambridge, Cambridge University Press) pp 658-659.

flows from the debt-recovery process for the creditor, who, at best, can expect to receive only a portion of what it is owed by the debtor.[2]

Third, where the debtor's liabilities exceed his assets, there may be more than one creditor. This scenario also permits only limited practical value for each creditor. This is because the proceeds from the sale of the debtor's assets must be shared equally among the creditors. Again, each creditor can receive only a portion of what it is owed by the debtor.[3]

To protect themselves against these disadvantages, many creditors (especially banks and financial institutions) lend money to a debtor only if he is willing and able to provide security for the repayment of the loan (the principal debt).

12.2 Personal and real security

South African law provides for several different forms of security, e.g. suretyship, pledge and mortgage. There are two broad categories, namely personal security rights and real security rights. A personal security right gives the creditor a personal right against a third person (someone who is not the debtor) who undertakes personally to settle the principal debt if the debtor fails to do so.[4] A real security right, on the other hand, gives the creditor a limited real right in property that belongs to the debtor.[5] A third party who is willing to provide security for the debtor may make her own property available as well. In other words, the property does not have to belong to the debtor to provide security. In terms of the limited real right, the debtor (or third party) agrees that the creditor can use the property to settle the principal debt if the debtor fails to do so.[6]

> **PAUSE FOR REFLECTION**
>
> **Distinction between personal security right and real security right**
>
> It is important to note the distinction between a personal security right and a real security right. The former gives rise to a claim against a person, while the latter gives the creditor an interest in the property of the debtor, i.e. a limited real right in the property is created for the creditor. A real security right, therefore, is considered to be a much stronger form of security than a personal security right.[7]

Personal security rights are regulated by the law of obligations (contract and delict), while real security rights are governed by the law of property. The main focus here is on real security rights.

---

2   Scott, S 'The Law of Real and Personal Security' (2009) in Scott, J (ed) *The Law of Commerce in South Africa* (hereafter in this chapter referred to as Scott *Commerce*) p 250.
3   Clarke, A & Kohler, P (2005) *Property Law Commentary and Materials* (Cambridge, Cambridge University Press) pp 658–659.
4   *Silberberg & Schoeman Property* p 357; *Wille's Principles* p 631.
5   *Silberberg & Schoeman Property* p 357; *Wille's Principles* p 631.
6   *Silberberg & Schoeman Property* p 357; *Wille's Principles* p 631.
7   Scott *Commerce* p 250.

12.3 Real security

This section contains a discussion of the general characteristics of real security. It deals with the different categories of real security rights, the function of real security rights and the nature thereof. It also deals with the different components comprising a real security right, namely the parties, the object and the transaction.

12.3.1 Categories of real security rights

Real security rights may be divided into three categories: express real security rights, such as pledges and mortgages, created by express agreement between the creditor and the debtor; tacit real security rights, such as tacit hypothecs and liens, created by operation of law; and judicial real security rights, such as judicial pledges and mortgages, created by a court order.[8]

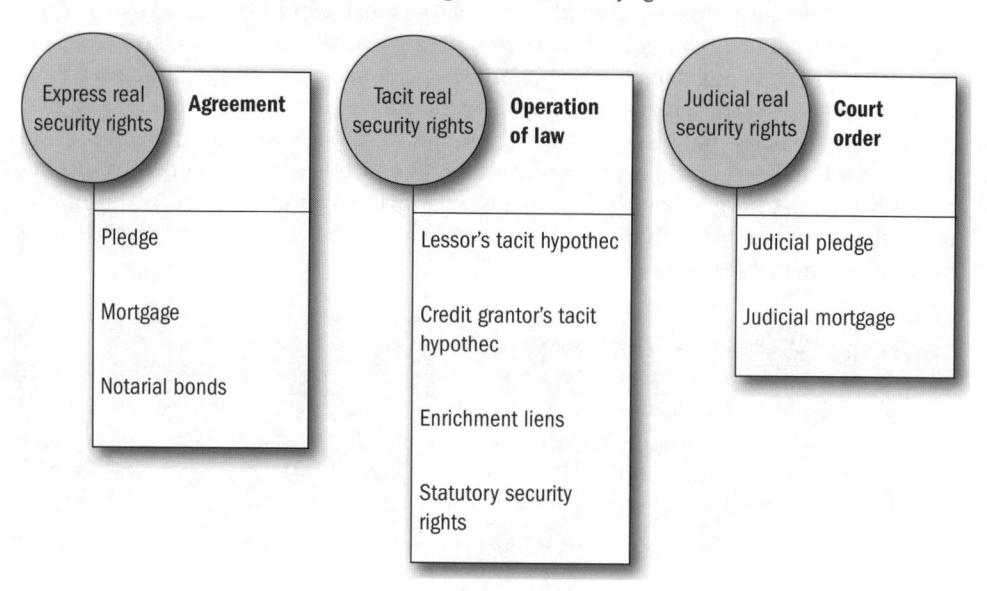

Figure 12.1: Categories of real security rights

Express real security rights — Agreement	Tacit real security rights — Operation of law	Judicial real security rights — Court order
Pledge	Lessor's tacit hypothec	Judicial pledge
Mortgage	Credit grantor's tacit hypothec	Judicial mortgage
Notarial bonds	Enrichment liens	
	Statutory security rights	

12.3.2 Functions of real security rights

Real security rights are popular in South Africa. The primary reason is that they give a secured creditor a 'right of first preference' over the property in question (the security object). This means that where a debtor is unwilling to repay the principal debt, the secured creditor can, after the security object has been attached and sold in execution, claim the proceeds from that sale before any other creditor.[9] Note, however, that a prior secured creditor with a real security right in the same security object, outranks the later creditor. In other words, the first-created real security right takes precedence.[10]

---

8 *Wille's Principles* p 631.
9 *LAWSA* Vol 17(2) at para 367.
10 See *Wille's Principles* pp 638–639 in relation to the ranking of various mortgage bond holders over the same property.

The right of first preference also applies in cases when the debtor is insolvent.[11] After the trustee has sold the debtor's assets, the secured creditor can claim the proceeds from the sale of the security object before any other creditor may do so. Only when the secured creditor's claim has been satisfied, can unsecured creditors claim from the free residue. The amount left over after the secured creditors have been paid is called the free residue. The enforcement of real security rights is thus a deviation from the principle that all creditors must be treated equally, i.e. the principle of *paritas creditorium*.

> **PAUSE FOR REFLECTION**
>
> **Functions of real security rights**
>
> Apart from conferring a right of first preference on a secured credit grantor, real security rights also perform a number of other functions:[12]
>
> First, a real security right helps the creditor to distinguish between debtors who are creditworthy and those who are not. A debtor who is willing and able to put up a valuable asset as security for a loan, e.g. his motor car, is more likely to be creditworthy. In addition, the creditor does not have to spend time and money checking the debtor's creditworthiness. This function is referred to as the 'signalling function'. The debtor's preparedness to put up a valuable asset as security sends out a signal that he is creditworthy.
>
> Second, a real security right forces the debtor to prioritise his obligations to the creditor. A debtor who has put up his home as security for a loan, would be reluctant to lose that asset. In most cases, therefore, the debtor would repay secured debts before unsecured debts. Furthermore, the debtor is likely to go to greater lengths to repay a secured debt than he would for an unsecured debt. This function is called the 'hostage function'. The threat of loss of the asset acts as an incentive to repay the principal debt.
>
> Third, a real security right confers on the creditor the power to prevent the debtor from disposing of the security object. In the case of a special mortgage in immovable property, the real security right is registered against the title deeds of the property concerned. A pledge puts the creditor in physical control of the security object. This function is known as the 'preservative function'. The fact that the debtor cannot dispose of the security object without the creditor's co-operation, preserves the creditor's rights and interests in that object.

12.3.3 Nature of real security rights

As was pointed out above,[13] real security rights are limited real rights. This means they have certain characteristics in common with other limited real rights. However, they also have certain characteristics that distinguish them from other limited real rights.

---

11 Meskin, PM (1990) *Insolvency* (Durban, Butterworths) at para 9.1.2.
12 Clarke, A & Kohler, P (2005) *Property Law Commentary and Materials* (Cambridge, Cambridge University Press) pp 660–661.
13 See p 297 above.

Characteristics in common with other limited real rights are that they are *iura in re aliena*, i.e. rights in the property of another. They confer limited and specific entitlements on their holders, and are enforceable against third persons, having an absolute nature.

Several characteristics distinguish real security rights from other limited real rights. The most important is that real security rights are said to be 'accessory' in nature. This means that the creation and continued existence of real security rights depends upon the existence of a valid underlying principal debt.[14] If there is no such principal debt, there can be no real security right. The principal debt and the real security right are, therefore, inextricably linked. An important consequence of this relationship is that if the underlying principal debt is invalid, the real security right will not come into existence. Similarly, when the principal debt is extinguished (repaid in full), the real security right is automatically terminated.

In *Kilburn v Estate Kilburn*,[15] a husband agreed to pay his wife an amount of £500. To secure this debt, he passed a notarial bond in her favour over his movable property. Some years later, the husband died insolvent and the widow claimed £500 from the insolvent estate. She argued that in terms of the notarial bond, she had a preferential claim to the proceeds of the sale of her late husband's movable property. The then Appellate Division, however, refused to enforce the notarial bond. The court explained that the existence of a real security right is dependent on a valid underlying principal debt:

> It is true that you can secure any obligation whether it be present or future, whether it be actually claimable or contingent. The security may be suspended until the obligation arises, but there must always be some obligation even if it only be a natural one to which the security obligation is accessory.[16]

The Appellate Division held that the husband had not seriously intended to pay his wife £500. He had agreed to the notarial bond simply to give her a preferential claim should he ever be declared insolvent. The principal debt was therefore invalid, which meant that the notarial bond was also invalid and, consequently, the widow had no preferential claim.

In most cases, the principal debt arises out of a contract, but it can also arise out of a delict or because of unjustified enrichment. In addition, the principal debt may arise out of a natural obligation or an obligation that is subject to a condition. A natural obligation is valid, but not legally enforceable, e.g. a gambling debt.

The principal debt may be intended to come into existence in the future.[17] For example, a businessman may establish an overdraft facility with his bank and secure this facility with a mortgage, but intend to use the overdraft facility only if and when it becomes necessary to do so. In the case of a future principal debt, the real security right is regarded as being suspended. That is, it has force only when the principal debt comes into existence.

The principal debt does not have to be an obligation to pay money.[18] It is possible to secure an obligation to perform an act or a series of acts. In practice, however, it is customary to express the principal debt as one sounding in money for a liquid amount. This is to gain the advantages of provisional sentencing proceedings to facilitate satisfaction of the creditor's claim if the debtor defaults or becomes insolvent.[19]

---

14 *Silberberg & Schoeman Property* p 358.
15 1931 AD 501.
16 *Kilburn v Estate Kilburn* 1931 AD 501 at 506.
17 *Silberberg & Schoeman Property* p 359.
18 *Silberberg & Schoeman Property* p 359; *Wille's Principles* p 633.
19 *LAWSA* Vol 17(2) at paras 329, 331.

Finally, it is important to note that unless the parties agree otherwise, a real security right secures the principal debt together with all its 'incidents'. These include any interest charged by the creditor; any costs incurred by the creditor in preserving the security; and any costs incurred by the creditor in enforcing her rights.[20]

Apart from their accessory nature, real security rights also have several other unique characteristics that distinguish them from other limited real rights. Among these are that real security rights do not confer on the creditor the entitlement to use and enjoy the security object, unless the parties agree otherwise.[21] The creditor is entitled to demand that the security object be attached and sold in execution, and that the proceeds be used to repay the principal debt.[22] Furthermore, real security rights are indivisible, which means that they secure the entire debt. The security object remains bound by the real security right until the whole debt has been paid, unless the parties agree otherwise.[23]

12.3.4 The security object

The property that secures the principal debt is referred to as the 'security object'. It is the object of the real security right. It may be movable, e.g. a diamond ring, or immovable property, e.g. a house. It may also be a single entity (*res singularis*), e.g. a horse, or a collection of things (*res universitatis*), e.g. a herd of cattle. It may even be incorporeal property, e.g. a servitude. The security object must be clearly determined and described in the security agreement in accordance with the specificity principle.[24] Note that the property may not belong to the creditor. By definition, one cannot have a limited real right in one's own property.[25]

12.3.5 The security parties

The security parties are the debtor and the creditor. Sometimes a third party is involved too. The person who provides the security object is usually the debtor. However, it can be provided by a third person. The debtor or the third party is known as the security grantor. Importantly, the security grantor must be the owner of the security object or a duly authorised representative of the owner. This is because only the owner is entitled to burden property with a real security right. The person in whose favour the security is provided is always the creditor, known as the security holder.

12.3.6 The legal transactions

Different legal transactions are involved when parties create a real security right. These transactions may be categorised as follows: the credit agreement; the security agreement; and the act that creates the real security right.

---

20 *Silberberg & Schoeman Property* p 359.
21 *LAWSA* Vol 17(2) at para 328.
22 *LAWSA* Vol 17(2) at para 328.
23 *Silberberg & Schoeman Property* p 358.
24 *Silberberg & Schoeman Property* p 360.
25 *Silberberg & Schoeman Property* p 360.

Figure 12.2: Overview of legal transactions giving rise to real security

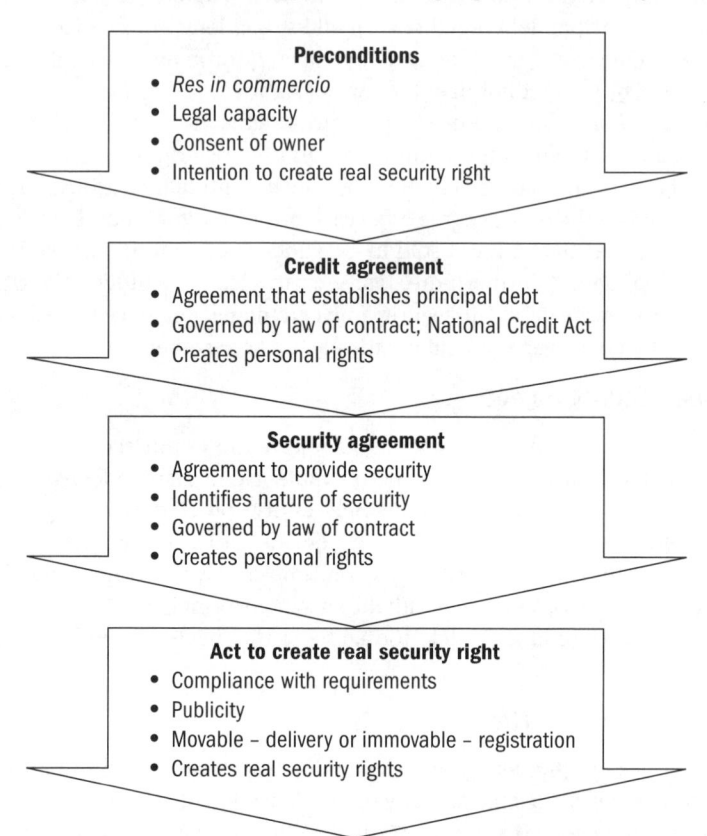

Preconditions
- *Res in commercio*
- Legal capacity
- Consent of owner
- Intention to create real security right

Credit agreement
- Agreement that establishes principal debt
- Governed by law of contract; National Credit Act
- Creates personal rights

Security agreement
- Agreement to provide security
- Identifies nature of security
- Governed by law of contract
- Creates personal rights

Act to create real security right
- Compliance with requirements
- Publicity
- Movable – delivery or immovable – registration
- Creates real security rights

A number of preconditions must be fulfilled before a real security right can come into existence.[26] These include that the property must be *res in commercio*; the parties must have capacity to enter into a legal transaction; the owner of the property must consent to the creation of the real security right; and the parties must intend to create a real security right.

The credit agreement describes the agreement between the creditor and the debtor, in terms of which the creditor lends a sum of money or makes credit available to the debtor. In other words, this agreement establishes the principal debt. The credit agreement is governed by the law of contract and the provisions of the National Credit Act.[27] It gives rise to personal rights.

The security agreement is that in which the debtor agrees to provide security for the debt created by the credit agreement. This agreement determines the nature of the security, e.g. whether it is pledge or mortgage. The security agreement is also governed by the law of contract and gives rise to personal rights.[28]

The security agreement by itself is insufficient to create a real security right. To create a real security right, the parties must comply with the requirements for establishing a limited

---

26 Silberberg & Schoeman *Property* pp 359-360.
27 Act 34 of 2005.
28 Scott *Commerce* p 261.

real right.[29] The most important requirement is that the creation of the real security right must be publicised. The manner in which the creation must be publicised differs depending upon whether the security object in question is movable or immovable. A movable security object must be delivered to the creditor. An immovable security object requires registration of the real security right in the Deeds Registry.

Consequently, a real security right in respect of movable property comes into existence when the security object has been delivered to the creditor and the other requirements have been fulfilled. With regard to immovable property, a real security right comes into existence when the real security right has been registered in the Deeds Registry and the other requirements have been fulfilled.[30]

12.4 Express real security rights: created by agreement

Real security rights created expressly, by agreement, form the bulk of the real security created in commercial activity today.[31] The two most frequently used forms are the special mortgage in respect of immovable property, and the pledge in respect of movable property. In this section, various facets of the special mortgage in immovable property are discussed. This section also deals with pledge of movables, being another type of real security that can be created expressly, by agreement. A third category of real security discussed in this section is notarial bonds.

12.4.1 Special mortgage in immovable property

The term 'mortgage' has both a wide and a narrow meaning.[32] In its wide sense, 'mortgage' refers to all limited real rights in movable or immovable property that would secure payment of a debt. The term encompasses express, tacit and judicial real security rights. This type of real security right is created by agreement between the creditor and debtor. In its narrow sense, 'mortgage' refers to specific limited real rights in immovable property to secure payment of a debt, also referred to as a 'special mortgage in immovable property'.[33] The term as it is used in this section refers to the latter use.

12.4.1.1 Definition

A special mortgage in immovable property may be defined as a limited real right in immovable property of another person to secure payment of a debt, created by registration in the Deeds Registry, pursuant to an agreement between the parties.[34] The parties to a special mortgage in immovable property are known as the 'mortgagor' and the 'mortgagee'. The mortgagor is the person whose immovable property is burdened by the mortgage, usually the debtor. The mortgagor must be the owner or the holder of a limited real right in the immovable property. The mortgagee is the person in whose favour the mortgage is created, always the creditor.[35]

---

29 See ch 3 above.
30 Scott *Commerce* pp 260–261.
31 See ch 3 above.
32 *Silberberg & Schoeman Property* p 357.
33 *LAWSA* Vol 17(2) at para 327.
34 *Wille's Principles* p 631.
35 *Silberberg & Schoeman Property* p 359.

As its title indicates, a special mortgage in immovable property is created only in respect of immovable property. In principle, both corporeal and incorporeal immovable property may be mortgaged. Land, sectional title units, a co-owner's undivided share in land, and the limited ownership of a fiduciary under a *fideicommissum* are all considered as corporeal immovable property and may, therefore, be mortgaged. The immovable property must be in existence at the time the mortgage is created and it must be *res in commercio*.

More than one immovable property can be mortgaged at the same time and in the same mortgage bond, provided that each asset is described clearly and specifically in separate paragraphs in that bond. It is not possible to register a mortgage bond that refers generally to all the debtor's (or third party's) immovable assets. This sort of global mortgage bond is specifically prohibited by s 53(1) of the Deeds Registries Act.[36] The principle of specificity requires precise description of each property.

Incorporeal immovable property, in the form of a limited real right in land (such as a usufructuary interest), may also be mortgaged. The limited real right must be capable of being dealt with separately from the land.[37]

12.4.1.2 Constituting the mortgage

A special mortgage in immovable property comes into existence as a real security right when a mortgage bond is registered in the Deeds Registry.

> **PAUSE FOR REFLECTION**
>
> **Hypothecation**
>
> The act of registering a mortgage bond in the Deeds Registry is often referred to as an 'act of hypothecation' and the mortgage bond as an 'instrument of hypothecation'.[38] The verb 'hypothecate' means 'to create a real security right in the form of a mortgage'.[39] It is important to note, however, that the word 'hypothec' does not mean the same thing as the word 'mortgage'. A mortgage is a real security right created by agreement, while a hypothec is a real security right created by operation of law.

The mortgage bond must be prepared by a conveyancer who practises in the province in which the Deeds Registry in question is located, and executed by the owner of the immovable property or by a duly authorised conveyancer. The mortgage comes into existence as a real security right as soon as the mortgage bond has been attested to (witnessed) by the Registrar of Deeds. After the Registrar of Deeds has attested to the mortgage bond, he must enter the details of the mortgage in the appropriate register and endorse the fact of the mortgage on the title deed of the immovable property.[40]

As was pointed out earlier,[41] it is important to distinguish the act of creating a real security right from the security agreement itself. This is because the security agreement gives rise to personal rights only. It cannot create a real security right by itself. To create a real security right and, specifically, a real security right in the form of a mortgage, the parties must publicise the fact that a mortgage has been created by registering a mortgage bond

---

36 Act 47 of 1937.
37 *Silberberg & Schoeman Property* p 360.
38 Kritzinger, KM (1999) *Principles of the Law of Mortgage, Pledge and Lien* (Cape Town, Juta) p 1.
39 *LAWSA* Vol 17(2) at para 327; *Wille's Principles* p 631.
40 *Silberberg & Schoeman Property* p 361. The procedure for registering a mortgage bond is set out in ss 13, 50(1) and 50A of the Deeds Registries Act 47 of 1937.
41 See p 302 above.

in the Deeds Registry. In the case of a mortgage, the security agreement is usually referred to as a 'mortgage agreement'. It may be defined as an agreement in terms of which the mortgagor agrees to secure a valid underlying principal debt by passing a mortgage bond over his immovable property in favour of the mortgagee. The mortgage agreement must comply with all requirements for a valid contract. It need not, however, comply with any formalities.[42] For instance, it need not be in writing or be signed by the parties.

> **PAUSE FOR REFLECTION**
>
> **National Credit Act**
>
> A mortgage agreement is considered to be a 'large credit agreement' for the purposes of the National Credit Act.[43] This Act regulates large credit agreements by providing, inter alia, that every such agreement must include certain information, e.g. the credit provider's details, the amounts that make up the cost of the credit, the duration of the agreement, and the consumer's rights. These requirements are set out in the regulations promulgated under the Act.
>
> Apart from prescribing the information that must be contained in a large credit agreement, the Act also prohibits certain unlawful credit agreements. For example, one may not enter into a credit agreement with an unregistered credit provider. Furthermore, credit agreements may not contain certain unlawful provisions, e.g. a provision that waives the consumer's statutory rights or common law rights.
>
> Finally, the Act also imposes restrictions on the cost of credit and regulates the manner in which interest may be calculated as well as the rates at which interest and other fees may be charged.

The creation of a mortgage as a real security right usually has two distinct stages.[44] During the first stage, the parties enter into a valid and binding mortgage agreement. This stage is governed by the law of contract and gives rise to personal rights only. In the second stage, the parties register the mortgage bond in the Deeds Registry. This stage is governed by the law of property and gives rise to real rights.

> **PAUSE FOR REFLECTION**
>
> **Stages in the creation of a mortgage bond**
>
> Although the creation of a mortgage usually takes place in two stages, it is important to note that the act of creating a mortgage as a real security right does not depend on the existence of a valid mortgage agreement.[45] Provided the real agreement and act of registration of the mortgage are valid, the real security right will come into existence even if the mortgage agreement is invalid. This is because the abstract system of transfer of real rights applies in South Africa.[46]
>
> The distinction between the mortgage agreement and the loan (or credit) agreement must be noted. A valid mortgage is dependent upon the existence of a valid loan (or credit) agreement because a mortgage is an accessory right. It can come into existence only if there is a valid underlying principal debt. If there is no such principal debt, there can be no valid mortgage. However, the existence of a valid mortgage agreement is not a necessary element for establishing a valid mortgage, as was explained above.

---

42 *LAWSA* Vol 17(2) at para 349.
43 Act 34 of 2005.
44 *Wille's Principles* p 634.
45 *LAWSA* Vol 17(2) at para 349.
46 See p 190 above.

Although a written agreement is not a legal requirement, it is common to reduce the terms of the mortgage agreement to writing by setting them out in the mortgage bond. Where this is the case, the mortgage bond performs more than one function. It acts not only as an **instrument of hypothecation**, but serves also as a **record of the mortgage agreement**. The terms of the principal debt, together with an acknowledgement of the principal debt, may also be included in the mortgage bond. When this happens, the mortgage bond also serves as a **record of the principal debt** and acts as an **instrument of debt**. These different functions were highlighted by the then Appellate Division in *Thienhaus NO v Metje and Ziegler Ltd*.[47]

In this matter, the factual detail regarding the principal debt was inaccurately recorded in the mortgage bond. A company (G Merjenberg (Pty) Ltd) owed money to the respondent, Metje and Ziegler Ltd. The debt was secured by a mortgage bond passed over the property of another company, The Batchelors (Pty) Ltd, in favour of the respondent. The mortgage bond incorrectly stated, however, that the debt was owed, not by the company G Merjenberg (Pty) Ltd, but rather by the sole shareholder of the company (one Gerrit Merjenberg). Thienhaus was later appointed as liquidator when The Batchelors (Pty) Ltd was declared insolvent. Metje and Ziegler Ltd claimed that they had a preferential right, in terms of the mortgage bond, to any proceeds generated by the sale of the land secured by the mortgage. The liquidator rejected this claim on the ground that the mortgage had never come into existence, due to the factual inaccuracy recorded in the mortgage bond. It was argued that Mr Merjenberg did not owe money in his personal capacity to the respondent, and thus that no principal debt and consequently no real security right existed.

The Appellate Division rejected the liquidator's argument. The court explained that a mortgage bond can clearly be used both as an instrument of hypothecation, and as a record of the terms and conditions of the obligation in respect of which the hypothecation is to create security; and in addition it is a 'matter of common and usual custom in the drafting of bonds'[48] to incorporate an unqualified admission of liability by the mortgagor. The court pointed out that the acknowledgment is certainly not required for the validity of the bond as a means of creating a real right by hypothecation in favour of the creditor: 'The origin and prime purpose of the custom is the facilitation of the obtaining of a quick and easy remedy, such as provisional sentence, against the mortgagor in case of his default.'[49]

The real object of a mortgage bond as an instrument of hypothecation is to publicise the fact that a limited real right has been established in the immovable property in question. It is not to publicise the amount, nature, or origin of the principal debt.[50] Furthermore, the requirements for a valid instrument of hypothecation remain the same irrespective of whether the mortgage bond functions only as an instrument of hypothecation, or as both an instrument of hypothecation and an instrument of debt. There is no authority for the argument that a description of the details of the amount, nature, or origin of the principal debt is an essential requirement that must be satisfied before a mortgage bond can act as a valid instrument of hypothecation. However, although the details of the amount, or nature, or origin of the principal debt do not need to be set out in the mortgage bond itself, the principal debt must exist. This is because a mortgage is an accessory right. If a defect in the bond rendered the principal debt invalid, the mortgage itself would be invalid.[51]

---

47 1965 (3) SA 25 (A).
48 *Thienhaus NO v Metje and Ziegler Ltd* 1965 (3) SA 25 (A) at 31D–E.
49 *Thienhaus* at 31D–E.
50 *Thienhaus* at 31H–32A.
51 *Thienhaus* at 32E–F.

In respect of the facts of *Thienhaus NO v Metje and Ziegler Ltd,* the court found that the mortgage bond in question satisfied all the requirements for a valid instrument of hypothecation because it accurately described the immovable property in question and clearly identified the parties to the mortgage. In addition, there was no doubt that the underlying principal debt was in existence. The fact that the principal debtor had been described mistakenly as G Merjenberg rather than G Merjenberg (Pty) Ltd was irrelevant. A description of the origin of the principal debt is not an essential requirement for a mortgage bond as an instrument of hypothecation.[52]

> **PAUSE FOR REFLECTION**
>
> **Summary judgment**
>
> The custom of including the acknowledgement of debt in a mortgage bond is to facilitate a quick and easy remedy for the mortgagee should the mortgagor fail to perform his obligations. The mortgagee can apply for summary judgment, which permits the plaintiff (mortgagee) to claim that the defendant (mortgagor) does not have a valid defence in law. The defendant is then required to show that his defence is legally valid. If the defendant is unable to do so, the court will immediately give judgment for the plaintiff.
>
> A summary judgment is considered a drastic remedy because it allows a court to give a final judgment without first having a trial. This obviously benefits the plaintiff. He wins without having to prove his case. To prevent this process from being abused, therefore, a plaintiff may only apply for summary judgment if he satisfies certain requirements. One requirement is that the plaintiff's claim must be based on a liquid document. A liquid document is 'one in which the debtor unconditionally acknowledges that he owes the creditor a fixed sum of money'.[53]
>
> An acknowledgement of debt clause is, as its name suggests, 'one in which the mortgagor unconditionally acknowledges that he or she owes the mortgagee a fixed sum of money'.[54] A mortgage bond which contains such a clause may, therefore, be classified as a liquid document.

12.4.1.3 Form and content of a mortgage bond

It is important to know the typical content of a mortgage bond and to understand that certain clauses would be invalid if they were to be incorporated in such a mortgage bond. With some exceptions,[55] no specific form is prescribed by law for a mortgage bond. The form and content of a mortgage bond, therefore, is based largely on the intentions of the parties, and the practices followed by bankers and conveyancers. Standard forms have been developed over time, however, for different types of bonds, particularly by banks and other financial institutions. Most of these standard forms contain similar provisions.

---

52 *Silberberg and Schoeman Property* p 362.
53 Van Winsen, L, Cilliers, AC & Loots, C (1997) *Herbstein and Van Winsen The Civil Practice of the Supreme Court of South Africa* 4 ed (Cape Town, Juta) p 960.
54 Van Winsen, L, Cilliers, AC & Loots, C (1997) *Herbstein and Van Winsen The Civil Practice of the Supreme Court of South Africa* 4 ed (Cape Town, Juta) p 960.
55 E.g. Collateral Mortgage Bonds, which are set out in Form KK, and Surety Mortgage Bonds, which are set out in Form LL in the Regulations issued in terms of s 9 the Deeds Registries Act 47 of 1937 (see Government Notice R474 of 29 March 1963 in *GG* 177). See also Sectional Mortgage Bonds, which are set out in Form Z in the Regulations issued in terms of s 55 of the Sectional Titles Act 95 of 1986.

Apart from identifying the parties and describing the immovable property, most mortgage bonds also contain a clause in which the mortgagor unconditionally acknowledges his debt to the mortgagee, and a clause in which the amount, the nature and the origin of the principal debt are set out. In addition, mortgage bonds usually contain clauses in which the contractual aspects of the principal debt and the mortgage relationship are set out.[56] In particular, note that, as a general rule, the mortgagee is not entitled to use and enjoy the mortgaged property, nor to take its fruits.[57] However the parties may agree that, in return for not charging interest, the mortgagee may use and enjoy the property, and take its fruits. This type of clause is called a *pactum antichresis*.

Insofar as the contractual aspects of the principal debt are concerned, mortgage bonds usually contain clauses dealing with the repayment of the capital amount;[58] the finance charges (which must conform to the provisions of the National Credit Act[59]);[60] and the possibility of foreclosure.[61] The latter entails a provision that if the mortgagor fails to perform any of his obligations, the capital amount of the principal debt together with any interest will immediately become repayable, and that the mortgaged property may be declared executable by a court to satisfy the mortgagee's claim.[62]

Mortgage bonds usually contain clauses dealing with the use and enjoyment of the mortgaged property (and may include a *pactum antichresis*);[63] the maintenance of the mortgaged property;[64] and procedural matters, such as where the mortgagor's *domicilium citandi et executandi* is.[65]

Certain types of clauses may not be included in a mortgage bond. The first is the *pactum commissorium* or forfeiture clause, and the second is an agreement of *parate executie* or summary execution clause. The *pactum commissorium* is a type of clause that provides that the mortgagee may keep the mortgaged property as her own if the debtor fails to perform his obligations.[66] This arrangement is not permitted because it may severely prejudice the mortgagor. For example, the value of the mortgaged property may be much greater than the outstanding amount of the principal debt. A *pactum commissorium* must be distinguished from an agreement that permits the mortgagee to acquire ownership of the mortgaged property at a fair price if the debtor fails to perform his obligations. This latter agreement is valid. The price, however, must be determined at the time that the debtor fails to perform his obligations and not at the time the credit agreement was entered into. After the principal debt has fallen due, the parties may also agree that the mortgagee can take over the mortgaged property at a specified fair price.[67]

Parate executie amounts to a clause providing that if the debtor fails to perform his obligations, the mortgagee may take possession of the mortgaged property and sell it

---

56 *LAWSA* Vol 17(2) at para 353.
57 *LAWSA* Vol 17(2) at para 360.
58 For further detail, see *LAWSA* Vol 17(2) at para 362.
59 Act 34 of 2005.
60 For further detail, see *LAWSA* Vol 17(2) at para 363.
61 For further detail, see *LAWSA* Vol 17(2) at para 364.
62 *LAWSA* Vol 17 (2) at paras 362-364.
63 For further detail, see *LAWSA* Vol 17(2) at para 365.
64 For further detail, see *LAWSA* Vol 17(2) at para 365.
65 Sharrock, R (2007) *Business Transactions Law* 7 ed (Cape Town, Juta) pp 568-569.
66 *National Bank of South Africa Ltd v Cohen's Trustee* 1911 AD 235 at 242; *Graf v Beuchel* 2003 (4) SA 378 (SCA) at paras 9-11.
67 *Wille's Principles* p 636.

privately to settle the principal debt.[68] This is not permitted in a mortgage bond because it allows the mortgagee to take the law into her own hands. A mortgagee must obtain a court order before she can have the mortgaged property attached and sold in execution.[69] Note that the position regarding pledge is different.[70]

12.4.1.4 Operation of a mortgage bond

To understand how a mortgage bond operates, it is necessary to take note of at least the following three aspects: first, the mortgagee's preferential right; second, the mortgagee's entitlement to immediate execution; and third, the rights and duties of the mortgagor. These are discussed below.

The mortgagee's right of preference. A special mortgage in immovable property comes into existence as a real security right as soon as a mortgage bond has been registered in the Deeds Registry.[71] The real security right of mortgage confers certain entitlements on the mortgagee. The most important is that the mortgagee has a preferential claim to the proceeds of the sale in execution of the mortgaged property. Only after the mortgagee's claim has been settled, may the remaining proceeds (the surplus) be used to settle other creditor's claims. The other creditors, therefore, will share in the proceeds of the sale of the mortgaged property only if there is a surplus.[72]

A sale in execution may take place either when the mortgagee himself has levied execution against the mortgaged property or when another creditor has done so.[73] In other words, a mortgage does not prevent another creditor from levying execution against the mortgaged property. It simply gives the mortgagee the right to claim the proceeds from the sale of the mortgaged property before other creditors may do so. This is what is meant by the term 'preferential claim'.

A mortgage also confers a right of preference on the mortgagee when the debtor is declared insolvent. The mortgaged property is considered to be an asset in the insolvent estate, and the mortgagee is considered to be a secured creditor.[74]

If the mortgaged property secures more than one claim, the order in which the competing claims must be paid depends upon how they are ranked. The rule is that only a lien ranks higher than a mortgage.[75] The lien holder, therefore, enjoys preference over a mortgagee. Where more than one mortgage exists in respect of the same immovable asset, each mortgage is ranked according to the date and time at which it was registered. A prior mortgagee, therefore, is preferred over a later mortgagee.[76]

By way of illustration, consider the following: Henry buys a house of which R1 million is financed by Homes24 Bank against a mortgage of the property. Henry has also taken out

---

68   *Osry v Hirsch, Loubser and Company Ltd* 1922 CPD 531 at 541; *Bock v Duburoro Investments (Pty) Ltd* 2004 (2) SA 242 (SCA) at para 7.
69   *Wille's Principles* p 636.
70   See pp 314*ff* below.
71   *LAWSA* Vol 17(2) at para 367.
72   See *Roodepoort United Main Reef Gold Mining Company Ltd (in liquidation) v Du Toit* 1928 AD 66 at 71.
73   *LAWSA* Vol 17(2) at para 373.
74   See ss 2 and 95(1) of the Insolvency Act 24 of 1936.
75   See *United Building Society v Smookler's Trustees and Galombik's Trustee* 1906 TS 623 at 633; *D Glaser and Sons (Pty) Ltd v The Master* 1979 (4) SA 780 (C) at 792.
76   *LAWSA* Vol 17(2) at para 374.

a second mortgage of R500 000 on the house from another financial institution, Enterprise Bank, to finance his new business, a yoga school. He has engaged a builder, Bob, to convert the loft of his house into a yoga studio, from where he wants to run the school. While he waits for the renovations to be completed, he runs the school from the premises next door, which he leases from Joe. If Henry is declared insolvent at this point, the creditors would rank as follows:

Figure 12.3: Illustration of the ranking of security rights

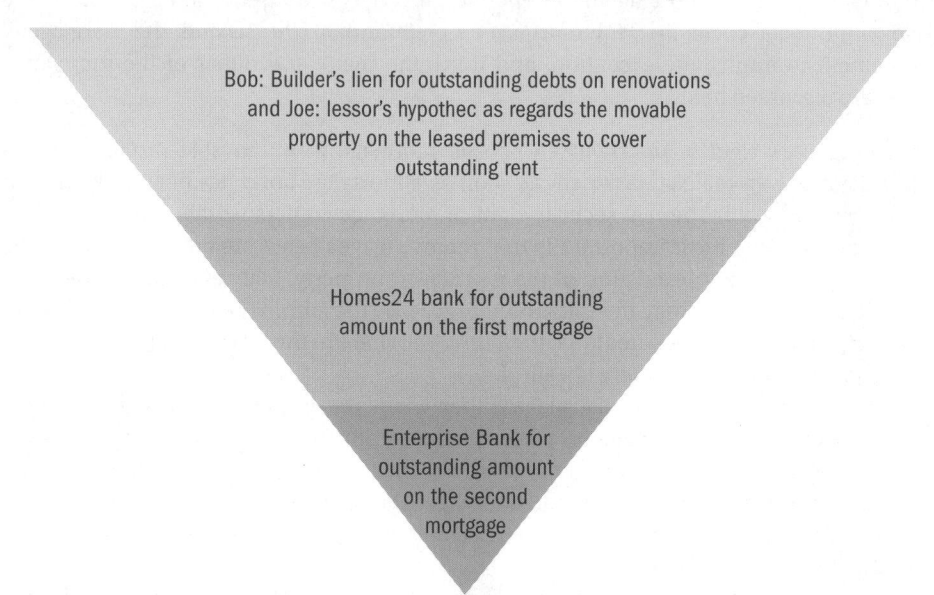

Bob: Builder's lien for outstanding debts on renovations and Joe: lessor's hypothec as regards the movable property on the leased premises to cover outstanding rent

Homes24 bank for outstanding amount on the first mortgage

Enterprise Bank for outstanding amount on the second mortgage

The mortgagee's entitlement to immediate execution. A mortgage also confers the entitlement to immediate execution against the mortgaged property on the mortgagee.[77] A mortgagee need not comply with the general rules governing attachment and sale in execution of a debtor's property. The general rules provide that a creditor must levy execution against a debtor's movable property first, and only if the proceeds of the movable property are insufficient to satisfy the judgment debt, may the creditor levy execution against a debtor's immovable property.[78] Where the debt is secured by a mortgage, however, the mortgagee does not have to levy execution against the debtor's movable property first. Instead, the mortgagee may levy execution immediately against the mortgaged property.

> **PAUSE FOR REFLECTION**
>
> **Distinction between right to levy execution immediately and *parate executie* (summary execution)**
>
> It is important to distinguish between a right of *parate executie* (summary execution) and a right to levy execution immediately against the mortgaged property. A right of summary execution allows the mortgagee to seize the mortgaged property and sell it without first having to obtain a court order, while a right to levy execution immediately does not. A right to levy execution immediately simply allows the mortgagee to apply to court for an

---

77 *Standard Bank of South Africa Ltd v Saunderson* 2006 (2) SA 264 (SCA) at para 3.
78 *Saunderson* at para 3.

> order instructing the sheriff to levy execution immediately against the mortgaged property without having to go through the normal process of levying execution first against the mortgagor's movable property, and only thereafter, if the movables are insufficient, against the immovable property. A right of summary execution, therefore, infringes the rule of law, while a right to levy execution immediately does not. This is because a right of summary execution allows the mortgagee to take the law into her own hands, while a right to levy execution immediately does not.

When the mortgagee does levy execution immediately against the mortgaged property, the mortgagee can protect his interests by setting a reserve price which must be obtained for the sale in execution to be effective. The mortgagee may also buy the mortgaged property at the sale in execution. In such a case, the mortgagee can set off the amount owed to him by the debtor against the purchase price.[79]

In *Standard Bank Ltd v Saunderson*,[80] the Supreme Court of Appeal explained that a mortgagee's right to levy execution immediately against the mortgaged property may, in certain rare cases, infringe the right of access to adequate housing guaranteed in s 26(1) of the Constitution.[81] A defaulting mortgagor does not have a defence to the claim for payment and, in most cases, will not seek legal advice. Consequently, the Supreme Court of Appeal explained that it is important to draw the mortgagor's attention to the fact that s 26(1) of the Constitution could affect the mortgagee's right to levy execution.[82] Thus, every summons in which an order for execution is sought against immovable property that is used for residential purposes, must inform the mortgagor that she has a constitutional right to access housing and if the mortgagor believes that an order for execution will infringe that right, then she must place information to this effect before the court.[83]

In *ABSA Bank v Ntsane*,[84] the court found that the mortgagee's right to levy execution immediately did infringe the mortgagor's constitutional right of access to adequate housing. The mortgagee was seeking to deprive the mortgagors of their only home when the amount outstanding on the bond (R18.46) was so small that it could easily have been settled by attaching and selling the mortgagors' movable property.

Finally, it is important to note that where a defaulting mortgagor's home has been attached and sold in execution, she may be evicted only in accordance with the provisions of s 26(3) of the Constitution and the Prevention of Illegal Eviction from and Unlawful Occupation of Land Act (PIE).[85]

The mortgagor's rights and duties. Unlike a pledge,[86] a mortgage does not deprive the mortgagor of his right to possess the mortgaged property nor to continue to use and enjoy it. However, the mortgagor may not exercise these entitlements in a manner that infringes

---

79 *LAWSA* Vol 17(2) at para 368.
80 2006 (2) SA 264 (SCA).
81 *Standard Bank of South Africa Ltd v Saunderson* 2006 (2) SA 264 (SCA) at para 19.
82 *Saunderson* at para 25.
83 *Saunderson* at para 27.
84 2007 (3) SA 554 (T).
85 Act 18 of 1998. In *Ndlovu v Ngcobo; Bekker v Jika* 2003 (1) SA 113 (SCA), the Supreme Court of Appeal decided that s 4 of PIE applies to a mortgagor whose home has been attached and sold in execution.
86 See pp 314*ff* below.

the mortgagee's security. In addition, the mortgagor's entitlement to use and enjoy the mortgaged property is often restricted by the terms of the mortgage bond.[87]

The mortgagor retains the entitlement to deal with the mortgaged property, unless the mortgage bond provides otherwise.[88] This means that the mortgagor may lease the mortgaged property, encumber it with further mortgages, or use it for mining purposes (subject to the provisions of the Mineral and Petroleum Resources Development Act[89]), without first obtaining the mortgagee's consent.[90] Any dealings with the mortgaged property occur subject to the preferential right of the mortgagee.

Certain dealings with the mortgaged property are restricted. For example, the mortgagor cannot alienate the mortgaged property nor burden it with a servitude without obtaining the mortgagee's written consent first.[91] If alienation or burdening of the mortgaged property occurs without the necessary consent, the existing mortgage remains in operation in accordance with the maxim, *qui prior est tempore, potior est iure*.[92] The mortgagee may, therefore, obtain judgment against the debtor on the principal debt and then bring an action (the *actio hypothecaria*) against the transferee or holder to obtain a judicial attachment and sale of the mortgaged property. In other words, the mortgagee has a right to 'follow up the mortgaged property.'[93]

In *Standard Bank van Suid-Afrika Bpk v Breitenbach*,[94] Breitenbach passed a third mortgage over his farm in favour of Standard Bank (the Bank). The purpose of the mortgage was to secure a debt Breitenbach owed to the Bank. Although the mortgage was properly registered, officials in the Deeds Registry mistakenly failed to endorse the fact of the mortgage on the title deed of Breitenbach's farm, as is common practice. A few years later, Breitenbach sold and transferred ownership of his farm to another person. At the time of transfer, the first and second mortgages were cancelled, but not the third mortgage.

Following the transfer, the Bank applied for an order declaring that the third mortgage was still valid and that it was still entitled to have the farm attached and sold in execution should Breitenbach default on his debt. The court granted the order, explaining that endorsement of the title deed of the mortgaged property is not a requirement for the creation of a valid mortgage. It is simply a practice followed in the Deeds Registry. The failure to endorse the title deed, therefore, could not affect the validity of the mortgage. Given that the third mortgage was still in existence, the Bank was entitled to have the farm attached and sold in execution should Breitenbach default on his debt.[95]

---

87 *LAWSA* Vol 17(2) at para 369.
88 *LAWSA* Vol 17(2) at para 369.
89 Act 28 of 2002.
90 *LAWSA* Vol 17(2) at paras 371, 372.
91 Sections 56(1), 65(3) and 75(3) of the Deeds Registries Act 47 of 1937.
92 Translation: 'First in time is stronger in law'. See *Barclays Nasionale Bank Bpk v Registrateur van Aktes, Transvaal* 1975 (4) SA 936 (T).
93 *LAWSA* Vol 17(2) at para 370.
94 1977 (1) SA 151 (T).
95 *Standard Bank van Suid Afrika Bpk v Breitenbach* 1977 (1) SA 151 (T) at 156C.

> **PAUSE FOR REFLECTION**
>
> **Effect of negative registration system**
>
> The decision in *Standard Bank van Suid-Afrika Bpk v Breitenbach*[96] is consistent with the policy choice to use a modified negative registration system. This type of system does not guarantee the accuracy of the records in the Deeds Registry. Consequently, a properly registered limited real right that is subsequently omitted from the title deed does not cease to exist. Even though it does not appear on the title deed, it is still effective. This was confirmed in *Cape Explosive Works Ltd v Denel (Pty) Ltd*.[97]

Finally, the mortgagor is also obliged to maintain the mortgaged property in a state of good repair. This does not mean, however, that he must put the mortgaged property to its best use.[98]

12.4.1.5 Types of mortgages

There are various types of mortgages, of which only a few receive attention here.[99] A **kustingsbrief** is a special mortgage in immovable property that provides security for the payment of the purchase price of the mortgaged property, commonly a house.[100] It is registered at the same time as the deed of transfer of the immovable property. The mortgagee is the seller (to secure payment of the purchase price), or a third party, usually a bank or financial institution (to secure the loan the third party has made to help the purchaser pay the purchase price).

A **covering bond** is a special mortgage in immovable property that provides security for the payment of a future debt. It must state expressly that it is intended to secure a future debt and include the maximum amount of the future debt.[101] A covering bond may be general or specific. A general covering bond is one that provides security for any future debt that may arise out of the relationship between the creditor and the debtor. A specific covering bond provides security for a specific debt that may arise out of the relationship between the creditor and the debtor. This type of mortgage is commonly used to secure the funds a client may withdraw from an overdraft facility.[102]

A **participation bond** is a special mortgage in immovable property that provides security for funds various individuals have invested in a company that runs a collective investment scheme. A collective investment scheme is one in which various individuals invest money in a nominee company and the company lends the combined amount to a borrower. The money invested in the company and lent to the borrower is secured by a mortgage passed over the borrower's immovable property. The bond is registered in the company's name, but it is the participants who acquire the real security right, not the company. These bonds are regulated by the Collective Investment Schemes Act.[103]

---

96 1977 (1) SA 151 (T).
97 2001 (3) SA 569 (SCA).
98 *LAWSA* Vol 17(2) at para 360.
99 For a more comprehensive discussion, see *LAWSA* Vol 17(2) at paras 396–398.
100 *Wille's Principles* p 642.
101 Section 51 of the Deeds Registries Act 47 of 1937.
102 *Wille's Principles* p 642.
103 Act 45 of 2002. See *Wille's Principles* p 642.

12.4.1.6 Termination of the mortgage

A special mortgage in immovable property may be terminated in different ways. First, given its accessory nature, a mortgage is terminated when the principal debt has been paid or terminated by compromise, merger, novation, prescription, release, and set-off. It is not necessary to cancel the registration of the mortgage bond first. The mortgage is terminated automatically by operation of law.[104]

Second, if the mortgaged property is totally destroyed, the mortgage is terminated. If, however, the mortgaged property is only partially destroyed, the mortgage continues to burden the remaining part. A mortgagor does not have to replace, restore or substitute the mortgaged property if the destruction was not his fault.[105]

Third, a mortgage is terminated when the mortgagee acquires ownership of the mortgaged property or becomes the holder of a limited real right burdened by a mortgage. This is referred to as 'merger' or '*confusio*'. The mortgagee who acquires ownership of the mortgaged property may continue to exercise her rights against subsequent mortgagees.[106]

Fourth, if a mortgage is granted for a specific period of time or subject to a resolutive condition, it terminates when the period of time expires or the condition is fulfilled. A mortgage may also, in the fifth place, be terminated by agreement, e.g. when the mortgagee agrees to release the mortgaged property from the mortgage, or agrees that the mortgagor may alienate the property free from the mortgage. Finally, a mortgage is also terminated when the mortgaged property is sold in execution or by the trustee of the debtor's insolvent estate.[107]

12.4.2 Pledge

A pledge may be distinguished from a special mortgage in at least two respects. First, it pertains to movable property, whereas a special mortgage pertains to land. Second, it does not give the debtor the option of retaining the property while burdening it with the real security right. In the following paragraphs, the definition of a pledge, the parties to the pledge, its operation and the manner in which it may be constituted and terminated are discussed in more detail.

12.4.2.1 Definition

A pledge is defined as a limited real right that one person acquires in another person's movable property to secure payment of a debt. It is created by delivery of the movable object, pursuant to an agreement between the parties.[108] The parties to a pledge are known as the pledgor and the pledgee. The pledgor is the person whose movable property is burdened by the pledge. He is usually the debtor. It is possible, however, for a third person to provide security on behalf of the debtor. In such a case, the third person will be the pledgor. The pledgor must be the owner of the movable property or the holder of a personal right. The pledgee is the person in whose favour the pledge has been created. The pledgee is always the creditor.

---

104 *LAWSA* Vol 17(2) at para 380.
105 *LAWSA* Vol 17(2) at para 382.
106 *Wille's Principles* p 641.
107 *Wille's Principles* p 641.
108 *LAWSA* Vol 17(2) at para 406.

Unlike a mortgage, a pledge may be created only in respect of movable property. In principle, both corporeal and incorporeal movable property may be pledged. The movable property must be in existence at the time the pledge is created and must be *res in commercio*. A pledge may be established over an individual thing, e.g. a horse, or over a collection of individual things, e.g. a herd of cattle.[109]

Pledge of incorporeal movable property occurs when a creditor (pledgor) cedes (pledges) a claim in the form of a personal right to her own creditor (pledgee) as security for a debt. This is commonly known as cession *in securitatem debiti*.[110] In other words, the pledgor has a claim against a third party, which is ceded to the pledgee. Following cession, quasi-control of the personal right vests in the pledgee. The type of control that vests in the pledgee is referred to as quasi-control rather than control. This is because it is factually impossible for a person to exercise control over an incorporeal such as a personal right. The primary claim, however, remains vested in the pledgor. Since transfer of quasi-control of a personal right cannot be observed by third parties, a further act of publicity is required. This can be achieved by sending notice of the cession to the pledgor's debtor.[111]

> **COUNTER POINT**
>
> **Pledge of personal rights**
>
> Although the courts generally have accepted that a personal right can be pledged to secure a debt, some legal scholars reject these decisions on dogmatic grounds.[112] These scholars argue that, conceptually, it is not possible to acquire a real right (such as a pledge) in a personal right. This is because the object of a real right is a thing, the definition of which is restricted to corporeal objects. An incorporeal such as a personal right cannot, therefore, be defined as a thing.[113]
>
> The problem with this argument is that it puts dogmatic considerations above the practical needs of society. As the courts have pointed out, people and, in particular, business people, want to be able to use their incorporeal assets as security for loans. One of the ways in which this practical need can be satisfied, the courts have held, is by extending the concept of a pledge to incorporeals.[114] It is, therefore, not surprising that the courts have refused to accept the dogmatic argument set out above. On the other hand, the decision to elevate expediency above a principled approach must be taken cautiously.[115]

12.4.2.2 Constituting a pledge

Creation of a pledge as a real security right usually has two distinct stages. First, the parties enter into a valid and binding pledge agreement, in terms of which the pledgor agrees to secure a valid underlying principal debt by pledging his movable property to the pledgee. The pledge agreement must comply with all requirements for a valid contract, but it need not comply with any formalities. This stage is governed by the law of contract and gives rise to personal rights only.

---

109 *LAWSA* Vol 17(2) at para 413.
110 Sharrock, R (2007) *Business Transactions Law* 7 ed (Cape Town, Juta) p 577; Collier-Reed, D & Lehmann, K (eds) (2009) *Basic Principles of Business Law* (Durban, LexisNexis Butterworth) pp 311–312.
111 *LAWSA* Vol 17(2) at para 414.
112 De Wet, JC & Van Wyk, AH (1992) *Die Suid-Afrikaanse Kontraktereg en Handelsreg Vol 1* 5 ed pp 415–424.
113 Van der Merwe *Sakereg* p 652.
114 *Britz NO v Sniegocki* 1989 (4) SA 372 (D) at 377G–H.
115 See discussion re *cessio iuris vindicationis* above.

During the second stage, the pledged object must be delivered or, in the case of an incorporeal, ceded to the pledgee. Delivery may be actual or constructive. Some forms of constructive delivery are accepted by the courts, namely *clavium traditio, traditio brevi manu, traditio longa manu* and attornment;[116] while others are not, namely *constitutum possessorium*.[117] This stage is governed by the law of property and gives rise to real rights.

Although the creation of a pledge usually takes place in two stages, it is important to note that the establishment of a pledge as a limited real right does not depend on the existence of a valid pledge agreement. Provided the pledged object has been delivered to the pledgee, the pledge will come into existence even if the pledge agreement is invalid in accordance with the abstract theory of transfer.[118] However, a valid underlying principal debt is essential. Similarly to mortgage, pledge has an accessory nature.[119]

12.4.2.3   Form and content

No formalities are prescribed by law for a pledge agreement. The form and content of a pledge agreement, therefore, are based largely on the intentions of the parties.[120] Like a mortgage agreement, a pledge agreement may contain a *pactum antichresis*. This means that parties to a pledge may agree that, in return for not charging interest, the pledgee may use and enjoy the pledged object, and take its fruits.

In addition, a pledge agreement may include a clause of *parate executie* (a summary execution clause).[121] This means that the parties to a pledge may validly agree that if the debtor fails to perform his obligations, the pledgee may sell the pledged object privately. In other words, the pledgee may sell the pledged object without having to obtain a court order first. This is contrary to the position of a mortgagee because a mortgage bond may not include a *parate executie* clause.[122] If the pledgee acts in a manner that prejudices the pledgor's interests, the pledgor may approach a court for protection.

> **PAUSE FOR REFLECTION**   **Summary execution clauses**
>
> In *Lesapo v North West Agricultural Bank*[123] and *First National Bank of SA Ltd v Land and Agricultural Bank of Southern Africa Ltd*,[124] the Constitutional Court held that statutory provisions that authorised certain state-owned banks to seize a debtor's property and sell it in execution without having to obtain a court order first, infringed the constitutional right of access to court (s 34 of the Constitution), and were therefore constitutionally invalid.
>
> Relying on these two judgments, the Eastern Cape High Court held, in *Findevco (Pty) Ltd v Faceformat SA (Pty) Ltd*,[125] that summary execution (*parate executie*) clauses in pledge agreements also infringed the constitutional right of access to court and were therefore

---

116   See pp 198*ff* above.
117   See p 198*ff* above.
118   See p 190 above.
119   *Wille's Principles* p 646.
120   *LAWSA* Vol 17(2) at para 418.
121   *Bock v Duburoro Investments (Pty) Ltd* 2004 (2) SA 242 (SCA) at para 15; *Juglal NO v Shoprite Checkers t/a OK Franchise Division* 2004 (5) SA 248 (SCA) at para 9; *SA Bank of Athens Ltd v Van Zyl* 2005 (5) SA 93 (SCA) at para 15.
122   See p 308 above.
123   2000 (1) SA 409 (CC).
124   2000 (3) SA 626 (CC).
125   2001 (1) SA 251 (E).

> invalid. This judgment introduced uncertainty about the well-established legal principles governing the law of pledge and was severely criticised by some legal scholars.[126]
>
> Subsequently, it was overruled by the Supreme Court of Appeal in *Bock v Dubororo Investments (Pty) Ltd*.[127] In this case, the Supreme Court of Appeal confirmed the important distinction between a special mortgage in immovable property and a pledge regarding summary execution clauses. A summary execution clause is invalid in the case of a special mortgage, but valid in the case of a pledge. In addition, the court reiterated that in the case of a pledge, the debtor may seek the protection of the court if the creditor has exercised her rights in a manner that has prejudiced the debtor.
>
> The Supreme Court of Appeal explained that summary execution clauses in pledges do not infringe the constitutional right of access to court because the movable property is already in the lawful possession of the creditor. A summary execution clause does not, therefore, authorise the creditor to bypass the courts and seize the property from a debtor who was lawfully in possession of it. In addition, the fact that the debtor may seek the protection of the court also means that the creditor is not a judge in her own cause.

A pledge agreement may not, however, include a *pactum commissorium* (a forfeiture clause).[128] This means that the parties to a pledge may not agree that if the debtor fails to perform his obligations, the pledgee may keep the pledged property as her own property. The parties may, however, agree that if the debtor fails to perform his obligation, the pledgee may acquire ownership at a fair price. The price must be determined at the time the debtor fails to perform. In addition, the parties may, after the principal debt has fallen due, agree that the pledgee can take over the pledged object at a specified fair price.[129]

12.4.2.4 Delivery

A pledge comes into existence as a real security right when the pledged object is delivered to the pledgee.[130] After it has been delivered to the pledgee, the pledgee must retain possession of the pledged object. If the pledgee voluntarily gives up possession of the pledged object, the pledge is terminated.[131]

The transfer of possession from the pledgor to the pledgee is intended to publicise the fact that a real security right in the form of a pledge has been established over the pledged object. It also serves to protect the pledgee's real security right by preventing the pledgor from alienating the pledged object or pledging it to some other person.[132] This requirement is also the reason why delivery may not take place by *constitutum possessorium*.

Delivery by means of *constitutum possessorium* occurs when the transferor retains possession of the object throughout, but acknowledges the transferee's rights and agrees

---

126 Scott *Commerce* p 656.
127 2004 (2) SA 242 (SCA).
128 *Bock v Dubororo Investments (Pty) Ltd* 2004 (2) SA 242 (SCA) at paras 6-9; *Graf v Buechel* 2003 (4) SA 378 (SCA).
129 *LAWSA* Vol 17(2) at para 427.
130 *Zandberg v Van Zyl* 1910 AD 302 at 318; *Vasco Dry Cleaners v Twycross* 1979 (1) SA 603 (A) at 611.
131 *Heydenrech v Fourie* (1896) 13 SC 371; *Zandberg v Van Zyl* 1910 AD 302 at 313; *Vasco Dry Cleaners v Twycross* 1979 (1) SA 603 (A) at 611.
132 *LAWSA* Vol 17(2) at para 421.

to hold the object on behalf of the transferee.[133] Given that physical control of the movable property is not actually transferred to the pledgee, this form of delivery not only undermines the principle of publicity, but also opens the door to fraud on the part of the pledgor. This is because the pledgor may fraudulently claim that his movable property is subject to a pledge and cannot, therefore, be attached.[134]

Although transfer of possession promotes the principle of publicity and protects the pledgee's security, it also has certain disadvantages. The most significant disadvantage is that it reduces the usefulness of a pledge as a real security right in the commercial world.[135] Most businesses cannot afford to give up possession of their movable property, particularly if it is a source of income. To avoid the requirement of transfer of possession, the parties sometimes enter into a 'simulated transaction'. This is a transaction that appears to be one type while actually it is something different. For instance, the parties intend to enter into a pledge but they do not wish to transfer possession, and so they claim the transaction is a sale and transfer of ownership. They claim that delivery takes the form of *constitutum possessorium*. This transaction is then followed immediately by a resale at the same price, transfer of ownership being reserved by the second sale until payment is made. Similarly, a transaction may also be 'disguised' by a leaseback following the purported sale and transfer of ownership.

In these sorts of cases, the courts will not give effect to the sale and transfer of ownership. The parties do not have a true intention to enter into a sale and transfer of ownership. This means that the real agreement is defective. Furthermore, the courts cannot give effect to the (hidden) true intention of the parties, namely to create a pledge, because possession of the movable property has not transferred to the pledgee and, thus, the requirements for a valid pledge have not been fulfilled.[136]

The courts' treatment of simulated transactions is illustrated well in the classic case of *Vasco Dry Cleaners v Twycross*.[137] The case involved Basil Carides who owned a dry-cleaning business. He sold the business and certain dry-cleaning machines to Air Capricorn (Pty) Ltd (Air Capricorn), which was controlled by Duff. The contract of sale provided that the purchase price would be paid in instalments and that ownership of the machines would not transfer from Carides to Air Capricorn until the last instalment had been paid. In other words, ownership was reserved to Carides until full payment had been made.

Before the last instalment had been paid, however, Air Capricorn ran into financial difficulties. Worried that Carides would reclaim the dry-cleaning machines, Duff approached his brother-in-law, Twycross, and asked for help. Following the request, Twycross entered into an agreement with Air Capricorn. This agreement provided that Twycross would buy the machines from Air Capricorn for a purchase price equivalent to the amount that Air Capricorn still owed to Carides. It also provided that Twycross would pay the 'purchase price' directly to Carides, and not to Air Capricorn.

At the same time, Air Capricorn and Twycross entered into another agreement, in terms of which Twycross 'resold' the machines to Air Capricorn for exactly the same purchase price. In addition, the contract provided that this purchase price would be paid to Twycross in instalments and that Twycross remained the owner of the machines until the last instalment had been paid. No actual delivery took place in terms of either the 'sale' or the 'resale'; Air Capricorn remained in physical control of the machines at all times.

---

133 See p 203 above.
134 *Silberberg & Schoeman Property* p 392.
135 *Wille's Principles* p 644.
136 *Silberberg & Schoeman Property* p 391.
137 1979 (1) SA 603 (A).

Approximately four months later, Air Capricorn sold and delivered the dry-cleaning machines to Vasco Dry Cleaners. In this sale, Air Capricorn warranted that it owned the machines. However, Air Capricorn had not paid any instalments to Twycross, as per the 'resale' agreement, which meant, of course, that Air Capricorn could not have acquired ownership. Twycross then claimed the machines from Vasco Dry Cleaners on the grounds that they belonged to him. In support of his claim, Twycross argued that when he bought the machines from Air Capricorn and paid the purchase price to Carides, ownership in the machines had been transferred from Carides to Air Capricorn by means of *traditio brevi manu*, and then from Air Capricorn to him by means of *constitutum possessorium*.

The Appellate Division rejected Twycross's argument. In arriving at this conclusion, the Court explained that the key question was whether the transaction between Air Capricorn and Twycross was a sale and resale, or a pledge. The evidence demonstrating the existence of a simulated transaction was to be found in the following facts: Duff did not want to dispose of the dry-cleaning machines; Twycross did not need the machines; the 'purchase price' for the dry-cleaning machines was not based on their market value, but rather on the amount Air Capricorn still owed Carides; the contract of sale between Air Capricorn and Twycross did not state expressly how ownership of the dry-cleaning machines was to be transferred to Twycross; Air Capricorn warranted that it owned the dry-cleaning machines when it sold them to Vasco Dry Cleaners.

These facts, the Appellate Division explained, clearly showed that the parties did not intend seriously to enter into a sale and resale, but rather to create a pledge. No pledge was created, however, because Twycross did not actually possess the dry-cleaning machines at any time.

> **PAUSE FOR REFLECTION**
>
> **Implication of the rule against simulations**
>
> The implication of the rule against simulation is that real security can only be established in accordance with established legal principles, and only with reference to acknowledged forms. An agreement to establish security over movables by a sale and resale or a leaseback transaction will not comply with the requirement that the movable must be in possession of the creditor, and so the attempt to establish real security will fail.

12.4.2.5 Operation

A pledge comes into existence as a real security right as soon as the pledged object has been delivered to the pledgee. Once it has come into existence, a pledge confers certain entitlements on the pledgee. The most important is the pledgee's right of preference to the proceeds of the sale in execution of the pledged property or upon the insolvency of the debtor.[138]

Given that the pledgee is required to retain possession of the pledged property, it is difficult to create more than one pledge in the same movable asset. This means that the problems associated with ranking the different holders of real security rights in the same asset do not usually arise in the case of a pledge.[139]

---

138 *LAWSA* Vol 17(2) at para 430.
139 *Wille's Principles* p 648.

Rights and duties of the pledgee. Although the pledgee is entitled to possess the pledged property, he is not entitled to use and enjoy it, nor to take any of its fruits.[140] The parties may, however, vary these restrictions by, including a *pactum antichresis* in the pledge agreement and so on.

The pledgee is obliged to take reasonable care of the pledged property. Upon the termination of the pledge, the pledgee is obliged to restore possession of the pledged property together with all its fruits (including those that would have been gathered if the pledgee had exercised due diligence) to the pledgor.[141]

The pledgee is entitled to protect his possession by means of an interdict.[142] If the pledgee has incurred necessary expenses in maintaining the pledged property, he may claim those expenses from the pledgor upon the termination of the pledge, and may retain possession of the pledged property until he has been paid.[143]

The movables cannot be followed or pursued rule. The principle, *mobilia non habent sequelam ex causa hypotheca* (a movable cannot be followed or pursued), governs the situation where possession is given up voluntarily by the pledgee.[144] This means the property may not be reclaimed from a bona fide third party. However, if the pledgee is deprived of possession involuntarily, e.g. if it is stolen or has been lost, then it may be reclaimed, even from a bona fide third party.

It is important to note also that giving up possession of the pledged property voluntarily terminates the pledge.[145] Possession by the pledgee is a necessary element of pledge. Consequently, a third party may exercise possession on behalf of the pledgee without terminating the pledge. Similarly, the pledged property may be returned to the pledgor for a temporary purpose without affecting the pledge.[146]

12.4.2.6 Termination of the pledge

A pledge may be terminated in the same ways that a special mortgage in immovable property may be terminated,[147] namely discharge of the principal debt; destruction of the pledged property; confusion or merger; effluxion of time or fulfilment of a condition; agreement; and sale in execution or upon insolvency.

In addition, a pledge is terminated when the pledgor loses ownership of the pledged property, or when the pledgee voluntarily gives possession of the pledged property to a third party in terms of the principle, *mobilia non habent sequelam ex causa hypotheca.*[148]

---

140 *Wille's Principles* p 649.
141 *Wille's Principles* p 650.
142 *Theron v Gerber* 1918 EDL 288.
143 *Silberberg & Schoeman Property* p 393.
144 *Heydenrech v Fourie* (1896) 13 SC 371; *Zandberg v Van Zyl* 1910 AD 302 at 313; *Vasco Dry Cleaners v Twycross* 1979 (1) SA 603 (A) at 611.
145 *LAWSA* Vol 17(2) at para 434.
146 *LAWSA* Vol 17(2) at para 431.
147 See p 314 above.
148 See above.

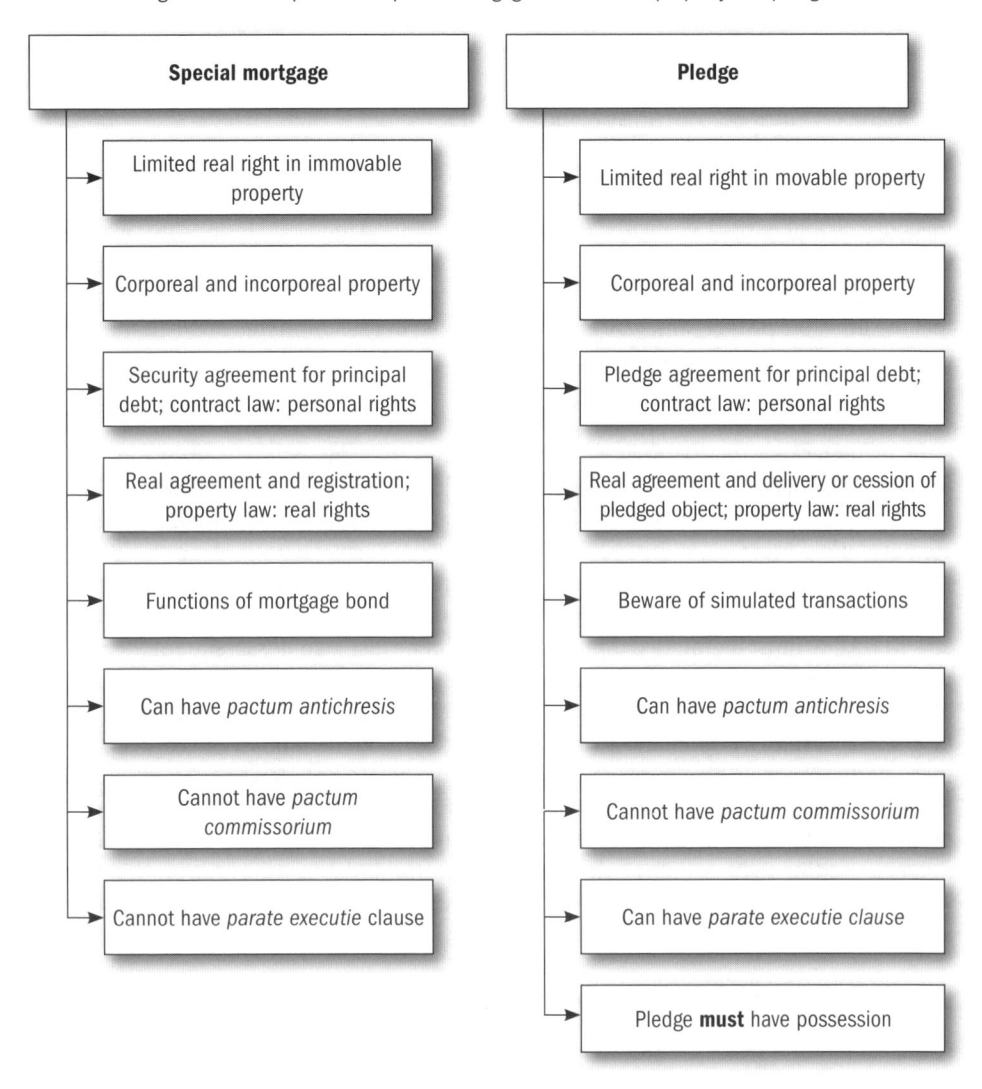

Figure 12.4: Comparison of special mortgage in immovable property and pledge

Special mortgage	Pledge
Limited real right in immovable property	Limited real right in movable property
Corporeal and incorporeal property	Corporeal and incorporeal property
Security agreement for principal debt; contract law: personal rights	Pledge agreement for principal debt; contract law: personal rights
Real agreement and registration; property law: real rights	Real agreement and delivery or cession of pledged object; property law: real rights
Functions of mortgage bond	Beware of simulated transactions
Can have *pactum antichresis*	Can have *pactum antichresis*
Cannot have *pactum commissorium*	Cannot have *pactum commissorium*
Cannot have *parate executie* clause	Can have *parate executie* clause
	Pledge **must** have possession

12.4.3 Notarial bonds

A notarial bond may be defined as a bond, attested to by a notary public, which hypothecates movable property and which has been registered in the Deeds Registry.[149] Most of the rules and requirements that apply to a mortgage bond also apply to a notarial bond. The most important difference between a mortgage bond and a notarial bond is that a mortgage bond may be registered only over immovable property, while a notarial bond may be registered only over movable property.

Notarial bonds have two forms, namely general notarial bonds and special notarial bonds. A general notarial bond applies generally to all movable property of the notarial bond debtor, while a special notarial bond is registered over a specific corporeal movable

---
149 S 102 of the Deeds Registries Act 47 of 1937.

thing that belongs to the notarial bond debtor. The common law governs general notarial bonds, while special notarial bonds are creatures of statute and are subject to the Security by Means of Movable Property Act.[150]

12.4.3.1 General notarial bonds

A general notarial bond is registered over all the corporeal and incorporeal movable property that belongs to the notarial bond debtor. Despite registration in the Deeds Registry, no real right of security is conferred by a general notarial bond.[151] This means that the movable property may be alienated without the consent of the bond holder, and that the bond does not bind a third party who acquires the movable property. It also means that the movable property may be attached and sold in execution free of the bond. In other words, the holder of a general notarial bond does not have a right of preference following a sale in execution.

However, when the debtor is declared insolvent, the bond holder does have a limited right of preference.[152] It simply provides that the proceeds of the sale of the movable property that form part of the free residue of the insolvent estate must be used to settle the bond holder's claim first, and only thereafter can those proceeds be used to settle other concurrent creditors' claims.

For a general notarial bond holder to acquire a real right of security in the movable property in question, the claim must be 'perfected'.[153] This means that the requirements for a valid pledge must be fulfilled, i.e. the bond holder must take possession of the movable property. Note, however, this can occur only if the parties have included a perfection clause in the bond. A perfection clause entitles the bond holder to take possession of the movable property in certain circumstances (usually when the debtor defaults). The courts have held that a perfection clause amounts to an agreement to create a pledge.[154] As soon as the bond holder exercises the right under a perfection clause and takes possession of the movable property, the pledge comes into existence. It is important to note that a bond holder may not exercise this right without either the consent of the debtor or a court order. In other words, the bond holder may not take the law into her own hands and simply attach the movable property herself.[155]

12.4.3.2 Special notarial bonds

A special notarial bond is registered over a specific corporeal movable asset that belongs to the bond debtor. The legal requirements are set out in the Security by Means of Movable Property Act.[156] There is an important distinction between the position that applied before the Act came into operation on 7 May 1993 and that which prevails since the Act came into operation.

Before the Security by Means of Movable Property Act came into operation, the legal principles governing special notarial bonds in Natal differed from the legal principles governing special notarial bonds in the rest of South Africa. In Natal, the principles

---

150 Act 57 of 1993.
151 *LAWSA* Vol 17(2) at para 405.
152 *Chesterfin (Pty) Ltd v Contract Forwarding (Pty) Ltd* 2003 (2) SA 253 (SCA) at para 3.
153 *Chesterfin* at para 4.
154 *Development Bank of Southern Africa Ltd v Van Rensburg* 2002 (5) SA 425 (SCA) at para 20.
155 *LAWSA* Vol 17(2) at para 405.
156 Act 57 of 1993.

governing special notarial bonds were set out in the Notarial Bonds (Natal) Act.[157] This Act provided that a corporeal or incorporeal movable that had been specially described and enumerated in a registered notarial bond was deemed to have been delivered to the bond holder in pledge. The Act thus created a fictitious (non-possessory) pledge and the bond holder was considered to be a pledgee, even though she was not in possession of the movable property.[158] This fictitious pledge only burdened the movable property while it was located within the borders of Natal.

In the rest of South Africa, the principles governing special notarial bonds were set out in *Cooper NO v Die Meester*.[159] In this case, the Appellate Division rejected the generally accepted view that a special notarial bond conferred the same preference on the bond holder that the general notarial bond did regarding an insolvent debtor. Instead, the court found that in terms of the Insolvency Act,[160] a preference was conferred only on the holder of a general notarial bond and not on the holder of a special notarial bond. According to the court, it followed that the holder of a special notarial bond should be ranked equally with other concurrent creditors.[161]

Following the decision in *Cooper NO v Die Meester*, Parliament intervened and passed the Security by Means of Movable Property Act.[162] Section 1 provides that a corporeal movable asset, which has been specified and described in a registered special notarial bond so that it is readily recognisable, shall be deemed to have been pledged as if it had expressly been pledged and delivered.[163] The Security by Means of Movable Property Act, therefore, extended the principles applicable in Natal to the rest of the country. This means that a special notarial bond, passed in terms of the Act, operates in exactly the same way as a pledge, notwithstanding that the corporeal movable asset is not delivered to the bond holder. The common law principles applicable to a real pledge apply also to a special notarial bond.[164]

The importance of specifying and describing the movable asset in the notarial bond was illustrated in *Ikea Trading and Design AG v BOE Bank Ltd*.[165] A close corporation, Woodlam Industries CC, registered a special notarial bond in favour of Ikea Trading, purportedly in terms of the Security by Means of Movable Property Act. The movable assets concerned were listed in a schedule attached to the bond, rather than specified and described in the bond itself. Approximately a year later, Woodlam Industries CC was declared insolvent and BOE Bank, one of the creditors, contested the validity of the special notarial bond on the grounds that the movable assets were not described in a manner that rendered them 'readily recognisable'. It was not possible to identify them without referring to external evidence such as invoices, other documents and even testimony from a former employee familiar with the insolvent's assets.

The Supreme Court of Appeal held the special notarial bond to be invalid because the test for determining whether a movable asset is readily recognisable is whether a third party can identify the movable without having to refer to any extrinsic evidence. The property must be identifiable from the terms of the bond itself.[166] The reason for this requirement is

---

157 Act 18 of 1932.
158 Scott *Commerce* p 268.
159 1992 (3) SA 60 (A).
160 Act 24 of 1936.
161 Scott *Commerce* p 269.
162 Act 57 of 1993.
163 *Silberberg & Schoeman Property* p 386.
164 Sharrock, R (2007) *Business Transactions Law* 7 ed (Cape Town, Juta) pp 574–576.
165 2005 (2) SA 7 (SCA).
166 *Ikea Trading and Design AG v BOE Bank Ltd* 2005 (2) SA 7 (SCA) at para 21.

that one of the bond's functions is to publicise that a real security right has been established. The bond can fulfil this function only if a third party can identify the movable asset by reading the bond itself, rather than by having to refer to external evidence.

The court explained that because s 1(1) of the Act states that the movable property bonded is 'deemed to have been pledged' as 'effectually as if it had expressly been pledged and delivered to the mortgagee', the bond must, as far as possible, have the same characteristics as a pledge. This means that outsiders (third parties) must be able to tell that the creditor has a right in the property pledged without having to rely on extrinsic evidence. For a pledge to be valid, the creditor (pledgee) must be in possession of the property. A pledge cannot be effected by *constitutum possessorium* because of the likelihood that third parties, such as other creditors or prospective purchasers, would be deceived if there is no outward manifestation of the security relationship created. Actual physical control of the pledged property constitutes notice to the world that someone other than the owner has a right in the property. In particular, such a person has the power to control the property. Accordingly, the court held that for property to be deemed pledged under s 1(1) of the Act, the bond in question must, without reference to the owner or anyone else, make readily identifiable the property so pledged. Any person seeking to establish from information in a deeds office whether a debtor's property is encumbered, must be able to do so from the bond itself.[167]

The table below summarises the position as regards the different types of notarial bonds, their objects and the circumstances under which they give rise to limited real rights.

Table 12.1: Summary of notarial bond categories

Category	Source of law	Object	Limited real right
General notarial bond	Common law	The notarial bond debtor's corporeal and incorporeal movable property in general	Does not create a real right, but does confer a slight preference on insolvency
Special notarial bond pre-1993 (within Natal)	Notarial Bonds (Natal) Act 18 of 1932	A specific corporeal or incorporeal movable asset(s) belonging to the notarial bond debtor.	Does create a real right in the form of a fictitious (non-possessory) pledge
Special notarial bond pre-1993 (outside Natal)	Common law	A specific corporeal or incorporeal movable asset(s) belonging to the notarial bond debtor	Does not create a real right and neither does it confer a preference on insolvency
Special notarial bond post-1993	Security by Means of Movable Property Act 57 of 1993	A specific corporeal movable asset(s) belonging to the notarial bond debtor	Does create a real right in the form of a fictitious (non-possessory) pledge

---

167 *Ikea Trading* at para 22.

12.5 Tacit real security rights: created by operation of law

The types of real security rights created explicitly by agreement have been discussed above. It is also necessary to pay attention to the kinds of real security rights that may be created tacitly by operation of law. In this section, tacit security rights, namely tacit hypothecs and rights of retention are discussed.

12.5.1 Tacit hypothecs

Tacit hypothecs are real security rights that arise by operation of law. In Roman-Dutch law, several tacit hypothecs were recognised, but only one common law tacit hypothec is still recognised in South Africa, namely the tacit hypothec of the lessor of immovable property. In addition, a number of statutory tacit hypothecs exist, the most important being the tacit hypothec of the seller under an instalment sale agreement.[168] The discussion here is limited to the common law hypothec and the most important statutory hypothec, namely that of a seller under an instalment sale agreement.

12.5.1.1 Lessor's tacit hypothec

As its title indicates, the lessor's tacit hypothec (also known as the landlord's tacit hypothec) arises out of the relationship between a lessor and a lessee. Its purpose is to secure the lessee's obligation to pay the rent stipulated in the lease agreement.[169] It comes into existence by operation of law as soon as the rent is in arrears. In other words, without any action on the lessor's part, as soon as the lessee fails to pay the rent, the lessor's tacit hypothec is triggered. This hypothec is accessory to the obligation to pay rent and, accordingly, terminates by operation of law as soon as the rent is paid.[170]

The property subject to the lessor's tacit hypothec is called *invecta et illata*. This term describes the corporeal movable goods brought onto the leased premises by the lessee, and includes any fruits of the property that the lessee has collected but not yet removed from the property. The goods must have been brought onto the premises for the permanent use of the lessee, and they must be present on the premises at the time the hypothec is enforced. The lessor does not need to be aware of the fact that the movable goods were present on the premises before enforcing the hypothec.[171]

Although the lessor's tacit hypothec is triggered by operation of law as soon as the rent is in arrears, a real right of security is not automatically created for the lessor at that time. Instead, the hypothec provides the lessor with a preferential claim upon the insolvency of the lessee. However, the lessee is not prevented from removing the *invecta et illata* from the leased premises and thus nullifying the hypothec.[172]

To create a real security right, the lessor must perfect the tacit hypothec by obtaining a court order that interdicts the alienation or removal of the *invecta et illata*, or attaches the *invecta et illata*. The lessor may attach only the property present on the premises or that which is in the process of being removed but has not yet reached its new destination (this is known as the right of quick pursuit).[173]

---

168 *LAWSA* Vol 17(2) at para 435.
169 *LAWSA* Vol 17(2) at para 438.
170 *Wille's Principles* p 656.
171 *Wille's Principles* p 657.
172 *LAWSA* Vol 17(2) at para 439.
173 *LAWSA* Vol 17(2) at para 441.

Once the lessor's tacit hypothec has been perfected, the lessor acquires a real security right. This is a right of preference following a sale in execution of the movable property. In addition, the lessor is entitled to prevent the lessee from removing the *invecta et illata* from the premises or to claim their return if they have been removed.[174]

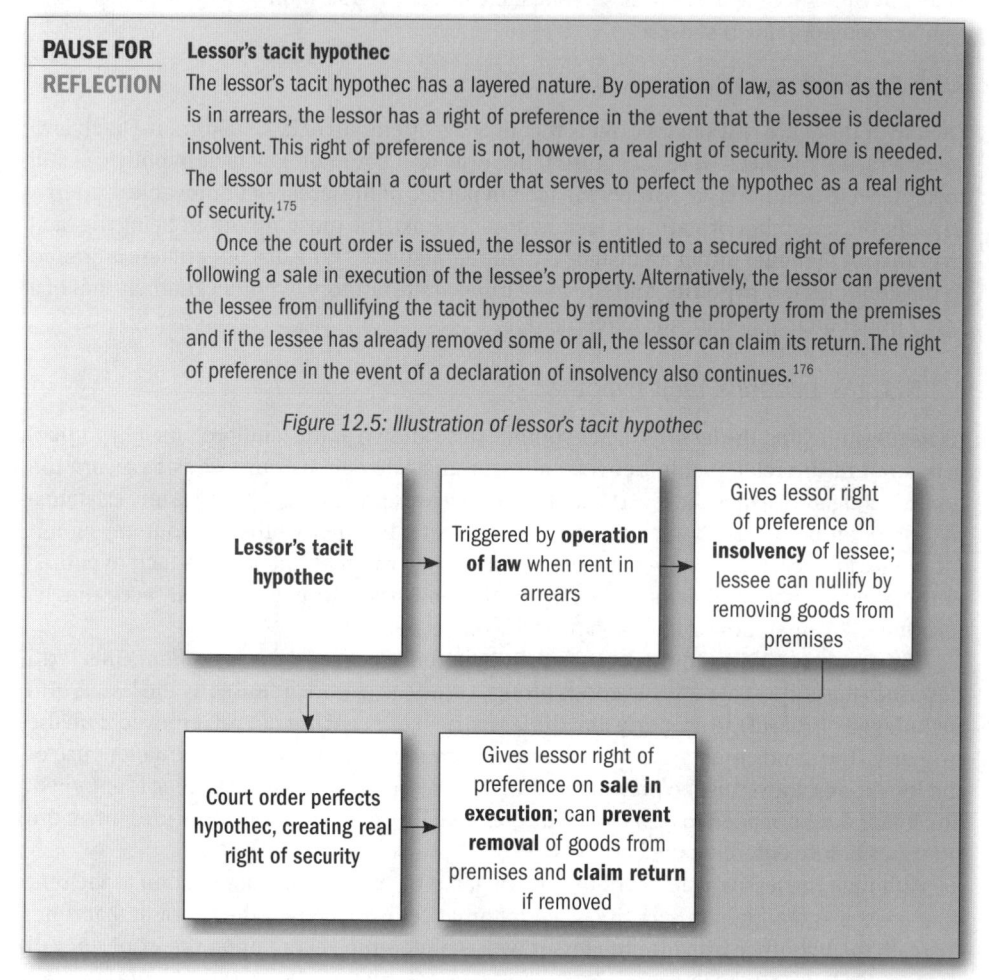

> **PAUSE FOR REFLECTION**
>
> **Lessor's tacit hypothec**
>
> The lessor's tacit hypothec has a layered nature. By operation of law, as soon as the rent is in arrears, the lessor has a right of preference in the event that the lessee is declared insolvent. This right of preference is not, however, a real right of security. More is needed. The lessor must obtain a court order that serves to perfect the hypothec as a real right of security.[175]
>
> Once the court order is issued, the lessor is entitled to a secured right of preference following a sale in execution of the lessee's property. Alternatively, the lessor can prevent the lessee from nullifying the tacit hypothec by removing the property from the premises and if the lessee has already removed some or all, the lessor can claim its return. The right of preference in the event of a declaration of insolvency also continues.[176]
>
> Figure 12.5: Illustration of lessor's tacit hypothec
>
> ```
> ┌──────────────┐    ┌──────────────────┐    ┌──────────────────────┐
> │ Lessor's     │ →  │ Triggered by     │ →  │ Gives lessor right   │
> │ tacit        │    │ operation of law │    │ of preference on     │
> │ hypothec     │    │ when rent in     │    │ insolvency of lessee;│
> │              │    │ arrears          │    │ lessee can nullify by│
> │              │    │                  │    │ removing goods from  │
> │              │    │                  │    │ premises             │
> └──────┬───────┘    └──────────────────┘    └──────────────────────┘
>        ↓
> ┌──────────────┐    ┌──────────────────────┐
> │ Court order  │    │ Gives lessor right of│
> │ perfects     │ →  │ preference on sale in│
> │ hypothec,    │    │ execution; can       │
> │ creating real│    │ prevent removal of   │
> │ right of     │    │ goods from premises  │
> │ security     │    │ and claim return if  │
> │              │    │ removed              │
> └──────────────┘    └──────────────────────┘
> ```

Where the lessee's *invecta et illata* are not sufficient to cover the rent arrears, the lessor's tacit hypothec may be extended to *invecta et illata* that belong to a sub-lessee, but only to the extent that the sub-lessee owes rent to the lessee under the sublease.[177] Similarly, where the *invecta et illata* of both the lessee and the sub-lessee are insufficient, the hypothec may be extended to property belonging to a third party, subject to certain requirements. The property must have been brought on to the leased premises by the lessee with the express or implied knowledge and consent of the third party. It must have been intended for the permanent use of the lessee. The lessor must not be aware that the property belongs to a

---

174 *LAWSA* Vol 17(2) at para 442.
175 *Webster v Ellison* 1911 AD 73 at 86–87.
176 *Webster* at 86–87.
177 *Wille's Principles* p 657.

third party.[178] The lessor's tacit hypothec will be nullified if the third party informs the lessor of his ownership of the property concerned.[179] It will also be nullified if by taking reasonable steps, the lessor could have discovered that the property did not belong to the lessee.[180]

In *Bloemfontein Municipality v Jacksons*,[181] the then Appellate Division held that where a third party has not taken reasonable steps to protect his property from the lessor's tacit hypothec, the courts will infer that the property was brought onto the leased premises with the implied knowledge and consent of the third party. In this case, one Smit bought furniture on hire purchase from the respondent. The hire-purchase agreement provided that the purchase price would be paid in instalments and that Jacksons reserved ownership until the last instalment was paid. At the time that Smit bought the furniture, he was living in an area called Shannon Valley. Then, without informing Jacksons, he moved to Bloemfontein and leased a house from Bloemfontein Municipality. Shortly after moving to Bloemfontein, Smit began to experience financial difficulties. He fell into arrears with the instalments he owed Jacksons and also rental payments to the Bloemfontein Municipality. The municipality then had the furniture attached in execution of the debt. When Jacksons discovered that the furniture, which still belonged to them, had been attached, they applied for an order declaring that the furniture was not subject to the lessor's tacit hypothec. In support of its application, Jackson's argued that the furniture had been brought onto the leased premises without its consent.

The Appellate Division rejected this argument and found that the furniture was indeed subject to the lessor's tacit hypothec. The court took the view that although Smit did not inform Jacksons that he was moving to Bloemfontien, Jacksons could quite easily have discovered where its furniture was, and informed the Bloemfontein Municipality that it was the owner of the furniture if it had simply taken reasonable steps to do so. Instead, for more than a year and despite the fact that Smit kept falling into arrears with his instalments, Jacksons had done nothing. It took no steps at all to discover where its furniture was, nor to inform the Bloemfontein Municipality that it was the owner of the furniture. In the circumstances, given Jacksons' failure to take steps to protect its property from the lessor's tacit hypothec, the inevitable inference was that Jacksons had consented impliedly to its furniture being subject to the lessor's tacit hypothec.

PAUSE FOR REFLECTION	Implications of *Bloemfontein Municipality v Jacksons*
	The judgment in *Bloemfontein Municipality v Jacksons* has serious implications for a third party whose property has been brought onto leased premises without her knowledge. This is because it essentially provides that even when a third party does not know that her property has been brought onto the leased premises, a court may nevertheless still find that the third party has through her conduct consented impliedly to her property being subject to the lessor's tacit hypothec. The judgment in *Bloemfontein Municipality v Jacksons* has consequently widened the scope of the lessor's tacit hypothec and made it easier for a lessor to attach a third party's property. Apart from favouring the lessor over the owner, the judgment may also be criticised on the grounds that it is difficult to understand how a person can consent, either expressly or impliedly, to something which she does not actually know about.

---

178 *Bloemfontein Municipality v Jacksons* 1929 AD 266 at 271; *TR Services (Pty) Ltd v Poynton's Corner Ltd* 1961 (1) SA 773 (D) at 775B–C; *Paradise Lost Properties v Standard Bank of South Africa (Pty) Ltd* 1997 (2) SA 815 (D) at 818G.
179 *LAWSA* Vol 17(2) at para 440.
180 *Paradise Lost Properties v Standard Bank of South Africa (Pty) Ltd* 1997 (2) SA 815 (D) at 822G–H.
181 1929 AD 266.

It is important to note that the advent of the Security by Means of Movable Property Act[182] excludes the lessor's tacit hypothec in respect of property bought in terms of an instalment sale agreement.[183] Similarly, movable property subject to a special notarial bond and in the possession of a person other than the bond holder is excluded from the lessor's tacit hypothec[184] unless the hypothec was perfected before the bond was registered.

12.5.1.2 Tacit hypothec of a seller under an instalment sale agreement

An instalment sale agreement allows the purchase price to be paid in periodic instalments after delivery of the property has occurred. In other words, the seller extends credit to the purchaser notwithstanding that the property is delivered into the physical control of the purchaser.[185] To secure payment of the purchase price, such an agreement contains a clause that reserves ownership of the property to the seller (credit grantor) until the last instalment has been paid by the buyer (credit grantee).[186]

If the credit grantee is declared insolvent before the last instalment is paid, the Insolvency Act[187] provides that the instalment sale agreement creates a tacit hypothec in favour of the credit grantor. This hypothec secures the credit grantor's claim to the outstanding instalments. The credit grantor has a preferential claim to the proceeds of the sale of the movable property in question.[188] It must be noted, however, that an important consequence is that the credit grantor loses ownership of the property in question because one cannot have a limited real right in one's own property. Ownership is transferred to the trustee of the insolvent estate and the credit grantor acquires a real security right in the form of the tacit hypothec.[189]

Lastly, it is important to note that the definition of an instalment sale agreement in the Insolvency Act[190] is not the same as the definition of an instalment sale agreement in the National Credit Act.[191] This means that the tacit hypothec of a seller under an instalment sale agreement applies to every instalment sale agreement which falls into the definition of an instalment sale agreement in the Insolvency Act, and not only to those instalment sale agreements which fall into the definition of an instalment sale agreement in the National Credit Act.[192]

12.5.2 Right of retention or lien

A lien may be a real security right that arises by operation of law or it may be a personal right. In both cases, the right is coupled with a right of retention. The underlying purpose of a lien is to secure repayment of money or labour that the lien holder has expended on

---

182 Act 57 of 1993.
183 Section 2 of the Security by Means of Movable Property Act, read with the definition of 'instalment sale agreement' per s 1 of the National Credit Act 34 of 2005.
184 Section 2 of the Security by Means of Movable Property Act.
185 As per the definition of 'instalment agreement' in s 1 of the National Credit Act 34 of 2005.
186 *Brooklyn House Furnishers (Pty) Ltd v Knoetze and Sons* 1970 (3) SA 264 (A) at 270F and *Bombay Properties (Pty) Ltd v Ferrox Construction* 1996 (2) SA 853 (W) at 856C and 858I.
187 Section 84 of the Insolvency Act 24 of 1936.
188 *Wille's Principles* p 659.
189 Scott *Commerce* p 272.
190 Act 24 of 1936.
191 Act 34 of 2005.
192 *Potgieter NO v Daewoo Heavy Industries (Edms) Bpk* 2003 (3) SA 98 (SCA).

the owner's movable or immovable property. It functions as a defence to the owner's *rei vindicatio* and entitles the lien holder to retain possession of the property until compensated for the expenditure incurred. It does not include the right to have the property sold in execution.[193]

Like other real security rights, a lien is accessory in nature. As soon as the lien holder's claim has been paid, the lien terminates automatically.[194] A lien differs from a tacit hypothec in certain respects. Most notably, the lien holder must exercise physical control over the property. This requirement and others are discussed in the following paragraphs.

12.5.2.1 Requirements

Possession is an essential requirement for the existence of a lien.[195] A lien comes into existence only if the property in question was in the lien holder's possession at the time the expenditure was incurred.[196] Both elements of possession must be satisfied, i.e. the lien holder must exercise exclusive physical control over the property (*corpus* element) with the intention to hold the property as security for the payment of the principal debt (*animus* element).[197]

To sustain the lien, the lien holder must continue to possess the property until payment occurs. If the lien holder loses possession, the lien is terminated automatically. Voluntary loss of possession terminates the lien irrevocably, i.e. permanently. Unlawful deprivation of possession, however, does not terminate the lien permanently, i.e. the lien terminates with loss of possession but, if the lien holder lawfully regains possession at a later stage, the lien can be revived.[198]

In *Singh v Santam Insurance Ltd*,[199] the Supreme Court of Appeal emphasised the rule that the lien holder must have been in possession of the property at the time the expenditure was incurred. Singh owned a motor car that was damaged in an accident while being driven by Muthusamy who was insured with the respondent (Santam). Santam instructed a panel beater to carry out the necessary repairs to the car, for which Santam paid. Then it discovered that Muthusamy had not paid premiums on his insurance policy. Consequently, Santam cancelled the policy and took possession of the motor car. Singh instituted a claim for return of the car on the ground that she was the owner. Santam countered on the basis that it had acquired a lien over the car because it had spent money to repair it.

The court rejected Santam's argument, explaining that a lien is acquired only if the person has the property in question in his possession when money or labour is expended on it. The repairs had been carried out and paid for before Santam acquired possession of the motor car, which meant that Santam could not have acquired a lien. The court underscored that '[w]hat the law requires for a lien is that the outlay should occur while the party claiming it is in possession of the subject matter.'[200]

---

193 See generally *Wille's Principles* pp 661–665.
194 *Wille's Principles* pp 661–662.
195 *LAWSA* Vol 15(2) at para 51.
196 *Singh v Santam Insurance Ltd* 1997 (1) SA 291 (SCA).
197 *LAWSA* Vol 15(2) at para 52.
198 *LAWSA* Vol 15(2) at para 53.
199 1997 (1) SA 291 (SCA).
200 *Singh v Santam Insurance Limited* 1997 (1) SA 291 (SCA) at 295.

A lien thus comes into existence when the lien holder has expended money or labour on property that belongs to another person. This expenditure must give rise to a valid claim for compensation in terms of the law of unjustified enrichment, or for payment in terms of the law of contract. The lien holder must have been in possession of the property at the time he expended the money or labour on it, and must have retained possession of it.

Note that a lien is a discretionary remedy. This means that a court must be persuaded by evidence that shows the justness of recognising the lien. This is because even if all requirements are met, a court may decide that, in the particular circumstances, it would not be just to recognise a lien.[201]

12.5.2.2 Operation

A lien confers a right of retention on the lien holder. It does not in itself confer a right on the lien holder to have the property attached and sold in execution.[202] In addition, it gives the lien holder a preferential claim upon insolvency of the owner. The ranking of this preferential claim depends on whether it is an enrichment lien, or a debtor and creditor lien.[203]

In the case of an enrichment lien, the lien holder's claim is ranked above those of all the other creditors, including those creditors who have a real security right in the property. In the case of a debtor and creditor lien, the lien holder's claim is ranked above those of the concurrent creditors, but below the claims of those creditors who have a real security right in the property.[204]

Although the lien holder is entitled to possess the property, she is not entitled to use it. While the property is in the possession of the lien holder, she is also required to take reasonable care of it.[205]

12.5.2.3 Types of liens

Liens are divided into two categories, namely enrichment liens and debtor and creditor liens. **Enrichment liens** are based on the principle of unjustified enrichment, and are usually classified as either salvage liens or improvement liens. **Debtor and creditor liens** flow from a contractual relationship between parties.

Enrichment liens arise in those cases where one person has spent money or labour on another person's property without the owner's consent or without a legal obligation to do so.[206] An enrichment lien comes into existence when the expenses incurred were necessary or useful, but not where they were luxurious.[207] Consequently, it is important to distinguish between necessary, useful, and luxurious expenses.

Necessary expenses are those which preserve or protect the property, while useful expenses are those which increase the market value of the property, and which are considered useful according to the economic and social views of the community. Luxurious expenses are those expenses which are incurred at the whim of a particular person, and

---

201 Van der Walt, AJ & Pienaar, GH (2002) *Introduction to the Law of Property* 4 ed (Cape Town, Juta) p 317.
202 *Brooklyn House Furnishers (Pty) Ltd v Knoetze and Sons* 1970 (3) SA 264 (A) at 270F; *Bombay Properties (Pty) Ltd v Ferrox Construction* 1996 (2) SA 853 (W) at 856C and 858I.
203 *LAWSA* Vol 15(2) at para 83.
204 *LAWSA* Vol 15(2) at para 83.
205 Sharrock, R (2007) *Business Transactions Law* 7 ed (Cape Town, Juta) p 592.
206 *Wille's Principles* pp 662–663.
207 *Wille's Principles* pp 663–664.

which are considered luxurious according the economic and social views of the community. They may also increase the market value of the property.[208]

As the definitions set out above indicate, the mere fact that an expense increases the market value of the property does not mean that it is a useful expense. This is because both useful and luxurious expenses may increase the market value of the property. The classification of an expense as either useful or luxurious depends, therefore, upon the economic and social views of the community. This means that it may be difficult to distinguish between useful and luxurious expenses in practice.[209]

The distinction between **salvage liens** and **improvement liens** is based on the difference between necessary and useful expenses. A salvage lien secures a claim for necessary expenses, while an improvement lien is associated with a claim for useful expenses.[210] Both salvage and improvement liens are real security rights, enforceable against the owner, successors in title, as well as holders of other limited real rights in the property, even if the latter were created before the lien came into existence.[211]

Debtor and creditor liens arise when a person (the creditor) expends money or labour on an owner's (the debtor's) property in terms of a valid contract, and serve to secure the creditor's claim for payment of the full contract price, regardless of whether the expenses were necessary, useful, or luxurious.[212] The amount secured by a debtor and creditor lien may therefore be greater than the amount secured by an enrichment lien.[213]

Unlike salvage and improvement liens, a debtor and creditor lien is a personal right, not a real security right.[214] This means that it is enforceable only against the other party to the contract, namely the debtor. An important consequence of this rule is that a debtor and creditor lien is not enforceable against the owner of the property unless the owner is also the debtor, or has consented to the expenditure. In those cases where the debtor is the owner, the lien is also enforceable against a gratuitous successor in title and a successor in title who knew about the existence of the lien at the time the transfer of ownership took place.[215]

12.5.3 Termination

A lien may be terminated in the same way as other real security rights,[216] namely by discharge of the principal debt; destruction of the property; *confusio* and merger; and waiver. A lien will also be terminated if the lien holder loses possession of the property.

The owner of the property or any person with a possessory right to the property may defeat the lien by furnishing adequate security for the payment of the lien holder's claim. A court will, however, take into account all the circumstances before exercising its discretion to order restoration of the property.[217]

---

208 Visser, D (2008) *Unjustified Enrichment* (Cape Town, Juta) pp 600–602.
209 Visser, D (2008) *Unjustified Enrichment* (Cape Town, Juta) p 601.
210 *LAWSA* Vol 15(2) at para 54.
211 *LAWSA* Vol 15(2) at para 62.
212 *Wille's Principles* p 663.
213 *LAWSA* Vol 15(2) at para 68.
214 *Wille's Principles* p 663.
215 *LAWSA* Vol 15(2) at para 72.
216 See pp 314, 320 above.
217 *Wille's Principles* p 665.

12.6 Judicial real security rights: created by court order

When a creditor has taken judgment against a debtor who has failed to comply, the creditor may enforce the judgment by applying for a writ of execution. The writ serves as a warrant that authorises the sheriff to attach the debtor's movable or immovable property.[218] Attachment of the debtor's property creates a real security right in favour of the creditor. This real security right is usually referred to as a **judicial pledge** where the attached property is movable, and as a **judicial mortgage** where the attached property is immovable.[219] These real security rights provide the creditor with a preferential claim to the proceeds of the sale of the attached property. This preferential claim ranks above the claims of unsecured creditors, but below those of creditors who acquired real rights of security in the property prior to attachment. The creditor's preferential claim ranks equally with claims of other creditors who also have writs of execution against the same property.[220] Additional writs of execution, therefore, diminish the first preferential right of a creditor to a **pro rata** share in the proceeds of the sale in execution. It should be noted, also, that s 98 of the Insolvency Act[221] provides that insolvency of the debtor after attachment terminates the creditor's preferential claim, except for the costs of the execution.[222]

Attachment of immovable property is possible only if the movable property is not sufficient.[223] Note, however, that in *Jaftha v Schoeman*,[224] the Constitutional Court held that a writ of execution may not be issued against a debtor's home unless consideration has been given to whether the sale in execution would infringe the debtor's constitutional right of access to housing.[225] Such infringement occurs when the sale in execution would cause the hardship and prejudice suffered by the debtor to far outweigh the benefit to the creditor.

On attachment, possession of the debtor's property passes into the hands of an officer responsible for executing the writ of execution, who must take reasonable care of it. At this stage, the debtor may redeem the property by paying the full judgment debt and the costs involved in attachment. If the debtor fails to redeem the property, it is sold by public auction and the proceeds are used to settle the judgment debt. Any surplus proceeds or property that remains after the debt has been settled must be paid over or returned to the debtor.[226]

---

218 *Silberberg & Schoeman Property* p 407.
219 *LAWSA* Vol 17(2) at para 449.
220 *Wille's Principles* pp 638–639.
221 Act 24 of 1936.
222 *LAWSA* Vol 17(2) at para 452.
223 *Wille's Principles* p 660. Except if the debt is secured by a special mortgage of immovable property: see p 309.
224 *Jaftha v Schoeman and Others; Van Rooyen v Stolz and Others* 2005 (2) SA 140 (CC).
225 In terms of s 26 of the Constitution.
226 *Wille's Principles* p 661.

12.7 Concluding remarks

Real security is important to commercial activity. It provides the mechanism that allows owners to maximise the potential to generate wealth by offering their existing property as security for credit. Simultaneously, real security binds owners who choose to use their property in this way, thus affording creditors limited real rights over the bonded property. It is not surprising, therefore, that there has been significant judicial activity involving security rights and constitutional property protection,[227] and security rights and the guarantee against eviction.[228] The manner in which such jurisprudence is changing the face of property law forms part of the analysis in the following, final chapter.

---

227 *First National Bank t/a Wesbank v Commissioner, South African Revenue Service* 2001 (3) SA 310 (C).
228 *Jaftha v Schoeman and Others; Van Rooyen v Stoltz and Others* 2005 (2) SA 140 (CC).

12.7 Concluding remarks

Few issues... It is important to contrast approaches that take these characteristics flows into account... the mechanics of the interaction, and so on... which is modeling these systems is open as is each of the simulations. We note that the fields... in the changes to see that it comes to the way... modeling techniques until a relatively... the interplay between the ... fluxes, the mechanics and electro... that there has been significant activity involving examples of their... occupational elastic... property processing... and so on... ... the manner in which this work is underway is changing the... the implications for some of the subjects including... engineering.

PART FOUR

OVERVIEW OF THE PRINCIPLES OF PROPERTY LAW IN ITS NEW CONTEXT

CHAPTER 13 Prospects of property law 337

Chapter 13

Prospects of property law

'... the more thought we give to basic familiar things – sex, friendship, life and death; and landownership I suggest is in that class – the more our sense of wonder grows. And the deeper we probe, the more we find that error, at times paraded as learning, has to be pruned away.'

DV Cowen 'New Patterns of Land Ownership: The Transformation of the Concept of Ownership as *Plena in re Potestas*' (paper read at the University of the Witwatersrand on 24 April 1984)[1]

13.1	Retrospect	337
13.2	Property law recontextualised	338
13.3	Principles and challenges	340
13.3.1	Transmissibility	340
13.3.2	*Numerus clausus*	341
13.3.3	Publicity	343
13.3.4	Abstraction	344
13.3.5	Absoluteness	345
13.3.6	Specificity	346
13.3.7	Responsibility and trust	347
13.4	Concluding remarks	349

13.1 Retrospect

The preceding chapters have provided an overview of the principles of property law as they are understood and applied currently within the specific historic, socio-economic, and constitutional context of South African law. The aim has been to provide a strong foundation on which to build a good understanding of the principles of property law to foster the skills needed to engage with them independently and judiciously.

The continued efficacy and legitimacy of the law depends largely on the calibre of the lawyers who design, drive and utilise it. To that end, future lawyers should acquire not only knowledge of property law, but also a sound understanding of its context, challenges and imperatives. We do not propose that this book is a 'critical' text in the legal-theoretical sense,

---

[1] Now published as Cowen, DV (2008) 'New Patterns of Land Ownership: The Transformation of the Concept of Ownership as *Plena in re Potestas*' in Cowen, S (ed) *Cowen on Law – Selected Essays* (Cape Town, Juta) p 280.

which would mean that the critique it offers would be 'either abstract/conceptual or social/transformative or, ideally, both'.[2] Yet, the very nature of property law in South Africa makes it impossible to engage with its principles in a non-conceptual way, oblivious to its role in the social-transformational imperative.[3] It would be remiss not to impart this approach to a new generation of property lawyers.

13.2 Property law recontextualised

Property is 'a fundamentally social and political institution'[4] and, as such, has notable features. First, it is predominant. Davies explains that 'our laws, our political communities, our lives, are very much shaped by the presence, the boundaries and the weight of property.'[5] This posits that property is central to the model of social organisation prevalent in our context.[6] Second, property has value because it is, fundamentally, a wealth-creating commodity. Land rights, for instance, make secure homes and business places possible because one of the entitlements associated with land rights is exclusivity. Third, property is inherently exclusionary. Exclusivity ensures that the other entitlements of property, such as use and enjoyment, disposal, and encumbrance can be practised. Fourth, property can be used as security to access finance.[7] In this context, the mortgage bond has been described as 'an indispensable tool for spreading home ownership'.[8] The downside of predominance, exclusivity, value, and security in this combination is that they render the institution of property highly likely to cause or to exacerbate hardship and suffering for those who cannot access it.

It is true that few people can acquire a home without using a mortgage bond to secure a loan. What is also true, however, is that use of this tool is not open to many South Africans. Widespread poverty and landlessness in the country prevent this kind of access to financial markets. It should also be noted that customary law provides an alternative mode of access to land and thus a home without engaging the formal financial sector.[9] This is possible within strictly confined parameters.

The fact that our understanding of property is contextual, that it relies on social, economic and political factors, means that it is affected by processes to bring about change.[10] Intervention in entrenched positions is necessary for all kinds of reasons, many of them unspectacular: for instance, no home owner should raise an eyebrow about the need for planning permission and approval from the municipal building authorities to extend his existing residence. Planning and building controls are regarded as a normal exercise of the state's regulatory capacity in the interests of other home owners and society at large. Similarly, the requirement that liquor dealers must have a valid licence or that tobacco dealers must comply with strict conditions is accepted as a legitimate intervention. What makes these interventions unspectacular is that they do not affect the stability of the system in which property law operates. Such interventions 'allow a measure of flexibility that can

---

2   Davies, M (2007) *Property – Meanings, Histories and Theories* (Abingdon, Routledge-Cavendish GlassHouse) p 6.
3   Davies, M (2007) *Property – Meanings, Histories and Theories* (Abingdon, Routledge-Cavendish GlassHouse) pp 4–7.
4   Van der Walt, AJ (2009) *Property in the Margins* (Oxford, Hart Publishing) p 211.
5   Davies, M (2007) *Property – Meanings, Histories and Theories* (Abingdon, Routledge-Cavendish GlassHouse) p 116.
6   Compare Cowen, DV, (2008) 'New Patterns of Land Ownership: The Transformation of the Concept of Ownership as *Plena in re Potestas*' in Cowen, S (ed) *Cowen on Law – Selected Essays* (Cape Town, Juta) p 280.
7   See ch 12 above.
8   *Standard Bank of Southern Africa Ltd v Saunderson* 2006 (2) SA 264 (SCA) at para 1.
9   Bennett, TW (2004) *Customary Law in South Africa* (Cape Town, Juta) p 409.
10 Van der Walt, AJ (2009) *Property in the Margins* (Oxford, Hart Publishing) p 212.

accommodate some regulatory change, without challenging or reconsidering existing values or assumptions about the place and role of property in society.[11]

The situation is significantly different and more contentious where reforms undermine 'central certainties or values' of the system; where they challenge existing property doctrine fundamentally or place 'issues or values that are considered irrelevant or marginal at the centre of [a] new policy focus'.[12] For instance, the reaction to judicial intervention that prevents a landowner from enforcing her rights of ownership against someone without any property rights simply because of his poverty and vulnerability, has been widespread and vociferous.[13] Likewise, the government's attempts to reform the system of mineral holding in South Africa by replacing private law property based entitlements with administrative rights, elicited extensive and extremely diverse reactions.[14]

These kinds of transformative efforts force a reconsideration of property law from the perspectives of both poor and rich.[15] They may wonder what to expect from property law in the future: will aspirations be realisable? From another perspective, one may ponder the responsibilities of everyone currently with or without property interests. At the rich, high-value end of the spectrum, the expectation remains that property law must secure and protect vested property interests. But as the preceding discussion has shown, there is burgeoning awareness, and concomitant expectations, that property law must serve the poor, low-value end of the spectrum as well: it is expected to address vulnerability and hardship. Can property law meet such high expectations and thus be 'all things to all men (and women)'? We posit that it can – under certain conditions.

The most important condition is the realisation that expectations cannot be divorced from responsibilities, whether individual or state. Another condition is the recognition that transformative property law challenges not only normative assumptions about its own purpose on the rich-poor spectrum, but also established views about its own scope and function within the arenas of private law, public law and customary law. The notion that property is a matter of private law is no longer accurate:[16] although the rules governing acquisition, protection and transfer of property are based in private law,[17] they are inevitably and undeniably influenced by public law and, increasingly, by customary law so as to give effect to the paramount constitutional values of dignity, equality and freedom.

In a pluralist legal system, by definition, it would be idealistic (if not naïve) to expect an exact match between the different property regimes. Nevertheless, the current efforts[18] to harmonise the rules of property law with those of customary law are important. Both systems utilise property as a central organising concept, which admits of different rules and principles. However, the paramount values and expectations of the Constitution must have increasing visibility in both systems. Consequently, a reasonable expectation might be an increasing similarity in the visible **values** of these different systems, if not in the actual **rules**.[19]

The ability to hold and control property, especially land, is fundamental to economic

---

11 Van der Walt, AJ (2009) *Property in the Margins* (Oxford, Hart Publishing) p 213.
12 Van der Walt, AJ (2009) *Property in the Margins* (Oxford, Hart Publishing) p 213.
13 See e.g. Cox, A 'Squatters can't be evicted in one go' 15.04.2007 *The Star* 5; SamaYende, S 'Burial tradition challenged' 27.01.2003 *www.news24.com* viewed on 17.09.2009.
14 See e.g. Macleod, F 'Landowners haul miners over the coals' 28.06.2007 *Mail & Guardian* p 12.
15 Van der Walt, AJ (2009) *Property in the Margins* (Oxford, Hart Publishing) p 214.
16 See ch 1 above.
17 See ch 5 and 7 above.
18 See e.g. *Alexkor (Pty) Ltd and Another v Richtersveld Community and Others* 2004 (5) SA 460 (CC) at paras 51, 62.
19 See further ch 5 above.

development, wealth creation (in the broad sense), and the consequent alleviation of poverty.[20] This strongly held idea underlies the transformative property efforts. We suggest that, for all the diversity of need, class, race and rank in our society, the common goal is to maximise wealth. But this must be done in a responsible and socially responsive manner. Different views may exist on how this goal is to be achieved. New political realities are relevant to future implementation of property law principles, and new policies affect the manner in which such established principles are likely to be understood.

13.3 Principles and challenges

Writing about South African property law in the twentieth century, Van der Merwe[21] began his seminal discussion of the topic by listing the principles of property: the *numerus clausus* principle (i.e. that property law adheres to closed categories or systems); absoluteness; publicity; abstraction; specificity; and transmissibility. These same principles underpin the discussion in the preceding chapters, demonstrating that they are still at the heart of South African property law. Their meaning and implementation may, however, be significantly different in this modern, twenty-first century context of transformation and change.

Van der Walt points out that considerations that were marginal to any enquiry based in property law a few decades ago, now take central stage in particular circumstances, forcing a review of established assumptions.[22] For example, factors such as social or economic vulnerability may inform a redetermination of the functions and purposes of property law in current circumstances, such as when eviction is at stake. Throughout this book, we have attempted to accentuate these considerations. In this section, we revisit the principles of property with these socially responsive considerations in mind. We simultaneously highlight some of the inevitable challenges raised by the constitutional prism through which these principles must be viewed.

In reviewing these principles, it will be obvious that some still are very much at the core of South African property law. So, for instance, publicity and abstraction are as important today as they were in the previous century. Other principles have been diluted or displaced to a significant extent due to the transitional paradigm in which property law now operates. This renders it necessary to revisit the principles of absoluteness and specificity in view of recent judicial and constitutional developments.[23] In addition, we argue that the conventional principles must be supplemented by core social and democratic values, as expressed most significantly by what we regard as hitherto unacknowledged principles of property, such as 'responsibility' and 'trust'. The principles of property are vulnerable when the responsibilities that accompany them and the trust underpinning them are not fully understood and acknowledged.[24]

13.3.1 Transmissibility

It is uncontentious that real rights are freely alienable and transmissible.[25] Exceptions are acknowledged, e.g. where real rights follow the person of their holder closely, such

---

20 De Soto, H (2001) *The Mystery of Capital: Why Capitalism Triumphs in the West and Fails Everywhere Else* (London, Black Swan) pp 6-9.
21 Van der Merwe, CG (1979) *Sakereg* 1 ed (Durban, Butterworths) pp 9-16; Van der Merwe *Sakereg* pp 10-18.
22 Van der Walt, AJ (2009) *Property in the Margins* (Oxford, Hart Publishing) pp 211-212, 214-215.
23 See the discussions at pp 220*ff* and pp 76*ff*.
24 See pp 344*ff* below.
25 Van der Merwe *Sakereg* p 16.

as personal servitudes (usufruct, *habitatio* etc.).[26] These are inalienable. Furthermore, a servitude generally cannot be alienated separately from the dominant tenement.[27] The alienability of land may be limited contractually or statutorily. In the case of a limitation on alienation per agreement, the conditions must be registered against the title deed to the land.[28] If property is the subject of a real security right, the parties may agree that alienation of the relevant property is excluded until the debt is extinguished.[29]

Indigenous land rights are transmissible in terms of and within the parameters of customary law. One might say, thus, that these rights are conditionally transmissible because most alienation takes place within the extended family grouping rather than freely.[30]

13.3.2 *Numerus clausus*

Relatively uncontentious at first sight is the reliance of South African property law on closed categories or systems.[31] Doctrinally, there is a *numerus clausus* of constructive modes of delivery[32] and of modes of original acquisition of ownership. Where the *numerus clausus* principle is applicable, high levels of certainty are possible: any attempt at acquiring ownership unilaterally must fulfil the requirements of one of the established original modes to succeed.[33] By contrast, in the absence of a closed system, the law is inherently more flexible, and the options inherently less certain. The fact that a *numerus clausus* of real rights does not exist enables users to customise arrangements to suit their specific needs. This possibility, however, leads to greater uncertainty as to whether customised arrangements translate into registrable land rights.[34] Although a closed systems approach advances legal certainty, adaptation to modern conditions is made more difficult.[35] The continuing debate about whether *cessio iuris vindicationis* should be regarded as a new form of constructive delivery illustrates the dilemma: to permit transfer of ownership merely by 'ceding' the power to vindicate the property may provide a useful tool for commercial purposes, but, equally, it may disadvantage those it is meant to serve, especially if abused.[36]

Several challenges arise from the constitutional imperative to transform particularly land holding. The conventional common law view of landownership is hierarchical and, in this way, manifests the principle of closed systems: ownership is regarded as the most extensive, comprehensive right in land, at the pinnacle of the hierarchy, and the only right one can hold in one's own property. Limited real rights are held in others' property and are registrable. But these rights (ownership and limited real rights) represent but a small percentage of the rights in land currently utilised in South Africa. Yet, most land reform laws aspire to broadening access to land by expanding the base of landowners in the

---

26 See pp 248*ff* above.
27 See p 243 above.
28 See ch 3 and 6 above.
29 *Wille's Principles* p 411.
30 Bennett, TW (2004) *Customary Law in South Africa* (Cape Town, Juta) pp 402–409.
31 Van der Merwe *Sakereg* p 11.
32 See pp 198*ff* above. Note the divided opinion about cession of the *rei vindicatio* as a mode of transfer of ownership.
33 See ch 7 above.
34 See pp 49*ff* above.
35 *Wille's Principles* p 410.
36 See p 209 above.

conventional sense of the word.[37] It has been suggested that such forms of 'titling' (i.e. formalising land holding to match the conventional patterns of landownership) cannot appropriately address the demands placed on land reform, especially redistribution.[38] Alternative solutions are sought, to some extent, by recognising the diverse forms of tenure that have crystallised under customary law, but reinforcing them statutorily. This reinforcement affords greater security of title than was the case under apartheid.[39] This approach is referred to the 'tenure' option in land reform circles.[40]

> **PAUSE FOR REFLECTION** **Titling and tenure within a closed systems approach**
>
> With reference to the closed systems principle, the developments around communal land[41] in South Africa serve as an example of the difficulties of giving effect to s 25(6) of the Constitution while managing legal pluralism in the manner envisaged by the Constitutional Court.[42] Claassens demonstrates convincingly that people living in rural areas often 'have no option but to engage with customary law because of its impact on power relations at the local level.'[43] Consequently, users within the customary tenure paradigm are restricted to that system unless the law provides exit routes from customary tenure arrangements.[44] However, the justification for an exit route would not easily fit with the Constitutional Court's direction to recognise the parallel system of customary tenure as having equivalent status with conventional land title.[45] The result is two parallel, doctrinally closed systems of land holding, one that we term common law title and the other customary land tenure.

In recognising the parallel systems of common law title and customary tenure, a further challenge arises. At stake is one of the inherent tensions underlying property law, namely that between individual interests and those of third parties (or the public). From the public interest point of view, a utilitarian approach would improve the socio-economic circumstances of relatively large numbers of people by adopting a particular form for securing land interests (e.g. by acknowledging customary tenure and protecting it via statute). From an individual point of view, however, it might be that this approach does not improve the position in reality, unless land rights of particular interest groups (e.g. rural black women) are specifically attended to statutorily.

Moreover, any solution that does not utilise land registration suffers from at least two defects: one is the inherent lack of certainty that flows from disregard for the publicity

---

37 Mostert, H (2003) 'The Diversification of Land Rights and its Implications for a New Land Law in South Africa' in Cooke, EJ *Modern Studies in Property Law* (Oxford, Hart Publishing) p 20.
38 Cousins, B (2008) 'Contextualizing the Controversies: Dilemmas of Communal Tenure Reform on Post-Apartheid South Africa' in Claassens, A & Cousins, B (eds) *Land, Power & Custom: Controversies generated by South Africa's Communal Land Rights Act* (Cape Town, UCT Press) pp 15*ff*.
39 Cousins, B '"Embeddedness" versus Titling: African Land Tenure Systems and the Potential Impacts of the Communal Land Rights Act 11 of 2004' (2005) 3 *Stell LR* 488 at 512.
40 Pienaar, GJL 'The Land Titling Debate in South Africa' (2006) 3 *TSAR* 435 at 436–439.
41 See ch 5 above.
42 See discussion in *Alexkor (Pty) Ltd and Another v Richtersveld Community and Others* 2004 (5) SA 460 (CC) at para 51 in ch 1.
43 Claassens, A (2008) 'Customary Law and Zones of Chiefly Sovereignty: Impact of Government Policy on whose Voices Prevail in the Making and Changing of Customary Law' in Claassens, A & Cousins, B (eds) *Land, Power & Custom: Controversies generated by South Africa's Communal Land Rights Act* (Cape Town, UCT Press) p 357.
44 See e.g. s 5 of the Communal Land Rights Act 11 of 2004.
45 *Alexkor (Pty) Ltd and Another v Richtersveld Community and Others* 2004 (5) SA 460 (CC) at para 62.

principle;[46] the other is the lack of transparency which hinders the ability to give effect to the rights to dignity, equality and freedom, particularly for interest groups such as rural black women. For example, the Extension of Security of Tenure Act[47] includes provisions that give rise to statutory limited real rights for 'occupiers' in particular circumstances. These real rights are not registered, but were intended to give secure rights to their holders. It is common knowledge that, notwithstanding their existence, 'occupiers' have been evicted and effectively stripped of such rights.[48] Part of the problem lies in the fact that these statutory real rights do not form part of the land registration system, which leads to the fact that they are not public or transparent. 'Occupiers' have difficulty in proving their claims to such rights. This results in evictions that are unfair, unjust and inequitable.

13.3.3 Publicity

A major tenet of property law is that property transactions must be publicised in the interests of certainty and protection.[49] For this reason, South African law requires registration of landownership and real rights in land.[50] For the same reason, constructive modes of delivery require consonance between outwardly manifested conduct and a particular mindset in order to effect transfer of movable property.[51] Publicity is also the reason for the 'openly as if owner' requirement of prescription.[52] Further, physical control is an important manifestation of the publicity principle in matters relating to the acquisition of property.[53] It gives rise to the presumption of ownership of movables in the same way that registration gives rise to the presumption of ownership of land.

Yet, the efficacy of publicity in the context of movables is dubious. The modern economy is highly reliant on credit sales and hire-purchase agreements as recent legislative activity confirms.[54] Since there is no register of items purchased on credit or hire purchase, possession as a form of publicity in case of movables becomes impossible to assess. Possession is essential to the creation of real security rights (i.e. pledge) in respect of movables. But, even in this sphere, ingenious plans can be made to avoid the restrictive effect that the requirement of possession in the case of pledge places on the owner.[55]

---

46 Pienaar, GJ 'The Land Titling Debate in South Africa' (2006) 3 *TSAR* 435 at 448–449.
47 The Extension of Security of Tenure Act 62 of 1997.
48 See e.g. Roodt, MJ 'Security of tenure and livelihood options in South Africa: a case study of a rural community facing eviction under post-apartheid legislation in the Eastern Cape Province' (2007) 37 *Africanus* at 3–12.
49 Van der Merwe *Sakereg* p 13.
50 See ch 3 and ch 6 above.
51 See pp 198*ff* above.
52 See pp 179*ff* above.
53 See ch 7 above.
54 See ch 12 above and more generally the National Credit Act 34 of 2005.
55 See pp 314*ff* above.

> **PAUSE FOR REFLECTION**
>
> **The ethical dimension[56] of publicity**
>
> Cooke cautions that for all the advantages posed by land registration, it has 'an appalling potential for oppression'.[57] She illustrates this claim by reference to the abuse of the registration system under apartheid that was used to create a system of spatial racial segregation based on the distinction between secure and protected registered 'white' land rights, and insecure and unprotected unregistered 'black' land rights. The call is to 'somehow harness' the registration system to achieve a position of security and marketability for all land users.
>
> In the past, the Deeds Registry was forced to march to a particular political tune. The music has changed and yet the Deeds Registry still does its work. This phenomenon points to the neutrality of the institution and to the lack of neutrality of those who determine its role and function. In relation to customary tenure, claims are made that registration would be an alien notion and would serve to undermine the integrity of customary land rights.[58] As was pointed out above, inherent dysfunctionality results from attempts to bypass the registration system.[59] What ought to be obvious is that the objectives of land reform, specifically secure tenure, necessarily involve policy choices, sometimes difficult choices. The need to analyse conceptually as well as to include consideration of relevant values and norms is foundational to making good policy choices.

13.3.4 Abstraction

The principle of abstraction underlies the theory of transfer prevalent in South African law. As indicated, transfer of ownership depends on a valid real agreement and an appropriate mode of delivery.[60] The presence of an underlying contract (i.e. the reason for transfer) is acknowledged but is not a prerequisite for transfer to occur.[61] The existence of the real agreement is decisive for an effective transfer. Importantly, as a component of the real agreement, the parties must intend to transfer ownership. If this is the case, infirmities in the underlying contract cannot frustrate the transfer. This illustrates the principle of abstraction.[62] This principle simplifies the legal position in that the moment at which transfer occurs is easily determinable, hence supporting legal certainty as well as the principle of publicity.

The challenge here (in the context of land reform especially) is to impart knowledge and understanding of a particularly abstract notion of transfer to a constituency of users who (for reasons of ignorance, illiteracy or inexperience) rely on the visible manifestations of what they regard as legal acts, rather than their doctrinal consequences. This educative approach is in line with the views of De Soto, who points out that when property rights and interests are not adequately documented:

---

56 Cooke, EJ (2003) *The new law of land registration* (Oxford, Hart Publishing) pp 12-13.
57 Cooke, EJ (2003) *The new law of land registration* (Oxford, Hart Publishing) p 13.
58 Kingwill, R (2008) 'Custom-building Freehold Title: The impact of family values on historical ownership in the Eastern Cape' in Claassens, A & Cousins, B (eds) *Land, Power & Custom: Controversies generated by South Africa's Communal Land Rights Act* (Cape Town, UCT Press) p 185.
59 See pp 342-343 above.
60 See pp 191*ff* above.
61 See pp 189*ff* above.
62 Van der Merwe *Sakereg* p 17.

these assets cannot readily be turned into capital, cannot be traded outside of narrow local circles where people know and trust each other, cannot be used as collateral for a loan and cannot be used as a share against an investment.[63]

The example of Nodyose in chapter 1[64] is a case in point: by informally selling on the plot simply by handing over the document and accepting payment, she effectively nullifies the possibility of protection and certainty that the formal system could provide her and subsequent users. The crux of the matter here is that efforts to facilitate access to adequate housing and to address landlessness are frustrated, not so much by the usual complaints of lack of service delivery, etc., but by ignoring the protection already offered by the formal system and the need to abide by it.

On another front, a solid understanding of the principle of abstraction helps to clarify doctrinal issues around the inclusion of *cessio iuris vindicationis* as an independent mode of constructive delivery. The difficulties with the inclusive position have been pointed out already.[65] It is worth noting here that inclusion of cession as a mode of transfer of ownership points to a conflation of the transactions that make up transfer: the underlying contract and the real agreement with delivery. Cession refers to the transfer of the (personal) rights and obligations in terms of the underlying contract. To include the entitlement to vindicate, ownership must necessarily also be transferred. This can be done only in the accepted way, with delivery (actual or constructive) accompanying the real agreement.

13.3.5 Absoluteness

Absoluteness was regarded (by some) as a major feature of property law.[66] So, for instance, real rights were taken to provide absolute certainty as to the control over property and the ability to protect this control. In the past, an owner could be quite sure that, with recourse to the law, he would be able to rid his property of someone who occupies it unlawfully. We have shown that this no longer is the case.[67] Besides, absoluteness as a principle of property law has always been somewhat contentious. Visser[68] and Birks[69] indicated convincingly that the absoluteness of ownership is based on a misunderstanding of the civilian principles that underpin South African property law.

Although owners may still have extensive remedies to protect their property, their rights are curtailed now by considerations of equity and fairness. These considerations provide practical standards by which to measure compliance with the constitutional values of dignity, equality and freedom. This is aptly demonstrated with regard to the law on eviction[70] which undermines the core idea that property law protects property holders in an hierarchical fashion: those with acknowledged rights better than those with no rights at all; and owners better than non-owners.[71]

---

63 De Soto, H (2001) *The Mystery of Capital: Why Capitalism Triumphs in the West and Fails Everywhere Else* (London, Black Swan) p 6.
64 See p 4 above.
65 See pp 209*ff* above.
66 Van der Merwe *Sakereg* p 12.
67 See pp 217*ff* above.
68 Visser, DP 'The "Absoluteness" of Ownership: The South African Common Law in Perspective' (1985) *Acta Juridica* at 39.
69 Birks, P 'The Roman Law Concept of Dominium and the Idea of Absolute Ownership' (1985) *Acta Juridica* at 31 indicates that to describe the content of ownership as absolute is inappropriate since this suggests a degree of immunity. Conceptually, Roman law ownership was absolute in the sense that it was distinct, singular and exclusive, although even this understanding was subject to qualification.
70 See pp 220*ff* above.
71 Van der Walt, AJ (2009) *Property in the Margins* (Oxford, Hart Publishing) p 227.

In reality, the law may expect owners to tolerate even severe inroads on their rights for considerations that may be labelled as extraneous or subjective: 'the historical, social or economic context within which eviction takes place, and the personal or social circumstances of the [unlawful] occupier and the effect that eviction will have on her and her family or community.'[72] On the other hand, these considerations do not afford absolute protection for the unlawful occupier. In *Transnet Ltd v Nyawuza and Others*,[73] despite obvious hardship and the vulnerability of the unlawful occupiers, the public interest in their removal outweighed the individual interests of the occupiers.

13.3.6 Specificity

The specificity principle links particular property to particular real rights in such property. This translates, for instance, in the rule that a real right pertains to specific property of a person, not her property in general.[74] Specificity thus delineates the legal position of a person in respect of property in which she has rights and determines that alienation can occur only in respect of specifically identified property.[75] Thus, a clear and detailed description of the land forming the subject of a transfer must be contained in the deed of transfer. Also, the *rei vindicatio* requires that the property to be vindicated must exist and be identifiable. It is not possible to restore the owner's position by substituting a similar object.[76]

In this respect, fungibility of certain kinds of property may represent a qualification to the specificity principle. This is best seen in the context of the *mandament van spolie*,[77] where some courts adopted the stance that where the possessor cannot be restored to possession of the original property that had been damaged, restoration of something which is of 'similar size and quality' may be sufficient.[78] This development was influenced by the historical and political context in which these decisions were made. As a general proposition, however, the principle of specificity prevents substitution on the basis of fungibility.[79]

13.3.7 Responsibility and trust

The transformative context of property law has revealed another underlying truth about this discipline – one that we have attempted to highlight in the preceding chapters. Though not conventionally counted as a 'principle', 'no system of private property can ignore ... that property ... involve[s] responsibilities to others as well as privileges.'[80]

Ownership involves responsibility. For example, the owner is obliged to pay various rates and taxes relating to his landownership and must prevent harms from emanating from his property.[81] Ideally, responsibilities should be carried out willingly in a context

---

72 Van der Walt, AJ (2009) *Property in the Margins* (Oxford, Hart Publishing) p 226.
73 2006 (5) SA 100 (D) at 112F-H.
74 Van der Merwe *Sakereg* p 15.
75 See ch 7 above.
76 See ch 8 above.
77 See ch 4 above.
78 *Fredericks v Stellenbosch Divisional Council* 1977 (3) SA 113 (C); *Ierse Trog CC v Sultra Trading CC* 1997 (4) SA 131 (C); *Rikhotso v Northcliff Ceramics* (Pty) Ltd 1997 (1) SA 526 (W).
79 See *Wille's Principles* p 460; Van der Walt, AJ 'Squatting, spoliation order and the new constitutional order – casenote: *Rikhotso v Northcliff Ceramics* 1997 (1) SA 526 (W)' (1997) 60 *THRHR* 522-528; *Tswelopele Non-Profit Organisation and Others v City of Tshwane Metropolitan Municipality and Others* 2007 (6) SA 511 (SCA) at para 24; Van der Walt 'Developing the Law on Unlawful Squatting and Spoliation' (2008) 125 *SALJ* at 24-36.
80 Alexander, GS (1998) 'Critical Land Law' in Bright, S and Dewar, J *Land Law – Themes and Perspectives* (Oxford, Oxford University Press) p 77.
81 See further pp 145*ff*.

where social and economic infrastructure exists and functions well. This implies a relationship of trust: the owner trusts that payment of taxes will result in service delivery which permits optimal use and enjoyment of his property. Where this infrastructure does not function well, the first casualty is the trust relationship, followed by a reluctance to carry out the responsibilities. For example, in *Mkontwana v Nelson Mandela Metropolitan Municipality*,[82] the failure by the municipality to send out invoices for consumption charges timeously led to a backlog in the payment of such revenues. This in turn affected the ability of the landowners to alienate their properties because of the statutory obligation on the owner to ensure that all charges are paid up before alienation can be attempted.[83]

The role of responsibility and trust is demonstrated also by the Constitutional Court's eviction jurisprudence. Legislative mechanisms protect unlawful occupants from severe eviction practices[84] to avoid apartheid-style forced removals from land.[85] Invariably, the interests of landowners clash with those of the unlawful occupants. This means that in disputes between the state and landowners or between the state and unlawful occupants, inevitably there is a third dimension, in that the opposing interests of **two** different private stakeholders must be weighed against those of the public. This task requires the balancing of the conventional rights of ownership against the new, equally relevant right not to be arbitrarily deprived of a home,[86] without creating hierarchies of privilege. In addition, landlessness and homelessness (at the root of unlawful occupation of land) are social phenomena that can and have been manipulated to gain access to government-provided housing. By invoking dire circumstances, unlawful occupiers sometimes hope to obtain preferential treatment in the allocation of housing. This is generally referred to as 'queue-jumping'.[87]

The involvement of trust may be illustrated by the following. Arguably, unlawful occupiers have lost trust in the ability of the state to give effect to their fundamental right to access to adequate housing,[88] while, on the other hand, owners trust the existing legal mechanisms to protect their property interests.[89] The double irony is that having lost trust in the system, the unlawful occupiers are required to trust that the protective eviction measures put in place by the system will assist them. Notwithstanding their trust of existing legal mechanisms, owners have to come to terms with the fact that these mechanisms do not provide absolute protection.

The function of responsibility is reflected in the Constitutional Court's attempts to engage the state and to encourage individuals to fulfil their civic duties.[90] On the one

---

82 2005 (1) SA 530 (CC) at paras 19-20.
83 E.g. s 118(1) of the Local Government: Municipal Systems Act 32 of 2000.
84 See pp 220*ff* above.
85 But see *Tswelopele Non-Profit Organisation and Others v City of Tshwane Metropolitan Municipality and Others* 2007 (6) SA 511 (SCA) at para 16, which demonstrates that the existence of the legal mechanisms does not prevent authorities from engaging in apartheid-style removal.
86 *Tswelopele* at para 23.
87 *Port Elizabeth Municipality v Peoples Dialogue on Land and Shelter and Another* 2000 (2) SA 1074 (SE) at 1085H-J; *Port Elizabeth Municipality v Various Occupiers* 2005 (1) SA 217 (CC) at para 26.
88 See e.g. *President of the Republic of South Africa and Another v Modderklip Boerdery (Pty) Ltd (AgriSA and Others, Amici Curiae)* 2005 (5) SA 3 (CC) at para 15; *Port Elizabeth Municipality v Various Occupiers* at para 33.
89 *Modderklip Boerdery* at para 25.
90 *Port Elizabeth Municipality v Various Occupiers* at para 41; *Mkontwana v Nelson Mandela Metropolitan Municipality and Another; Bissett and Others v Buffalo City Municipality and Others; Transfer Rights Action Campaign and Others v MEC, Local Government and Housing, Gauteng, and Others (KwaZulu-Natal Law Society and Msunduzi Municipality as Amici Curiae)* 2005 (1) SA 530 (CC) at para 59.

hand,[91] municipalities must fulfil their constitutional duty to improve access to housing systematically for all within their areas.[92] On the other hand, individuals must contribute to the evolution of a society that has regard for 'the need for human interdependence, respect and concern.'[93] This means that those wishing to evict squatters should not engage in social stereotyping, relying on 'concepts of faceless and anonymous squatters automatically to be expelled as obnoxious social nuisances.'[94] Justice and equity require that 'everyone is to be treated as an individual bearer of rights entitled to respect for his or her dignity.'[95] *Port Elizabeth Municipality v Various Occupiers*[96] emphasises the responsibilities of landless people by stating that:

> those who find themselves compelled by poverty and landlessness to live in shacks on the land of others, should be discouraged from regarding themselves as helpless victims, lacking the possibilities of personal moral agency. ... Justice and equity oblige them to [be] resourceful ... in seeking a solution to their plight and to explore all reasonable possibilities of securing suitable alternative accommodation or land.

By engaging with the idea of 'civic' and state duty in this manner, the court illustrates precisely what is meant by the statement that property involves not only privileges but, importantly, also responsibilities.

As demonstrated, responsibility and trust are concepts that hitherto have not been raised in the context of the principles of property law, but a principled approach to property law cannot deny the impact of these notions on the content and function of this area of the law. This is evident from the increasingly aspirational eviction jurisprudence such as *Port Elizabeth Municipality v Various Occupiers*,[97] *Occupiers of 51 Olivia Road, Berea Township and Others v City of Johannesburg and Others*[98], *Thubelisha Homes v Various Occupants*[99] and *Blue Moonlight Properties 39 (Pty) Limited v Occupiers of Saratoga Avenue and Another*.[100] The challenge that these judgments raise is the heightened expectation of (free) housing delivery among the currently homeless. They also create opportunities for activism and political point-scoring,[101] while simultaneously diminishing the ability of local authorities to conduct themselves in coherent and efficient ways. In other words, these aspirations are hampered by the current realities of service delivery and the constraints on municipal capacity in all respects.

All interested parties, including municipalities, are expected to put meaningful information before the court[102] to allow it to reach a just and equitable decision regarding eviction. Municipalities must fulfil multiple roles, including ensuring that the rule of law

---

91 *Port Elizabeth Municipality v Various Occupiers* at paras 29, 31, 52-55.
92 See *Government of the Republic of South Africa and Others v Grootboom and Others* 2001 (1) SA 46 (CC) for more detail.
93 *Port Elizabeth Municipality v Various Occupiers* 2005 (1) SA 217 (CC) at para 37.
94 *Port Elizabeth Municipality v Various Occupiers* at para 41.
95 *Port Elizabeth Municipality v Various Occupiers* at para 41.
96 2005 (1) SA 217 (CC) at para 41.
97 2005 (1) SA 217 (CC).
98 2008 (3) SA 208 (CC).
99 2008 JOL 21559 (C).
100 2009 (1) SA 470 (W).
101 *Ritama Investments v The Unlawful Occupiers of Erf 62, Wynberg and Others* (2007) JOL 18960 (T) at 10 (TPD case NO 2005/30782).
102 *Port Elizabeth Municipality v Various Occupiers* at para 32.

prevails, that access to housing is facilitated,[103] that temporary accommodation (especially for the poor and vulnerable) is available,[104] and they must engage and mediate with unlawful occupiers, especially in relation to the availability of alternative accommodation.[105] These roles must be fulfilled in the face of adversities such as budgetary constraints, lack of competencies etc.[106] This state of affairs severely impedes the ability to give effect to the demands placed on municipalities by aspirational jurisprudence.[107] It should be noted, however, that:

> [w]hile judicial activism is decreed by the Constitution, it is also clearly circumscribed and limited only to the extent that is necessary to achieve the objects of the Constitution.[108]

It is worth noting, therefore, that the obligation imposed in *Government of the Republic of South Africa and Others v Grootboom and Others* is vis-à-vis individuals with no access to land, no roof over their heads, or who live in intolerable conditions or crisis situations, rather the homeless in general.[109] Subsequent judgments[110] seem to overlook the qualifications articulated in *Government of the Republic of South Africa and Others v Grootboom and Others* and *Port Elizabeth Municipality v Various Occupiers*, where Sachs J made it clear that alternative accommodation is desirable, but not an inflexible requirement.

Another challenge is that land is a finite resource. Consequently, the harsh reality is that there will never be enough housing, especially in urban areas. In addition, the idea of using all available land, also arable land, for housing raises the spectre of threats to food security.

13.4 Concluding remarks

In the preceding discussion and analysis, many themes and issues have been raised. Three interrelated themes emerge. The first is that the matrix of modern South African property law has changed significantly and continues to change; consequently, property lawyers should be aware of the new frontiers of the discipline. The second is the challenge of managing change and simultaneously ensuring legal certainty. Third, preconceived ideas about the purpose and place of property law and about the individual and social interests it expresses, challenge property lawyers.

Much of the discussion has focused, on the one hand, on individual interests, which express autonomy, freedom and certainty. On the other hand, it has also highlighted third party interests in property, which express the utilitarian and social responsibility aspects of

---

103 Sections 3(1), 6(5), 9–10B, 15, 16 of the Housing Act 107 of 1997; see also s 153 and Schedule 4 to the Constitution.
104 *Government of the Republic of South Africa and Others v Grootboom and Others* 2001(1) SA 46 (CC) at paras 89–92. See also the Local Government: Municipal Systems Act 32 of 2000 which obliges municipalities to engage in developmentally orientated planning, and to promote social and economic development of the community.
105 *Occupiers of 51 Olivia Road, Berea Township and Others v City of Johannesburg and Others* 2008 (3) SA 208 (CC) at paras 9–23; *Port Elizabeth Municipality v Various Occupiers* 2005 (1) SA 217 (CC) at para 39.
106 Citizen Reporter 'Massive Service Delivery Mess' 28.07.2008 *Citizen* 5; *Blue Moonlight Properties 39 (Pty) Ltd v Occupiers of Saratoga Avenue and Another* 2009 (1) SA 470 (W) at paras 28–29.
107 *Ritama Investments v Unlawful Occupiers of Erf 62 Wynberg* [2007] JOL 18960 (T) at 10 (TPD Case No: 2005/30782).
108 *Ritama Investments* at 13.
109 *Government of the Republic of South Africa and Others v Grootboom and Others* 2001(1) SA 46 (CC) at para 52.
110 *Occupiers of 51 Olivia Road, Berea Township and Others v City of Johannesburg and Others* 2008 (3) SA 208 (CC); *Dada and Others NNO v Unlawful Occupiers of Portion 41 of the Farm Rooikop and Another* 2009 (2) SA 492 (W); *Sailing Queen Investments v The Occupants La Colleen Court* 2008 (6) BCLR 666 (W); *Lingwood and Another v The Unlawful Occupiers of R/E of Erf 9 Highlands* 2008 (3) BCLR 325 (W).

property, including fulfilling the constitutional mandate to reform land holding and tenure security. In essence, the tension between individual interests and third party interests must be balanced against the other tension of property law, namely that between principle and policy. Whichever system's principles are used, and whatever policy is implemented, both must visibly reflect the core values of dignity, equality and freedom. Thus policy cannot only be pragmatic. It must also remain true to the principles of its system, which in our case are dignity, equality and freedom. This shift in consciousness can provide new generations of property lawyers with a reflective foundation upon which to base implementation of principles and formulation of policy in a critical but sensible manner.

Bibliography

BOOKS

ALEXANDER, GS. 1998. 'Critical land law' in Bright, S & Dewar, J *Land law – Themes and perspectives*. Oxford: Oxford University Press.

ALLEN, T. 2000. *The right to property in commonwealth constitutions*. Cambridge: Cambridge University Press.

BADENHORST, PJ & MOSTERT, H. 2004. *Mineral and petroleum law of South Africa*, Revision Service 3 (2007). Cape Town: Juta.

BADENHORST, PJ, PIENAAR, JM & MOSTERT, H. 2006. *Silberberg and Schoeman's Law of Property*. Durban, LexisNexis Butterworths (cited as *Silberberg and Schoeman Property*).

BENNETT, TW. 1996. 'African land – A history of dispossession' in Zimmerman, R & Visser, D *Southern cross: Civil law and common law in South Africa*. Cape Town: Juta.

BENNETT, TW. 2004. *Customary law in South Africa*. Cape Town: Juta.

BENNETT, TW. 2008. '"Official" vs "Living" customary law: Dilemmas of description and recognition' in Claassens, A & Cousins, B (eds) *Land, power & custom: Controversies generated by South Africa's Communal Land Rights Act*. Cape Town: UCT Press.

BORKOWSKI, A & DU PLESSIS, P. 2005. *Textbook on Roman law*, third edition. Oxford: Oxford University Press.

BRADBROOK, AJ, MACCULLUM, SV & MOORE, AP. 2007. *Australian real property law*. Rozelle NSW: Thomson Lawbook Co.

BUDLENDER, G. 1998. 'Constitutional protection of property rights' in Budlender, G, Latsky, V & Roux, T (eds) *Juta's new land law*. Cape Town: Juta.

BUTT, P. 2006. *Land law*, fifth edition. Sydney: Thomson Lawbook Co.

CAREY MILLER, DL & POPE, A. 2004. 'Acquisition of ownership' in Zimmermann, R, Visser, D & Reid, K (eds) *Mixed legal systems in comparative perspective: Property and obligations in Scotland and South Africa*. Cape Town: Juta.

CAREY MILLER, DL & POPE, A. 2000. *Land title in South Africa*. Cape Town: Juta.

CHAMBERS, R. 2008. *An introduction to property law in Australia*, second edition. Rozelle NSW: Thomson Lawbook Co.

CHASKALSON, M & LEWIS, C. 1996. 'Property' in Chaskalson, M, Kentridge, J, Klaaren, J, Marcus, G, Spitz, G & Woolman, SL (eds) *Constitutional law of South Africa*, Vol 2. Cape Town: Juta.

CLAASSENS, A. 2008. 'Customary law and zones of chiefly sovereignty: Impact of government policy on whose voices prevail in the making and changing of customary law' in Claassens, A & Cousins, B (eds) *Land, power & custom: Controversies generated by South Africa's Communal Land Rights Act*. Cape Town: UCT Press.

CLAASSENS, A & COUSINS, B (EDS). 2008. *Land, power & custom: Controversies generated by South Africa's Communal Land Rights Act*. Cape Town: UCT Press.

CLARKE, A & KOHLER, P. 2005. *Property law commentary and materials*. Cambridge: Cambridge University Press.

COLLIER-REED, D & LEHMANN, K (EDS). 2009. *Basic principles of business law*. Durban: LexisNexis Butterworths.

COOKE, E. 2006. *The new law of land registration*. Oxford: Hart Publishing.

COOKE, EJ. 2006. *Land law.* Oxford: Oxford University Press.

COUSINS, B. 2008. 'Contextualizing the controversies: Dilemmas of communal tenure reform on post-apartheid South Africa' in Claassens, A & Cousins, B (eds) *Land, power & custom: Controversies generated by South Africa's Communal Land Rights Act.* Cape Town: UCT Press.

COWEN, DV. 2008. 'New patterns of land ownership: The transformation of the concept of ownership as *plena in re potestas'* in Cowen, S (ed) *Cowen on law – Selected essays.* Cape Town: Juta.

CURRIE, I & DE WAAL, J. 2005. *Bill of rights handbook, fifth* edition. Cape Town: Juta.

DALE, MO, BEKKER, L, BASHALL, FJ, CHASKALSON, M, DIXON, C, GROBLER, GJ & LOXTON, CDA. 2005. *South African mineral and petroleum law.* Durban: LexisNexis Butterworths.

DAVIES, M. 2007. *Property – Meanings, histories and theories.* Abingdon: Routledge-Cavendish GlassHouse.

DE SOTO, H. 2001. *The mystery of capital: Why capitalism triumphs in the West and fails everywhere else.* London: Black Swan.

DE WAAL, J, CURRIE, I & ERASMUS, G. 2001. *Bill of Rights Handbook, fourth* edition. Cape Town: Juta.

DE WAAL, MJ. 1996. 'Servitudes' in Zimmermann, R & Visser, DP *Southern cross: Civil law and common law in South Africa.* Cape Town: Juta.

DE WET, JC & VAN WYK, AH. 1992. *Die Suid-Afrikaanse kontrakteg en handelsreg Vol 1, fifth* edition. Butterworths: 1992.

DU PLESSIS, LM. 1999. *An introduction to law.* Cape Town: Juta.

ELTON MILLS, HE & WILSON, M. 1952. *Land tenure (Keiskammahoek rural survey Vol IV).* Pietermaritzburg: Shuter and Shooter.

FRANKLIN, BLS & KAPLAN, M. 1982. *The mining and minerals laws of South Africa.* Durban: Butterworths.

GIBSON, JTR (ED). 1977. *Wille's Principles.* seventh edition. Cape Town: Juta (cited as Wille's Principles).

GILDENHUYS, A. 2001. *Onteieningsreg, second* edition. Durban: LexisNexis Butterworths.

GLAZEWSKI, J. 2000. *Environmental law in South Africa.* Durban: LexisNexis Butterworths.

HALL, CG & KELLAWAY, EA. 1942. Servitudes. Cape Town: Juta.

HALL, CG. 1973. *Servitudes,* third edition. Cape Town: Juta.

HONORÉ, AM. 1961. 'Ownership' in Guest, AG (ed) *Oxford essays in jurisprudence.* Oxford: Oxford University Publishers.

JAMES, D. 2007. *Gaining ground? 'Rights' and 'property' in South African land reform.* Oxford: Routledge-Cavendish.

JONES, RJM & NEL, HS. 1991. *Conveyancing in South Africa, fourth* edition. Cape Town: Juta.

KINGWILL, R. 2008. 'Custom-building freehold title: The impact of family values of historical ownership in the Eastern Cape' in Claassens, A & Cousins, B (eds) *Land, power & custom: Controversies generated by South Africa's Communal Land Rights Act.* Cape Town: UCT Press.

KRITZINGER, KM. 1999. *Principles of the law of mortgage, pledge and lien.* Cape Town: Juta.

LAWSA Vol 15(2): Scott, TJ. 'Lien' in *Law of South Africa,* second edition. Durban: LexisNexis Butterworths.

LAWSA Vol 17: Lubbe, G. (revised by Scott, TJ) 'Mortgage and pledge' in *Law of South Africa,* second edition. Durban: LexisNexis Butterworths.

LAWSA Vol 18(2): Badenhorst, PJ, Mostert, H & Dendy, M. 'Minerals and petroleum' in *Law of South Africa,* second edition. Durban: LexisNexis Butterworths.

LAWSA Vol 19: Church, J & Church, J. 'Nuisance' in *Law of South Africa*, second edition. Durban: LexisNexis Butterworths.

LAWSA Vol 24: Van der Merwe, CG & De Waal, MJ. 'Servitudes' in *Law of South Africa*, first reissue. Durban: LexisNexis Butterworths.

LAWSA Vol 27(1): Van der Merwe, CG. 'Things' in *Law of South Africa* first reissue. Durban: LexisNexis Butterworths.

LAWSA Vol 28: Van Wyk, J. Year? 'Townships and town planning' in *Law of South Africa* first reissue. Durban: LexisNexis Butterworths.

LOXTON, CDA. 2005. *South African mineral and petroleum law.* Durban: LexisNexis Butterworths.

MESKIN, PM. 1990. *Insolvency.* Durban: Butterworths.

MOSTERT, H. 2002. *The constitutional protection and regulation of property and its influence on the reform of private law and landownership in South Africa and Germany – A comparative analysis.* Heidelberg: Springer.

MOSTERT, H. 2003. 'The diversification of land rights and its implications for a new land law in South Africa' in Cooke, EJ *Modern studies in property law Vol II.* Oxford: Hart Publishing (sometimes cited as Mostert, H. *Modern Studies II).*

MOSTERT, H & PIENAAR, JM. 2005. 'Formalization of South African communal land title and its impact on development' in Cooke EJ (ed) *Modern studies in property law* III. Oxford: Hart Publishing.

MURPHY, J. 1996. 'The restitution of land after apartheid: The constitutional and legislative framework' in Rwelamira, MR & Werle, G (eds) *Confronting past injustices, approaches to amnesty, punishment, reparation and restitution in South Africa and Germany.* Durban: Butterworths.

NEETHLING, J, POTGIETER, JM & VISSER, PJ. *2006. Law of delict, fifth edition.* Durban: LexisNexis Butterworths.

NONYANA, MR. December 2002. 'The Communal Land Rights Bill 2002 and related legislation' in *Butterworths Property Law Digest 4. Durban: Butterworths.*

NTSEBEZA, L. 2008. 'Chiefs and the ANC in South Africa: The reconstruction of tradition?' in Claassens, A & Cousins, B (eds) *Land, power & custom: Controversies generated by South Africa's Communal Land Rights Act.* Cape Town: UCT Press.

OKOTH-OGENDO, HWO. 2008. 'Nature of land rights under indigenous law in Africa' in Claassens, A & Cousins, B (eds) *Land, power & custom: Controversies generated by South Africa's Communal Land Rights Act.* Cape Town: UCT Press.

Oxford University Press. 2005. Oxford Dictionary of English, second revised edition. Oxford: Oxford University Press.

ROUX, T. 2002. 'Property' in Woolman, SL, Chaskalson, M & Roux, T (eds) *Constitutional Law of South Africa,* second edition. Cape Town: Juta.

SCHOLTENS, JE. *1960.* 'Law of property' in Hahlo, HR & Kahn, E. *The Union of South Africa: The development of its laws and constitution.* Cape Town: Juta.

SCOTT, S. 2009. 'The law of real and personal security' in Scott, J (ed) *The law of commerce in South Africa.* Cape Town: Oxford University Press.

SHARROCK, R. 2007. *Business transactions law, seven*th edition. Cape Town: Juta.

SMITH, H. 2008. 'An overview of the Communal Land Rights Act 11 of 2004' in Claassens, A & Cousins, B (eds) *Land, power & custom: Controversies generated by South Africa's Communal Land Rights Act.* Cape Town: UCT Press.

SONNEKUS, JC. 2003. *Sectional titles, share blocks and time-sharing* Vol 2. Durban: LexisNexis Butterworths.

SONNEKUS, JC & NEELS, JL. 1994. *Sakereg vonnisbundel.* Durban: Butterworths.

SOUTHWOOD, MD. 2000. *The compulsory acquisition of rights.* Cape Town: Juta.

THOMAS, JAC. 1976. *Textbook of Roman law.* Oxford: New Holland.

THOMPSON, H. 2006. *Water law: A practical approach to resource management and the provision of services.* Cape Town: Juta.

VAN DER MERWE, CG. 1979. *Sakereg,* first edition. Durban: Butterworths.

VAN DER MERWE, CG. 1989. *Sakereg,* second edition. Durban: Butterworths (cited as Van der Merwe *Sakereg*).

VAN DER MERWE, CG. 1996. *Sectional titles, share blocks and time-sharing Vol I.* Durban: LexisNexis Butterworths.

VAN DER MERWE, CG. 1996. 'Neighbour law' in Zimmermann, R & Visser, DP *Southern Cross: Civil law and common law in South Africa.* Cape Town: Juta.

VAN DER MERWE, CG & BUTLER, DW. 1985. *Sectional titles, share blocks and time-sharing.* Durban: LexisNexis Butterworths.

VAN DER MERWE, CG & PIENAAR, JM. 1997. 'Land reform in South Africa' in Jackson, P & Wilde, DC (eds) *The reform of property law.* Dartmouth: Ashgate.

VAN DER MERWE, CG & SONNEKUS, JC. 2008. *Sectional titles, share blocks and time-sharing Vol I and Vol II.* Durban: LexisNexis Butterworths.

VAN DER WALT, AJ. 1991. 'The future of common law landownership' in Van der Walt, AJ (ed) *Land reform and the future of landownership in South Africa.* Cape Town: Juta.

VAN DER WALT, AJ. 2005. *Constitutional property law.* Cape Town: Juta (cited as Van der Walt *Constitutional property law*).

VAN DER WALT, AJ. 2006. *Law of property casebook for students,* sixth edition. Cape Town: Juta.

VAN DER WALT, AJ. 2009. *Property in the margins.* Oxford: Hart Publishing.

VAN DER WALT, AJ & PIENAAR, GJ. 2002. *Introduction to the law of property,* fourth edition. Cape Town: Juta.

VAN DER WALT, AJ & PIENAAR, GJ. 2006. *Introduction to the law of property,* fifth edition. Cape Town: Juta.

VAN WINSEN, L, CILLIERS, AC & LOOTS, C. 1997. *Herbstein and Van Winsen: The civil practice of the Supreme Court of South Africa,* fourth edition. Cape Town: Juta.

VAN WYK, J. 1999. *Planning law – Principles and procedures of land-use management.* Cape Town: Juta.

VAN ZYL, DH. 1983. *Geskiedenis van die Romeins-Hollandse Reg.* Durban: Butterworths.

VILJOEN, HP & BOSMAN, PH. 1979. *A guide to mining rights in South Africa.* Johannesburg: Lex Patria Publishers.

VISSER, D. 2008. *Unjustified Enrichment.* Cape Town: Juta.

WOOLMAN, SL. 2002. 'Limitations' in Woolman, SL & Chaskalson, M (eds) *Constitutional law of South Africa,* second edition. Cape Town: Juta.

WOOLMAN, SL. 2002. 'Application' in Woolman, SL & Chaskalson, M (eds) *Constitutional law of South Africa,* second edition. Cape Town: Juta.

ZIMMERMANN, R & VISSER, DP. 1996. 'Introduction: South African law as a mixed legal system' in Zimmermann, R & Visser, DP (eds) *Southern cross: Civil law and common law in South Africa.* Cape Town: Juta.

Journal articles

BADENHORST, PJ. 2005. 'Nature of new order rights to minerals: A Rubikian exercise since passing the Mayday Rubicon with a cubic circonium.' *Obiter* 26:505.

BADENHORST, PJ & COETSER, PPJ. 1989. 'Die berging van skeepswrakke – Enkele aspekte – *Mills v Reck and Others* 1988 (3) SA 92 (K).' *Tydskrif vir die Suid-Afrikaanse Reg/Journal for South African Law*:137.

BADENHORST, PJ & MOSTERT, H. 2004. 'Revisiting the transitional arrangements of the Mineral and Petroleum Resources Development Act 28 of 2002 and the constitutional property clause (Part Two).' *Stellenbosch Law Review* 15:22.

BADENHORST, PJ & MOSTERT, H. 2007. 'Artikel (3)(1) en (2) van die *Mineral and Petroleum Resources Development Act* 28 of 2002: 'n Herbeskouing.' *Tydskrif vir die Suid-Afrikaanse Reg/Journal for South African Law* 3:469.

BADENHORST, PJ & MOSTERT, H. 2008. 'Duelling prospecting rights: A non-custodial second?' *Tydskrif vir die Suid-Afrikaanse Reg/Journal for South African Law* 4:819-833.

BADENHORST, PJ & SHONE, RW. 2008. '"Minerals", "petroleum" and "operations" in the Mineral and Petroleum Resources Development Act 28 of 2002: A geologist as devil's advocate for a change?' *Obiter* 29(11):33-52.

BIRKS, P. 1985. 'The Roman law concept of *dominium* and the idea of absolute ownership.' *Acta Juridica:* 31.

BOBBERT, MCJ. 1996. 'Kennisleer.' *Tydskrif vir Regswetenskap.* 21(1): 36.

BURGER, A. 2007. 'Roman water law (part 1).' *Tydskrif vir die Suid-Afrikaanse Reg/Journal for South African Law* 1:72-95.

BUTLER, DW. 1992. 'The statutory protection of investors in retirement schemes.' *Tydskrif vir die Suid-Afrikaanse Reg/Journal for South African Law*:12.

CLAASSENS, A. 1993. 'Compensation for expropriation: The political and economic parameters of market value compensation.' *South African Journal on Human Rights* 9:422.

CLOETE, R. 2005. 'Die historiese onderskeid tussen stoflike en onstoflike sake in die Suid-Afrikaanse sakereg: 'n Sinopsis.' *De Jure* 38(2):314.

COUSINS, B. 2005. '"Embeddedness" versus titling: African land tenure systems and the potential impacts of the Communal Land Rights Act 11 of 2004.' *Stellenbosch Law Review* 3:488.

COUSINS, T & HORNBY, D. 2003. 'Communal property institutions: Adrift in the sea of land reform' in Greenberg, S (ed) *Piecemeal Reforms and Calls for Action. Development Update* 44:127-148.

CRONJE, DSP. 1979. 'Die verkryging van eiendomsreg deur 'n huurkoopkoper.' *Tydskrif vir die Suid-Afrikaanse Reg/Journal for South African Law*:16.

CROSS, C. 1992. 'An alternate legality: The property rights question in relation to South African land reform.' *South African Journal on Human Rights* 8:305.

DALE, MO. 2002. 'Mining Law.' *Annual Survey:* 573.

DE VISSIER, J, COTTLE, E & METTLER, J. 2003. 'Realizing the right of access to water: Pipe dream or watershed?' *Law, Democracy & Development* 1:27-54.

DE WET, JC. 1958. 'Die resepsie van die Romeins-Hollandse reg in Suid-Afrika.' *Tydskrif vir Hedendaagse Romeins-Hollandse Reg/Journal of Contemporary Roman-Dutch Law* 21:84-97.

DU PLESSIS, JE. 1998. 'The promises and pitfalls of mixed legal systems: The South African and Scottish Experiences.' *Stellenbosch Law Review* 9:338.

DU PLESSIS, W, OLIVIER, N & PIENAAR, J. 2003. 'Expropriation, restitution and land redistribution: An answer to land problems in South Africa?' *SA Public Law* 18:491-514

EISENBERG, A. 1993. 'Different constitutional formulations of compensation clauses.' *South African Journal on Human Rights* 9:412.

ERASMUS, HJ. 1994. 'Thoughts on private law in a future South Africa.' *Stellenbosch Law Review* 5:105.

GILDENHUYS, A. 1996. 'Editorial.' *Human Rights and Constitutional Law Journal of South Africa*, 1:2-3.

JANSE VAN RENSBURG, AM. 2002. 'Access to ancestral burial sites – Recent decisions.' *Obiter* 23:175-185.

KOK, JA. 2000. 'An occupier's right to bury relatives on land.' *De Jure* 161-174.

LEWIS, C. 1979. '*Superficies solo cedit – sed quid est superficies.*' *South African Law Journal* 96:94.

LEWIS, C. 1985. 'The modern concept of ownership of land.' *Acta Juridica*:241.

MILTON, JRL. 1969. 'The law of neighbours in South Africa.' *Acta Juridica*:123.

MILTON, JRL. 1985. 'Planning and property.' *Acta Juridica*:267-288.

MOSTERT, H. 2002. 'The alienation of transfer of rights of exclusive use in sectional title law.' *Stellenbosch Law Review* 13(2):265.

MOSTERT, H. 2003. 'The distinction between deprivations and expropriations and the future of the "doctrine" of constructive expropriation in South Africa.' *South African Journal on Human Rights* 19(4):567-592.

PAUW, P. 1980. 'Die Romeins-Hollandse reg in oënskou.' *Tydskrif vir die Suid-Afrikaanse Reg/Journal for South African Law* 01:32-46

PIENAAR, GJ. 2000. 'Registration of informal land-use rights in South Africa: Giving teeth to (toothless?) paper tigers.' *Tydskrif vir die Suid-Afrikaanse Reg/Journal for South African Law* 3:442.

PIENAAR, GJ. 2006. 'The land titling debate in South Africa.' *Tydskrif vir die Suid-Afrikaanse Reg/Journal for South African Law* 3:435.

PIENAAR, J. 1992. 'Die regsaard van beperkende voorwaardes.' *Tydskrif vir Hedendaagse Romeins-Hollandse Reg/Journal of Contemporary Roman-Dutch Law* 55:50

PIENAAR, JM. 2001. 'Wisselwerking tussen die Wet op die Beheer van Aandeleblokke 59 van 1980 en die Wet op Uitbreiding van Sekerheid van Verblyfreg 62 van 1997.' *Tydskrif vir die Suid-Afrikaanse Reg/Journal for South African Law*:134

PIENAAR, JM & MOSTERT, H. 2005. 'The balance between burial rights and landownership in South Africa: Issues of content, nature and constitutionality.' *South African Law Journal* 3:633-660.

POPE, A. 2002. 'Eviction and the protection of property rights: A case study of *Ellis v Viljoen*.' *South African Law Journal* 119:709-720.

POPE, A. 2007. 'Encroachment or accession? The importance of the extent of encroachment in light of South African constitutional principles.' *South African Law Journal* 124:537-556.

RENS, A. 2004. '*Telkom SA Limited v Xsinet (Pty) Ltd.*' *South African Law Journal* 120:749-756.

ROEDERER, CJ. 2003. 'Post-matrix legal reasoning: Horizontality and the rule of values in South African law.' *South African Journal on Human Rights* 19(1):57-81.

ROODT, MJ. 2007. 'Security of tenure and livelihood options in South Africa: A case study of a rural community facing eviction under post-apartheid legislation in the Eastern Cape Province.' *Africanus* 37:3-12.

SCOTT, S. 2005. 'Recent developments in case law regarding neighbour law and its influence on the concept of ownership.' *Stellenbosch Law Review* 16(3):351.

Scott, S. 2009. 'The law of real and personal security' in Scott, J (ed) *The law of commerce in South Africa*. Cape Town: Oxford University Press.

Sonnekus, JC. 2000. 'Eiendomsregte op grafte – en dan die gevolge daarvan?' *Tydskrif vir die Suid-Afrikaanse Reg/Journal for South African Law*. 90(1):103–109.

Van der Schyff, E. 2008. 'Who "owns" the country's mineral resources? The possible incorporation of the public trust doctrine through the Mineral and Petroleum Resources Development Act, 2002.' *Tydskrif vir die Suid-Afrikaanse Reg/Journal for South African Law*:757.

Van der Vyver, JD. 1988. 'Expropriation, rights, entitlements and surface support of land recent cases.' *South African Law Journal* 105:1–16.

Van der Walt, AJ. 1990. 'Developments that may change the institution of private ownership so as to meet the needs of a non-racial society in South Africa.' *Stellenbosch Law Review* 1(1):26–48.

Van der Walt, AJ. 1992. 'The South African law of ownership: A historical and philosophical perspective.' *De Jure* 25:446.

Van der Walt, AJ. 1995. 'Marginal notes on powerful(l) legends: Critical perspectives on property theory.' *Tydskrif vir Hedendaagse Romeins-Hollandse Reg/Journal of Contemporary Roman-Dutch Law* 58:396–420.

Van der Walt, AJ. 1995. 'Subject and society in property theory: A review of property theories and debates in recent literature: Part II.' *Tydskrif vir die Suid-Afrikaanse Reg/Journal for South African Law*:322-345

Van der Walt, AJ. 1995. 'Tradition on trial: A critical analysis of the civil-law tradition in South African property law.' *South African Journal on Human Rights* 11:169.

Van der Walt, AJ. 1995. 'Unity and pluralism in property theory – A review of property theories and debates in recent literature: Part I.' *Tydskrif vir die Suid-Afrikaanse Reg/Journal for South African Law*:15.

Van der Walt, AJ. 1997. 'Squatting, spoliation order and the new constitutional order – casenote: *Rikhotso v Northcliff Ceramics* 1997 (1) SA 526 (W).' *Tydskrif vir Hedendaagse Romeins-Hollandse Reg/Journal of Contemporary Roman-Dutch Law* 60:522–528.

Van der Walt, AJ. 1999. 'Compensation for excessive or unfair regulation: A comparative overview of constitutional practice relating to regulatory takings.' *SA Public Law* 14:273–331.

Van der Walt, AJ. 1999. 'Property rights and hierarchies of power: A critical evaluation of land reform policy in South Africa' *Koers, Potchefstroom University* 64:259.

Van der Walt, AJ. 2001. 'Dancing with codes – Protecting, developing and reconstructing property rights in a constitutional state!' *South African Law Journal* 118:258.

Van der Walt, AJ. 2002. 'Moving towards recognition of constructive expropriation? *Steinberg v South Peninsula Municipality* 2001 (4) SA 1243 (SCA).' *Tydskrif vir Hedendaagse Romeins-Hollandse Reg/Journal of Contemporary Roman-Dutch Law* 65:459–473.

Van der Walt, AJ. 2005. 'The state's duty to protect property owners v the state's duty to provide housing: Thoughts on the Modderklip case.' *South African Journal on Human Rights* 21:144–161.

Van der Walt, AJ. 2006. 'Reconciling the state's duties to promote land reform and to pay "just and equitable" compensation for expropriation.' *South African Law Journal* 123:23.

VAN DER WALT, AJ. 2008. 'Developing the law on unlawful squatting and spoliation.' *South African Law Journal* 125:24-36.

VAN DER WALT, AJ. 2008. 'Property, social justice and citizenship: Property law in post-apartheid South Africa.' *Stellenbosch Law Review* 19(3):325.

VAN DER WALT, AJ. 2008. 'Replacing property rules with liability rules: Encroachment by building.' *South African Law Journal* 125:592-626.

VAN DER WALT, AJ. 2009. 'Regulation of building under the Constitution.' *De Jure* 42:32-47.

VAN DER WALT, JWG. 1997. 'Perspectives on horizontal application: *Du Plessis v De Klerk* revisited.' *SA Public Law* 12:1-31.

VAN DER WESTHUIZEN, JM. 1990. '*Locus standi in judicio* van persone wat nakoming van beperkende voorwaardes eis.' *Tydskrif vir Hedendaagse Romeins-Hollandse Reg/Journal of Contemporary Roman-Dutch Law* 53:130-136.

VAN MAANEN, G. 1993. 'Ownership as a constitutional right in South Africa – Articles 14 & 15 of the *Grundgesetz*: The German experience.' *Recht & Kritiek* 19:74.

VAN WYK, J. 1992. 'The historical development of restrictive conditions.' *Tydskrif vir die Suid-Afrikaanse Reg/Journal for South African Law*:280-297.

VAN WYK, J. 1992. 'The nature and classification of restrictive covenants and conditions of title.' *De Jure* 25:270-288.

VAN WYK, J. 1992. 'Removing restrictive conditions and preserving the residential character of the neighbourhood.' *Tydskrif vir Hedendaagse Romeins-Hollandse Reg/Journal of Contemporary Roman-Dutch Law* 55:369-385.

VAN WYK, J. 1995. 'Preserving the character of the neighbourhood – A German perspective.' *De Jure* 28:396-404.

VAN DER WALT, AJ. 2001. 'Negating Grotius – The constitutional validity of statutory security rights in favour of the state: *First National Bank t/a Wesbank v Commissioner of South African Revenue Service* 2001 (7) BCLR 715 (C).' *South African Journal of Human Rights* 18:86-113.

VAN WYK, J. 2002. 'Revaluation of conditions of title.' *Tydskrif vir Hedendaagse Romeins-Hollandse Reg/Journal of Contemporary Roman-Dutch Law* 65:642-649.

VAN WYK, J. 2004. 'Developers, municipalities, wrong decisions, liability and the Constitution.' *SA Public Law* 19:422-432.

VAN WYK, J. 2007. 'Contravening a condition of title can lead to a demolition order.' *Tydskrif vir Hedendaagse Romeins-Hollandse Reg/Journal of Contemporary Roman-Dutch Law* 70:658-662.

VAN WYK, J. 2008. 'Restrictive conditions – why fiddle with a recipe that works?' *SA Public Law* 23:38-58.

VISSER, DP. 1985. 'The "absoluteness" of ownership: The South African common law in perspective.' *Acta Juridica*:39.

WEST, A. 2003. 'Consent or no consent? The Subdivision of Agricultural Land Act 70 of 1970.' *De Rebus* Feb:59.

ZIMMERMANN, R. 1986. 'Synthesis in South African private law: Civil law, common law and *usus hodiernus Pandectarum*.' *South African Law Journal* 103:259-289.

Conference proceedings

MAYSON, D, MICHAEL, B & CRONWRIGHT, R. 1998. 'Elandskloof land restitution: Establishing membership of a communal property association' in Barry, M (ed) *Proceedings of the International Conference on Land Tenure in the Developing World*. University of Cape Town.

Theses

VAN DER SCHYFF, E. 2006. *The constitutionality of the Mineral and Petroleum Resources Development Act 28 of 2002*. LLD thesis, Potchefstroom University of the North-West.

Newspaper articles

CITIZEN REPORTER. 28.07.2008. 'Massive service delivery mess' *Citizen:* 5.

COX, A. 15.04.2007. 'Squatters can't be evicted in one go' *The Star:* 5.

MACLEOD, F. 28.06.2007. 'Landowners haul miners over the coals' *Mail & Guardian:* 12.

Internet

SAMAYENDE, S. 27.01.2003. Burial tradition challenged. Available from *www.news24.com* (accessed 17.09.2009).

Table of cases

A

Absa Bank t/a Bankfin V Jordasche Auto CC 2003 (1) SA 401 (SCA) ... 225
Absa Bank v Ntsane 2007 (3) SA 554 (T) ... 311
Administrator, Cape v Ntshwaqela 1990 (1) SA 705 (A) ... 76
African Farms and Townships Ltd v Cape Town Municipality 1961 (3) SA 392 (C) ... 126
AgriSouth Africa v Minister of Minerals and Energy; Van Rooyen v Minister of Minerals and
 Energy Case No: 55896/2007, Case No: 102351/2008 unreported
 (N&S Gauteng) ... 94, 266, 267, 268, 272, 274
AGS van Suid-Afrika (Maitland) v Capes 1978 (4) SA 48 ((C) ... 223, 226
Air-Kel h/a Merkel Motors v Bodenstein 1980 (3) SA 917 (A) ... 190, 191, 194, 207, 208
Alderson & Flitton (Tzaneen) (Pty) Ltd v EG Duffeys Spares (Pty) Ltd 1975 (3) SA 41 (T) ... 228
Aldine Timber Co v Hlatwayo 1932 TPD 337 ... 176
Alexander v Johns 1912 AD 431 ... 248
Alexkor (Pty) Ltd and Another v Richtersveld Community and
 Others 2004 (5) SA 460 (CC) ... 16, 17, 339, 342
Allaclas Investments (Pty) Ltd v Milnerton Golf Club and Others 2008 (3) SA 134 (SCA) ... 115, 137
Andrews v Rosenbaum & Co 1908 EDC 419 ... 179
Anglo Operations Ltd v Sandhurst Estates (Pty) Ltd 2007 (2) SA 363 (SCA) ... 269, 279
Associated South African Bakeries (Pty) Ltd v Oryx & Vereinigte
 Bäckereien (Pty) Ltd 1982 (3) SA 893 (A) ... 59
Aussenkjer Diamante (Pty) Ltd v Namex (Pty) Ltd 1983 (1) SA 263 (A) ... 267

B

Badenhorst v Balju, Pretoria Sentraal, en Andere 1998 (4) SA 132 (T) ... 8
Bank of Lisbon and South Africa v The Master 1987 (1) SA 276 (A) ... 22
Barclays Nasionale Bank Bpk v Registrateur van Aktes, Transvaal 1975 (4) SA 936 (T) ... 211, 312
Barclays Western Bank Ltd v Ernst 1988 (1) SA 243 (A) ... 207
Beck v Premier, Western Cape 1998 (3) SA 487 (C) ... 260
BEF (Pty) Ltd v Cape Town Municipality 1983 (2) SA 387 (C) ... 146
Benade v Minister van Mineraal en Energiesake 2002 JDR 0769 (NC) ... 269
Bennett NO v Le Roux 1984 (2) SA 134 (Z) ... 39
Ben-Tovim v Ben-Tovim and Others 2001 (3) SA 1074 (C) ... 8
Berdur Properties (Pty) Ltd v 76 Commercial Road (Pty) Ltd 1998 (4) SA 62 (D) ... 240
Beyers v McKenzie 1880 Foord 125 ... 191
Bhe v Magistrate, Khayalitsha 2005 1 SA 580 (CC) ... 110
Bingham v City Council of Johannesburg 1934 WLD 180 ... 143
Bisschop v Stafford 1974 (3) SA 1 (A) ... 182, 240
Bissett v Buffalo City Municipality Case No: 903/02 (unreported) ... 125
Bloemfontein Municipality v Jacksons 1929 AD 266 ... 327
Blue Moonlight Properties 39 (Pty) Ltd v Occupiers of Saratoga Avenue and the
 City of Johannesburg 2009 (1) SA 470 (W) ... 222, 348, 349
Bock v Duburoro Investments (Pty) Ltd 2004 (2) SA 242 (SCA) ... 309, 316, 317
Boiler Efficiency Services CC v Coalcor (Cape) Pty (Ltd) 1989 (3) SA 460 (C) ... 146, 150
Boland Bank Bpk v Engelbrecht 1996 (3) SA 537 (A) ... 105

Bombay Properties (Pty) Ltd v Ferrox Construction 1996 (2) SA 853 (W) 328, 330
Bon Quelle (Edms) Bpk v Munisipaliteit van Otavi 1989 (1) SA 508 (A) 77, 78, 254
Bouwer v Stadsraad van Johannesburg 1978 (1) SA 624 (W) 128
Bowring v Vrededorp Properties CC 2007 (5) SA 391 (SCA) 61, 62, 63
Briers v Wilson 1952 (3) SA 423 (C) 240
Brits v Eaton NO 1984 (4) SA 728 (T) 191
Britz NO v Sniegocki 1989 (4) SA 372 (D) 315
Brooklyn House Furnishers (Pty) Ltd v Knoetze and Sons 1970 (3) SA 264 (A) 328, 330
Bührmann v Nkosi and Another 2000 (1) SA 1145 (T) 31

C

Caledon & Suid-Westelike Eksekuteurskamer Bpk v Wentzel 1972 (1) SA 270 (A) 209
Campbell v Hall 1774 1 Cowp 204 98 ER 1045 10
Camps Bay Ratepayers and Residents' Association and Others v Minister of Planning,
    Culture and Administration, Western Cape, and Others 2001 (4) SA 294 (C) 153, 256, 257, 258
Cape Explosive Works Ltd v Denel (Pty) Ltd and
    Others 2001 (3) SA 569 (SCA) 49, 53, 54, 55, 57, 197, 213, 242, 313
Cape Town and District Waterworks v Executors of Elders (1890) 8 SC 9 31
Chesterfin (Pty) Ltd v Contract Forwarding (Pty) Ltd 2003 (2) SA 253 (SCA) 322
Chetty v Naidoo 1974 (3) SA 13 (A) 216, 217, 218, 219
Christie v Haarhof (1886) 4 HCG 349 140
City of Johannesburg and Others v Mazibuko and Others 2009 (3) SA 592 (SCA) 293
City of Tshwane Metropolitan Municipality v Grobler 2005 (6) SA 61(T) 156
Clifford v Farinha 1988 (4) SA 315 (W) 227
Colonial Development (Pty) Ltd v Outer West Local Council 2002 (2) SA 589 (N) 117
Commissioner of Customs & Excise v Randles, Brothers & Hudson Ltd 1941 AD 369 191
Concor Construction (Cape) (Pty) Ltd v Santambank Ltd 1993 (3) SA 930 (A) 193
Consistory of Steytlerville v Bosman (1893) 10 SC 67 236
Contract Forwarding (Pty) Ltd v Chesterfin (Pty) Ltd 2003 (2) SA 253 (SCA) 59
Cooper NO v Die Meester 1992 (3) SA 60 (A) 323
Corium (Pty) Ltd v Myburgh Park Langebaan (Pty) Ltd 1995 (3) SA 51 (C) 147
Cussons v Kroon 2001 (4) SA 833 (SCA) 58, 59

D

Dada and Others NNO v Unlawful Occupiers of Portion 41 of the Farm Rooikop and
    Another 2009 (2) SA 492 (W) 349
De Beer v Firs Investments Ltd 1980 (3) SA 1087 (W) 81, 82, 83
De Beer v Zimbali Estate Management Association (Pty) Ltd 2007 (3) SA 254 (N) 70, 71, 72, 77
De Beers Consolidated Mines Ltd v Ataqua Mining (Pty) Ltd and
    Others (OPD) Case No: 3215/06 .... 170, 265, 272, 274
De Charmoy v Day Star Hatchery 1967 (4) SA 188 (D) 134, 135
De Chazal De Chamarel's Estate v Tongaat Group Ltd 1972 (1) SA 710 (D) 35
De Kock v Hänel and Others 1999 (1) SA 994 (C) 241
Denel (Pty) Ltd v Cape Explosive Works Ltd 1999 (2) SA 419 (T) 276
Development Bank of Southern Africa Ltd v Van Rensburg 2002 (5) SA 425 (SCA) 322
Diepsloot Residents' and Landowners' Association v Administrator, Transvaal 1993 (3) SA 49 (T) 146
Diepsloot Residents' and Landowners' Association v Administrator, Transvaal 1993 (1) SA 577 (T) 146

Diepsloot Residents' and Landowners' Association v Administrator, Transvaal 1994 (3) SA 336 (A) 146
Die Vereniging van Advokate (TPA) v Moskeeplein (Edms) Bpk 1982 (3) SA 159 (T) 135
Director, Mineral Development, Gauteng v Save the Vaal
　　Environment 1999 (2) SA 709 (SCA) 146, 152
D Glaser and Sons (Pty) Ltd v The Master 1979 (4) SA 780 (C) 309
Dorland and Another v Smits 2002 (5) SA 374 (CPD) 137, 138, 139
Dreyer and Another NNO v AXZS Industries (Pty) Ltd 2006 (5) SA 548 (SCA) 191, 194
Drummond v Dreyer 1954 (1) SA 306 (N) 100
Dunn v Bowyer 1926 NPD 516 .... 30, 163
Du Randt v Du Randt 1995 (1) SA 401 (O) 77, 79
Durban City Council v Woodhaven Ltd 1987 (3) SA 555 (A) 249
Du Toit v De Bot, Du Toit v Zuidmeer (1883) 2 SC 213 135
Du Toit v Minister of Transport 2003 (1) SA 586 (C) 128
Du Toit v Visser 1950 (2) SA 93 (C) 253, 254

E
Eichelgruen v Two Nine Eight South Ridge Road (Pty) Ltd 1976 (2) SA 678 (D) 253
Electrolux (Pty) Ltd v Khota 1961 (4) SA 244 (W) 224
Elektrisiteitsvoorsieningskommissie v Fourie en Andere 1988 (2) SA 627 (T) 93
Ellis v Viljoen 2001 (5) BCLR 487 (C) 217
Enslin v Vereeniging Town Council 1976 (3) SA 443 (T) 259
Eriksen Motors Ltd v Protea Motors Warrenton and Another 1973 (3) SA 685(A) 195
Erlax Properties (Pty) Ltd v Registrar of Deeds and Others 1992 (1) SA 879 (A) 54, 252
Eskom v Rollomatic Engineering (Edms) Bpk 1992 (2) SA 725 (A) 202
Estate Marks v Pretoria City Council 1969 (3) SA 227 (A) 128
Esterhuyse v Jan Jooste Family Trust 1998 (4) SA 241 (C) 146
Etkind v Hicor Trading Ltd 1999 (1) SA 111 (W) 8, 209, 210
Ex parte Eloff 1953 (1) SA 617 (T) 21, 33
Ex parte Former Highland Residents: In re Ash v Department of Land
　　Affairs 2000 (2) All SA 26 (LCC) 128
Ex parte Geldenhuys 1926 OPD 155 .... 41, 49, 50, 51, 52, 53, 55, 57, 238, 243
Ex parte Menzies et uxor 1993 (3) SA 799 (C) 192
Ex parte Nader Tuis (Edms) Bpk 1962 (1) SA 751 (T) 258
Ex parte Optimal Property Solutions CC 2003 (2) SA 136 (C) 256, 257, 258, 262
Ex parte Pierce 1950 (3) SA 628 (O) 44, 267
Ex parte Rovian Trust (Pty) Ltd 1983 (3) SA 209 (D) 256, 257
Ex parte Saiga Properties (Pty) Ltd 1997 (4) SA 716 (E) 262
Ex parte Uvongo Borough Council 1966 (1) SA 788 (N) 253
Ex parte Vinkati Investments (Pty) Ltd 1965 (4) SA 421 (W) 255, 256

F
Faircape Property Developers (Pty) Ltd v Premier, Western Cape 2000 (2) SA 67 (C) 260
Faircape Property Developers (Pty) Ltd v Premier, Western Cape 2002 (6) SA 180 (C) 260
Felix v Nortier [1996] 3 All SA 143 (SE) 251
Findevco (Pty) Ltd v Faceformat SA (Pty) Ltd 2001 (1) SA 251 (E) 316

First National Bank of SA Ltd t/a Wesbank v Commissioner, South African Revenue Service,
First National Bank of SA Ltd t/a Wesbank v Minister of
Finance 2002 (4) SA 768 (CC) 27, 28, 120, 121, 122, 123, 124, 129, 130, 131
First National Bank of SA Ltd v Land and Agricultural Bank of
Southern Africa Ltd 2000 (3) SA 626 (CC) 316
First National Bank t/a Wesbank v Commissioner, South African Revenue
Service 2001 (3) SA 310 (C) 333
Forsdick Motors v Lauritzen and Another 1967 (3) SA 249 (N) 205
Fourie v Marandellas Town Council 1972 (2) SA 699 (R) 246
Frankel Pollak Vinderine v Stanton 2000 (1) SA 425 (W) 57, 228
Fredericks v Stellenbosch Divisional Council 1977 (3) SA 113 (C) 81, 346
Frye's (Pty) Ltd v Ries 1957 (3) SA 574 (A) 211
Fuel Retailers Association of Southern Africa v Director-General Environmental Management,
Department of Agriculture, Conservation and Environment,
Mpumalanga Province and Others 2007 (6) SA 4 (CC) 155

G

Gardens Estate Ltd v Lewis 1920 AD 144 245
Geue v Van der Lith 2004 (3) SA 333 (SCA) 147
Geyser and Another v Msunduzi Municipality and Others 2003 (5) SA 18 (N) 28, 125
Gibbons v SAR&H 1933 CPD 521 135
Gien v Gien 1979 (2) SA 1113 (T) 91, 116, 135
Gien v Gien 1984 (3) SA 54 (T) 134
Glaffer Investments (Pty) Ltd v Minister of Water Affairs and Forestry 2000 (4) SA 822 (T) 245, 254
Glatthaar v Hussan 1912 TPD 322 91
Gore NO v Parvatas (Pty) Ltd 1992 (3) SA 363 (C) 168
Government of the Republic of South Africa and Others v Grootboom and
Others 2001 (1) SA 46 (CC) 348, 349
Graf v Beuchel 2003 (4) SA 378 (SCA) 308, 317
Grant v Stonestreet 1968 (4) SA 1 (A) 58
Groenewald v Van der Merwe 1917 AD 233 .... 202, 204
Groengras Eiendomme (Pty) Ltd v Elandsfontein Unlawful Occupants 2002 (1) SA 125 (T) 221
Grosvenor Motors (Potchefstroom) Ltd v Douglas 1956 (3) SA 420 (A) 195, 217, 225

H

Hargovan v Minister of Agriculture 1971 (1) SA 858 (A) 128
Harksen v Lane NO 1998 (1) SA 300 (CC) 131
Hassam v Shaboodien 1996 (2) SA 720 (C) 58
Hawkins v Munnik (1830) 1 Menz 465 240
Hayes and Another v Minister of Finance and Development Planning, Western
Cape 2003 (4) SA 598 (C) 146, 155, 156, 255
Hayes v Harding Town Board 1958 (2) SA 297 (N) 181
Hearn & Co (Pty) Ltd v Bleiman 1950 (3) SA 617 (C) 207, 208
Heydenrech v Fourie (1896) 13 SC 371 .... 317, 320
Hichange Investments (Pty) Ltd v Cape Produce Co (Pty) Ltd t/a Pelts Products and
Others 2004 (2) SA 393 (E) 271
Hochmetals Africa (Pty) Ltd v Otavi Mining Co (Pty) Ltd 1968 (1) SA 571 (A) 201

Holland v Scott 1882 EDC 307 135
Hollmann and Another v Estate Latre 1970 (3) SA 638 (A) 245
Hudson v Mann 1950 (4) SA 485 (T) 278

I
Ierse Trog CC v Sultra Trading CC 1997 (4) SA 131 (C) 346
Ikea Trading and Design AG v BOE Bank Ltd 2005 (2) SA 7 (SCA) 324
Illing v Woodhouse 1923 NPD 166 247
Info Plus v Scheelke and Another 1998 (3) SA 184 (SCA) 205
In re Elandskloof Vereniging 1999 (1) SA 176 (LCC) 107

J
Jackson NO and Others v Aventura Ltd and Others [2005] 2 All SA 518 C 247
Jaftha v Schoeman and Others; Van Rooyen v Stolz and Others 2005 (2) SA 140 (CC);
    2005 (1) BCLR 78 ....220, 332, 333
Janse van Rensburg v Grieve Trust CC [1993] 3 All SA 597 (C) 22
Johaadien v Stanley Porter (Paarl) (Pty) Ltd 1970 (1) SA 394 (A) 225
Jonordan Investment (Pty) Ltd v De Aar Drankwinkel (Edms) Bpk 1969 (2) SA 117 (C) 248
Juglal NO v Shoprite Checkers t/a OK Franchise Division 2004 (5) SA 248 (SCA) 316

K
Kangra Holdings (Pty) Ltd v Minister of Water Affairs 1998 (4) SA 330 (SCA) 127
Kazazis v Georghiades 1979 (3) SA 886 (T) 59
Kerksay Investments (Pty) Ltd v Randburg Town Council 1997 (1) SA 511 (T) 128
Khan v Minister of Law and Order 1991 (3) SA 439 (T) 8, 37, 38, 165, 167
Khumalo and Others v Holomisa 2002 (5) SA 401 (CC) 118
Khumalo v Potgieter 2000 (2) All SA 456 (LCC) 128
Kia Motors (SA) (Edms) Bpk v Van Zyl 1999 (3) SA 640 (O) 225
Kilburn v Estate Kilburn 1931 AD 501 300
Kirsh v Pincus 1927 TPD 199 ....116, 135, 138
Klerck NO v Van Zyl and Maritz NNO and Related Cases 1989 (4) SA 263 (SE) 191
Kleyn v Theron 1966 (3) SA 264 (T) 258
Knop v Johannesburg City Council 1995 (2) SA 1 (A) 146, 147
Knysna Hotel CC v Coetzee NO 1998 (2) SA 743 (A) 211
Konstanz Properties (Pty) Ltd v Wm Spilhaus en Kie (WP) (Bpk) 1996 (3) SA 273 (A) 172, 174
Kotzé v Minister van Landbou 2003 (1) SA 445 (T) 147
Kriel v Terblanche NO 2002 (6) SA 132 (NC) 191

L
Land- en Landboubank van Suid-Afrika v Die Meester 1991 (2) SA 761 (A) 22
Laskey and Another v Showzone CC and Others 2007 (2) SA 48 (CPD) 136
Lazarus and Jackson v Wessels, Oliver and the Coronation Freehold Estates, Town and
    Mines Ltd 1903 TS 499 (T) 44, 266
Leal & Co v Williams 1906 TS 554 218
Lebowa Mineral Trust Beneficiaries Forum v President of the Republic of
    South Africa 2002 (1) BCLR 23 (T) 126
Legator McKenna Inc and Others v Shea and Others [2008] JOL 22819 (SCA) 191
Leith v Port Elizabeth Museum Trustees 1934 EDL 211 135

Lendalease Finance (Pty) Ltd v Corporacion de Merçadeo Agricola 1975 (4) SA 397 (C) 201
Le Riche v PSP Properties CC 2005 (3) SA 189 (C) 78, 81
Le Roux and Others v Loewenthal 1905 TS 742 267
Le Roux v Odendaal 1954 (4) SA 432 (N) 58
Lesapo v North West Agricultural Bank 2000 (1) SA 409 (CC) 316
Leyds v Noord-Westelike Koöperatiewe Landboumaatskappy Bpk 1985 (2) SA 769 (A) 22
Ley v Ley's Executors 1951 (3) SA 186 (A) 236
Lief NO v Dettmann 1964 (2) SA 252 (A) 34
Lindiwe Mazibuko and Others v City of Johannesburg and Others CCT 39/09 [2009] ZACC 28 293
Lingwood and Another v The Unlawful Occupiers of R/E of Erf 9
    Highlands 2008 (3) BCLR 325 (W) 349
Lingwood and Schon v The Unlawful Occupiers of Erf 9, Highlands
    (Case No: 2006/16243, 16 October 2007) 222
Linvestment CC v Hammersley and Another 2008 (3) SA 283 (SCA) 235, 245, 263
Lombard v Fischer [2003] 1 All SA 698 (O) 116, 140, 141
Lorentz v Melle 1978 (3) SA 1044 (T) 49, 51, 52, 53, 236, 241, 248
Low Water Properties (Pty) Ltd v Wahloo Sand CC 1999 (1) SA 655 (SE) 242, 243
Lucas v South Carolina Coastal Council 505 US 1003 (1992) 131

M

Macdonald Ltd v Radin NO and the Potchefstroom Dairies and
    Industries Co Ltd 1915 AD 454 .... 168, 169, 170, 171, 172, 173, 174
Malan v Ardconnel Investments (Pty) Ltd 1988 (2) SA 12 (A) 146, 255, 256, 257, 258
Malan v Nabygelegen Estates 1946 AD 562 182
Malherbe v Ceres Municipality 1951 (4) SA 510 (A) 135, 138, 143
Mans v Loxton Municipality 1948 (1) SA 966 (C) 81, 82
Marcus v Stamper and Zoutendijk 1910 AD 58 72
Mbuku v Mdinwa 1982 (1) SA 219 (Tk) 71
Meepo v Kotze 2008 (1) SA 104 (NC) 266, 270, 274, 276, 278, 279
Meintjies v Wilson 1927 OPD 183 205
Melcorp SA v Joint Municipal Pension
    Fund (Transvaal) 1980 (2) SA 214 (W) 164, 170, 171, 172, 174
Menqa and Another v Markom and Others 2008 (2) SA 120 (SCA) 220
Meyer v Glendinning 1939 CPD 84 .... 70, 71, 72, 75, 76, 77, 80
Mills v Reck and Others 1988 (3) SA 92 (C) 77
Minister of Public Works and Others v Kyalami Ridge Environmental Association and
    Others 2001 (3) SA 1151 (CC) 146, 152
Minister of the Interior v Lockhat 1961 (2) SA 587 (A) 13
Minister of Water Affairs v Mostert 1966 (4) SA 690 (A) 128
Minister van Landbou v Sonnendecker 1979 (2) SA 944 (A) 182
Minister van Lande v Swart 1957 (3) SA 508 (C) 181
Minister van Verdediging v Van Wyk 1976 (1) SA 397 (T) 227
Mkontwana v Nelson Mandela Metropolitan Municipality and Another; Bissett and
    Others v Buffalo City Municipality and Others; Transfer Rights Action Campaign and
    Others v MEC, Local Government and Housing, Gauteng, and Others (KwaZulu-Natal Law
    Society and Msundzi Municipality as *Amici Curiae*) 2005 (1) SA 530 (CC) 121, 124, 125, 347
Mkontwana v Nelson Mandela Municipality Case No: 1238/02 (unreported) 125, 156, 347

Mlombo v Fourie 1964 (3) SA 350 (T) 219
Mngadi NO v Ntuli 1981 (3) SA 378 (D&C) 217
Mocke v Beaufort West Municipality 1939 CPD 135 254
Modderfontein Squatters, Greater Benoni City Council v Modderklip Boerdery (Pty) Ltd;
  (AgriSA and Legal Resources Centre, *Amici Curiae*); President of the Republic of
  South Africa and Others v Modderklip Boerdery (Pty) Ltd (AgriSA and
  Legal Resources Centre, *Amici Curiae*) 2004 (6) SA 40 (SCA) 119, 132
Modderklip Boerdery (Edms) Bpk v President van die Republiek van
  Suid-Afrika 2003 (6) BCLR 638 (T) 119
Modderklip Boerdery (Pty) Ltd v Modder East Squatters 2001 (4) SA 385 (W) 132, 156
Moleta v Fourie 1975 (3) SA 999 (O) 82
Molteno Bros and Others v SAR and Others 1936 AD 321 84
Morkels Transport (Pty) Ltd v Melrose Foods (Pty) Ltd 1972 (2) A 464 (W) 182
Morobane v Bateman 1918 AD 460 229
Morum Bros Ltd v Nepgen 1916 CPD 392 224
Mpunga v Malaba 1959 (1) SA 853 (W) 76
Muller v Muller 1915 TPD 28 .... 75, 77
Municipality City of Port Elizabeth v Rudman 1999 (1) SA 665 (SE) 152

N

Nach Investments (Pty) Ltd v Yaldayi Investments (Pty) Ltd and Another 1987 (2) SA 820 (A) 245
Naidoo v Moodley 1982 (4) SA 82 (T) 79
National Bank of South Africa Ltd v Cohen's Trustee 1911 AD 235 .... 22, 308
Naude v Bredenkamp 1956 (2) SA 448 (O) 139
Naudé v Ecoman Investments 1994 (2) SA 95 (T) 247
Ndauti v Kgami and Others 1948 (3) SA 27 (W) 84
Ndlovu v Ngcobo, Bekker v Jika 2003 (1) SA 113 (SCA) 217, 221, 311
Nel NO v Commissioner for Inland Revenue 1960 (1) SA 227 (A) 49, 54, 55
Ness v Greeff 1985 (4) SA 641 (C) 81, 82
Nhlabathi v Fick [2003] 2 All SA 323 (LCC) 31
Nino Bonino v De Lange 1906 TS 120 .... 75, 77, 80
Nkosi and Another v Bührmann 2002 (1) SA 372 (SCA) 31
Nolte v Johannesburg Consolidated Investment Co Ltd 1943 AD 295 .... 44, 267
Northview Properties (Pty) Ltd v Lurie 1951 (3) SA 688 (A) 236

O

Oakland Nominees (Pty) Ltd v Gelria Mining and Investment
  Co (Pty) Ltd 1976 (1) SA 441 (A) 215, 224
Occupiers of 51 Olivia Road, Berea Township and Others v City of Johannesburg and
  Others 2008 (3) SA 208 (CC) 348, 349
Opera House (Grand Parade) Restaurant (Pty) Ltd v Cape Town Municipality 1989 (2) SA 670 (C) 127
Osry v Hirsch, Loubser and Company Ltd 1922 CPD 531 309

P

Paola v Jeeva 2004 (1) SA 396 (SCA) 145, 151, 154
Paradise Lost Properties v Standard Bank of South Africa (Pty) Ltd 1997 (2) SA 815 (D) 327
Pearly Beach Trust v Registrar of Deeds 1990 (4) SA 614 (C) 52, 53

Pennefather v Gokul 1960 (4) SA 42 (N) 205
Pennsylvania Coal Co v Mahon 260 US 393 (1922) 131
Philip Robinson Motors (Pty) Ltd v NM Dada (Pty) Ltd 1975 (2) SA 420 (A) 228
Phoebus Apollo Aviation CC v Minister of Safety and Security 2003 (2) SA 34 (CC) 119
Pick 'n Pay Stores and Others v Teazers Comedy and Revue CC and
    Others 2000 (3) SA 645 (WLD) 146, 150
Pietermaritzburg Corporation v South African Breweries Ltd 1911 AD 501 .... 35, 128
Plaatjie and Another v Olivier NO and Others 1993 (2) SA 156 (O) 78, 79
Port Elizabeth Municipality v Peoples Dialogue on Land and Shelter and
    Another 2000 (2) SA 1074 (SE) 347
Port Elizabeth Municipality v Various Occupiers 2005 (1) SA 217 (CC) 15, 16, 221, 222, 347, 348, 349
Potgieter NO v Daewoo Heavy Industries (Edms) Bpk 2003 (3) SA 98 (SCA) 328
Premier of the Western Cape v Faircape Property Developers (Pty) Ltd 2003 (6) SA 13 (SCA) 260
President of the Republic of South Africa and Another v Modderklip Boerdery (Pty) Ltd
    (AgriSA and Legal Resources Centre, *Amici Curiae*) 2005 (5) SA 3 (CC) 132, 221, 222, 347
Pretoria City Council v South African Organ Builders (Pty) Ltd 1953 (3) SA 400 (T) 151
Pretorius v Nefdt & Glas 1908 TS 854 99
Prinsloo v Shaw 1938 AD 570 .... 134, 135, 137
Prophet v National Director of Public Prosecutions 2007 (6) SA 169 (CC) 95
Provincial Heritage Resources Authority, Eastern Cape v Gordon 2005 2 SA 283 (EC) 153
PS Booksellers (Pty) Ltd v Harrison 2008 (3) SA 633 (C) 256

Q

Qualidental Laboratories (Pty) Ltd v Heritage Western Cape and Another 2008 (3) SA 160 (SCA) 153
Quathlamba (Pty) Ltd v Ministry of Forestry 1972 (2) SA 783 (N) 145
Quenty's Motors (Pty) Ltd v Standard Credit Corporation Ltd 1994 (3) SA 188 (A) 224, 225

R

Rand Water Board v Bothma 1997 (3) SA 120 (C) 139
Receiver of Revenue, Cape v Cavanagh 1912 AD 459 35
Reck v Mills 1990 (1) SA 751 (A) 8
Redelinghuys v Bazzoni 1976 (1) SA 110 (T) 144
Regal v African Superslate (Pty) Ltd 1963 (1) SA 102 (A) 116, 138
Residents of Joe Slovo Community, Western Cape v Thubelisha Homes 2009 JDR 0580 (CC) 222
Richtersveld Community v Alexkor (Pty) Ltd 2001 (3) SA 1293 (LCC) 16, 17
Richtersveld Community v Alexkor 2003 (6) SA 104 (SCA) 16, 17
Rikhotso v Northcliff Ceramics (Pty) Ltd 1997 (1) SA 526 (W) 81, 82, 346
Ritama Investments v The Unlawful Occupiers of Erf 62, Wynberg and
    Others (2007) JOL 18960 (T) 348, 349
RMS Transport v Psicon Holdings (Pty) Ltd 1996 (2) SA 176 (T) 228
Rocher v Registrar of Deeds 1911 TPD 311 267
Rondebosch Municipal Council v Trustee of Western Province Agricultural Society 1911 AD 271 126
Roodepoort United Main Reef Gold Mining Company Ltd (in liquidation) v Du Toit 1928 AD 66 309
Rubidge v McCabe & Sons and Others; McCabe & Sons and Others v Rubidge 1913 AD 433 245
Ruskin NO v Thiergen 1962 (3) SA 737 (A) 219
R v Mafohla 1958 (2) SA 373 (SR) 8

S

SA Bank of Athens Ltd v Van Zyl 2005 (5) SA 93 (SCA) 316
Sailing Queen Investments v The Occupants La Colleen Court 2008 (6) BCLR 666 (W) 349
Samsudin v De Villiers Berange NO [2006] SCA 79 (RSA) 5
Samuel v Pagadia 1963 (3) SA 45 (D) 35
Sasfin (Pty) Ltd v Beukes 1989 (1) SA 1 (A) 22
Saunders v Executrix of Hunt (1828-1849) 2 Menz 313 254
Scheepers v Robbertse 1973 (2) SA 508 (N) 35
Schwedhelm v Hauman 1947 (1) SA 127 (E) 241, 242, 243
Secretary for Inland Revenue v Sturrock Sugar Farms (Pty) Ltd 1965 (1) SA 897 (A) 35
Secretary for Lands v Jerome 1922 AD 103 167
Senekal v Roodt 1983 (2) SA 602 (T) 36
Sentraalwes Personeel Ondernemings (Edms) Bpk v Wallis 1978 (3) SA 80 (T) 147
Serole v Pienaar 2000 (1) SA 328 (LCC) 31
Setlolego v Setlolego 1914 AD 221 84
Shell South Africa (Pty) Ltd v Alexene Investments (Pty) Ltd 1980 (1) SA 683 (W) 258, 259
Silvermine Valley Coalition v Sybrand van der Spuy Boerderye and Others 2002 (1) SA 478 (C) 154
Simmer and Jack Mines Ltd v GF Industrial Property Co (Pty) Ltd 1975 (2) SA 654 (W) 170
Singh v Santam Insurance Ltd 1997 (1) SA 291 (SCA) 329
Slabbert v Minister van Lande 1963 (3) SA 620 (T) 126
Smith v Basson 1979 (1) SA 559 (W) 143
Smith v Martin's Executor (1899) 16 SC 148 182
South African Railways and Harbours v Transvaal Consolidated Land and
　Exploration Co Ltd 1961 (2) SA 467 (A) 267
South African Shore Angling Association and Another v Minister of Environmental
　Affairs 2002 (5) SA 511 (SE) 271
Southern Tankers (Pty) Ltd t/a Unilog v Pescana D'Oro Ltd (Velmar Ltd
　Intervening) 2003 (4) SA 566 (C) 207, 208
Stadsraad van Vanderbijlpark v Uys 1989 (3) SA 528 (A) 147, 255
Stalwo (Pty) Ltd v Wary Holdings (Pty) Ltd 2008 (1) SA 654 (SCA) 154
Standard Bank of SA Ltd v Stama (Pty) Ltd 1975 (1) SA 730 (A) 225
Standard Bank of South Africa Ltd v Saunderson 2006 (2) SA 264 (SCA) 295, 338
Standard Bank of Southern Africa Ltd v Saunderson 2006 (2) SA 264 (SCA) 310, 311
Standard Bank van SA Bpk v Breitenbach 1977 (1) SA 151 (T) 211, 312, 313
Standard Bank v O'Connor (1888) 6 SC 32 206
Standard-Vacuum Refining Co of SA (Pty) Ltd v Durban City Council 1961(2) SA 669 (A) .. 169, 170
Steinberg v South Peninsula Municipality 2001 (4) SA 1243 (SCA) 131
Strydom v De Lange 1970 (2) SA 6 (T) 71
S v Frost, S v Noah 1974 (3) SA 466 (C) 163
S v Riekert 1977 (3) SA 181 (T) 176, 178

T

Telkom SA Ltd v Xsinet (Pty) Ltd 2003 (5) SA 309 (SCA) 22, 78, 79
Theatre Investments (Pty) Ltd v Butcher Brothers Ltd 1978 (3) SA 682 (A) 169, 170, 172, 173
Theron v Gerber 1918 EDL 288 320
Thienhaus NO v Metje & Ziegler Ltd 1965 (3) SA 25 (A) 58, 306, 307
Thubelisha Homes v Various Occupants 2008 JOL 21559 (C) 348

Tigon v Bestyet Investments (Pty) Ltd 2001 (4) SA 634 (N) 22, 78
Total South Africa (Pty) Ltd v Xypteras 1970 (1) SA 592 (T) 58
Transnet Ltd v Nyawazu and Others 2006 (5) SA 100 (D) 346
Trojan Exploration Co (Pty) Ltd and Another v Rustenburg Platinum Mines Ltd and
    Others 1996 (4) SA 499 (A) 237, 267, 269, 273
TR Services (Pty) Ltd v Poynton's Corner Ltd 1961 (1) SA 773 (D) 327
Trustees of the Brian Lackey Trust v Annandale 2004 (3) SA 281 (C) 142
Tswelopele Non-Profit Organisation and Others v City of Tshwane Metropolitan Municipality and Others
    2007 (6) SA 511 (SCA) 82, 347
Tuckers Land and Development Corporation (Pty) Ltd v Truter 1984 (2) SA 150 (SWA) 147
Turkstra Ltd v Richards 1926 TPD 276 135

U

Underwater Construction and Salvage Co (Pty) Ltd v Bell 1968 (4) SA 190 (C) 71
Unimark Distributors (Pty) Ltd v Erf 94 Silvertondale (Pty) Ltd 1999 (2) SA 986 (T) 164, 173
United Building Society v Smookler's Trustees and Galombik's Trustee 1906 TS 623 309

V

Van Boom v Visser (1904) 21 SC 360 140
Van der Bijl v Louw 1974 (2) SA 493 (C) 147
Van der Merwe v Wiese 1948 (4) SA 8 (C) 242, 243
Van Rensburg v Coetzee 1979 (4) SA 655 (A) 247
Van Rensburg v Nelson Mandela Metropolitan
    Municipality 2008 (2) SA 8 (SECLD) 255, 256, 257, 258
Van Rensburg v Taute 1975 (1) SA 279 (A) 246
Van Vuren and Others v Registrar of Deeds 1907 TS 289 .... 44, 267, 273
Van Wyk v Louw 1958 (2) SA 154 (C) 181
Vasco Dry Cleaners v Twycross 1979 (1) SA 603 (A) 204, 317, 318, 320
Venter v Minister of Railways 1949 (2) SA 178 (E) 241
Vereeniging City Council v Rhema Bible Church 1989 (2) SA 142 (T) 146
Victoria & Alfred Waterfront v Police Commissioner, Western Cape, and Others
    (Legal Resources Centre as *Amicus Curiae*) 2004 (4) SA 444 (C) 30, 84
Vogel v Crewe [2004] 1 All SA 587 (T) 135, 138

W

Wahloo Sand Bpk v Trustees, Hambly Parker Trust 2002 (2) SA 776 (SCA) 59, 60, 61, 62
Warren v MEC of Housing, Local Government and Traditional Affairs
    unreported case EL220/07; ECD520/07 256
Wary Holdings (Pty) Ltd v Stalwo (Pty) Ltd 2009 (1) SA 337 (CC) 154
Webster v Ellison 1911 AD 73 326
Webster v Mitchell 1948 (1) SA 1186 (W) 84
Welgemoed v Coetzer 1946 TPD 71
Wightman t/a JW Construction v Headfour (Pty) Ltd and Another 2008 (3) SA 371 (SCA) 71, 77
Wilderness (1921) Ltd v Union Government 1927 CPD 455 181
Willoughby's Consolidated Co Ltd v Copthall Stores Ltd 1918 AD 245, 251
Windhoek Municipality v Lurie & Co (SWA) (Pty) Ltd 1957 (1) SA 164 (SWA) 135
Winshaw v Miller 1916 CPD 439 135
Wright v Cockin 2004 (4) SA 207 (E) 135

X
Xsinet (Pty) Ltd v Telkom SA Ltd 2002 (3) SA 629 (C) 79

Y
Yeko v Qana 1973 (4) SA 735 (A) 76, 77

Z
Zandberg v Van Zyl 1910 AD 302 .... 317, 320
Zinman v Miller 1956 (3) SA 8 (T) 76
Zondi v MEC for Traditional and Local Government Affairs 2005 (3) SA 25 (N) 27
Zulu v Minister of Works, KwaZulu 1992 (1) SA 181 (N) 78, 79

Table of legislation

Acts

Advertising on Roads and Ribbon Development Act 21 of 1940 152
    section 2 152
    section 9 152
Alienation of Land Act 68 of 1981 197
Black Administration Act 38 of 1927 .... 14, 155
Black Land Act 27 of 1913 13
Cape Town Foreshore Act 26 of 1950 163
Collective Investment Schemes Act 45 of 2002 313
Communal Land Rights Act 11 of 2004 .... 105, 110, 111, 112, 113
    section 5 342
    section 39 111
Communal Property Associations Act 28 of 1996 105
    section 5 106
    section 6 106
    section 7 106
    section 8 .... 105, 106
    section 9 106
    section 11 107
    section 12 107
    section 13 107
Constitution of the Republic of South Africa, 1996 .... 5, 9, 15, 16, 17, 106, 128, 132
    chapter 2 118
    section 8 .... 118, 259
    section 9 107
    section 10 22
    section 24 .... 151, 155, 287
    section 25 .... 14, 27, 91, 111, 117, 118, 119, 120, 121, 122, 123, 125, 126, 127, 129, 130, 140, 143, 150, 151, 174, 188, 220, 221, 258, 261, 275, 287, 290, 342
    section 26 .... 14, 117, 118, 119, 151, 217, 220, 221, 311, 332
    section 27 .... 151, 284, 287, 293
    section 29 151
    section 33 188
    section 36 .... 120, 121, 122, 124, 125, 129, 130
    section 39 119
    section 152 151
    section 153 .... 151, 349
    schedule 4 .... 148, 349
    schedule 5 148
Customs and Excise Act 91 of 1964
    section 114 120
Deeds Registries Act 13 of 1918 12

Deeds Registries Act 47 of 1937 .... 12, 15, 197, 212, 213, 290, 291
    section 9 307
    section 13 304
    section 16 .... 45, 47, 211
    section 50 304
    section 50A 304
    section 51 313
    section 53 304
    section 56 .... 22, 33, 312
    section 60 .... 22, 33
    section 63 .... 45, 47, 49, 50, 52, 55, 243
    section 64 22
    section 65 312
    section 68 .... 22, 33, 254
    section 69 .... 22, 33
    section 71 .... 22, 33
    section 75 .... 239, 252, 312
    section 76 252
    section 77 33
    section 81 22
    section 102 .... 35, 321
    section 132 290
Development Facilitation Act 67 of 1995 .... 15, 105, 146, 197
    section 3 152
    section 62 35
Environment Conservation Act 73 of 1989 136
    section 73 136
Expropriation Act 63 of 1975 .... 126, 140, 188, 279
    section 12 127
Extension of Security of Tenure Act 62 of 1997 .... 100, 105, 146, 197, 217, 222, 343
    section 1 222
    section 4 96
    section 6 31
    section 9 222
    section 10 .... 222, 223
    section 11 222
    section 12 222
Fencing Act 31 of 1963 144
Firearms Control Act 60 of 2000
    chapter 6 95
Game Theft Act 105 of 1991 .... 163, 164, 218
    section 1 30
    section 2 30
Group Areas Act 36 of 1966 .... 13, 14
Group Areas Act 41 of 1950 13

Housing Act 107 of 1997
    section 3 349
    section 6 349
    section 9 349
    section 10 349
    section 10B 349
    section 15 349
    section 16 349
Housing Development Schemes for Retired Persons Act 65 of 1988
    section 1 105
Insolvency Act 24 of 1936 323
    section 2 309
    section 36 220
    section 84 328
    section 95 309
    section 98 332
Interim Protection of Informal Land Rights Act 31 of 1996 105
Irrigation and Conservation of Water Act 8 of 1912 286
Land Reform (Labour Tenants) Act 3 of 1996 .... 100, 105, 197, 222
    chapter III 96
    section 1 222
    section 5 222
    section 7 .... 222, 223
    section 15 .... 222, 223
    section 15A 222
    sections 16–28 96
Land Survey Act 8 of 1997 .... 15, 197
    section 14 23
Less Formal Township Establishment Act 113 of 1991 153
Local Government: Municipal Structures Act 117 of 1998 292
Local Government: Municipal Systems Act 32 of 2000 .... 151, 156, 349
    section 23 151
    section 25 151
    section 35 152
    section 118 .... 124, 347
Local Government Transition Act 209 of 1993 288
Magistrates' Courts Act 32 of 1944
    section 66 220
    section 70 220
Marine Living Resources Act 18 of 1998 163

Mineral and Petroleum Resources
    Development Act 28 of 2002 .... 127, 250, 265, 268, 271, 275, 282, 312
        section 1 .... 273, 274, 275, 276, 277, 278, 281
        section 3 .... 31, 266, 269, 270, 272, 274, 278
        section 4 270
        section 5 .... 274, 276, 277, 278
        section 11 279
        section 15 277
        section 19 276
        section 25 276
        section 27 277
        section 32 277
        section 35 277
        section 38 280
        section 41 280
        section 43 280
        section 54 279
        section 55 279
        section 56 .... 279, 280
        section 69 .... 278, 279, 280
        section 78 277
        section 82 276
        section 86 276
        section 93 278
        section 106 278
        section 123 281
        schedule II 129, 268, 275, 279, 281
Mineral and Petroleum Resources Royalty Act 28 of 2008 278
Minerals Act 50 of 1991
        section 5 267
        section 6 268
        section 9 268
Mining Rights Act 20 of 1967
        section 2 268
Mining Titles Registration Act 16 of 1967 268
        section 3 276
        section 5 .... 276, 280
        section 15 276
Mining Titles Registration Amendment Act 24 of 2003 268
        section 53 22
National Building Regulations and Building Standards Act 103 of 1977 139
        section 4 154
        section 7 154
National Credit Act 34 of 2005 .... 194, 302, 305, 308, 343
        section 1 .... 206, 328

National Environmental Management Act 107 of 1998 .... 154, 155
    chapter 3 152
    section 2 .... 152, 271
    section 28 271
    section 30 271
National Health Act 61 of 2003 23
National Heritage Resources Act 25 of 1999 .... 94, 153, 163
    section 34 .... 122, 153
    section 38 153
National Water Act 36 of 1998 .... 31, 127, 277, 284, 287, 288, 293
    section 2 288
    section 3 .... 271, 288
    section 4 289
    section 22 289
    section 127 .... 289, 290, 292
    section 128 291
    section 129 .... 290, 291, 292
    section 130 290
    section 132 .... 290, 291
    section 133 .... 254, 291
    section 136 289
    schedule 1 289
    schedule 2 290
Notarial Bonds (Natal) Act 18 of 1932 323
Physical Planning Act 125 of 1991 152
Precious Stones Act 73 of 1964
    section 2 268
Prescription Act 18 of 1943 .... 180, 181, 183, 184, 186
Prescription Act 68 of 1969 .... 179, 180, 181, 182, 184, 186, 187
    section 2 183
    section 3 185
    section 6 252
    section 7 253
Pre-Union Statutes Law Revision Act 44 of 1968 269
Prevention of Illegal Eviction from and Unlawful Occupation of Land
    Act 19 of 1998 .... 16, 105, 132, 146, 217, 311
    section 4 .... 221, 223, 311
    section 5 221
    section 6 .... 221, 223
Prevention of Organised Crime Act 121 of 1998 95
Promotion of Administrative Justice Act 3 of 2000 188
Property Time-sharing Control Act 75 of 1983
    section 1 104
Provision of Land and Assistance Act 123 of 1993 105

Removal of Restrictions Act 84 of 1967 .... 153, 155, 262
    section 2 153
    section 3 .... 262, 263
    section 4 263
Restitution of Land Rights Act 22 of 1994 .... 16, 100, 105, 197
Road Traffic Act 29 of 1989 95
Sea-shore Act 21 of 1935 163
Sea Transport Documents Act 65 of 2000
    section 2 31
    section 3 201
Sectional Titles Act 66 of 1971
    section 23 252
Sectional Titles Act 95 of 1986 .... 23, 100, 101, 103
    section 25 248
    section 28 252
    section 55 307
    Annexure 8 102
    Annexure 9 102
Security by Means of Movable Property Act 57 of 1993 .... 322, 324
    section 1 .... 323, 324
    section 2 328
Security of Tenure Act 62 of 1997
Share Blocks Control Act 59 of 1980 103
    section 1 104
    section 5 113
State Land Disposal Act 48 of 1961
    section 3 188
Subdivision of Agricultural Land Act 70 of 1970 .... 38, 147
    section 3 154
Subdivision of Agricultural Land Act Repeal Act 64 of 1998 154
Traditional Leadership and Governance Framework Act 41 of 2003 112
Transformation of Certain Rural Areas Act 94 of 1998 105
Water Act 54 of 1965 .... 284, 285, 286
    section 1 286
    section 5 286
    section 6 286
Water Services Act 108 of 1997 .... 287, 288, 293
    section 1 287
Wreck and Salvage Act 94 of 1996 163

Foreign statutes

Mineral Resources Act 1989 (Qld)
    section 310 273
Mineral Resources (Sustainable Development Act 1990 (Vic)
    section 11 273
Mining Act 1992 (NSW)
    section 11 273

Mining Act 1978 (WA)
      section 85 273
Mining Right Act (SA)
      section 18 273

Bills

Land Use Management Bill [B 27-2008] 152, 153
      section 1 255

Provincial legislation

Gauteng Local Government Ordinance 17 of 1939
      section 49 124
      section 50 124
Gauteng Removal of Restrictions Act 3 of 1996 .... 153, 262
      section 5 .... 262, 263
      section 6 263
      section 35 262
Land Use Planning Ordinance 15 of 1985 (C) 152, 155, 156
Northern Cape Planning and Development Act 7 of 1998 .... 152, 155
Provincial Notice 627 of 1998 (PG 5309 of 20 November 1998)
Town-planning and Townships Ordinance 15 of 1986 (T) 152, 155, 156
Town Planning Ordinance 27 of 1949 (N) 152, 155, 156
Townships Ordinance 9 of 1969 (OFS) 152, 155

Subordinate legislation

Environmental Impact Assessment Regulations, 2006 154
Government Notice R474 of 1963 307
Government Notice R1886 of 1990 155
Government Notice R1888 of 1990 152
Government Notice 1639 of 2004 281
Government Notice No R385 of 2006 154
Government Notice No R386 of 2006 154
Government Notice No R387 of 2006 154
Land Redistribution for Agricultural Development Plan (LRAD), 2000 15
Noise Control Regulations (Western Cape) PN 627 of 1998 136
Proclamation on Conversion of Loan Places to Quitrent Tenure, 1813 .... 12, 269
Proclamation R293 of 1962 .... 14, 155
Proclamation R188 of 1969 111
Proclamation R1897 of 1986 155
Regulations in terms of the Sectional Titles Act 95 of 1986 307

White Paper

White Paper on a National Water Policy for South Africa, 1997 287
White Paper on Land Policy, 1997 .... 14, 15, 105

Index

Please note: page numbers in italics refer to tables and figures.

A

absolute rights 48
abstract theory 190
accession *(accessio)* 161, 164–165
    and art 166
    immovable to immovable property 175
    movable to other movable property 165–167
    movables to immovable property 167–175
accessory things 37–38
acquired possession 71
acquisition
    of a thing *(iura in personam ad rem acquirendam)* 59
    see also original acquisition of ownership
acquisitive prescription 179–180
actions
    in damages 137
    personal *(actiones in personam)* 48
    real *(actiones in rem)* 48
    right to bring an action *(locus standi)* 80
Acts of Parliament 10
actual knowledge of prior personal right 59
administrative law 10
Advertising on Roads and Ribbon Development Act 152
Afrikaans terminology 12
ancestral land 16
apartheid 13
    statutory rights and obligations 13–53
Appellate Division 54–55
appropriability 23–24
appropriation (occupatio) 161
arbitrary deprivation of property 123
attachment (join) 166
    of immovable property 332
    manner and degree 169
    permanency 169, 171, 172
auxiliary things (appurtenances) 36, 37

B

bare (factual) possession 73, 75
Black Economic Empowerment 281
Black Land Act 13n49
body corporate 101, 102
bound co-ownership 97
    see also tied co-ownership
building *(inaedificatio)* 168–175
    analysis of approaches 173–175
    omne quod inaedificatio solo credit 168, 169, 170
    restrictions 34
    right to build on another's land *(superficies)* 48, 237
    superficies solo credit 168
bundle of rights 28, 28n54
burden of proof 57

C

capitalist system 4
case law (precedent) 15, 16, 58
causal theory 190–191
cession of the right of vindication *(cessio iuris vindicationis)* 198, 345
Civil Law 9
'classical squatting' ('holding over') 221
closed category *(numerus clausus)*
    45, 341–343
    titling and tenure 342
collection
    or aggregate 35–36
    of things *(res universitatis)* 301
Collective Investment Schemes Act 313
colonisation 10, 10n26
common law 8, 9, 15, 16
    ownership 97–98
    South African 10
commonly owned property 99
common property 102
common to all *(res omnium communes)* 31
Communal Land Rights Act (CLRA) 111–112
communal property association (CPA) 105–107
    dispute resolution 107
    dissolution of 107

Communal Property Associations Act 105
communal tenure 107-108, 111
communist system 4
compensation 8, 127-129, 247
    market value 127-128
    unjustified enrichment basis 139
composite things 35-38
conceptual severance 28
Constitution 188, 217, 259, 287
constitutional concept of property 27, 27-47
Constitutional Court 15, 16, 27, 347-348
constitutional limitations on ownership
    compensation 127-129
    interference/infringement 119-122
    law of general application 125
    non-arbitrariness 123-125, 129
    proportionality of interferences 129-132
    public purpose/public interest 126-127
    Section 25 of Constitution 118-132
constitutional property clause 5, 14
constitutional remedies 259
constructive knowledge 57, 59
consumable things 39
contract of service 203
contractual or delictual obligation 40, 45
control-based possession 69
conventional title 104
co-ownership 96-97
corporate bodies *(res universitatis)* 29
corporeal immovable property 304
corporeality 21-22
corporeal things 32-35, 78
counterspoilation (self-help) 82
covering bond (special mortgage) 313
Cradock, Sir John 12
credit agreement 302
creditor (holder) 44, 296-297
    paritas creditorium principle 299
crime, commission of a 8
currently owned *(res alicuius)* 29, 30
customary law 341
    and common law 17
    ownership 16
customary tenure 342

D

debt
    contract 300
    instrument of 306
    natural obligation 300
    record of principal debt 306
    rights attached in execution of 32
debtor 44, 296
    liabilities 297
declaratory order (declaration of rights) 259
Deed of Transfer 213
Deed's Office 8, 47, 197
Deeds Registries Act 35, 47, 50, 52-53, 55, 243, 291, 304
Deeds Registry 179, 211, 212
delictual action
    circumstances for applicability 85
    defences 86
    relief available 86
    requirements 85
    use of 86
delictual or contractual obligation (performance) 40, 45
delictual remedies 215-216
    actio ad exhibendium 228
    actio legis Aquillae 229
    condictio furtiva 227
delivery 47
    attornment 198, 206, 207, 206, 206-210
    attornment and cession 209-210
    constitutum possessorium 198, 203-4, 318, 324
    constructive delivery 198, 199, 200, 341, 345
    elements 197
    or registration 197-200
    symbolic *(clavium traditio)* 198, 201
    way of *(traditio)* 197
    with long hand *(traditio longa manu)* 198, 201-202
    with short hand *(traditio brevi manu)* 198, 204-206
Department of Minerals and Energy 279
derivative acquisition of ownership 188-189
developing countries 4-5
Development Facilitation Act 35, 35n94, 152
divisible things 38-39

doctrine
    of constructive knowledge 57
    of notice 58-61

E

economic unit 35
encroacher
    'approved' 141
    in bad faith *(mala fide)* 139
    in good faith *(bona fide)* 139
encroachment
    and accession 142-143
    by building 139-142
    overhanging branches 143
English Common Law 10
enrichment liens 330
entitlement(s) 94, 338
    to alienate or encumber property *(ius disponendi)* 94
    civil and natural 94-95
    to control property physically *(ius possidendi)* 84, 94
    of ownership 92
    to possession 73
    to use property *(ius utendi)* 94
    to vindicate property *(ius vindicandi)* 94
Environmental Conservation Act 136
Environmental Impact Assessment Regulations 154
equalisation 131-132
estate 25-26
    components 26
estoppel 223-226
    requirements 224
European Civil Law 10
eviction 13
    Constitutional Court's jurisprudence 347-348
    instruments 223
    orders 221-223
    squatters 348
    unlawful occupiers 221
exclusivity 338
ex parte (from one side only) application proceedings 85

express real security rights (by agreement)
    constituting the mortgage 304-307
    definition 303
    special mortgage in immovable property 303
Expropriation Act 127-128, 188, 279
expropriation of property 188, 274-175
    purpose of 129
Extension of Security of Tenure Act (ESTA) 100, 217, 222
extracted (severed) minerals and petroleum 273

F

factual identity 164, 171
forced removals 13
Free Basic Water Strategy 287
free co-ownership 97
freehold title, see conventional title 104
fungible things 39-40

G

Game Theft Act 30, 164
good faith *(bona fides)* 177
Group Areas Act 13
group rights 6

H

hire-purchase agreement 171
Housing Development Schemes for Retired Persons Act 105
human body parts 23
human rights 118-119, 259
hypothecation 304
    instrument 306

I

immovable property (land) rights 49
    coram judice rei sitae principle 210
immovable things 33-35, 76n28, 197
impersonal nature of law 22-23
incidental use rights 79
incorporeal movable property 315
incorporeality 21-22
incorporeal things 32-35
    application to remedy 78-79
    mobility of 34
independent legal existence 23
indigenous customary law 11

indigenous land rights 107–110, 341
    and common law landholding 109–110
indigenous property rights 13–14
individual
    co-ownership 101
    interests of 161
    title 96
individual rights 6
    assets or estate 7
indivisible things 38–39
infringement 59
    see also interference with property
Insolvency Act 328, 332
instanter (acting immediately) 82
intangible objects 7–8
integrated development plans
    (IDPs) 149, 151–152
intention
    to benefit self *(animus ex re commodum*
        acquirendi) 76, 80
    to be owner *(animus domini)* 163, 181
    inferred 169
    real 169
    subjective *(ipse dixit)* 169
interdict
    audi alterum principle 85
    circumstances for applicability 84
    defences 85
    relief available 85
    requirements 84–85
interest in close corporation 7
interference with property
    non-arbitrariness 123–125
    of property rights 119–122
    proportionality 129–130
    proportionality test 130
    sufficient reason for 123
    that goes too far 130–132
interruption of prescriptive period 183–184
    civil (judicial) 184
    natural 183
interventions in entrenched positions 338–339
intrinsic pecuniary value 32
irregular servitudes 248

J

join, see attachment
judicial mortgage 332
judicial pledge 332
judicial real security rights 332
juristic persons 6, 7

K

knowledge 243
kustingsbrief mortgage 313

L

land
    control 13
    discriminatory law 14
    law 12–13
    limited rights in 47
    reform laws 222, 342
    registration 342–343
    rights 338
    rights of use or habitation 34, 341
    title 14
land development objectives (LDOs) 149
landlord's tacit hypothec, see lessor's tacit
    hypothec
    landownership 13
    minerals and petroleum 269
Land Reform (Labour Tenants) Act 96, 100, 222
land use management
    national legislation 153–154
    provincial legislation 155
Land Use Management Act 152
land use schemes 152
lateral support 143–144
law
    of contract 7
    of general application 125
    of succession 7
    of things ('sakereg') 11
Law of Contract 40
Law of Property 3, 4, 133
Law of Succession 40
leases 21, 32
legal identity 164, 166–167
legal meaning of property 5
legal object 5, 7, 12
legal system and property law 7

Less Formal Township Establishment Act 153
lessor's tacit hypothec 325–328
    property subject *(invecta et illata)* 325, 326–327
lien (right of retention) 328–329
    debtor and creditor liens 331
    luxurious expenses 330, 331
    necessary expenses 330
    operation 330
    possession 329
    requirements 329–330
    salvage and improvement liens 331
    termination 331
    useful expenses 330, 331
limitations of ownership 116–117
    categories and examples 117
    public law 145–156
    types 117–118
    see also constitutional limitations
limited real rights *(iura in re aliena)* 42, 43, 78, 117, 235
    property 92
    water 284
    see personal servitues
liquidation 279–280
loan (principal debt) 297
Local Government: Municipal Systems Act 151–152
Local Government Transition Act 288
lost things *(res deperditae)* 30, 66, 163

M

Magistrates' Court Act 220
mandament van spoilie (possessory remedy) 71, 73, 82, 84, 346
    application of remedy to incorporeals 78–79
    circumstances for applicability 75–77
    defences 80–83
    relief available 80
    requirements 77–78
    use of 83
mandatory interdict 259
    order *(mandamus)* 259
market economy, role in 6
marriage in community of property 97
mental element *(animus possidendi)* 66, 70, 72–73, 80, 191, 192

mercantile law 10
Mineral and Petroleum Resources Development Act (MPRDA) 129, 265–266, 268, 312
    concepts used in 273–274
    content of rights 277–8
    environmental provisions 280
    ownership of minerals and petroleum 269–273
Mineral and Petroleum Resources Royalty Act (MPRPA) 278
Mineral and Petroleum Titles Registration Office 276
mineral industry
    environmental provisions of MPRDA 280
mineral law
    history of 266–269
    part of property law 266, 267, 281
mineral rights 21, 265, 274–275
    activities and requirements 278
    cancellation or abandonment of 280
    common law understanding 267
    content of 276–277
    deregistration 280
    expropriation 274–275
    holder (nominee) 267–268
    leases of 22, 22n15
    nature of 276
    to prospect and mine 268
    as real rights *(sui generis)* 44
    surface owner 278–279
    termination of 279–280
    transfer and encumbrance 279
minerals
    permissions to remove 274
    prospecting rights 274
    reconnaissance permissions 274, 277
    retention permits 275
mining
    access to 281
    ecological degradation 280
    environmental liability 280
    permits 274, 277
    pollution 280
    rights 274
    subordinate rights of extraction 268
    see also Black Economic Empowerment 281

Mining Titles Registration Act (MTRA) 268, 276
misrepresentation 225
monetary debts and obligations 296
mortgage 44, 298
    binding agreement 305
    creation of bond 305
    record of agreement 306
    right of preference 309
    termination of 314
    types of 313
    written agreement 306
mortgage bond 304, 306, 338
    forfeiture clause *(pactum commissorium)* 308
    form and content 307–308
    operation 309
    summary execution *(parate executie)* 308–309
mortgagee
    entitlement to immediate execution 310–311
    pactum antichresis 308
    right of preference 309–310
    rights and duties 311–313
movable things 33–35
municipalities 125, 125n53
    access to housing 348
    eviction 348–349
Municipal Structures Act 292

N

National Building Regulations and Building Standards Act 154
National Credit Act 305, 328
National Environmental Management Act 152, 154
National Heritage Resources Act 153
National Water Act 31, 277, 284, 287, 292, 293
    abstracting and/or leading water *(aquaehaustus)* 289
    access and use 288–289
    cancellation of servitudes 291
    common law and statutory servitudes 292
    rights and rules of relevant parties 291
    servitude of *aquaeductus* 289
    servitudes 289–290
    state as trustee 288
    statutory procedure 290–291
natural persons 6, 7
nature of things 32, 32
negative registration system 313
negotiability 28–31
    things based on 29
negotiable *(res in commercio)* 28–29, 192, 302, 304
neighbour law 132–134
    elimination of dangers 145
    encroachment 139–143
    lateral support 143–144
    motive to annoy *(animo vicino nocendi)* 135
    nuisance in narrow sense 134–137
    nuisance in wide sense 137–139
    party walls and fences 144
    scope of *133*
    surface water 144
    traditional rules 139–145
nemo plus iuris rule (nobody can give what he does not have) 193–194, 195, 202, 217, 282
Noise Control Regulations (Western Cape) 136
non-consumable things 39
non-fungible things 39–40
non-physical types of property 27
Northern Cape Planning and Development Act 155
notarial bonds 321–322
    categories *324*
    general 322
    special 322–324
Notarial Bonds (Natal) Act 323

O

objective law (legislation and neighbour law) 95
objects 45
obligations, law of 47
'ordinary person' 135
original acquisition of ownership 160, 161
    accession *(accessio)* 161, 164–165
    acquisitive prescription (long possession) 161
    appropriation *(occupatio)* 161, 163–164
    general requirements 165
    limited real right 160
    manufacture *(specificatio)* 161, 166, 177–178

mingling/mixing *(confusio/commixtio)* 161, 178-179
  recognised modes *162*
original owner (transferor) 190
ownership 17
  completeness of 94
  content of 89-91, 93
  content and entitlements 92-95
  definition 91-92
  enforceability of entitlements 90
  limitations 95-96
  minerals and petroleum 269-73
  most complete real right in property 92
  nemo plus iuris in alium principle 91, 160
  plena in re potestas principle 116, 145
  relocation of rights 166-167
  responsibility and trust 346-349
  see also transfer of ownership
ownership, forms of
  co-ownership 96-100
  individual title 96
own property right *(ius in re propria)* 43

P

Pandectist method 11, 11n36
Pandectists 90
  German 11
participation bond (mortgage) 313
patrimonial assets 12
patrimonial law 7
patrimonial loss 133, 231
patrimonial rights 26
patrimonial value 25
payment
  cash 194
  credit 194
  with delivery 194
performance, *see* delictual or contractual obligation
personalist theory 45-46
personal rights 12, 25, 34, 235
  see also real and personal rights
personal security rights 297
  and real security rights 297
personal servitudes 21, 248-251, 341
petroleum law
  environmental provisions of MPRDA 280
  exploration 278
  ownership under MPRDA 269-273
petroleum rights 265, 274-275
  activities and requirements 278
  cancellation or abandonment of 280
  content of 276-277
  content under MPRDA 277-278
  deregistration 280
  exploration rights 274, 277
  nature of 276
  production rights 274, 277
  reconnaissance permits 274, 277
  surface owner 278-279
  technical co-operation permits 274, 277
  termination of 279-280
  transfer and encumbrance 279
physical element *(corpus/detentio)* 66, 70-72, 75, 76, 191
planning law 145-148
  content 149
  enforcement of measures 156
  land use 149
  national legislation 151-152
  position *148*
  provincial legislation 152
  scope 148-149
  structure *147*, 147-148
  sub-disciplines *149*
  town scheme *150*
  zoning 150-151
planting and sowing 167-168
pledge 44, 298
  cession *(in securitatem debiti)* 315
  constituting of 315-316
  definition 314-315
  delivery 317-319
  form and content 316-317
  and immovable property *321*
  movables cannot be followed or pursued rule 320
  operation 319
  of personal rights 315
  termination 320
pledgee, rights and duties of 320
pluralist legal system 339-340
political issues 3
possession 41

animus elements 66, 70, 77, 80
corpus elements 70–73, 75, 77
detentio element 66, 71, 75, 78
explanation 67–68
nature of possessory rights 66
remedies for protection 74
requirement of 181–182
retained 71
right of *(ius possessionis)* 66–67
right to *(ius possidendi)* 66–67, 85
rights-based approach 69
possessory action
    circumstances for applicability 83
    defences 83
    relief available 83
    requirements 83
    use of 83
possessory delictual action
    circumstances for applicability 85
    defences 86
    requirements 85
    use of 86
possessory interdict
    circumstances for applicability 84, 85
    defences 85
    delictual action 85
    relief available 85
    requirements 84–85
possessory remedy, *see mandament van spolie*
possessory rights 66–70
praedial servitudes 34, 252
    and flexibility 244–245
    and personal servitudes 238, 238–239
    requirements 240
    restrictive condition 257
precedent law 15
Prescription Acts (1943 and 1969) 179–185, 186, 187
Prevention of Illegal Eviction from and Unlawful Occupation of Land Act (PIE) 16, 217, 221
previously owned property *(res derelictae)* 163
prima facie right 84
principle of publicity 318
principles and challenges of property law 17, 340–341
    absoluteness 345–346
    abstraction principle 344–345

    ethical dimension of publicity 344
    modes of delivery 341
    numerus clausus of real rights 341–343
    publicity 343–344
    responsibility and trust 346–349
    specificity 346
    transmissibility 340–341
prior personal right 59
    first in time *(prior in tempore rule)* 59
private law 7, 8
    limitations 132–145
privately owned *(res extra commercio)* 28–29, 221
privately owned, cannot be *(res extra commercium)* 31
private ownership *(res nullius)* 163
private property 6
    deprivation 119–122, *121*
    expropriation 119–122, *121*
private stakeholders 268
procedural law 10
prohibitory interdict 259
Promotion of Administrative Justice Act 188
property 4–5
    current use of 128
    direct state investment and subsidy 129
    exclusivity 338
    history of acquisition 129
    history of use of 128–129
    lawyers 5
    physical control of 95
    relationships relating to 42
    right to dispose of *(ius disponendi)* 52–53
    as security to access finance 338
property, connotations of
    Constitutional concept 27
    context 6
    meaning 4–5
property, framework and sources of
    function 6
    place 7–9
property, roots of 9–11
    scope 11–15
    sources 15–17
Property Time-sharing Control Act 104
proprietary relationships 41–42
    relating to property *42*

proprietary remedies 7–8
prospecting or mining right 277
    retention permit 277
protected from desecration (actio iniuriarium) 31
protection
    constitutional 5
    of ownership 168
    of possession 73
proven facts (facta probanda) 76, 80, 85
provincial legislation 152, 155
public
    access to private things 29–30
    interest 8, 161, 342
    law 7, 8
    things (res publicae) 31, 272
publicity principle 56–57, 168
public law limitations, see planning law
public purpose/public interest 126–127

Q

quasi-possession 66, 78
quasi-usufruct 39

R

racial diversity 13
real agreement (subjective mental
    element) 192–194
real and personal rights 45
    courts' approach to distinction 50–56
    distinction between 46–49
real remedies 215, 216
    actio negatoria 216, 226
    rei vindicatio 217–226, 329, 346
real rights 12, 34, 340–341
    acquired gratuitously (ex titulo lucrativo) 59
    closed list (numerus clausus) 48, 49, 340,
        341–343
    conventional categories 42–44
    in own property (ius in re propria) 42, 43
    in property 235
    owned by another (ius in re aliena) 42, 43
    see also limited real rights
real security rights 44, 45
    categories 298, 298
    functions 298–299
    legal transactions 301, 302, 302–303
    nature of 299–301

    security object 301
    security parties 301
reasonableness
    concept of 134
    and fairness 140
redistribution 222
registrability of rights
    intention to bind successors in title test
        50, 54–56
    subtraction from dominium test 50–54
Registrar of Deeds 47, 52, 304
registration 47, 57
    of documents 8
    see also transfer of immovable property
rei vindicatio
    and damages 219
    defences against 219
    immovable property and eviction 220–223
    limitations on use 219
    requirements 218
    statutory limitations 220
relative rights 48
religious things (res divini iuris) 31
remedies
    choosing 231
    co-ownership 99–100
    owners 216
    protection of ownership 230
    see also delictual remedies; real remedies
remedy, see possessory remedy
Removal of Restrictions Act 153–154, 155
requirement of vicinity (vicinitas) 246
reserving ownership 196
respondent (spoliator) 80
restitution 14
Restitution of Land Rights Act 16, 100
restoration 81–82
restore unlawful dispossession (spoliatus ante
    omnia restituendus est) 77
restrictions on ownership, see limitations on
    ownership
restrictive conditions 254–255
    classified as 'property' 258
    defences 261
    definition and examples 255–256
    enforcements and defences 259–260, 260
    ex parte application 262

judicial remedies 259-260
nature, character and status 256-259
public law character 258
removal by court application 262
removal or amendment 261, 261
status 258-259
statutory procedures for removal 262-263
statutory remedies 261
terminology 256
retirement schemes 104-105
rezoning and environmental clearance 155
right of way 244, *244*
after subdivision 244, *244*
permanent *(ius viae plenum)* 247
precarious *(ius viae precario)* 247
right(s)
and duties 245-246
hierarchy of 47-48
to occupy a house *(habitatio)* 248
of ownership 5
of ownership 92
of quick pursuit 325
of retention (lien) 328-329
of servient owner *(civiliter modo)* 245-246
to tribal land 14
of use *(usus)* 248
see also under possession
rights in property 17, 42-56
of another *(iura in re aliena)* 300
categories 43
conventional categories of real rights 42-44
see also real and personal rights
Roman-Dutch law 9, 14
legal principles 10, 15
Roman law 9
rule of vicinity *(vicinitas)* 240
rural praedial servitudes 246

S

sale of movables 194-196
sectional ownership 101-102
Sectional Titles Act 100, 101, 248, 252
sectional title schemes 100, 102-103
modified uses of 104-105
sectional title unit 36
security agreement 302-303
Security by Means of Movable Property Act 322

security rights 17, 44
ranking of 310
sequestration 279-280
servitudes 43-44, 45, 341
acquisition 252
creation of 251-253
definition and classification 236-237, *237*
enforcement 254
existing *(servitutus esse non potest)* 239
extinction or termination 253-254
good state of repair *(servitus oneritus ferendi)* 241
holder of 236
imposed on a servitude *(servitus servitus esse non potest)* 240
over own property *(nemini res sua servit)* 239
owner of servient property 236-237
passivity principle *(servitus in faciendo consistere nequit)* 241
positive and negative 253
rule of passivity 242
servitus altius tollendi 241
servitutes perpetua causa habere dabent 241
types of 246-247
unregistered 62, 62-63
servitutal nature 78
severed (extracted) minerals and petroleum 273
share-block schemes 103-104
modified uses 104-105
shares 8
simulated transactions 318-319
rule against 319
single entity *(res singularis)* 36, 301
single things 35-38
slavery 22
social function 6
socially appropriate activity *(secundum bonos mores)* 134
socio-economic issues 3, 342
South African Constitution 5, 14, 15-16
private and public law 9
see also Constitution
South African Law of Property, *see* Law of Property
spatial development frameworks (SDFs) 149

spoliation 77
    order 76
state
    authority 7, 8
    grant 252
    held things 29–30
    property 31
State Land Disposal Act 188
state of affairs previously *(status quo ante)* 76, 80, 226, 254
statutes 16
statutory law 15
Subdivision of Agricultural Land Act 147, 154
Subdivision of Agricultural Land Act Repeal Act 154
subjective rights 7
    of others (limited real or personal rights) 95
subtraction from *dominium* test 50–54
successive sales 61–62
    example *61*
summary execution clauses 316–317
summary judgment 307
surface water 144

T

tacit hypothec 325
    seller under instalment sale agreement 328
tacit real security rights 325
tangible objects 7–8
temporal requirement of acquisition
    interruption 183–184
    suspension 184–185
    uninterrupted period 182–183, *186*
temporary interdict 259
tenure
    option 342
    security 222
    systems, pre-1991 110–111
terminology, use of 170
theft of financed vehicle (example) 69–70
things, concept of
    characteristics of 20–21
    classification 28–40
    definition 24–25, *25*
    never been owned (*res nullius* proper) 30, 163, 164
    not currently owned *(res nullius)* 29

    owned but abandoned *(res derelictae)* 30, 164
    owned by individuals *(res singulorum)* 29
    rights and property 25–28
tied co-ownership 101
time-share schemes 104
title, alternative forms of 100–112
town planning 149, 152
    scheme *150*
trading rights 248
traditional leaders 293
transfer
    context of 60
    elements of *192*
    order for 140
    possession 318
    process *193*
    and underlying contract *189*
transferee (acquirer) 192
transfer of immovable property, registration
    conveyance principle *(coram judice rel sitae)* 210
    effects of registration 211–213
    publicity and certainty 210–211
transfer of ownership 160, 188–189, 217
    as abstract juristic act 190–191
    intention 191
    postponed 205
    requirement for validity 191–192
    and sale of movables 194–196

U

undivided co-ownership share 98
unjustified enrichment 216, 229
unreasonable delay 81
unsevered (*in situ*) minerals or petroleum 269
urban servitudes 246
use
    rights (licences) 284
    and value of things 24
usufruct *(usufructus)* 21, 32–33, 39, 240, 341
    essentially intact *(salva rei substantia)* 250–251
    personal servitude of 175–176 250–251
usufructuary interest 249
utilitarian approach 342
utility *(utilitas)* 240, 241

W

water 284-284
- historical background 285
- landowners 286
- new paradigm 286-287
- non-perennial water 285
- ownership entitlements 284
- perennial streams 285
- property law and human rights law 284
- riparian ownership 285, 286
- state control over resources 286

Water Act 285, 286

water dispensation
- implications for general public 293
- structural implications 292-293

Water Services Act 287-288, 293

ways of necessity *(via necessitatis)* 247

White Paper on a National Water Policy for South Africa in 1997 287

White Paper on Land Policy (1997) 14-15

Z

zoning 149, 150-151, 152